Alternative DNS Servers

Alternative DNS Servers

Choice and deployment, and optional SQL/LDAP back-ends

Jan-Piet Mens

UIT CAMBRIDGE LTD.

CAMBRIDGE, ENGLAND

First published in England in 2009.
UIT Cambridge Ltd.
PO Box 145
Cambridge
CB4 1GQ
England

Tel: +44 1223 302 041
Web: www.uit.co.uk

ISBN 978-0-9544529-9-5

10 9 8 7 6 5 4 3 2 1

To Alexandra

For your interest, support, and enthusiasm (as well as relentless page-count-checking) during this project, and for being my greatest fan.

Related Titles

Practical TCP/IP – Designing, using, and troubleshooting TCP/IP networks on Linux and Windows, (Second edition) Niall Mansfield

The Exim SMTP Mail Server – Official Guide for Release 4, (Second edition) Philip Hazel

Exim by Example – Getting started, with configurations for common scenarios, Jason Meers

The Joy of X – The architecture of the X window system, Niall Mansfield

Contents at a glance

Contents

List of Tables

List of Listings

Preface

What's different about this book

This book concentrates on two particular aspects of using the DNS:

1. Whereas most DNS documentation discusses only the BIND program (Berkeley Internet Name Daemon), there *are* other implementations, which might be better suited to your requirements. For example, MaraDNS is amazingly easy to set up, and NSD has wonderful performance. We cover all the important alternative programs (and some special features of BIND as well). We explain what environments they are particularly suited for, and their advantages and disadvantages, and describe in detail how to implement and manage them.

2. Traditionally, DNS data is kept in flat, plain text, files. Many of the servers we cover, and the extensions to BIND, let you store your DNS data in SQL databases, LDAP directories, or other special formats. We explain why you might want to do this – primarily because it lets you automate your DNS management, and integrate it with the rest of your systems – and how to implement these back-end data stores.

In addition we cover many other interesting topics, such as secure DNS (DNSSEC), Dynamic DNS with DHCP, DNS blacklists especially for mail system administrators, load balancing with the DNS, and implementing your own DNS servers in Perl.

Who should read this book

This book is aimed at three broad groups of people:

1. Systems administrators setting up a new DNS infrastructure, redesigning an existing one, or who just want to manage an existing system better.

2. Consultants recommending or implementing DNS solutions for customers, perhaps running them as an outsourced service.

3. IT or Network managers who need to understand what's involved in getting a DNS infrastructure up and running.

We cover the needs of all sizes of organization, from small Small Office / Home Office networks requiring simple DNS services, to corporate networks and ISPs requiring high performance and very reliable services for public Internet use and for internal systems. Whichever group you belong to, this book addresses you requirements:

- If you haven't implemented a DNS server yet, or are considering moving to a different server:
  - We show what's involved, from installation through to ongoing management.
  - We help you choose the server best suited to your environment. For each server we include a feature chart, showing you at a glance the particular server's benefits and drawbacks.
  - We show you how to build a simple test environment to evaluate the different servers. We show how to run the performance tests, and give you our test results.
- If you have an existing DNS system:
  - You may be using only basic features, and want to investigate further facilities that might be useful.
  - You may want to investigate whether a change of server would improve performance, or streamline your system management or allow you to automate it.
- Installing your chosen server is only the first step – there's a lot more to running a professional DNS setup. Whether you are managing a new or existing DNS system:
  - You may want to simplify your system administration, or automate it, and/or integrate your DNS data into a corporate database or LDAP directory. We discuss the storage schemes used by DNS servers that support relational databases or LDAP directories, and show you how to add and modify DNS entries
  - If you are currently expanding your network, we show you how to configure standalone internal servers for private networks, as well as providing public DNS service to users on the Internet connecting to your public services such as Web and e-mail servers.
  - We explain how to implement dynamic DNS, and provide workarounds if the server software of your choice doesn't support the standard for updating DNS directly. We explain how to get Dynamic DNS and DHCP to work together.
  - We show you how to implement DNS blacklists, to reduce the spam load on your e-mail system.
  - If you like programming, we show you how you can create your own name special-purpose servers in Perl.
  - In addition to the security requirements of the individual programs, we show you how to protect your DNS servers by implementing TSIG, and how you protect and validate DNS replies with DNSSEC.
  - We explain how to handle Internationalized Domain Names (IDNA).

All configurations tested are included in the book or on the companion Web site, so you can use them as a basis for your own implementation. Sample code is provided where appropriate, as well as detailed configuration descriptions.

Organization of the book

The book is in three parts, as shown in the Figure. On first reading you should read Part I, i.e. chapters 1–3, in order, although you can skip chapters 1 and 2 if you are a DNS expert. If you haven't decided which server to implement, skim through the individual servers in Part II, to familiarize yourself with what's available, and then concentrate on the relevant server(s). Finally, but before you start your implementation – so you're aware of the whole picture in advance – read Part III, which tells you about operational issues that you should factor in right from the beginning.

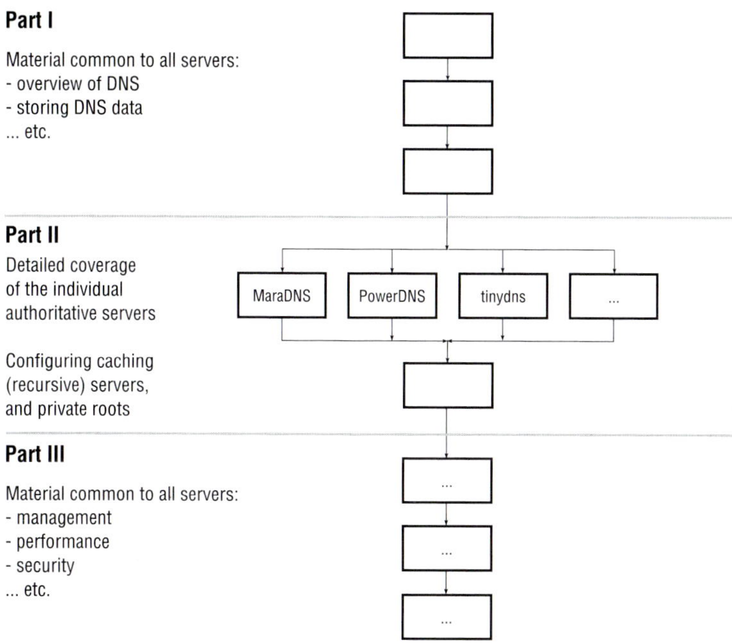

At the end of each chapter, a section called *Related topics* points you to other chapters that relate to what you are currently reading. For example, when we discuss a programmable back-end for one brand[1] of name server, we point you to other brands that have similar capabilities, or to a chapter where we discuss a different way of solving a similar problem.

Installation instructions for servers are in the *Notes* sections at the end of each chapter, rather than in the chapter proper. This is for two reasons. First, many UNIX and GNU/Linux distributions have pre-built packages for the various brands of server, so you can install using your distribution's standard installation manager instead of using server-specific procedures. Secondly, you're likely to install only one or two of the servers, so the installation instructions for most of the servers will be irrelevant to you.

[1] We use the term "brand" of name server to distinguish between MyDNS, BIND, tinydns etc. Phrases such as "type of name server" could be ambiguous, perhaps suggesting a particular feature (such as SQL support), rather than meaning "brand X".

by a number of large organizations. A collection of published papers can be found at `www.skills-1st.co.uk`.

David Jones began programming on the 8-bit micros of the 1980s and has been programming professionally since 1994. He has written garbage collectors, video games, embedded control software, and the odd language implementation or two. Currently he lives on the edge of the Peak District National Park in England, and is a senior consultant at Ravenbrook Limited.

Copyrights etc.

Part

I

Preparation

Chapter 1 introduces you to the Domain Name System. Chapter 2 shows you how DNS resource records are stored. (You can skip these chapters if you are a DNS expert.) Chapter 3 explains what you will need to set up the name servers that we cover, and introduces you to dig, the DNS lookup tool.

Chapter

1 Introduction to the DNS

When you have disciplined thought, you don't need bureaucracy.

Jim Collins

Introduction

This chapter is a quick introduction to the Domain Name System. We fast-forward you over the terminology we'll need throughout the book, and in particular explain the different types of functions performed by name servers, how they are commonly named, and where you locate your servers on your network.

1.1 The Domain Name System – overview and terminology

The *Domain Name System* (*DNS*) denotes both the worldwide system that your computers use to translate between machine names and network addresses, and also the software that you use to perform and manage these translations. For example, the name google.com maps to the address 72.14.207.99 and vice versa; it is the DNS that enables this mapping.

A survey taken in October 2007 (see Notes) estimates that there are over eleven million DNS name servers on the public Internet, excluding the private name servers on networks within organizations. DNS is a *very* important technology.

1.1.1 The DNS tree

Remember what the DNS is all about: we want to refer to machines at remote sites on the Internet by name rather than IP number, e.g. to connect to the Web site www.tcpdump.org or send e-mail to `fred@example.com`. (DNS is also used internally, within your organization, but we'll ignore that for now while we concentrate on the big issue of using DNS on the Internet.)

Before domains were thought of, there was a single file called `HOSTS.TXT` that contained the names and IP numbers of every host on the Internet. This was maintained centrally by a couple of volunteers. Machine names were simple one-part names without any dots. When you gave a name to a new machine, it had to be unique across the whole Internet. To add a new machine to your site you had to coordinate with the `HOSTS.TXT` file maintainers, who entered the changes in the `HOSTS.TXT` file for you. Every site on the Internet had to download a fresh copy of the `HOSTS.TXT` file periodically (Figure 1.1). Translating a name to

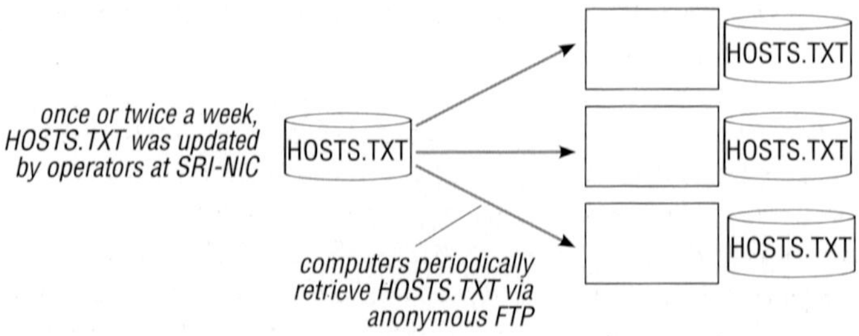

Figure 1.1: `hosts.txt` was distributed via FTP

an IP address involved looking up names and IP numbers in this file. As the Internet grew, this arrangement became unmanageable and the DNS was introduced instead, in the 1980s.

How domains are named in the DNS

DNS names are organized hierarchically in a tree structure (Figure 1.2) like the names of files and directories on disk. In Unix and Linux, the full "pathname" of a file is the basic filename (for example `readme.txt`), combined with the path to the file from the root (e.g.

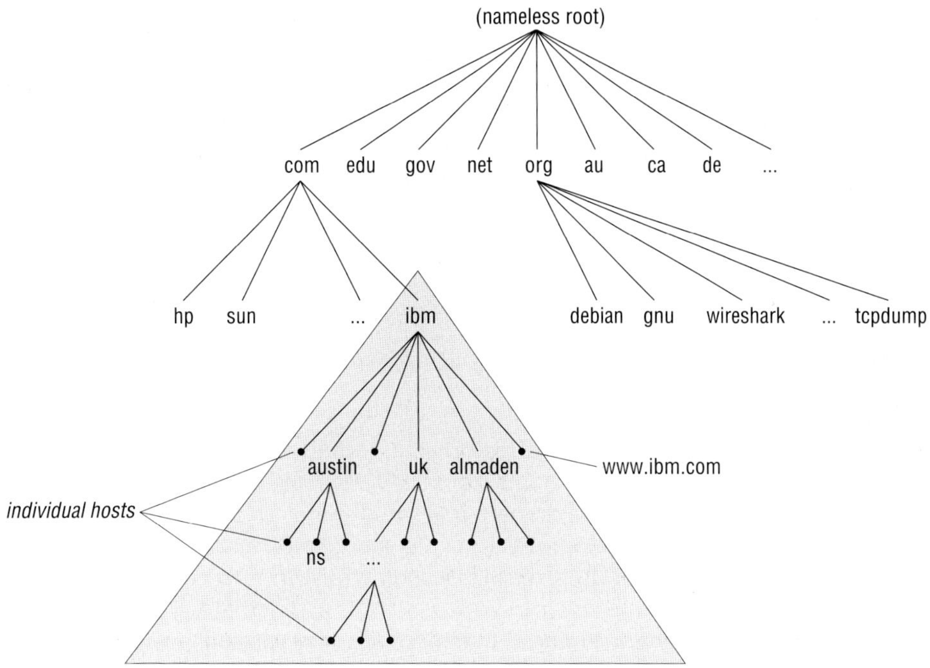

Figure 1.2: Tree structure of DNS names

`/usr/local/doc/readme.txt`). DNS naming works in much the same way. The basic name of a node in the DNS tree is called its *simple name*.

A node's *fully-qualified domain name* (*FQDN*), i.e. its full name, is its simple name followed by the names of each of its parents in turn, separated by dots instead of slashes. In Figure 1.2 the FQDN of the node ns is ns.austin.ibm.com. Note that in DNS the most significant parts are on the right, whereas in a file pathname they are on the left.

An individual node in the DNS tree is also called a *label*; it's limited to 63 characters and must not contain a period (just as in the *nix file system a filename must not contain a slash). The depth of the DNS tree is limited to 127 levels, and a fully qualified domain name is limited to 255 characters (including the dot separators).

A *domain* is a node in the naming tree, plus all its children, grandchildren, etc., if it has any; its domain name is the full name of the node. E.g. ibm.com is the name of the domain consisting of the whole sub-tree highlighted in gray in Figure 1.2, including the ibm node itself, right down to the individual machines. Your DNS domain is a specific part of the name space that is dedicated to you, so you can create your own names without clashing with anyone else's.

A hierarchy or tree structure avoids name clashes if you simply insist that no two children of the same parent have the same name. E.g. two different children of .com can't have the same name, so you're not allowed to have two separate domains called ibm.com and ibm.com. However, IBM can have a machine called www and you can have one called www too, because they are *not* children of the same parent; their full domain names are www.ibm.com and www.example.com so there's no ambiguity. (Files name work in exactly the same way: you can't have two files of the same name in the same directory. However, you *can* have the same basic filename, e.g. `readme.txt`, in many different directories, because the full pathname of the file *is* unique. Pathnames let you refer unambiguously to any file.)

The root of the tree has no name but is sometimes represented as a single dot (which, in this chapter only, we often show as • to make it more visible), for ease of reference or to emphasize the "tree-ness" of a name. Similarly, fully-qualified domain names (FQDNs) are often written with a trailing dot, e.g. "bob.example.com•" to emphasize or indicate that they are fully-qualified and go all the way back to the root.

Subdomains

Just as a file directory can contain sub-directories, a domain can contains *subdomains*. The root domain • contains all the subdomains .com, .edu, .org, .uk, etc. (and therefore contains the entire DNS tree). In turn, the .com domain has subdomains hp.com, ibm.com, sun.com, etc. and each of these has its own subdomains too. E.g. ibm.com contains every domain whose name ends with ".ibm.com", including zurich.ibm.com, which in turn contains anything that ends with ".zurich.ibm.com".

By the way, the name of an individual machine, e.g. mx3.sun.com, is a "domain name" because the name is a node in the DNS tree. The only thing in this domain is the machine itself. In practice the name of a single machine isn't usually referred to as a domain, even though we frequently *do* refer to the "domain name of a host".

1.1.2 Name resolution

When you visit a Web site, you enter the domain name of the site in the browser's address bar. The Web site name must be translated to a numeric IP network address for the browser to be able to connect to the Web server, because, at the lowest level, TCP/IP can use only numeric addresses. This process of translating a domain name to an address is called *resolving* or *name resolution*; it is performed in a number of steps via a number of DNS servers, as we'll see in the example in Section 1.1.4.

1.1.3 DNS packets

One of the DNS standards documents, RFC 1035, requires that DNS messages are sent over the UDP protocol, and that their data payload is at most 512 octets (8-bit bytes) – to reduce the chance of fragmentation occurring, which would render the message useless. Because of this, most modern DNS software will not use larger UDP datagram packets.

However, some queries *can* require larger answers. (For example, queries that return multiple address records for a single domain name, or large DNS security keys.) If the answer to a query won't fit in 512 octets, the server returns whatever will fit, and sets the *TC* (*content truncated*) bit in the answer header. This should cause the DNS client to retry the query over TCP instead of over UDP. TCP is an "expensive" protocol, in network resource terms, to use for a simple thing like a DNS query, and it should be avoided wherever possible.

We discuss in Chapter 22 that larger UDP datagrams are possible with DNS extensions. We rarely have to consider whether TCP needs to be used, except when one server is transferring to a backup server all the data about a whole domain, and we'll cover that explicitly.

1.1.4 An example – translating domain name www.qupps.biz to an address

To illustrate the various functions and components of the DNS, we're going to look in detail at an example of how a client computer uses the DNS to translate a name. After that we'll examine each of the steps in more detail, referring back to this example when required.

Assume you want to visit the Web site www.qupps.biz, a site remote from you on the Internet. Your desktop PC, which has address 192.168.1.11, must translate this name to an IP address. (For simplicity, we assume that all the client and server programs involved have just started, so they don't contain any information cached from previous sessions.) Figure 1.3 shows the steps and the software components involved:

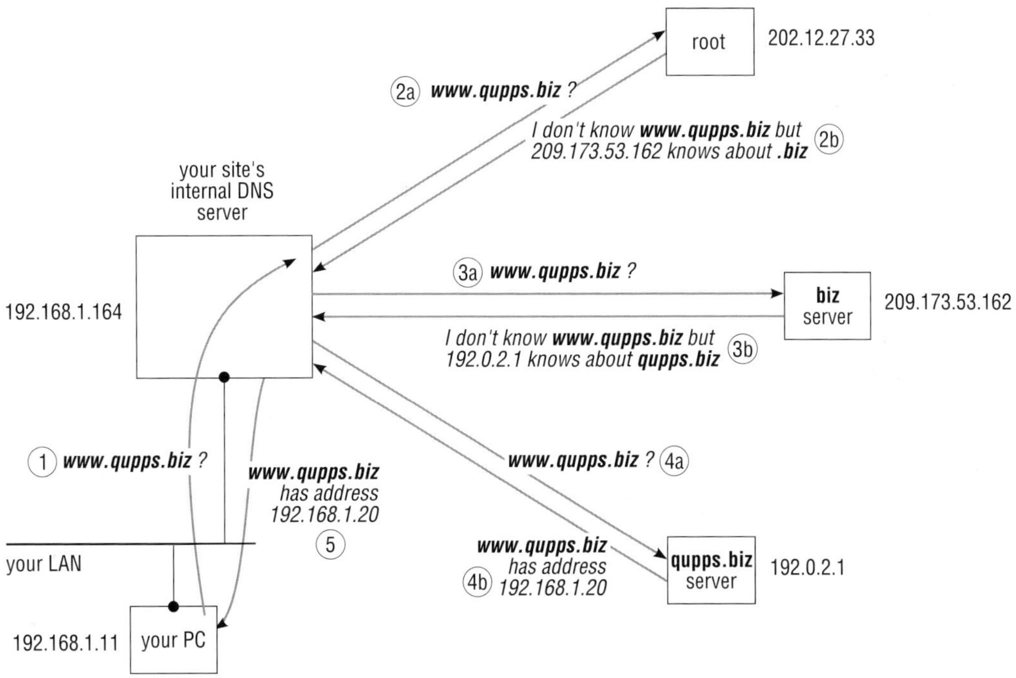

Figure 1.3: The different steps in resolving the name www.qupps.biz

1. Your client PC contains software to send DNS queries to a server. This software is called the *resolver* (Section 1.1.5 on page 9). The system administrator (oh: that is you!) configures the resolver with the address of the DNS server that the client will send its queries to, to be *resolved*, i.e. translated from name-to-address, or address-to-name. In

our example, the client's resolver is configured to use the server 192.168.1.164, which is our internal DNS server, so the client sends to 192.168.1.164 the DNS query requesting the IP address for name www.qupps.biz.

2a. Server 192.168.1.164 receives the query for name www.qupps.biz. This is a domain name owned by someone else. Your server has no knowledge of it, so your server has to use one or more other DNS servers to resolve the query. How does your server go about this?

We said that all the servers have just started up, so the only information 192.168.1.164 has is whatever is in its configuration files. This includes a list of *root servers* that know about the root – the highest level of the DNS.

192.168.1.164 chooses a root server at random from its list, 202.12.27.33, say, and sends the query for www.qupps.biz to that.

2b. The root servers know about the root domain (•), and very little else. However, what they *do* know is addresses of other name servers that handle domains the next level down from the root – .com, .edu, .biz, .uk, .au, etc. (These are called *top level domains, TLD.*) And when queried for any domain ending in biz, for example, while a root server can't return the answer (because it doesn't know it), it *will* return the addresses of the name servers that know about .biz

So, root server 202.12.27.33 looks up, in the information its administrators configured it with, the addresses of name servers that know about .biz, and it returns this list to the server that sent it the query, i.e. to our internal DNS server 192.168.1.164.

3a. Our server 192.168.1.164 receives the list of servers for domain .biz, and randomly chooses one from the list, 209.173.53.162, say. Our server sends the same query as before, for www.qupps.biz, to 209.173.53.162.

3b. 209.173.53.162 knows about .biz, but just as we've seen above, it doesn't know everything about it. However, it certainly does know the addresses of other name servers that handle domains the next level down, i.e. domains of the form *anything*.biz. Server 209.173.53.162 looks up, in the information its administrators configured it with, the addresses of name servers that know about qupps.biz, and it returns this list to our server.

4a. Once more, our server chooses a server (192.0.2.1, say) from the list it has just received, and sends to it the query for www.qupps.biz

4b. Server 192.0.2.1 *does* know about www.qupps.biz. Remember: we said this is one of the servers that knows about domain qupps.biz; in practice, this is almost certainly a server that's run either by the owner of this domain, or by someone on the owner's behalf, so it's not surprising that it knows a lot about the internals (i.e. lower down names) of qupps.biz.

Server 192.0.2.1 looks up www.qupps.biz in its data and returns the address 192.168.1.20 to our DNS server.

5. Our server 192.68.1.164 sends, to the client in our desktop PC, the address 192.168.1.20 as the answer to the query for domain name www.qupps.biz.

In other words, our server repeatedly sends queries to carefully chosen name servers, and gets progressively more information about www.qupps.biz each time, until finally it contacts the server that either has the information or can definitely say that there is no such domain name. (Looking at it the other way round, the remote servers queried in Steps 2 and 3 replied: "I don't know what you want, but here's a man who probably does know – ask him instead".)

Now we're going to go through each of the above steps in more detail, looking at how the various DNS servers and other components perform their functions.

1.1.5 Step 1 – the resolver

The *resolver* is the DNS client code that an application program uses to perform DNS queries. "The resolver" is not a separate program. (And later on, when we talk about a "DNS client", the client isn't a separate program either – it's just the resolver in the application program that wants to use the DNS.)

Where the resolver code resides depends on the implementation.

- On *nix the resolver is a set of functions in a library linked into the program (Figure 1.4). The *nix resolver does *not* remember (or "cache") any names or addresses it looked up in the past. When an application program uses the resolver to resolve www.qupps.biz a name, the resolver sends a query over the network to the DNS server, and waits for the answer. If the application immediately calls the resolver again to resolve www.qupps.biz, the resolver will send another query over the network, and wait for its reply, which might not be what you want on a very busy application. We'll see later (Section 1.1.6 on page 10) how you can get over this. This kind of resolver is called a *stub resolver*; it doesn't really do the work of resolution itself but hands it off to to a DNS server that does.

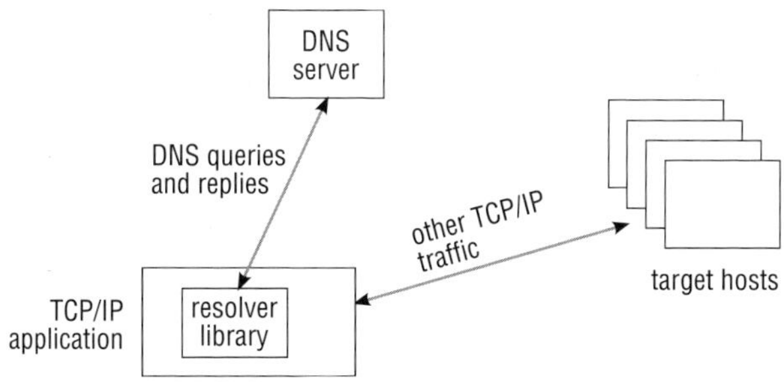

Figure 1.4: The resolver on *nix is implemented as a library

- On Microsoft Windows, resolution is performed in a similar fashion. An application invokes functions in a dynamic link library (DLL) which hands off the work of performing resolution to one or more name servers. When the server(s) return an answer, the functions pass that answer back to the application. It is worth noting that although this stub resolver does not cache, programs such as the Internet Explorer will unfortunately cache results themselves; this can be a cause of woe if you are debugging your DNS.

Recent versions of Microsoft Windows include a caching resolver service called the DNS Client, designed to reduce DNS network traffic by providing a local DNS cache for all applications. If this service is enabled, the library routines attempt to "talk to" it via an internal communications channel. The DNS Client service itself communicates with DNS servers, and caches answers, including negative answers, to speed up client processing. If you disable this service, workstations will use the stub resolver as before.

Irrespective of how it's implemented, the resolver is configured with the addresses of one or more DNS servers, that it should use to perform queries for clients. In the next section we look more closely at those servers.

1.1.6 Step 1, contd. – caching DNS servers

Your client resolver is, as we said above, configured with the addresses of one or more DNS servers, that it should use to perform queries for your client. In an organization of a reasonable size, these are usually internal servers run by the organization itself (and we show how to set up these servers later in the book). By contrast, for a Small Office / Home Office network, these are probably servers provided by the ISP, at the ISP's site (but we show you that you might want to have your own caching servers in this case also).

As we saw in the example in Section 1.1.4, these servers often have to query many other servers in succession, to resolve the name for the client. We also saw that the resolution process is "recursive" – getting information from one server may require the server to issue another query, and so on. For this reason, servers fulfilling this function are called *recursive servers*.

Consider what happens if a different client on our example network queries our recursive server, 192.168.1.164, for the same domain, www.qupps.biz, as before. It would clearly be very slow, and very wasteful of Internet bandwidth, if our server went through the whole procedure as before. Instead, our server *caches* (keeps a note of) the address it got in the previous answer, and serves up this address immediately, whenever it receives a query for www.qupps.biz, giving much better performance. All "internal" DNS servers that handle queries for clients as above, use caching, and so are called *caching (name) servers*. The terms "caching server" and "recursive server" are often used synonymously.

Note that the cache is built up from *all* the queries this server issues, including those in Step 2, where we got the address of the .biz servers. That means that if our server now receives a query for ftp.example.biz, it will be able to skip out at least Steps 2a and 2b, because it has cached the list of .biz servers from earlier.

1.1.7 Step 2 – root DNS servers

In the example, the first external server that our caching server contacted when it began resolving a name, was a root server. A root name server is one that answers requests for the root name-space (which is called •) and in effect "redirects" requests for a particular top-level domain to the name servers of that domain. In our example, the root server 202.12.27.33 returned the list of servers for the top-level domain .biz, so we could continue resolving www.qupps.biz.

There are 13 root server installations for the public DNS, called a.root-servers.net... m.root-servers.net. All initial queries are directed to a root server determine the addresses of the lower level DNS servers. We said 13 "installations": in fact there are far more than 13 servers (Figure 1.5); for example, i.root-servers.net consists of servers spread across 31 different sites.

As a matter of interest, at the time of this writing, the total number of DNS queries arriving at all the root servers, is about 118 000 per *second*, equivalent to about 10 billion (10^{10}) per day[1].

If you are on an large isolated network (i.e. one without an Internet connection) but need a working DNS, then you have to fake the infrastructure (root servers, etc.) found on the Internet. This sounds much more difficult than it actually is; we show you how to set it up in Chapter 18. But don't worry: most sites don't need to do this, and you certainly won't if you are on a small network and want to set up DNS for your Small Office / Home Office.

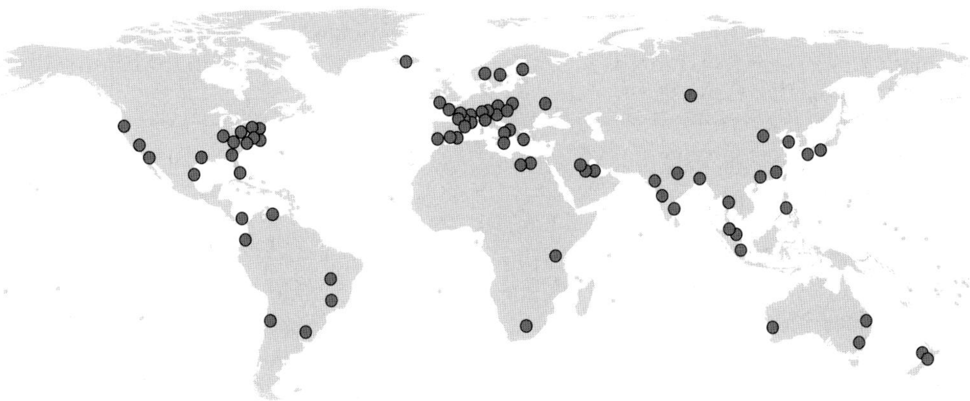

Figure 1.5: Distribution of root name servers

1.1.8 Step 3 – authoritative DNS servers

In our example, the next server that our own server (192.168.1.164) contacted, after the root, was a server that "knows about" the .biz domain. To be more precise, each of the .biz servers returned in the list from the root server is *authoritative* for the .biz domain. This means that each server can, from its own internal database or configuration files, answer the question: "does domain *something*.biz" exist, and if so, what is the associated address?". (The *something* must not contain a dot; if it does, the .biz might have to pass us along to yet another server, as we saw in Step 4.) The server doesn't need to ask any other server: if its own database doesn't have a record of the requested domain name, then the domain name definitely does

[1] `http://www.isoc.org/briefings/020/`

not exist, and the authoritative server sends a negative reply saying so. Note that this is *not* the same as saying "I don't know if it exists – go ask someone else".

In our example, we were querying for www.qupps.biz, which did exist, so the .biz servers gave us the address, 192.0.2.1, of a server that "knows about" (is authoritative for) qupps.biz. But how is that authoritative status set up, and who does it? When the domain qupps.biz was allocated to its owner – the QUPPS company – control over it (and all its sub-domains, by definition) was given to QUPPS. This assignment of the responsibility for a domain to someone else is called *delegation*. Two thing are needed for delegation to work. First, you must configure your name servers so that they believe themselves authoritative for your domains, and contain the data for your domain. Secondly, the name server "above" yours (i.e. your parent server) must be configured with the information that it is your server that is authoritative for your domain. (This configuration is performed with Name Server records, which we discuss in Chapter 2.) In our example above, the following chain of events have made our servers authoritative for the qupps.biz domain:

- The root server operators have made the servers for biz authoritative for biz by configuring the root servers to point to the biz-servers whenever queries for biz are issued.
- The operators of the biz domain have made the qupps.biz servers authoritative for qupps.biz by setting up records on the biz servers which define them to be authoritative.
- We configured our name servers to contain the DNS data for qupps.biz.

QUPPS had to decide whether to run their own authoritative server, or whether they would get their ISP to make the ISP's server authoritative for qupps.biz. For simplicity, we assume QUPPS run their own server, which has address 192.0.2.1. QUPPS informed the .biz server administrators of this address, and they configured the .biz servers to say that server 192.0.2.1 "knows more about" (is authoritative for) qupps.biz. This process of configuring one server (for .biz) with a list of authoritative domains for a sub-domain (qupps.biz) is also called delegation. (We discuss the process of delegation and how you delegate in Chapter 18.) Each and every domain has at least one authoritative server responsible for it.

Distribution of responsibility

Delegation devolves the responsibility and authority for assigning IP addresses to domain names. For example, if QUPPS want to change the IP address of www.qupps.biz they change it themselves on their own server (192.0.2.1). They don't have to tell the .biz server administrators about this. In other words, responsibility has been devolved to a lower level as part of the the delegation process, so the worldwide DNS ends up as a hierarchical, distributed database of information.

The only truly central part of the DNS is the root servers, which provide the initial entry point into the DNS tree.

1.1.9 Steps 1&5 v. 2-4 – authoritative and caching servers contrasted

There are fundamental differences between authoritative and caching servers, both in their function and how they operate. Whereas a caching name server will always attempt to find the answer to a query, an authoritative server behaves differently. An authoritative name server will not answer queries for a zone it is not authoritative for, and will not pass the query to other name servers. As an example, suppose you ask the authoritative[2] servers for qupps.biz a question about google.com. The qupps server cannot answer the query as it has no knowledge of the content of google.com's DNS database and can therefore not tell whether such a name exists or not. How the server responds depends on the implementation:

- Some servers send back a "no error" status packet, but include information telling you where to go and start looking, by providing additional hints with pointers to the root name servers.

- Some implementations simply drop the query for zones for which they are not authoritative, causing the DNS client to time-out waiting for the answer.

To make the differences between authoritative and caching name servers clear we'll consider things from the point of view QUPPS's network (Figure 1.6).

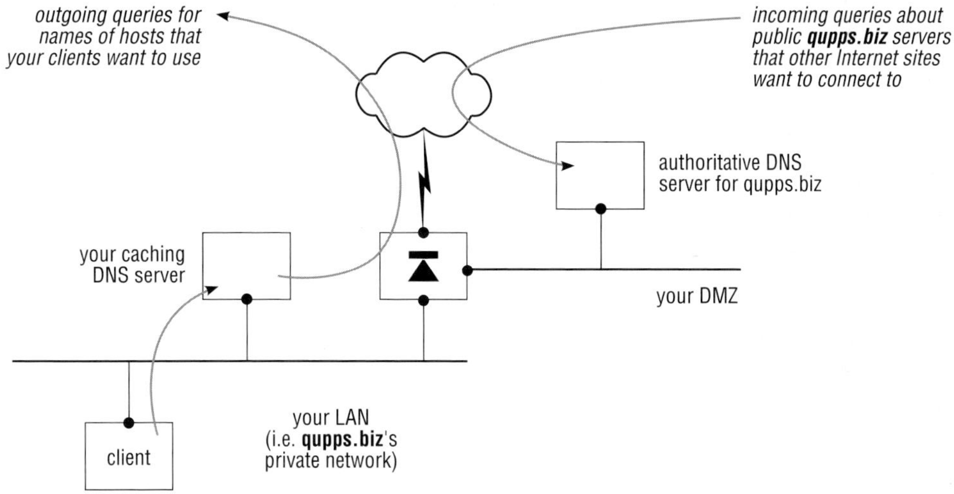

Figure 1.6: Different functions of authoritative and caching servers

QUPPS's internal DNS server is a caching server that all the internal hosts use, to get the IP addresses of hosts elsewhere on the Internet that they want to access. For example, a browser on a desktop PC will use this internal server, to resolve the name of the site the user wants to visit.

By contrast, QUPPS's authoritative server is used only by outsiders, who want to find out addresses of our public servers, so they can connect to smtp.qupps.biz, for example, to send us e-mail. (If you have been paying attention, you will have noticed that the description

[2]Here we assume that the authoritative servers are authoritative-only, although you can configure some servers to be both authoritative and recursive. Even so, what we say is still true of the authoritative part of a server configured to be both authoritative and recursive.

is not strictly correct: QUPPS's caching server will also, by way of referrals from the root servers, be able to query QUPPS's authoritative server, but we'll ignore that for now).

Now reverse the perspective, and consider what happens at a site that a user in qupps.biz wants to connect to, www.example.com, say. Our caching internal server queries *their* authoritative server.

Recursive v. iterative queries

In Step 1 our caching server, 192.168.1.164, received a query from our DNS client. Our server wasn't able to answer the query immediately, so it started the recursive procedure of querying other servers. However, in Step 2, root server 202.12.27.33 received a query that it couldn't answer fully and all it did was send back a single partial answer; it did *not* start a recursive resolution process. To see why, we need to look at DNS queries in a little more detail.

There are two different types of DNS query: recursive and non-recursive (iterative). The application (DNS client) sending the query specifies the type, by setting or clearing a 1-bit *Recursion Desired* (*RD*) flag in the query packet.

- A *non-recursive query* (*iterative query*) is typically sent by a caching DNS server acting as a recursive resolver for local clients. In our example, the queries sent in Steps 2–4 were all iterative, i.e. the RD bit was cleared in all these queries. Note that in each of these steps, host 192.168.1.164 is acting as a client, whereas in Steps 1 and 5 it is acting as a server.

  As we saw, the answer to an iterative query can be either a definitive one, as in Step 4, where the server returned the requested IP address, or an incomplete one, as we saw in Steps 2 and 3, which require our server to ask other servers for progressively more detail.

- *Recursive* queries have the RD bit set. They are typically sent by application programs (strictly, the resolver used by the program) calling the `gethostbyname()` or `gethostbyaddr()` library functions. The recursive query asks the server to do everything possible to determine the answer to the query, including iteratively querying other servers if need be. The answer to a recursive query is either the final answer to the original question or a message indicating that the answer couldn't be found.

In other words, application programs send recursive queries to caching servers, whereas caching servers send iterative queries to authoritative servers.

There is another reason why we sent non-recursive queries to the authoritative servers in Steps 2–4. Most authoritative servers are configured not to perform recursion, because recursive queries would be sent to them only by badly configured or malicious clients or servers.

1.2 Deployment issues with DNS servers

So far we've explained how DNS clients and the various server functions interact. Now we need to consider how name servers are deployed, and some of the system management issues involved.

1.2.1 Where domain information is stored – "zones"

In the example we saw that, to resolve the domain name www.qupps.biz, we had to obtain information from three different external servers, each of which only held part of the overall picture. Each server returned only the information that it was authoritative for – information about its own domains, or delegations direct from its own domains. If we assume that QUPPS has delegated further internally, as described below, it will be easier to see what information is stored where.

QUPPS's head office is in Germany, with subsidiaries in the UK and in Spain. They have decided to split up their name space (i.e. the part of the DNS tree that they "own") into sub-domains for each country. The advantages are:

- DNS maintenance is handled by system administrators who are closer to the relevant part of the business. Why should, for example, an administrator in Germany have to maintain DNS data for a machine in Spain?

- By setting up name servers in different geographic regions, the DNS is more resilient.

QUPPS have decided to delegate their sub-domains to name servers in two countries, as follows:

- es.qupps.biz and uk.qupps.biz are handled by the server in Spain, because there are no technical staff in the UK.

- The German head office holds information about the rest of the qupps.biz domain, i.e. anything that isn't in uk.qupps.biz or es.qupps.biz. This includes corporate wide resources, such as www,qupps.biz, as well as the German sub-domain de.qupps.biz.

The sub-tree of information that a server holds for a domain is a called a *zone*. Working from the bottom up, in Figure 1.7, the es.qupps.biz zone overlaps exactly with the es.qupps.biz domain. The same is true for uk.qupps.biz. However, there is no de.qupps.biz zone: this domain wasn't delegated, so it's just part of the qupps.biz zone, which consists of everything apart from the es.qupps.biz and ukqupps.biz zones.

Note that a domain is always a full tree or sub-tree, whereas a zone can have chunks missing – lower down sub-trees that have been delegated. The missing pieces can be at different levels (which we haven't shown in Figure 1.7), because you can delegate at different levels. For instance, example.com might delegate au.example.com to an Australian server, but delegate sales.alaska.us.example.com to a server in Canada.

A different definition of a zone is that it is the collection of related records for a domain or sub-domain, and usually stored in a file. Because this is the definitive version of the data for the zone, the file is called a "master file". (However, a zone doesn't *have* to be stored in a file: as we show you in later chapters, it can be stored in databases or LDAP directories instead, but that's only a detail.)

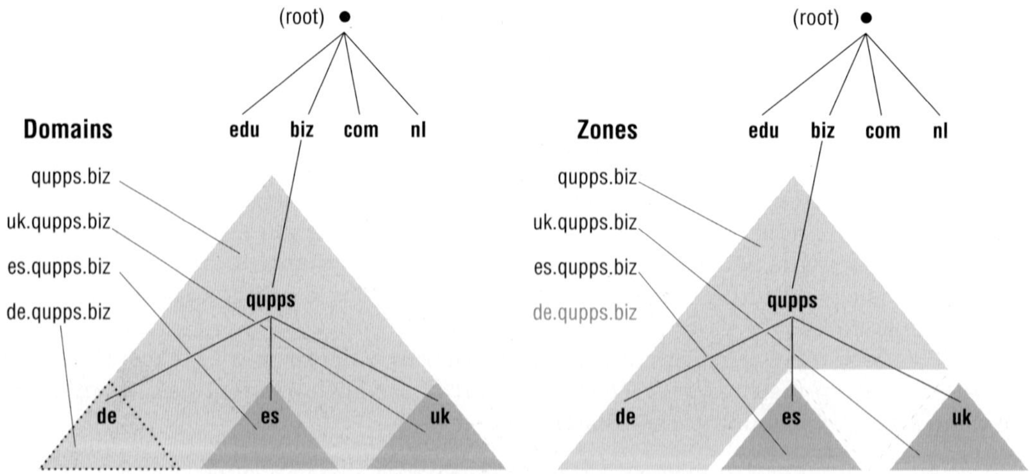

Figure 1.7: DNS domains and zones

1.2.2 Creating redundancy – master/slave, primary/secondary servers

What happens when the authoritative name server for your domain is down and cannot answer queries? Client hosts elsewhere on the Internet wishing to connect to your Web and e-mail servers can't find those servers' addresses: your site is effectively down, even though only the DNS server is unavailable.

To provide reliable service you want redundant servers – i.e. more than one server with identical content. You must also ensure that these servers give identical answers to identical queries. (Imagine your domain qupps.biz has two DNS name servers, but they supply different addresses as answers to queries for www.qupps.biz!) There are two different ways to ensure that all servers have the same content and keep in sync:

A. Set up "master" and "slave" name servers, with some mechanism for the primary to copy its data to the secondary, to keep it in sync.

B. Set up name servers that access a replicated database store. In this case it is the database software, not the name servers, that replicate the zone data.

Now let's look at each of these in detail. (Before we go on, remember that this only applies to authoritative servers; caching servers don't maintain zone data, so there are no issues about getting out of sync.)

A. Master and slave name servers

The QUPPS administrators have decided to set up the name server in Spain so it can also serve the DNS data normally held in the zones in Germany (Figure 1.8), in order to give their DNS service greater resilience. They do this by configuring the authoritative name server located in Germany to be a "master" name server and the server in Spain to be a "slave" name server.

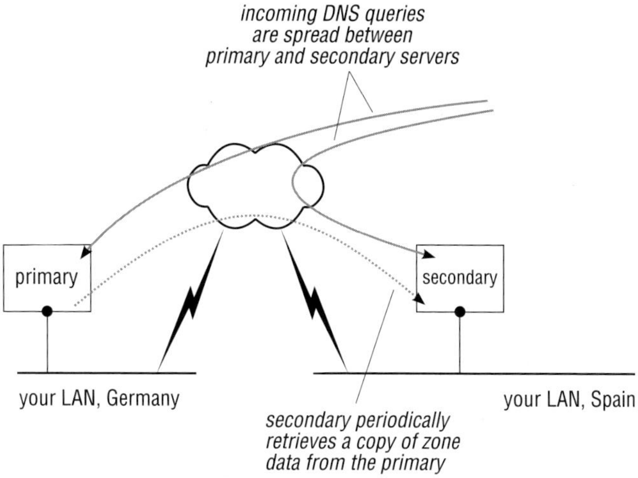

Figure 1.8: Secondary or slave name server

A *master name server* (or *primary name server*) is one that holds the definitive copy of information for one or more zones, which it uses to answer queries from clients. By contrast, a *slave name server* or *secondary name server* is never directly configured with the zone data. Instead, all changes to DNS data are made on the master name server, and the slave transfers this data from its master. A master can have multiple slaves.

In all cases, both master and slave server(s) are authoritative for the zone data. As far as authority is concerned, there is no difference between the master and the slave server(s) of a zone.

The data is transferred from master to slave by *zone transfer*, which duplicates the data from the master to the slave. A zone transfer is a special type of DNS request named AXFR, which allows master and slave to use the DNS protocol as the interchange mechanism, without having to add other special transfer facilities. In contrast to most DNS requests which are performed over UDP, zone transfers are carried out over TCP. Zone transfers performed by a slave server are called incoming or inward transfers. Zone transfers provided by master servers are called outgoing transfers. Note that whenever we say zone transfer or AXFR we use the term strictly (i.e. we mean a zone transfer using the DNS AXFR request) and not as a generic term for replication of DNS data from one name server to another.

There are two ways a zone transfer can be initiated:

1. A slave server periodically checks with its master server whether the zone has changed, by querying a special DNS record called the Start of Authority (Chapter 2). If this check indicates that the zone's content has changed, the slave transfers it by sending an AXFR query to the master server, requesting a copy of the zone data. This zone is then "downloaded" to the slave server via the DNS. Some server implementations offer so-called *incremental zone transfers*, which allow a slave server to receive only the changed DNS zone data, instead of a full copy of the zone.

2. Alternatively, when a master server detects that the content of a zone has changed (i.e. either because an operator has told it so, or because it is able to differentiate between before and after), it sends out a special DNS query to its slave servers. This request, called a DNS NOTIFY, instructs the slave servers that a modification has taken place. The slave servers then proceed as in item 1 above.

B. File or database replication

There are alternatives to zone transfers to replicate zone data between servers. When you use these, you effectively create not a primary and one or more secondary servers, but rather a set of primary name servers, because none is more special than any of the others. (Also, some DNS servers don't support zone transfers, so you *have to* use some non-DNS replication method to keep master and slave servers in sync.)

- MaraDNS and tinydns store zone data in files on a file system. These programs use file synchronization tools such as rsync to transfer zone data from one authoritative server to another.

- PowerDNS, ldapdns and Bind DLZ can store their zone data in a back-end LDAP directory. To keep two such servers in sync, you replicate the LDAP directory. (That's purely an LDAP-related operation; the front-end DNS servers don't know anything about it.)

- When the zone data is stored in a relational SQL database, such as MySQL, you can use the database server's replication facilities to replicate the SQL tables from one SQL server to another.

We cover each of these in detail in Part II.

1.2.3 Special authoritative server configurations – split horizon and hidden servers

Split horizon servers

An authoritative DNS server gives the same answers to queries irrespective of where the queries come from. However, if you have a name server in your DMZ which you want to use both for serving DNS data to public clients on the Internet and for use by internal clients, you might want a query for www.qupps.biz to return different answers depending on where the client is located. For example, in Figure 1.9, when an external client queries our server for www.qupps.biz, it should receive the reply 192.0.2.1, which is the "official", public, address of our Web server, whereas an internal client should get the reply 192.168.1.20, which is our Web server's "internal", private, address.

A *split horizon* DNS server lets you do this – it can serve one set of DNS content to one specified portion of the network, and serves different content to a different portion of the network. (DNS servers that offer split horizon are often seen in a DMZ, offering "official" authoritative content to clients on the Internet and "internal" content to clients on the internal network.)

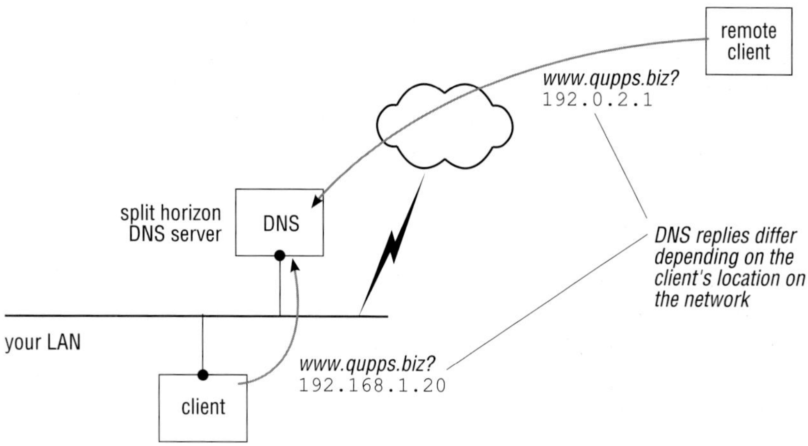

Figure 1.9: Split-horizon DNS

Two servers support split-horizon DNS services out of the box: BIND and tinydns. Some of the other name servers can be coerced into providing split-horizon service.

In all cases, split horizon must be done very carefully, as a small misconfiguration could publish on the Internet content about internal systems that should only be seen by internal machines. We recommend you don't use split horizon. Instead, deploy completely separate "internal" and "external" content DNS servers. This configuration requires two IP addresses, but these are easy to obtain. You get a more secure system. Another advantage is that you can use two different brands of DNS servers, if you have very different performance and management requirements for your internal server and for your external server.

Hidden name servers

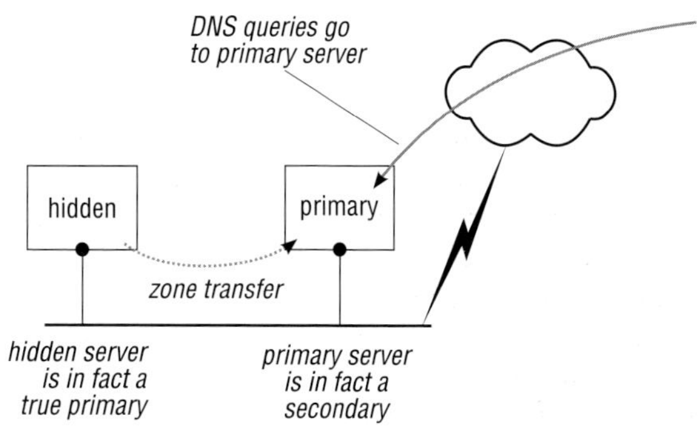

Figure 1.10: Hidden or stealth name server

You may decide to use a brand of name server that stores zone data in an SQL database or in an LDAP directory (e.g. MyDNS or PowerDNS). In order to be as resilient as possible, you decide that you don't want to have those accessible on the Internet, and deploy a "front-line" server which uses the file system as storage for the zone data, so that the front- line server can continue to operate even if the back-end fails.

You can do this by creating a *hidden name server* (Figure 1.10). A name server is called hidden (or *stealth*) if its address does not appear in the zone data anywhere on the network. Because no other servers point to the server, the public DNS has no knowledge of its existence. (However, the server that is slave to the hidden server *does* know about the hidden server, because the hidden server's address is included in the slave's *configuration* files, as opposed to its zone data files.)

Your "front-line" servers (e.g. NSD or BIND) are slave servers to your hidden servers, and they obtain a copy of the zone data via zone transfers.

1.2.4 Special caching server configurations – forwarding, forwarder, proxy

Your LAN clients use your own internal or your ISP's caching server to perform name-to-address translation. Caching name servers usually talk to authoritative name servers, as we saw in the example (Section 1.1.4). However, sometimes a caching server will want to talk to other caching name servers.

Suppose your organization works closely with the QUPPS organization. You have joined your networks (e.g. via a VPN – Virtual Private Network), and both organizations decide they need access to each other's private DNS zones. You configure your DNS server to send all recursive queries for the QUPPS zones to a selected list of name servers at QUPPS. The servers at QUPPS provide recursive service for QUPPS-related queries that your DNS server receives but cannot answer from its own database. In effect, your DNS server behaves like a DNS client with respect to the QUPPS servers, but normally when querying other non-QUPPS domains.

Name servers that pass requests on to other (upstream) resolving servers are called *forwarding servers* or *proxy servers*, whereas a *forwarder* is the server which is forwarded *to*. In forwarding mode, a server talks to caching servers only – never directly to authoritative servers. Forwarding servers usually cache answers to the queries they have processed. Figure 1.11 shows the forwarding and forwarder servers for the QUPPS example above.

Forwarders are used:

- When you want to forward queries for one or more zones to a specific server for resolution, as we have just seen.
- When access to the DNS is over a slow network link. Using a forwarder can cut down on traffic, because the (remote) forwarder does most of the DNS work.
- When the forwarder can build up a large cache which speeds up internal queries. For example, you might use a forwarder at your ISP because then you get the benefit of the caching of queries from all the ISP's customers.
- When you have several internal caching servers, but want only one server – the forwarder – to communicate directly with the Internet, for security reasons.

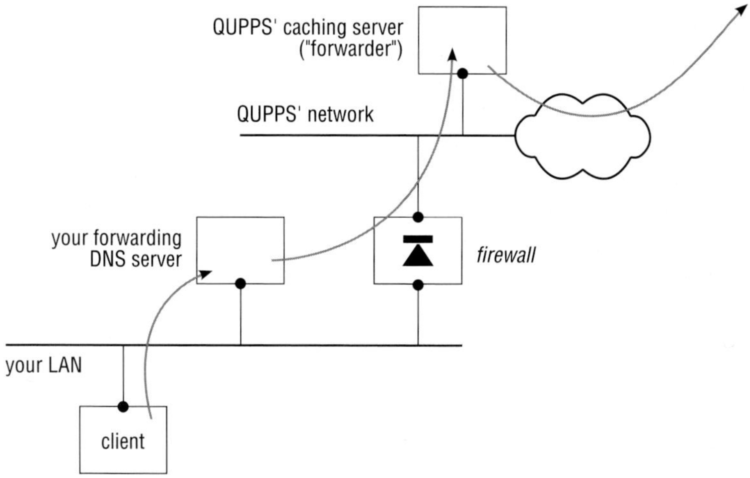

Figure 1.11: Forwarding/proxy name server

1.2.5 Special authoritative and caching server configurations

The tasks of providing authoritative DNS and caching (recursive) DNS should be clearly separated. We discuss in Chapter 22 that mixing both roles in a single name server can cause a carefully crafted malicious DNS query to "pollute" (i.e. corrupt) the authoritative replies served in a "mixed" server.

Nevertheless, there are cases in which you won't want to bother with setting up separate servers. Instead you will want to have both roles in a single name server program, such as in a branch office or Small Office / Home Office. This is called an *internal name server*. Your internal name server is a caching name server for your network, but it also offers a zone authoritatively, for the devices on your network.

1.3 Features you might want to have in a name server

The different brands of name server we discuss in this book implement some facilities that you might require. In this section we introduce some of them.

- DNS NOTIFY.

  We mentioned above that some brands of name server implement a special request called a DNS NOTIFY, which is sent by a master name server to its slave servers to inform them of changes to a zone.

  DNS NOTIFY is not easy to implement for two reasons:

  1. A master name server that implements NOTIFY needs some way to detect that a zone's data has changed. If it cannot detect a difference between "before" and "after" you've changed a zone, it won't be able to notify a slave server of a zone's change.

2. DNS NOTIFY requests are sent to slave servers but, as we discuss in Chapter 2, a master server typically only "knows" its slaves by their names in the zone data (the Name Server records). There may well be slave servers that aren't mentioned in a zone, which makes it impossible for a name server to notify them.

Not all brands of name servers with support for being master servers implement DNS NOTIFY. We discuss that when we discuss the individual name servers.

- Dynamic DNS updates.

  Some brands of name server allow DNS data to be modified in real time via a special DNS protocol called *dynamic DNS update*. The protocol is defined in RFC 2136, and it is mainly used by client workstations that use DHCP to obtain their IP address when starting up, and then "register" the address with the DNS (i.e. they "create" an Address record in it). We discuss dynamic updates in Chapter 19, where we also discuss methods you can use if the brand of name server you choose doesn't support "proper" dynamic DNS.

- DNSSEC – DNS Security Extensions.

  The Domain Name System is fragile in as much as answers to DNS queries can be "spoofed" or altered on their path from a name server to a client. DNSSEC adds a cryptographic layer to the DNS, allowing a client to determine whether the reply it has received is authentic. This very complex processing is implemented in only a few brands of name server.

- TSIG – Transaction Signatures.

  TSIG provides a means of authenticating zone transfers and Dynamic DNS Updates by using cryptographic keys exchanged between clients and name servers.

- Database back-ends.

  Some brands of name server allow you to choose the type of database you want it to use for zone data storage. These name servers support some or all of the following database systems:

  - PostgreSQL and MySQL, the two best known Open-Source database systems.
  - Berkeley DB (BDB) is an embedded non-relational database that can be used by applications for persistent storage and fast access to data. In contrast to SQL databases, that support a query language for accessing or modifying the data, and that often need a human to administer them, Berkeley DB offers programmers a high performance embedded database library with a number of language bindings, and no administration overhead. Berkeley DB stores arbitrary key/data pairs and offers a simple yet powerful API with a set of defined function calls for data manipulation.
  - SQLite is a library that implements an embeddable SQL database engine. It supports many SQL features from much larger systems (such as MySQL and PostgreSQL). Because it is embeddable into a program, it can give a name server ac-

cess to a relational database system without having to rely on a separate database server.

- LDAP back-ends.

  Some brands of name server allow DNS data to be retrieved from an LDAP directory server. If you already store information about people and configuration data in your organization, you might want to store your DNS data in your LDAP directory server, and have a DNS server use that as its back-end data source.

- Programmable back-ends.

  Some brands of name server allow you to extend them by providing a programming interface. You can "plug in" some code that receives a DNS query and can produce a reply to it. We often call this kind of reply a "dynamic answer" or "dynamic reply" because the code can produce the reply by almost any means, "on the fly". For example, if you are Web hoster you will have "standardized" zones for small customers (i.e. all zones have a Web server, a mail exchanger, etc.) and you can create code that gives similar answers irrespective of the zone queried, because all your small customers use the Web and mail servers that you provide. As another example, you may want the answer to a query for an Address (A) to depend on the availability of a particular machine; you can create code to do that, and we show you how to do so in Chapter 8 and Chapter 15.

  Adding code to your name server is not something most sites need to do. On the contrary, you extend a name server only if it cannot provide a specific functionality without you having to resort to programming.

1.4 Scenarios of name server deployment

Which DNS server functions you need depends on what your department or organization does. A corporation has to provide DNS for its presence (Web, e-mail, ...) on the Internet, as well as DNS for its private LAN. An ISP, on the other hand, is mainly concerned with Internet-facing name servers, which are part of the core of its business.

Below we discuss some common combinations of DNS requirements.

1.4.1 ISP

The ISP has several name servers that provide DNS services to its customers (Figure 1.12):

- An ISP providing dial-up services needs caching name servers for its customers to use. Consider Unbound as a caching name server or any of BIND, dnscache or MaraDNS.

- An ISP providing hosting services will typically have authoritative name servers providing DNS for the domains owned by its customers. If you allow your customers to maintain their own DNS data, consider:

  - Bind DLZ which provides a database or LDAP back-end.

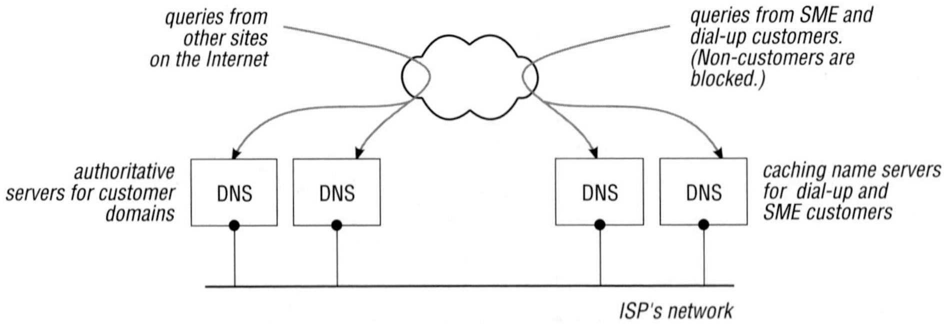

Figure 1.12: An ISP has many name servers

- BIND with a hidden primary master consisting of PowerDNS or MyDNS. This allows you to manage zone data in a database or LDAP directory and have BIND perform zone transfers from your hidden primary server.

Most Internet Service Providers have some sort of database in which they record customers, the zones these have, billing numbers, etc. in what is called a "registry" (we discuss this in Chapter 19). If you have such a system, you typically use it to create or "generate" zones from it. This is called *provisioning*. If you have specialized provisioning systems for your customer's DNS data, consider:

- tinydns (Chapter 11) which is a widely-used authoritative-only server.
- NSD (Chapter 10) if performance is very important.

1.4.2 SOHO network

Setting up your own name server in a *SOHO* (Small Office / Home Office) network might look like overkill, but many SOHO networks contain a increasing number of IP-addressable devices such as other computers, a printer, etc. If you want to be able to address these devices, you need a small authoritative name server for a zone or two and we recommend you install a caching name server too (Figure 1.13). This sounds like a complicated undertaking, but several of the programs we discuss in Part II make it easy:

- dnsmasq is an excellent choice, as it provides authoritative content from a simple and easy-to-administer `/etc/hosts` file, as well as a DNS cache for public DNS queries. It also provides your Small Office / Home Office network with a DHCP server, which allows you to configure your networking devices automatically.

- MaraDNS is an authoritative content server which can also be made to recurse.

- If you already have a MySQL or PostgreSQL database on your Small Office / Home Office network, MyDNS is easy to set up. Adding dnscache as a recursive resolver gives all the DNS services you need.

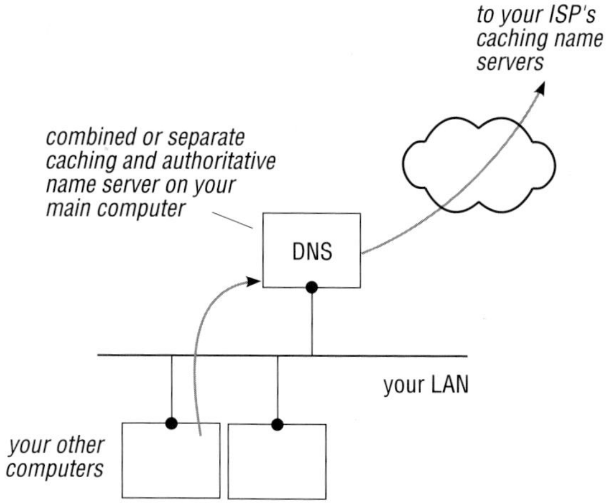

Figure 1.13: A possible SOHO scenario

1.4.3 Corporate environment

The corporate environment is the most difficult to describe, because there are so many possibilities.

Small to medium organizations

In a small to medium organization, you might use a couple of servers for DNS services to internal users, with separate authoritative servers to handle requests from the Internet for your public domain names (Figure 1.14).

- BIND can provide different sets of data (split-horizon) depending on whether queries are internal or external, by using views as we described in Section 1.2.3. Although we don't recommend you do so, BIND can simultaneously provide recursion for your internal clients.

- tinydns also provides split horizon DNS. Deployed together with dnscache it can fulfill all your DNS needs. If you have only one machine for both, you add dnsproxy to combine both services behind a single address.

- PowerDNS, with its multiple database back-ends, is the way to go if you want to integrate DNS services into an existing LDAP directory or SQL database. Its associated PowerDNS Recursor is a recursive name server which you use to provide recursive queries to your internal network.

Large organizations

Large organizations typically have many different name servers. As with smaller organizations (discussed above), they separate caching services from authoritative services. Apart

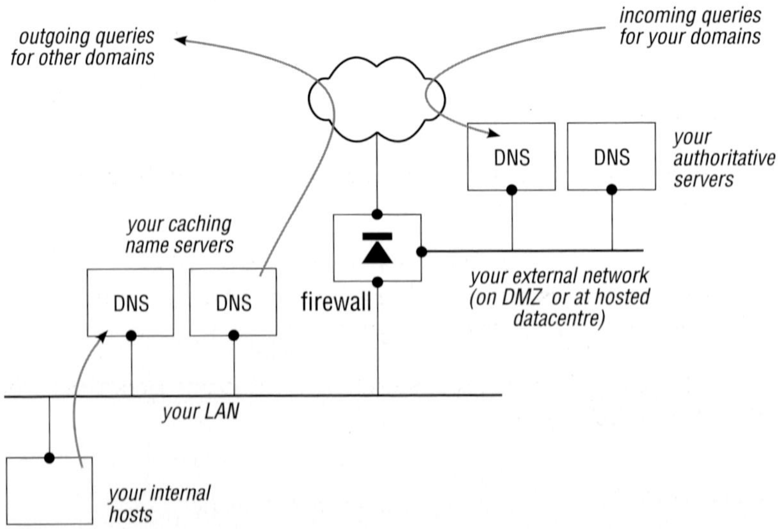

Figure 1.14: A typical setup for a small organization

from spreading their name servers over diverse geographical areas wherever possible, it is not unusual to find name servers on a departmental level. Large organizations often have a mixture of name server brands deployed, and many of the programs we discuss in Part II are sensible choices. Some suggestions:

- Bind DLZ integrates DNS with your LDAP directory server or SQL database environment.
- Bind DLZ with the Berkeley DB High Performance back-end provides database and high performance simultaneously.
- PowerDNS offers a large choice of back-end stores for DNS data, and you can also set it up to be master or slave server.
- Unbound or PowerDNS Recursor installed on separate machines provide your environment with fast recursive resolvers.
- BIND offers an incredible list of features and is often deployed in large organizations.
- If you require great performance, consider the NSD authoritative server.

A large number of combinations of the programs we discuss are possible, and many of them make good sense; the choice is yours. As an example, the DNS infrastructure for a real-life large corporation is shown in detail in the Notes.

This concludes our fast-forwarding over the terminology we'll be using throughout the book. In the next chapter, we discuss how you configure zone data and how different brands of server store it.

Summary

- The Domain Name System is a vital network service on the Internet as well as within corporate networks.
- Name servers that are configured with "knowledge" about the hosts in a domain are called authoritative for that domain.
- Caching name servers perform the hard work of query resolution, and they contact authoritative name servers in sequence to determine whether a queried name exists, and if it does, to obtain its requested DNS records.
- How you deploy DNS servers depends on the size of your organization, the knowhow available and the topology of your network.

Notes and further reading

- DNS Survey (see `http://dns.measurement-factory.com/surveys/200710.html`)
- ICANN's root-server map (see `http://www.icann.org/maps/root-servers.htm`)

Example of large corporate DNS implementation

For one of our large corporate customers we designed the following DNS environment. It consists of a public server that serves authoritative data for the domains owned by the company, and a separate private DNS environment including a private root, isolated from the Internet. The environment (Figure 1.15) has the following characteristics:

- Addressing on the internal networks is based on RFC 1918 Private IP addresses. Devices on the internal networks cannot communicate directly with the Internet.

  Internal users can surf the Internet only via a squid proxy server in the DMZ. User's workstations therefore do not require the public DNS. Instead, the squid proxy server uses a DNS cache to resolve host names.
- A set of BIND name servers with hidden PowerDNS servers provide authoritative public DNS services. Another pair of authoritative servers (not shown) are of a different brand: we do this to lower the risks involved due to possible software bugs and security problems.
- Separate dnscache servers provide caching name services to the machines in the DMZ.
- Because Mail Transfer Agents (MTA) on the internal network don't have access to the public DNS, they cannot resolve target host names via the DNS. Instead, the internal MTA use an external MTA in the DMZ as a *smart host* for transferring e-mail.
- Internal DNS is handled with a private root and a group of PowerDNS servers.

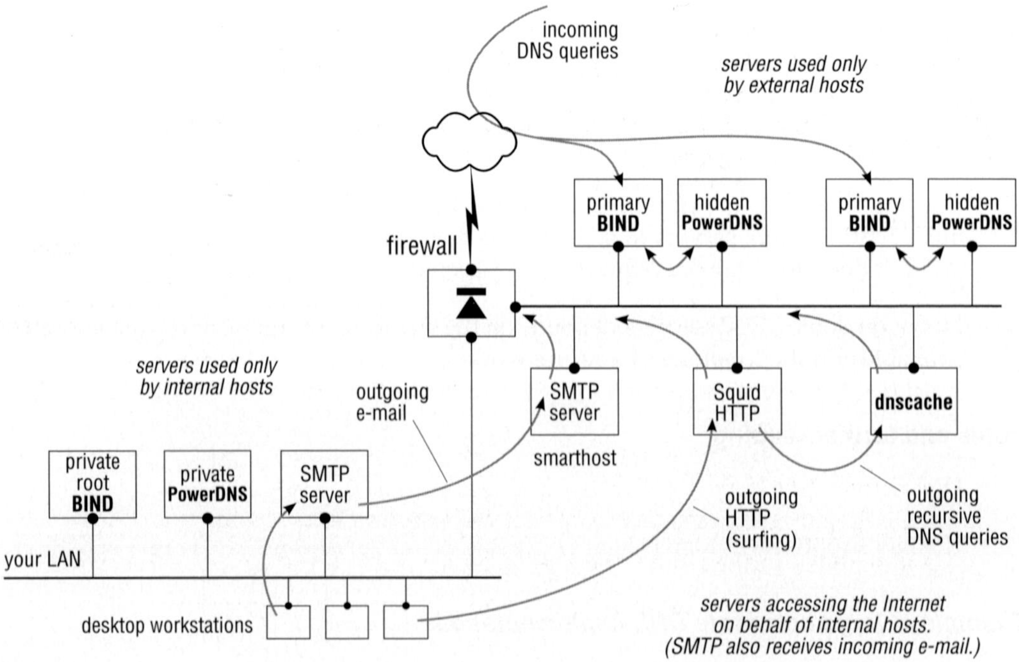

Figure 1.15: Sample of corporate DNS infrastructure

Practical TCP/IP

We highly recommend the companion book in this series, *Practical TCP/IP* by Niall Mansfield. This book is a must-have if you want to have a detailed insight into the workings of TCP/IP and its related protocols. The author dissects the protocols, shows you the content of data packets and gives hands-on tips on how to configure individual services on your network. The book contains three chapters on DNS.

Chapter

2 How to represent zone data and where to store it

The Internet works because a lot of people cooperate to do things together.

Jon Postel

Introduction

In the previous chapter we described how a Web browser, and a caching name server, sent DNS queries to a series of authoritative name servers to resolve the domain name qupps.biz. In this chapter we explain in detail the information that the client specifies in the query, the information the server returns in the answer, and how an authoritative server stores the information that it creates the answer from.

2.1 dig – a DNS lookup utility

When working with DNS, you need a tool that lets you issue queries to DNS servers. The commonly used tools are:

- The program of choice in all things DNS is dig.
- host is simpler than dig but written by the same people, isc.org.
- nslookup. This has been deprecated for many years. (Older versions on *nix warn you that it will be obsoleted; in newer versions of the BIND source distribution, the warning has been removed.) Don't use it, because it sometimes gives weird or un-useful error messages; use dig instead.
- The djbdns package has some nifty command-line tools, which are particularly useful in scripts. We discuss these in Chapter 11.
- unbound-host, from the Unbound distribution, is similar to host, but it can additionally verify DNSSEC keys (Chapter 17).

2.1.1 dig overview

dig is the only lookup utility we use throughout this book. It's readily available on most *nix platforms; if it's not already on your system, you can get it free via the BIND utilities (Chapter 7). In Chapter 14 we tell you how you get dig for Microsoft Windows.

dig is flexible about how it parses options and arguments, and you can pretty much intermix those however you like. The general syntax is:

dig @*server* *name* *type* *class* *opt*

where the arguments are:

server — *server* is the name or address of the server you want dig to send its queries to. If you omit @*server*, dig uses the system's resolver to find the address(es) of the DNS servers it should send queries to. The system's resolver typically consults `/etc/resolv.conf` to determine the addresses of the name servers it should use (Chapter 20).

We recommend you specify this as an IP address while testing. (If you specify a hostname, dig will have to use the system's resolver, i.e. use the DNS, to look up *server*'s IP address before performing the query you asked for, and this may be confusing.)

name — *name* is the domain name or IP address you want information about.

type — *type* is the type of query you want to perform – A, MX, etc. (Don't worry if these types don't mean a lot to you yet; we explain them fully later in the chapter.) *type* defaults to Address (A).

class — *class* is the query class. This is an historical item. It arose before TCP/IP became the dominant networking system; the class is now always "IN", for "Internet", which is the default. However, we have to mention it because you will see it all the time in DNS query listings and server configurations.

options — *options*, which control details of dig's operation. `dig -h` lists the available options. You enable an option by prefixing it with a plus sign (+); you disable an option by prefixing it with a minus sign (–).

2.1.2 Looking up an IP address (A record)

Use dig to query a name server for an Address. In the following example, we use no special dig *options*, and you'll notice we don't specify a *type* either, because dig's default query *type* is for an Address:

```
$ dig @127.0.0.1  ldap.qupps.biz
; <<>> DiG 9.2.4 <<>> @127.0.0.1 ldap.qupps.biz
; (1 server found)
;; global options:  printcmd
;; Got answer:
;; ->>HEADER<<- opcode: QUERY, status: NOERROR, id: 28350
;; flags: qr aa rd ra; QUERY: 1, ANSWER: 1, AUTHORITY: 2, ADDITIONAL: 2

;; QUESTION SECTION:
;ldap.qupps.biz.                        IN      A

;; ANSWER SECTION:
ldap.qupps.biz.         86400   IN      A       192.168.1.20

;; AUTHORITY SECTION:
qupps.biz.              86400   IN      NS      ns2.qupps.biz.
qupps.biz.              86400   IN      NS      ns1.qupps.biz.

;; ADDITIONAL SECTION:
ns1.qupps.biz.          86400   IN      A       192.168.1.20
ns2.qupps.biz.          86400   IN      A       192.168.1.173

;; Query time: 3 msec
;; SERVER: 127.0.0.1#53(127.0.0.1)
;; WHEN: Sun Jan 27 13:45:43 2008
;; MSG SIZE  rcvd: 116
```

The example above is typical of dig output:

- dig prints results in "master file" format, which is used by the BIND and NSD name servers, which we discuss later. (This is handy; you can use dig's output to create those files if you need to.)
- Lines beginning with a semicolon (`;`) are of an informative nature only, and indicate how you invoked dig and which options it used to query the name server. (In a master file semicolons indicate comments, which is why they indicate "for information only" here.)
- The *answer section* contains the answer to a query.
- The *authority section* shows the authoritative name servers for the queried domain.

- The *additional section* may contain additional DNS records supplied by the name server.

dig's output format is a very close representation of the content of a DNS reply packet. (If you want to learn in great detail what DNS packets contain, we recommend you read *Practical TCP/IP*; see Notes in Chapter 1.) The authority sections are populated by authoritative DNS servers to inform DNS clients whom to contact for authoritative information, and some name servers add the "additional section" to the reply, foreseeing that clients will want that information.

In our examples we often edit dig's output to show only the sections relevant to what we're discussing at the time.

2.1.3 Find version of remote name server, using dig

Most brands of name servers can be made to advertise their brand and version number, via a special domain called BIND (even on non-BIND name servers). The information is stored in a Text (TXT) record (page 44). You query this using the DNS to determine the version information. For historical reasons, the information is provided for the *Chaosnet* (a protocol over coax), so you must use the Chaos class (CH) when querying:

```
$ dig @127.0.0.1 version.bind ch txt
; <<>> DiG 9.2.4 <<>> @127.0.0.1 version.bind ch txt
; (1 server found)
;; global options:  printcmd
;; Got answer:
;; ->>HEADER<<- opcode: QUERY, status: NOERROR, id: 11872
;; flags: qr aa rd; QUERY: 1, ANSWER: 1, AUTHORITY: 1, ADDITIONAL: 0

;; QUESTION SECTION:
;version.bind.                  CH      TXT

;; ANSWER SECTION:
version.bind.           0       CH      TXT     "9.2.4"

;; AUTHORITY SECTION:
version.bind.           0       CH      NS      version.bind.

;; Query time: 0 msec
;; SERVER: 127.0.0.1#53(127.0.0.1)
;; WHEN: Sun Jan 27 13:53:38 2008
;; MSG SIZE  rcvd: 62
```

For security purposes, name servers can be, and often are, configured to hide their version information, so frequently the above will not work.

2.1.4 Transfer a zone with dig

By default, dig uses UDP to send queries to name servers. For testing purposes you can force dig to use TCP by giving the +tcp switch:

```
$ dig +tcp @127.0.0.1 domain_name qtype
```

If you set *qtype* to AXFR, dig initiates an incoming zone transfer for the specified zone, printing the result in master zone file format to standard output. (AXFR transfers are always done over TCP, so you don't have to specify the `+tcp` switch.)

```
$ dig @127.0.0.1 qupps.biz axfr
qupps.biz. 86400 IN SOA ns1.qupps.biz. jp.qupps.biz. 196205286 10800 900 604800 3600
qupps.biz. 86400 IN NS  ns1.qupps.biz.
qupps.biz. 86400 IN NS  ns2.qupps.biz.
qupps.biz. 86400 IN A   192.168.1.20
qupps.biz. 86400 IN MX  10 mail.qupps.biz.
...
...
```

This enables you to test zone transfers from your (or other people's) name servers. Note that the name server must support outgoing zone transfers and it must permit[1] you to transfer zones. (Most servers are configured *not* to allow zone transfers except to other servers owned by the same organization.)

2.1.5 Trace recursion using dig

If you want to trace how a host is resolved recursively, use the `+trace` option to dig:

```
$ dig +trace www.fupps.com
; <<>> DiG 9.2.4 <<>> +trace www.fupps.com
;; global options:  printcmd
.                   343211    IN   NS    F.ROOT-SERVERS.NET.
.                   343211    IN   NS    E.ROOT-SERVERS.NET.
...
;; Received 512 bytes from 127.0.0.1#53(127.0.0.1) in 0 ms

com.                172800    IN   NS    F.GTLD-SERVERS.NET.
com.                172800    IN   NS    E.GTLD-SERVERS.NET.
...
;; Received 491 bytes from 192.5.5.241#53(F.ROOT-SERVERS.NET) in 39 ms

fupps.com.          172800    IN   NS    ns49.1und1.de.
fupps.com.          172800    IN   NS    ns50.1und1.de.
;; Received 77 bytes from 192.31.80.30#53(D.GTLD-SERVERS.NET) in 141 ms

www.fupps.com.      10800     IN   A     82.165.102.119
;; Received 47 bytes from 195.20.224.149#53(ns49.1und1.de) in 37 ms
```

This shows how our caching server queries the various authoritative servers in order: first the root servers, then the .com servers, and finally the fupps.com servers which return the full answer we wanted.

2.2 Contents of a DNS query

When a DNS client queries an authoritative server for a domain, it supplies three pieces of information in the query:

[1] In 2008 a court in North Dakota, USA, ruled that performing a zone transfer as an unauthorized outsider, to obtain information that was not publicly accessible, constitutes trespass under U.S. law (see `http://www.spamsuite.com/node/351`).

1. The domain name of the object it is querying for (e.g. ldap.qupps.biz).
2. The "class" of the object it is querying for. This is the same as the "class" we explained in Section 2.1.1, so it will always be IN.
3. The type of information it wants about the domain – for example, the A record for the domain. This type is called the *query type* or *qtype*.

These three items are clearly shown in the QUESTION SECTION of dig's output:

```
$ dig @127.0.0.1  ldap.qupps.biz
...
;; QUESTION SECTION:
;ldap.qupps.biz.                         IN      A
```

Now we'll examine how a name server uses these items when it answers the query.

2.3 Resource records define information about a domain name

When you query a DNS server about a domain name, the server answers with pieces of information of a particular type about that domain name; each separate piece is shown on a line on its own in the one of the ANSWER, AUTHORITY, or ADDITIONAL sections of dig's output. Each piece describes one characteristic or *resource* of a node in the DNS tree, and is stored in a separate record in the the server's zone data file or database, so it's known as a *resource record* (*RR*). A zone file is just the set of all the resource records for the zone.

You can consider resource records from a slightly different perspective. Above we implicitly assumed that the resource records in the zone file just describe nodes in the tree that somehow exist in their own right. In fact, the resource records *define* the nodes in the tree (Figure 2.1), as well as containing descriptive information about them. If a node doesn't appear in the zone file of the server that's authoritative for the zone, then the node doesn't exist in the DNS tree.

To see how this works, consider dig querying for a particular type of information, MX say, about qupps.biz. quppz.biz's authoritative server receives the query, and checks its zone data as follows:

- If the server isn't authoritative for qupps.biz, the server returns an error code "I can't serve this" in the reply. You can recognize this because dig shows `status:REFUSED` in its output.
- If the domain qupps.biz doesn't exist, i.e. qupps.biz has no RRs anywhere in the zone file, the server returns an error code "non-existent domain" in the reply. You can recognize this because dig shows `status:NXDOMAIN` in its output.

  The NXDOMAIN indicates an authoritative negative answer (i.e. "Sorry, but this domain is non-existent").
- If qupps.biz does exist, the server now looks in its database for records that match the *type* specified in the query, MX in this case:

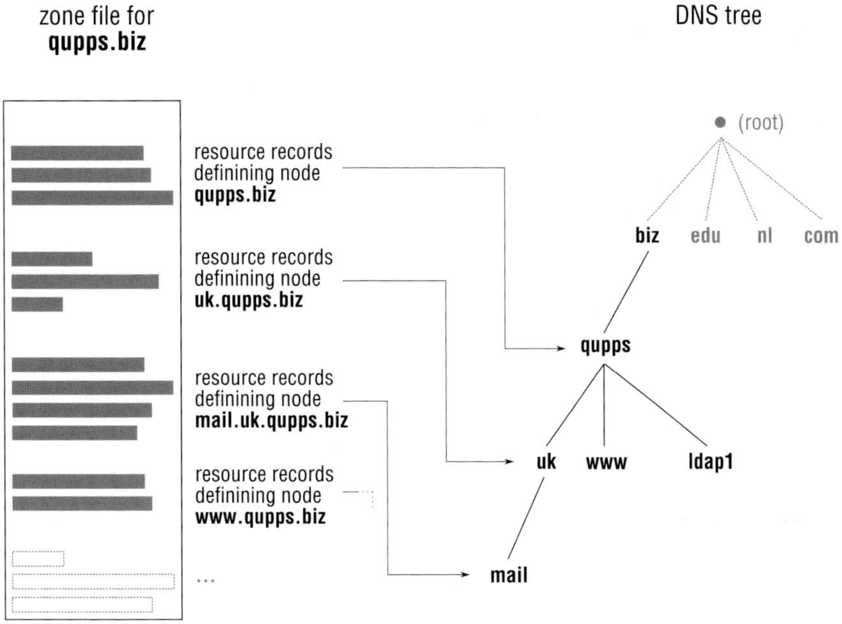

Figure 2.1: Resource records in the zone file define the nodes in the DNS tree

- If it finds any matching records, it returns them in the reply. dig shows them, one per line, in its ANSWER SECTION, and also shows the number of ANSWERs, in its `;; flags` output line.
- If there are no matching records, the server returns a reply containing zero ANSWERs.

Even if there were no matching records, dig outputs `status:NOERROR`: the server successfully found the requested domain, but it happened not to have any RRs of the type we were interested in.

Now we're going to explain in detail the types of resource records you're likely to come across, their contents, and what they are used for. But before we do that, we need to look at the format that's common to all resource records.

2.3.1 The format of a Resource Record

A resource record consists of five fields:

name *TTL* *class* *type* *rdata*

name The name of the domain that this resource record describes. This name is sometimes called an *owner* or the *origin*.

If *name* has a trailing period (e.g. qupps.biz.), it is usually taken to be a fully qualified domain name (FQDN, see Section 1.1.1). If you don't include a trailing period in *name*, it's interpreted as "unqualified" – relative to the current zone name. For example, in the qupps.biz file, the unqualified name mail is interpreted as mail.qupps.biz. If you specify a name as mail.qupps.biz (without the trailing period) in the qupps.biz zone file, it will be fully qualified for you, so the result will be a domain mail.qupps.biz.qupps.biz., which is probably not what you wanted.

Different brands of DNS server handle the qualification of *name* differently: some consider any *name* in the zone to be fully qualified, others don't require the trailing period. We discuss this wherever it is relevant.

In this chapter we fully qualify all domain names, for clarity. (Later on we relax the rule, because it will become obvious to you when we mean fully-qualified.)

Note that if you omit the *name*, the record is a defined with the same name as the previous record. We show you examples below.

TTL The "Time to Live" of the resource record, in seconds, i.e. how long this record is valid for. It is primarily used by caching name servers to decide how long they may cache the resource record for, before they discard it because it is out of date.

If you omit the *TTL* on a resource record, the zone's *TTL* is used (i.e. the *TTL* of the zone as defined in the Start of Authority record, see below).

class We already saw this in Section 2.1.1; this is always "IN", for "Internet".

type Specifies the kind of information this resource record describes, and has the same meaning as the qtype of a query. You've seen type A records in the dig examples (Section 2.1.2), and you're probably familiar with MX and PTR records too. We cover all the interesting types in the following sections.

rdata The data that describes the resource. The format and content of *rdata* are specific to the record type. For example the rdata of an A resource record contains a single IP address, whereas the *rdata* for an some other types contain multiple items, as we'll see later. Because the *rdata* field is the last field in a DNS resource, it's often referred to as the "right hand side".

The above specifies the format of records as entered in the flat-text zone data files used by the BIND and NSD servers. Some other servers can and do use other formats. However the BIND server has been so closely involved with the growth of the Internet that many of the DNS RFCs define standards in terms of BIND-specific syntax, and zones are often described using BIND's "zone master file" format. Consequently, you need to be familiar with this format, and it's what we use in the rest of this chapter. In later chapters, when covering servers that use different formats, we give full details of those formats.

2.3.2 Resource record sets

We said that a server returns zero or more resource records in reply to a query, and that dig displays these one per line. A single domain name, i.e. a node in the DNS tree, can have multiple resource records of the same type, and all of them will be returned in the answer to a query. For example, a multi-homed host (one with multiple network interfaces, each with its own IP address) will often have more than one A record, one for each IP address. Querying for such a name with dig shows something like:

name	*TTL*	*class*	*type*	*rdata*
www.qupps.biz.	3600	IN	A	192.168.1.20
www.qupps.biz.	600	IN	A	10.0.12.1
www.qupps.biz.	1800	IN	A	192.0.2.40
www.qupps.biz.	3600	IN	A	192.168.1.46

We expect the *rdata*, i.e. the IP addresses, to be different in each of the records, but note that the TTLs can also differ, although the other three fields of all the RRs are the same. A set of resource records with the same *name*, *class* and *type* is called a *resource record set* or *RRset*.

2.3.3 Resource records in detail

Address (A) resource records

An *Address* (type A) resource record associates an IP address with a domain name. For many nodes in the DNS tree, their single A record is the only entry in the zone file, so in these cases it is the A record that both creates the node (i.e. the domain name or hostname) in the tree, and gives it its IP address. The *rdata* portion of the record contains the single address in the usual dotted-quad notation:

name	*TTL*	*class*	*type*	*rdata*
www.qupps.biz.	3600	IN	A	192.168.1.20

A node can have more than one A record, as we saw for a multi-homed host, above. In such cases, you just add as many A records as necessary for that domain in your zone file. (And what would the resulting group of records be called? Right: a resource record set.)

Mail Exchanger (MX) resource records

When you e-mail `alexi@qupps.biz`, your e-mail server (or your ISP's e-mail server) must send it to "qupps.biz's e-mail server". How does your server find out which server that is, or even whether qupps.biz have a server? That's where MX records come in. Your e-mail server queries the DNS for a *Mail Exchanger* resource record for the qupps.biz domain. Mail Exchanger records define which hosts are willing to receive (and subsequently ensure delivery of) mail to qupps.biz. This might be one of qupps.biz's own mail servers on the Internet, or they might have arranged that their ISP's server will receive and forward qupps.biz's mail. You can have multiple MX records for a domain.

An MX's *rdata* consists of two parts: a decimal *preference* number, and a domain name of a host willing to accept e-mail for the domain. The host must be a hostname, not an IP address: an IP address in an MX record is illegal, and will cause conforming servers to ignore that MX record when they attempt to deliver mail. When there is more than one MX record, those with a low preference value will be used before those with a high preference. (If there's only one MX record for the domain, the preference has no effect.) If you have two or more records with the same preference, they are typically used in a pseudo-random order (i.e. the sending mail server uses them on a "first come, first served" basis). The preference is also called the *priority*.

In the example below, two mail servers are willing to handle incoming mail for qupps.biz. The host bigiron.qupps.biz is preferred (it has a lower preference value) over the mail server at the ISP. (QUPPS want mail to be delivered to their own server when possible, but if their server isn't reachable, mail should be sent to their ISP – who will presumably deliver to QUPPS later.)

name	*TTL*	*class*	*type*	*rdata*
`qupps.biz.`	`3600`	`IN`	`MX`	`70 my-isp.example.net.`
`qupps.biz.`	`3600`	`IN`	`MX`	`10 bigiron.qupps.biz.`

We strongly recommend you choose preference values that are "far apart" (e.g. 10, 20, 30... or even 100, 200, 300...) rather than "close together" (1, 2, 3...). The reason is that you can then easily "shove" another MX in between those, in case you have to quickly switch mail servers.

Do note that Mail Exchanger records are not a panacea; you still have to correctly configure your mail server to handle and accept incoming e-mail for domains you set up in Mail Exchanger records.

Pointer (PTR) resource records

A DNS client queries for a domain's A record to get the address for that name; this is called a *forward lookup* or *forward query*. A *reverse query* or *inverse query* is the opposite: it gets the domain name for an IP address. Reverse queries are performed by querying for the *Pointer* (PTR) resource record in a special domain called the in-addr.arpa domain. A client wishing to determine the domain name of an IP address reverses the octets of the IP address, and appends in-addr.arpa to form the domain name to query, and then it queries the DNS for a PTR record for that domain. For example, to reverse lookup the address 192.168.1.20, the name queried for is 20.1.168.192.in-addr.arpa:

name	*TTL*	*class*	*type*	*rdata*
`20.1.168.192.in-addr.arpa.`	`3600`	`IN`	`PTR`	`www.qupps.biz.`

With dig you use the `-x` option to query for a Pointer record, saving you from having to reverse the address's octets manually:

```
$ dig @127.0.0.1 -x 192.168.1.20
...
```

Because these resource records are in the in-addr.arpa domain and not in the qupps.biz domain, your authoritative server must be configured for an in-addr.arpa zone, and that must be delegated to it for reverse lookups to function (Chapter 18).

Forward and reverse queries

Many people think of two different types of queries, forward queries and reverse queries. However, if you look at the Address (A) and Pointer (PTR) records we discussed above, you see there is little difference in them:

- A *forward query* is one that performs name-to-address lookup, by querying the DNS for an A resource record.

- A *reverse query* or *inverse query* is one which performs address-to-name lookup, by querying the DNS for a PTR resource record.

Both of these search the DNS for a domain name: the difference is which domain is queried – the domain you specified, or the in-addr.arpa domain.

Canonical name (CNAME) resource records

CNAME records let you create an alias for a machine in your DNS. "CNAME" stands for *"canonical name"* – the "real" or "official" name of a host. (This term is a little watery, because basically any domain name with an A record is a canonical name.) Suppose you have a host with an Address record of:

```
name                  TTL       class   type    rdata
bigiron.qupps.biz.    3600      IN      A       192.168.1.17
```

You can make that domain name available under different names by creating aliases for it:

```
name                    TTL       class   type     rdata
imapserver.qupps.biz.   3600      IN      CNAME    bigiron.qupps.biz.
webserver.qupps.biz.    3600      IN      CNAME    bigiron.qupps.biz.
```

In the example above, bigiron.qupps.biz is the canonical name, and imapserver.qupps.biz and webserver.qupps.biz are aliases for it.

When a server is queried for a domain name and finds a CNAME for that name, the server replaces the name with the canonical ("real") name and looks up the new name instead, repeating this step as often as needed until the server finds an A record rather than a CNAME, and it replies with the canonical names, and the A records of those names. For example, a query of webserver.qupps.biz results in:

```
$ dig webserver.qupps.biz.
;; ->>HEADER<<- opcode: QUERY, status: NOERROR, id: 9628
;; flags: qr aa rd; QUERY: 1, ANSWER: 2, AUTHORITY: 2, ADDITIONAL: 2

;; ANSWER SECTION:
webserver.qupps.biz.    3600     IN      CNAME bigiron.qupps.biz.
bigiron.qupps.biz.      86400    IN      A     192.168.1.17
```

Common uses of CNAME records are:

- To give "nicer-looking" names to hosts.
- The extra level of indirection allows you to easily migrate webserver.qupps.biz to a different host without any reconfiguration of the hosts. If you change the CNAME of webserver.qupps.biz to point at bigtank.qupps.biz, all your clients would subsequently connect to the bigtank host.
- To have a number of web sites (www.example.net, www.qupps.biz, www.example.org) all reside on a single machine but give the impression that they are different machines.
- To create host names that represent different services, even though they (currently) run on a single host. Suppose you are starting off small and have a single machine

running mail services (SMTP, POP3, IMAP, LDAP) as well as a Web server, you create CNAME records for each of these services, which point to your host smallbox:

```
name                   TTL     class   type    rdata
smallbox.qupps.biz.    3600      IN    A        192.168.1.44
qupps.biz.             3600      MX    10       smallbox.qupps.biz.
pop3.qupps.biz.        3600      IN    CNAME smallbox.qupps.biz.
imap.qupps.biz.        3600      IN    CNAME smallbox.qupps.biz.
www.qupps.biz.         3600      IN    CNAME smallbox.qupps.biz.
ldap.qupps.biz.        3600      IN    CNAME smallbox.qupps.biz.
```

After some time, you realize that your Web server is very popular, and you decide to migrate it onto larger hardware. You acquire new hardware, give the machine a canonical name (newerbox) and get your Web server running. As soon as you have completed that task, you change your DNS and have the CNAME for www.qupps.biz point to the new box. We highlight the changes to your zone's data in bold:

```
name                   TTL     class   type    rdata
smallbox.qupps.biz.    3600      IN    A      192.168.1.44
newerbox.qupps.biz.    3600      IN    A      192.168.1.46
qupps.biz.             3600      MX    10     smallbox.qupps.biz.
pop3.qupps.biz.        3600      IN    CNAME smallbox.qupps.biz.
imap.qupps.biz.        3600      IN    CNAME smallbox.qupps.biz.
www.qupps.biz.         3600      IN    CNAME newerbox.qupps.biz.
ldap.qupps.biz.        3600      IN    CNAME smallbox.qupps.biz.
```

There are some things you must note about CNAME records:

- RFC 1034 explicitly states:

  If a CNAME RR is present at a node, no other data should be present

  For example, if you have a CNAME for host printer.example.net aliased to *anything*, then printer.example.net must not have any other DNS resource records associated with it[2]. This is a source of woe for many an administrator, and it is something you must look out for.

- You should never use the new alias in the *rdata* portion of a record – i.e. never put it on the right-hand-side of a resource record. In other words, the new alias webserver we created above must never be on the right hand side of a resource record; only place the canonical name there.

- For the same reason, an alias must not be used in a Name Server (page 43) or a Mail Exchanger record. (Using CNAMEs in MX records is a very common mistake.)

- You can use Address (A) records instead of CNAME records at any time. In fact, as they save the server from performing a level of indirection (searching for the Address of the canonical name), they are actually "faster".

[2]RFC 4034 allows for one exception to the rule: a resource of type RRSIG may coexist with a CNAME resource record.

The Start of Authority (SOA) resource records

The *Start of Authority* resource record can be thought of as a "header" for a zone. It contains management data, such as the e-mail address of the zone maintainer. It is called Start of Authority because it specifies the server which provides authoritative information about an Internet domain.

Every DNS zone *must* have exactly one SOA resource record. (There are brands of name servers that create a zone's SOA record automatically, without you having to explicitly enter it, but the end result is the same – the zone has an SOA.) The TTL of the SOA record defines the Time to Live for all records in a zone which don't override the SOA's TTL. In other words, you can set a TTL on the SOA record and "forget" about setting individual TTLs on each record.

The SOA record's *rdata* format differs from most other RRs. There are two different formats for expressing the same information:

- A single line, containing whitespace- separated values, as in:

```
example.com.  3600  IN SOA  dns.example.com. hostmaster.example.com.↩
       2007122401 86400 7200 3600000 172800
```

- Multiple lines, with each value on its own line, but with the set of values enclosed in parentheses (which is how a program recognizes this format), as in:

```
example.com.  3600  IN SOA  dns.example.com. hostmaster.example.com. (
       2007122401    ; serial YYYYMMDDnn
       86400         ; refresh (  24 hours)
       7200          ; retry   (   2 hours)
       3600000       ; expire  (1000 hours)
       172800 )      ; minimum (    2 days)
```

Most of the values in the Start of Authority record are necessary for the management of slave servers. You recall from Chapter 1, that a slave server "periodically" queries its master server whether the zone data has changed, in order to initiate a zone transfer if it has. The fields within the SOA define how often this check is performed.

The Start of Authority resource has the following seven values associated with it:

mname The *mname* is the name of the primary master name server for the zone. It is relevant only for Dynamic DNS updates; we discuss it in Chapter 19.

rname The *rname* is the e-mail address of the person responsible for the zone. Replace the "at" character (`@`) in the e-mail address by a period.

Good practice, recommended in RFC 2142, is to define (and maintain) a dedicated mail alias "hostmaster" for DNS operations, and ensure that that address is monitored. (Unfortunately, hostmaster addresses, like postmaster addresses, are a good target for spammers. The only thing you can do to avoid this spam is run a good spam filter.)

serial The serial number is an integer value that represents the "version number" of a zone. In practice, the serial number is often represented as a date in "YYYYMMDD" format with an additional "version per day" which caters for more than one modification in a day, as in:

```
2008052801
```

but you might prefer to start your serial numbers at 1 and simply increment them every time you modify a resource in your zone. Another format often encountered is the UNIX time (the number of elapsed seconds since the 1st of January 1970 at 00:00:00 UTC).

The serial number is important when you provide the zone to slave servers using AXFR zone transfer. Slaves use the serial number to detect whether a zone has changed, so they can initiate a zone transfer if required. The slave checks whether the current serial is greater than the last time it checked; if so, the zone file has changed. If you forget to *increase* the serial number when you add, delete or update any record in the zone, the slave will think the zone is unmodified, and will not transfer it; the slave will then be out of sync with the master.

If you don't provide the zone to slave servers, or if you have more than one primary server that uses native database replication to transfer zone data, then the serial number is never used for anything. Even so, we recommend that you always update it when you modify the zone, if only as an indication to yourself that you have modified the zone's data.

refresh The *refresh* value – the time, in seconds, after which a slave server should check with the master server whether the serial number in the zone's SOA has changed, to decide if the slave should initiate a zone transfer.

retry If a slave server failed to contact the zone's master (e.g. because it was down for maintenance, or because of a network failure), the slave will try again every *retry* seconds. It will continue do so at *retry* intervals until the expiry time (*expire*) has elapsed (see next item).

expire The time in seconds after which a zone is *expired*, i.e. the zone's data is too old to be of any value. A slave will not answer queries for a zone that has expired.

There are differing opinions as to how long the *expiry* time should be set; we recommend you set it to a very long period to cater for network outages that might last more than a week.

minimum The *minimum* field has had a number of different meanings in the past, but RFC 2308 (*Negative Caching of DNS Queries*) has obsoleted those, and now defines *minimum* to be how long, in seconds, that a (caching) name server may cache a negative answer returned for a query. (In other words, *minimum* is the Time to Live for a NXDOMAIN answer.)

Note that the *serial* number as well as the *refresh*, *retry*, and *expire* times, are all defined in the zone database on the primary server, but they are *used* by the secondary or slave server to determine when and how often to perform an incoming zone transfer for the zone.

The *refresh* and *retry* values affect zone maintenance and have to be negotiated between zone maintainer and secondary service operators. Modern DNS servers implement the NOTIFY protocol making these values less important, but if notifications are neither available nor implemented or perhaps even get lost in transit, the slave server will attempt to transfer the zone automatically. We recommend you use SOA values as in the examples above.

Name Server (NS) resource records

The resolution example in Section 1.1.4 showed a series of authoritative name servers being queried in turn, to obtain the final answer for a query. The root server had delegated .biz to the .biz servers, which in turn delegated qupps.biz to QUPPS. Delegation is implemented by means of *Name Server* (NS) resource records. The zone file on the parent server contains, in NS records, the addresses of the name servers that the child domain is delegated to (i.e. the NS records contain the names of the servers authoritative for the child domain). Figure 2.2 shows the three delegations from the root to es.qupps.biz.

There can, and should, be more than one Name Server resource record in a zone, each containing the host name of a different authoritative server. As we said in Section 1.2.2, you typically want to create resilience for your name servers, and there are DNS registries that insist on having more than one name server (e.g. the DENIC in Germany).

The name server specified in an NS record must be a canonical name (i.e. a real hostname as you define with an A RR), not an IP address or an alias.

```
name           TTL      class   type   rdata
qupps.biz.     3600     IN      NS     ns1.qupps.biz.
qupps.biz.     3600     IN      NS     dns.my-isp.example.net.
```

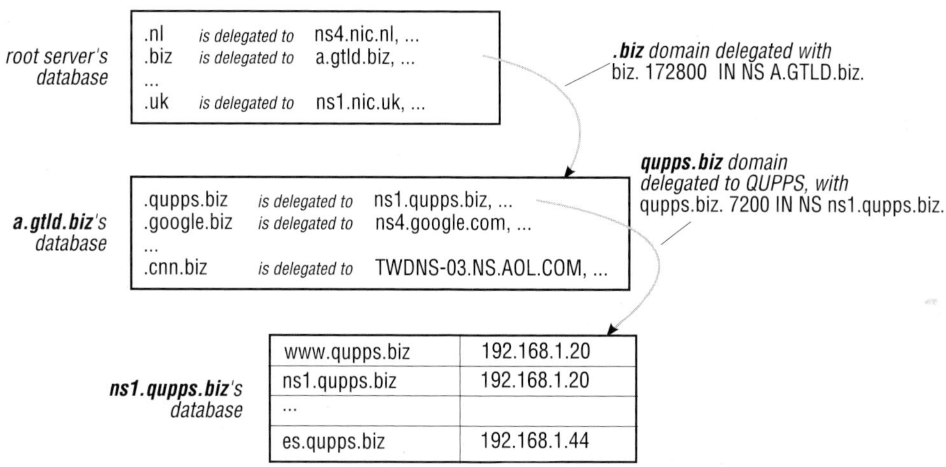

Figure 2.2: How NS resource records are used to delegate sub-domains

If a zone contains an NS record for, say ns9.example.com, but that name server does not exist, or does not answer authoritatively for the zone, you have what is called a *lame delegation*. You have wrongly delegated authority to a name server that isn't (or doesn't believe it is) authoritative for the zone.

Text (TXT) *resource records*

A *Text* (TXT) resource record contains arbitrary text strings with a total length of less than 256 characters.

```
name              TTL        class    type     rdata
qupps.biz.        3600                TXT      "contact Fred for details"
t.qupps.biz.      3600                TXT      one two three
x.qupps.biz.      3600                TXT      "had a little" "lamb"
```

Strings in text records are typically specified within double quotes as in the first example above. If you omit the quotes, each white-space separated word is quoted in the DNS reply. The following examples show the results of queries on the TXT records defined above:

```
$ dig @127.0.0.1 qupps.biz txt
;; ANSWER SECTION:
qupps.biz.        3600    IN   TXT "contact Fred for details"

$ dig @127.0.0.1 t.qupps.biz txt
;; ANSWER SECTION:
t.qupps.biz.      3600    IN   TXT "one" "two" "three"

$ dig @127.0.0.1 x.qupps.biz txt
;; ANSWER SECTION:
x.qupps.biz.      3600    IN   TXT "had a little" "lamb"
```

You can use TXT resource records for all sorts of things (Section G.1) but do remember, that anyone who can query your DNS can see your TXT records, so make sure they don't contain confidential or security-related information.

Service (SRV) *resource records*

SRV (*Service*) records let applications query the DNS to find the server(s) providing a particular service. For example, suppose you have three LDAP servers called ldap1, ldap5 and ldap7. Normally you'd configure your LDAP client by specifying the hostnames and TCP port numbers of each of the three servers servers. However, using DNS SRV records, you define a domain name, _ldap._tcp and in this domain create three SRVs, one for each of ldap1, ldap5 and ldap7. (The name *_service._protocol* is a convention.) A client that supports SRV records then queries domain _ldap_tcp for SRV records, and gets the three server names as answer.

The format of the RR is

_service._proto.name ttl class SRV *priority weight port target*

The *rdata* for SRV records contains:

service — *service* is the symbolic name of the desired service, such as `ldap` or `http`. An underscore ("_") is prepended to the service identifier to avoid collisions with existing DNS names you may have defined.

proto — *proto* is the symbolic name of the desired protocol (i.e. "`tcp`" or "`udp`") with an underscore prepended to it.

name — *name* is the domain name.

priority indicates the order in which this host should be used, in the same way MX uses its own preference field.

weight The weight field specifies a relative weight for entries with the same priority. If you have two SRV records with the same priority, you might specify 60 as the weight for the first and 40 for the weight of the second RR. This would cause the first target (see below) to be used 60% of the time and the second target to be used for 40% of the requests. If there is only one SRV record for a domain, it should use a weight of zero.

port The TCP or UDP port number of the service on the target host.

target The domain name of the target host. This must be a canonical name, not an alias or an Address, i.e. the domain name must have at least one Address (A) record. If *target* contains a single period (`.`), the service is explicitly not available at the domain, but you may well have other SRV records for the same service pointing to other targets.

Here's an example that lets clients who want to connect to an LDAP server over TCP find our three LDAP servers.

name	*TTL*	*class*	*type*	*rdata*
`ldap1.qupps.biz.`	`3600`	`IN`	`A`	`192.168.2.31`
`ldap5.qupps.biz.`	`3600`	`IN`	`A`	`192.168.2.35`
`ldap7.qupps.biz.`	`3600`	`IN`	`A`	`192.168.2.37`
`_ldap._tcp.qupps.biz.`	`3600`	`IN`	`SRV`	`30 0 389 ldap1.qupps.biz.`
`_ldap._tcp.qupps.biz.`	`3600`	`IN`	`SRV`	`30 0 389 ldap5.qupps.biz.`
`_ldap._tcp.qupps.biz.`	`3600`	`IN`	`SRV`	`30 0 389 ldap7.qupps.biz.`

A SRV-conforming client that wants to discover an LDAP directory server and speak to it via TCP, would perform a query for _ldap._tcp.qupps.biz with a query type of SRV. As we've specified the same priority for all three it will use one of the servers at random.

Unfortunately, DNS SRV records are catching on only slowly. The Name Service Switch (NSS), which we discuss in Chapter 20 uses them, and recent versions of Microsoft Windows use them extensively.

That concludes our discussion of the individual resource records. In the next section we show how you gather all these individual records together to form a correctly-constructed zone file.

2.4 Creating zones from resource records

So we now have a bunch of typical DNS records, but what do we do with them? We use the records described earlier to create a zone. As we said in Section 2.3.1, the record syntax we have used so far is what BIND and NSD use for zone files, so the rest of this chapter will use the same syntax. Other servers use different formats, which we explain fully when dealing with those servers, but the following illustrates the basic principles in constructing a zone, no matter which brand of server you're using.

2.4.1 Define a minimal zone

A zone *must* contain at least a Start of Authority (SOA) resource record, so you can define a full zone by creating just that. Some brands of name server (e.g. BIND) require that a zone also contain NS records, so we add one of these as well.

```
name          TTL   class type   rdata
qupps.biz. 3600    IN   SOA    dns.qupps.biz.    jp.foo.bar.   1 86400 7200 3600 1800
qupps.biz. 3600    IN   NS     dns.qupps.biz.
```

Although this zone can be loaded by a name server, it's not very useful:

- The SOA defines the *mname* to be dns.qupps.biz, but there is no such address defined in the zone.
- We have defined a Name Server (NS) record for the zone, but we don't have an Address for it.

2.4.2 A more realistic "minimal" zone

One of the name servers is our own, so we add an Address (A) record for that. The other name server is located at our ISP and they have set up an A record for my-isp.example.net.

```
name              TTL  class  type  rdata
qupps.biz.        3600 IN     SOA   dns.qupps.biz. jp.foo.bar. 2 86400 7200 3600 1800
qupps.biz.        3600 IN     NS    dns.qupps.biz.
qupps.biz.        3600 IN     NS    my-isp.example.net.
dns.qupps.biz.    3600 IN     A     192.168.1.20
```

2.4.3 Add desktop hosts, and Web and e-mail servers

The zone we defined above still isn't very useful. Let's make it more realistic:

- We have several hosts we want to access by name, so we add A records for them:

  ```
  name               TTL    class type   rdata
  ns1.qupps.biz.     3600   IN    A      192.168.1.20
  pc1.qupps.biz.     3600   IN    A      192.168.1.18
  ldap.qupps.biz.    3600   IN    A      192.168.1.164
  ```

  Note that we now have two hostnames (ns1 and dns) with the same IP address; that is perfectly legal.

- We also want to have a neat name for our Web server, but we don't have a separate machine for it – it currently runs on 192.168.1.164. We could add an Address (A) record for it, but we'll do it with an Alias (CNAME), because that better reflects the real configuration of our network:

  ```
  name               TTL   class  type   rdata
  www.qupps.biz.     3600   IN    CNAME ldap.qupps.biz.
  ```

- Our mail server software has also been installed on the same machine as the Web server. We want the world to know we can receive mail on this, so we add an MX for it:

```
name          TTL   class  type   rdata
qupps.biz.    3600  IN     MX     100 ldap.qupps.biz.
```

  Note:

  - We have to use the host's canonical name and we must not use the newly created Alias (www) on the Mail Exchanger (MX) record.
  - The right hand side of the record (i.e. the *rdata* field) must not contain an IP address.
  - As we only have one server capable of accepting e-mail, the preference value is irrelevant at this point.

2.4.4 Add a reverse zone

So far, our zone lets people query to find the address of our named hosts. For example, `dig pc1.qupps.biz.` will return 192.168.1.18. We would also like to be able to query an IP address to get its name: i.e. we'd like to be able to `dig -x 192.168.1.18` and get the answer pc1.qupps.biz. To do this we must set up a reverse zone.

The real difference between a "forward" and a "reverse" or inverse zone is the domain name you use, both in the query and the zone file. In Section 2.3.3 we explained address-to-name lookups query for the reversed IP address octets in the in-addr.arpa domain. The address space allocated to our domain qupps.biz is 192.168.1/24, so we have to set up a zone file for 1.168.192.in-addr.arpa. We are assuming that a delegation to our domain has already been set up. (Remember that being authoritative means that we have configured our name servers correctly and that a delegation to our zone exists.) We set up the zone file as follows:

```
$ORIGIN .
$TTL 86400        ; 86400 seconds = 1 day
1.168.192.in-addr.arpa    IN SOA  ns1.qupps.biz. hostmaster.mens.de. (
                  200612688  ; serial
                  28800      ; refresh (8 hours)
                  14400      ; retry (4 hours)
                  3600       ; expire (5 weeks 6 days 16 hours)
                  86400      ; minimum (1 day)
                  )
                                  NS      ns1.qupps.biz.

20.1.168.192.in-addr.arpa.        PTR   ns1.qupps.biz.
17.1.168.192.in-addr.arpa.   3600 PTR   bigiron.qupps.biz.

$ORIGIN 1.168.192.in-addr.arpa.
51                                PTR   dom.mens.de.
```

There are several points to note:

- The first two lines contain special directives which are typical of zone master files:

$ORIGIN — This takes a string as argument. It defines the "origin" for the zone file: all *names* within the file have the string automatically appended unless they are FQDNs, i.e. unless you ended them with a period. The third line above (1.168.192.in-addr.arpa) is not fully qualified, so the origin (which we specified to be " . ", qualifies it, giving 1.168.192.in-addr.arpa. (qualified with a terminating period). On line 15 we change the origin, and as a result the name `51` on line 16 is interpreted as 51.1.168.192.in-addr.arpa..

$TTL — The Time To Live in this directive specifies a default TTL for each resource record in the file. You can override the TTL for a record, as we have done for the PTR to bigiron on line 13.

- The Name Server (NS) record on line 10 appears not to have a *name* associated with it, but it has: as we said on page 36, if you omit *name*, it defaults to the last one used, 1.168.192.in-addr.arpa. in this case.

- On line 16 we have a Pointer to a domain name (dom.mens.de) that doesn't belong to us. Is that allowed? Yes, it is. Since you are authoritative for the inverse zone 192.168.1, you can create whatever records you think necessary.

2.4.5 Inconsistencies

You will note that there are several inconsistencies in the two zones we created above for qupps.biz and for 1.168.192.in-addr.arpa:

- The serial numbers in the SOA records don't match. That is quite normal and they do not have to match; you may have updated one file more often than the other.

- We have A records with no matching Pointers (PTR). The DNS standards don't demand that you have matching pairs, although you will probably want to.

- Because the forward and reverse domains are handled with two completely separate zone files, if you are going to have matched forward/reverse zones, you will usually have to do it "manually" yourself – by editing one file to take account of any changes you make in the other. (However, the MaraDNS and tinydns servers do manage this automatically for you, and we will discuss easy ways to keep forward/reverse zones in sync on other brands of name server.)

Notes on master file syntax

- There is no specific order in which resource records must appear in a master zone file. You can put them in any order, but resource records in zone master files are typically ordered as shown in our examples.

- The master file can contain a domain named * (asterisk):

```
name              TTL   class  type   rdata
*                 3600  IN     CNAME  bigiron.qupps.biz.
```

This is a *wild card* for the domain. A query for any domain name, in this zone, that has no explicit record in the zone file, is matched by the wild card. For example, a request for the domain frobizz.qupps.biz would receive the CNAME record as answer.

- A semi-colon (`;`) indicates a comment. Comments can start anywhere on a line and continue until the end of the line.

2.5 How and where zone data is stored

An authoritative name server has to store its definition of zones and resource records somewhere, so it can access the data when it needs it, to respond to incoming DNS queries. There are two ways to store zone data:

1. In flat files on the local file system. We can sub-divide this classification according to the syntax used in the zone file:
   (a) Zone master files, used by BIND, NSD, and PowerDNS (with the BIND back-end).
   As we said, the format of resource records we showed you in the earlier sections is zone master file format.
   (b) Program-specific file format. Instead of using master-file format, the program's author has defined his own. (As master file syntax is messy, defining a simpler but equivalent representation for the data is a good idea.)
   MaraDNS uses a text format similar to that of a zone master file with a number of shortcuts. tinydns uses a text format consisting of lines with colon-separated fields. We'll describe each format in detail when we come to it.
2. In external databases or directories.

In the rest of this chapter we look at the advantages and disadvantages of the two approaches, and give an overview of what's involved in using back-end databases or directories.

2.5.1 Advantages and disadvantages of text files for zone data

Good reasons for storing zone data in text files include:

- You can enter or modify zone data using any text editor. No special-purpose data maintenance program has to be developed, ported to different platforms, and maintained.
- Plain text files are easy to maintain and to store. They can be put into a version control system for tracking changes and alterations.
- Plain text files are easily transferred over networks by e-mail or by using tools like rsync, rdist, scp (but this applies to any type of file really).

- Plain text files can easily be generated from other sources of data. We discussed above how you might use dig to get answers to DNS queries which you store in master zone files.

  You might also be interested in storing your zone data in an SQL database and generating zone text files from that; we discuss that in Chapter 19.

On the other hand, storing zone data in text files has downsides:

- All the text formats for zone files have complicated syntax. It's easy to make errors – e.g. by omitting a punctuation or separator character – that render a zone useless and prevent it being processed by the name server.
- Many text editors don't lock the file you are editing, so you could inadvertently undo or overwrite a modification recently performed on the same file by a colleague.
- File-locking issues make it difficult to implement tools that allow several administrators to update zone data simultaneously.
- Replication of text files from one machine to another, though easy, has to be implemented on a case-by-case basis.

For these reasons, you might either choose a brand of name server that doesn't use text files, or even if your server does use text files, store the definitive copy of your zone data in some other way, and then automatically generate the text file with a suitable program.

2.5.2 Zone data in databases and directories

As we said, the alternative to storing zone data in text files is to use some form of back-end data store instead. The two commonly-used back-ends are: Relational Database Management Systems (RDBMS), also called SQL databases, and LDAP directory servers. Reasons for using a back end include:

- You may already have integrated a lot of your infrastructure into an SQL database or an LDAP directory. For example, it's very common to use an LDAP directory to store e-mail addresses of all employees and clients, configuration data, etc. Tying in your DNS system with this makes sense (Microsoft Windows does this with Active Directory.)
- Using a data source separate from your DNS server can reduce duplication and ease your maintenance tasks. If you intend to (or already have) data such as e-mail addresses, host configuration, etc. in your LDAP directory or database, adding DNS data to it keeps all this diverse data centralized, and you can use the same management tools and backup procedures to handle it.
- You can automate addition and modification of DNS records in a way that isn't possible (without a lot of fancy work) using zone master files. (We discuss this further in Section 2.5.5.)

On the other hand:

- An external database means you have to learn about it. If you want to store zone data in an LDAP directory, you need to know about that directory, how to manage it, how to add entries to it, etc. Similarly, if you want to use an SQL database, you will need to have an understanding of SQL, you will need to learn how to manage the SQL database, create backups, etc. We show you how to implement an LDAP directory server in Appendix A.

- An external database adds an extra level of software to your DNS infrastructure, which needs to be maintained and cared for, and it makes your setup more complex.

- Using an external data source will *not* make your DNS servers answer queries faster.

- Unfortunately, there is no standard for how to represent DNS resource records in databases or LDAP directories. There are several different methods to choose from. We recommend you consider this carefully when planning your implementation, as moving from one brand of DNS server to another might involve changing the format of all the data in your back-end.

Now we'll consider what's involved in using, first, an SQL back-end, and then, an LDAP back-end.

2.5.3 SQL databases

Next to ordinary file systems, relational database management systems (RDBMS) are the most common data storage technology today, and have been for the last 30 years. RDBMS have become even more popular with the advent of GNU/Linux and FreeBSD systems which come with the MySQL and PostgreSQL databases more or less as standard. An advantage of SQL databases over LDAP directories is that many SQL systems support atomic transactions, making it possible to *roll back* out of a mass-update gone wrong.

DNS resource records are represented differently in an SQL database than in a text-file, although the information content is equivalent. A zone is represented by one or more *rows* of data in one or more database *tables*. Individual components of a resource record are usually contained in different *columns* of a row. The database *schema* that is used is defined by the DNS server's author. We will explain the format when we discuss the brands of name server that support SQL.

Databases supported by DNS servers

- MySQL and PostgreSQL are supported by: MyDNS, BIND SDB, Bind DLZ, and PowerDNS.

- PowerDNS' OpenDBX back-end supports a number of database systems, including Firebird, Interbase, Sybase, Oracle and SQLite.

- PowerDNS has a (deprecated) DB2 back-end.

Replication of zone data stored in an SQL back-end

It is imperative to ensure that more than one name server doesn't access only one database back-end or you would create a single point of failure: if your database server collapsed, all your DNS servers accessing it would be left without a data store. You should use database replication to ensure timely duplication of data from your single master database to one or more slave databases (Figure 2.3). MySQL possibly has a small advantage over PostgreSQL because MySQL has replication built in, whereas with PostgreSQL you need add-ons such as Slony-I (see `http://slony.info/`) or pgpool-II (see `http://pgpool.projects.postgresql.org/`).

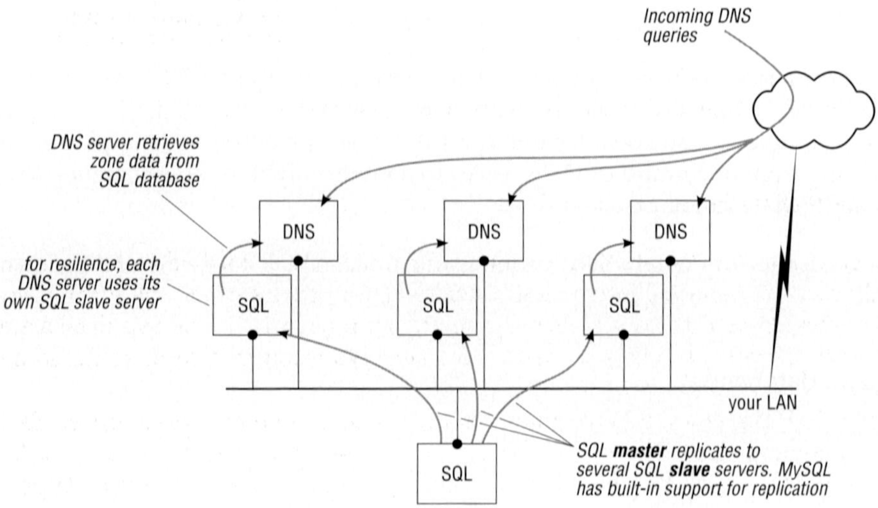

Figure 2.3: Database replication ensures resilience

Figure 2.3 shows each DNS server accessing its own database server, but we recommend you keep the data as close as possible to the DNS server (from a network point of view) and that you deploy both the DNS name server and its SQL database server on the same machine (Figure 2.4).

Manipulating records in an SQL database

There are several ways to add, update or delete records in an SQL database:

- Most SQL databases have a command-line interface that let you submit SQL statements to manipulate data. MySQL has the mysql program; PostgreSQL has psql.
- MySQL provides the MySQL Administrator and MySQL Query browser tools. A good Web-based utility is phpMyAdmin (see `http://www.phpmyadmin.net`).
- For PostgreSQL, pgAdmin III is a cross-platform administration tool, and PhpPgAdmin is a Web-based administration tool (see `http://phppgadmin.sourceforge.net/`).

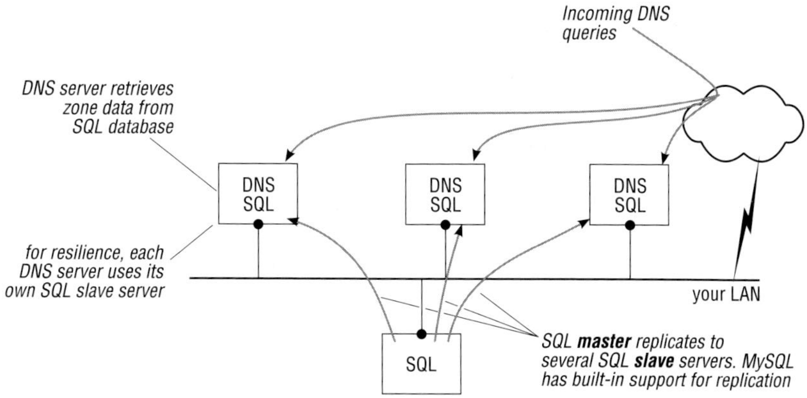

Figure 2.4: Database server and SQL server on one machine

2.5.4 LDAP Directories

Many organizations integrate their configuration data, and security data for authentication and authorization services, into a single, consolidated, data store in the form of an LDAP directory. The LDAP directory is then the single point from which all this data is managed. In such environments it makes sense to store the DNS resource records in the same LDAP directory.

In an LDAP directory, a DNS zone is represented as one or more entries. Each entry contains several attribute types, each representing a specific DNS resource record. (If you are new to LDAP, or want to refresh your memory, we discuss these terms in Appendix A.)

DNS servers that support LDAP

The following name servers can store zone data in LDAP directories: BIND SDB, Bind DLZ, PowerDNS, and ldapdns.

Microsoft Windows DNS Server can be made to store zone data in Active Directory. (Although Active Directory is accessible via LDAP, the format of the entries containing DNS resources is undocumented, which means you cannot manipulate DNS zone data in an Active Directory via LDAP.)

Choice of LDAP directory servers

If you already have a directory server, such as Novell eDirectory, Microsoft Active Directory or similar, you will use that. If you don't yet have a directory server, we recommend OpenLDAP, an Open Source implementation of an LDAP directory server and associated programming libraries and utilities (see `http://www.openldap.org`). We show you in Appendix A how you acquire, install and configure a ready-built package of OpenLDAP.

Replicating LDAP data

To avoid a single point of failure, to spread the performance load, or to service geographically dispersed clients, you can run multiple identical copies of an LDAP directory server (Figure 2.5).

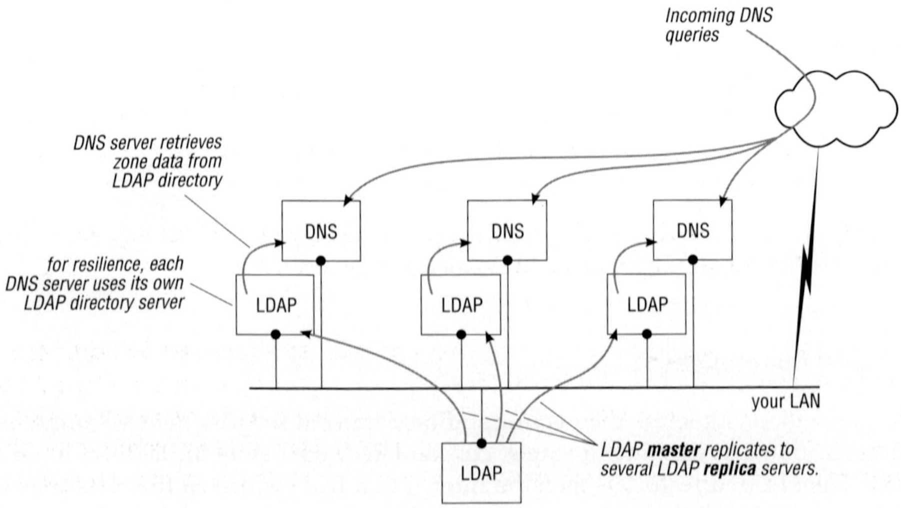

Figure 2.5: Directory server replication ensures resilience

Figure 2.5 shows each DNS server accessing its own directory server, but we recommend you keep the data as close as possible to the DNS server (from a network point of view) and that you deploy both the DNS name server and its LDAP directory server on the same machine, as we showed you above for the SQL databases.

If you're going to use an LDAP directory server as the back-end for a DNS server, replication is essential. You should *never* have more than one name server accessing a single directory server; that would create a single point of failure: if your directory server goes down, all DNS servers querying it are left without a data store. Having more than one DNS server reading entries from a single LDAP directory server is a sure road to disaster.

Manipulating entries in an LDAP directory

The following are editors ("*LDAP browsers*") for creating, modifying or deleting entries in an LDAP directory: task:

- phpLDAPadmin is a Web-based LDAP browser that you can install on a Web server (see `http://phpldapadmin.sourceforge.net/`).
- LDAP Browser/Editor is written in Java. It runs on a variety of platforms (see `http://www-unix.mcs.anl.gov/~gawor/ldap/`).

- The Apache Directory Project has released an Eclipse-based application called Apache Directory Studio which runs on a multitude of platforms (see `http://directory.apache.org/studio/`).
- If you use Microsoft Windows, you may be interested in the commercial *Softerra LDAP Administrator* (see `http://www.ldapadministrator.com/`).
- *ldapadmin* also runs on Microsoft Windows; it lets you browse, search, modify, create and delete objects on an LDAP server. It also supports more complex operations such as directory copy and move between remote servers and extends the common edit functions to support specific object types (such as DNS zones and records) with templates (see `http://ldapadmin.sourceforge.net/`)
- web2ldap is a WWW to LDAP gateway by Michael Ströder. It lets you access and manipulate the content of an LDAP directory server, and also includes a schema browser (see `http://www.web2ldap.de/`).
- We prefer command line tools, and recommend ldapvi by David Lichteblau. This searches an LDAP directory for entries, and drops you into your preferred text editor with an LDIF (LDAP Data Interchange Format) representation of the entries. When you save the file in your editor, ldapvi asks whether you want to commit the changes, and if so, it updates the directory (see `http://www.lichteblau.com/ldapvi/`).

2.5.5 How you maintain zone data stored in a back-end

In this book we show you how you create zones and DNS resource records for servers that use a database or an LDAP directory back-end. We do this using utilities that are readily available:

- For the MySQL database examples, we use the mysql command-line interface supplied as part of the MySQL package.
- For the LDAP directory examples, we use ldapadd or ldapmodify because you will have these installed as the basic utilities provided by your LDAP directory server software.

These basic tools are fine for experimenting, and you can (and should) use them to "look" at the contents of your back-end data store. But we don't recommend you use these tools for the day-to-day operational tasks of adding new zones and resource records to your DNS. Apart from easily introducing errors, you simply won't *want* to use them as the primary interface to your DNS data. There are, however, a number of alternatives you can consider:

- We discussed above that you can use graphical or Web-based utilities to manage the data. These are only slightly better than the command-line programs because they force you to "think" about the data you are entering (does the TTL value go in this table column?, must I fully qualify the domain name?, etc.).
- We discuss some other Web-based utilities you can use, in Chapter 19. These are typically a bit better because they isolate you from the structure of the underlying data.

Unfortunately they are often not the perfect solution because some of the tools are simply not comfortable or "clever" enough. For example, most Web interfaces allow you to add a CNAME for a domain even if there is "other data" present, and that is not allowed by the DNS specification.

- Simple shell scripts you whip up often provide great flexibility and comfort, particularly for repetitive tasks. For example, suppose you frequently add new zones to your LDAP directory; instead of maintaining an LDIF file and remembering how to run that through ldapadd to add entries to your directory, create a tiny shell script to do so:

```
#!/bin/sh

[ $# -ne 1 ] && { echo "Usage: $0 zonename" >&2; exit 1; }
ZONE=$1

ldapadd -x -D cn=manager,dc=qupps,dc=biz -W << !EndZone
dn: relativeDomainName=@,zoneName=${ZONE},dc=qupps,dc=biz
objectClass: dNSZone
zoneName: ${ZONE}
dNSTTL: 86400
...
!EndZone
```

  Although it may be obvious to you that small tools like these greatly simplify daily tasks, time and time again many people forget to use these time-savers.

- Custom made tools that you create to solve a particular task are most flexible. They give you fine control over how you update DNS data stored in a database or LDAP directory. Most modern programming languages have APIs for MySQL (or PostgreSQL) and LDAP, so you can use whatever language you feel most comfortable with.

  For example, if you often create DNS zones with similar resource records in them, you write a program that issues the corresponding SQL `INSERT` or LDAP `add` commands; invoking, say:

```
$ my-addzone example.net
```

  is much faster than messing about with most utilities, and, with a bit of extra work, you can make the program available to colleagues or users who don't have access to a login shell, as a CGI script which they invoke through a Web browser.

- If you have to provide DNS management tools for inexperienced users, we strongly recommend you take the time to create tools (whether Web-based, command-line, or graphical) that very carefully inspect the data before your utility adds it to the back-end data store. Say, for example, a user enters a domain name and doesn't fully qualify it with a period. If the brand of DNS server you deploy expects it to be qualified, you might spend quite some time looking a reason why the domain is not being resolved by your DNS server.

2.5.6 Provisioning text files from a database back-end

Even if you decide to use a DNS server that stores its zone data in text files, you can store the definitive copy of the data in an SQL or LDAP back-end, and periodically generate working copies of the necessary text files from the back-end (Figure 2.6).

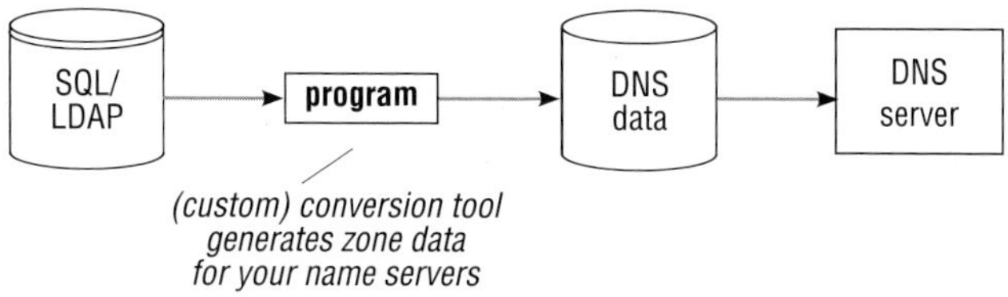

Figure 2.6: Generating zone data from SQL/LDAP

The benefit of this approach is that maintenance of the zone data is easier (you can use similar tools to manage users and DNS data in your database or directory), and your DNS server always has access to its zone data, even if the back-end goes down for a while. We discuss this in Chapter 19.

Summary

- A zone consists of a set of resource records, each of which has a specific content format.
- Depending on the brand of name server you choose, it will retrieve its zone data from text files or from an SQL or LDAP back-end.
- Using a database back-end has advantages and disadvantages.

Notes and further reading

SQL

- Wikipedia defines SQL: "Structured Query Language is a computer language designed for the retrieval and management of data in relational database management systems, database schema creation and modification, and database object access control management" (see `http://en.wikipedia.org/wiki/SQL`).
- A small tutorial on SQL (data definition statements, functions, statements, etc.) is at Wikibooks (see `http://en.wikibooks.org/wiki/Programming:SQL`).

OpenLDAP

- OpenLDAP is an Open Source implementation of the Lightweight Directory Access Protocol. It boasts a very good *Administrator's Guide* (see `http://www.openldap.org/doc/admin/`) and a list of *Frequently Asked Questions* (see `http://www.openldap.org/faq/`).
- *Mastering OpenLDAP* by Matt Butcher (Packt Publishing) is a good introduction to OpenLDAP and its configuration.

Reserved domain names

When you create a fictitious domain we recommend you use one of the following:

- The reserved names example.net, example.org or example.com.
- A TLD explicitly reserved in RFC 2606 for testing and documentation. The reserved TLDs are .test, .example, .invalid and .localhost.
- Alternatively, you can use a ccTLD with one of the reserved country codes. ISO 3166 specifies[3]:

> If users need code elements to represent country names not included in this part of ISO 3166, the series of letters `AA`, `QM` to `QZ`, `XA` to `XZ`, and `ZZ`, and the series `AAA` to `AAZ`, `QMA` to `QZZ`, `XAA` to `XZZ`, and `ZZA` to `ZZZ` respectively [...] are available.

[3]`http://www.iso.org/iso/customizing_iso_3166-1.htm`

Chapter

3 Preparing for your implementation

At Your Name Service

Diane M Boling

Introduction

We show you how to plan your name server implementation, and explain the factors you need to consider when deciding which DNS server program you should use, taking into account whether or not you want to use an SQL/LDAP back-end.

In Part II of this book we will discuss in detail the various brands of server you can use to provide authoritative and/or caching name services on your network. However, before you start your implementation, you need to plan it, and you need to decide which brand of server is the most suitable for your environment. You must decide how you're going to store your zone data – in flat files or in an SQL/LDAP back-end. As many of these factors are interconnected, we recommend you read this chapter to get a feel for the process as a whole, and then read Part II to see which server and back end are best for you. Then re-read this chapter and plan your implementation accordingly.

3.1 Planning your implementation

Implementing a reliable DNS name service is non-trivial. Your planning will typically involve several "passes", as you may want to experiment with different servers before finally choosing which to implement.

1. Choosing your server and back-end:

   (a) Either you've chosen an operating system platform for your name servers already, or you will have to choose one now. It may come as a surprise, but not all platforms are equal (see Notes).

   (b) The name server you choose determines the choices open to you for storing your zone data; for example, only some servers support LDAP back-ends. Contrariwise, if you definitely want/need to use a particular type of back end, that in turn limits your choice of name server (Figure 3.1). (See also Section 3.4 for more detail about back-end support.)

   (c) If you want to use an SQL (or LDAP) back-end, but have no prior experience of SQL (or LDAP), we strongly recommend you start acquiring knowledge in that area before you start implementing a name server that uses such a back-end. Otherwise, you could spend hours or days in a futile attempt to get your name server running.

   (d) If you want an SQL back-end but don't have any preference for which RDBMS to use, decide which of the freely available database systems (PostgreSQL vs. MySQL) is best for you. We recommend you stay away from benchmark comparisons. Much more important are ease of use (does it have good tools?), platform availability (will it run on *your* platform?), standards compliance (will it run with *your* application?). Good places to start are `http://troels.arvin.dk/db/rdbms/` and `http://www.wlug.org.nz/PostgresVsMysql`, and a Web search of "PostgreSQL vs MySQL" reveals more. Mind however, that some documents are very dated and possibly don't take account of the huge progress that both MySQL and PostgreSQL have made in terms of features.

       On the other hand, If you want an SQL back-end, and are already using an SQL RDBMS for other purposes, you will probably want to use the same RDBMS for your DNS. Support for your chosen RDBMS will influence which brand of name server you choose.

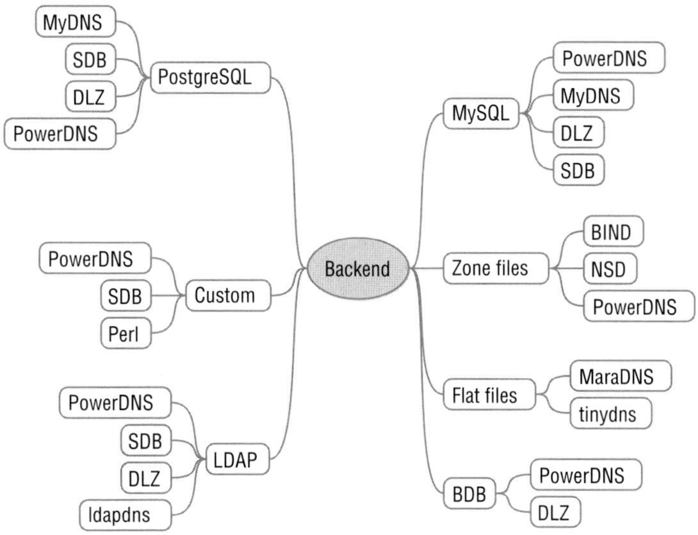

Figure 3.1: Choosing a brand of name server by back-end

(e) If you have demanding performance requirements, that will probably be the dominant factor in your choice of name server. Having chosen a server, you are then of course limited to the zone data storage options supported by that server.

In any case, we recommend you run your own tests before deploying a system, to ensure that your capacity requirements can be satisfied. We explain how you do that in Chapter 23.

When considering performance, you *must* take into account the performance of any SQL/LDAP back-end if you chosen to use one. Allocate time and resources for tuning the back-end.

2. Provide at least two of "everything":

   (a) If you provide authoritative name servers on the Internet for your public domain names, you'll need at least two servers.

   Some DNS registries, such as the German DENIC, require that the two name servers are on different class-C networks, which can involve providing additional networking resources, and/or using a hosting service where you place your second name server.

   (b) If you are setting up caching name servers for your private network, provide at least two of them.

   (c) For name servers that have an SQL database or LDAP directory back-end, you will need one back-end server per name server, so you have no single point of failure. We discuss this in more detail in Chapter 23.

3. Implement a caching name server on every machine that makes heavy use of the DNS – your mail servers and HTTP proxy servers, for example.

4. If you are operating in an environment in which you have to create your own private root name servers, allow additional time to set those up.

5. Depending on the back-end you choose to deploy, you might have to find an ideal storage schema for your back-end. We explain how you are often able to adapt an existing schema, but you might decide to create a new schema to make it easier to integrate into your existing systems. We cover this in detail for name server brands that you can adapt, when we discuss the brands of name servers.

6. If you plan on using incoming or outgoing AXFR zone transfers, security considerations may limit your choice of name server: only a few name servers support transaction signatures (TSIG) for authorizing zone transfers, and this could be a decision maker or breaker for you.

7. Implement monitoring of your name services (Chapter 24).

8. If you want statistics on your DNS usage, you will need additional software to gather and analyze the statistics. We show you which brands of server produce their own statistics, and in Chapter 24 we show you a program that you can use independently of a specific brand of server.

9. If you plan on implementing one of the back-ends that allow you to add your own program code to them, you will need some time for programming and testing. This can turn out to be non-negligible, depending on the amount of experience you have.

10. If you are a mail system administrator, and want to implement a DNS blacklist, you will need to be proficient with your mail server configuration.

11. Do you need DNSSEC security? This greatly restricts your choice of name server: currently only two authoritative servers (NSD and BIND), and two caching servers (Unbound and BIND) support DNSSEC.

12. If you want to integrate DHCP with your DNS, decide which of the methods we discuss in Chapter 19 is best for you.

13. If you intend to implement internationalized domain names, make sure you have the required tools with which to test them. We discuss this in Chapter 21.

14. Secure the host machines on which you run your name servers. Apart from the initial configuration effort, allocate ongoing resources to keep the operating system and DNS software up to date with the latest security patches.

15. Set up a backup system for your DNS servers and perform regular backups of the zone data and relevant configuration files. Create disaster-recovery plans (and test them!).

16. You may want to implement two different brands of server to provide name services. The downside of using different programs on each server is that you have to know the different programs and maintain them separately; the upside is that they are unlikely to fail for the same reasons, so you system is more resilient in the face of widespread bugs or DNS problems or security holes.

17. If you use private IP networks as specified by RFC 1918, you might need to configure some of the caching name servers specifically to handle AS112 zones. The *AS112* zones are the reverse DNS zones for the networks described by RFC 1918. If you use private IP addresses, this is important to you.

18. Many sites implement DNS on a server with an SQL/LDAP back-end, but have a different brand of server acting as a "front-end" server. Although this is quite easy to implement, it does mean you have to learn and maintain two different programs.

3.1.1 Planning your name server placement

Where, from the network point of view, are you going to place your new DNS servers?

- Authoritative servers that handle from the Internet for your public domain names are positioned in your DMZ.
- If you need an authoritative name server for internal (i.e. non-public) zones within your network, or you decide to implement "internal" name servers with authority and caching function like we described in Section 1.2.5, you place the servers on any convenient part of your internal network.
- Unless you are an Internet Service Provider, you will typically not have a caching server facing the Internet, as you won't want others to use your caching name server, just as you wouldn't want others to use your HTTP proxies or (gasp!) your e-mail server.
- We recommend you place the back-end's replica as close as possible (from a network point of view) to the DNS server, ideally on the same machine. While this increases the load on the machine, the advantages are:
  - You reduce the *latency* (i.e. the delay in sending the DNS answer back to the requesting client) caused by the DNS server querying the back-end.
  - You can reduce the overhead (and thus also some latency) in the communication between the DNS server and its database back-end by using UNIX domain sockets, instead of network sockets, wherever possible.
  - Diagnosing errors is easier as you can eliminate network errors from the equation.

3.1.2 Capacity planning

- It is probably difficult to predict how many queries your DNS servers will receive. If you know of a site comparable to yours, contact its system administrators: they may be willing to give you an idea.

As a rule of thumb, you can calculate one DNS query for each visit to your Web site by a browser client; the Web browser will have to determine the IP address of your Web site before it can connect to it. The Web browser will probably be querying your DNS server via a caching name server, so it won't have to query your DNS again until the TTL of the DNS reply expires.

You can typically apply a similar rule of thumb for an e-mail sent to your site.

- If you know how many zones you will be publishing you can estimate the disk capacity you will need based on our examples in Chapter 23. Zones stored in text files are compact, because DNS resource records are very small. However, an SQL or LDAP back-end adds a lot of storage overhead. For example, the 100 000 zones we use in our performance tests (Chapter 23) occupy 400 MB of disk space when stored as zone master files, compared with 2 GB, including indexes, when stored in OpenLDAP.
- The CPU requirements for running a name server are typically not very high, but depend on a number of factors:
  - The brand of name server.
  - How your server stores its zone data. For example, an SQL back-end uses more resources than zone data stored in local flat files.
  - The number of queries your name servers receive..
  - The load caused by any other services you run on the same machine.
  - If you deploy DNSSEC, your name servers will utilize more CPU.
- In general, the higher you set the Time to Live (TTL) on your DNS records you serve, the less frequently your DNS servers will be queried, because caching name servers will cache the answers for a long time.
- If you use low TTL values on your records, your authoritative servers are queried more often, but you know that a change of, say an Address of one of your mail or Web servers, will propagate quickly.
- You might want to load-balance services using the DNS. Consider using Service (SRV) or Mail Exchanger (MX) records to give priorities to services. Round-robin answers to Address (A) resource records are also a kind of load-balancing. We discuss how you might implement load-balancing of services by implementing custom DNS servers in Chapter 6 and in Chapter 8.

3.1.3 Business continuity

DNS is mission critical for almost every organization. It is terribly embarrassing (and costly due to lost revenue) if customers get a "can't find the server" error message when they try to visit your Web site (Figure 3.2). To make sure your DNS is highly available, you have to build in resilience to failure, but you also have to avoid downtime for inevitable system maintenance. Points to consider are:

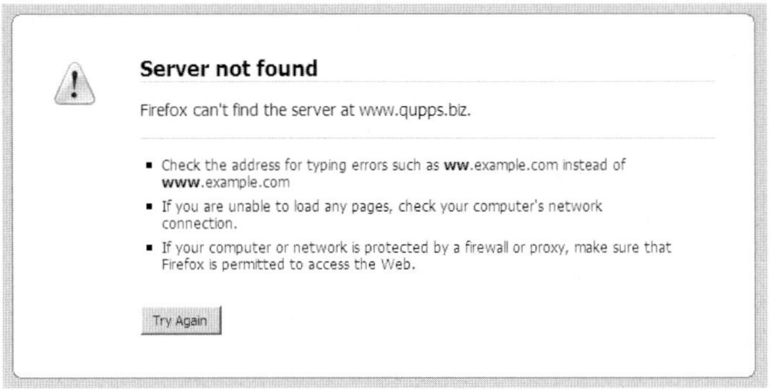

Figure 3.2: What your customer sees when your DNS fails

- Plan changes well in advance. For example, if you know that in two weeks you'll be moving one of the Web servers on www.qupps.biz to a new host with a new IP address, lower the TTL of www.qupps.biz's A record *now*. Set the TTL to a low a value, say 60 or 120 seconds;. this will increase the number of queries you get, but when you change the Address record, the new value will be propagated very quickly. As soon as you know that the change was successful, raise the TTL to its normal value.

- Within your organization, provide at least two caching name servers on your network, and ensure that all your workstations and (non-DNS) servers include them in their network configuration (`/etc/resolv.conf` on *nix, and TCP/IP properties on Microsoft Windows). Believe us: at some point in time, one of the machines on which the recursive resolvers run will fail; this will cause havoc on your local network if you don't have a second server.

  Remember: *use at least two of everything.*

- Even though you have more than one DNS server, consider "duplicating" it onto a machine (perhaps even a virtual machine) that you can bring on-line in the unlikely event of a catastrophe. Ensure you document procedures for bringing it on-line in a rush.

- Spread your name servers over different geographical regions if your organization's network allows it. Or, convince a friendly neighboring organization to be a secondary to your zones if you do the same for them. Then your public DNS can continue to operate even if one of your sites goes down. A DNS service can fail for many different reasons: *how* it fails is important:

  - A simple DNS server daemon might just have crashed. As long as you have more than one server (you do, don't you?) that is, surprisingly, very satisfactory: the crashed daemon won't answer at all, leaving the other daemon to answer requests correctly. The reason this is acceptable, and in fact the best thing that can happen, is that we know the crashed server will not answer incorrectly: a wrong answer is *much* worse than no answer at all.

  - In a more complex setup, you might have a DNS server which relies on a database back-end on a remote system. When the database server crashes, how does your front-end DNS server react? Will it answer queries sent to it? Will it answer correctly, by sending a SERVFAIL error answer, or will it answer all queries with NXDOMAIN as answer? The latter is disastrous: one of your DNS servers is saying, *authoritatively*, that the domain names do not exist! That must not happen. When we say that the best case is the DNS daemon crashing, we aren't kidding.

- DNS is a vital service for the workstations and servers on your own internal network. Ensure that the caching name servers you set up actually work, and monitor them continuously. We discuss this in Chapter 24.

- Use DHCP settings to distribute alternating name server addresses to your workstations to distribute the load on your internal name servers.

3.2 The programs and why we chose them

Is BIND the only name server implementation? The answer to this question is a resounding "perhaps not", although it *is* the most widely used. There are other programs which may very well be better suited to *your* environment. BIND is the most feature-rich of all the servers we discuss, and this is probably what makes BIND a daunting beast: its documentation is huge. If you won't need all its features, there are several very good alternatives. You might also decide to use both BIND in conjunction with a different server, and we show you how to do so.

The programs we cover are: MaraDNS, PowerDNS and PowerDNS Recursor, MyDNS, BIND (with BIND SDB and Bind DLZ), djbdns (which consists of tinydns and dnscache), ldapdns, NSD, Unbound, dnsmasq, dnsproxy, Perl name servers, and rbldnsd. We selected these programs for several different reasons:

- Most of these programs are in widespread use. They are usually well maintained and you will find plenty of people willing to help you deploy them. They have active mailing lists where you can ask for support if you need it.

- All the programs are special in some way. For example, MyDNS, PowerDNS and Bind DLZ can access SQL back-ends to retrieve zone data. PowerDNS, Bind DLZ, BIND SDB, and ldapdns can read their DNS zone data from LDAP directories, and MaraDNS has a special resource record type which allows you to have the server automatically create an inverse entry (i.e. a PTR RR in the in-addr.arpa domain) for each domain name you define.

- BIND SDB and Bind DLZ are add-ons to the BIND name server rather than servers of in their own right. They enable BIND to retrieve zone data from external data sources.

- rbldnsd is very specialized: you use it to publish DNS blacklists for your e-mail systems.

- Some of the programs allow you to extend their functionality. For example, BIND SDB allows you to create a custom interface in the C programming language, with which you "produce" answers to DNS queries from any source you come up with, and PowerDNS's Pipe back-end lets you easily solve a similar task with a simple shell or Perl script. If you want to, you can even create your own specialized name server in Perl; we show you how to do that as well.

- One of the programs, NSD, offers incredible performance, which you might need if you are an Internet Service Provider, for instance.

- Unbound is a "new kid on the block". It is a caching and validating name server developed by the people who wrote NSD, and it supports DNSSEC validation.

- With the exception of a short discussion of Microsoft Windows DNS Server, all the programs we discuss are Open Source. The quality of these programs is very high; because they are so widely used, bugs are found quickly; because people can download the source code of the programs, bugs are usually fixed quickly too.

Some of the programs we discuss in this book haven't been maintained for a while, which is a shame. Still, we think all the programs have valuable characteristics, which is why we discuss them. Take ldapdns for example; an LDAP-based DNS name server that does its job reasonably well. What future does it have? We can't answer that question, and we believe the same question can be asked for most software packages. Software comes and goes, and if there is nobody who undertakes to maintain a program, it typically slides into oblivion. As another example, suppose the Internet quickly moves to DNSSEC, what future would be in store for djbdns or PowerDNS? If the maintainers of these packages aren't willing to add DNSSEC to them (and they don't appear to be, at the time of this writing), what future is there for the programs? The question is a bit rhetorical perhaps, but it is something we hope you'll keep in mind.

3.3 Operating system and software requirements

Name servers impose few special requirements on the operating system:

- All the programs we discuss run on *nix, and consume moderate amounts of resources.

  We tested all the Open Source programs on a modern Linux distribution without any special software added. (See Chapter 23 for the software we used in our tests.)

- Microsoft Windows versions of the code are available for some of the programs, and there are ready-made binary packages of MaraDNS and BIND for Microsoft Windows.

- Obviously, if you want to use an SQL or LDAP directory back-end, you need the respective server software (and perhaps extra hardware to run it on). (We show you how to set up an LDAP directory back-end easily, in Appendix A.)

3.3.1 Using pre-built packages

Modern *nix system software distributions provide individual *packages* (or *ports* in the case of FreeBSD) of software. This is a great way to get started quickly. You can compile from scratch later, when you may want to tailor your build, and when you have a better understanding of what the various components of a package provide.

However, the package content is at the whim of the packager and is sometimes quite outdated. Of course, not all software is available as a pre-built package for all platforms. If there isn't one for your chosen platform, you'll have to build from source (see below).

You will have to consult your system documentation on how to install a package, but you will typically have a program with which you can browse or search for a package by name and then install it. On Red Hat systems this would be yum or rpm, on Suse Linux you might use yast, or dpkg or apt-get on Debian Linux.

Building software from source

We always prefer building from source, because:

1. You specify exactly which features of a program you want compiled, without having to live with what a package maintainer thinks you want.

2. You, not your operating system's package management system, decide when to update this software.

3. You have a handy copy of the source that you can consult if something goes wrong. Even if you yourself don't know how to "read" or "fix" source code, you can readily employ somebody else to do it for you. Think of it as "protecting your investment" (one of the major benefits of Open Source!).

4. You can specify exactly where you want your programs installed.

5. The source packages often contain additional and valuable documentation which isn't installed by packages.

6. You can compile a program on a platform for which no pre-built package is available (for Cygwin on Microsoft Windows, for example).

Compiling the Open Source name servers is not difficult. Most use the GNU autoconf and automake tools, which simplify the task. The program's documentation will instruct you how to build it, and we also cover each program's compilation in its respective chapter.

Upgrading the programs is usually simply a matter of compiling a newer version and installing it instead of a previous version. It is always important to backup previous programs and configuration files of course, and we strongly recommend you read at least the program's `Changelog` to find out about new requirements or features the program supports.

3.4 Back-ends supported by the various servers

Many of the name servers give you a choice of where to store their zone data. Some of the more "exotic" ones are Bind DLZ, with its Berkeley DB back-end. (Berkeley DB is an in-process database – think of a database system embedded into the program. We discuss this in greater detail in Chapter 9.)

Again others (BIND SDB, PowerDNS, Stanford::DNSserver) are so flexible that you can program your own answers to DNS queries by attaching a back-end you code yourself, if you have some programming skill. For example, we show you in Chapter 8 how you can implement your own load-balancer, and in Chapter 15 we show you how you query details of people in your LDAP directory via the DNS!

The alternatives are summarized in Table 3.1. (If you are not familiar with some of the abbreviations such as BDBHPT, BDB, etc. don't worry: we explain them when we cover them in their respective chapters.)

Name server	LDAP	SQL	Files	Other
MaraDNS			•[a]	
PowerDNS	•	•	•[b]	•[c]
MyDNS		•		
BIND			•[d]	
BIND SDB	•	•		•
Bind DLZ	•	•		•[e]
tinydns			•[f]	
ldapdns	•			
NSD			•[g]	

[a]Program specific
[b]Standard master file format
[c]Pipe, Random, Oracle, SQLite, DB2, ODBC, XDB
[d]Standard master file format
[e]BDB, BDBHPT, ODBC, File system
[f]Program specific
[g]Standard master file format

Table 3.1: Back-end support in authoritative name servers

3.5 Setting up a test environment

Before you plan your implementation, we recommend you create a test environment so you can evaluate and experiment with the programs. (Even when your system has gone live, a separate test environment lets you try out new configurations and techniques with impunity.)

- You will need access to a modest machine on which you install software, create configuration files and possibly wreak havoc without affecting anything important. If you don't have a spare machine, we recommend you use VMware (see `http://vmware.`

com), VirtualBox (see http://www.virtualbox.org/) or Parallels (see http://www.parallels.com/). These programs let you create sand-boxed environments, called virtual machines, where you can experiment to your heart's content; they also let you reset a virtual machine back to its initial state, making re-installation a snap if you make a big mess and need to start over. The fear of damaging something important is a huge barrier to becoming really proficient in complex systems.

- Use a recent version of your favorite operating system. GNU/Linux or FreeBSD are excellent platforms for name services.
- If you are going to experiment with DHCP, make sure your test DHCP server is completely isolated from your live network. It is very easy to cause havoc in an organization by setting up a DHCP server that starts doling out (duplicate) addresses to your live machines.

  Unlike DHCP, installing an extra DNS server is not dangerous, because no clients will know about it, or use it, until you explicitly configure them to. (Extra DHCP servers *are* a problem, because clients locate them automatically by broadcasting for them.)
- You do not need Internet connectivity for testing the programs; a Local Area Network suffices.
- When testing in a sand-boxed environment, use IP addresses rather than hostnames when querying your name server. If you don't, you can be misled by your system using its /etc/resolv.conf which might contain incorrect entries.

Summary

- When planning your implementation, choose your server and back-end, and carefully plan their placement on your network.
- BIND is the most widely used name server, but there are many good reasons why you might decide to choose a different brand of server.
- Make sure you have at least "two of each".
- Identify machines which make heavy use of the DNS, and place a caching name server on those.
- You can easily set up an environment in which you test name servers for their functionality, and we strongly recommend you do so.

What's next?

This concludes Part I of the book, where we introduced you to the DNS, to zones and their data. Part II is quite different: it discusses the Open Source DNS servers, how you compile them (if necessary), and most importantly, how you configure them. We show you some of their outstanding features, and help you decide what they are best used for.

- If you want to set up DNS in a branch or Small Office / Home Office environment, we recommend you learn about:
  - MaraDNS (Chapter 4)
  - tinydns (Chapter 11)
  - dnsmasq (Chapter 13)
- If you are planning to deploy DNS authoritative and/or caching name services in your organization, we recommend you read the chapters in order to get an overview. Ideally then go back and re-read in detail the chapters that are important to you.

Notes and further reading

Database transactions

In a relational database system such as PostgreSQL or MySQL, a *transaction* is a sequence of operations performed as a single unit of work. A transaction has four key properties, abbreviated as "ACID":

1. Atomic. This means that all the work (i.e. all the modifications) in a transaction are treated as one. Either they are *all* performed, or *none* are.
2. Consistent. This means that a completed transaction leaves the datbase in a consistent internal state.

3. Isolated. This means that a transaction sees the database in a consistent state. It will not "see" a partial update performed by another transaction until that is complete.

4. Durable. This means that the results of the transaction are permanently stored in the system and will not "somehow disappear".

In PostgreSQL transactions are part of the database system, whereas for MySQL only certain so-called "engines" offer transactional capabilities. We recommend you use the InnoDB engine for MySQL.

Choosing a platform

- The ISC has a benchmark that shows that not all platforms are equal in terms of running a specific program. Case in point is a benchmark conducted on a number of different operating systems. Even GNU/Linux distributions differ in the performance attained (see `http://new.isc.org/proj/dnsperf/OStest.html`).

Part II

The DNS servers

This Part of the book covers the different brands of name servers in detail. We start off with the authoritative name servers and show you how you implement them. Even if you are not interested in a particular program, we suggest you at least skim its chapter, as we do point out things you might wish to implement with a different brand of name server.

After the authoritative servers, we cover the caching name servers, and finally we discuss how you set up delegation, and create your own private root name space if you need that.

Chapter

4 MaraDNS

BIND9 is the emacs of DNS servers: It includes everything but the kitchen sink. This results in a full-featured DNS server that has about 5,000 features you will never use.

MaraDNS documentation

Introduction

MaraDNS has just about the smallest configuration file possible: four lines of configuration turn it into an authoritative DNS server. It can automatically create PTR records for hosts, which simplifies zone maintenance.

MaraDNS, created by Sam Trenholme, is designed to be a lightweight, secure authoritative, recursive and caching multi-threaded name server. Security is based on a special string library designed to be resistant to buffer overflows. MaraDNS must run as a non-privileged user, and it refuses to run without a `chroot()` directory (`chroot()` replaces the view a process has regarding the / directory, effectively limiting that process' view of the file system).

Pros	• Special line types that create both A and PTR records • Optional on-the-fly generation of SOA and NS records • Recursion can be disabled at compile time to make an authoritative-only server • Native Win32 support • Versatile access control lists • Manual (man-) pages
Cons	◦ Limited slave support ◦ Threaded model limits scalability
Scenarios	Small environments that want a DNS server that is easy to set up and configure.

Table 4.1: MaraDNS at a glance

MaraDNS reads its zone data from files in the file system. Its zone files slightly resemble zone master files, but the syntax is different, and it provides some nice shortcuts. If you are a beginner with DNS you will greatly appreciate a record type that automatically sets up PTR records when you define a host's A record.

MaraDNS runs as one of the following:

- An authoritative-only server. You define this when compiling MaraDNS (see Notes). If you build MaraDNS as authoritative-only, the installation procedure appropriately names the executable maradns.authonly.

- An authoritative and recursive name server. You use this to set up a DNS name server in your Small Office / Home Office environment. When running as a recursive name server, MaraDNS restricts the use of its recursive cache, by means of ACLs (Access Control Lists), preventing unauthorized clients using it for recursion.

- MaraDNS can also act as a custom root name server.

A strength of MaraDNS is its native support for running on *nix and on Microsoft Windows (i.e. without Cygwin). The Microsoft Windows implementation is fully featured; we describe how you install it in Chapter 14. The threaded model currently used by MaraDNS means it doesn't scale well with high traffic loads (which could make MaraDNS unsuitable for use by ISPs).

4.1 Getting results quickly

(This section is just to give you an overview of the program. Don't worry too much about the detailed syntax for now – we cover that in Sections 4.2 onwards.)

MaraDNS is probably the easiest of all name servers to set up. A three-line configuration makes a recursive name server, and a four-line configuration makes an authoritative one. There are many options that can be set in the configuration file, of course, and we discuss some of them later on in this chapter.

After installing the programs (see Notes) you set up MaraDNS either as a recursive resolver, as an authoritative server, or both, as we show in the following sections.

4.1.1 Set up MaraDNS as a caching name server

To set up MaraDNS as a caching name server, you create a minimal configuration in a file named `/etc/mararc`. This is MaraDNS's default configuration file, and it is separate from any zone files you might define (see below). The configuration file contains:

```
chroot_dir = "/etc/maradns"
ipv4_bind_addresses = "127.0.0.1, 192.168.1.164"
recursive_acl = "127.0.0.0/8, 192.168.1.0/24"
```

The above three lines in `mararc` will cause MaraDNS to:

- `chroot()` into the specified directory when it starts running, for security.
- Listen on the specified addresses for incoming queries.
- Allow its recursor to be used as a caching name server by clients on the local machine (127.0.0.1) as well as those with network addresses 192.168.1.1 – 192.168.1.255.

We discuss below how you modify MaraDNS's behavior.

4.1.2 Set up MaraDNS as a caching and authoritative server

MaraDNS can operate as a caching name server and as an authoritative name server simultaneously, i.e. as an "internal" server (Section 1.2.5). In a Small Office / Home Office environment, this enables you to publish the content of one or more zones for your internal network and to use MaraDNS as a caching name server for the public DNS. In order to configure it as such, you add one or more zone definitions to the configuration, as shown in the next section.

4.1.3 Set up MaraDNS as an authoritative name server

MaraDNS can serve the content of one or more DNS zones authoritatively, whether you run it as a caching name server or as an authoritative-only server. Zone files are read once, when the maradns daemon starts up. If the files' content changes, you must restart the server to reload them. During the reloading, the server is unavailable to answer queries.

Modify or create `/etc/mararc` and add this content:

```
chroot_dir = "/etc/maradns"
ipv4_bind_addresses = "127.0.0.1, 192.168.1.164"

csv2 = {}
csv2["soho."] = "soho.csv"
```

The line csv2={} indicates that the daemon will be authoritative and initializes an internal list of zones, and the second csv2 line configures the daemon as authoritative for a zone called soho with zone data in a file named `soho.csv`. We use the zone called soho because then our internal hosts will be named printer.soho, pc2.soho, etc. which cannot clash with public domain names.

You create the `soho.csv` file in the `/etc/maradns` directory, and give it this content:

```
printer.soho.        FQDN4        192.168.4.17
```

Note that white space separates the three fields, but you can use a vertical bar (|) instead if you prefer.

4.1.4 Automatic zones

Now launch the daemon, maradns (or maradns.authonly if you built it authoritative-only), and send it queries. If you query it for the address of your printer, you see:

```
$ dig @192.168.1.164 printer.soho
;; ANSWER SECTION:
printer.soho.              86400 IN   A   192.168.4.17

;; AUTHORITY SECTION:
soho.                      86400 IN   NS synth-ip-c0a801a4.soho.

;; ADDITIONAL SECTION:
synth-ip-c0a801a4.soho. 86400 IN   A   192.168.1.164
```

The Address (A) record of your printer is correctly returned, and you can see that MaraDNS has automatically "completed" the zone for you:

- It has provided a Name Server (NS) record for the zone, with a synthesized name – constructed from the hexadecimal value of the IP address of the maradns machine.
- If you query your MaraDNS DNS server for the inverse (reverse) pointer to your printer, you might be pleasantly surprised:

  ```
  $ dig @192.168.1.164 -x 192.168.4.17
  ;; QUESTION SECTION:
  ;17.4.168.192.in-addr.arpa.        IN        PTR

  ;; ANSWER SECTION:
  17.4.168.192.in-addr.arpa. 86400 IN        PTR        printer.soho.
  ```

  MaraDNS automatically created a reverse pointer (PTR) because of the FQDN4 record type in the `soho.csv` file.

- If you query the Start of Authority (SOA) of your new zone, you see sensible values:

```
;; AUTHORITY SECTION:
soho.        86400   IN   SOA   soho. hostmaster.soho. 151655571↩
                    7200 3600 604800 3600
```

Technically neither the Start of Authority (SOA) nor the Name Server (NS) records are required in a zone file. The SOA, including its serial number and RNAME, is synthesized, and synthetic records are created for the Name Servers as shown above. Nevertheless, we recommend you explicitly set the records to the values you want (and we will show you to set the SOA, NS and PTR records explicitly).

That concludes our "getting results quickly". In the next three sections we explain in detail the format of MaraDNS's zone files, its configuration file, and how to launch it.

4.2 Format of MaraDNS zone files

MaraDNS uses a format called csv2 for its zone files. This is a simple format consisting of lines of "tokens" separated by white-space or pipe (|) characters. Empty lines and lines starting with a hash symbol are ignored. Starting in MaraDNS version 1.3, the tilde character (~) is used to delimit records in csv2 files, but this is only enabled if a tilde is placed between the first and second record; otherwise tildes are not allowed in zone files, except in comments. You can use pipe, tabs, or spaces to separate fields in zone files. Any combination of tabs and spaces can separate fields, and there can be a single vertical bar in that whitespace. Zone files in csv2 format contain lines in the following form:

name [*+ttl*] [*rtype*] *rdata* ~

where the values have the following meanings:

name This is the domain name of the record to be added, such as www.qupps.biz. (qualified with a terminating period). It must be placed at the beginning of a line. It must be either fully qualified (with a terminating dot), or qualified with a percent sign (%), which stands for the current zone name. For example, if the csv2 file being loaded is for zone qupps.biz, and you specify "*name*.%", then the domain name will be "*name*.qupps.biz.", with the terminating period.

+ttl The Time to Live (TTL) of the record in seconds. If it is not set on a line, it defaults to 86400 seconds (1 day), unless overridden in the csv2 file with the `/ttl` command:

```
www.qupps.biz.   +60 A 192.168.1.20
w4.qupps.biz.        A 192.168.1.21
/ttl 3600
mail.qupps.biz.      A 192.168.1.24
```

The first host has its TTL explicitly set to 60 seconds; the second gets the default of one day. The third line sets the new default of 3 600 seconds; subsequent records inherit that TTL until it is overridden by a further `/ttl` command.

rtype The type of the DNS resource record. The default is an Address record (A).

rdata The data for the resource record; its format depends on *rtype*.

~ The tilde is optional; if it is included at the end of the line, it defines the record separator for the whole csv2 file – instead of a newline.

Typical resource records

We list some of the more common resource records here with examples, but MaraDNS supports others as well (consult the documentation):

A — An Address record contains an IPv4 Address. This is the default rtype, so you can omit the type, if you like:

```
host.qupps.biz.  A 192.168.3.23
host2.qupps.biz.   192.168.3.123
```

PTR — A Pointer for an inverse lookup in an in-addr.arpa zone. Its content is a domain name.

```
21.1.168.192.in-addr.arpa.  PTR www.qupps.biz.
```

MX — The Mail Exchanger *rdata* contains two fields: a preference (or priority) and a domain name.

```
qupps.biz.  MX 10 mail.qupps.biz.
```

AAAA — This record contains an IPv6 Address.

```
server.%  AAAA 3ffe:ffff:ffe:501:ffff::b:c:d
```

SRV — Service definition. The *rdata* must have four fields: priority, weight, port and target host.

```
_ldap._tcp.%   SRV  0 10 389 ldap.%
```

NS — Name server. This contains a domain name (*not* an IP address).

```
qupps.biz.  NS dns2.%
```

SOA — The Start of Authority *rdata* in MaraDNS contains the usual seven fields:

```
qupps.biz. SOA ns.% mail@% 200801010 7200 3600 604800 1800
```

Note that the RNAME field contains a real e-mail address with an `@` character.

If the serial number is specified as the string `/serial`, the serial number is synthesized from the modification time of the file containing the zone.

TXT — The Text record can contain an arbitrary string, which is placed between two single quotes:

```
printer6.%   TXT 'on second floor behind ping-pong machine'
```

FQDN4 — This type is specific to MaraDNS. It creates an Address (A) with an associated Pointer (PTR) record:

```
www.%   FQDN4 192.168.1.17
```

but you still have to create the in-addr.arpa zone (see below). The example above could have been specified as:

```
www.qupps.biz.                A  192.168.1.17
17.1.168.192.in-addr.arpa.  PTR www.qupps.biz.
```

FQDN6 Like the FQDN4 record for IPv4 addresses, MaraDNS has the FQDN6 record for IPv6:

```
big.qupps.biz   FQDN6 3ffe:ffff:ffe:501:ffff::b:c:d
```

CNAME Sets up an alias.

```
www.%  CNAME webserver.qupps.biz.
```

An example zone in csv2 *format*

The following shows a zone file including SOA and NS records:

```
%       SOA    % hostmaster@% 1 7200 3600 604800 1800
%       NS     ns1.%
%       NS     ns2.%

%       FQDN4 192.168.1.20
%       MX    10 mail.%

ns1.%  FQDN4 192.168.1.164
www.%  A     192.168.1.21
mail.% FQDN4 192.168.1.20
```

Reverse zones

A line type FQDN4 in MaraDNS sets up an Address (A) and its associated PTR record for you, but it does not automatically create authority for the appropriate reverse in-addr.arpa zone. In order to do that you still have to:

1. Set up the zone in `mararc` by adding it to the csv2 variable:

   ```
   csv2["4.168.192.in-addr.arpa."] = "reverse.csv"
   ```

   As we'll see in Section 4.4, `csv2[]` is a " dictionary" variable that can take multiple values, so you can use this in addition to the `csv2["soho."]` line we saw earlier.

2. Create the file `reverse.csv` with a Start of Authority (SOA). We show this here with the pipe separators:

   ```
   %|SOA|% email@soho. 1 7200 3600 604800 1800
   ```

   A dig query for this shows:

   ```
   $ dig @127.0.0.1 4.168.192.in-addr.arpa.  soa
   ;; ANSWER SECTION:
   4.168.192.in-addr.arpa. 86400   IN      SOA 4.168.192.in-addr.arpa.↩
                 email.soho. 1 7200 3600 604800 1800
   ```

3. If you want to add additional records to the in-addr.arpa zone, you append them to the `reverse.csv` file:

   ```
   6.%|PTR|router.soho.
   ```

4.3 Launch the maradns daemon

The configuration we created above together with the csv2 zone file suffice to authoritatively serve DNS for the qupps.biz domain. Upon starting the MaraDNS daemon, we see:

```
# /usr/local/sbin/maradns.authonly
 Log: Root directory changed
 Log: Binding to address 127.0.0.1, 192.168.1.164
 Log: Socket opened on UDP port 53
 Log: Root privileges dropped
Processing zone qupps.biz. right now.
Filename: db.qupps.biz
MaraDNS proudly serves you 11 DNS records
MaraDNS maximum memory allocation set to 2638336 bytes
Log: All RRs have been loaded
```

The diagnostic error-messages issued by maradns are sometimes a bit misleading. For example, a misplaced comma (instead of a period) in ipv4_bind_addresses can produce:

```
Fatal error: Problem binding to port 53.
System said: Cannot assign requested address
```

If you get an error like that, we recommend you go over your configuration once more. There are no surprises when querying the server:

```
$ dig @127.0.0.1 qupps.biz
;; flags: qr aa rd; QUERY: 1, ANSWER: 1, AUTHORITY: 2, ADDITIONAL: 1

;; ANSWER SECTION:
qupps.biz.              86400    IN       A        192.168.1.20

;; AUTHORITY SECTION:
qupps.biz.              86400    IN       NS       ns1.qupps.biz.
qupps.biz.              86400    IN       NS       ns2.qupps.biz.

;; ADDITIONAL SECTION:
ns1.qupps.biz.          86400    IN       A        192.168.1.164
```

4.4 Configuring MaraDNS behavior with the mararc file

As seen above, you configure the behavior of the MaraDNS daemons, either maradns or maradns.authonly, with the `mararc` file (which is completely separate from the csv2 files that contain zone data). Edit the file with a text editor. Lines that begin with a hash character (#) and lines that contain only white space are ignored. Otherwise, lines contain variable/value pairs. Variables in `mararc` are of two types:

1. *Normal variables* take only a single value, although that single value can indicate multiple things. E.g. admin_acl takes a single string value, but that string can specify multiple IP addresses, netblocks or aliases. The syntax for setting a normal variable is:

   name = "*value*"

2. *Dictionary variables.* These are arrays that can have multiple elements, indexed by strings. (Think associative arrays in PHP, or Perl hashes). The syntax of a dictionary variable is:

   name["*index-1*"] = "*value-1*"
   name["*index-2*"] = "*value-2*"

   where *name* is the name of the dictionary variable, *index* is the index of the array, and *value* is the value stored at that index. Dictionary variables must be initialized before their first use with:

   name = {}

   We showed a simple example starting in Section 4.1.3:

```
csv2                                  = {}
csv2["soho."]                         = "soho.csv"
csv2["1.168.192.in-addr.arpa."] = "reverse.csv"
```

4.4.1 Normal variables

The most commonly required normal variables are:

admin_acl Netblocks specifying the addresses that are allowed to query the server for administrative information, including the MaraDNS version number and the number of threads it is running. The comma-separated list of networks, specified as individual IP addresses or CIDR networks, may retrieve server information, depending on the setting of debug_msg_level (see below). If admin_acl is unset, nobody may query the server for these values.

```
admin_acl = "127.0.0.1, 192.168.1/24"
```

This administrative information is served as TXT resource records on special domain names, so they can be queried with a standard TXT DNS query.

Instead of specifying individual netblocks here, you can also specify an ipv4_alias (see page 86).

```
admin_acl = "127.0.0.1, bossMachines"
```

chroot_dir The directory to which MaraDNS `chroot()`s when you launch it.

debug_msg_level A number specifying the level of information a running MaraDNS process should make public:

0 No information should be made public.

1 or higher (this is the default). MaraDNS's version number is available as a TXT RR on domain name version.maradns.

```
$ dig @127.0.0.1 version.maradns. txt
;; ANSWER SECTION:
version.maradns. 770616 IN TXT "MaraDNS version 1.3"
```

2 or higher: the number of currently running threads is available as a TXT RR on domain name numthreads.maradns, and the number of elements in its cache as a TXT RR for the domain cache-elements.maradns.

```
$ dig @127.0.0.1 cache-elements.maradns. txt
;; ANSWER SECTION:
cache-elements.maradns. 770616 IN TXT "Elements in ↩
                   DNS cache: 223"
```

A query for domain memusage.maradns returns the amount of memory that MaraDNS has allocated, if you compiled the program with "`make debug`" (not recommended).

```
$ dig @127.0.0.1 memusage.maradns. txt
;; ANSWER SECTION:
memusage.maradns. 770616  IN TXT "Memory usage, in ↩
                          bytes: 85377"
```

3 or higher: the current time on the server on which maradns is running is returned in traditional UNIX seconds if you query domain timestamp.maradns:

```
$ dig @127.0.0.1 timestamp.maradns. txt
;; ANSWER SECTION:
timestamp.maradns. 770616 IN TXT "Timestamp: 914..."
```

dns_port
: Port that MaraDNS listens on. It defaults to 53.

hide_disclaimer
: Whether or not to hide the disclaimer that MaraDNS issues upon startup. After you have read that once, for the future you may wish to set:

```
hide_disclaimer = "yes"
```

ipv4_bind_addresses
: A comma-separated list of the IPv4 addresses the MaraDNS server should listen on.

```
ipv4_bind_addresses = "127.0.0.1, 192.168.1.164"
```

ipv6_bind_address
: The single IPv6 address MaraDNS should listen on. For this to work, the server must be bound to at least one IPv4 address.

maradns_uid

maradns_gid
: The numeric UID and GID respectively that the server should run as. The default for both number is 99.

```
maradns_uid = 103
maradns_gid = 98
```

max_total
: The maximum number of records that the server will include in a DNS reply. (For example, if you have a host with many A records, you can limit the number of records returned in a query for it.)

random_seed_file
: MaraDNS needs 16 random bytes to seed its pseudo random number generator. This value specifies the name of a file from which the 16 bytes will be read. The file name is relative to the system's

root directory (and not to the directory `chroot()`ed to). The default is `/dev/urandom`.

```
random_seed_file = "/etc/maradns/rnd"
```

recursive_acl
Comma-separated netblocks specifying addresses that are permitted to query the server for recursive queries. If this variable is unset, the recursor is effectively disabled.

```
recursive_acl = "localhost, ip/netmask"
```

ip is an IP address; *netmask* can be in one of two formats:

1. A single number between 1 and 32, which indicates the number of leading bits in the netmask (CIDR representation).
2. A 4-digit dotted decimal netmask.

remote_admin
If remote_admin is set to 1 and admin_acl is set, any IP address listed in admin_acl is allowed to modify the value of verbose_level by querying the server for a TXT record of *n*.verbose_level.maradns, to set the value of verbose_query to *n*.

```
$ dig @127.0.0.1 4.verbose_level.maradns. txt
;; ANSWER SECTION:
4.verbose_level.maradns. 770616 IN TXT ↩
                        "Verbose level is now 4"
```

upstream_port
The port number (default is 53) that the MaraDNS recursive resolver should use to contact other DNS servers.

verbose_level
Specifies what should be logged to standard output. There are five possible values:

- `0` No messages except for the legal disclaimer and fatal file parsing errors.
- `1` Only startup messages (default).
- `2` Error queries and level `1` messages.
- `3` All queries and level `2` messages.
- `4` All actions, including adding and removing records from the cache, are logged.

verbose_query
Whether to verbosely output all DNS queries that the recursive DNS server receives. If this is set to 1, then all recursive queries sent to MaraDNS are logged. This is mainly used for debugging.

4.4.2 Dictionary variables

The dictionary variables currently supported by MaraDNS are:

csv2
The set of all zone-name/filename pairs that MaraDNS serves. The named files are read after the program `chroot()`s, so paths are relative to the chroot_dir directory.

```
csv2 = {}
csv2["qupps.biz."]   = "qupps.biz.csv"
csv2["soho."]        = "soho.csv"
csv2["example.net."] = "db.example.net"
```

Note how the zone name is specified as the index into the csv2 variable, and that its name is qualified with a terminating period.

ipv4_alias

This lets you give nicknames or aliases to netblocks for IPv4 addresses. You can then use these aliases in ACLs (as we showed you for admin_acl above).

```
ipv4_alias = {}
ipv4_alias["laptop"]        = "192.168.2.178"
ipv4_alias["office"]        = "laptop,192.168.1/24"
ipv4_alias["bossMachines"] = "192.1.1.1, 192.168.1.20"
```

Aliases can nest as shown in the above example: the alias `office` contains all the hosts in the range 192.168.1.1 – 192.168.1.255 and the single host 192.168.2.178.

An ipv4_alias can also be "appended to" with an operator that concatenates additional values to it. The alias for "bossMachines" above could have been written as:

```
ipv4_alias["bossMachines"] = "192.1.1.1"
ipv4_alias["bossMachines"] += "192.168.1.20"
```

You typically use this when defining an alias with many values to allow for a neat layout of your `mararc` file.

root_servers

When acting as a caching name server, MaraDNS uses a compiled-in set of root name servers. If you are in an environment in which you have to access your own private root servers (Chapter 18), you will have to change the default set, by using this variable. The value you set consists of one or more IP addresses, netblocks, or ipv4_aliases:

```
ipv4_alias = {}
ipv4_alias["myown"] =  "198.41.0.4, 192.228.79.201,"
ipv4_alias["myown"] += "128.8.10.90, 192.203.230.10,"
...
ipv4_alias["myown"] += "202.12.27.33"

root_servers = {}
root_servers["."]        = "myown"
```

root_servers must point to root servers; if you want MaraDNS to act as a forwarding server, use the upstream_servers variable instead.

root_servers is an array, so it can have more than one element, each with a different index, of course; The index is a zone name qualified with a terminal period. Extending on the example above, if we add:

```
root_servers["example.net."] = "192.168.1.1"
root_servers["org."]         = "192.168.1.20"
```

then queries for www.example.net will be resolved via the server at 192.168.1.1 – i.e. 192.168.1.1 will be the first name server contacted by MaraDNS when progressing along the chain of delegations. Queries for *anything*.org will use the name server you configured at 192.168.1.20, and all other domains will be resolved via the servers defined for the "." element of the array (i.e. the servers in the "myown" variable).

upstream_servers — Syntactically, this variable is identical to the root_servers variable above, but upstream_servers lists forwarders (i.e. servers MaraDNS should forward *to*). So, if you want MaraDNS to forward queries for domain example.net to two specific forwarders, you would define:

```
ipv4_alias = {}
ipv4_alias["boxes"] =  "192.0.2.4, 192.168.1.401"

upstream_servers["example.net."] = "boxes"
```

Having upstream_servers and root_servers in the same `mararc` file causes a fatal error.

4.5 Zone transfers

MaraDNS supports zone transfers (AXFR) using two ancillary programs:

zoneserver — This handles outgoing zone transfers. (In fact it handles all queries/responses sent over TCP instead of UDP.)

fetchzone — Performs incoming zone transfers, printing whatever it receives, to standard output.

Both programs use the same configuration file as the main maradns program.

4.5.1 Using MaraDNS as a master DNS server

The zoneserver program handles TCP/IP traffic for MaraDNS as follows:

1. When zoneserver receives an incoming DNS query over TCP, if it isn't an AXFR request, it forwards it via UDP to main maradns daemon at the address specified in the tcp_convert_server variable. The main maradns program replies to zoneserver, over UDP, and zoneserver sends the reply to the original client over TCP (Figure 4.1, left).

   Only clients listed in the variable tcp_convert_acl may send zoneserver non-AXFR requests over TCP. If a client whose address is not in the ACL, attempts to connect via TCP, zoneserver closes the connection.

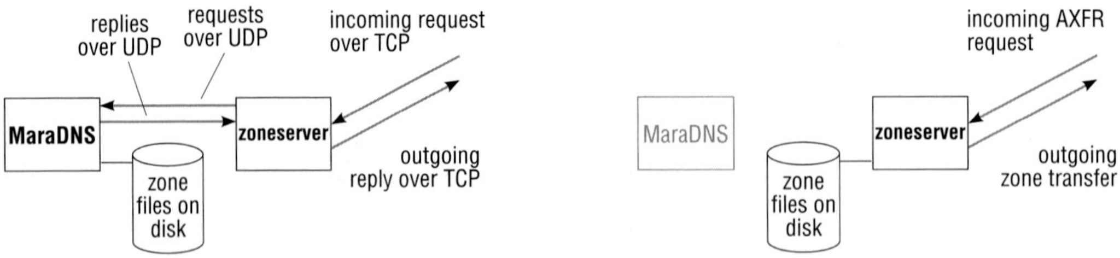

Figure 4.1: zoneserver handling non-AXFR requests (left) and AXFR (right)

2. If the incoming TCP query is an AXFR request, zoneserver itself handles the request (Figure 4.1, right), reading the zone files as necessary from disk. The zone_transfer_acl variable defines the list of clients that are allowed to perform zone transfers. Once you have authorized a client to perform a zone transfer, it may transfer all zones offered by MaraDNS; there is no provision to limit the zones a specific client may transfer. Setting:

   ```
   zone_transfer_acl = "0.0.0.0/0"
   ```

   allows any client to transfer zones from your server. We do not recommend this.

3. You enable zone transfers by adding the IP addresses of the requesting clients to zone_transfer_acl.

A snippet from `/etc/mararc` illustrates the variables:

```
tcp_convert_server        = "127.0.0.1"
tcp_convert_acl           = "office"
zone_transfer_acl         = "laptop"
```

A potential problem with MaraDNS as a master server to non-MaraDNS slaves is that resources specified with MaraDNS's `FQDN4` format have their reverse in-addr.arpa PTR records returned mixed in with their forward zone, as illustrated; there are slave servers that don't like that very much (e.g. MaraDNS's own fetchzone), because the zone contains "foreign" data.

```
$ dig @127.0.0.1 qupps.biz axfr
qupps.biz.                  86400    IN      SOA     qupps.biz.  hostmaste...
qupps.biz.                  86400    IN      NS      ns1.qupps.biz.
qupps.biz.                  86400    IN      NS      ns2.qupps.biz.
20.1.168.192.in-addr.arpa.  86400 IN         PTR     qupps.biz.
qupps.biz.                  86400    IN      A       192.168.1.20
qupps.biz.                  86400    IN      MX      10 mail.qupps.biz.
164.1.168.192.in-addr.arpa.  86400 IN        PTR     ns1.qupps.biz.
ns1.qupps.biz.              86400    IN      A       192.168.1.164
...
```

zoneserver handles incremental zone transfer (IXFR) requests as if they were full (i.e. AXFR) requests.

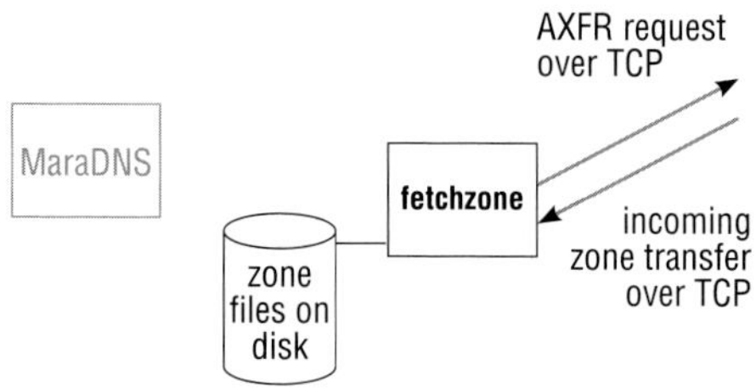

Figure 4.2: fetchzone, not MaraDNS, handles incoming zone transfers

4.5.2 Using MaraDNS as a slave DNS server

MaraDNS relies on fetchzone to transfer zone files from other servers. MaraDNS can't automatically initiate transfers; instead, you invoke fetchzone with the name of a zone and the IP address from which the zone should be loaded. The source name server (i.e. the master server from which the zone transfer will be received) must obviously be willing to handle zone transfers, or fetchzone will fail.

Incoming zone transfers are rudimentary: fetchzone performs the AXFR and dumps the result in CSV2 format on standard output, leaving it up to you to do something with it. For MaraDNS that would mean saving the CSV2 formatted output to a zone file, to be served up by the main daemon. Under no circumstances should you shell-redirect data into a production file; if the zone transfer should fail, the state of the resulting zone would be indeterminate. Instead, you should use something along the lines of:

Listing 4.1: Safe fetchzone for MaraDNS

```
#!/bin/sh
fetchzone=/usr/local/bin/fetchzone

[ $# -ne 2 ] && { echo "Usage: $0 zone IP" >&2; exit 2; }

zone=$1
ip=$2
tmpz=/tmp/zone.$$

${fetchzone} ${zone} ${ip} > ${tmpz} &&
        mv ${tmpz} /etc/maradns/db.${zone}

rm -f ${tmpz}       # unlink anyway; file exists even
                    # if transfer failed
```

MaraDNS doesn't notice when a zone file changes. This means that you must restart maradns for changes to take effect.

Steffen Beyer has written a Ruby script that enables MaraDNS to operate as a slave server, by automating the tasks you'd otherwise have to perform manually. The script, run via cron, fetches the master zones, checks their serial numbers against those in the local zones, sorts in the new records, and restarts MaraDNS if necessary (see `http://teralink.net/misc/fetchzones/`).

4.6 Recursion, roots and forwarders

Unless it has been built as authoritative-only, MaraDNS can also act as a recursive name server with support for IP-based access control to the recursor. By default, the name of the recursive-enabled server binary is maradns instead of maradns.authonly. As we mentioned before, even when built with recursion enabled, MaraDNS can still act as an authoritative name server if you specify zones to be served in the csv2 dictionary variable.

Access to the recursive portion of the MaraDNS server is controlled by an ACL set up in mararc. The variable recursive_acl contains a list of IP addresses or alias names that define the addresses of the clients allowed to perform recursive queries. For example,

```
recursive_acl = "127.0.0.1"
```

allows only localhost to use the server for recursion.

4.6.1 Setting up private root servers

When acting as a recursive name server, MaraDNS loads a compiled-in list of root name servers by default. To override this, you set the root_server variable. Here's an example of how:

```
ipv4_alias = {}
ipv4_alias["myroots"] = "192.168.1.20"
ipv4_alias["myroots"] += "192.168.9.53"

root_servers = {}
root_servers["."] = "myroots"
```

MaraDNS's powerful ipv4_alias mechanism is used to create a named array of local authoritative root servers, and this is then assigned to the root_servers variable, effectively overriding MaraDNS's compiled-in list. The root_servers may point only to root servers; as we said before, if a forwarding server is needed, use the upstream_servers variable instead.

4.6.2 Forwarding queries

MaraDNS can act as a forwarding server by setting the variable upstream_servers to point to a list of caching servers willing to act as forwarders, either for all zones or on a zone by zone basis. Similar to what we did in the section on private roots, we create an array of our (QUPPS') servers named myown. Forwarding for all domains is set up to point to those servers; however, we specify an exception for domain mens.de, for which it is to use two different forwarders, which are queried in the specified order:

```
ipv4_alias = {}
ipv4_alias["myown"]              = "192.168.1.20"
ipv4_alias["myown"]              = "192.168.9.53"

upstream_servers = {}
upstream_servers["."]            = "myown"
upstream_servers["mens.de."] = "192.168.1.21, 192.168.1.45"
```

4.7 Logging and utilities

4.7.1 Logging and monitoring

If you define verbose_level in `mararc` to an appropriate value, MaraDNS logs queries to standard output in the format shown in Figure 4.3. The `Z` in the following example log entry indicates the query type as per the list in Table 4.2.

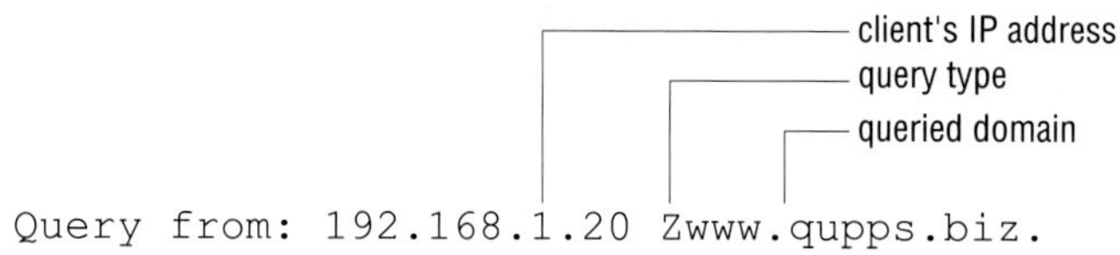

Figure 4.3: Query logging in MaraDNS

Qtype	Log code
A	A
NS	N
CNAME	C
SOA	S
PTR	P
TXT	T
ANY	Z
MX	@
other	U

Table 4.2: MaraDNS query types and logging codes

If MaraDNS's main configuration `/etc/mararc` contains an admin_acl that allows it, a few metrics can be retrieved from a running MaraDNS server via DNS (see description of debug_msg_level in Section 4.4.1).

4.7.2 Converting BIND master zone files to csv2 format

The bind2csv2 program included in later versions of MaraDNS converts master zone files, such as those used by the BIND name server, to the csv2 zone file format used by MaraDNS, and which you typically place in a directory from which MaraDNS can find them. For example, the following converts the BIND zone master file for qupps.biz, and creates a new CSV2 file `qupps.biz.csv2`:

```
$ bind2csv2.py -c qupps.biz
Processing zone file qupps.biz
qupps.biz.csv2 written
```

bind2csv2 does not yet handle BIND's `$ORIGIN`, nor does it handle wild-card names, ignoring them during conversion.

4.7.3 The duende utility

The duende utility (included in MaraDNS's distribution) is a program that can "daemonize" MaraDNS main program or the zoneserver. After spawning the servers, it logs the standard output of the child processes via syslog.

If duende is sent a HUP signal it restarts the child. You can use this to force maradns to re-read its configuration file, for example after fetchzone has finished writing an incoming zone transfer.

4.7.4 Querying DNS servers with askmara

askmara is a small program that queries remote name servers for DNS records and outputs these in a csv2-compatible format. Whereas with dig you specify the query type with `-t`, or as the last argument on the command line, with askmara you specify the query type by prefixing the domain name with one of the mnemonics from table 4.2:

```
$ askmara -n @qupps.biz. 127.0.0.1
# Querying the server with the IP 127.0.0.1
# Question: @qupps.biz.
qupps.biz. +86400 mx 10 mail.qupps.biz.
...
```

Summary

- You can compile MaraDNS as an authoritative-only or as an authoritative and recursive name server.
- Setting up and configuring MaraDNS is easy. One of its best features is the automatic creation of PTR resource records with the `FQDN4` and `FQDN6` line types.
- MaraDNS also runs on Microsoft Windows; we show you how to install it in Chapter 14.

Related topics

In this section of each chapter, we point you to other Chapters in this book where we discuss topics or other name servers you may wish to implement together with what you are currently reading. Don't worry if the terms don't mean anything to you. We recommend you ignore these "pointers" on first reading.

- tinydns (Chapter 11) is an authoritative-only server you may want to consider as it too is easy to set up. We discuss its caching counterpart, dnscache, in Chapter 17.
- dnsmasq in Chapter 13 is an easy-to-setup caching name server, suitable for Small Office / Home Office environments.

Notes and further reading

MaraDNS's home page is at `http://www.maradns.org/`. The program is released under a BSD-type license. News about new snapshots are usually published at the MaraDNS blog `http://maradns.blogspot.com/`

Building MaraDNS

Interestingly, MaraDNS does not use autoconf during the build process because, to quote its author, "autoconf is designed to solve a problem that existed in the mid 1990s but does not exist today". Admittedly, the diversity of C compilers and environments is nowhere near as large as it was.

To build MaraDNS as an authoritative name server, use a procedure like this:

```
$ wget http://www.maradns.org/download/1.3/1.3.07.08/maradns-1.3.07.08.tar.gz
$ tar xvzf maradns-1.3.07.08.tar.gz
$ cd maradns-1.3.07.08
$ ./configure --authonly
$ make
# PREFIX=/usr/local make install
```

Built as above, the main binary server is installed as maradns.authonly in `/usr/local/sbin`. To build MaraDNS with recursion enabled, omit the `--authonly` switch to configure; the main server is then called maradns.

The installation procedure creates a minimal `mararc` configuration file in `/etc` (but you will certainly want to adapt this to your environment) and installs MaraDNS's manual pages and a script that launches maradns and its zoneserver at startup.

If you want to tweak the locations of the installation directories, either set `$PREFIX` as shown in the example above, or modify the `build/install.locations` file in the source before invoking `make install`.

Further reading

- The MaraDNS Web site has a few good tutorials and guides (see `http://www.maradns.org/tutorial/tutorial.html`).
- The record types supported by MaraDNS are listed both in the manual pages and online at `http://www.maradns.org/tutorial/man.csv2.html`
- A paper by Sam Trenholme on the *Security design of MaraDNS* can be found at `http://www.tisc-insight.com/newsletters/42.html`

Chapter

5 MyDNS

Life would be so much easier if only we had the source code.

anonymous

Introduction

MyDNS stores its zone data in a MySQL or PostgreSQL database. It is currently the only server with a database back-end that has support for RFC 2136 Dynamic DNS Updates. It includes a lean and mean Web-based administration tool, and tools for migrating to and from MyDNS.

MyDNS is an authoritative DNS server created by Don Moore. It uses an SQL database back-end to store zone data. The program is easy to install, and it supports both MySQL and PostgreSQL. It boasts a very neat Web-based administration script contained in a single PHP file, which makes its deployment trivial. MyDNS supports Dynamic DNS updates, allowing it to work in conjunction with a DHCP server that registers DHCP clients in the DNS. MyDNS has support for outgoing zone transfers (but not incoming), and it supports DNS over TCP if you enable it.

Pros	• RFC 2136 Dynamic DNS updates are written to the back-end database • Tunable cache • Normalized database schema • Web interface in a single PHP file • *nix manual pages
Cons	◦ Future development uncertain (see Notes) ◦ No incoming zone transfers
Scenarios	Small to medium DNS servers.

Table 5.1: MyDNS at a glance

5.1 Getting MyDNS up and running

To get started with MyDNS, proceed in the following order:

1. Decide which SQL database back-end (MySQL or PostgreSQL) you want to use. (See Section 3.1 for guidance if necessary.)
2. Download and install MyDNS (see Notes).
3. Create the database and the tables required for MyDNS. We show you how to do this in Section 5.1.1.
4. Create a zone and some resource records in the database. We show you how to do this in Section 5.1.3.
5. Launch MyDNS:

   ```
   # /usr/local/sbin/mydns  --background --verbose
   ```

   Check the log file (the default on our system is `/var/log/messages`) to ensure that MyDNS started successfully. Common errors that prevent a successful MyDNS launch include:

   - You have another DNS server listening on the same IP address/port numbers, making it impossible for MyDNS to acquire access to it (see Notes on using netstat).
   - The username and/or password used to access the MySQL database are incorrect.

5.1.1 Creating the MySQL database tables for MyDNS

MyDNS has a facility to print the list of commands you need to create the tables in the MySQL or PostgreSQL database for use with MyDNS. For example, you can feed this list of commands to the mysql command line tool:

```
$ mysqladmin create ourdnsdb
$ mydns --create-tables | mysql ourdnsdb
```

(Throughout this chapter we assume the name of the database you're using for MyDNS is `ourdnsdb`.)

You will then want to create a user and its associated password with which MyDNS access the MySQL database:

```
$ mysql ourdnsdb
mysql> GRANT ALL on ourdnsdb.* TO fred@'localhost' IDENTIFIED BY 'hah!';
mysql> \q
```

Change the username ("fred") and password ("hah!") appropriately in `mydns.conf`.

5.1.2 The MyDNS database tables

MyDNS stores zones in one database table and the zones' resource records in a separate table. The two database tables used by MyDNS are:

soa This table defines a zone and its Start of Authority (SOA) resource record.

rr This table defines the resource records (RR) that make up a DNS zone.

In the following discussion, columns marked as being "optional" are just that: optional. If you want MyDNS to use these, you have to create the columns, by altering the database schema. We discuss the use of these optional columns when we discuss the feature they relate to.

The soa table

The `soa` table is used to store the Start of Authority (SOA) of a zone. Each zone is defined by a single row (a single record) in this table. The table definition has sensible defaults for most values, so you don't have to insert them explicitly when defining a new zone. The columns in the default schema are:

id A unique numeric ID for the record. The database schema provides an auto increment column for this, which means you can `INSERT` a NULL value to have it increased automatically.

origin The name of the zone, such as "`qupps.biz.`". Note that this value *must* be terminated by a period. If you omit the terminating period, the zone will not exist.

ns The name of the primary name server (MNAME) for the zone.

mbox The RNAME of the Start of Authority.

serial The serial number of the zone (default: 1).

refresh The SOA refresh value in seconds (default: 28800 = 8 hours).

retry The SOA retry value in seconds (default: 7200 = 2 hours).

expire The SOA expire time in seconds (default: 604800 = 1 week).

minimum The SOA minimum time in seconds (default: 86400 = 1 day).

ttl The SOA TTL (default: 86400 = 1 day).

xfer This optional column contains IP access lists specifying which clients may transfer zones (Section 5.3.1).

update_acl This optional column contains IP access lists specifying which clients may perform RFC 2136 dynamic DNS updates (Section 5.4).

active If this optional column exists, whenever rows are selected from the table, its value is honored. It should contain a boolean value (integer 1/0, or string "Y"/"N", "1"/"0", or "Active"/"Inactive"). If the row is marked as inactive, MyDNS will react as though the row didn't exist at all. If you use this optional column, you normally set it to a "true" value, and set it "false" to temporarily "delete" the respective zone, which can be easily undeleted later if necessary.

The `rr` table

The `rr` table for "Resource Records" stores individual DNS resources for all the zones. The zone to which a record belongs is specified by the `zone` column. The default schema for this table is:

id A unique number that identifies this record. The database schema provides an auto increment column for this, which means you can `INSERT` a NULL value to have it increased automatically.

zone The `id` in the `soa` table of the zone to which this record belongs. In other words, the value of this column (`rr.zone`) corresponds to the value of the `soa.id` column.

name The domain name that this record describes. This column may contain a host name, a fully qualified domain name (terminated by period), or an asterisk (*) for wild cards.

type The type of resource record. The following types are implemented:

A An Address in dotted-decimal format.

```
192.168.1.20
```

AAAA An IPv6 Address.

```
fe80::2ff:52ff:fee7:4c4e
```

ALIAS A server-side alias. It is handled like a CNAME, but the client only sees an Address (A).

```
print.qupps.biz
```

CNAME Canonical name.

www

MX — Mail Exchanger. The preference value for an MX is set in the `aux` column.

mail.qupps.biz

NS — Name Server.

ns1.qupps.biz

PTR — Pointer record; used only within in-addr.arpa zones.

www.qupps.biz

SRV — Service location. The `data` column contains three space-separated values: The first is the weight, the second is the port number on the server, and the third is the target host.

0 389 ldap.qupps.biz

TXT — Text record.

hello world

data The data associated with the DNS resource record `type`.

aux An auxiliary numeric value in addition to `data`. For Mail Exchanger records (MX) this column specifies the preference, for SRV records, the priority.

ttl The value, in seconds, of the Time to Live (TTL) for the resource record.

active As with `active` in the `soa` table, if this optional column exists, whenever records are retrieved from the table, its value is honored. It should contain a boolean value which can be an integer (1/0) or a string ("Y"/"N", "1"/"0", or "Active"/"Inactive"). If MyDNS detects that the row is inactive (because the column exists and you have set it to a "false" value) it will react as though the row didn't exist at all.

You can add as many additional columns as you wish to either of the two tables, and you can change column lengths too, if you want. Do not, however, change the names of the columns.

5.1.3 Example – Create a zone and its resource records

To create a new zone with some records in it, you can use the MySQL command-line tool, mysql, to perform appropriate inserts into the database tables:

```
$ mysql ourdnsdb
mysql> INSERT INTO soa (origin, ns, mbox)
    ->    VALUES ('qupps.biz.', 'ns.qupps.biz.', 'jp');

mysql> INSERT INTO rr (zone, name, type, data)
    ->         VALUES (1, 'ns', 'A', '192.168.1.20');

mysql> INSERT INTO rr (zone, name, type, data)
    ->         VALUES (1, 'www', 'CNAME', 'ns');
```

There are several points to note:

- In the first `INSERT` we insert our very first zone into the `soa` table – as `id` is not specified, and thus `NULL`, MySQL gives the "automatic" `id` column an integer value of 1.

  In the two next `INSERT` statements, we use this to associate the records in `rr` to the zone in table `soa`.

- The zone name in the `origin` column of the `soa` table must be qualified with a trailing period.

- If you don't fully qualify names in both the `ns` and `mbox` columns, they are qualified with `origin`. In the example above, the `mbox` column is unqualified; this will cause MyDNS to return the RNAME of this zone as jp.qupps.biz..

- MyDNS has sensible values for the Start of Authority (SOA) resource record fields, so we didn't enter them. However you can override these on a zone by zone basis by inserting (or later updating) the appropriate columns of the `soa` table.

- As soon as you have inserted a row into the `soa` or `rr` tables, it is there for MyDNS to serve via DNS. That is, after all, the whole point in having a database back-end on a DNS server. This of course means that if you "accidentally" incorrectly mass-update one of the database tables, your DNS clients will immediately "see" the results. This isn't a problem in itself: it is simply a word of caution that you should be careful with your SQL queries.

If you now query your MyDNS server, the DNS resources you entered are immediately visible:

```
$ dig @127.0.0.1 www.qupps.biz
;; flags: qr aa rd; QUERY: 1, ANSWER: 2, AUTHORITY: 0, ADDITIONAL: 0
;; WARNING: recursion requested but not available

;; ANSWER SECTION:
www.qupps.biz.          86400   IN      CNAME   ns.qupps.biz.
ns.qupps.biz.           86400   IN      A       192.168.1.20
```

5.2 Changing the way MyDNS works

5.2.1 Configuration in `mydns.conf`

There are several configuration variables to alter MyDNS behavior. The following sections detail the available configuration variables. Most of these variables have sensible default values. To add or modify a variable, edit the `mydns.conf` file, usually located in `/etc`, and save the file. You must restart the MyDNS daemon (mydns) for changed variables to take effect. The syntax for variables is:

variable = *value*

On any line, text following a hash sign (#) is ignored unless it is escaped with a backslash (\#). Empty lines are ignored.

If you invoke mydns with the `--dump-config` option, it prints a default configuration to standard output, merging it with whatever settings you already have in your `mydns.conf`.

Basic database information

The following variables define how MyDNS accesses the underlying database:

db-host
: The domain name (i.e. hostname) or address of the MySQL server. Note that the name you specify should be in your `/etc/hosts` because otherwise the name couldn't be resolved – to resolve the name MyDNS would have to use itself before it had started itself! We recommend you use an IP address. The default is localhost.

```
db-host = 192.168.1.178
```

database
: The name of the database from which MyDNS reads its zone data.

```
database = ourdnsdb
```

db-user
: The username to use for authenticating with the back-end database server. There is no default.

```
db-user = fred
```

The user you specify in db-user needs `SELECT` privileges on the database you specified with the database variable. If you use RFC 2136 dynamic updates, the specified user will additionally require `INSERT`, `UPDATE` and `DELETE` privileges.

db-password
: The password to use for authenticating to the back-end database server.

```
db-password = hah!
```

Server options

The following variables control the general behavior of the server:

user

group
: The server will drop privileges and run with the permissions of the specified user or group.

```
user = nobody
group = nogroup
```

listen
: The server should listen on the specified address(es). If the value of this variable is `*`, the server will bind to all interfaces of the system. We recommend, however, that you explicitly specify which addresses to use. The variable may have a comma-separated list of IP addresses, or you may specify multiple listen variables. To use a port other than the default (53), append the desired port number to the IP address, preceded by a colon (`:`).

```
listen = 127.0.0.1
listen = 192.168.1.164:593
```

no-listen
: The server should *not* listen on the given IP address, even if it is specified in the listen variable. This sounds a bit pointless, but if you run MyDNS on a host with many interfaces, you can specify listen = * and "remove" the interfaces you don't want MyDNS to listen on with one or more no-listen settings.

Options to control internal caching

MyDNS answers incoming queries with records obtained from the database back-end. In order to lower both the load on the back-end database and the time taken to answer the query, MyDNS can cache replies for queries it answers.

When MyDNS receives a question it can answer, MyDNS stores the positive results (i.e. found records) in its *zone cache*.

Once a complete reply has been constructed for a specific query (for example, `IN A www.qupps.biz.`), this complete reply is stored in the *reply cache*. The reply cache is especially useful because if it contains a match for a specific query, MyDNS does not need to perform any database queries or even very much internal computation in order to return the reply.

The following options alter the behavior of the cache:

zone-cache-size
: The maximum number of entries the zone cache may contain at any time. Default 4 096. (The average entry in the cache has a size of about 128 bytes, so a zone-cache-size of 8 192 gives a cache of approximately 8 192 x 128 bytes = 1 MB.)

```
zone-cache-size = 8192
```

A large cache improves performance but can cause MyDNS to serve out-of-date answers to queries for resource records that have been recently modified. You can disable the zone data cache completely by setting its size to 0.

zone-cache-expire
: Entries that have been in the cache for this number of seconds (default 60) are expired from the cache. If the Time to Live (TTL) for any resource record in the zone is less than the cache expiry time, the TTL is honored (i.e. it overrides the zone-cache-expire time).

```
zone-cache-expire = 120
```

If you set this to zero, the zone data cache is disabled. The higher you set this value, the longer it will be before MyDNS has to query the back-end database to find out if a record has changed. If you have a fairly static DNS with few changes being made to your zones, increasing this value will increase the overall performance of your system.

reply-cache-size
: When MyDNS has constructed a complete reply for a specific query, this complete reply is stored in the reply cache. This variable defines how large the reply cache should be (default 1 024 entries).

```
reply-cache-size = 2048
```

Setting the value of this variable to zero disables the reply cache.

reply-cache-expire
: Entries in the reply cache expire once they are this number of seconds old. Default 30.

```
reply-cache-expire = 120
```

Setting this value to zero disables the reply cache.

Options that affect the name server

The variables in this section affect the operation of the MyDNS name server. You will usually not need these, but they do allow you to create interesting configurations. Variables defined as being of type boolean are enabled by specifying their value as being "true" or "yes", and they are disabled by using "false" or "no".

allow-axfr
: (boolean) Whether outgoing zone transfers are allowed (default: "no"):

```
allow-axfr = yes
```

You can specify IP-based access rules for outgoing zone transfers by adding an optional column to the `soa` table (Section 5.3.1).

allow-tcp
: (boolean) Whether DNS requests over TCP are allowed (default: "no"). This variable does not affect zone transfers (which are always over TCP).

allow-update
: (boolean) Whether dynamic updates are allowed (default: "no"). We discuss this in Section 5.4.

soa-table
: Specifies the name of the database table containing the Start of Authority records for zones. The default value is `soa` and you shouldn't need to modify this.

soa-where
: If set, this variable contains an extra `WHERE` clause to append to queries selecting records from the soa-table.

For example, if you're an ISP, you might have a policy that you disable a customer's zone if he hasn't settled his invoice. You define:

```
soa-where = paid=1
```

and create the additional column `paid` in the `soa` table:

```
mysql> ALTER TABLE soa
    -> ADD COLUMN paid INTEGER NOT NULL DEFAULT 1;
```

To disable customer QUPPS's zone, for example, use:

```
mysql> UPDATE soa SET paid = 0 WHERE origin = 'qupps.biz.';
```

and MyDNS will hide this zone, until `paid` is set to `1` again when QUPPS pay their bill. This approach is clearer and more flexible than deleting QUPPS's zone when they don't pay, and then having to recreate it later.

Note that a similar functionality (i.e. disabling of a zone) can be implemented with the optional `active` column on both the `soa` and `rr` database tables.

rr-table
: Specifies the name of the database table containing the resource records for zones. The default value is `rr` and you shouldn't need to modify this.

rr-where
: Analogous to soa-where, this contains an additional `WHERE` clause to append to queries selecting records from the rr-table. You can use this to selectively enable or disable individual resource records.

recursive
: The IP address of a DNS server that accepts recursive DNS queries. If MyDNS receives a query where recursion is desired, and the zone is not local (i.e. MyDNS is not authoritative for it), MyDNS will forward the query to the server at the specified and return the result to the client.

```
recursive = 192.168.1.20
```

If your MyDNS server is Internet-facing, do *not* set this option: you should not make recursive DNS available to the whole Internet.

5.3 Replicating zones

MyDNS can replicate zone data in two ways:

1. Replication by the back-end database system. (This is what PowerDNS calls "native" replication.)

   For two or more peer MyDNS servers serving the same zone data, set up each mydns server with its own SQL back-end. Then use SQL database replication from the master database to the slave database (Figure 5.1).

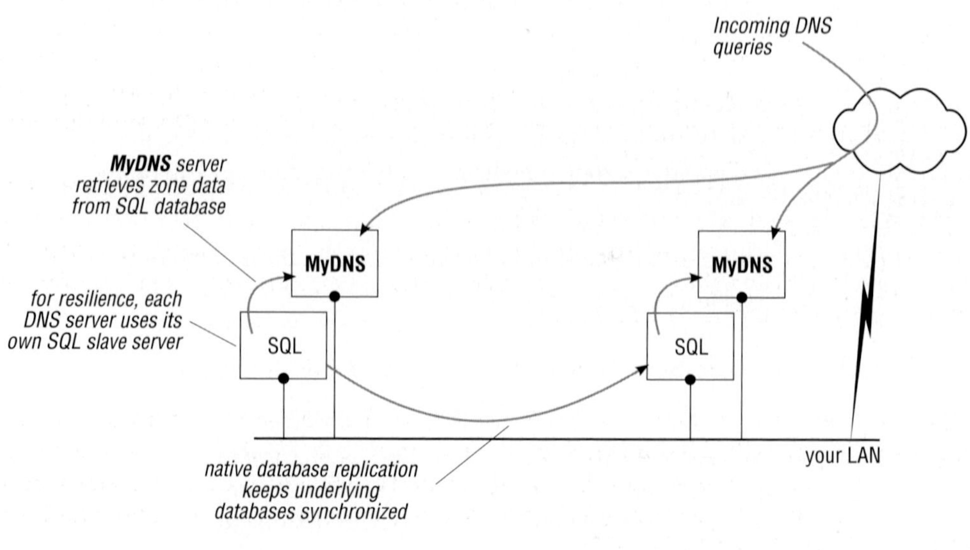

Figure 5.1: MyDNS with "native" database replication

2. AXFR zone transfer: use this where you have a MyDNS master server and a different brand of server as slave(s) (Figure 5.2). MyDNS doesn't support incoming zone transfers, so it can't act as a slave server.

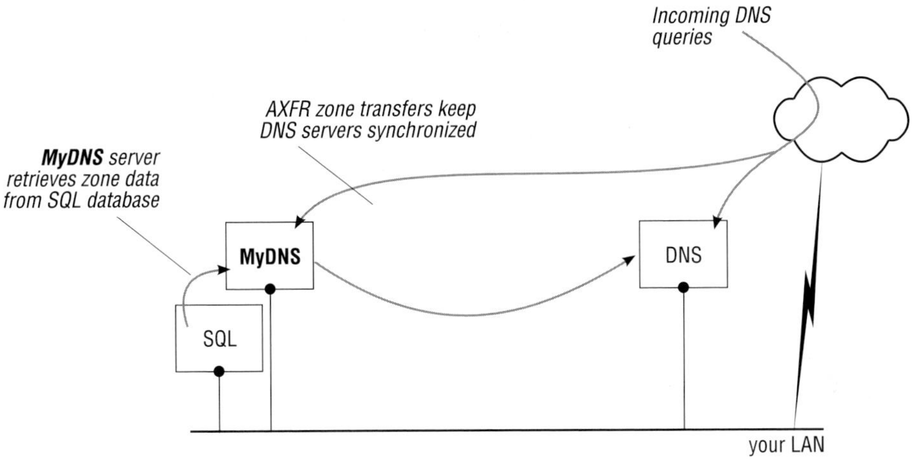

Figure 5.2: MyDNS as a master server

5.3.1 Zone transfers

Zone transfers are allowed only if the allow-axfr variable is "true" in the server configuration. MyDNS supports only outgoing AXFR zone transfers; it does not support incremental transfers (IXFR) or incoming zone transfers. If you enable zone transfers, any client may perform a transfer for any zone in the database. As this is not a good idea, MyDNS provides access controls to limit who may transfer zones.

You can enable IP-based access control in MyDNS by adding a predefined (but optional) column called `xfer` to the `soa` table. The server examines the value of this column when a client requests a zone transfer to determine whether the client is allowed to transfer the zone. If you want to add the column to your database, use mysql (or any other program you normally use to alter a database schema):

```
mysql> ALTER TABLE soa ADD COLUMN xfer CHAR(255) NOT NULL;
```

The `xfer` column contains either an asterisk (*), or a comma-separated list of individual IP addresses and/or CIDR *network*/*netmask* pairs, specifying which addresses are allowed to perform AXFR zone transfers. (The asterisk means "allow any client to transfer zones".) For example, to allow zone transfer requests for zone qupps.biz, from hosts with addresses 127.0.0.1 or 192.168.1.1–192.168.1.255:

```
mysql> UPDATE soa SET xfer='127.0.0.1,192.168.1/24' WHERE origin = 'qupps.biz.';
```

If MyDNS is running as a hidden or stealth master to a slave, it will not notify its slave servers when data in a zone has changed – it has no support for NOTIFY. There are currently three ways a slave can detect that data on the master has changed:

1. The slave server waits for the Start of Authority (SOA) retry timer to expire, and then checks the SOA serial number on the master: if that number has increased, the slave initiates a zone transfer.
2. Perform notification manually using a program like dnsnotify (see Notes.)
3. A new experimental version of MyDNS (see Notes) now *does* support slave notification. Use that.

5.4 Dynamic DNS updates in MyDNS

A big advantage of MyDNS is that it supports RFC 2136 Dynamic DNS updates. These update requests are received as DNS queries and cause the database server (MySQL or PostgreSQL) to modify or create the relevant resource records (i.e. records in the `rr` database table) in the database back-end. We discuss dynamic DNS in detail in Chapter 19, but we want to show you how this works for MyDNS here.

Before enabling dynamic DNS updates, ensure the db-user user specified in `mydns.conf` has permission to insert and update rows on the `rr` table (or the table you specified in the rr-table variable). If MyDNS cannot update the tables, dynamic DNS updates fail.

We strongly recommend you use a transactional database back-end if you allow dynamic updates, so that MyDNS can roll back (i.e. undo) a transaction if an update fails. Without a transactional back-end, your database could be left in an inconsistent state if an update should fail (see Notes on page 71).

5.4.1 Enable dynamic DNS updates

MyDNS allows dynamic DNS updates by clients if the boolean configuration variable allow-update in your `mydns.conf` is "true" (Remember that you must restart mydns for a changed setting to take effect.)

```
allow-updates = yes
```

5.4.2 IP access rules for dynamic DNS updates

By default dynamic DNS updates are allowed from localhost only. You can override this by specifying IP based access rules for DNS updates. Enable IP-based access rules in MyDNS by adding a predefined (but optional) column called `update_acl` to the `soa` table. `update_acl` controls dynamic updates in the same way that `xfer` controls zone transfers. The server examines the value of this column when a client performs an DNS update to determine whether the client is allowed to. If this column does not exist, updates are allowed from localhost only. If you want to add the column to your database, use mysql (or any other program you normally use to alter a database schema):

```
mysql> ALTER TABLE soa ADD COLUMN update_acl VARCHAR(254);
```

The `update_acl` column contains either an asterisk (*), or a comma-separated list of individual IP addresses and/or CIDR *network/netmask* pairs, specifying which addresses are allowed to perform updates. (The asterisk means "allow any client to update".) For example, to allow update requests for zone qupps.biz, from hosts with addresses 127.0.0.1 or 192.168.1.1–192.168.1.255:

```
mysql> UPDATE soa SET update_acl = '127.0.0.1,192.168.1/24' WHERE ↩
                                 origin = 'qupps.biz.';
```

We show you an example of dynamic DNS updates using MyDNS in Section 19.6.2.

5.5 Utilities included with MyDNS

MyDNS includes several useful utilities:

mydnsimport
: to import zones via zone transfer (AXFR), or from a tinydns-data file as used by tinydns.

mydnsexport
: export any amount of zones either to master file format, or to tinydns-data format for use with tinydns.

admin.php
: a Web interface for managing zone data.

5.5.1 Importing zones into MyDNS with mydnsimport

This utility is great if you are migrating from tinydns or BIND to MyDNS, because it can import zone data into MyDNS from either of two sources:

1. From a DNS server via the zone transfer (AXFR) protocol.

2. From an existing data file in tinydns-data format.

During import, you can specify with the `--replace` flag whether existing records in the SQL database should be replaced with data from the import source; if you omit the flag, mydnsimport refuses to change existing zones. For example, to import a zone via zone transfer:

```
$ mydnsimport  --axfr=192.168.1.20 example.net
```

5.5.2 Exporting zones from MyDNS with mydnsexport

mydnsexport exports zone data for one or more zones, extracting the zone data from MyDNS' underlying SQL database and providing it in either master zone file format, suitable for use by BIND or NSD, or tinydns-data format, suitable for conversion and consumption by tinydns.

1. To create master file format:

   ```
   $ mydnsexport  --bind qupps.biz
   $TTL 86400
   ; Zone: qupps.biz. (#1)
   ```

```
; Created by "mydnsexport --bind qupps.biz"
; Sun Dec 30 18:15:33 2007
$ORIGIN qupps.biz.

@       IN SOA  ns.qupps.biz.   jp.mens.de. (
        1                ; Serial
        28800            ; Refresh
        7200             ; Retry
        604800           ; Expire
        86400          ) ; Minimum

ns                      86400   IN A            192.168.1.20
pc.qupps.biz.           86400   IN A            192.168.1.178
www                     86400   IN CNAME        ns.qupps.biz.
```

2. To create tinydns-data format:

```
$ mydnsexport --tinydns qupps.biz
#
# Created by "mydnsexport --tinydns qupps.biz"
# Sun Dec 30 18:18:28 2007
#
Zqupps.biz:ns.qupps.biz:jp.mens.de:1:28800:7200:604800:86400:86400
=ns.qupps.biz:192.168.1.20:86400
=pc.qupps.biz:192.168.1.178:3600
Cwww.qupps.biz:ns.qupps.biz:86400
```

5.5.3 The MyDNS Web interface: admin.php

MyDNS has a Web-based administration utility (Figure 5.3) contained in a single file. It is located in the `contrib` directory of the source distribution. (For other Web-based administration programs, see Notes.) A very nice feature of the program is that it can automatically increment the serial number in the SOA record for a zone whenever a client modifies any record in that zone – a great convenience. If you are offering outgoing zone transfers.
Installation is simple: copy the admin.php file to a suitable location on a Web server, and modify the database parameters at the top of admin.php to suit your setup. You may wish to change some of the other variables as well:

- If `$auto_update_serial` is "true", admin.php will automatically update the zone's serial number whenever a record is modified.

- If `$auto_update_ptr` is "true", admin.php will automatically create PTR records for you when a user adds, modifies or deletes an Address (A) record. admin.php will automatically create the zone in the database, adding a record to the `soa` table if necessary. For this to work, `$default_ns` and `$default_mbox` have to be set as well.

- If you use PostgreSQL, set `$use_pgsql` to "true".

admin.php doesn't have built-in authentication, because it relies on the Web server to allow users to access it. If you use an Apache Web server, you can use one of the many available authentication modules to control access to admin.php.

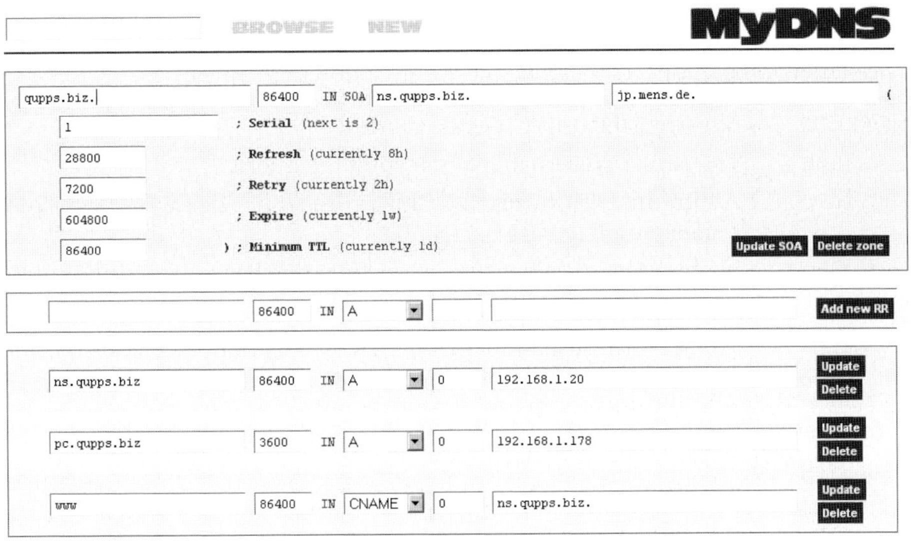

Figure 5.3: MyDNS admin.php

5.6 Monitoring MyDNS

5.6.1 Logging queries

If you start mydns with the verbose option (`-v`), it logs each query it receives, in a format like:

```
30-Dec-2007 15:28:04+163961 #2 42597 UDP 127.0.0.1 IN A ↩
      www.qupps.biz. NOERROR - 1 2 0 0 LOG N QUERY ""
```

Each log line consists of 17 space-separated fields:

1. The date the query was received (`30-Dec-2007`).
2. The time the query was received as *hour:minutes:seconds+microseconds*.
3. A hash symbol followed by an incrementing internal ID number for the query (`#2`).
4. The query ID provided by the client (`42597`). This is usually a seemingly-random 16-bit number used by the client to make sure the answer it receives matches the question it asked.
5. The transport used (`UDP`); this is either TCP or UDP.
6. The client's IP address (`127.0.0.1`).
7. The query class. Always `IN` (Internet).
8. The query type (`A`), such as `MX`, `NS`, etc.

9. The name being requested (`www.qupps.biz.`).

10. The status of the query. This can be one of the following values:

NOERROR	No error; the query was successful.
FORMERR	The server was unable to interpret the query.
SERVFAIL	An internal error occurred; this is probably due to incorrect data in the underlying database back-end.
NXDOMAIN	Nonexistent domain: the requested name has no matching resources.
NOTIMP	The requested type of query is not implemented.
REFUSED	The server refused the query. This usually happens when a zone transfer is requested by a client not allowed to do so.

11. If the previous field was anything but NOERROR, this is a human-readable reason why the query failed, with space characters converted to underscores (_). If the previous field was NOERROR, this field contains a dash (–).

12. The number of resource records included in the question section of the reply.

13. The number of resource records included in the answer section of the reply.

14. The number of resource records included in the authority section of the reply.

15. The number of resource records included in the additional section of the reply.

16. The word `LOG`.

17. The character "Y" if this was a cached reply, "N" if it was not.

Summary

- MyDNS is an authoritative-only server, although it can forward recursive queries to a nominated server.
- It uses either a MySQL or a PostgreSQL back-end.
- MyDNS includes tools both for migrating to, and away from, MyDNS.
- MyDNS implements support for RFC 2136 dynamic DNS updates.

Related topics

In this section we point you to other Chapters in this book in which we discuss topics or other name servers you may wish to implement together with what you are currently reading. Don't worry if the terms don't mean anything to you on first reading. If you are reading this book sequentially, we recommend you ignore these "pointers".

- dnsmasq (Chapter 13)
- In Chapter 18 we discuss how to set up a private root name server with MyDNS.
- In Chapter 19 we discuss RFC 2136 Dynamic DNS Updates and show you an example using MyDNS.

Notes and further reading

MyDNS' *home*

The home of MyDNS is at `http://mydns.bboy.net/`. Its author, Don Moore, considers MyDNS to be complete, so he has stopped developing it.

At the time of this writing, the development of MyDNS has restarted with a new name: MyDNS-NG. Development of MyDNS-NG is being coordinated by Howard Wilkinson and the project is hosted at `http://sourceforge.net/projects/mydns-ng/`.

Building MyDNS

Building MyDNS is straightforward:

```
$ wget http://mydns.bboy.net/download/mydns-1.1.0.tar.gz
$ tar xvzf xvzf mydns-1.1.0.tar.gz
$ cd mydns-1.1.0
$ ./configure --prefix=/usr/local --with-mysql-lib=/usr/lib64/mysql
$ make
$ make install
```

After installing MyDNS the command:

```
$ make conf
```

creates a commented `/etc/mydns.conf` which you can edit and tailor to your environment: at the very least, you will have to change the database connection settings in the file. To view a commented configuration file use:

```
$ mydns --dump-config
```

The netstat utility

netstat is a program that prints information on network connections. You can also use it to determine whether a specific port is already in use. For example, to see whether there is already a DNS server running on your system, you use:

```
# netstat -anp | grep 53
tcp    0   0 0.0.0.0:53        0.0.0.0:*        LISTEN       5204/pdns_server
udp    0   0 0.0.0.0:53        0.0.0.0:*                     5204/pdns_server
```

The two lines in the sample output above show a program called pdns_server running on PID 5204. It is listening on TCP port 53 and on UDP port 53. Note how we use the `-n` option to netstat to have IP addresses printed instead of hostnames. (When you are investigating problems with the DNS, it's clearly best not to use diagnostic tools that inadvertently use the DNS to resolve hostnames.)

DNS notify

You can use a tool like dnsnotify to manually send out a notification request to a slave server (see Section 1.3 for a discussion of NOTIFY). In doing so, you "pretend" to be a master DNS name server (see `http://people.debian.org/~pkern/dnsnotify`).

MyDNSConfig

MyDNSConfig (see `http://www.mydnsconfig.org/`) is another Web based administration tool built upon MyDNS' MySQL schema (my, there are a lot of "My"s in that sentence!).

lochDNS

lochDNS is a self-contained package of operating system and tools (sometimes called a "virtual appliance", as for Xen, VMware, etc.) that provides an installation of MyDNS. It is packaged together with MyDNSConfig and MySQL, so it is ready to run (see `http://wiki.rpath.com/wiki/Appliance:LochDNS`).

Chapter

6 PowerDNS Authoritative Server

Not all DNS servers run BIND. There are other ones.

anonymous

Introduction

The PowerDNS server is a feature-rich program that can fulfill most DNS server requirements. It supports several different back-ends from which it retrieves DNS zone data, including MySQL, LDAP, BIND and the Pipe back-end. It can support several back-ends simultaneously, making it very flexible.

PowerDNS is a DNS server that serves DNS zone data from a large number of supported database systems. PowerDNS was developed by the Dutch company PowerDNS B.V. as a commercial product. In November 2002 they released PowerDNS under an Open Source License (GPL version 2), although they still offer commercial support for it. Bert Hubert is its main author.

Pros	• Multiple database back-ends supported simultaneously • Supports LDAP, SQL databases, and BIND zone files • Separate versatile, high-performance, caching server (PowerDNS Recursor) • Full master/slave semantics including NOTIFY • Automatic provisioning of slaves • Packet cache increases throughput and lowers load on back-ends • Programmable back-end • Built-in Web server for statistics and monitoring
Cons	○ No DNS security (TSIG) ○ No RFC 2136 Dynamic DNS
Scenarios	Medium to large environments that need the widest range of options for DNS zone data storage.

Table 6.1: PowerDNS at a glance

PowerDNS is rich in features, so we recommend you get an overview of its capabilities before digging in. To get the most out of PowerDNS:

1. Read the following sections to become familiar with PowerDNS, how it stores data, and its configuration directives and settings.
2. Choose one (or more) back-ends that you are interested in and look at their capabilities.
3. Download, build and install the software (see Notes).

You will also want to familiarize yourself with PowerDNS' control (Section 6.8.1) and init (Section 6.8.3) programs which you use for day-to-day administration.

6.1 How PowerDNS stores zone data

PowerDNS supports various back-ends for storing zone data (Figure 6.1). Note that a back-end consists of two distinct parts. A database back-end, for example, consists of:

(a) The back-end code within PowerDNS.

(b) The database that the back-end communicates with.

You can configure PowerDNS to use more than one back-end in the same PowerDNS instance – you might want to use LDAP for some zones, and an RDBMS for some other zones, say.

When PowerDNS receives a query, it has to obtain from one of its configured back-ends the information it needs for the answer. If more than one back-end is configured, PowerDNS queries each back-end in turn (in the order you configured them): if a back-end satisfies the query, PowerDNS returns the answer, and the procedure terminates; otherwise the next back-end is queried, and so on.

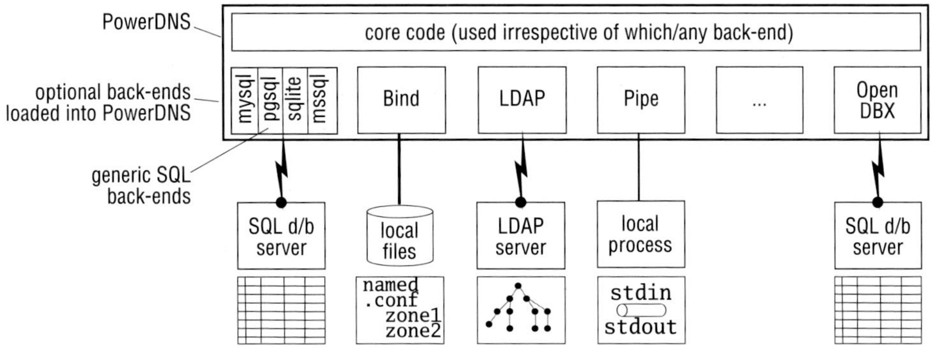

Figure 6.1: PowerDNS architecture

PowerDNS currently supports the following back-ends:

BIND Reads zone data from zone master files that you might already have from a previous BIND or NSD installation, for example.

SQL Reads zone data from relational databases. You can choose from several different SQL back-ends. We discuss two here:

- OpenDBX is a versatile SQL-database back-end. This is our SQL back-end of choice.
- The generic MySQL (gmysql), PostgreSQL (gpgsql) and Oracle (goracacle) back-ends allow you to connect PowerDNS to a MySQL, PostgreSQL or Oracle database respectively for zone storage. We introduce you to gmysql, but we recommend you familiarize yourself with the more flexible OpenDBX back-end, as it has more features.

  PowerDNS can use the gsqlite and gsqlite3 back-ends to store zone data in SQLite databases. SQLite support is also provided by the OpenDBX back-end. (We don't discuss SQLite any further.)

LDAP Retrieves zone data from an LDAP directory.

Pipe Enables you to create a so-called "coprocess" (somewhat like a *nix filter) in almost any programming language, with which you create a programmable back-end to PowerDNS. The coprocess receives a query and produces an answer which PowerDNS returns to the DNS client.

ODBC The Microsoft Windows port of PowerDNS uses this to retrieve zone data from a database via ODBC. Currently, there is no up-to-date Microsoft Windows port of PowerDNS, so we don't discuss this back-end.

6.1.1 Generic SQL or OpenDBX for SQL back-ends?

As you can see above, if you are planning to deploy PowerDNS with either a PostgreSQL or a MySQL database, you have a choice of two different database back-ends – you can use either of:

- The generic MySQL (gmysql) or generic PostgreSQL (gpgsql) database back-end.
- The OpenDBX back-end.

There appears to be little distinction between the two – they even use almost identical database schemas to store zone information. However, closer examination shows that the OpenDBX back-end has several advantages, even though it is another library that your server now requires. The advantages of OpenDBX are:

- It supports multiple database drivers[1].
- It supports connections to more than one database, enabling the driver to provide load balancing across several databases.
- It supports master/slave databases, with `UPDATE` queries directed at one database server, and `SELECT` queries being retrieved from a second. Update queries are performed on incoming AXFR zone transfers, when PowerDNS acts as a slave name server.
- It reacts very cleanly if connection errors occur when accessing the databases, and in the case where you have defined more than one database to use, it will seamlessly connect to the next.

Binary distributions of PowerDNS typically include the gmysql back-end which is why we will start you off with that back-end in Section 6.3.2. Our back-end of choice however is opendbx, which we discuss in Section 6.4.

6.2 Server roles – master/slave, superslave, native

PowerDNS offers full master and slave semantics for replicating DNS zones. It can be configured as a slave server to any DNS server that supports outgoing AXFR zone transfers. It can be configured as a master server, offering outgoing AXFR zone transfers to capable clients servers. It can simultaneously be a slave for some zones and a master for others. (PowerDNS also has "superslave" and "native" roles, which we explain later.) Table 6.2 lists the available back-ends and their master/slave features.

6.2.1 Master

When operating as a master (Figure 6.2), if the employed back-end supports detection of zone changes, PowerDNS notifies its slaves whenever changes to a zone have been performed. The way this works is that PowerDNS periodically asks its back-ends to check the

[1] The OpenDBX developers permitted us to call them "drivers" to avoid overloading the term "back-end"

Back-end	Native	Master	Slave	Superslave
bind	●	●	●	○
db2	●	○	○	○
gmysql	●	●	●	●
gpgsql	●	●	●	●
gsqlite3	●	●	●	●
ldap	●	●	○	○
odbc	●	●	●	○
opendbx	●	●	●	●
oracle	●	○	○	○
pipe	●	○	○	○

Table 6.2: Roles in PowerDNS back-ends

freshness of their data, which they do by querying their databases. If the back-ends detect a changed record, they inform the main PowerDNS code, and it then notifies its slaves. (Table 6.2.)

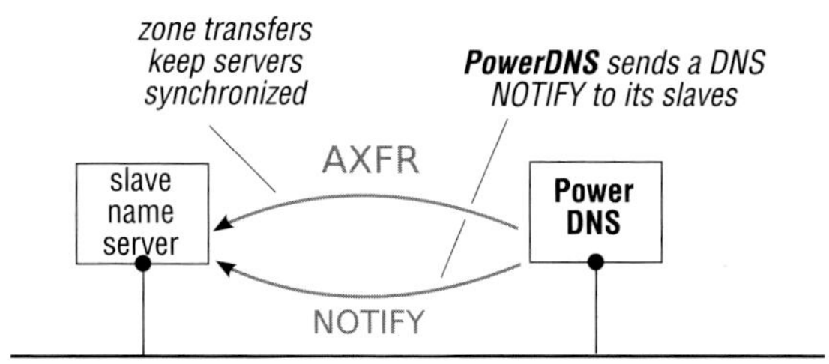

Figure 6.2: PowerDNS as a master server

6.2.2 Slave

PowerDNS can also act as a slave DNS server (Figure 6.3), retrieving zones via incoming zone transfers.

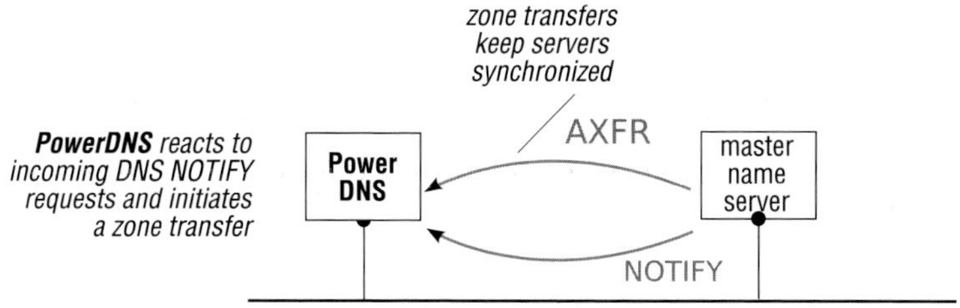

Figure 6.3: PowerDNS as a slave server

When PowerDNS starts, and at regular intervals, it requests, from all its back-end(s) that support incoming zone transfers, a list of zones that have not been checked to see if they have changed. For each "unfresh" zone, PowerDNS queries the zone's master server for the zone's Start of Authority (SOA) record and then checks the serial number in the SOA: if it has increased, PowerDNS initiates an incoming zone transfer.

PowerDNS also reacts to incoming NOTIFY requests: as above, it checks whether the zone has changed, and if so, initiates an incoming zone transfer. You must explicitly configure support for PowerDNS being a slave server if you need the functionality (Section 6.3.4).

6.2.3 Superslave

A unique feature of PowerDNS is that you can configure it to accept notifications from specified "trustworthy" master servers for which it does not yet carry slave zones, and have it create the slave zone(s), and provision them from the master via incoming zone transfers, all automatically (Figure 6.4). In this role, the server is said to be a *Superslave.* (By contrast, a normal slave will accept/action NOTIFYs only if you have manually pre-configured it as a slave for the zone. You have to create a zone on the slave, giving it the name of the zone, and create an NS record in the zone pointing to this slave itself.)

PowerDNS can operate as a Superslave for any brand of DNS server running as a normal master, as long as the master supports sending DNS NOTIFY requests, or at least can send them out "manually". When the foreign master loads or reloads a zone, it informs its slaves by sending NOTIFYs.

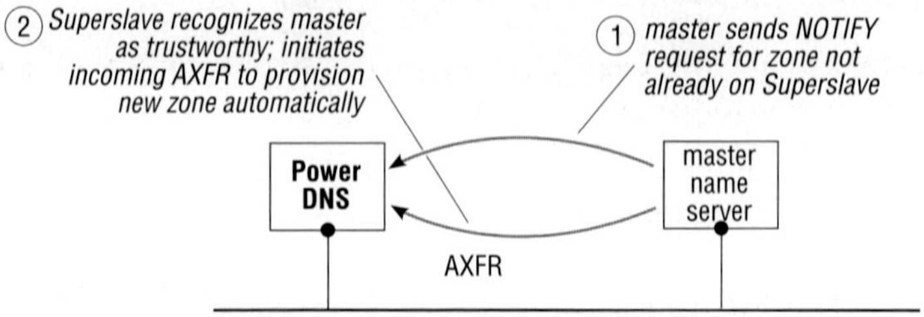

Figure 6.4: PowerDNS as a Superslave server

6.2.4 Native

PowerDNS can also make good use of native database replication (Figure 6.5), with back-ends that support it. A zone is called *native* if it is replicated by means other than AXFR zone transfers.

For example, when using PowerDNS with an LDAP back-end, primary and secondary servers use LDAP replication to ensure the data is kept up to date on both servers. (We have to call the servers primary/secondary, rather than master/slave, because master/slave implies AXFR replication.) This type of PowerDNS configuration is termed native, and it is the default in all database and LDAP back-ends. Native zones never generate any NOTIFYs to be sent to slave servers. Even so, outgoing zone transfers are still possible, and you could for example NOTIFY slaves using pdns_control (Section 6.8.1 on page 149).

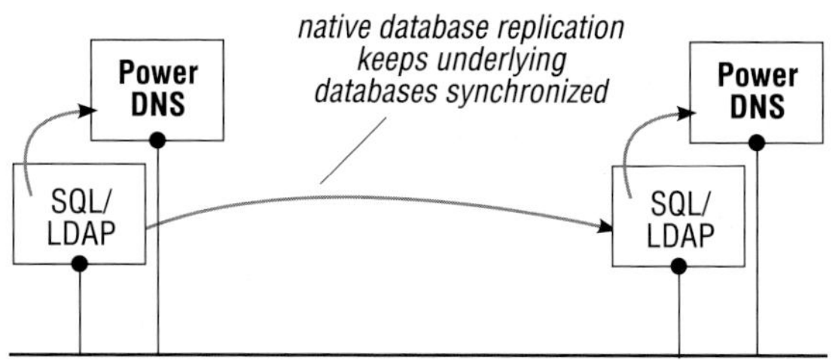

Figure 6.5: PowerDNS with native replication

6.2.5 Mixing roles

One of the great advantages of PowerDNS is its flexibility: you are free to mix roles, creating quite complex scenarios. For example:

- You set up a pair of PowerDNS machines with native replication, to provide authoritative name services for a number of zones.
- Simultaneously, you provide slave service for a couple of zones to a friendly company.
- You use PowerDNS as a master for a zone that belongs to a department in your organization, while they use a different brand of server as a slave.

You can implement all this in a single instance of a PowerDNS server, although we recommend you use two servers for resilience.

6.3 Getting started quickly

PowerDNS is a very versatile program, but it has so many features and back-ends that it's hard to understand at first. Therefore, we'll start off with the easiest scenario, even if it isn't the one most likely to be of interest. Then, we'll cover the more advanced features as we go along.

After installing PowerDNS (see Notes) proceed as follows:

A. Configure PowerDNS to serve one or more zones using the BIND back-end.

B. Configure PowerDNS to serve one or more zones using the generic MySQL back-end.

When we've covered these steps, we will move on to show you how to configure the LDAP, OpenDBX, and Pipe back-ends. At that point, you can discard any configuration for back-ends you used only for familiarizing yourself with PowerDNS.

6.3.1 A. Configure the BIND zone file back-end

The BIND back-end (Figure 6.6) is compiled into PowerDNS by default, enabling it to serve BIND-compatible zone master files.

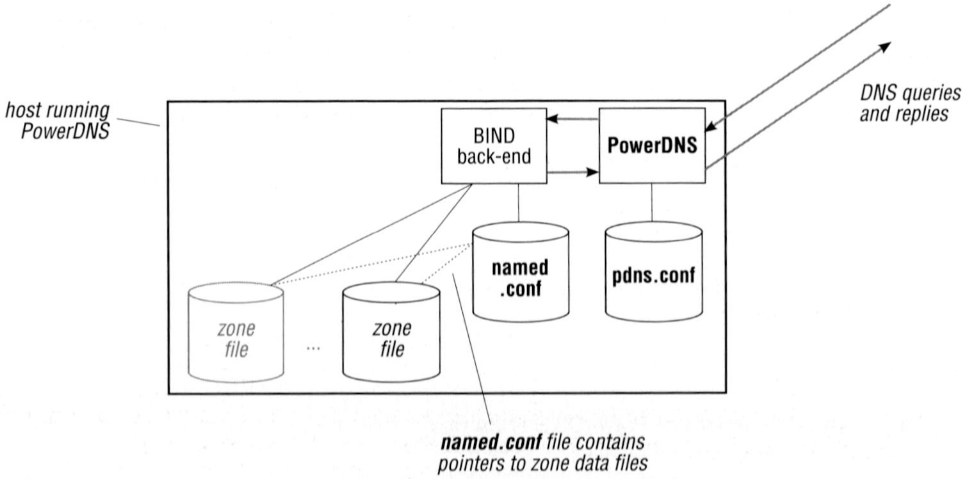

Figure 6.6: PowerDNS BIND back-end

Using PowerDNS with the BIND back-end is probably not the most common way to deploy PowerDNS; most people use it with a database back-end (which we cover later). However, we start with this back-end for three reasons:

(a) It's the easiest to understand, and to configure.

(b) You may already be familiar with BIND.

(c) You have some BIND zone files, and want to configure PowerDNS as quickly as possible to serve those zones.

To configure PowerDNS to serve a zone with the BIND back-end:

1. Section 2.4 showed how you create a zone master file from individual resource records. Create this file in a convenient directory; in this example we create a file in the directory `/etc/powerdns`, called `qupps.biz.zone`:

```
# cd /etc/powerdns
# cat qupps.biz.zone
qupps.biz. 84600  IN SOA  ns1.qupps.biz.  jp.qupps.biz. (
        200803160  ; serial
        10800      ; refresh (3 hours)
        900        ; retry (15 minutes)
        604800     ; expire (1 week)
        3600       ; minimum (1 hour)
        )
                    NS    ns1.qupps.biz.
                    NS    ns2.qupps.biz.
                    MX    10 mail.qupps.biz.

ns1                 A     192.168.1.20
ns2                 A     192.168.1.173
mail                A     192.168.1.20
```

2. The BIND back-end to PowerDNS needs an additional configuration file which is used

only by the BIND name server. This file is usually called `named.conf`, although in this initial example we need a minimal file, so we call it `mini-named.conf`. (We defer discussing the syntax of this file until Chapter 7, BIND, because only a tiny amount of `named.conf` is relevant to PowerDNS's BIND back-end.) Create the file:

```
# cat /etc/powerdns/mini-named.conf
options {
    directory "/etc/powerdns";
};

zone "qupps.biz" {
    type master;
    file "qupps.biz.zone";
};
```

Note all the braces and the semicolons ("`;`") which you must enter as shown; this is *not* PowerDNS syntax, but the syntax required by the BIND name server.

This minimal configuration will enable PowerDNS' BIND back-end to locate and read the zone file created in step 1 above; the name of the zone is specified in the configuration above in the `zone` clause, and the file containing the zone's data in the `file` statement. Zone files are relative to the directory specified in the `directory` statement of the `options` clause.

3. Edit PowerDNS' configuration file, which is called `pdns.conf`. The file contains a lot of lines of text which are all commented out (the lines start with a hash ("#") character). We recommend you simply rename the file and start afresh, for clarity.

   Create the following lines of configuration in `/etc/powerdns/pdns.conf`:

   ```
   launch=bind
   bind-config=/etc/powerdns/mini-named.conf
   ```

   These directives configure PowerDNS as follows:

   launch — Which back-end(s) PowerDNS should enable (i.e. "launch") when it starts up. We specify `bind` to use the BIND back-end.

   bind-config — The PowerDNS back-ends have various back-end-specific configuration directives that modify their behavior. This is one of the very few BIND back-end directives. It specifies the name of the BIND configuration file; we use the name of the file `mini-named.conf` that we created in step 2, above.

4. Start the PowerDNS daemon (i.e. the name server proper):

   ```
   # /etc/init.d/pdns start
   ```

   Even if you get a message that the name server has started, we recommend you check your log file. (On our system it is `/var/log/messages`, but your system might use `/var/log/daemon.log`.) If you have a syntax error in your `pdns.conf`, the server will log an error and exit immediately, but without any message on the terminal. For example, if you get an error such as:

```
Unable to launch, no back-ends configured for querying
```

check that you don't have spaces before the equals ("=") sign in your lines. Similarly, don't surround the value to the right of the equals sign with quotes of any kind; this almost always causes syntax errors.

5. When PowerDNS launches the BIND back-end, it reads in the `mini-named.conf` and very quickly loads all master and slave zones, serving those up as soon as they are loaded, and then logs the following information:

```
[bindbackend] Parsing 1 domain(s), will report when done
[bindbackend] Done parsing domains, 0 rejected, 1 new, 0 removed
```

At this point, your PowerDNS server is ready to answer queries from the zones you configured with the BIND back-end.

Using the BIND *back-end as a slave server*

To use the BIND back-end to PowerDNS in a slave role, add the slave keyword to your configuration (Section 6.7). PowerDNS queries the master servers for each zone and transfers each zone into a temporary file. If the zone transfer is successful, it renames the file and starts answering queries for the zone.

That completes the setup of PowerDNS with the BIND back-end. In the following section we show you how to configure and use the MySQL back-end for PowerDNS.

6.3.2 B. Configure the generic MySQL back-end

PowerDNS gets interesting when you configure it to use a database back-end (Figure 6.7). We discussed on page 115 that there are several you can use. The easiest to start with are probably the generic PostgreSQL or the generic MySQL back-ends, because they are often provided as part of a PowerDNS installation when you install a ready-made binary PowerDNS package. We'll initially use the generic MySQL back-end, to get you started quickly.

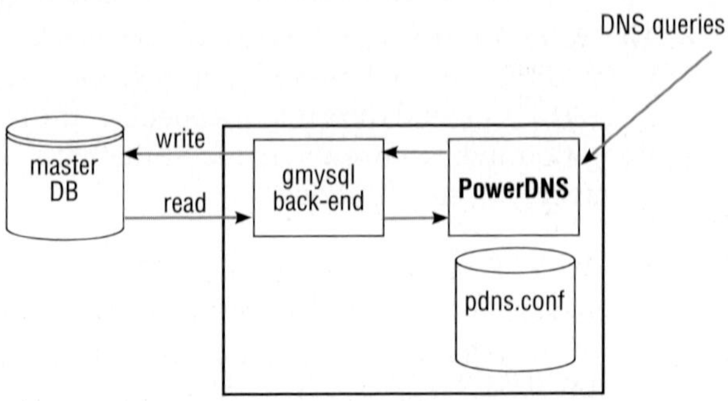

Figure 6.7: The gmysql back-end for PowerDNS

To use the generic MySQL back-end:

1. We assume you already have your MySQL server running, and that you have some basic SQL knowledge.

2. Set up the database and its tables.

   (a) Depending on the version of your MySQL server and PowerDNS binary, you may have to configure your MySQL server to accept passwords using its "old" protocol by setting a variable in `/etc/my.cnf` and restarting the MySQL daemon:

   ```
   ...
   [mysqld]
   old_passwords = true
   ...
   ```

   (b) You need a database in which to store zone data. You can use an existing one, but we recommend that for initial testing you create a new one. We'll create the database `ourpdns`:

   ```
   # mysqladmin -p create ourpdns
   Enter password:
   ```

   (c) Create the tables within the database, and use SQL `GRANT` queries to enable PowerDNS to access the tables. We provide a script that does this, on our Web site (☞ D064). Retrieve the script and edit the two variable settings in the first few lines: *user* and *pass* are the MySQL username and password respectively you use to allow PowerDNS to access your database. In the examples that follow, we assume the username is `pdnsadmin` and the password is `hah!`.

   ```
   $ wget http://fupps.com/dnsbook/pdns/pdns-tables.sh
   $ edit pdns-tables.sh
   $ sh pdns-tables.sh | mysql -p ourpdns
   ```

3. Configure PowerDNS to use the gmysql back-end.

   (a) Create the following lines of configuration in `pdns.conf`, replacing the values in the last four lines to match what you specified when creating the database in step 2 above:

   ```
   launch=gmysql
   gmysql-host=localhost
   gmysql-dbname=ourpdns
   gmysql-user=pdnsadmin
   gmysql-password=hah!
   ```

   These directives configure PowerDNS as follows:

launch	Which back-ends to launch. This time we want to use the generic MySQL back-end, so we specify `gmysql`.
gmysql-*something*	The configuration directives specific to gmysql all begin with `gmysql-`. The four directives shown specify the MySQL host, database name, username and password respectively.

   (b) Invoke PowerDNS by launching the binary program pdns_server (but also see Section 6.8.3). You should see output resembling this:

```
# pdns_server
This is a standalone pdns
Listening on controlsocket in '/var/run/pdns.controlsocket'
It is advised to bind to explicit addresses with the --local-address...
UDP server bound to 0.0.0.0:53
TCP server bound to 0.0.0.0:53
PowerDNS 2.9.21 (C) 2001-2006 PowerDNS.COM BV (Nov 12 2007, 10:06:14
PowerDNS comes with ABSOLUTELY NO WARRANTY. This is free software, ...
Creating backend connection for TCP
gmysql Connection succesful
About to create 3 backend threads for UDP
gmysql Connection succesful
gmysql Connection succesful
gmysql Connection succesful
```

(c) Ensure that the connection to the database is successful, as in the example above. If PowerDNS cannot connect to the MySQL back-end it will issue appropriate diagnostic messages, like these:

```
gmysql Connection failed: Unable to connect to database:
Access denied for user 'pdnsadmi'@'localhost' (using password: YES)
Caught an exception instantiating a backend, cleaning up
```

Such messages usually indicate a mismatch between the username and password you configured in `pdns.conf` and those you specified when you created the MySQL database, specifically when executing the `GRANT` statements on the tables, but they can also be an indication that you have to use MySQL's "old password" protocol, as in step 2 above.

Configured as in the example above, the pdns_server will run in the foreground. If you don't see errors, you can use the pdns script to start it instead (Section 6.8.3).

(d) PowerDNS is now ready to answer queries. If you send it a query for, say, qupps.biz, you see it print:

```
Not authoritative for 'qupps.biz', sending servfail to ↩
        127.0.0.1 (recursion was desired)
```

and the DNS client will receive a SERVFAIL error. Why does that happen? Because PowerDNS' database tables do not contain any data, until we complete the next step.

4. Add DNS data to the database tables.

   You add zones and zone data to PowerDNS by inserting records into its database tables. Both the gmysql and opendbx back-ends use similar database tables. We cover this in the next section.

6.3.3 Database schema used by the gmysql and opendbx back-ends

When we created the tables in Section 6.3.2, we used the database schema of the opendbx back-end. (You can download the schema from the book's Web site at (☞ D061).) You can use this for both the gmysql and the opendbx back-ends (Figure 6.8).

There are two tables, `domains` and `records`, that contain all the DNS data for your zones.

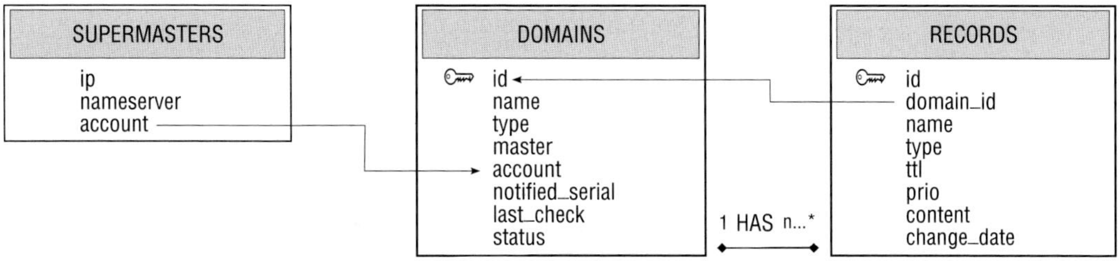

Figure 6.8: PowerDNS database schema

The `domains` table

The `domains` table specifies which zones PowerDNS will serve. It contains one record per zone. The columns of this table are:

`id` A unique identifier for this record. (If you `INSERT` a `NULL` value, MySQL automatically increments this `id` for you.)

`name` The name of the zone (qupps.biz). The name must *not* be qualified with a terminating period. This column has a constraint defined on it to ensure you keep domain names unique; if you try to add a zone name that already exists you will get an error.

`type` The type of zone. Possible values are:

- MASTER — PowerDNS is a master for this zone, and it will NOTIFY slaves when changes to the zone's Start of Authority (SOA) serial number are detected.
- SLAVE — PowerDNS is a slave for the zone.
- NATIVE — PowerDNS uses native replication. No SOA checks are performed, no NOTIFYs are sent, and received NOTIFYs are not processed. Superslaves don't use these zones either.

`master` The IP address of the master server for this zone. (Applies to slaves only.)

`notified_serial` The serial number from the Start of Authority (SOA) that was used to notify a slave. PowerDNS updates this column when it sends out a NOTIFY.

`account` This is an arbitrary string which is copied from the `account` column of the `supermasters` table when a master provisions your Superslave (Section 6.3.4).

`last_check` The UNIX time stamp when a slave zone was last checked for freshness.

`status` A single character which defaults to `A` (for Active). This column was designed to indicate whether a record is active or inactive. Neither the gmysql nor the opendbx back-ends use this column[2], but that doesn't matter: you can have as many additional columns in your tables as you want.

The `records` table

The `records` table stores all resource records of all zones. The columns in this table are:

id A unique identifier for the record. (If you `INSERT` a `NULL` value, MySQL automatically increments this `id` for you.)

domain_id The `domain_id` identifies the record in the `domains` table to which this resource record belongs. To join the tables, you can use an equality statement

```
... WHERE domains.id = records.domain_id ...
```

name The domain or host name of the DNS resource. The domain is always fully qualified, but is not terminated with a period. For example, you use a value of `www.qupps.biz` and *not* just `www`.

type The DNS resource type (SOA, A, NS, MX, ...).

ttl The Time to Live (TTL) of the DNS resource. This value defaults to NULL, in which case the value of default-ttl is used.

prio For records of type MX, this is the Mail Exchanger preference. If the value of this column is NULL, the preference will be zero.

content The data portion of the DNS resource: IP Address for an A record, host name for the NS record, ...

change_date Unused by PowerDNS.

You are free to add any other columns you wish. For example, you might want to add a `comment` column to the `records` table to help you identify why you created or updated a record, or, if you are an ISP, you may wish to add a `customerID` column to `domains` to associate a domain with a specific customer.

The default SQL queries that PowerDNS issues rely on the tables above having the names and columns shown, i.e. as defined in the standard schema. You can change the tables and/or or column names, but if you do, you also have to rewrite the queries that PowerDNS issues. This is possible for both SQL back-ends; we show you how to do it for OpenDBX (see Notes).

6.3.4 Managing zones in the database

Zones and their data are managed in the SQL back-ends by adding, deleting or updating records in the database tables. You do this either manually with the database management tool of your choice, or via command-line scripts that you craft to ease your administrative chores, or via a Web-based interface. (We discuss this in Section 2.5.5 and Section 19.4.)

[2] See the home page of the OpenDBX project for information on how to use the column.

A zone consists of a single record in the `domains` database table and one or more records (probably more) in the `records` table. The exact SQL syntax needed to add these records depends on the database vendor; unfortunately, there are differences in the dialects, but we will attempt to remain ANSI-SQL compliant in the examples that follow.

Create a new master or native zone in the database

To create a master or native zone we have to insert a new row into the `domains` table, specifying the zone name, as well as its type:

```
mysql> INSERT INTO domains (name, type) VALUES('qupps.biz', 'NATIVE');
mysql> SELECT id,name,type,status  FROM domains;
+----+-----------+--------+--------+
| id | name      | type   | status |
+----+-----------+--------+--------+
|  1 | qupps.biz | NATIVE |  A     |
+----+-----------+--------+--------+
```

At this point, the domain is still not active, as it doesn't contain any records. DNS queries on the domain would fail, as the zone does not yet contain a Start of Authority (SOA) record.

Adding resource records to the database

You add DNS resource records to the `records` table and ensure that the column `domain_id` contains the identifier `id` from the `domains` table. This is the value `1` shown in the example above.

We now insert three records to make the zone operative. The columns we need to set are: `domain_id` with the corresponding `id` from the `domains` table, `name` with the fully qualified host or domain name, the DNS `type` (one of SOA, A, TXT, NS, MX, etc.), and `content` which is the data to be returned for the specified `name` (i.e. the right-hand side of the resource record).

```
mysql> INSERT INTO records (domain_id, name, type, content)
     > VALUES (1, 'qupps.biz', 'SOA',
     > 'ns.qupps.biz. jp.qupps.biz. 1 10800 900 604800 7200');
mysql> INSERT INTO records (domain_id, name, type, content)
     > VALUES (1, 'qupps.biz', 'NS', 'ns.qupps.biz');
mysql> INSERT INTO records (domain_id, name, type, content)
     > VALUES (1, 'ns.qupps.biz', 'A', '192.168.1.20');
mysql> SELECT id, domain_id AS Did, name, type, ttl, content FROM records;
+----+-----+--------------+------+------+------------------------------------+
| id | Did | name         | type | ttl  | content                            |
+----+-----+--------------+------+------+------------------------------------+
|  1 |   1 | qupps.biz    | SOA  | NULL | ns.qupps.biz. jp.qupps.biz. 1 1080...
|  2 |   1 | qupps.biz    | NS   | NULL | ns.qupps.biz                       |
|  3 |   1 | ns.qupps.biz | A    | NULL | 192.168.1.20                       |
+----+-----+--------------+------+------+------------------------------------+
```

As that looks good, we'll now attempt to query our PowerDNS:

```
$ dig +norecurs @127.0.0.1 ns.qupps.biz A
;; flags: qr aa; QUERY: 1, ANSWER: 1, AUTHORITY: 0, ADDITIONAL: 0

;; ANSWER SECTION:
ns.qupps.biz.          3600    IN      A       192.168.1.20
```

If you have query-logging enabled in `pdns.conf` (Section 6.7), you will see the SQL queries being issued to the database by the back-end. The TTL that PowerDNS returns is the default-ttl (see Section 6.7 on page 146), unless you have defined a TTL specific to this record, in the `ttl` column.

Automating record inserts

We saw above that you have to set `records.domain_id` to the value of `domains.id`. You can "automate" this during an `INSERT` by using a sub-query, supported by many SQL dialects:

```
mysql> INSERT INTO domains (name, type) VALUES('qupps.biz', 'NATIVE');
mysql> INSERT INTO records (domain_id, name, type, content)
     > VALUES (
     >        (SELECT id FROM domains WHERE name = 'qupps.biz') ,
              'qupps.biz',
              'SOA',
              'ns.qupps.biz. jp.qupps.biz. 1 10800 900 604800 7200'
               );
mysql> INSERT INTO records (domain_id, name, type, content)
     > VALUES (
     >        (SELECT id FROM domains WHERE name = 'qupps.biz') ,
              'qupps.biz',
              'NS',
              'ns.qupps.biz'
               );
mysql> INSERT INTO records (domain_id, name, type, content)
     > VALUES (
     >        (SELECT id FROM domains WHERE name = 'qupps.biz') ,
              'qupps.biz',
              'A',
              '192.168.1.20'
               );
```

While the SQL statements are now much longer, you don't have to manually look up a zone's `id` in the `domains` table. This makes it much easier to create scripts to automatically add zones or records to your database.

Adding a slave zone

Adding a slave zone to the `domains` database table is very similar to adding a native zone, but you have to add one extra piece of data: the IP address of the zone's master server. PowerDNS will use this to retrieve the zone via AXFR zone transfer.

```
mysql> INSERT INTO domains (name, type, master)
     >    VALUES ('mens.de', 'SLAVE', '192.168.1.20');
```

Every slave-cycle-interval seconds (default 60s), PowerDNS checks for new slave zones, by performing an SQL query to check for unfresh slaves, i.e. slaves that need to be primed with an incoming zone transfer. If this query determines that there is an unfresh slave, then:

- It performs an SQL query to determine the IP of the master server from either the `domains` table or from an existing SOA resource in the `records` table. As soon as those have been found, all subsequent queries are wrapped in an SQL transaction which is committed to the database if the zone transfer succeeds (or is rolled back and attempted at a later time if it fails).

The reason for a transactional database back-end becomes clear now: all records in the database for the current zone are deleted, effectively emptying the zone if it contained data.

- Then a sequence of `INSERT`s is run, one for each of the resource records on the incoming zone.

So, after a short while, the `domains` table is updated to reflect when the last check was performed:

```
mysql> SELECT * FROM domains WHERE name = 'mens.de';
*************************** 1. row ***************************
             id: 2
           name: mens.de
           type: SLAVE
         master: 192.168.1.20
        account:
notified_serial: NULL
     last_check: 1195049242
         status: A
```

and the `records` table now contains our zone data:

```
mysql> SELECT id,name,type,prio,content FROM records
         WHERE domain_id =
            (SELECT id FROM domains WHERE name = 'mens.de');
+----+--------------------+-------+------+-----------------------------------+
| id | name               | type  | prio | content                           |
+----+--------------------+-------+------+-----------------------------------+
|  4 | mens.de            | SOA   |    0 | mens.de. jp.mens.de.  200705537 108...
|  5 | mens.de            | NS    |    0 | home.mens.de                      |
|  8 | home.mens.de       | A     |    0 | 192.168.1.20                      |
|  6 | dom.mens.de        | A     |    0 | 192.168.1.51                      |
| 21 | pr.mens.de         | CNAME |    0 | printer.mens.de                   |
| 22 | printer.mens.de    | A     |    0 | 192.168.1.78                      |
+----+--------------------+-------+------+-----------------------------------+
```

How you configure a Superslave

When a PowerDNS superslave receives a notification from a known master, it can automatically configure itself as a slave for the zone and provision itself via an incoming zone transfer. When PowerDNS acts as a master to Superslaves, it calls itself a *Supermaster*, for lack of a better term.

Configuring a PowerDNS server to be a Superslave is easy with the back-ends that have Superslave capabilities (Table 6.2). The `supermasters` table contains a record for each Superslave you create:

`ip` This column contains the IP Address of the DNS master server which is allowed to provision your Superslave.

nameserver This column contains the NS name of the DNS master name server which is allowed to provision your Superslave. This value must either be the official host name or the IP address of the DNS server that sends the NOTIFY.

account This is an arbitrary string that allows you to identify a DNS master. When a master DNS server has notified your PowerDNS of the existence of a new zone, PowerDNS will provision itself with the zone. The value of `supermasters.account` will be copied into the `account` column of the `domains` table for the zone. This allows you to track how a slave zone entered your system.

Add a record to the `supermasters` table to define a Superslave:

```
mysql> INSERT INTO supermasters VALUES ('192.168.1.20', 'home.mens.de', 'JP');
```

If you then add a domain on your master (in this case host 192.168.1.20), it will send a NOTIFY to our PowerDNS server thinking the latter is a normal slave. At that point, the PowerDNS Superslave receives the NOTIFY and notices that is has no data on the zone but recognizes the IP address of the master name server as being allowed to provision it. It will creates a new slave zone, adding the zone to the `domains` table, and it performs an incoming zone transfer for the zone, storing the data in the `records` table:

```
mysql> SELECT * FROM domains WHERE account = 'JP';
*************************** 1. row ***************************
             id: 2
           name: mens.de
           type: SLAVE
         master: 192.168.1.20
        account: JP
notified_serial: NULL
     last_check: 1195039983
         status: A
```

and PowerDNS records the creation of the zone, in the system log file:

```
Created new slave zone 'mens.de' from supermaster 192.168.1.20, queued axfr
```

If a zone is removed from the master server, there is no way to remove it automatically from the PowerDNS slave; this is not a limitation of PowerDNS – there is simply no defined protocol to announce zone removal to slaves.

We have discussed how the SQL-capable back-ends in PowerDNS use the database tables to organize zones and their data, and we discussed that both the gmysql and opendbx back-ends can use the same database schema. If you don't want to learn about the OpenDBX, LDAP or Pipe back-ends, you can skip to Section 6.7 on page 143, where we discuss the PowerDNS configuration in detail. In the following section we discuss the OpenDBX back-end.

6.4 The OpenDBX database back-end

The OpenDBX back-end was created by Norbert Sendetzky. It utilizes the similarly-named OpenDBX package, which is a library of routines written in the C programming language

(C++ is also available), that hides the database-specific APIs, by presenting a unified and consistent API to an application. OpenDBX favors speed and therefore doesn't attempt to unify the SQL query language; the application programmer must submit SQL queries in the dialect of the supported database system. This offers a significant performance increase over systems (such as ODBC) that try to encapsulate all SQL dialects by providing a translation system between the query a program uses and the database system used.

The authors claim that the OpenDBX back-end to PowerDNS is marginally faster than the gmysql or gpgsql back-ends, and we have been able to reproduce the numbers with some reservations, depending on the test cases (see Chapter 23). We favor the OpenDBX back-end over the generic SQL back-ends because of its homogeneous interface to different database systems (Table 6.3), some of which may require additional software (see the OpenDBX documentation). OpenDBX itself should compile on all UNIX-based platforms (see Notes), although as yet, no port to Microsoft Windows has been released, unfortunately.

Firebird	PostgreSQL
Interbase	SQLite
Microsoft SQL Server	SQLite3
MySQL	Sybase
Oracle	

Table 6.3: OpenDBX drivers

A most interesting feature of the OpenDBX back-end is its support for reading and updating zones from different database servers (Figure 6.9). Cluster environments in which database nodes are not equal can benefit from this. You specify which is the master database, and PowerDNS directs all updates (e.g. during incoming zone transfers) to that copy of the database. PowerDNS directs only read requests to the other (replica) servers.

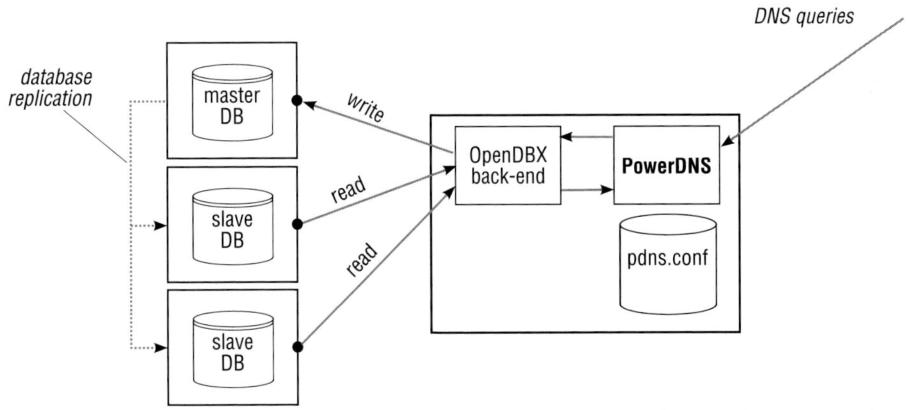

Figure 6.9: The OpenDBX back-end for PowerDNS

6.4.1 Getting started with the OpenDBX back-end

Getting started with the OpenDBX back-end is very similar to what we discussed in Section 6.3.2 for the gmysql back-end:

1. If your binary PowerDNS package doesn't contain the opendbx back-end, you have to build OpenDBX and PowerDNS yourself, but that isn't difficult (see Notes).

2. You provide a database for the OpenDBX back-end to use and create tables for it. Copy the procedure we showed you for MySQL in Section 6.3.2; it works just the same for OpenDBX with the MySQL driver.

3. The database tables and their content are also exactly the same as we described in Section 6.3.3; if you've already set them up for gmysql and are now just moving to the opendbx back-end, you don't have to change anything: the opendbx back-end will happily use the data you previously used with gmysql.

The opendbx back-end has a number of additional configuration options, mainly pertaining to the fact that it can (but doesn't have to) use multiple database servers for resilience. We discuss these settings next.

6.4.2 Configuration options for the OpenDBX back-end

The OpenDBX back-end introduces two sets of configuration options to the main PowerDNS configuration: (A) General options, and (B) options that affect queries (see Notes).

6.4.3 A – General options

launch
: Which back-end(s) PowerDNS should launch. This must include the keyword opendbx to initialize the OpenDBX back-end.

opendbx-backend
: Name of the database driver you want to use (default: `mysql`). The OpenDBX library must support it on your platform (see Notes).

opendbx-host-read
: Contains one or more host names[3] or IP addresses of the database servers (default is 127.0.0.1). These database servers will be used for retrieving queries that involve `SELECT` statements (i.e. zone and resource record lookups performed by PowerDNS). The default for this option is localhost.

```
opendbx-host-read=192.168.1.20,192.168.1.24
```

For the SQLite and SQLite3 drivers, this variable should be set to the name of the directory containing the SQLite database file, and it must include the trailing slash.

```
opendbx-host-read=/var/pdns/db/
opendbx-host-write=/var/pdns/db/
opendbx-database=powerdns.sqlite
```

[3]Careful with host names: they have to be resolved, and we are launching a DNS server!

opendbx-host-write
: Contains one or more addresses of database servers which will be used for SQL `INSERT`, `UPDATE` or `DELETE` statements (default is 127.0.0.1). These are invoked by PowerDNS only for incoming zone transfers. In a setup that involves a master database server with one or more read replicas, opendbx-host-write contains the address of the master database server. The default for this option is localhost.

```
opendbx-host-write=192.168.1.49
```

opendbx-port
: The TCP port number (or name from `/etc/services`) used to contact the database server. (Default is empty string). Most databases will use their default port number if this is left empty.

opendbx-database
: The name of the database. (Default: "`powerdns`".)

opendbx-username
: Username which is sent to the database for authentication (together with opendbx-password). (Default: "`powerdns`".)

opendbx-password
: Clear text password sent in combination with opendbx-username to connect to the database engine. (Default: "".)

For a MySQL database engine running on the same host as the PowerDNS server itself, our configuration is:

```
opendbx-backend=mysql
opendbx-host-read=127.0.0.1
opendbx-host-write=127.0.0.1
opendbx-port=3306
opendbx-database=ourpdns
opendbx-username=pdnsadmin
opendbx-password=hah!
```

whereas for SQLite3, a configuration would be

```
launch=opendbx
opendbx-backend=sqlite3
opendbx-host-read=/usr/local/var/db/
opendbx-host-write=/usr/local/var/db/
opendbx-port=
opendbx-database=power.db
opendbx-username=
opendbx-password=
```

This completes our discussion of the OpenDBX back-end. You can skip to Section 6.7 to learn about the other PowerDNS configuration directives, if you want. In the next section we discuss the LDAP back-end.

6.5 The LDAP directory server back-end

The LDAP back-end was created by Norbert Sendetzky. With it, you enable PowerDNS to retrieve DNS resource records from an LDAP directory server, fully integrating your DNS with LDAP (Figure 6.10).

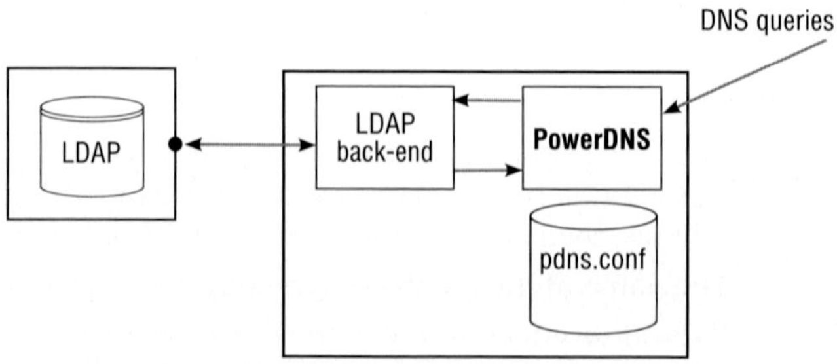

Figure 6.10: PowerDNS LDAP back-end

Before rushing off to add appropriate entries to your LDAP directory, we strongly recommend you take some time to design the tree in which you will be storing DNS entries, as a mis-design now can be painful to correct later on, so we cover that next.

6.5.1 Designing the LDAP directory tree

The LDAP back-end is very flexible: you can keep your DNS related entries in almost any tree structure you want to. The back-end supports three tree styles:

`simple` For any requested domain, the LDAP back-end searches the LDAP directory for an attribute type `associatedDomain` matching the requested domain name. As the hierarchy of your LDAP directory tree is not used at all in the `simple` method, you are free to organize your DNS entries as you wish.

`tree` With the `tree` style, the PowerDNS LDAP back-end maps the requested domain into a distinguished name. This means that for a query of www.qupps.biz, your LDAP directory must have an entry named `dc=www,dc=qupps,dc=biz` under the base of the tree you keep your DNS data in.

`strict` The `strict` form is identical to the `simple` form, but the LDAP back-end is able to generate PTR records for any LDAP `aRecord` (IPv4 Address) or for any `aAAARecord` (IPv6 Address) entries: when a query for a PTR arrives, the back-end checks if it has a forward entry for the IP address; if so it answers the PTR query.

However, if you use `strict`, PowerDNS with the LDAP back-end can't act as a master server for any zone, so we don't discuss this form any further.

Our tests show there is no noticeable difference in performance using the "simple" or "tree" styles, leaving the decision of how to structure your tree to a matter of taste. We show you the "simple" style.

6.5.2 LDAP schema used by the LDAP back-end

The schema used by the LDAP back-end of PowerDNS builds on elements found in the Cosine schema. (Download the dNSDomain2 schema (☞ D062).) We show you an example LDIF file for the zone qupps.biz:

```
dn: dc=qupps.biz,ou=pdns,ou=dns,dc=qupps,dc=biz
dc: qupps.biz
objectClass: dcObject
objectClass: dNSDomain2
objectClass: domainRelatedObject
sOARecord: ns1.qupps.biz. hostmaster.mens.de. 196205281 10800 900 604800 3600
NSRecord: ns1.qupps.biz
NSRecord: ns2.qupps.biz
mXRecord: 10 mail.qupps.biz
mXRecord: 20 mail.uit.co.uk
aRecord: 192.168.1.20
tXTRecord: "v=spf1 a:mail.qupps.biz a:mail.uit.co.uk mx:qupps.biz ~all"
LOCRecord: 52 2 2.76 N 8 28 37.919 E 118m
dNSTTL: 86400
associatedDomain: qupps.biz
```

To define an entry for a DNS wild card domain, use an LDIF like this example:

```
dn: dc=wild,dc=qupps.biz,ou=pdns,ou=dns,dc=qupps,dc=biz
dc: wild
objectClass: top
objectClass: dNSDomain2
objectClass: domainRelatedObject
associatedDomain: *.qupps.biz
cNAMERecord: qupps.biz
```

Table 6.4 shows the most frequently used DNS records and their corresponding LDAP attribute types as implemented by the LDAP back-end.

DNS RR	Attribute type	Sample content
A	aRecord	192.168.1.20
AAAA	aAAARecord	fe80::200:ff:fe00:0
CNAME	cNAMERecord	www.somewhere.org
class	dNSClass	IN
TTL	dNSTTL	3600
HINFO	hInfoRecord	"PC P5/700" "Ubuntu 7.04"
LOC	LOCRecord	52 2 2.760 N 8 28 37.919 E
MX	mXRecord	10 mail.qupps.biz
NS	NSRecord	ns.qupps.biz
PTR	PTRRecord	www.aa01.net
SOA	sOARecord	f.q. e.f.q. 2 10800 900 604800 3600
SRV	sRVRecord	0 0 389 ldap.qupps.biz
TXT	tXTRecord	hello world

Table 6.4: Attribute types used by PowerDNS LDAP back-end

6.5.3 Defining an LDAP back-end in `pdns.conf`

To set up an LDAP back-end, you configure the following parameters in `pdns.conf`: Note that quotes (`""`) in `pdns.conf` are almost always wrong; while quoting a DN might appear to be the right thing to do, it will not work.

launch
: Which back-end(s) to launch. This must contain the word `ldap` to launch the LDAP back-end.

```
launch=ldap
```

ldap-host
: Host name or IP address list of the LDAP directory server(s), optionally followed by a colon and the TCP port number. Note that a host name is probably not useful here if you need *this* DNS server to resolve it to an IP address. (Default: `127.0.0.1:389`.)

```
ldap-host=192.168.1.20:389
```

ldap-host may take a comma- or space-separated list of addresses, with which you provide fail-over capabilities to the LDAP back-end. The LDAP client libraries attempt to connect to the LDAP directory servers in the order you specify; the first successful connection is used. (In other words, this is *not* a way to spread your load across multiple LDAP directory servers.)

SSL connections can only be established by setting this parameter to a valid LDAP URI such as

```
ldap-host=ldaps://192.168.1.20:636/
```

If you are using TLS (see next parameter), the `subjectAltName` flag of your SSL certificate will almost certainly have to contain an `IP:a.b.c.d` for TLS to function correctly.

ldap-starttls
: Whether to use TLS to encrypt the connection to your directory server (default is no). TLS is enabled by the underlying LDAP libraries to which the LDAP back-end was linked during building.

```
ldap-starttls=yes
```

ldap-basedn
: Distinguished name (DN) of the directory entry under which the LDAP back-end should start searching. The default setting is `""`.

```
ldap-basedn=ou=pdns,ou=dns,dc=qupps,dc=biz
```

ldap-binddn
: The distinguished name (DN) with which the back-end binds to the LDAP directory. If it is not required, it can be left at the default of an empty string (anonymous bind); otherwise it should be set to a valid DN, whose password is given as ldap-secret.

```
ldap-binddn=cn=dnsAdmin,dc=qupps,dc=biz
```

ldap-secret
: The clear-text password which the LDAP back-end will use with ldap-binddn as credentials to bind to the LDAP directory. As the

password is given in clear text, the file containing it must be adequately protected from prying eyes, by file system permissions.

```
ldap-secret=hah!
```

ldap-method — The style of tree on the LDAP directory. Valid settings are `simple` (the default), `tree` or `strict`.

```
ldap-method=tree
```

ldap-filter-axfr — If set, this filters which LDAP entries will be returned as records in a zone transfer.

Normally the LDAP back-end will return all DNS resource records found in the LDAP entries of the directory, but this filter may be used to limit them. The default is the string `(:target:)`, which includes the default search specification, but you can augment that with any valid LDAP filter by And/Or-ing it with any desired attribute=value.

```
ldap-filter-axfr=(&(:target:)(dNSDomainFlags=axfr))
```

The `dNSDomainFlags` attribute type is defined in the object class `dNSDomainFlags`, and you can download the schema for that from (☞ D063). It could be used to offer split-horizon DNS by setting the flag to either "internal" or "external" and adjusting the ldap-filter-axfr and ldap-filter-lookup settings.

ldap-filter-lookup — This filter is used to perform individual lookups, and it too may be augmented to allow or disallow lookups.

```
ldap-filter-lookup=(&(:target:)(!(dNSDomainFlags=nolook)))
```

The `dNSDomainFlags` attribute type is defined in the object class `dNSDomainFlags`, as explained in the previous item.

(You typically won't have to alter ldap-filter-lookup or ldap-axfr-lookup, as the defaults are quite sensible.)

6.5.4 The zone2ldap utility

Instead of manually crafting LDIF files for zones, you can use the zone2ldap utility provided with PowerDNS. It converts zone master files to LDIF, which you can feed directly to ldapmodify to update your LDAP directory. The utility supports the `simple` and `tree`-styles as defined by the PowerDNS LDAP back-end. If you give it just a `named.conf`, it will look in there to find the names of the zone data files and use those. Assume a master zone file for qupps.biz contains:

```
$ORIGIN .
$TTL 86400     ; 1 day
qupps.biz     IN SOA    ns1.qupps.biz. hostmaster.mens.de. (
                 196205281  ; serial
                 10800      ; refresh (3 hours)
                 900        ; retry (15 minutes)
```

```
                604800      ; expire (1 week)
                3600        ; minimum (1 hour)
                )
            NS      ns1.qupps.biz.
$ORIGIN qupps.biz.
            A       192.168.1.20
            MX      10 mail.qupps.biz.
*           CNAME   qupps.biz.
```

If you run zone2ldap with the "tree" style on this zone file, it produces the following output:

```
$ zone2ldap --basedn=ou=dns,dc=qupps,dc=biz \
      --dnsttl=yes \
      --layout=tree \
      --zone-file=qupps.biz  \
      --zone-name=qupps.biz
dn: dc=biz,ou=dns,dc=qupps,dc=biz
changetype: add
objectclass: dNSDomain2
objectclass: domainRelatedObject
dc: biz
associatedDomain: biz

dn: dc=qupps,dc=biz,ou=dns,dc=qupps,dc=biz
changetype: add
objectclass: dnsdomain2
objectclass: domainRelatedObject
dc: qupps
dNSTTL: 86400
associatedDomain: qupps.biz.
sOARecord: ns1.qupps.biz. hostmaster.mens.de. 196205281 10800 900 604800 3600

dn: dc=qupps,dc=biz,ou=dns,dc=qupps,dc=biz
changetype: modify
add: NSRecord
NSRecord: ns1.qupps.biz

dn: dc=qupps,dc=biz,ou=dns,dc=qupps,dc=biz
changetype: modify
add: aRecord
aRecord: 192.168.1.20

dn: dc=qupps,dc=biz,ou=dns,dc=qupps,dc=biz
changetype: modify
add: MXRecord
MXRecord: 10 mail.qupps.biz

dn: dc=qupps,dc=biz,ou=dns,dc=qupps,dc=biz
changetype: add
objectclass: dnsdomain2
objectclass: domainRelatedObject
dc: qupps
associatedDomain: qupps.biz

dn: dc=*,dc=qupps,dc=biz,ou=dns,dc=qupps,dc=biz
changetype: add
objectclass: dnsdomain2
```

```
objectclass: domainRelatedObject
dc: *
dNSTTL: 86400
associatedDomain: *.qupps.biz
cNAMERecord: qupps.biz
```

If you don't have access to the master zone files but are able to perform a zone transfer for the designated zone(s), use dig to retrieve the zone and feed its output to zone2ldap. The following listing is an example of how to do that.

Listing 6.1: Feed a zone transfer to zone2ldap

```
#!/bin/sh

NS=192.168.1.20
ZONES="mens.de example.com example.net"
BASE="ou=dns,o=qupps.biz"

for z in ${ZONES}
do
    dig @${NS} "${z}" axfr > z.tmp
    zone2ldap --basedn="$BASE" --dnsttl=yes \
        --layout=tree \
        --zone-file=z.tmp \
        --zone-name="${z}"
done
```

6.5.5 Limitations of the LDAP back-end

The LDAP back-end is powerful; if you want to store DNS data in your LDAP directory, it will probably satisfy your needs. Two points to note are:

- You can use the LDAP back-end to provide zone master DNS services, and if you need to be a slave for some zones, we recommend you add slave support to PowerDNS for an SQL database with the OpenDBX back-end, or a BIND-style file with the BIND back-end.

- The LDAP back-end cannot be used as a slave. When PowerDNS is a slave, it has to store the DNS records of an incoming zone transfer in a back-end database. Because LDAP is (currently) non-transactional, the authors decided (correctly) not to implement slave functionality, because a failed incoming zone transfer could potentially damage the LDAP directory with writes on an incomplete zone.

6.6 The Pipe back-end

The Pipe back-end lets you add dynamic resolution to PowerDNS by writing a custom program that reads queries sent to it by PowerDNS and generates the answers. You can write this program, called a *coprocess*, in any language that can read from standard input and write to standard output in an unbuffered method.

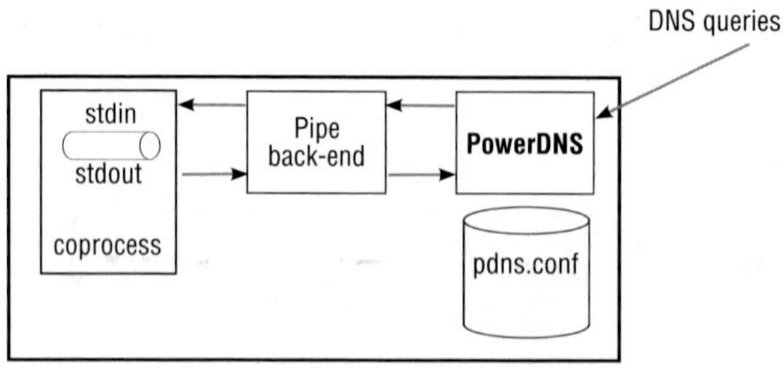

Figure 6.11: PowerDNS Pipe back-end

6.6.1 How PowerDNS and the coprocess communicate

The PowerDNS server and the coprocess communicate using a simple protocol:

- They exchange messages in the form of tab-separated lines of text.
- The first line the coprocess receives is a `HELO` with the protocol version number.
- After that, they enter an infinite loop: PowerDNS server sends the coprocess a line containing a request, and waits for for an answer.

The server can send three types of request. The request type is specified as the first tab-separated field in the request line:

PING: check whether the coprocess is alive.

AXFR: PowerDNS wants to perform a zone transfer from the Pipe back-end. This command does not report for which zone an AXFR is being requested, so you can't implement a Pipe back-end that satisfies multiple zones.

Q: a regular DNS query which contains seven fields, which we'll cover in a moment.

The coprocess answers with one or more lines containing tab-separated fields. The first field in each line indicates the type of response:

FAIL: the lookup failed.

DATA: the lookup succeeded, and additional fields. in the line contain responses to queries.

END: no more DATA lines to come in response to this query.

LOG: the server should log the text in the rest of this line.

Regular "Q" requests contain seven fields:

1. The record *type* – `Q` in this case.
2. *qname*, the query name, e.g. www.qupps.biz

3. The type of query (*qtype*); one of A, NS, SOA, ... Note however, that, in order to optimize communication with the Pipe coprocess, PowerDNS always passes an ANY query.

   As PowerDNS translates a query for an Address record (A) into an ANY query, the coprocess should be prepared to answer accordingly. If the answer contains a CNAME, PowerDNS will follow its indirection, but if it contains any other record such as an A, it will return that as an answer.

4. The class of the query (*qclass*), which is always `IN`.
5. An identifier *id*, that you can specify to help your coprocess identify an earlier query, but you typically ignore this.
6. The remote IP of the querying client (*remote_ip*). This will usually be the IP of the caching name server the query was received from.
7. The local_address of the PowerDNS process.

6.6.2 Directives for the Pipe back-end

The Pipe back-end has only a few configuration directives:

pipe-command
: This string contains the name of the coprocess program that should be forked by PowerDNS. It is invoked once for each of the configured distributor-threads plus three times.

pipebackend-abi-version
: This defines the protocol spoken between PowerDNS and the Pipe coprocess, and may be set to 1 or 2. The only difference is that in version 2, the server adds an extra field to the queries it sends to the coprocess; this extra field contains the IP address of the client requestor.

pipe-timeout
: Determines the number of milliseconds that PowerDNS should wait for an answer from the coprocess. If the timeout is exceeded, the coprocess is considered dead and PowerDNS forks another.

pipe-regex
: A regular expression that determines which queries are sent by PowerDNS to the Pipe back-end. When deploying the Pipe back-end with other back-ends, this expression can help limit the load on the Pipe back-end, by avoiding giving it queries which it will never be able to answer.

  For example, a query for an Address (A) resource record for qupps.biz will be presented to the regular expression parser as `qupps.biz;A`, so to enable just that query to reach the back-end you would use a regular expression like `^qupps\.biz;A$`.

For the pseudo load-balancer we describe in the next section, the configuration we use is:

```
launch=pipe
pipe-command=/etc/powerdns/pipe/loadb.pl
pipebackend-abi-version=2
pipe-regex=example\.com;
```

6.6.3 An example load balancer coprocess for the Pipe back-end

The program in the following listing is a coprocess for the Pipe back-end of PowerDNS, providing simple load balancing. (We provide similar functionality for BIND SDB in Chapter 8.) When it receives a query for www.example.com, the program reads a single IP address from the file `/tmp/load` and returns that as a reply. (We assume that a separate monitoring process is writing the address of the least-laden Web server into `/tmp/load`.)

Listing 6.2: PowerDNS Pipe back-end: load-balancer

```
#!/usr/bin/perl

use strict;

my $ipfile = '/tmp/load';
my $soarr  = 'foo.bar email.qu 1 10800 3601 608400 3600';

$|=1;   # disable buffering

chomp(my $line = <>);

unless($line eq "HELO\t2") {
    print "FAIL\n";
    <>;
    exit;
}
print "OK\tHere is $0\n";

while(chomp($line = <>))
{
    # print STDERR "Received: $line\n";
    print "LOG\tGot {$line}\n";
    my @pq = split(/\t/, $line);

    if ($pq[0] eq 'AXFR') {
        reply('example.com', 'IN', -1, 86400, 'SOA', $soarr);
        reply('example.com', 'IN', -1, 86400, 'NS', 'ns.qupps.biz');
        reply('example.com', 'IN', -1, 60, 'A', '1.0.0.2');
        reply('example.com', 'IN', -1, 60, 'TXT', "Served by PowerDNS and $0");
        print "END\n";
        next;
    } elsif (@pq < 6) {
        print "LOG\tPowerDNS sent unparseable line\n";
        print "FAIL\n";
        next;
    }

    my ($type,$qname,$qclass,$qtype,$id,$client,$ip) = @pq;

    if (($qname eq 'example.com') && (($qtype eq 'SOA') || ($qtype eq 'ANY'))) {
        reply($qname, $qclass, $id, 86400, 'SOA', $soarr);
        reply($qname, $qclass, $id, 86400, 'NS', 'ns.example.com');
        reply($qname, $qclass, $id,  9600, 'MX', "10\tmail.qupps.biz");
    }
    if (($qname eq 'www.example.com') && ($qtype eq 'ANY')) {
```

```
        my $ip = undef;
        if (open(IP, "$ipfile")) {
            chomp($ip = <IP>);
            close(IP);
        }

        reply($qname, $qclass, $id, 60, 'A',
                ($ip) ? $ip : '127.0.0.1');
    }

    print "END\n";
}

sub reply {
    my ($qname, $qclass, $id, $ttl, $qtype, $rr) = @_;

    print "DATA\t$qname\t$qclass\t$qtype\t$ttl\t$id\t$rr\n";
    print "LOG\treturning $rr for $qname/$qtype\n";
}
```

When PowerDNS starts up, it logs the banner issued by the coprocess:

```
Backend launched with banner: OK        Here is .../pipe/loadb.pl
Done launching threads, ready to distribute questions
```

If we now query this back-end with:

```
$ dig @localhost www.example.com a
www.example.com.            60      IN      A       10.51.3.4

$ echo 45.1.3.29 > /tmp/load
$ dig @localhost www.example.com a
www.example.com.            60      IN      A       45.1.3.29
```

we see this printed to the log:

```
Coprocess: Got Q    www.example.com    IN    ANY  -1    127.0.0.1  0.0.0.0
Coprocess: returning 10.51.3.4 for www.example.com/A
Coprocess: Got Q    www.example.com    IN    ANY  -1    127.0.0.1  0.0.0.0
Coprocess: returning 45.1.3.29 for www.example.com/A
```

For an alternative solution, see *Related topics* on page 161.

That completes our discussion of the back-ends provided by PowerDNS. In the following section we show you how to configure PowerDNS (although you know a bit about that already).

6.7 Global PowerDNS configuration directives

PowerDNS is configured via a `pdns.conf` file or via command-line switches. The location of `pdns.conf` depends on how the software was built (see Notes), but it is typically either `/etc/powerdns/pdns.conf` or `/usr/local/etc/pdns.conf`. Names of the command-line switches are identical to the name of directives in the configuration file but have a double hyphen ("`--`") prepended to them; for example, a configuration file setting of:

```
local-address=127.0.0.1
launch=pipe
```

is equivalent to invoking the PowerDNS binary with:

```
# pdns_server --local-address=127.0.0.1 --launch=pipe
```

To display a list of all configuration settings and options:

```
# pdns_server --launch=gmysql --help
```

and to display the list of supported options for a specific back-end, use:

```
# pdns_server --launch=gmysql --help=gmysql
```

To see which modules are compiled in to your copy of PowerDNS:

```
# pdns_server --list-modules
Modules available:
bind
geo
ldap
opendbx
pipe
random
```

Most of the back-ends require some form of TCP/IP to access their databases, and you may be tempted to use hostnames when configuring them. Keep in mind, however, that these names have to be resolved to IP addresses via the host's resolver. Since it is quite likely that your resolver talks to a caching server, which in turn requires the PowerDNS server you are configuring, you are creating a problem: PowerDNS can't connect to its back-end database because it cannot access the database to perform the resolution[4]. In case of doubt, use IP addresses when specifying the hosts on which your SQL or LDAP servers run, or configure these names locally in `/etc/hosts`.

We now show you some of PowerDNS' more interesting global configuration settings. All others are documented at `http://doc.powerdns.com`. We have already described settings pertinent to the individual database back-ends, in their respective sections.

allow-axfr-ips
: Which clients are allowed to request a zone transfer from PowerDNS, specified as a comma-separated list of IP addresses or IP/subnet pairs.

```
allow-axfr-ips=127.0.0.1,192.168.1.0/24
```

Unfortunately it is not possible to control access to zone transfers via data in the back-end database, forcing you to list IP addresses of the slave servers here. In other words, this is an all-or-nothing proposition: in the example above, the client 192.168.1.23 can transfer all zones hosted by PowerDNS.

allow-recursion
: PowerDNS allows recursion by default. However, PowerDNS itself cannot act as a full recursive name server; instead, it implements recursion

[4]See the novel *Catch 22* by Joseph Heller.

by forwarding queries to a separate caching name server, at the address specified by the recursor variable (Figure 6.12). We recommend this feature as a last-resort only, because all queries sent to PowerDNS will first cause a database back-end to look up the query; if it cannot answer it, PowerDNS hands the query off to the external recursor. This will cause an unnecessary load on the PowerDNS, which is after all an authoritative name server.

If you do use this feature, you can forward to any brand of caching name server, although since you are using PowerDNS, you might want to use PowerDNS Recursor, as it is written by the same authors as PowerDNS (Section 17.3).

You can restrict recursion to a specified set of clients, by specifying allow-recursion with a comma-separated list of IP addresses or subnets:

```
allow-recursion=127.0.0.1 ,192.168.0.0/16
```

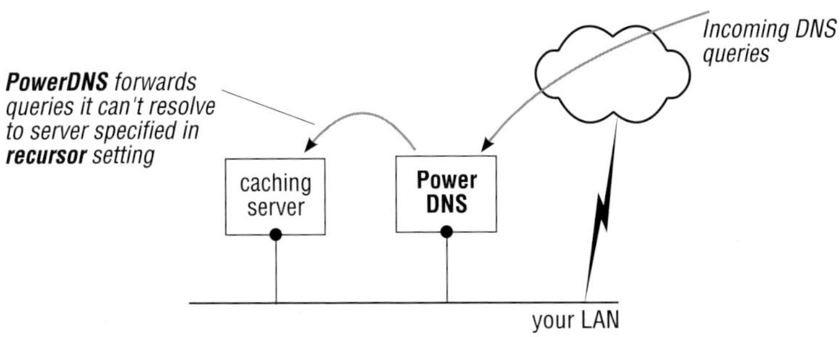

Figure 6.12: PowerDNS can forward queries to a cache

cache-ttl

PowerDNS caches entire packets it sends out, to save time on querying back-ends for the data. This variable specifies the number of seconds (default 20) that PowerDNS should store packets in the packet cache before dropping them.

If cache-ttl is 0, PowerDNS will consult the back-end databases for each incoming query, thereby increasing the load on the database, but ensuring very fresh replies. A value of 60 is a good compromise. (This means that it can take up to 60 seconds before a record you update on a back-end database is seen by a DNS client.)

```
cache-ttl=60
```

You can check the size of the packet cache with:

```
# pdns show packetcache-size
```

config-name

This setting lets you run multiple instances of a PowerDNS on a single machine. This best way to use this is by renaming the pdns startup script to pdns-*something*; that causes the startup script to use the word *something* as the value of config-name when it starts the binary:

```
# pdns_server --config-name=foob
$ ps ax | grep pdns
........    pdns_server-foob-instance ....
```

We use this as a kind of virtual hosting to run more than one instance of PowerDNS on a single machine. We define two different config-names to run two different PowerDNS instances, each listening on a separate IP address and accessing different back-ends.

default-ttl The TTL that should be returned in answers for records retrieved from a database that have no TTL defined for them. (Default: 3600.)

The OpenDBX back-end performs slightly better if you have NULL values in the `ttl` column of the `records` database, as it does not have to convert strings to numbers.

Not having the `dNSTTL` attribute type in your LDAP entries also gives a slight performance improvement, because the LDAP back-end doesn't have to convert the numbers; it uses the value of default-ttl.

```
default-ttl=7200
```

Tests indicate that you can attain a performance increase of up to seven percent by using default-ttl instead of specifying a TTL per record.

disable-axfr Do not allow zone transfers, not even to those listed in allow-axfr-ips.

disable-tcp Do not listen to TCP queries. This effectively disables the TCP port and PowerDNS can then no longer be used to serve zone transfers, nor can it accept queries over TCP, effectively breaking RFC compliance. This matters if you serve large resource record sets (RRset) that don't fit into a single UDP packet.

distributor-threads If your database back-ends are latency-bound, you might want to increase the number of parallel instances, by increasing the setting of this variable. The server will then be able to send queries in parallel to the back-end databases for processing. We recommend you set this to a value of 3.

Depending on your operating system and system architecture, setting this variable to 1 might actually increase performance as PowerDNS then effectively reverts to unthreaded operation.

guardian When PowerDNS is launched from the pdns init script (Section 6.8.3) it wraps itself up in a so-called guardian process that monitors a forked pdns_server instance (see config-name above). It is this guardian process that pdns_control communicates with. This setting should be enabled on production systems because it restarts PowerDNS automatically if necessary.

```
guardian=yes
```

Sending the guardian a SIGTERM signal will cause it to exit and terminate its children as well.

launch
List of the back-ends that this instance of PowerDNS should activate. The order is important because it determines the order in which back-ends are sent queries. As soon as one back-end answers the query successfully, no further back-ends are asked (for this query).

```
launch=opendbx,ldap,opendbx:qdb
```

The example shows how you can rename a back-end, by appending a colon and an arbitrary string to the name. If you do this, all the related options are renamed too, so you can define options specific to the back-end instance. E.g. opendbx-host-read becomes opendbx-*string*-host-read (opendbx-qdb-host-read in the example above). This lets you load a back-end more than once. So, if you want to set up a PowerDNS which has most of its zones in a MySQL database, and some legacy zones in a Sybase system, you could use:

```
launch=opendbx:mysql ,opendbx:sybase
...
opendbx-mysql-backend=mysql
opendbx-mysql-host-read=127.0.0.1
...
opendbx-sybase-backend=sybase
opendbx-sybase-host-read=192.168.3.44
...
```

local-address
A comma-separated or whitespace-separated list of addresses of the local machine, on which the PowerDNS instance should listen. We recommend you specify this list and not have PowerDNS listen to all interfaces (the default).

log-dns-details
PowerDNS usually logs informative details on DNS queries. Set this variable to "no" to disable the logging.

logging-facility
Set this to a single digit, *n*, to syslog with facility LOCAL*n*, instead of the default DAEMON.

loglevel
Controls how detailed PowerDNS logs should be. Set this to an integer between 1 and 9. A value of 9 prints debugging information. On a production machine, we recommend you run with a low loglevel setting.

master
To allow PowerDNS to act as a DNS master, you must enable this variable. (Default is no.)

```
master=yes
```

When PowerDNS is running as a master, it will send out DNS notifications to all slaves of the zones. Master and slave support may be enabled simultaneously.

query-cache-ttl
Each DNS query leads to a number of back-end queries. Consider a request for the address (A) of www.qupps.biz. This could be a CNAME, so PowerDNS must first check if there is a CNAME record before checking

for the A record. These complete queries to the back-ends and their answers are stored in the query cache if they result in zero or one answer, and expire after the number of seconds specified in this variable.

```
query-cache-ttl=120
```

The query cache saves hitting the database back-ends, but the packet cache (see cache_ttl above) saves a lot of CPU because no processing needs to be done at all.

query-logging Tells a back-end that it should log a textual representation of queries it performs. We recommend you use this for debugging only.

recursive-cache-ttl How long, in seconds, to store recursive packets in the packet cache. (default: 10)

recursor Set to the address of a caching name server to which PowerDNS sends queries it cannot answer from its back-ends. See allow-recursion above.

slave To allow PowerDNS to act as a DNS slave or superslave, you must enable this variable. (Default is no.)

```
slave=yes
```

Master and slave support may be enabled simultaneously. Since both default to `no`, PowerDNS supports only native zones by default.

slave-cycle-interval PowerDNS periodically checks its slave zones, to see if they are up-to-date. This option specifies how long, in seconds, that PowerDNS should wait between these checks. If a zone is out-of-date (i.e. its SOA *refresh* has elapsed), PowerDNS contacts the master server and queries the SOA resource record to determine whether or not the zone must be refreshed. If you don't use PowerDNS as a slave, this option is ignored.

At the same time, if configured as a master, PowerDNS asks its back-ends to check whether any records have recently been modified; if so, PowerDNS sends DNS NOTIFYs to the zones' slave servers.

version-string When queried via DNS for its version, PowerDNS normally responds with a full version string. This variable controls the answer. There are four possible settings:

`full` The server answers with :

```
Served by POWERDNS 2.9.21 ... 20:43:14Z ahu
```

`powerdns` The server answers with:

```
Served by PowerDNS - http://www.powerdns.com
```

`anonymous` The server sends a SERVFAIL reply instead of a text string.

string The server answers with *string*.

wildcards DNS wild cards enable a query for *something*.qupps.biz to be satisfied if there exists a record for *.qupps.biz. Wild cards are enabled in PowerDNS by default, and cause a query for *something*.qupps.biz to be searched for as *something*.qupps.biz, qupps.biz, *.qupps.biz and even *.biz. If you know that you do not use wild cards, disabling wild card support can lower the load on your back-end databases.

```
wildcards=no
```

6.8 Monitoring PowerDNS

Monitoring is an integral component of PowerDNS, making it easy to see what the program is doing. The program provides three tools for monitoring:

- pdns_control which "talks" to a running pdns_server and requests information from it.
- A built-in Web server which shows vital numbers (i.e. metrics).
- MRTG-capabilities of the pdns script.

which we cover in the following sections.

6.8.1 pdns_control

You can launch the PowerDNS binary using the pdns script (preferred), or manually by invoking pdns_server. When the PowerDNS server starts, it creates a control socket to allow two-way communication with a special utility called pdns_control. pdns_control can pass commands to the server, requesting information or instructing the server to terminate. When you run pdns_control, it expects a command and optional parameters. The currently supported commands are:

ccounts Returns statistics on the current content of the cache, unless the cache TTLs are zero (in which case no caching is performed by the server):

```
# pdns_control ccounts
negative queries: 1367, non-recursive packets: 2048
```

notify Adds a specified zone name to the notification list, causing PowerDNS to send out NOTIFYs to the Name Servers (NS) of a zone. Use this command manually if you detect that a slave has missed a previous (automatic) notification:

```
# pdns_control notify mens.de
Added to queue
```

notify-host The same as `notify`, except you specify an IP address as destination for the notification packet.

```
# pdns_control notify-host mens.de 192.168.1.20
Added to queue
```

purge Tells pdns_server to purge the packet cache. You can specify an optional argument *recordname* in which case only entries for the exact record name are purged. If you specified it as *recordname*$ it purges cache entries *ending* in this name – effectively purging an entire domain.

```
# pdns_control purge www.qupps.biz
4
# pdns_control purge 'qupps.biz$'
9
```

rediscover Instructs back-ends that new domains may have appeared in the databases. In most cases this does nothing. For the BIND-back-end however, pdns_server rechecks `named.conf` and loads new or unloads unused domains.

```
# pdns_control rediscover
Ok. Done parsing domains, 0 rejected, 1 new, 0 removed
```

reload Tells back-ends that the contents of domains may have changed. Many back-ends ignore this, but the BIND back-end will check timestamps for all zones and reload them if needed.

```
# pdns_control reload
Ok
```

retrieve Tells PowerDNS that it should retrieve a slave domain from its master. This operation is performed almost immediately (i.e. as soon as PowerDNS gets around to doing it).

```
# pdns_control retrieve mens.de
Added retrieval for 'mens.de' from master 192.168.1.20
```

set Sets a server variable at runtime. Currently the only variable you can set is query-logging:

```
# pdns_control set query-logging 0
done
```

show Displays a variable from the current pdns_server instance. The list of metric names is in Table 6.5.

```
# pdns_control show packetcache-hit
7
```

This command is also available via the pdns script (see Section 6.8.3 on page 152).

uptime Shows the uptime of the PowerDNS server.

```
# pdns_control uptime
6.7 hours
```

version Prints the version of the running PowerDNS instance.

```
# pdns_control version
2.9.21
```

corrupt-packets	recursing-questions
deferred-cache-inserts	servfail-packets
deferred-cache-lookup	tcp-answers
latency	tcp-queries
packetcache-hit	timedout-packets
packetcache-miss	udp-answers
packetcache-size	udp-queries
qsize-q	udp4-answers
query-cache-hit	udp4-queries
query-cache-miss	udp6-answers
recursing-answers	udp6-queries

Table 6.5: pdns_control variable (metric) names

bind-domain-status Outputs status of one or more domains but only after the BIND back-end has successfully loaded.

```
# pdns_control bind-domain-status aa01.net aal01.org
aa01.net:   parsed into memory at Sat Nov 17 21:19:23
aal01.org:  parsed into memory at Sat Nov 17 21:19:23
```

bind-list-rejects Lists all zones that have problems and indicates what the problems are.

```
# pdns_control bind-list-rejects
qupps.biz   error at Sat Nov 17 21:23:19 2007 parsing ↩
    'qupps.biz' from file 'qupps.biz':↩
            Can't parse zone line '$RIGIN .'
```

bind-reload-now Reloads one or more specified zones from disk immediately, reporting results of the reload.

```
# pdns_control bind-reload-now notfound.com qupps.biz
notfound.com no such domain
qupps.biz:  parsed into memory at Sat Nov 17 21:26:41
```

6.8.2 Built-in Web server

PowerDNS has a built-in Web server that shows what the server is doing at the moment (Figure 6.13). To configure the Web server, use the following configuration variables in pdns.conf:

webserver Start the Web server. (Default: no)

```
webserver=yes
```

webserver-address The IP address on which the Web server should listen for incoming connections. Set it to 0.0.0.0 to listen on all the machine's addresses. (Default: 127.0.0.1)

```
webserver-address=192.168.1.143
```

webserver-password The password for HTTP basic authentication for the Web server. A username is not required, but you can enter anything when asked to. If this is not set (default), you won't be asked for a password.

```
webserver-password=hah2!
```

webserver-port The TCP port number on which the built-in Web server should listen for HTTP requests. (Default: 8081.)

```
webserver-port=8080
```

Total queries: 780212. Question/answer latency: 0.26ms

Top-10 of 4: Log Messages		
Reset Resize: 10 100 500 1000 (10000) 500000		
gmysql Connection succesful	5	62%
About to create 3 backend threads for UDP	1	12%
Creating backend connection for TCP	1	12%
Launched webserver on 192.168.1.164:8080	1	12%
Total:	**8**	**100%**

Figure 6.13: An excerpt of PowerDNS' built-in web server

If you require stronger authentication or want to allow different users to access the PowerDNS monitor using their own passwords, you can have the Web server listen on the host's loopback interface and give users access to it via a Web proxy with stronger authentication.

6.8.3 pdns init.d script

An easy way to control PowerDNS is via its pdns script; this script is built when the software is compiled, and you usually install it in `/etc/init.d/pdns`. It accepts the following commands:

`start` Starts PowerDNS. When you first start the server, or after any change in its configuration, make sure you carefully watch the system's log for any errors you may have introduced into its configuration, that prevent the server from starting. The location of these logs depends heavily on your setup, but typically is `/var/log/messages`.

`stop` Stops PowerDNS.

`restart` Stops and starts the server. This is identical to performing a `stop` followed by a `start`. A synonym is `force-reload`.

`status` Shows whether or not the server is running.

`dump` Dumps a list of all metrics and their current values. A list of these is shown in Table 6.5 on page 151.

show Displays the value of an individual metric. (See the list in Table 6.5 on page 151.)

```
# pdns show udp4-queries
udp4-queries=2166
```

mrtg Displays the value of an individual metric in a form suitable for feeding to the MRTG system (see Notes).

```
# pdns mrtg udp4-queries
2166
0
5.8 minutes
PowerDNS daemon
```

Figure 6.14 shows a sample MRTG graph of the packet cache hit rate taken from a live system.

cricket Displays the value of an individual metric in a form suitable for feeding to the Cricket monitoring system (see Notes).

```
# pdns cricket udp4-queries
2166
```

monitor Start PowerDNS with an option enabling full debugging. PowerDNS runs un-daemonized, without a guardian attached, and it opens a monitoring console at which you can type control commands to PowerDNS.

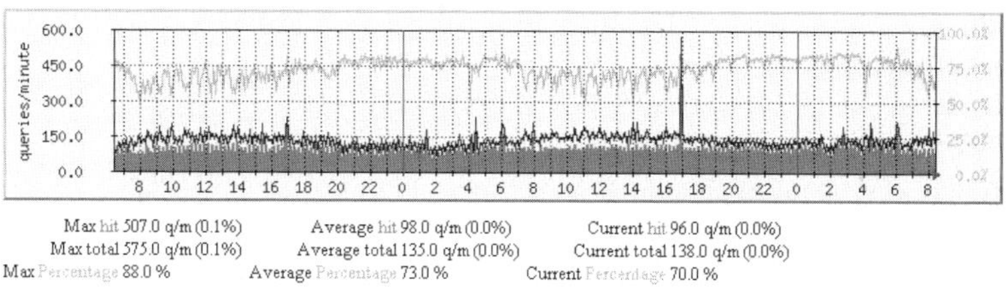

Figure 6.14: MRTG graph of PowerDNS' packet cache

6.9 Deployment and provisioning scenarios

6.9.1 Don't create a single point of failure

Do *not* set up two PowerDNS servers that access a single SQL or LDAP back-end, or else you will create a single point of failure (SPOF). No matter how stable you think your back-end is, a full file system, two disks gone bad, or a network problem will bite you some day. Believe us. If that happens, all your PowerDNS servers – and any other services you may have – that rely on that single back-end will be "kaput".

The general rule of thumb is: one back-end server for one PowerDNS server, and we very strongly recommend putting both on a single box (Figure 6.15), provisioning the database or directory back-ends from a central location.

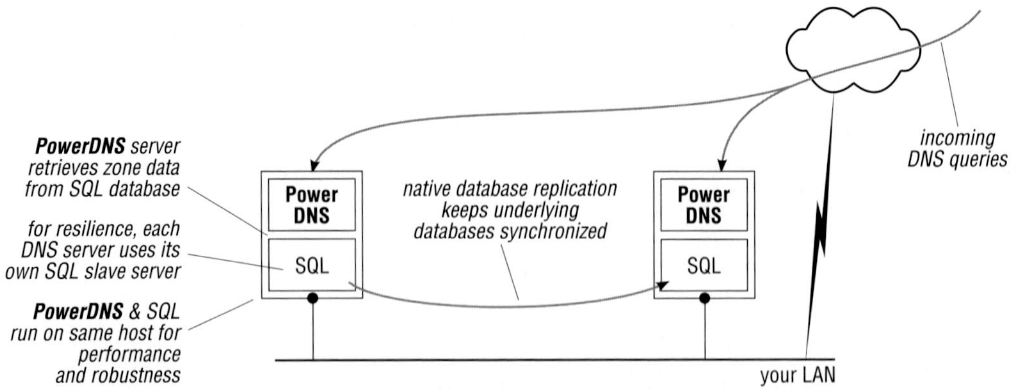

Figure 6.15: Each PowerDNS has its own back-end

6.9.2 Domain hoster

If you are a domain hosting organization, you often register new domains for customers, and assign NS entries for the newly registered domain to your PowerDNS, because you are going to provide public DNS services for them. Unfortunately, some registries insist on your DNS servers returning correct answers to queries, even though you might not yet be ready to provide the real data.

A fairly simple Pipe back-end solves this problem. Get PowerDNS to launch both a database and a Pipe back-end:

```
launch=opendbx,pipe
...
```

This causes the OpenDBX back-end to be queried first, and if it cannot find the answers in the database, PowerDNS then asks the Pipe back-end. The program you write for the Pipe back-end should give standard SOA, NS and A answers which will satisfy the registry, until you can set up the zone's final data in the OpenDBX back-end database. When you do add the zone data to the OpenDBX back-end, PowerDNS queries that first, finds the data, and answers the query, avoiding the Pipe back-end completely.

6.9.3 Set up NSD or BIND with a hidden/stealth MySQL PowerDNS

Running PowerDNS as a hidden or stealth primary to an NSD or BIND name server is straightforward. However, you first have to configure `zone` clauses manually in both BIND and NSD. If you have PowerDNS with an OpenDBX or gmysql database back-end, you can use a small program to automatically create a file containing the necessary `zone` clauses, which you then `include` in BIND's `named.conf` or in NSD's `nsd.conf` file. The program below generates a file from the `domains` table of the database. The program can also be made to generate BIND ACLs or NSD `provide-xfr` statements if you want it to.

Listing 6.3: Enumerate zones from MySQL for NSD with PowerDNS::Backend::MySQL

```
#!/usr/bin/perl
# enumzonessql (C)2008 by Jan-Piet Mens
# Generate zones to include in named.conf or nsd.conf

use strict;
use PowerDNS::Backend::MySQL;

my $params = {
        db_user         => 'pdnsadmin',
        db_pass         => 'hah!',
        db_name         => 'ourpdns',
        db_port         => '3306',
        db_host         => '127.0.0.1',
        mysql_print_error => 1,
        mysql_warn        => 1 };

my %nic = (
    'hu'    => 'hu-nic',
    'dk'    => 'dk-nic',
);

my $pdns = PowerDNS::Backend::MySQL->new($params);

my $zones = $pdns->list_domain_names;

for my $name (@$zones) {
    $name = lc $name;
    my ($pfx, $tld) = split(/\./, $name, 2);

    my $xfer = "";
    $xfer = 'allow-transfer { "' . $nic{$tld} . '"; };' . "\n"
        if (defined($nic{$tld}));

#print <<ZoneEnd;
#zone "$name" {
# type slave;
# file "$name";
# masters { 127.0.0.2; };
# $xfer
#};
#ZoneEnd

print <<ZoneEnd;
zone:
  name: "$name"
  zonefile: "$name.zone"
  provide-xfr: 127.0.0.1 NOKEY

ZoneEnd

}
```

The program outputs stanzas of zone configurations. Here's an example for NSD:

```
zone:
  name: "example.net"
```

```
    zonefile: "example.net.zone"
    provide-xfr: 127.0.0.1 NOKEY
```

You direct the output of this program to a file:

```
$ enumzonessql.pl > /tmp/db.zones && mv /tmp/db.zones /etc/nsd/nsd.zones.incl
```

The disadvantage of this setup is obviously that the dynamic nature of PowerDNS is not utilized to its full extent, as zones will only be visible once you've created BIND or NSD's configuration and reloaded the slave server. (We show you how you can solve this problem with a MySQL trigger and a user defined function in Section F.2.)

6.9.4 Set up BIND with hidden/stealth PowerDNS and LDAP back-end

Similar to above, we can easily extract the list of zones from an LDAP directory server back-end, and create a file containing zone clauses to be included in BIND's `named.conf`:

Listing 6.4: Enumerate PowerDNS zones from LDAP for BIND

```
#!/usr/bin/perl

# Print a list of all dNSDomain2 zones in LDAP to
# include in BIND.

use strict;
use Net::LDAP;

my @masters = qw(192.168.1.20   192.168.2.56);

my $ldap = Net::LDAP->new('localhost') or die "$@";

my $mesg = $ldap->bind('cn=manager,dc=qupps,dc=biz', password=>'heh?');

$mesg = $ldap->search(
    base   => "ou=pdns,ou=dns,dc=qupps,dc=biz",
    filter => "(&(objectClass=dnsDomain2)(sOARecord=*))",
    attrs  => [ 'associatedDomain' ],
);

$mesg->code && die $mesg->error;

foreach my $e ($mesg->entries) {
    my $zone = $e->get_value('associateddomain');

    print "zone \"$zone\" IN {\n";
    print "  type slave;\n";
    print "  file \"$zone.zone\";\n";
    print "  masters { " . join('; ', @masters) . "; };\n";
    print "};\n";
}

$ldap->unbind;
```

The program's output is like:

```
zone "qupps.biz" IN {
  type slave;
  file "qupps.biz.zone";
  masters { 192.168.1.20; 192.168.2.56; };
};
```

6.9.5 Create your own provisioning tools

The back-end you choose determines what you can use to provision its data store with DNS records. Here are some ideas to get you started:

- If you decide to deploy an SQL database back-end such as OpenDBX, have a good look at Perl's DBI or PHP's Pear modules, which will help you get results quickly.
- Writing tools for the LDAP back-end is not much more difficult than for an SQL back-end. A good starting point is Perl's Net::LDAP. However, if performance is important, look at Net::LDAPapi or the C language if you are conversant with that: OpenLDAP has a very good client library with all functions you need.

Update your database with PowerDNS::Backend::MySQL

Augie Schwer has created a set of Perl modules for controlling PowerDNS. One of these is PowerDNS::Backend::MySQL, a powerful Perl interface to the MySQL database used by the OpenDBX and the generic MySQL back-ends. The module is available on CPAN. It provides methods to:

- Add, delete and list master zones.
- Add, delete, list and find records.
- Add slave zones.

The example below uses the module to add the example.com zone if it doesn't already exist. It then adds an SOA record and an A record, for www.example.com.

Listing 6.5: Create a zone in PowerDNS with PowerDNS::Backend::MySQL

```
#!/usr/bin/perl

use strict;
use PowerDNS::Backend::MySQL;

my $MNAME = 'ns.qupps.biz.';
my $RNAME = 'hostmaster.qupps.biz.';
my $refresh = 7200;          # Refresh 2 hours
my $retry   = 1800;          # Retry 30 minutes
my $expire  = 2592000;       # Expire 30 days
my $minimum = 14400;         # Minimum 4 hours


my $params = {
        db_user              => 'pdnsadmin',
```

```
        db_pass           => 'hah!',
        db_name           => 'ourpdns',
        db_port           => '3306',
        db_host           => '127.0.0.1',
        mysql_print_error => 1,
        mysql_warn        => 1 };

my $pdns = PowerDNS::Backend::MySQL->new($params);

my $domain = 'example.net';

if (! $pdns->domain_exists(\$domain)) {
        unless ($pdns->add_domain(\$domain) ) {
                die "Cannot add domain $domain";
        }
}

addrr($domain,  'www', 'A', '192.168.1.20');
addrr($domain, '', 'SOA', "$MNAME $RNAME 0 $refresh $retry $expire $minimum");

$pdns = undef;
exit;

sub addrr {
        my ($domain, $host, @rr) = @_;

        my $fqdn = ($host) ? "$host.$domain" : "$domain";
        my @rrset = ($fqdn, @rr);

        unless ($pdns->add_record(\@rrset, \$domain) ) {
                die "Cannot add RR to $domain";
        }
}
```

6.9.6 Enforce correct CNAME usage in your database

We discussed in Chapter 2 that RFC 1034 explicitly states:

> *If a CNAME RR is present at a node, no other data should be present*

However, it's easy to forget that, and if you insert an incorrect record, it could cause a slave server of your PowerDNS to fail, on a zone transfer. One solution to this is to use OpenDBX with its MySQL back-end, and set up a trigger in MySQL to prevent you from entering the bad data. (This technique should work with most SQL database systems that support triggers.)

Creating the trigger

The listing below shows our MySQL database trigger.

Listing 6.6: Trigger prevents CNAME and other data

```
-- cnametrigger.sql by Jan-Piet Mens
-- Do *not* create the two procedures CALLed below; they
-- should fail in order to RAISE an error.

DELIMITER $$

CREATE TRIGGER pdnsCNAMEtrigger
  BEFORE INSERT ON records
  FOR EACH ROW
BEGIN
  DECLARE nrows INTEGER;

  IF NEW.type = 'CNAME' THEN
    SELECT COUNT(*) INTO nrows
      FROM records
      WHERE name = NEW.name;

    IF nrows > 0 THEN
      -- there is an RR already (including CNAME):
      -- don't insert this one!
      --
      CALL NO_CNAME_AND_OTHER_DATA_OTHER_EXISTS();
    END IF;

  ELSE --       NEW.type <> 'CNAME'
    SELECT COUNT(*) INTO nrows
      FROM records
      WHERE name = NEW.name
        AND type = 'CNAME';

    IF nrows > 0 THEN
       -- there is already a CNAME: don't insert!
       --
      CALL NO_CNAME_AND_OTHER_DATA_CNAME_EXISTS();
    END IF;
  END IF;

END $$
DELIMITER ;
```

The trigger is executed before a row is inserted into the `records` table. The two procedures that are `CALL`ed from within the trigger don't exist and must not exist: as MySQL has no SQL `RAISE ERROR`, there is no elegant way of getting the trigger to produce an error; however, by calling procedures that have not been created in the database, we emulate a `RAISE ERROR`. In Appendix F we show you how to solve the problem more elegantly, using a User Defined Function (UDF).

Viewing the effects of the trigger

To demonstrate what happens on an `INSERT`, we create a new zone with a few records in it:

- Add a zone.

```
mysql> INSERT INTO domains (name,type) VALUES ('jp.xa', 'MASTER');
mysql> SELECT id,name FROM domains WHERE NAME = 'jp.xa';
+--------+-------+
| id     | name  |
+--------+-------+
| 100011 | jp.xa |
+--------+-------+
mysql> INSERT ... values (100011,'jp.xa','SOA', '1 1800  900 604800 86400');
mysql> INSERT ... values (100011,'jp.xa','NS', 'dns.jp.xa');
mysql> INSERT ... values (100011,'dns.jp.xa', 'A', '192.168.1.11');
mysql> SELECT id,name,type,content FROM records WHERE domain_id = 100011;
+---------+-----------+------+-------------------------+
| id      | name      | type | content                 |
+---------+-----------+------+-------------------------+
| 1000173 | jp.xa     | SOA  | 1 1800  900 604800 86400 |
| 1000174 | jp.xa     | NS   | dns.jp.xa               |
| 1000176 | dns.jp.xa | A    | 192.168.1.11            |
+---------+-----------+------+-------------------------+
```

This gives us a basic zone with a Start of Authority record (SOA) and a Name Server (NS) record.

- Add a first CNAME record. If you insert a CNAME record, it works:

```
mysql> INSERT ... values (100011,'www.jp.xa', 'CNAME', 'www.qupps.biz.');
mysql> SELECT id,name,type,content FROM records WHERE domain_id = 100011;
+---------+-----------+-------+-------------------------+
| id      | name      | type  | content                 |
+---------+-----------+-------+-------------------------+
| 1000173 | jp.xa     | SOA   | 1 1800  900 604800 86400 |
| 1000174 | jp.xa     | NS    | dns.jp.xa               |
| 1000176 | dns.jp.xa | A     | 192.168.1.11            |
| 1000177 | www.jp.xa | CNAME | www.qupps.biz.          |
+---------+-----------+-------+-------------------------+
```

- Try to add a CNAME record for an existing domain.

  Now we try to add a CNAME record for a domain that already exists, and it fails. The name of the procedure gives an indication of what went wrong:

```
mysql> INSERT ... values (100011,'dns.jp.xa', 'CNAME', 'www.qupps.biz.');
ERROR 1305 (42000): PROCEDURE opendbx.NO_CNAME_AND_OTHER_DATA_OTHER_EXISTS ↩
                    does not exist
```

- Try to add an "other" record for an existing CNAME.

  Similarly, if you attempt to add a record for which there already exists a CNAME, you get a similar error:

```
mysql> INSERT ... values (100011,'www.jp.xa', 'A', '127.0.0.3');
ERROR 1305 (42000): PROCEDURE opendbx.NO_CNAME_AND_OTHER_DATA_CNAME_EXISTS ↩
                    does not exist
```

The code presented isn't perfect, and it handles only `INSERT`s to the tables, not `UPDATE`s. However, it might give you a few ideas for your own implementation. Using non-existent procedures to indicate errors isn't ideal, and we show you how to create a MySQL user-defined function to handle the problem more elegantly in Appendix F.

Summary

- PowerDNS is a versatile DNS server with a number of database back-ends, (a) SQL (gmysql, opendbx, ...) (b) LDAP (c) BIND, and (d) Pipe, that you can use simultaneously if you want.
- PowerDNS's BIND back-end is useful if you want to slowly migrate to PowerDNS, and its Pipe back-end allows you to provide dynamic answers to DNS requests.
- PowerDNS has full support for being a master/slave name server, and it can be a Superslave, allowing it to be provisioned remotely.
- PowerDNS has good tools to control the server, and its built-in Web server provides statistics on its operation.
- The packet cache provides a good balance between throughput and dynamic back-ends.

Related topics

- PowerDNS Recursor is a powerful and fast caching name server, complimentary to PowerDNS. We discuss it in Section 17.3 on page 395.
- You like the idea of creating a program to generate answers to DNS queries on the fly with PowerDNS()'s Pipe back-end? Before you dive into that, read about the Stanford::DNSserver server implemented in Section 15.3 on page 362, which just might be better suited to your needs. Although it would be a standalone server running on its own IP address, Stanford::DNSserver will provide better performance, and you might find it easier to implement than handling the text protocol spoken by the PowerDNS Pipe back-end.

Notes and further reading

PowerDNS' home

PowerDNS home is at `http://www.powerdns.com/` and its documentation lives online at `http://wiki.powerdns.com/`.

Installing PowerDNS

You may already have PowerDNS installed on your system. If you don't, there are three ways you can obtain PowerDNS:

1. Install it via your package manager, if your *nix distribution has it.
2. Obtain a statically linked version directly from the `powerdns.com` download site.
3. Download the source and build it yourself (see Notes.) You typically build PowerDNS yourself if you want to add options not readily available in the binary packages.

Installing the PowerDNS *binary*

The following is an example of how to install PowerDNS on a GNU/Linux system using the pre-build binary package from the PowerDNS web site.

Download the package:

```
$ wget http://downloads.powerdns.com/releases/deb/stable/    \
                pdns-static_2.9.21-1_i386.deb
# dpkg -i pdns-static_2.9.21-1_i386.deb
```

The installation copies configuration files and programs to their appropriate locations. It specifically creates the following files:

- The file `/etc/powerdns/pdns.conf` contains a list of all valid configuration directives. They are commented out, and we recommend you rename the file, and create a new one containing only the directives you need, depending on the functionality you want PowerDNS to provide.
- `/etc/init.d/pdns` is the script you typically use to start, stop and control the name server.
- The file `/usr/sbin/pdns_server` is the name server binary, which you typically don't execute yourself, leaving it up to the pdns script.

Installing PowerDNS *from source*

When building PowerDNS from source, you must decide whether you prefer to have modules compiled in to the final binary, or have them dynamically loaded. These hints might help you decide:

1. Most GNU/Linux distribution maintainers seem to prefer the dynamically loaded modules.
2. There is no noticeable performance difference when running PowerDNS with dynamically loaded modules.
3. You configure PowerDNS to use statically linked modules with:

   ```
   --with-modules=...
   ```

   and to use dynamically loaded modules with:

   ```
   --with-dynmodules=...
   ```

4. If you statically link in libraries, your current binary can't break when you install a new version of the library. By contrast, if you have dynamic libraries, when you install a new version of the library, your DNS server *can* break, because of incompatibilities in the library.

To build PowerDNS with the OpenDBX, LDAP and Pipe back-ends, proceed as follows:

```
$ wget http://downloads.powerdns.com/releases/pdns-2.9.21.tar.gz
$ tar xvzf pdns-2.9.21.tar.gz
$ cd pdns-2.9.21
$ export LDFLAGS="-L/opt/symas/lib -L/usr/lib64/mysql" # LDAP & MySQL libraries
$ export CXXFLAGS="-I/opt/symas/include -I/usr/include/mysql"
$ ./configure \
  --prefix=/usr/local \
  --with-dynmodules="" \
  --with-modules="opendbx ldap pipe"
$ make
$ make install
```

Change the modules options as necessary, for the back-ends you want to use.

Installing OpenDBX

OpenDBX' lives at `http://www.linuxnetworks.de/doc/index.php/OpenDBX`

```
$ wget http://linuxnetworks.de/opendbx/download/opendbx-1.3.4.tar.gz
$ tar xzf opendbx-1.3.4.tar.gz
$ cd opendbx-1.3.4
$ export LDFLAGS="-L/usr/lib64/mysql"
$ export CFLAGS="-I/usr/include/mysql"
$ ./configure --prefix=/usr/local --with-backends="mysql sqlite3"
$ make
$ make install
```

Build PowerDNS with the OpenDBX back-end, making a static build

```
$ export CXXFLAGS="-I/opt/symas/include -DLDAP_DEPRECATED=1"
$ export CFLAGS="-I/opt/symas/include -DLDAP_DEPRECATED=1"
$ export LDFLAGS="-L/opt/symas/lib/ -L/usr/lib64/mysql/"

$ ./configure --prefix=/usr/local \
      --with-modules="" \
      --with-dynmodules="opendbx ldap pipe"
```

Retrieving the latest version of PowerDNS

You can obtain the bleeding edge version of the PowerDNS source code directly from its official Subversion repository.

```
$ mkdir pdnsSVN
$ cd pdnsSVN
$ svn co svn://svn.powerdns.com/pdns/trunk/pdns pdns
A    pdns/regression-tests
A    pdns/regression-tests/basic-hinfo
...
A    pdns/makerelease
U   pdns
Checked out revision 1123.

$ cd pdns
$ ./bootstrap
$ ./configure ...
```

OpenDBX *options that affect queries*

The SQL statements that OpenDBX uses in its queries are configurable. The standard ones are almost always adequate, but there are situations where you might wish to change them. For example, you might have to adapt them to accommodate a custom database schema. Or, an ISP might want to change the queries to check whether a specific zone may be served by the back-end – "if the customer hasn't paid his invoice, I won't serve his DNS".

Here's an example of how you might customize a query. The opendbx-sql-lookup parameter specifies the SQL used to lookup a resource record. The default is:

```
SELECT domain_id, name, type, ttl, prio, content
   FROM records WHERE name=':name'
```

By changing this, you can alter the behavior of a DNS reply. Suppose you have a zone with lots of Address (A) records, and you want to return only one in each answer, selected randomly. You could set this query to:

```
SELECT domain_id,name,type,ttl,prio,content
      FROM records where name = ':name'
      ORDER BY RAND() LIMIT 1
```

The client querying PowerDNS may then see different A records for two consecutive queries:

```
$ dig @127.0.0.1 www.ex.net
;; ANSWER SECTION:
www.ex.net.          360     IN      A         10.0.0.4

$ dig @127.0.0.1 www.ex.net
;; ANSWER SECTION:
www.ex.net.          360     IN      A         10.0.0.7
```

Do note however, that the packet-cache may "interfere": because it caches the answers, your client will see the next random record only when the previous packet expires from the cache.

Alternatively, you could add a column to the database, to assign a "weight" or preference to each server name. (You could even use the MX `pref` column for that). You would periodically set the value in the column for a "preferred" server (e.g. a server with the least load, the fastest machine, etc.) and return the two most preferred servers with:

```
ORDER BY pref LIMIT 2
```

Do note however, that the changes you make to the the SQL queries affect *all* zones served by the back-end instance. We recommend you consider carefully whether you really need to modify the queries, because you might introduce an error into PowerDNS if you do change them.

A list of all the SQL queries used by the OpenDBX (Table 6.6) back-end is at `http://www.linuxnetworks.de/` – search for "Configuring SQL statements".

Migrating from BIND-sdb-LDAP

If you are migrating from BIND-sdb-LDAP to PowerDNS, you might be interested in a migration script that allows you update your LDAP directory entries so that PowerDNS can use them. (See `http://tinyurl.com/6xyb6a`)

opendbx-sql-infomasters	opendbx-sql-master
opendbx-sql-infoslaves	opendbx-sql-supermaster
opendbx-sql-insert-record	opendbx-sql-transactabort
opendbx-sql-insert-slave	opendbx-sql-transactbegin
opendbx-sql-list	opendbx-sql-transactend
opendbx-sql-lookup	opendbx-sql-update-lastcheck
opendbx-sql-lookupid	opendbx-sql-update-serial
opendbx-sql-lookuptype	opendbx-sql-zonedelete
opendbx-sql-lookuptypeid	opendbx-sql-zoneinfo

Table 6.6: Options that affect OpenDBX queries

MRTG & Cricket

- MRTG is the Multi Router Traffic Grapher, which draws pretty pictures from data collected from all sorts of devices and programs on a network (see `http://oss.oetiker.ch/mrtg/`).
- Cricket is a system for monitoring trends in data. While it was developed to help network managers visualize network data, you can use it to visualize almost anything and as such it is also useful with PowerDNS (see `http://cricket.sourceforge.net/`).

Further reading

Andy Smith has implemented a Geographic load balancer using a custom back-end for PowerDNS. "Geographic load balancing" means tailoring the answer to a queries for a domain name according to where the query comes from. This lets you disperse services across different countries or continents, and then direct clients, via the DNS, to a server that is close to them (network-wise), to reduce network traffic and improve response. (See the article by Andy Smith, in `modules/geobackend/README` in the distribution source.) The geo back-end is now included in the PowerDNS distribution (see `http://wiki.blitzed.org/DNS_balancing`).

Chapter

7 An overview of BIND

BIND 9 is the Apache of nameservers

Stephane Bortzmeyer

Introduction

BIND is the most widely used implementation of the Domain Name System server. It is a reference implementation of all things DNS, and has a very impressive list of features. We give you an overview of the latest release, BIND9, here.

If there is one program that is associated with serving DNS data, it is the BIND name server. Created in 1986, the Berkeley Internet Name Domain (BIND) is the most widely used DNS name server implementation:

- In 2002, Daniel J. Bernstein (author of djbdns) determined that 70% of the name servers were running BIND to publish second level .com domains[1] (i.e. *anything*.com).
- In 2004, Don Moore (the author of MyDNS) surveyed[2] 646 524 name servers: 72% were running BIND.
- In a survey taken in October 2007[3], 91% of the world's DNS servers were running a version of BIND (84% had BIND version 9).

Irrespective of how accurate these figures may be, BIND is certainly the most widely used name server implementation.

Pros	• Reference implementation of all DNS RFCs • Full master/slave support • Programmable back-ends • Access Control Lists • DNS security (TSIG, DNSSEC) • Built-in Web server serves XML for viewing statistics (BIND 9.5) • Native port for Microsoft Windows
Cons	○ Zone data must be stored in zone master files. BIND has no in-built support for SQL/LDAP back-ends (but see: Bind DLZ). ○ Slow startup if configured with a large number of zones. ○ Complex configuration files and a huge number of options make BIND hard to learn.
Scenarios	Large environments that require all DNS features, including security and dynamic DNS updates.

Table 7.1: BIND at a glance

A huge amount has been written on the operation of BIND, and there are two books which you *must* have if you want to deploy it (see Notes). This *isn't* a beginners guide to BIND, and we are not even going to attempt to duplicate these excellent references; instead we will just summarize the important aspects of the BIND configuration. To do so, we are going to plunge you into a BIND configuration file, with the sole purpose of preparing you for BIND SDB (Chapter 8) and Bind DLZ (Chapter 9).

[1] `http://cr.yp.to/surveys/dns1.html`
[2] `http://mydns.bboy.net/survey/`
[3] `http://dns.measurement-factory.com/surveys/200710.html`

7.1 Why use the BIND name server?

People use BIND for many reasons:

- BIND is the most widely deployed name server software in the world.
- It is provided as standard on many operating systems.
- There is a huge amount of documentation on its use, with myriad examples for specific scenarios or problems that people have solved with BIND.
- BIND is very flexible: you can create very versatile configurations with authoritative and caching services combined (which we do not recommend).
- BIND has a huge number of features.
- BIND supports access control lists (ACLs) so you can restrict which DNS clients can perform what operations.
- BIND is extensible. With its application programming interface you can create interfaces between BIND and foreign data sources from which you retrieve answers to DNS queries. We discuss the simple database API in Chapter 8.
- Along with MyDNS (Chapter 5), BIND is one of the few name servers that have support for RFC 2136 Dynamic DNS Updates.

7.2 Scenarios for deployment of BIND

The BIND name server is monolithic: it implements all its functionality within a single binary program, called named. While there are certain features you can choose to include or exclude at compile-time, most of its functionality is automatically included.

7.2.1 Authoritative name server

BIND can simultaneously act as an authoritative master for some zones and as a slave server for other zones.

7.2.2 Caching name server

BIND can act as a caching name server. You can combine caching and authoritative services in a single named instance, but we don't recommend it (for reasons given in Section 1.2.5).

In addition to being a recursive resolver, you can configure BIND to forward queries for some or all zones to other servers.

7.2.3 Front-end to stealth server

BIND is frequently used as a front-end server to a stealth or hidden name server. You can run a hidden or stealth server (MyDNS, ldapdns, PowerDNS, ...) with BIND as your "official" name servers, i.e. the Name Server (NS) records in your zones point to your BIND servers. Reasons for doing this include:

- You might not want to have a DNS name server with a database or LDAP directory back-end directly connected to the public DNS.
- When you run BIND with its zone data stored in local master files, it doesn't depend on a complex SQL/LDAP back-end being available and operating correctly, so your system is less complex.
- Zone transfers from BIND servers might be easier for you to manage than MySQL or LDAP replication.

(Note that you can also use a different server such as NSD (Chapter 10), instead of BIND, as a front-end server to your database-powered hidden DNS server.)

7.3 Configuring zones in BIND

The BIND configuration file is typically called `/etc/named.conf`. You create or modify it with your favorite text editor, and we recommend you place it under a version control system, in order to track changes to it. The file itself may contain comments, in any of three formats:

1. C-style comments, enclosed in `/*` and `*/` which may span multiple lines.
2. Shell-style comments, which begin when a hash sign (`#`) is encountered and run to the end of the same line.
3. C++-style comments on a single line, initiated with a double forward slash (`//`).

7.3.1 A sample configuration of an authoritative BIND name server

In this section we construct a sample configuration file, to configure BIND as follows:

- BIND is to act as an authoritative server and will not perform recursion.
- It is a master for the qupps.biz and 1.168.192.in-addr.arpa zones.
- It is a slave server for the mens.de zone.
- Access Control Lists (ACL) specify which IP addresses may initiate zone transfers for the master zones.

The following *clauses* make up our configuration file:

acl The `acl` clause defines one or more access control lists that may be referenced in other clauses. We define two ACLs, `internal` and `qupps-xfer`, which we use later on in the `zone` clause, to limit access to zone transfers.

```
acl "internal" {
   127.0.0.1;
   192.168.1.20/32;
};

acl "qupps-xfer" {
   192.168/16;
   10.0.21.2/32;      # a friend
};
```

options The `options` clause contains statements that influence the behavior of the server. Some of the options in the `options` clause also apply to all `zone` clauses, except where locally overridden within one.

```
options {
   directory "/var/named";
   statistics-file "/var/run/named/stats";
   zone-statistics yes;

   version "[no-way-jose]";

   listen-on {
      127.0.0.1;
      192.168.1.164;
   };

   recursion no;
   auth-nxdomain yes;
   allow-transfer { none; };
   allow-update { none; };
   allow-recursion { none; };
};
```

Our configuration defines the options:

directory The base path for the server. All other paths in the configuration file are relative to this directory.

statistics-file The file in which the server records statistics (when instructed to do so with the rndc program). (Default: `named.stats` in the server's `directory`)

zone-statistics If this option is set, the server collects statistics on all zones (except zones explicitly disabled).

version The string the server answers with, when queried for version.bind in the CHAOS class:

```
$ dig @server ch version.bind txt
```

listen-on A list of the IPv4 addresses the server should listen on. The default is to use all interfaces the system provides, but we recommend you set this explicitly.

recursion If this option is set, the server will always provide recursive queries to clients. On an authoritative server, this option should be set to `no`.

auth-nxdomain If set to `yes`, allows the server to authoritatively respond with NXDOMAIN.

allow-transfer Specifies which source addresses (listed in an `acl` clause) are allowed to transfer zones (master or slave zones). We recommend you disable zone transfers globally (as we have shown above) and allow them on a per-zone basis only.

allow-update Specifies which clients (matched by an `acl` clause) are allowed to perform RFC 2136 Dynamic Updates to zones. We recommend disabling this globally, and enabling it on individual zones as required.

allow-recursion Specifies hosts which are allowed to issue recursive queries to the server. On an authoritative server this should be set to `none`, as shown.

Note that if the answer to the query already exists in the cache it will be returned irrespective of this statement. In other words, if you allow recursion for some hosts, they cause the cache to fill with answers that are returned to all hosts – also those *not* allowed to recurse.

include Interpolate the content of a separate file at this point. You typically use this to include external files containing the definition of keys (as in the example below), or to include a file containing externally generated `zone` clauses. `include` can appear anywhere in the `/etc/named.conf` file.

```
include "/usr/local/etc/rndc.key";
```

controls BIND sets up a *control channel* for communicating with the rndc program – the "remote name daemon control" program, that you can use to tell the named daemon to reload one or more zones or even to shut itself down. This clause configures the control channel.

```
controls {
   inet 127.0.0.1 port 953 allow {
      127.0.0.1;
      192.168.1.20;
   } keys { "admindns"; };
};
```

The `keys` statement specifies the names of the keys that this instance of named will accept from rndc for controlling it. You create keys with the rndc-confgen program: it creates a default key that will be used both by named and rndc.

zone The `zone` clause defines a zone that your server is authoritative for. You use a separate `zone` clause for each zone. We explain the `zone` clause in Section 7.3.2. Here is a brief example:

```
zone "qupps.biz" {
   type master;
   file "q/qupps.biz";
   allow-transfer {
      "internal";
      "qupps-xfer";
   };
};

zone "1.168.192.in-addr.arpa" {
   type master;
   file "rev/1.168.192";
};

zone "mens.de" {
   type slave;
   file "m/mens.de";
};
```

logging Configures the type of logging that BIND performs (default: logging via syslogd):

```
logging {
      channel "x_info" {
      file "/var/log/axfr.log";
      severity info;
      print-time yes;
      print-category yes;
      print-severity yes;
     };

     category "xfer-out"      { "x_info"; };
     category "xfer-in"       { "x_info"; };

   category default {
      default_syslog;
      default_debug;
   };
};
```

The clause defines a logging channel called `x_info` which writes to a file `/var/log/axfr.log`, adding a timestamp, the log category and the severity, to the log entry. This "channel" is used to log both outgoing and incoming zone transfers.

7.3.2 Defining zones

BIND lets you define five types of zones:

A. Master zones.

B. Slave zones.

C. Forwarding zones.

D. Stub zones.

E. Root hints.

Each zone is defined in a `zone` clause.

A,B. Master and slave zones

For a master zone you specify the name of the file containing the zone data.

```
zone "qupps.biz" IN {
     type master;
     file "qupps.biz";
};
```

For a slave zone, you must also specify the master servers from which this slave should transfer the zones:

```
zone "aa01.net" IN {
         type slave;
         file "aa01.net";
         masters { 192.168.1.164; 192.168.2.14; };
};
```

For master zones you provide the zone data *in* the specified file, whereas for slave zones, BIND will write the content of the transferred zone *to* the specified file.

C. Forwarding zones

If you want queries for certain zones to be resolved using a specific remote name server, set up a forwarding zone for it. For example:

```
zone "qupps.bl" {
     type forward;
     forward only;
     forwarders {
          127.0.0.3 port 53;
     };
};
```

With this configuration:

- All queries for qupps.bl and its sub-domains are sent for resolution to the name servers specified in the `forwarders` statement (optionally specifying a port number).
- Because we specify the `forward only` statement, BIND will not iteratively search for an answer to queries for this zone, but it will answer from data received by the forwarder only. If you omit this statement, BIND will forward the query to its forwarders, and if it doesn't receive a reply from them, BIND will recursively search for an answer.

D. Stub zones

When you delegate a zone to a subordinate name server, you normally have to provide Start of Authority (SOA) and Name Server (NS) records, together with the necessary glue, so that the subordinate zones can be found. (We discuss delegation in Chapter 18). However, BIND gives you an easier way to do this. You define a *stub zone*; this tells BIND to query the delegated name servers and load the SOA and NS records (plus the necessary glue) from those servers. You define a stub zone in `named.conf` like:

```
zone "es.qupps.biz" {
    type stub;
    masters { 192.168.1.20; 192.168.1.22; };
    file "es.qupps.biz";
};
```

In the `masters` statement you list the master servers. When BIND loads this stub zone, it queries the master servers for the necessary records for the zone and maintains them in the specified file. At every refresh interval (specified in the SOA record just retrieved), BIND checks with the masters whether the serial number of the zone has changed, and if so, updates the Start of Authority, Name Server and glue records. The master servers do not have to enable outgoing zone transfers for stub zones to work.

E. Root hints

If you configure BIND as a caching name server, it must know where to find the root name servers. BIND has a built-in list of root server addresses. You can get a fresh copy of the ICANN root hints with, for example:

```
$ dig @k.root-servers.net . ns  | tee root.hints
;; flags: qr aa rd; QUERY: 1, ANSWER: 13, AUTHORITY: 0, ADDITIONAL: 15

;; ANSWER SECTION:
.                       518400  IN      NS      a.root-servers.net.
.                       518400  IN      NS      b.root-servers.net.
...

;; ADDITIONAL SECTION:
a.root-servers.net.     518400  IN      A       198.41.0.4
b.root-servers.net.     518400  IN      A       192.228.79.201
...
```

You use the `root.hints` file created by the above command to configure the hints for the root zones:

```
zone "." IN {
    type hint;
    file "root.hints";
};
```

You must change the list of root servers BIND uses when deploying your own private root servers (Chapter 18).

7.4 Using TSIG to secure zone transfers and updates

RFC 2845, *Secret Key Transaction Authentication for DNS*, defines TSIG (Transaction SIGnature), a protocol used for authenticating:

- DNS queries, such as zone transfers.
- Dynamic DNS Updates (RFC 2136).

TSIG uses a shared secret key, a time-stamp and a one-way hashing function called HMAC (keyed-Hash Message Authentication Code) to provide a cryptographically secure means of identifying the endpoints of a connection. The use of a time-stamp means that all clients and servers that participate in TSIG transactions must have synchronized clocks. (Time synchronization of machines is beyond the scope of this book, but you typically use NTP, the Network Time Protocol, for keeping the clocks of machines in your network synchronized to a time source.)

You typically use TSIG to permit only hosts that you authorize with appropriate keys to update your zones, or to transfer zones – usually between your master and slave name servers (Figure 7.1).

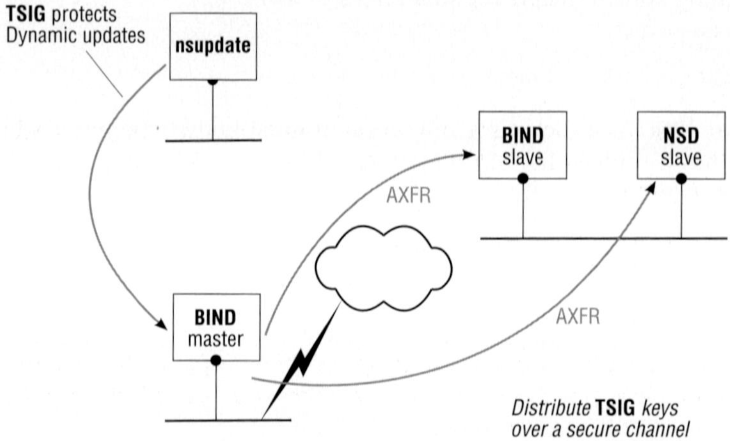

Figure 7.1: Securing your primary and slave name servers with TSIG

There are a number of points to consider when you use TSIG:

- As TSIG requires shared keys, you have to securely distribute the keys "out-of-band" to each of the name servers involved.
- We recommend you use a different key for each pair of hosts.
- If you use TSIG, any client with access to the shared secret key can impersonate a valid client.

To use TSIG, proceed as follows:

1. Generate the TSIG keys.

2a. Configure the zones with the TSIG keys to protect zone transfers.

2b. To protect updatable zones, add `allow-update` statements to them, and include your keys.

1 – Generating TSIG keys

You typically generate TSIG keys with one of:

- The ldns-keygen utility from the ldns package (see Chapter 10).
- The dnssec-keygen program from the BIND distribution.

For example, using dnssec-keygen to create a TSIG key:

```
$ dnssec-keygen -a HMAC-MD5 -b 256 -n HOST ma-clef
Kma-clef.+157+30764
```

produces two files:

i. The `.key` file

```
ma-clef. IN KEY 512 3 157 t3Q+wdd6Nzt0VnKslPuHk5JkE931QqPyntA33Z1AjEo=
```

ii. The `.private` file

```
Private-key-format: v1.2
Algorithm: 157 (HMAC_MD5)
Key: t3Q+wdd6Nzt0VnKslPuHk5JkE931QqPyntA33Z1AjEo=
Bits: AAA=
```

Note that the two base64-blobs (the long strings of apparently random characters) are identical. If you don't have access to ldns-keygen or dnssec-keygen, as a last resort you can use any valid base-64 encoded string instead of a key:

```
$ echo -n "DNS is vital!"  | openssl enc -a
RE5TIGlzIHZpdGFsIQ==

$ echo 'RE5TIGlzIHZpdGFsIQ==' | openssl enc -a -d
DNS is vital!
```

The first command takes a piece of plain text and encodes it in base 64 with the openssl utility. The result is a base64 blob that you use in lieu of a key. (We show you the second command just for completeness: it decodes a base64 string and prints the result on standard output.) Encoding can be useful if you want to exchange a TSIG key with a systems administrator over the telephone: you dictate a word or a a phrase and she can create the required base64 on the fly, adding it to a `key` clause in either BIND or NSD (which uses BIND-compatible zone master files).

2a – Configure zones with TSIG keys

We discuss how you set up TSIG to protect zone transfers between a Name Server Daemon (NSD) and a BIND server in Chapter 10.

2b – Protect updatable zones

- Create a `key` clause in `named.conf`:

```
key "ma-clef" {
   algorithm hmac-md5;
   secret "t3Q+wdd6Nzt0VnKslPuHk5JkE931QqPyntA33Z1AjEo=";
};
```

- Apply the key to a zone to allow updates to it:

```
zone "qupps.biz" IN {
    type master;
    file "qupps.biz";
    allow-update {
        key "ma-clef";
    };
};
```

- You can now use the key with nsupdate

```
$ nsupdate -y 'ma-clef:t3Q+wdd6Nzt0VnKslPuHk5JkE931QqPyntA33Z1AjEo='
>
...
```

7.5 Configuring BIND to accept dynamic DNS updates

Other than MyDNS, BIND is the only other program we discuss in this book that supports Dynamic DNS Updates as defined by RFC 2136. We discuss RFC 2136 in Chapter 19, but for now here's how you enable Dynamic DNS Updates in BIND:

A. Define a master zone for which you want to enable RFC 2136 Dynamic DNS Updates.

B. Add `allow-update` statements, to permit specific networks to update your zone.

C. Optionally create TSIG keys for authenticating the DNS updates, as described in the previous section.

The following example defines a zone qupps.biz (step A) that may be updated by the two hosts 127.0.0.1 and 192.168.1.20 (step B):

```
zone "qupps.biz" IN {
    type master;
    file "qupps.biz";
    allow-update {
        127.0.0.1;
        192.168.1.20;
    };
};
```

7.5.1 How your zone is updated

As soon as named receives the first Dynamic DNS update for your zone, BIND creates a journal file. The name of the journal is the zone's file name with "`.jnl`" appended. BIND records updates in the journal, and increments the zone's serial number in the Start of Authority (SOA) at each change. BIND processes the update request by modifying its in-memory data. It uses this in-memory data for answers to queries it receives. Modifications are not merged back into the zone's file on disk until either:

- named is stopped, or ...
- Dynamic Updates to the zone (or to all zones served by BIND) are frozen with the command:

  ```
  # rndc freeze qupps.biz
  ```

  When you subsequently thaw the zone with:

  ```
  # rndc thaw qupps.biz
  ```

  dynamic updates are allowed again and the first update causes named to create the journal file for the zone.

If your machine crashes, when named starts up again, it merges whatever it has in its journal file back into its in-memory copy and continues answering from there.

7.6 Split-horizon DNS using BIND views

You can configure BIND to give different answers to the same query, according to the IP address of the querying client, using BIND's *views* feature. It may sound a bit schizophrenic, to have a name server that doesn't answer consistently, but split-horizon DNS servers are useful. Recall from Section 1.2.3 that we had a Web server in the DMZ. From hosts within the DMZ, we can address the Web server called www.qupps.biz as 192.168.1.20, but for hosts on the public Internet, we want the same domain name to resolve to 192.0.2.1.

We illustrate how to configure views with an example:

```
acl "trusted" {
   127.0.0.1;
   192.168.1.20/32;
};

options {
   directory ".";
   listen-on {
      127.0.0.1;
      192.168.1.164;
   };
};

view "inside" IN {
   match-clients { "trusted"; };
```

```
        zone "qupps.biz" {
            type master;
            file "inside/qupps.biz";
        };
};

view "outside" IN {
        match-clients { any; };
        zone "qupps.biz" {
            type master;
            file "outside/qupps.biz";
        };
};
```

This provides the following features:

- An access control list, `trusted`, defines the clients on the internal network, for use in the next step.
- Two `view` clauses are defined with the same zones:

  inside The view `inside` is used when the querying client's address matches the `trusted` ACL. The zone loads its data from the file `inside/qupps.biz`.

  An internal client querying this server sees:

  ```
  $ dig @192.168.1.164 www.qupps.biz
  www.qupps.biz.          86400    IN       A 192.168.1.20
  ```

  outside The view `outside` matches any client including internal trusted hosts. However, internal hosts never "reach" this view because BIND accepts the first match it finds when processing views. Internal hosts match on the first view, `internal`, because it is defined first in `named.conf`. Therefore the ordering of views is very important: you place the view with the greatest restrictions first.

  An external client that queries this *same* DNS server sees:

  ```
  $ dig @192.168.1.164 www.qupps.biz
  www.qupps.biz.          86400    IN       A 192.0.2.1
  ```

7.7 Aspects of implementing a BIND name server

7.7.1 How you create your zone files

Instead of maintaining zone files manually, i.e. by modifying their content with a text editor, you may be interested in tools that allow you to generate them from content stored in an SQL database or in an LDAP directory server. In Chapter 19 we show you how to do this. In addition, Appendix B describes a system that can automatically increment serial numbers in your zone's SOA records when you modify your zone master file.

7.7.2 Monitoring your BIND name server

You can monitor BIND's operation using Statistics, Query logging, and its Statistics server (BIND 9.5). We look at each of these in turn, now.

Statistics

BIND can gather statistics on the number and type of queries it receives. You enable this with the `zone-statistics` statement in the `options` clause, and optionally specify the name of the file to which statistics are written, using the `statistics-file` statement (default: `named.stats` in named's directory):

```
options {
     ...
     zone-statistics yes;
     statistics-file "/var/named/stats";
     ...
};
```

This instructs named to collect in memory statistical data on all zones (unless specifically turned off on a per-zone basis by specifying `zone-statistics` "no" in the `zone` clause). You tell named to dump the in-memory data to its statistics file with:

```
# rndc stats
```

The statistics file then contains a list of global query statistics, followed by statistics on individual zones:

```
+++ Statistics Dump +++ (1203256530)
success 806705
referral 146981
nxrrset 286490
nxdomain 179147
recursion 0
failure 2
success 294034 qupps.biz
referral 0 qupps.biz
nxrrset 138001 qupps.biz
nxdomain 34677 qupps.biz
recursion 0 qupps.biz
failure 0 qupps.biz
...
...
--- Statistics Dump --- (1203256530)
```

We recommend dnsstats[4], a small Perl program written by Haw Loeung that uses MRTG to graph the output of the statistics file and produces query totals (Figure 7.2).

Query logging

If you are having trouble identifying whether queries are being satisfied by your named, you can have it (temporarily) log the queries it receives by toggling the `querylog` function at run-time:

[4] `http://sourceforge.net/projects/statusreport`

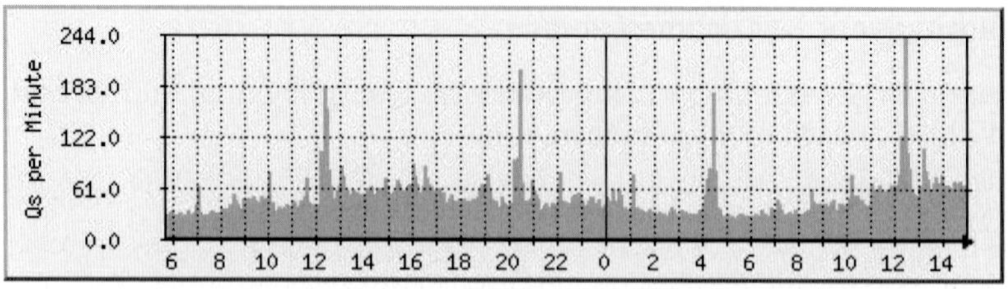

Figure 7.2: Using MRTG to graph BIND statistics

```
# rndc querylog
switch on query logging
wait a while or watch logs
# rndc querylog
stitch off query logging
```

By default, named logs its queries to syslog, which will show when you enabled and disabled query logging, as well as the queries named received:

```
query logging is now on
client 127.0.0.1#53178: query: www.qupps.biz IN A
client 127.0.0.1#53178: query: cnn.com IN MX
client 127.0.0.1#53178: query: www.cnn.com IN A
client 127.0.0.1#53178: query: www.yahoo.de IN A
...
query logging is now off
```

The BIND *9.5 stats Web server*

BIND version 9.5 includes an experimental built-in Web server that can output statistics about the server and the zones it serves, in XML format. An extract of the XML is shown below:

```
<?xml version="1.0" encoding="UTF-8"?>
<?xml-stylesheet type="text/xsl" href="/bind9.xsl"?>
<isc version="1.0">
  <bind>
    <statistics version="1.0">
  ...
  ...
      <server>
        <boot-time>2008-01-26T06:30:03Z</boot-time>
        <current-time>2008-01-27T14:56:31Z</current-time>
        <counters>
          <success>17511</success>
          <referral>0</referral>
          <nxrrset>5482</nxrrset>
          <nxdomain>0</nxdomain>
          <recursion>1</recursion>
          <failure>0</failure>
          <duplicate>0</duplicate>
          <dropped>0</dropped>
```

```
        </counters>
      </server>

  ...
```

The built-in Web server also provides an XSL style sheet on demand, so you can open the URL to BIND's "Web server" in a Web browser, and see a neatly styled view of what your server is currently doing (Figure 7.3).

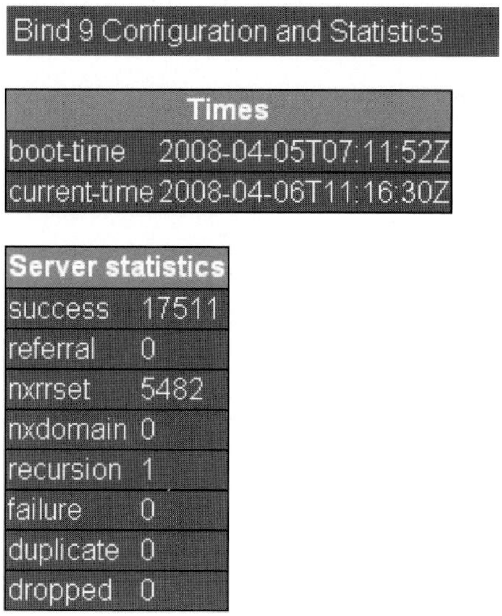

Figure 7.3: BIND's built-in statistics server

You enable the statistics server with the `zone-statistics` statement in `named.conf`. If you want BIND to also accumulate statistics on a zone by zone basis, you enable the `zone-statistics` option globally, or in the `zone` clause of each zone that is to log its statistics:

```
options {
    ...
    stats-server port 8000;
    zone-statistics yes;
    ...
};
```

You can use the XML produced by the BIND stats server to build tools to integrate into your monitoring environment (e.g. Nagios). As a small example, the listing below uses the XML shown above, to print the number of successful and failed queries in the current instance of named.

Listing 7.1: Parsing the XML produced by BIND's statistics server

```
#!/usr/bin/perl

use XML::Simple;
use strict;

my $xs = XML::Simple->new();
my $xml = $xs->XMLin('bind.xml');

my $counters = $xml->{bind}->{statistics}->{server}->{counters};

print "Success: ", $counters->{success}, "\n";
print "Failure: ", $counters->{failure}, "\n";
```

When you run this program, it prints something like:

```
Success: 17511
Failure: 0
```

7.8 Points to note when using BIND

- BIND is very memory-hungry. It loads all its zones into RAM upon startup. During startup, the server is "deaf" (i.e. it won't answer queries). You can use Bind DLZ to avoid this behavior.
- One of BIND's strengths is its ability to run as an authoritative and as a caching name server simultaneously. (We recommend you don't do this.)
- Another of BIND's strengths is that it is very flexible. However, the downside of that is that BIND's configuration language is very complex, with too many options and statements.
- BIND fully supports DNSSEC (Chapter 22).

Summary

- BIND is the most widely used name server implementation.
- BIND implements all DNS specifications in a single binary.
- BIND can, but should not, be configured as an authoritative and caching name server in one.
- BIND supports TSIG and DNSSEC.
- BIND supports RFC 2136 Dynamic DNS Updates.

Related topics

- Bind DLZ (Chapter 9) lets BIND use a number of different SQL databases, LDAP directory servers and Berkeley DB databases as back-ends for storing zone data.
- BIND SDB (Chapter 8) lets you create your own BIND back-end with a special programming interface.
- PowerDNS (Chapter 6) has a BIND back-end which reads master zone files.
- MyDNS (which stores zone data in a MySQL or PostgreSQL database) is the only other name server that supports RFC 2136 Dynamic DNS Updates (Chapter 5).
- NSD, the Name Server Daemon (Chapter 10), supports TSIG for controlling zone transfers. NSD uses BIND-compatible zone master files.
- We discuss running BIND on Microsoft Windows in Chapter 14.
- We show you how to configure BIND to serve or validate DNSSEC signed zones in Chapter 22.

Notes and further reading

Building BIND

The Internet Systems Consortium is the current maintainer and provider of the BIND software distribution (see `http://www.isc.org/`). It is quite likely that you won't have to build BIND yourself: most operating system vendors and distribution maintainers provide binary packages of BIND. If you do want to build it yourself, you can, as follows:

```
$ wget http://ftp.isc.org/isc/bind9/9.5.0b1/bind-9.5.0b1.tar.gz
$ tar xvzf bind-9.5.0b1.tar.gz
$ cd bind-9.5.0b1/
$ ./configure --prefix=/usr/local --enable-threads --with-libxml2=yes
$ make
$ make install
```

The XML2 library (specified in the `configure` line in the example) is needed for the built-in Web server.

Secure BIND *Template*

Rob Thomas maintains a template that can be used to securely deploy a BIND name server, mitigating some of the risks involved (see `http://www.cymru.com/Documents/secure-bind-template.html`).

GeoDNS for BIND

GeoDNS is a small patch to BIND to add geographical filters support to its views. Together with Maxmind's GeoIP, you can filter by countries' address blocks without specifying their IP address blocks (which would be a gargantuan task). For example, the following configuration in `named.conf` enables this view only for addresses that Maxmind reports as being from Spain and France:

```
view "SpainFrance" {
    match-clients { country_ES; country_FR; };
    recursion no;
    zone "qupps.biz" {
         type master;
         file "qupps.biz-es-fr.zone";
    };
};
```

After patching BIND, the `match-clients` statement triggers use of GeoIP when you use the literal string "`country_`" in the `match-clients` statement; the two-letter country codes (in the above example, `ES` and `FR`) define the countries' IP addresses (see `http://www.caraytech.com/geodns/`).

Further reading

- The first book we recommend is already in its 5th edition: Paul Albitz and Cricket Liu's, *DNS and BIND, Fifth Edition* (O'Reilly) covers BIND version 9.3.2
- Another book that should not be missing from your DNS bookshelf is: *Pro DNS and BIND*, by Ron Aitchison (Apress).
- The *BIND9 Administrator Reference Manual*, also known as ARM is part of the BIND distribution (see `http://www.isc.org/index.pl?/sw/bind/arm95/`).
- An advisory published by ISC on *Running An Authoritative-Only BIND Nameserver* explains why you shouldn't mix caching and authoritative functions (see `http://www.isc.org/pubs/tn/isc-tn-2002-2.txt`).

Chapter

8 BIND's Simplified Database Interface

When solving problems, dig at the roots instead of just hacking at the leaves.

Anthony J. D' Angelo

Introduction

The Simplified Database Interface (sdb) is one of the APIs provided by BIND in version 9.1 and above. It lets an administrator extend BIND by creating a driver that is linked into BIND. We discuss the BIND-sdb-LDAP driver and develop a simple load-balancer driver for BIND SDB.

The Simplified Database Interface for BIND 9 is an application programmer interface (API) with which a programmer can add a back-end (called a driver in BIND SDB) to the BIND name server. BIND uses that driver to provide answers to DNS queries. BIND 9.1 introduced this simplified database interface, or SDB, to make it easy to create specialized applications.

While many people have programmed SDB drivers and made them available as contributed software, Bind DLZ, described in the next chapter, is much more flexible, and SDB will probably be of interest to you only if you want to use the contributed LDAP driver, or to program your own, special-purpose, driver.

Pros	• Can provide answers to DNS requests from any data source • Programmable • Many available drivers in BIND's `contrib` directory • LDAP driver very stable • Supported natively on Microsoft Windows
Cons	○ Zones must be configured manually in `named.conf` ○ Slow startup if configured with a large number of zones
Scenarios	Users who want to add custom drivers to the BIND name server.

Table 8.1: BIND SDB at a glance

8.1 Overview of BIND SDB

SDB is one of the APIs that BIND provides, to allow its functionality to be extended. When a zone uses SDB, BIND answers queries for the zone, not by reading information from zone master files, but instead by using the driver specified in the zone's configuration. Standard drivers distributed with BIND SDB let you use a variety of databases and files from which to retrieve data. You can also program your own drivers for special purposes; for example, the demonstration timedb driver returns the date and time when you query for a TXT record in a zone configured to use timedb.

SDB doesn't remove any of BIND's features; on the contrary, it expands on what BIND has to offer. A single instance of BIND can have both normal zones and zones served by SDB drivers. An SDB zone has an SDB-specific `database` statement in a `zone` clause. If this is present when BIND receives a query for such a zone, BIND calls the SDB driver to resolve the query instead of using master files as for normal zones. Consider this example `named.conf`, which has two `zone` clauses:

```
zone "qupps.biz" {
   type master;
   file "qupps.biz.zone";
};
zone "example.net" {
   type master;
   database "my-back-end";
};
```

There are two master zones:

- qupps.biz is a "normal" master zone, loaded from a zone file `qupps.biz.zone`.
- example.net is also a master zone, but because of the `database` statement, queries on it will be satisfied by calling the `my-back-end` SDB driver, instead of from a zone master file. You can have two different zones each served by a different driver if you want. For example, a zone example.net served by the `my-back-end` driver, and a zone example.org served by the `another-back-end` driver.

SDB is extremely versatile as it allows you to add to BIND, almost any kind of functionality for retrieving zone data, with an easy API. A limitation is that zones still have to be added manually by configuring `zone` clauses in `named.conf`, because there are no "does this zone exist" and "add this zone" functions within BIND SDB.

8.1.1 Existing BIND SDB drivers

Current BIND source distributions include several SDB drivers in the `contrib` directory of the source distribution:

bdb Stores zones in Berkeley DB databases.

dir A database driver that returns basic information about files and directories in the *nix file system, as DNS data.

TCL A driver with a TCL back-end. TCL is a scripting language, created by John Ousterhout. The driver allows you to write your own back-end in TCL.

Time A simple driver that allows the server to return the current time in a DNS resource record.

PostgreSQL A database driver that interfaces to a PostgreSQL database, enabling BIND to retrieve answers to DNS queries from a database. Its design requires that each zone be contained in a separate database table.

MySQL The MySQL BIND SDB driver was derived from the PostgreSQL driver, and it is the MySQL equivalent of that. The MySQL driver for BIND SDB is not in the BIND source distribution; you can download it from `http://mysql-bind.sourceforge.net/`.

LDAP The LDAP driver allows BIND to answer queries from a suitably configured LDAP directory server. It is quite popular, and we discuss it below.

We don't discuss the contributed drivers, except for the LDAP driver in Section 8.2, because a lot of the functionality provided by the database drivers is available in Bind DLZ, and we recommend you use that instead, as it is easier to use and more versatile. We discuss Bind DLZ in Chapter 9.

One of the most popular SDB drivers is the LDAP driver, which we discuss next. After that, we show you how you develop your own SDB driver, in Section 8.4.

8.2 Overview of BIND SDB LDAP driver

Stig Venaas[1] created the LDAP SDB driver for BIND9 to store DNS zone data in an LDAP directory server, using a specialized schema called `dNSZone`. Why another schema? Because the `dNSDomain` object class defined in the Cosine schema (one of the standard LDAP schemas) didn't fulfill his needs, as it defines only very few resource record types. The `dNSZone` object adds attribute types for Time to Live (TTL), class, zone name and relative domain name, which make it easy to maintain and to organize the entries in an LDAP directory server.

BIND with BIND-sdb-LDAP can manage any number of zones stored in LDAP simultaneously with any number of different master or slave zones stored in zone master files.

8.2.1 Limitations of the BIND-sdb-LDAP driver

There are some limitations when using BIND-sdb-LDAP. These are caused not by the implementation of this driver, but rather by SDB's API:

- Starting named when configured with a large number of SDB zones is slow.
- New zones cannot be created "on the fly". Even if you create LDAP entries for a new zone, BIND recognizes the new zone only after you define the zone in a `zone` clause in `named.conf`, and reload named.

  If this is unacceptable to you, but you still want to use BIND, instead of SDB use BIND's DLZ add-on, which *does* let you add zones dynamically, i.e. on the fly. We cover Bind DLZ in Chapter 9.
- BIND-sdb-LDAP can serve only as a master name server and not as a slave. BIND's SDB API defines functions only for reading resource data from the driver, not for writing to it. Therefore, a BIND server can't act as a slave for a zone stored in SDB, because BIND can't do anything with a zone retrieved in a zone transfer. To avoid this problem, configure slave zones normally (i.e. configure them from files), and not as SDB zones.
- The original design of the BIND-sdb-LDAP driver did not implement support for wildcard domain names. For this book, we created a small patch to remedy that. The patch is easy to implement (see Notes) and adds support for wildcard domain names, and for some debugging output.

8.3 Installing BIND SDB and configuring your LDAP server

To deploy BIND SDB with the LDAP driver:

A. Download BIND, apply the BIND SDB LDAP patch, optionally applying the wildcard patch if you require support for DNS wild cards (see Notes), and compile BIND SDB.

[1] Turbo Fredriksson has taken over the project maintenance at `http://bind9-ldap.bayour.com/`

B. Configure your LDAP directory server. Add the schema definitions needed by the LDAP driver.

C. Optionally create indexes for the two LDAP attribute types the driver uses to search entries. We strongly recommend you do this to enhance performance of the driver.

D. Define the SDB zone(s) in `named.conf`.

E. Create entries in your LDAP directory for zones.

F. Create entries in your directory for resource records.

8.3.1 A – Compile BIND SDB with the LDAP driver

To download, compile and install BIND-sdb-LDAP, proceed as follows:

1. Download and unpack BIND into a temporary directory (e.g. `/tmp`):

```
$ wget http://ftp.isc.org/isc/bind9/9.4.2/bind-9.4.2.tar.gz
$ tar xvzf bind-9.4.2.tar.gz
```

2. Download and extract the latest release of the LDAP driver into the same temporary directory:

```
$ wget http://www.venaas.no/ldap/bind-sdb/bind-sdb-ldap-1.1.0.tar.gz
$ tar xvzf bind-sdb-ldap-1.1.0.tar.gz
```

3. Move or copy the source of the LDAP driver into named's source directory:

```
$ mv bind-sdb-ldap-1.1.0/ldapdb.? bind-9.4.2/bin/named/
```

4. Change into BIND's source directory:

```
$ cd bind-9.4.2
```

5. Edit named's `Makefile.in`, to add the dependencies to the LDAP driver:

```
$ edit bin/named/Makefile.in
```

   Locate lines that begin with the string `DBDRIVER_` near the top of the file and modify those as shown here:

```
#
# Add database drivers here.
#
DBDRIVER_OBJS = ldapdb.o
DBDRIVER_SRCS = ldapdb.c
DBDRIVER_INCLUDES = ldapdb.h
DBDRIVER_LIBS = -lldap -llber
```

6. Edit `main.c` to add the entry and exit points of the LDAP driver:

```
$ edit bin/named/main.c
```

   Search the file for the string "`xxdb`" and add the necessary lines:

```
/* #include "xxdb.h" */
#include "ldapdb.h"
...

/*
 * Add calls to register sdb drivers here.
 */
/* xxdb_init(); */
ldapdb_init();
...


/*
 * Add calls to unregister sdb drivers here.
 */
/* xxdb_clear(); */
ldapdb_clear();
...
```

7. Configure named with whichever options you need:

```
$ ./configure --prefix=/usr/local --enable-threads=no ...
$ make
$ make install
```

8.3.2 B – Configure your LDAP directory server

The LDAP schema used by BIND-sdb-LDAP relies on the `dNSZone` object class, which in turn builds on classes and attribute types defined in the Cosine schema. These dependencies mean that the LDAP directory server must load both the Cosine and `dNSZone` schemas. In OpenLDAP parlance, that would require at least the following `include` directives in `slapd.conf`:

```
include path/to/cosine.schema
include path/to/dnszone.schema
```

8.3.3 C – Indexes required by BIND-sdb-LDAP

Zones configured with the BIND-sdb-LDAP driver are not cached; each and every query for resource records in the zones is sent directly to the LDAP directory server back-end for answering. The advantages are of course, that the data is never out of date; as soon as an entry has been modified on the LDAP directory it is immediately visible to the BIND name servers that have the zone configured. The downside is that the directory server must be able to handle the load.

If we log the LDAP queries that are used by BIND-sdb-LDAP on the directory servers (Section 8.3.8), we see that a number of attribute types are requested of course, and the search filters indicate which attribute types should be indexed to get maximum performance for this back-end with an LDAP directory server. The indexes you should add to your directory server are for the `zoneName` and the `relativeDomainName` attribute types. In OpenLDAP, you would add these lines to your `slapd.conf`:

```
database      bdb
suffix        "o=qupps.biz"
directory     ...
index         objectclass     eq
index         zonename,relativedomainname       eq
```

8.3.4 D – Define the zone in `named.conf`

All zones, both SDB and non-SDB, are configured with a `zone` clause in `named.conf`. The SDB zones do not retrieve their zone data from files but rather from what SDB calls a "database". The `database` statement describes on one line (without line breaks or continuation lines) the name of the driver and the arguments that will be passed to it. In the case of the LDAP driver, the driver name is `ldap`, and the driver has two arguments:

1. The first argument is an LDAP URL (Section A.3.11) that specifies the hostname (or IP address) and the search base of your LDAP directory server. Because this hostname has to be resolved when *your DNS server* is starting up, we strongly recommend you use either an IP address or a hostname you define in the system's `/etc/hosts` file.

2. The second argument is the default Time To Live (TTL) that the LDAP SDB driver should return in DNS replies for LDAP entries which do not explicitly have a `dNSTTL` attribute type (see Section 8.3.6 below).

The zone clause we use for our example is:

```
zone "qupps.biz" {
   type master;
   database "ldap ldap://127.0.0.1/zoneName=qupps.biz,ou=forward,ou=zones,↩
            ou=sdb,ou=dns,o=qupps.biz 129600";
};
```

Note once again: the *whole* `database` statement must be written on one line.

Once you have reloaded named, you can start querying it for your new zone, but you won't get any replies until you add the zone to your LDAP directory server.

8.3.5 E – Creating DNS zones in your LDAP directory server

Before you can define your zones in your LDAP directory, you must set up your LDAP directory server to contain the `dNSZone` schema, which you can download from the book's Web site (☞ D081)).

BIND-sdb-LDAP searches your LDAP directory server for every query it gets on a master zone you configure with it in `named.conf`. The entries it searches for belong to the object class `dNSZone`. A `dNSZone` object can store a zone, or a single DNS record for a host.

The `dNSZone` class supports only a limited set of DNS resource record types, because its author didn't consider the implementation of all types necessary. Adding new types to the schema is trivial, and the maintainers of the project will probably help you do it if need be. The `dNSZone` object class (Table 8.2) duplicates a few types defined in the Cosine schema. Two attribute types are mandatory: `relativeDomainName` and `zoneName`.

Type	D[a]	C[b]	Usage
relativeDomainName	•		The starting labels of a domain name
zoneName	•		The name of a zone
dNSView	•		The view this record should show in
a6Record	•		A6 Record Type, RFC 2874
aAAARecord	•		IPv6 address, RFC 1886
aFSDBRecord	•		for AFS Data Base location, RFC 1183
aRecord		•	Address record
certRecord	•		certificate, RFC 2538
cNAMERecord		•	Canonical name
dNameRecord	•		Non-Terminal DNS Name Redirection, RFC 2672
dNSClass	•		The class of a resource record (IN)
dNSTTL	•		An integer denoting time to live
dSRecord	•		Delegation Signer, RFC 3658
hInfoRecord	•		host information, RFC 1035
KeyRecord	•		Key, RFC 2535
kXRecord	•		Key Exchange Delegation, RFC 2230
LocRecord	•		Location, RFC 1876
MDRecord		•	RFC 1274
mInfoRecord	•		mailbox or mail list information, RFC 1035
nAPTRRecord	•		Naming Authority Pointer, RFC 2915
nSECRecord	•		NSEC record, RFC 3755
NSRecord		•	Name server
nXTRecord	•		non-existant, RFC 2535
PTRRecord	•		PTR record, RFC 1035
rRSIGRecord	•		RRSIG record, RFC 3755
SigRecord	•		Signature, RFC 2535
sOARecord		•	Start of Authority
sRVRecord	•		service location, RFC 2782
sSHFPRecord	•		SSH Key Fingerprint, draft-ietf-secsh-dns-05.txt
tXTRecord	•		text string, RFC 1035

[a] dNSZone schema
[b] Cosine schema

Table 8.2: Resource records in the `dNSZone` & Cosine schemas

How you organize LDAP entries

The `dNSZone` schema is flexible in regard to the design of the LDAP tree with the BIND SDB LDAP driver, because it imposes neither a specific hierarchy nor specific naming of the relative distinguished names (RDNs) (Figure 8.1).

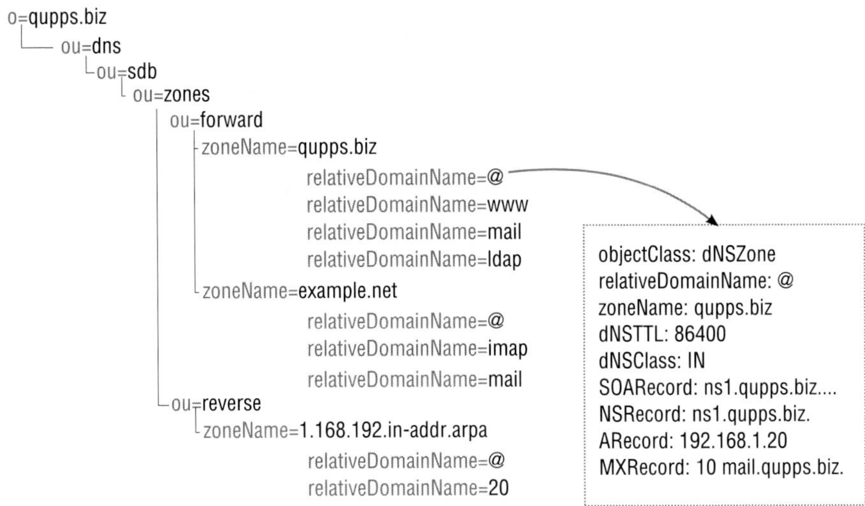

Figure 8.1: An LDAP tree for BIND SDB

How you store your zone data in the LDAP directory tree is unimportant to the workings of the BIND SDB LDAP driver. We recommend you put each zone in its own container as shown in Figure 8.1, but you don't have to. Here are some ways you can do it:

- Create an organizational unit (`ou`) named after the zone, and store all LDAP entries which belong to a zone in this:

  ```
  ou=qupps.biz,ou=DNS,...
  ```

- Use the `zoneName` as an RDN for the container and put all LDAP entries for a zone into that.

  ```
  zoneName=qupps.biz,ou=DNS,...
  ```

In the examples that follow, we choose to use `zoneName` as the container for zone data.

```
dn: zoneName=qupps.biz,ou=forward,ou=zones,ou=sdb,ou=dns,o=qupps.biz
objectClass: top
objectClass: dNSZone
relativeDomainName: qupps.biz
zoneName: qupps.biz
```

8.3.6 F – Adding a zone

To add a new zone to BIND-sdb-LDAP:

1. Create the LDAP entries to represent the zone. As a minimum you require one entry of object class `dNSZone` with the attribute types `sOARecord` containing the fields of a Start of Authority (SOA) record.

2. Add the zone to your `named.conf` and reload named so it sees the newly added zone definition. From this point on, you add LDAP entries for the zone to the directory server without reloading named.

A sample LDIF file that you might use to create zone qupps.biz in your directory server, using ldapadd or any program with which you load LDIF into your directory server, is:

```
$ cat zone.ldif
dn: relativeDomainName=@,zoneName=qupps.biz,ou=forward,ou=zones,
 ou=sdb,ou=dns,o=qupps.biz
objectClass: top
objectClass: dNSZone
relativeDomainName: @
zoneName: qupps.biz
dNSTTL: 86400
sOARecord: ns1.qupps.biz. hostmaster.qupps.biz. 1 10800 900 604800 3600
nSRecord: ns1.qupps.biz.
tXTRecord: "my first zone"

$ ldapadd ... < zone.ldif
```

You can directly query BIND SDB for the zone data. The new zone has the following characteristics which we illustrate with excerpts from the dig output of queries for the newly created zone:

SOA — The zone's Start of Authority (SOA) record, which you define with the attribute type `sOARecord`. It contains the seven fields of an SOA as defined in master zone file format. Remember to change the serial number of the SOA whenever you change, add or delete an entry from your LDAP directory for the zone, if you provide zone transfers for it.

```
;; ANSWER SECTION:
qupps.biz.  86400  IN SOA ns1.qupps.biz.  ↩
         hostmaster.qupps.biz. 1 10800 900 604800 3600
```

NS — The zone has a Name Server (NS) record, but no glue for it (i.e. the Address (A) for the Name Server is missing. You add that separately as a host entry with an IP address (see Section 8.3.7 below).

```
;; ANSWER SECTION:
qupps.biz.        86400     IN NS ns1.qupps.biz.
```

TXT — The Text (TXT) record is defined by the `tXTRecord` attribute type. This type is multivalued so you add as many of these attributes as you like.

```
;; ANSWER SECTION:
qupps.biz.        86400     IN TXT      "my first zone"
```

TTL The Time to Live (TTL) for these records is 86400 seconds as defined by the attribute type dNSTTL. If that is missing, the default TTL of the database statement is used (Section 8.3.4).

8.3.7 G – Adding a host

Adding a host to our zone is trivial: add an entry to your LDAP directory in the same container as you have the apex of the zone (i.e. the LDAP entry with a relativeDomainName of @): (Remember that whitespace at the beginning of a line in LDIF indicates a continuation line.)

```
$ cat host.ldif
dn: relativeDomainName=www,zoneName=qupps.biz,ou=forward,ou=zones,
 ou=sdb,ou=dns,o=qupps.biz
objectClass: top
objectClass: dNSZone
relativeDomainName: www
zoneName: qupps.biz
aRecord: 192.168.1.12
aRecord: 192.168.1.10
aRecord: 192.168.1.11
```

When you ldapadd host.ldif, the entry is immediately visible from the DNS server, without having to reload named, so you can:

```
$ dig @127.0.0.1 www.qupps.biz
;; ANSWER SECTION:
www.qupps.biz.     129600  IN    A 192.168.1.10
www.qupps.biz.     129600  IN    A 192.168.1.11
www.qupps.biz.     129600  IN    A 192.168.1.12

;; AUTHORITY SECTION:
qupps.biz.          86400  IN    NS ns1.qupps.biz.
```

Note:

- The TTL of the Address (A) records is the default as specified in named.conf for the zone, whereas the TTL for the NS is determined from the SOA.
- The addresses in the A records are returned in pseudo-random order.

8.3.8 Watching LDAP queries

When getting started with BIND-sdb-LDAP we recommend you enable debugging on your LDAP directory server, to "see" the LDAP searches being performed by BIND SDB.

- A DNS query for vino.qupps.biz causes our BIND SDB to search for the fully qualified name. BIND-sdb-LDAP knows the name of the zone (from the zone clause in named.conf) and uses the remainder as the relativeDomainName, so BIND-sdb-LDAP searches for:

  ```
  (&(zoneName=qupps.biz)(relativeDomainName=vino))
  (&(zoneName=qupps.biz)(relativeDomainName=@))
  ```

A query for tinto.**es**.qupps.biz would have resulted in these LDAP filters being applied during the search:

```
(&(zoneName=qupps.biz)(relativeDomainName=es))
(&(zoneName=qupps.biz)(relativeDomainName=tinto.es))
```

- If tinto.es.qupps.biz is not found, the Start of Authority (SOA) record is searched for at the apex of the zone:

```
(&(zoneName=qupps.biz)(relativeDomainName=@))
```

- With our wildcard patch applied (see Notes), a DNS query for leche.qupps.biz would have BIND SDB perform these LDAP searches:

```
(&(zoneName=qupps.biz)(relativeDomainName=leche))
(&(zoneName=qupps.biz)(relativeDomainName=~))
(&(zoneName=qupps.biz)(relativeDomainName=@))
```

Note the additional search for a `relativeDomainName` of ~ (tilde). The tilde represents a wildcard entry.

Zones in the in-addr.arpa domain are stored in a similar fashion, and they have the same `dNSZone` objectclass, with an attribute type `PTRRecord` pointing back to the appropriate domain name.

8.3.9 Miscellaneous features

LDAP over IPC

If the LDAP directory server is on the same host as BIND SDB, and it supports LDAP over *nix sockets, you can use the URL prefix `ldapi://` (note the **i** in `ldap`**`i`**) for communication between BIND SDB and your LDAP directory server, which may improve performance. For example:

```
zone "qupps.biz" {
    type master;
    database "ldap ldapi://%2fvar%2frun%2fslapd.sock /ou=dns,dc=qupps,dc=biz 600";
};
```

Note that the hex value %2F is a forward slash (/), so the bold text specifies a *nix path name `/var/run/slapd.sock`.

Views

We discussed in Chapter 7 that you can create views to allow a single named instance to serve differing content depending on the network location (IP address) of the querying client. The LDAP driver for BIND SDB implements this with an LDAP attribute type called `dNSView`, a single-valued type, which you can add to your directory entries to specify which entries should be used in which view.

Suppose you have a view called "`inside`" and another named "`outside`", and an ACL, `trusted`, that matches on IP addresses of your own trusted hosts. You would use the `dNSView` type as follows:

```
view "inside" IN {
  match-clients { "trusted"; };
   zone "qupps.biz" {
     type master;
     database "ldap ↩
       ldapi:///o=qupps.biz??sub?(&(objectClass=dNSZone)(dNSView=inside) ) 600";
   };
};

view "outside" IN {
  match-clients { any; };
   zone "qupps.biz" {
     type master;
     database "ldap ↩
       ldapi:///o=qupps.biz??sub?(&(objectClass=dNSZone)(dNSView=outside) ) 600";
   };
};
```

Zone transfers

BIND-sdb-LDAP supports outgoing zone transfers, just as for normal zones. You enable zone transfers in `named.conf` with `allow-transfer` statements, either globally, or on a zone-by-zone basis as in this example:

```
zone "qupps.biz" {
  type master;
  database "ldap ldap:// ... ";
  allow-transfer { 192.0.2.17; };
};
```

Controlling zone transfers

If you manage a large number of zones with BIND-sdb-LDAP, you might be interested in a feature we created specially for this book: an auxiliary LDAP object class that you can add to `dNSZone` entries, to specify BIND access control list (ACL) names on a zone-by-zone basis. You enable this schema with a few simple steps:

1. Add the schema for the `dNSZoneAXFR` object class to your server. For example, in OpenLDAP, you add this line to `slapd.conf`:

   ```
   include /path/to/dNSZoneAXFR.schema
   ```

2. Add the `dNSZoneAXFR` object class to entries. For example:

   ```
   $ cat qupps.modif
   dn: relativeDomainName=@,zoneName=qupps.biz,ou=forward,
    ou=zones,ou=sdb,ou=dns,o=qupps.biz
   changetype: modify
   add: objectClass
   objectClass: dNSZoneAXFR

   $ ldapmodify ... < qupps.modif
   ```

3. Populate the multi-valued attribute type `dNSZoneAXFRacl` with the name of one or more ACLs you have already declared in `named.conf`.

```
$ cat qupps.acl
dn: relativeDomainName=@,zoneName=qupps.biz,ou=forward,
 ou=zones,ou=sdb,ou=dns,o=qupps.biz
changetype: modify
add: dNSZoneAXFRacl
dNSZoneAXFRacl: hu-nic
dNSZoneAXFRacl: Acme-USA
dNSZoneAXFRacl: 192.168.1.14

$ ldapmodify ... < qupps.acl
```

A small program (see next section) reads your LDAP directory and creates a file with `zone` clauses and their ACLs, which you can include in your `named.conf`.

The following LDIF shows a sample entry for a zone with the new object class and attribute type:

```
dn: relativeDomainName=@,zoneName=qupps.biz,ou=forward,
 ou=zones,ou=sdb,ou=dns,o=qupps.biz
objectClass: top
objectClass: dNSZone
objectClass: dNSZoneAXFR
relativeDomainName: @
zoneName: qupps.biz
dNSTTL: 86400
dNSClass: IN
sOARecord: ns1.qupps.biz. hostmaster.qupps.biz. 1 10800 900 604800 3600
nSRecord: ns1.qupps.biz.
tXTRecord: "my first zone"
mXRecord: 10 mail.qupps.biz.
LocRecord: 52 2 2.76 N 8 28 37.919 E 118m
dNSZoneAXFRacl : hu-nic
dNSZoneAXFRacl : Acme-USA
dNSZoneAXFRacl : 192.168.1.14
```

You can download the schema for the `dNSZoneAXFR` object class from (☞ D082).

Create `zone` clauses for `named.conf` from LDAP

If you use the `dNSZoneAXFR` class, you will be interested in a utility we developed for this book, which generates `zone` clauses for inclusion in your `named.conf`. The program scans your LDAP directory for BIND SDB zones. It prints each zone to standard output in `named.conf` format; if the LDAP entry for a zone has an `dNSZoneAXFRacl` value, the program includes the appropriate `allow-transfer` statement in its output for that zone:

```
$ sdbldap2bind.pl
zone "qupps.biz" {
   type master;
   database "ldap ldap:// ... ";
   allow-transfer {
      "hu-nic";
      192.168.1.14;
```

```
        "Acme-USA";
    };
};
```

Your `named.conf` should contain the ACLs you specified on your zones:

```
acl "Acme-USA" {
    127.0.0.1;
    192.168.1.20/32;
};
acl "hu-nic" { ... };
acl "de-nic" { ... };

options {
    directory "/var/named";
    allow-transfer { none; };
    ...
};
...
include "/etc/ldapzones.inc";
...
```

Running the program is trivial, so you can automate the creation of the file you `include` in your `named.conf`, but do be careful that it isn't clobbered if an error occurs:

```
# sdbldap2bind.pl > zones.$$ && mv zones.$$ /etc/ldapzones.inc
# rndc reload
```

We show you the small program in Section C.1, and you can download it from the book's Web site (☞ D083).

Convert master zone files to LDIF

Roman A. Egorov created zone2ldif, a program that converts a zone master file into LDIF for import into an LDAP directory server. Before running the program, make sure that the `$ORIGIN` line before the SOA in master zone files contains the zone name. For example, the following produces LDIF for mens.de from the zone master file `mens.de.zone`:

```
$ zone2ldif.pl -b ou=dns,o=qupps.biz \
                      -z mens.de.zone \
                      -l mens.ldif

$ more mens.ldif
dn: zoneName=mens.de,o=qupps.biz
objectClass: top
objectClass: dNSZone
relativeDomainName: mens.de
zoneName: mens.de

dn: relativeDomainName=mens.de,zoneName=mens.de,o=qupps.biz
objectClass: top
objectClass: dNSZone
relativeDomainName: mens.de
zoneName: mens.de
dNSTTL: 86400
```

```
dNSClass: IN
SOARecord: mens.de. jp.mens.de. 200712127 10800 900
604800 86400
NSRecord: home.mens.de.
...
```

zone2ldif is available from `http://www.venaas.no/ldap/bind-sdb/zone2ldif.pl`.

Performance

BIND SDB with the LDAP driver is widely used, and many system administrators find it easy to set up. If you have trouble with performance, consider configuring BIND-sdb-LDAP as a hidden master to a non-SDB BIND slave.

That concludes our explanation of how to use BIND SDB with the contributed LDAP driver. In the next sections we explore how you can write your own driver.

8.4 Anatomy of a BIND SDB driver

This section describes how you can write your own driver for BIND SDB.

A BIND SDB driver is a module (typically written in the C programming language). There is currently no provision for BIND to load these driver modules at run time, so you must link them into the server at compile time.

A driver module interfaces with the standard SDB code in two ways, as shown in Figure 8.2:

1. SDB calls specially-named functions or *callbacks* to request data from the driver. For example, it calls `lookup()` to query for a resource record. The driver programmer has to write the callback functions in the driver, so that they are available for SDB to call.

2. The driver has retrieved the necessary information. It then calls a few standard-named functions to pass the information back to SDB. For example, the driver calls `dns_sdb_putrr()` to return ("put") a resource record ("rr"). These functions are provided by SDB; the driver programmer doesn't have to write them, but just uses them.

When domain names or resource records are passed between SDB and the driver, they are represented as ASCII text, which greatly eases the amount of coding you have to do. (Programmers wishing to access the SDB API should definitely consult `doc/misc/sdb` of the BIND source distribution, where the nitty gritty is explained.)

One important detail to note is that the current SDB interface does not implement zone lookup. So, when BIND needs to check if a zone exists when it starts to process an incoming query, it can't use SDB; instead, it has to look in `named.conf` to see if the zone exists. Consequently, to add a new SDB zone, you have to enter it in `named.conf` and restart or reload named as usual. An alternative package, Bind DLZ ("Dynamically Loadable Zones"), doesn't have this limitation; it lets you implement zones dynamically (i.e. without having to reload named). We discuss Bind DLZ in Chapter 9.

8.4.1 Writing a Driver

When a driver is registered with the SDB subsystem, it publicizes its name, list of callback functions and flags. There are five callback functions which can be provided (Figure 8.2):

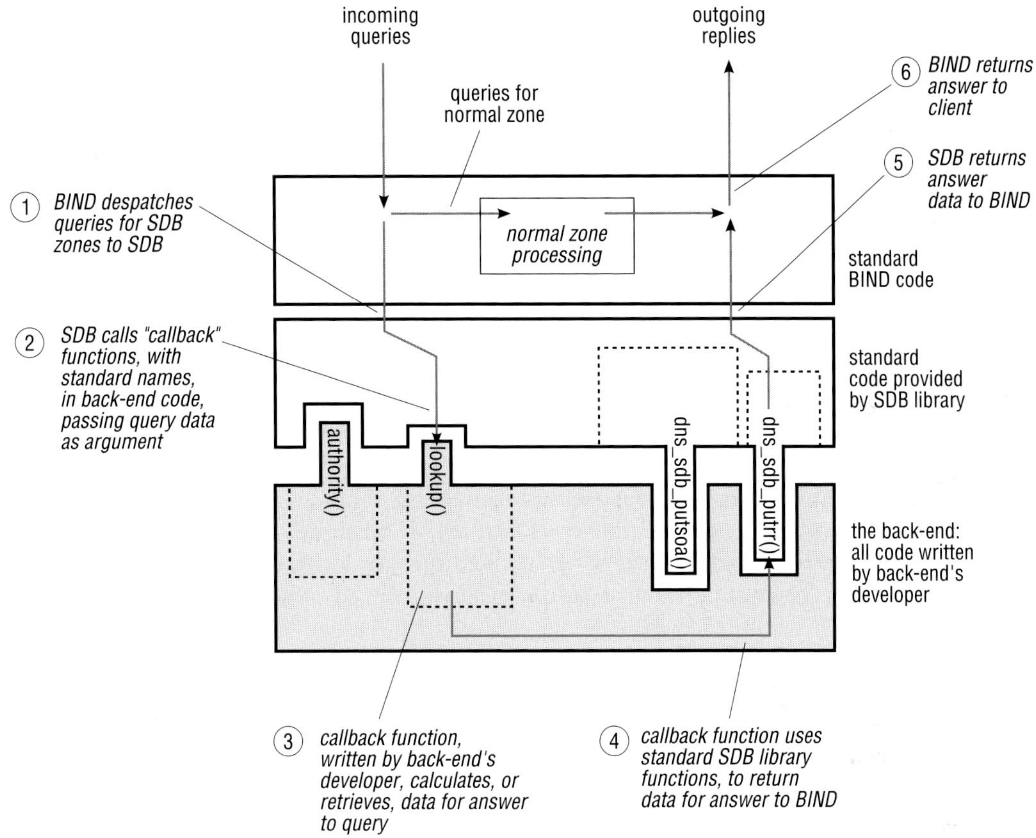

Figure 8.2: The named program, showing the SDB library and driver code

create() This is a convenience function that allows the programmer to initialize a zone by connecting to an external database, allocating resources, etc. If the `create()` function is provided, a corresponding `destroy()` can free whatever resources where reserved by `create()`.

lookup() The `lookup()` function is mandatory. It is invoked by BIND for each query it receives. The function may return whatever resource records are required by the query and, if no `authority()` function is provided, it must return Start of Authority (SOA) and Name Server (NS) records, when queried for the zone apex.

authority() The optional `authority()` function must be provided to return SOA and NS records, if the `lookup()` function does not or cannot provide answers to NS or SOA requests for a zone. If `authority()` is defined, `lookup()` must not supply NS or SOA records.

allnodes () This routine need be implemented only if zone transfers (AXFR) for this database are to be supported. `allnodes()` provides all records that are to be included in the zone transfer.

destroy () This is an optional function, called during destruction of the database (i.e. when named is terminating). You use this routine to free any resources you allocated allocated in the `create()` function.

These functions are how SDB calls your driver; writing the code for these functions (plus any ancillary functions you need) is how you implement the driver. The only callback function that *must* be implemented is `lookup()`; the others are optional and depend on the feature set you require in your driver. For example, if you don't want your driver to provide zone transfers, you don't implement the `allnodes()` function.

That completes our overview of the features of an SDB driver, and we show you an example, now.

8.5 Load balancing with DNS, implemented using SDB

Standard DNS is often used as load sharing mechanism, when a particular service is provided by more than one server. Suppose we run IMAP on three servers. We assign three Address (A) records to imap.qupps.biz. When a client queries for that name, our DNS server returns the answer, containing the three addresses in a pseudo-random order:

```
;; ANSWER SECTION:
imap.qupps.biz.          120      IN       A 192.168.1.61
imap.qupps.biz.          120      IN       A 192.168.1.63
imap.qupps.biz.          120      IN       A 192.168.1.62
```

Most IMAP clients use the first returned address, so returning the address records in random order in the answer effectively shares the load over the three servers that have the name imap.qupps.biz.

The above is load sharing but not load *balancing*: even if host 192.168.1.63 is very heavily loaded for some reason, or has crashed, it will still be returned first in the list on average 33% of the time. A better approach would be for the DNS to monitor, somehow, the availability and load of each of the IMAP servers. Then it could omit dead machines from the list of addresses returned for imap.qupps.biz, and could either return the addresses so that the least-loaded server is listed as the first, or indeed the only, item in the answer. BIND SDB lets you build this sort of functionality into your DNS, and that's what we cover in the next section.

8.5.1 Implementing a simple load-balancer driver

To illustrate how SDB works, we implement a simple load balancer driver for BIND.

- On our SDB DNS server we have a process that continually monitors the load on our three Web servers; it writes the IP address of the least loaded Web server into a text file (Figure 8.3). (How the process monitors the Web servers is irrelevant, and we don't cover it. All we need to know is that our file contains the address of the least loaded Web server.)

- When a client queries the BIND SDB server for address www.*yourdomain.name*, our driver opens the file, reads a line containing the IP address, and closes the file. It then returns the IP address as answer to the query. (You can download the full source code of our sample driver from (☞ D084).)

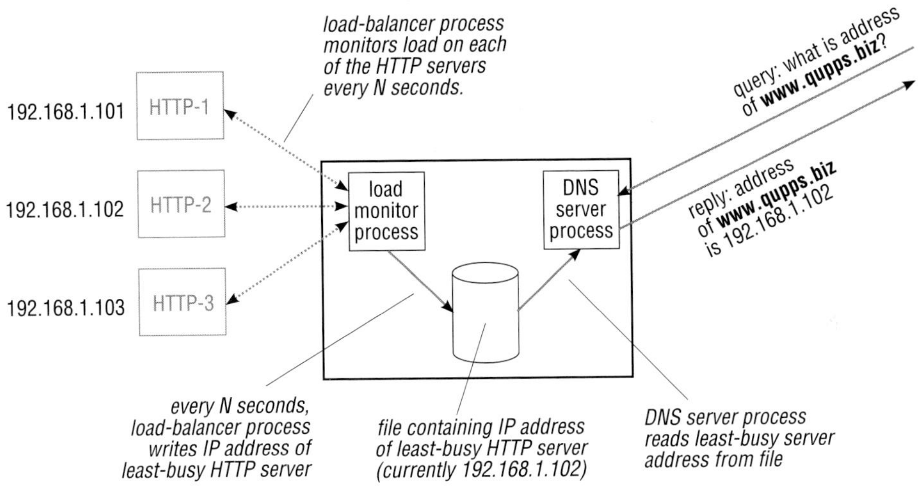

Figure 8.3: BIND SDB driver to load-balance DNS

Initializing the driver

The programmer-supplied `init()` function calls `dns_sdb_register()` which registers a simple database driver with BIND for the database type *drivername*. The name of the driver is the first argument to the `dns_sdb_register()` function and corresponds to the name specified in the `database` statement in `named.conf` (see Section 8.5.2).

Flags let you specify details of the driver's operation. For example, you can choose between relative or absolute domain names in the `lookup()`, `authority()`, and `putrr()` functions, and whether `lookup()` is thread-safe or must be serialized. The `create()` and `destroy()` functions can be `NULL` if no initialization or destruction code is required.

Performing lookups

The BIND name server performs lookups in the database by invoking `lookup()` with four parameters:

1. The name of the queried zone (e.g. qupps.biz), as a string.

2. The name of the queried domain (e.g. www), as a string.

3. A programmer-supplied, optional, pointer *dbdata*. This points to data which you set up earlier in your `create()` function. This is a way to pass arbitrary data to your callback functions.

4. An opaque data item which is passed in to `lookup()` when called by SDB, and which `lookup()` must pass on unchanged when it in turn calls `dns_sdb_putrr()`. This argument is used to return resource records to BIND.

The following listing shows a sample `lookup()` routine. The complete source code for the whole load balancing driver is in Section C.2.

```
static isc_result_t
jpload_lookup(const char *zone, const char *name, void *dbdata,
            dns_sdblookup_t *opq)
{
    struct jpinfo *jpi = dbdata;

    if (strcmp(name, "@") == 0) {

         /* If authority() is not defined, issue RR for SOA
          * and for NS here. (Not shown to save space.) */

    } else if (strcmp(name, "www") == 0) {
        char buf[BUFSIZ];
        FILE *fp;

        res = ISC_R_FAILURE;
        if ((fp = fopen(jpi->path, "r")) != NULL) {
                if (fgets(buf, sizeof(buf) - 1, fp) != NULL) {
                        buf[strlen(buf) - 1] = '\0';     /* strip newline */

                        res = dns_sdb_putrr(opq, "a", 60, buf);
                        if (res != ISC_R_SUCCESS)
                                res = ISC_R_FAILURE;
                }
                (void)fclose(fp);
        }
        return (res);
    }
    return (ISC_R_SUCCESS);
}
```

Lookups at the zone apex (when *name* contains the string `"@"`) will cause the server to also invoke the `authority()` function if it is defined. If it isn't, the `lookup()` function is responsible for returning SOA and NS resource records.

The functions `dns_sdb_putrr()` and `dns_sdb_putnamedrr()` are part of the SDB API; they send resource records from your function "back" to BIND, converting the ASCII values into BIND's internal representation.

Note how the lookup function has no method with which to determine what kind of query was issued (A, ANY, TXT, CNAME, etc.). The BIND SDB interface doesn't care; for example, if the programmer pushes TXT and A answers down the pipe when an Address (A) query was issued, BIND will simply discard the TXT answers and keep the A answers.

Returning all records in a zone transfer

The `allnodes()` function, if defined, should return the result for an AXFR zone transfer. (If it is not defined, a zone transfer is disabled.)

There will usually be a correlation between the records returned by `allnodes()` and the set of possible records returned by `lookup()`, but there need not be: the `allnodes()` function could return a completely different set of DNS records.

8.5.2 Adding an SDB zone to named.conf

To configure a BIND zone to use an SDB driver, include a `database` statement in its `zone` clause in `named.conf`, with the driver's name enclosed in double quotes as argument:

```
zone "load.local" {
   type master;
   database "jpload";
};
```

You can specify extra information which is to be passed to your driver's `create()` function. List the data you want passed, as whitespace separated arguments in the `database` statement. For example:

```
zone "load.qupps.biz" {
    type master;
    database "jpload /var/load/balance.ip dns1";
};
```

When `create()` is called, it retrieves the items you specified, via its *argc* and *argv* arguments:

```
jpload_create(const char *zone, int argc, char **argv,
              void *driverdata, void **dbdata)
```

In the example above, `create()` is passed:

argc Containing the integer value 2.

argv Contains two string (`char*`) pointers:

1. `argv[0]` contains the pathname to the file `/var/load/balance.ip`.
2. `argv[1]` contains the host name (`dns1`).

8.5.3 Building the driver and linking named

You provide the code for your SDB driver in one or more files that contain the source code, which must be compiled and linked to the binary named executable.

Our example consists of two files:

1. `jpload.h` declares the functions and includes header files required for the compilation of `jpload.c`.
2. `jpload.c` contains the source code of the driver.

There are a number of steps required to compile named with the SDB driver, and we recommend you proceed in this order:

1. Extract the source code of the BIND distribution and change into the newly extracted directory.

   ```
   $ tar xvzf bind-9.5.0a6.tar.gz
   $ cd bind-9.5.0a6/
   ```

2. Copy (or create) your source code in the following paths. Assuming your source files have the names used above, you provide the files in the following locations:

   ```
   $ edit bin/named/jpload.c
   $ edit bin/named/jpload.h
   ```

3. Edit named's `Makefile.in`, to add the dependencies of your source code.

   ```
   $ edit bin/named/Makefile.in
   ```

   Locate the lines that begin with the string `DBDRIVER_` near the top of the file and modify them to use your driver's source and object files names:

   ```
   #
   # Add database drivers here.
   #
   DBDRIVER_OBJS = jpload.o
   DBDRIVER_SRCS = jpload.c
   DBDRIVER_INCLUDES = jpload.h
   DBDRIVER_LIBS = -lmylib
   ```

   The last line is not required for our driver; we've added it as an example of how you would add linking options if your driver requires additional libraries.

4. Edit `main.c` to add the entry and exit points of your driver code.

   ```
   $ edit bin/named/main.c
   ```

   Search the file for the string "`xxdb`" and add your `#include` directives (if you need any) and the names of your functions.

   ```
   /* #include "xxdb.h" */
   #include "jpload.h"
   ...

   /*
    * Add calls to register sdb drivers here.
    */
   /* xxdb_init(); */
   jpload_init();
   ...


   /*
    * Add calls to unregister sdb drivers here.
    */
   ```

```
/* xxdb_clear(); */
jpload_clear();
...
```

5. Configure named with whichever options you need, but don't install it yet.

```
$ ./configure --prefix=/usr/local ...
$ make
```

6. Create a minimal `named.conf` containing only what you need to test your driver. Note how we define a high port number which allows us to test named without requiring "root" privileges.

```
$ cat test.conf
controls {
};

options {
  directory "/tmp";
  listen-on port 9953 { 127.0.0.1; };
  listen-on-v6 { none; };
  allow-query { any; };
};

zone "load.local" {
   type master;
   database "jpload /tmp/load  dns1 ";
};
```

Launch named, in debugging mode, in the foreground, with the configuration file you created above.

```
$ bin/named/named -d 1 -g -c test.conf
starting BIND 9.5.0a6 -f -d 1 -g -c test.conf
loading configuration from '/tmp/x/bind-9.5.0a6/bin/named/test.conf'
listening on IPv4 interface lo, 127.0.0.1#9953
automatic empty zone: 127.IN-ADDR.ARPA
ignoring config file logging statement due to -g option
load_configuration: success
...
zone load.local/IN: starting load
*** jpload_create start
*** jpload_create end
zone load.local/IN: loaded
*** jpload_lookup start: zone=load.local name=@
*** jpload_lookup start: zone=load.local name=dns1
*** jpload_allnodes start: zone=load.local
*** jpload_lookup start: zone=load.local name=@
...
running
```

7. We configured our **named** to listen on a non-standard port number (9953), so we must use that port number with dig as well:

```
$ dig -p 9953 @127.0.0.1 filename.load.local txt
;; flags: qr aa rd ra; QUERY: 1, ANSWER: 1, AUTHORITY: 1, ADDITIONAL: 1

;; ANSWER SECTION:
filename.load.local.    60      IN      TXT     "/tmp/load"

;; AUTHORITY SECTION:
load.local.             86400   IN      NS      dns1.load.local.

;; ADDITIONAL SECTION:
dns1.load.local.        100     IN      A       127.0.0.1
```

8. When you have finished writing your driver code and named works as intended, you can install it and its supporting tools into their final locations by running:

   ```
   # make install
   ```

   in the main directory of the distribution.

8.5.4 What happens when named starts?

After writing the code and building the named binary, launch the program by running:

```
# named
```

When named starts up, BIND loads all the SDB zones (and any other zones you may have) that have been defined in `named.conf`. When BIND loads an SDB zone, BIND calls the corresponding driver's `create()` function, if supplied, and then invokes the `lookup()` function, passing it the name of the configured zone and `@` as domain name, searching for the zone apex. If an `authority()` function is defined, BIND invokes that as well, to determine the Start of Authority (SOA) and Name Server (NS) resource records for the zone.

If no `authority()` function is defined, BIND invokes `lookup()` at load time on the zone apex (*name* is `@`) to retrieve NS and SOA records; if none exist, BIND issues diagnostic warnings and refuses to serve the zone:

```
zone load.local/IN: starting load
zone load.local/IN: loaded
zone load.local/IN: has 0 SOA records
zone load.local/IN: has no NS records
```

After querying the zone for its apex, and still as part of the zone-loading procedure, BIND invokes the `lookup()` function for all unqualified names that `lookup()` returned. As an example, if `lookup()` returns a name `dns1` for an Name Server (NS) query, BIND will call `lookup()` to find an address record for that name. You might keep in mind, that the `allnodes()` function, if you defined it, is also invoked at the start of BIND. This might considerably increase startup times.

In our example driver, for a query of www.load.local BIND invokes the `lookup()` function for these names:

```
zone=load.local name=www
zone=load.local name=@
zone=load.local name=dns1
```

8.5.5 Querying the new BIND SDB driver

At this point named and our SDB driver are fully initialized. Now let's see how our load balancer answers some queries. When we query it for a text (TXT) record, we get:

```
$ dig filename.load.local TXT
;; ANSWER SECTION:
filename.load.local.    60      IN      TXT     "/var/load/balance.ip"
```

We now query for the Address (A) record, then manually modify the `balance.ip` file, and re-issue the same query:

```
$ dig www.load.local
;; ANSWER SECTION:
www.load.local.         60      IN      A       10.51.0.2

$ echo 10.4.5.19 > /var/load/balance.ip

$ dig www.load.local
;; ANSWER SECTION:
www.load.local.         60      IN      A       10.4.5.19
```

The SDB driver works – it has correctly picked up the changed contents of the file. We would now launch whatever tool we need to monitor our Web or IMAP servers and insert the IP address of the least loaded one into the `balance.ip` file.

8.5.6 Retrieving a zone transfer from the BIND SDB driver

A zone transfer performed on our BIND SDB database calls our `allnodes()` routine which returns all the resource records you have programmed it to return. (See Section C.2 for the code that produces the example below.) Whether or not a zone transfer (i.e. `allnodes()`) is useful for such dynamic data is up to you to decide of course, but it is possible to implement.

```
$ dig load.local axfr
; <<>> DiG 9.2.3 <<>> @127.0.0.1 -p 9953 load.local axfr
;; global options:  printcmd
load.local.          86400 IN SOA   localhost. root.localhost. 7 28800 7200 604...
imap.load.local.      3600 IN A     192.168.2.1
googl.load.local.     3600 IN CNAME www.google.com.
poem.load.local.     86400 IN TXT   "These" "words" "will" "be" "individually"...
poem.load.local.     86400 IN TXT   "its fleece was white as snow"
ns.load.local.         100 IN NS    foo.load.local.
filename.load.local. 1800 IN TXT    "/var/load/balance.ip"
load.local.          86400 IN SOA   localhost. root.localhost. 7 28800 7200 604...
;; Query time: 0 msec
;; SERVER: 127.0.0.1#9953(127.0.0.1)
;; WHEN: Sat Nov 03 19:29:09 2007
;; XFR size: 8 records
```

Summary

- BIND SDB allows you to create your own interface to the BIND name server, providing answers to DNS queries for specific zones from any imaginable source.
- Writing an BIND SDB interface requires programming experience in the C language.
- BIND SDB provides a number of sample drivers in the BIND source distribution.
- The BIND SDB LDAP driver is in widespread use.

Related topics

- Bind DLZ (Chapter 9) extends the BIND name server with drivers that provide database and LDAP directory back-ends to BIND. In contrast to SDB, DLZ enables BIND to serve new zones, on the fly as they are added to the back-end without having to alter `named.conf`.
- If you enjoy programming, you will be interested in the PowerDNS' Pipe back-end (Chapter 6) and in DNS name servers you can implement in Perl (Chapter 15).
- We discussed in Chapter 1 that some organizations need their own private DNS root zones. We show you how to use BIND-sdb-LDAP for this in Chapter 18.

Notes and further reading

Wildcard domain patch for BIND SDB *LDAP*

For this book we have created a small patch which enables the BIND SDB LDAP driver to support wildcard DNS domains as in `*.qupps.biz`, and can log on the console a list of LDAP queries being used. The patch is simple to apply. After configuring BIND SDB with the LDAP driver as described above, get and apply the patch:

```
$ cd bind-9.4.2/bin/named
$ wget http://fupps.com/code/sundry/sdb/bind-sdb-ldap-wildcard3.patch
$ patch < bind-sdb-ldap-wildcard3.patch
$ make
```

Our patch has already been committed to the project's CVS tree, so you may prefer to get the code from there (see `http://bind9-ldap.bayour.com/`).

ISC's stand on load-balancing in BIND

The Internet Systems Consortium (ISC) is reluctant to include load-balancing in BIND. `www.isc.org/index.pl?/sw/bind/docs/bind-load-bal.php` explains why.

Chapter

9 Bind DLZ

Now you're coming back to Earth, and things are getting more and more dynamic.

Duane G. Carey

Introduction

Dynamically Loadable Zones (DLZ) is an add-on for the BIND name server that lets you store zone data in an external database, greatly reducing BIND's memory requirements and, more importantly, its startup time. DLZ lets you add zones to BIND on-the-fly without having to reconfigure or reload named.

Managing DNS data in zone master files, which are usually edited by hand, requires great care: whenever you modify a zone file, you have to remember to reload or restart BIND. And when editing a file it's easy to introduce errors, which are difficult to detect or can even prevent BIND's named from loading a zone at all.

BIND loads all configured zone master files into main memory when the named daemon starts up, so that when it's running it can answer queries quickly, without having to access disks. This of course has the side-effect that startup takes a long time, during which the server is unavailable to answer queries. Because the startup time is proportional to the number and size of the zone files, administrators are cautious of restarting or reloading BIND. Additionally, when serving a very large number of zones, BIND uses a lot of memory.

To overcome the long startup time and BIND's hunger for memory, and to let you store zone data in external databases, Rob Butler created *Dynamically Loadable Zones* (Bind DLZ) for BIND. Bind DLZ was sponsored by Stichting NLnet[1]; the project was completed in 2005; support and the mailing list are still active.

Because of the way DLZ handles its zones, it is dynamic – it serves zones you add to one of its database back-ends immediately, without you having to reconfigure or reload BIND. So, while it is more effort to get started with one of Bind DLZ's back-ends (SQL or LDAP, say), the great advantage is that zone data management can be automated, which is crucial for large organizations and ISPs.

Unfortunately, DLZ is not a panacea for DNS data management: it has limitations, some of which are due to BIND's design. DLZ has no support for RFC 2136 dynamic updates, nor does it support incremental zone transfers (IXFR).

Even so, you can set up BIND together with DLZ to solve most requirements you might have in terms of DNS serving. For example, you can configure BIND to serve some domains from zone master files, and others from an external database.

Pros	• Adds LDAP, SQL and Berkeley DB databases to BIND • BIND doesn't need to be reloaded when you add zones or zone data • Adaptable database schemas • Fast startup, lower memory consumption • Native Microsoft Windows port • Good documentation
Cons	○ No RFC 2136 Dynamic DNS (in back-ends) ○ No Web GUI or data management tools provided ○ BDBHPT driver difficult to implement
Scenarios	Large BIND environments that want to manage DNS using an external database, adding zones and DNS data on-the-fly.

Table 9.1: Bind DLZ at a glance

[1]NLnet Foundation is a non-profit organization committed to network (Internet) related research and development. As part of this commitment, they sponsor the development of software that would benefit the Internet, and make that software available as Open Source (see `http://www.nlnet.nl`).

9.1 Architecture of Bind DLZ

DLZ is a large add-on for BIND that is integrated into ISC's BIND9 and later distributions. It is similar in purpose to BIND SDB that we discussed in the previous chapter. DLZ consists of two main parts (Figure 9.1):

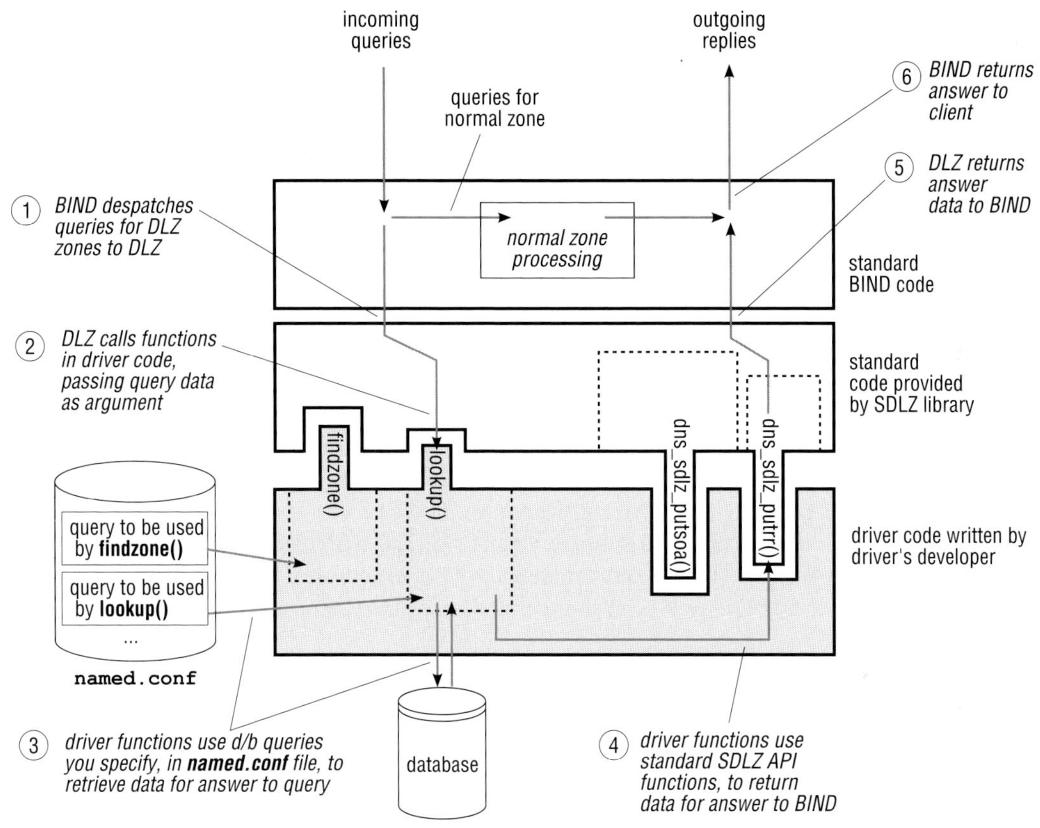

Figure 9.1: Inside DLZ

A. The SDLZ API is built into the BIND core. It allows BIND to ask (via a DLZ driver) whether a zone is contained in the database, and to retrieve the zone data when needed. This apparently small change is what gives DLZ its dynamic capabilities. (If you read the previous Chapter, recall that BIND SDB didn't have this feature, so you had to configure zones manually, in advance.) Compared to SDB, DLZ provides two new functions: `findzone()` to query the external database to determine if a zone exists, and `allowzonexfr()` to determine if a zone transfer for a specific zone is allowed.

   SDLZ acts as a driver adapter converting all data to and from plain ASCII text for use by the real DLZ back-end API, so that the answers are received from the back-end in exactly the same format as answers from zone master files.

B. A number of database *drivers*, that you enable with switches to the configure program when building Bind DLZ (see Notes). These drivers are located in the `contrib` directory of BIND's source distribution.

   A driver interfaces with a particular type of data store, which you use for your DNS zone data. For example, the DLZ MySQL driver lets you store your zone data in a MySQL database.

   DLZ provides many different drivers ready for you to use with SQL, LDAP, and Berkeley DB databases, as we explain in Section 9.4.

9.1.1 How a Bind DLZ driver works

Every Bind DLZ driver interfaces with BIND in a standard way. As shown in Figure 9.1, Bind DLZ calls just a few functions (`findzone()`, `lookup()`, ...) to tell the driver what to do – for example, "retrieve the MX records for example.com". There are only five of these functions. The driver uses other standard functions (`dns_sdlz_putrr()`, ...) to return answers to Bind DLZ.

The `findzone()`, `lookup()`, ... functions are part of the driver, and they interface with the back-end data store. For example, Figure 9.1 illustrates `lookup()` retrieving data from the back-end database. A very important feature of Bind DLZ and its drivers is that it doesn't force you to store you data in a particular place or a specific format. As long as the data is present and can be retrieved in the right format, Bind DLZ can use it. The small price for this flexibility is that you have to configure your Bind DLZ with enough information that it can successfully retrieve the data from the respective back-end database, which is what we cover next.

Configuring a Bind DLZ *driver – overview*

Configuring a Bind DLZ driver requires about ten lines of configuration information in your `named.conf` file. There's nothing particularly difficult involved, but you do need to know how Bind DLZ uses the configuration information. To make things concrete, let's assume you are using a MySQL back-end database.

What information does Bind DLZ need, in order to be able to retrieve DNS data from your MySQL database? First, you have to tell it that it will be a MySQL database that you're using; then DLZ needs the name of the database, the IP address of the machine it's on, and user ID/password details.

Next (and this is the only complicated part) you have to tell Bind DLZ how to perform queries against the database, to get the information required. Remember, Bind DLZ deliberately doesn't mandate any database schema, and therefore you have to give it all the necessary details. Each of the five different functions that we mentioned above – `findzone()`, `lookup()`, ...– will use a query to interrogate the database. You have to write a template for each of these five queries; when you've done that, you have finished configuring your driver.

Later on (Section 9.6.1), we'll give you full details of what data the five functions expect to receive back from their queries, but for now, we just want you to understand broadly how things work. Again to make things more concrete, let's look at an example. When you query Bind DLZ for the address of example.com, say, Bind DLZ first uses the `findzone()` function to decide whether it is authoritative for example.com. You have to write a template SQL statement that Bind DLZ can use for this. In your SQL statement you specify the database table and column names to use, and that's the crucial point: the template query you write gives Bind DLZ all the information it needs about the database schema, etc. For our `findzone()` example, your template SQL query might look like this:

```
SELECT zname FROM dns_records WHERE zname = '$zone$'
```

This example illustrates one other important point about Bind DLZ's query operation: there are a number of *tokens* that you can use in your template query. When Bind DLZ comes to use the query, it replaces the tokens with the relevant values for the current query. In the example above, Bind DLZ replaces `$zone$` with the name of the zone being queried. (Two other tokens are also used: `$record$`, which contains the host name of the domain being queried, and `$client$` which contains the IP address of a client requesting zone transfer.)

To summarize, configuring your Bind DLZ driver involves giving it enough information to connect to your back-end database of whatever type, and writing five template SQL (or LDAP or ...) queries, one for each of the five `findzone()`, `lookup()`, ... functions.

That's all we'll say about configuration for now. We'll cover it in all the detail you require in later sections.

9.2 Why should you use Bind DLZ?

If you are using BIND already, the benefits of DLZ are:

- DLZ does not *remove* any of BIND's capabilities or features; it *adds* to them.
- DLZ enables BIND to store zone data in a back-end database. Because you can use DLZ zones and normal master file zones in the same BIND, you don't have to convert all your current BIND zone files to database format; you can convert existing zones to DLZ as and when you want.
- DLZ makes BIND fully dynamic, meaning you don't have to reload the name server when you add zones. We discussed in Chapter 8 that BIND SDB adds dynamic record lookup to BIND. DLZ goes a step further: it can dynamically add new zones to BIND.
- DLZ starts very quickly and has low memory consumption, even when you have hundreds or thousands of zones.
- DLZ supports a variety of database drivers including SQL databases, LDAP directory servers and a special driver that uses Berkeley DB, an embedded non-relational database that offers high performance.
- As we've already mentioned, DLZ lets you use any database or LDAP schema you want, so you can layer your DNS systems on top of an existing database infrastructure if you need to.

9.2.1 Limitations of Bind DLZ

Bind DLZ has some limitations:

- Bind DLZ can serve only as a master name server and not as a slave. The SDLZ API defines functions only for reading resource data from the back-end, not for writing to it. Therefore, a BIND server can't act as a slave for a zone stored in DLZ, because BIND can't do anything with a zone retrieved in a zone transfer. To avoid this problem, configure slave zones normally (i.e. to use zone files), and not as DLZ zones.
- DLZ query performance is generally slower than with zone files. As the different drivers provided with DLZ have different performance characteristics, we recommend you test which driver offers the performance requirements you have to meet (see Chapter 23).
- BIND statements such as `allow-transfer`, etc. cannot be used in a DLZ zone. The only statement allowed within a DLZ zone is the `database` statement.

  However, this doesn't matter, because DLZ does let you control who can perform zone transfers, with ACL-like sets of addresses that you configure in your back-end database.
- You can't use Dynamic DNS (RFC 2136) in a DLZ-managed zone. However, a single instance of BIND can simultaneously have DLZ zones and normal zones which do have support for RFC 2136. Or you can use our "poor man's dynamic DNS" (Chapter 19).

9.3 Order of processing with multiple Bind DLZ back-ends

When Bind DLZ receives a query, it handles it as follows:

1. BIND checks its in-memory database, loaded from `master` and `slave` zone statements, to see if it has authoritative data for this zone. If there is no such in-memory database (because you are using only DLZ and have no other zone sources configured), this check will be completed very quickly. If an in-memory match is found, DLZ is bypassed – goto step 3.
2. BIND checks to see if the DLZ database back-end is authoritative for the queried zone by executing the `findzone()` query. This query can be executed several times, checking for shorter versions of the zone's name at each iteration until it finds a match or terminates; only if it gets a positive response is the domain considered authoritative. For example, if we are searching for www.qupps.biz, DLZ could call `findzone()` once for each of www.qupps.biz, qupps.biz, and biz in that order.
3. If neither BIND's in-memory database nor DLZ are authoritative, BIND then consults its cache, and returns the necessary data if it's there.
4. If BIND is configured to recurse (and we recommend it shouldn't be when acting as an authoritative server) it will query other DNS servers for the requested information, cache it, and return it as answer to the client.

In other words, you can mix DLZ zones and normal (master / slave) zones in BIND, but zone files have precedence over DLZ zones – they are queried before DLZ. Thus, if a DLZ database back-end contains data for a zone example.net and you have also configured a zone file for example.net, BIND will always answer queries for *anything*.example.net from the zone master file; BIND will never consult DLZ's back-end database. However, you *can* have DLZ serve data for example.net and use a master zone file for a sub-domain such as europe.example.net. A configuration like this may be of interest if you need RFC 2136 dynamic updates, for a sub-domain only; it's a workaround for DLZ's lack of support for dynamic DNS updates.

9.4 Choosing a DLZ driver

DLZ provides several drivers: choose the one that's best suited to your needs and your performance requirements. They are:

- The MySQL driver, which we cover in Section 9.7.
- A PostgreSQL driver, very similar in function to the MySQL driver. We don't cover this because it is so similar to the MySQL driver.
- The LDAP driver, which we cover in Section 9.8.
- The Berkeley DB High Performance Text (BDBHPT) driver, which we cover in Section 9.9.

  For the BDBHPT driver, you don't have to create any template queries, as these are built-in to the driver. As a result, the Bind DLZ configuration is much easier than for SQL and LDAP. On the other hand, you have to create the databases (which involves writing a program or script), and you have to write the programs that manipulate the data in those databases, so the overall implementation is a lot of work.
- The ODBC driver (Microsoft Windows only) can be used on supported platforms to access databases via ODBC, if there is no DLZ driver available for your specific database. We don't cover this driver, but you will find it documented on the Bind DLZ Web site (see Notes).
- The File System driver allows you to use a file system as a database for DNS data. Zones and hosts are represented by names of directories and (empty) files. The file system driver is the easiest to build as it doesn't have external library dependencies, but we do not recommend it, as it is quite slow.
- The BDB driver is the original Berkeley DB driver, which should not be confused with the newer BDBHPT driver, above. The BDB driver is deprecated because it is much slower than the BDBHPT driver, which is unfortunate as, unlike the BDBHPT driver, it comes with utilities for data management.

9.5 Getting started with Bind DLZ

Configuring DLZ is not trivial because it requires that *you* tell it what to do. Approach it in this order:

1. Read the next Section (9.6) irrespective of the back-end you plan to implement. It contains general information that you require for any back-end.
2. If you plan on using the MySQL driver, read Section 9.7. We show you how to configure the MySQL driver, and we give you three examples, with three different database schemas: (a) minimal, (b) Bind DLZ's default, and (c) the MyDNS schema.
3. If you plan on using an LDAP directory server as a back-end to Bind DLZ, read Section 9.8. We show you how to configure the LDAP driver, and we show you two schemas for doing so: (a) minimal and (b) Bind DLZ's default.
4. And finally, if you plan on using the High Performance Berkeley DB driver, read Section 9.9.

9.6 How Bind DLZ retrieves information from your SQL or LDAP server

As we outlined earlier, for the SQL and LDAP drivers, you have to instruct DLZ how it should find the answers to DNS queries, i.e. how the data in your back-end database is organized and how you want Bind DLZ to lookup and use that data. Because Bind DLZ doesn't know what your database schema is, part of the configuration that you specify is template queries that Bind DLZ should use. For example, if you are using an SQL database, you have to write template SQL `SELECT` statements, that contain the correct table and column names. You must also ensure that the data returned by the queries is in the correct format.

In the next two sections we go through this configuration process in detail, so you'll know exactly how to write the query templates. In the sections after that (Section 9.7 onwards) we cover the other configuration details – how you specify which database, on which host, etc.

9.6.1 The five template queries that you have to configure

DLZ uses five different queries, for five different purposes which we will now explain. These are the template queries that *you* have to configure. The five different queries are:

findzone() DLZ invokes this whenever it needs to find out if it is authoritative for a given domain. The only token translated in this query is `$zone$`, as the others don't make sense in this context.

`findzone`() uses neither the contents of the results, nor any attribute types/values returned by the query: what matters is the *number* of results the query returns. If the LDAP query returns zero entries (or the SQL query returns zero rows), DLZ considers it is not authoritative for the zone, and it will not answer queries about it. A non-zero number of results indicates to DLZ that the underlying database back-end is authoritative for the zone.

DLZ calls `findzone()` for each DNS query BIND receives, so the efficiency of this function affects the performance of the database back-end considerably. A single result by the query is enough to indicate that the zone exists, so you should phrase your queries to return *only one* result; doing so will speed up DLZ considerably. To speed up DLZ further, we recommend your query returns the shortest possible single field and not a whole row of data. Use the SQL syntax of your database back-end to return only one row, with a single (small) column, if the zone exists. In MySQL you can do this by adding:

```
... LIMIT 1
```

to the end of your SQL `SELECT` statement.

The `findzone()` query is mandatory; without it, DLZ doesn't do anything.

lookup() DLZ invokes the `lookup()` query once `findzone()` has determined that DLZ is authoritative for the zone. `lookup()` must return the zone data for the query, and in the order specified in Table 9.2.

If the `lookup()` query returns Start of Authority (SOA) and Name Server (NS) records, the `authority()` query (see below) must not return them.

The tokens supported by this query are `$zone$` and `$record$`; the former is set to the zone name (de.qupps.biz) and the latter to the host name portion (www) of the DNS query. Both tokens must be specified in the query; if you omit either, DLZ won't start up. When searching at the zone apex, `$record$` is set to `@` and when searching for a wild card host name, it is set to a special character:

- For LDAP, the special character is a tilde (~).
- For SQL, the special character is an asterisk (*).

Your `lookup()` query must *not* return the *host* field (see Table 9.2) because if it did, for a query of, say, www, you would illegally return a line consisting of:

```
www       86400 A www 192.168.7.4
```

The `lookup()` query is mandatory.

authority() DLZ calls the optional `authority()` query, replacing the `$zone$` token with the zone's name, to find the zone's Start of Authority (SOA) and Name Server (NS) records. If your `lookup()` function already returns NS and SOA records, this query must not be defined.

allnodes() DLZ invokes the `allnodes()` query to gather the DNS records that will be returned in an outgoing zone transfer. Only the `$zone$` token is interpolated and `allnodes()` will work only if an `allowzonexfr()` query has "permitted" the zone transfer.

Your `allnodes()` query must return values in the order specified in Table 9.2, *including* the *host* field.

`allowzonexfr` () Bind DLZ uses this query to determine if a specific client is allowed to request a zone transfer for the zone. The name of the requested zone (e.g. qupps.biz) is interpolated into the `$zone$` token and a string representation of the IPv4 or IPv6 address of the requesting client in `$client$` (e.g. 192.168.1.1). In this context, the client will commonly be a slave DNS server requesting a zone transfer.

The contents of results returned by this query are not used by DLZ. It is rather the *number* of LDAP entries (or SQL rows) that determines whether a zone transfer is allowed or not. If the LDAP search finds zero entries (or the SQL `SELECT` returns zero rows), the zone transfer is denied; otherwise it succeeds. Here again, to speed up DLZ, we recommend you phrase your queries in such a way as that a maximum of one row (or entry) is returned.

Those are the five queries you have to configure, and we have just explained when DLZ uses them. In the next section we explain the format in which the functions must return the data. section

9.6.2 Format of data returned by queries to the DLZ drivers

Bind DLZ connects to your back-end database and performs searches with queries you provide: for an SQL back-end, these are SQL `SELECT` statements, and for an LDAP directory server back-end, they are LDAP URLs (Section A.3.11). In both SQL and LDAP queries, you name the fields[2] that you want to retrieve. The names you give your fields don't matter, as long as the values returned by your queries are in the right format and in the right order. For example, the drivers expect the TTL value of a DNS resource record to be returned as the first whitespace-separated value, and the value must be convertible to an integer. The field might be called `timeToLive` or `mySpecialTimer`; that doesn't matter, but it *must* be the first item on the line returned by your query.

When developing your own schema, you may decide to use fewer or more fields than those described. That is perfectly in order as long as the concatenation of the returned values makes sense to Bind DLZ. If you really want to, you can store the whole DNS data record in a single field, separating the individual values with a single space.

DLZ expects at least three items to be returned for every entry in an LDAP search (or for every row in an SQL query). In order, these are:

1. The TTL of the host. This string must be able to be transformed to a positive integer by a call to `strtol()`. The TTL of all records in an RRset (resource record set) must be the same. (Remember, that an RRset comprises all the records of the same type for the same host.) So, for example, if your host has two MX records, they must both have the same TTL value. Failure to observe this rule can result in "bad ttl" errors issued by `dns_sdlz_putrr()`.

[2]We hate doing this, but we have to to make your reading easier: as you know, SQL has "columns" and LDAP has "attribute types", but we call them both "fields" in this section only.

Order	Name	Type	Description
1	ttl	number	Time to Live
2	type	string	DNS record type (A, NS, ...)
3	host	string	Hostname or IP address
4	mx_prio	number	MX priority (for MX records)
5	data	string	Record content
6	primary_ns	string	MNAME of SOA
7	resp_person	string	RNAME of SOA
8	serial	number	SOA Serial number
9	refresh	number	SOA Refresh time
10	retry	number	SOA Retry time
11	expire	number	SOA Expiry time
12	minimum	number	SOA Minimum time

Table 9.2: DLZ driver attribute type order

2. The type of the resource record, as an ASCII string (SOA, A, MX, etc).
3. All subsequent items are concatenated to form the *"rdata"* that is returned to BIND. The concatenation of values forms what you would use on the right-hand side of a zone master file record. Some examples for commonly used records:

SOA — For the Start of Authority record, the data consists of the primary name server for the zone (MNAME), followed by the usual values in the SOA record.

```
ns1.qupps.biz. hostmaster.mens.de. 196205281 10800 900 604800 3600
```

A — For an Address record, the data consists of a dotted quad IP address.

```
192.168.1.20
```

MX — A Mail Exchanger must contain a decimal priority followed by a single space and the host name of the mail exchanger.

```
10 mail.qupps.biz.
```

SRV — For a Service record, the data contains the priority, weight, port and target, each separated by a space.

```
0 0 636 ldap.qupps.biz.
```

For example, for a Name Server record, either of these two SQL queries:

```
SELECT ttl,type,mx_prio,data FROM tablename WHERE ...
SELECT ttl,type,rest FROM tablename WHERE ...
```

is valid if the concatenation of the values returned by the query produce:

```
84600 NS ns.qupps.biz.
```

So, now that you know what queries you have to write, and the format of the data they should return, we can show you a sample Bind DLZ configuration. (We still have to explain the database connections lines in the configuration, but ignore those for now – we'll cover them shortly. For now, we just want you to look at the five `SELECT` statements which are the template queries for `findzone()`, `lookup()`, `authority()`, `allnodes()` and `allowzonexfr()`.)

```
dlz "minimalDB" {
  database "mysql
  {host=127.0.0.1 dbname=dlzmini user=dnsadmin pass=hah!}
  {SELECT id FROM zones WHERE zone = '$zone$' LIMIT 1}
  {SELECT ttl,type,data FROM zones z,rrset r WHERE z.id=r.zid ↩
       AND zone='$zone$' AND host='$record$' AND type NOT IN ('SOA','NS')}
  {SELECT ttl,type,data FROM zones z,rrset r WHERE z.id=r.zid ↩
       AND zone='$zone$' AND type IN ('SOA','NS')}
  {SELECT ttl,type,host,data FROM zones z,rrset r WHERE z.id=r.zid↩
       AND zone='$zone$'}
  {SELECT '$zone$', '$client$'}";
};
```

9.6.3 Using tokens in your queries

As we explained in Section 9.1.1, in your template queries Bind DLZ replaces the three tokens `$zone$`, `$record$` and `$client$`, with the appropriate real values. By default (i.e. in the DLZ code as distributed), the tokens you use when configuring DLZ in `named.conf` are surrounded by percent characters (`%`), but that doesn't work for LDAP URLs, so we have written a small patch (see Notes):

- If you apply the patch, you surround the token name with dollar characters, e.g. `$zone$`.
- If you don't apply the patch, surround the token name with percent characters, e.g. `%zone%` as normal. Note however, that you will not be able to use the LDAP driver.

In this chapter we assume you *have* applied the patch so we've used `$`*token*`$` throughout.

That completes our discussion of how DLZ uses the queries you describe for the SQL and LDAP back-ends, and the type of data it expects. Now, we start discussing the individual back-ends.

9.7 The Bind DLZ MySQL driver

9.7.1 Configuration

Bind DLZ's MySQL driver lets you store zone data in a MySQL database (Figure 9.2). As we mentioned, the DLZ MySQL driver doesn't specify which database schema to use; you use any schema you want. This means that DLZ doesn't know the details of your schema. Therefore, your configuration must give DLZ enough information that it can query the database for the resource record data it needs. You give DLZ this information by specifying five SQL `SELECT` statements – one for each of the `findzone()`, `lookup()`, ...functions that we described in Section 9.5. (If you use the schema suggested by the DLZ authors, you can get the necessary `SELECT` statements from the DLZ Web site (see Notes).)

To define a zone for Bind DLZ with the MySQL driver, and to configure the MySQL driver, create a `dlz` clause in `named.conf`:

```
dlz "descriptive name" {
    database "mysql
```

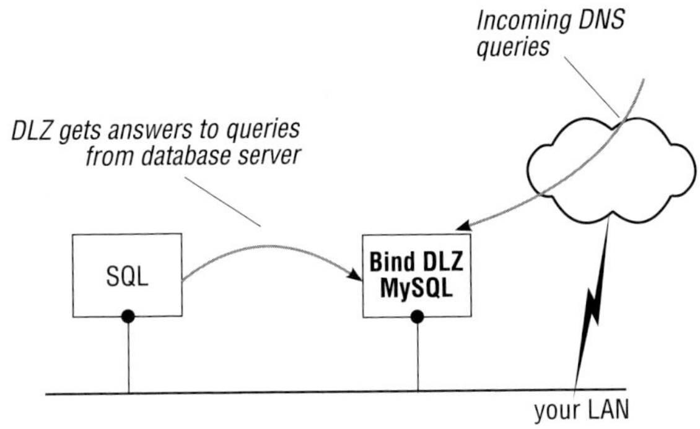

Figure 9.2: Bind DLZ MySQL driver

```
3         database connection
4         SELECT ... definition of findzone() ...
5         SELECT ... definition of lookup() ...
6         SELECT ... definition of authority() ...
7         SELECT ... definition of allnodes() ...
8         SELECT ... definition of allowzonexfr() ...
9         UPDATE ... ";
10 };
```

Lines 3–9 are best written in braces. Each pair of braces with their enclosed characters make up an argument to the `database` statement, shown in line 2. The meaning of the various lines is:

1. The keyword `dlz` specifies that this is a Bind DLZ driver. The *descriptive name* is an identifier you choose, such as `"Spain's data"`, and the opening brace must be on this first line. It is closed on line 10.

2. Specify which DLZ driver to use. Enter the keyword `database` followed by the string `"mysql` after the opening quote; note that we don't close the double quote until line 9.

   This is the only place where we specify that this zone is a MySQL-driver zone, and that Bind DLZ should therefore load that driver.

3. Specify the database connection parameters. The line contains a set of *keyword=value* pairs that describe the connection to the back-end database.

   ```
   { host=127.0.0.1 dbname=dns }
   ```

   The allowed keywords are:

   `host` The IP address of the host where the MySQL database is located.

   `port` The MySQL port number; if not defined, it defaults to 3306.

   `dbname` The name of the MySQL database.

user The username with which Bind DLZ authenticates against the MySQL database.

pass The password for *user*.

socket The filename of the UNIX socket to use instead of connecting via TCP to *host:port*.

compress Flag: if "true", MySQL uses the compression protocol. (Default: false.)

ssl Flag; if "true", the connection to the MySQL database should be SSL-encrypted. (Default: false.)

space Flag: if "true", spaces are allowed in MySQL function names. (Default: false.)

A *keyword=value* pair may not include whitespace. Anywhere.

4. Your definition of the `findzone()` query.
5. Your definition of the `lookup()` query.
6. Your definition of the `authority()` query.
7. Your definition of the `allnodes()` query.
8. Your definition of the `allowzonexfr()` query.
9. If the `findzone()` query returns a row, this optional query is invoked. This allows you to gather statistics on how many queries have been performed for a zone. Since `findzone()` is also invoked by `allowzonexfr()`, this query is also run when a zone transfer is initiated, even if the client is not allowed to transfer the zone.

   If you don't want to update a table when `findzone()` is called, simply omit the query.

   Note the closing double quotes and the semicolon (`;`) at the end of the line.

   For maximum performance, we recommend you omit this query completely.
10. This last line in `/etc/named.conf` closes the `dlz` clause started on line 1. Note the terminating semicolon.

Remember that each of the queries in lines 4–9 must be written on a single line.

9.7.2 Minimal MySQL schema

We demonstrate the use of the MySQL driver by creating a small schema which you can download from the book's Web site (☞ D091). Our schema uses two tables: `zones` and `rrset`.

zones This table contains a single row per zone. The `id` column is a primary key and is referenced from the `rrset` table. The zone's name is in the column `zone`.

```
mysql> SELECT * FROM zones;
+----+-----------+
| id | zone      |
+----+-----------+
|  1 | qupps.biz |
|  2 | jp.de     |
+----+-----------+
```

rrset The table `rrset` contains all the resource records for all zones and has the following columns:

id A unique identifier for the record.

zid This is the `id` from the `zones` database table; it identifies the zone this record belongs to.

ttl Defines the Time to Live (TTL) of this DNS resource.

host The host name for the DNS domain. It must be a value like `www`, a single "at" character (`@`) for the zone apex, or an asterisk (`*`) for a wild-card record.

type The type of DNS resource record (SOA, NS, A, ...).

data This column contains the "right hand side" of a DNS resource, as in a zone master file.

```
mysql> SELECT * FROM rrset;
+----+-----+-------+------+-------+---------------------------------+
| id | zid | ttl   | host | type  | data                            |
+----+-----+-------+------+-------+---------------------------------+
|  1 |   1 | 86400 | @    | SOA   | mens.de. jp.mens.de. 1 10800 ...
|  2 |   1 | 86400 | @    | NS    | ns.qupps.biz.                   |
|  3 |   1 | 86400 | @    | NS    | ns2.qupps.biz.                  |
|  4 |   1 | 86400 | www  | A     | 192.168.1.20                    |
|  5 |   2 | 86400 | @    | SOA   | jp.de. jp.mens.de. 1 10800 90...
|  6 |   2 | 86400 | @    | NS    | jp.de.                          |
|  7 |   2 |    67 | @    | A     | 10.0.0.1                        |
|  8 |   2 | 86400 | www  | CNAME | www.qupps.biz.                  |
+----+-----+-------+------+-------+---------------------------------+
```

Configure the minimal schema in `named.conf`

The configuration for this schema is easy. We specify an SQL query for each of the five functions we want to implement. Note again, that you have to write each query on a single line:

```
dlz "minimalDB" {
  database "mysql
  {host=127.0.0.1 dbname=dlzmini user=dnsadmin pass=hah!}
  {SELECT id FROM zones WHERE zone = '$zone$' LIMIT 1}
  {SELECT ttl,type,data FROM zones z,rrset r WHERE z.id=r.zid ↩
       AND zone='$zone$' AND host='$record$' AND type NOT IN ('SOA','NS')}
  {SELECT ttl,type,data FROM zones z,rrset r WHERE z.id=r.zid ↩
       AND zone='$zone$' AND type IN ('SOA','NS')}
  {SELECT ttl,type,host,data FROM zones z,rrset r WHERE z.id=r.zid↩
       AND zone='$zone$'}
```

```
    {SELECT '$zone$', '$client$'}";
};
```

The five queries specified in the `dlz` clause do the following:

1. This query is used by `findzone()` to determine whether a zone actually exists. The SQL `LIMIT` is overkill, as `zone` is a unique key and by design can return only a single row, but we leave it in to remind you that returning even a single row indicates that a zone exists: this improves Bind DLZ's performance.

2. This is the `lookup()` query. As we wanted to demonstrate the `authority()` query on the next line, this query should not return the SOA and NS records, which is why we add:

   ```
   AND type NOT IN ('SOA','NS')
   ```

   to the `SELECT` statement.

   To increase performance, return the SOA and NS records in the `lookup()` function if possible, and don't use the `authority()` function at all. That way, you reduce the number of database queries.

3. This is the `authority()` query, which determines the Start of Authority and the Name Servers for a zone, and it returns only those resource records to BIND, due to the:

   ```
   AND type IN ('SOA','NS')
   ```

4. This is the `allnodes()` query, which is utilized for outgoing zone transfers. It returns all the records of a zone. Note that it also selects the `host` column.

5. This last query is the `allowzonexfr()` query, which you use to limit who can perform zone transfers. As an example, we open our BIND name server to all by ensuring the query returns exactly one row. Note how we have to use the `$zone$` and `$client$` tokens in the query: Bind DLZ does not start without them.

   This simple `SELECT` will always return one row.

Note that we have omitted the `UPDATE` query, for two reasons: we aren't interested in gathering statistics on the number of queries DLZ receives, and we want maximum performance.

Observing queries

After launching Bind DLZ (see Notes) you populate the database tables, and then Bind DLZ is ready to answer queries. A query for an Address record:

```
$ dig @127.0.0.1 www.qupps.biz
;; ANSWER SECTION:
www.qupps.biz.          86400    IN       A 192.168.1.20

;; AUTHORITY SECTION:
qupps.biz.              86400    IN       NS ns2.qupps.biz.
qupps.biz.              86400    IN       NS ns.qupps.biz.
```

will cause named to submit the following SQL queries. (For clarity we omit the column and table names in the `SELECT` statements.)

```
1 SELECT zone FROM zones WHERE zone = 'www.qupps.biz' LIMIT 1
2 SELECT zone FROM zones WHERE zone = 'qupps.biz' LIMIT 1
3 SELECT ... AND zone='qupps.biz' AND host='www' AND type NOT IN ('SOA','NS')
4 SELECT ... AND zone='qupps.biz' AND host='@' AND type IN ('SOA','NS')
5 SELECT ... AND zone='qupps.biz' AND host='*' AND type NOT IN ('SOA','NS')
6 SELECT ... AND zone='qupps.biz' AND type IN ('SOA','NS')
```

1. `findzone()` query to determine whether www.qupps.biz is in fact a zone.

2. Bind DLZ removes a label from the name and again uses `findzone()` to find the zone. This time it finds it.

3. `lookup()` query to find the host `www`.

4. `lookup()` query to find SOA and NS records.

5. The Name Server (NS) records in the `rrset` table contain names which cannot be resolved. This `lookup()` query checks for a wild-card entry.

6. `authority()` query to determine the SOA and NS records for the zone.

Adding an in-addr.arpa *zone to Bind DLZ*

If you query Bind DLZ for a Pointer (PTR) to the address 192.168.1.20 you would see the following queries issued by the MySQL driver, when it uses `findzone()` to determine whether Bind DLZ is authoritative for the zone:

```
SELECT zone FROM zones WHERE zone = '20.1.168.192.in-addr.arpa' LIMIT 1
SELECT zone FROM zones WHERE zone = '1.168.192.in-addr.arpa' LIMIT 1
SELECT zone FROM zones WHERE zone = '168.192.in-addr.arpa' LIMIT 1
SELECT zone FROM zones WHERE zone = '192.in-addr.arpa' LIMIT 1
SELECT zone FROM zones WHERE zone = 'in-addr.arpa' LIMIT 1
SELECT zone FROM zones WHERE zone = 'arpa' LIMIT 1
```

To add an in-addr.arpa zone to your minimal schema database, add the following records to your database:

```
mysql> INSERT INTO zones (zone) VALUES ('1.168.192.in-addr.arpa');

mysql> INSERT INTO rrset (zid, host, type, data)
         SELECT id, '@', 'SOA',
         'ns.qupps.biz. jp.qupps.biz. 1 10800 900 604800 86400'
         FROM zones
         WHERE zone = '1.168.192.in-addr.arpa';

mysql> INSERT INTO rrset (zid, host, type, data)
         SELECT id, '@', 'NS', 'ns.qupps.biz.'
         FROM zones
         WHERE zone = '1.168.192.in-addr.arpa';

mysql> INSERT INTO rrset (zid, host, type, data)
```

```
SELECT id, '20', 'PTR', 'www.qupps.biz.'
FROM zones
WHERE zone = '1.168.192.in-addr.arpa';
```

These records added to the `zones` and `rrset` tables set up an authoritative zone 1.168.192.in-addr.arpa, and an inverse Pointer to 192.168.1.20:

```
$ dig @127.0.0.1 -x 192.168.1.20
;; ANSWER SECTION:
20.1.168.192.in-addr.arpa. 86400 IN     PTR www.qupps.biz.

;; AUTHORITY SECTION:
1.168.192.in-addr.arpa. 86400   IN      NS ns.qupps.biz.
```

Limitations of the minimal schema

The minimal schema just discussed works very well and has good performance. However:

- Updating the DNS resources in the `rrset` table is complicated by the fact that the data portion (right hand side) of a record is a one long string in the `data` column. If you create tools to update the tables, you have to keep this in mind.
- Any client can perform zone transfers because the query in `allowzonexfr()` always returns a row. A simple way to control zone transfers is to create a table (called `axfr`, say) containing zone names and IP addresses of clients allowed to transfer those zones:

```
mysql> select * FROM axfr;
+----+-----------+--------------+
| id | zone      | ip           |
+----+-----------+--------------+
|  1 | qupps.biz | 192.168.1.20 |
|  2 | qupps.biz | 127.0.0.1    |
+----+-----------+--------------+
```

Then change the `allowzonexfr()` query to read:

```
{SELECT id FROM axfr WHERE zone='$zone$' AND ip='$client$'}";
```

When Bind DLZ gets a request for a zone transfer, it uses `findzone()` to determine whether the zone exists, and if it does, it issues the `allowzonexfr()` query, which produces:

```
SELECT id FROM axfr WHERE zone='qupps.biz' AND ip='192.168.1.20'
```

If this query returns a row, the `allnodes()` query is invoked to return the actual data. Do *not* use the following as it always returns a row:

```
SELECT COUNT(*) FROM axfr WHERE ...
```

The minimal schema is functional and fast, but there is another schema: the one designed by the Bind DLZ author. We discuss that next.

9.7.3 MySQL schema proposed by Bind DLZ

The Bind DLZ project has its own suggested MySQL schema, as documented on the project's Web site (see Notes). The suggested configuration is:

```
dlz "mysqlzone" {
 database "mysql
 {host=127.0.0.1 dbname=dlzdns ssl=false}
 {SELECT zone FROM dns_records WHERE zone = '$zone$' LIMIT 1}
 {SELECT ttl, type, mx_priority, CASE↩
    WHEN lower(type)='txt'↩
    THEN concat('\"', data, '\"')↩
    WHEN lower(type) = 'soa'↩
    THEN concat_ws(' ',data,resp_person,serial,refresh,retry,expire,minimum)↩
    ELSE data END↩
    FROM dns_records↩
    WHERE zone = '$zone$' AND host = '$record$'}
 {}
 {SELECT ttl, type, host, mx_priority, CASE↩
    WHEN lower(type)='txt'↩
    THEN concat('\"', data, '\"')↩
    ELSE data END,↩
    resp_person, serial, refresh, retry, expire, minimum↩
    FROM dns_records↩
    WHERE zone = '$zone$'}
 {SELECT zone FROM xfr_table WHERE zone = '$zone$' AND client = '$client$'}
 {INSERT INTO hits (zone) VALUES ('$zone$') ON DUPLICATE KEY UPDATE nr=nr + 1}";
};
```

Note that all lines beginning with an opening brace ({) *must* be continued on the same line until the closing brace (}); wrapping is not supported and is not allowed, and it would cause Bind DLZ to fail when it tried to load its configuration.

The `data` column contains the data of the DNS resource record which will be returned by Bind DLZ: the equivalent of the right hand side of a zone master file. For an address record (A), it is the IP address; for a Name Server record (NS) it is the hostname of the name server (possibly qualified with a terminating period: BIND rules).

You can download the project-suggested schema from (☞ D092). We have added a `hits` table to it to illustrate the optional update query that Bind DLZ submits whenever a zone is requested.

Adding a zone and resource records with the Bind DLZ *MySQL schema*

1. Adding a new Start of Authority (SOA) record creates a new zone:

```
mysql> INSERT INTO dns_records (zone,host,ttl,type,data,resp_person,
    ->    serial,refresh,retry,expire,minimum)
    -> VALUES ('qupps.biz','@',3600,'SOA','ns.qupps.biz.', 'jp.mens.de.',
    ->    '1', '10800', '900', '604800', '86400');
```

2. To illustrate how to add other record types, we now add a Name Server (NS):

```
mysql> INSERT INTO dns_records (zone,host,ttl,type,data)
    ->   VALUES ('qupps.biz', '@', 3600, 'NS', 'ns.qupps.biz.');
```

```
mysql> INSERT INTO dns_records (zone,host,ttl,type,data)
    ->    VALUES ('qupps.biz', 'ns', 1800, 'A', '192.168.1.20');
```

Note that we have not added any values to the other columns in the database table. Their values will be inserted as `NULL`, which is fine, because the MySQL driver will not use them.

If we now query our new Bind DLZ server for the newly added host:

```
$ dig @127.0.0.1 ns.qupps.biz
;; flags: qr aa rd; QUERY: 1, ANSWER: 1, AUTHORITY: 1, ADDITIONAL: 0

;; ANSWER SECTION:
ns.qupps.biz.            1800     IN      A 192.168.1.20

;; AUTHORITY SECTION:
qupps.biz.               3600     IN      NS ns.qupps.biz.
```

we see the following queries being performed (edited for clarity):

```
SELECT zone FROM dns_records WHERE zone = 'ns.qupps.biz'
SELECT zone FROM dns_records WHERE zone = 'qupps.biz'
INSERT INTO hits VALUES ('qupps.biz') ON DUPLICATE KEY UPDATE nr = nr + 1
SELECT ttl, type, ..... WHERE zone = 'qupps.biz' AND host = 'ns'
SELECT ttl, type, .....  WHERE zone = 'qupps.biz' AND host = '@'
```

Also note, that the `hits` table now shows:

```
mysql> SELECT * FROM hits;
+-----------+------+
| zone      | nr   |
+-----------+------+
| qupps.biz |    1 |
+-----------+------+
```

3. To enable a zone transfer, insert the client's IP address into the table, remembering that, in this context, a client will usually be a secondary DNS server that is requesting a zone transfer:

```
mysql> INSERT INTO xfr_table (zone,client) VALUES ('qupps.biz','127.0.0.1');
```

and we see on the debugging console:

```
SELECT zone FROM dns_records WHERE zone = 'qupps.biz'
INSERT INTO hits (zone) VALUES ('qupps.biz') ON DUPLICATE KEY UPDATE nr = nr + 1
SELECT zone FROM xfr_table WHERE zone = 'qupps.biz' AND client = '127.0.0.1'
SELECT ttl, type, mx_priority, ....... WHERE zone = 'qupps.biz' AND host = '@'
SELECT ttl, type, host, .... FROM dns_records WHERE zone = 'qupps.biz'
SELECT ttl, type, .... WHERE zone = 'qupps.biz' AND host = '@'
```

as well as BIND itself logging successful zone transfers on its logging channel (Chapter 7).

9.7.4 Alternative database queries with the MySQL driver

As explained in Section 9.5, Bind DLZ doesn't mandate a specific database schema; instead, you can configure Bind DLZ to use any schema you want. As a final example of how flexible Bind DLZ can be, in this section we configure it to use the database schema of the MyDNS server (Chapter 5). Just to be clear, we are using a schema from a different DNS server, MyDNS, which is not to be confused with the MySQL schema for Bind DLZ we discussed above!

Recall that MyDNS uses two separate database tables to represent zones:

1. The `soa` table contains the data required for a zone's Start of Authority (SOA).
2. The `rr` table contains all other resource records of a zone.

Finding the resource records of a zone means joining both tables. Once again, note that on the following lines, each SQL query enclosed in braces *must* be written on a single line!

```
dlz "mydns-schema" {
  database "mysql
  {host=127.0.0.1 dbname=mydns user=dnsadmin pass=hah!}
  {SELECT origin FROM soa WHERE origin = '$zone$.'}
  {SELECT rr.ttl, rr.type, CASE↩
     WHEN rr.type='TXT' THEN concat('"',rr.data,'"')↩
     WHEN rr.type='MX' THEN concat(rr.aux, ' ',rr.data)↩
     ELSE rr.data END, '', '', '', '', '', ''↩
     FROM rr,soa↩
     WHERE soa.origin = '$zone$.'↩
        AND rr.name = REPLACE('$record$','@','')↩
        AND rr.zone = soa.id↩
   UNION ↩
   SELECT ttl, 'SOA', ns, mbox, serial, refresh, retry, expire, minimum↩
     FROM soa
     WHERE origin = '$zone$.'}";
};
```

There are a few points worth noting in the example above:

- MyDNS qualifies zone names in the `origin` column by appending a period so we have to include the terminating period in the query. (The period follows the `$zone$` token.)
- The `authority()` query is not specified, because the `lookup()` query returns the SOA and NS records.
- The other two queries (`allnodes()` and `allowzonexfr()`) are not specified either. (We could have made this more obvious by including pairs of empty braces {}.)

The example above uses many SQL functions, which is bad for performance, but there's nothing we can do about it.

9.8 The Bind DLZ LDAP driver

The LDAP driver of Bind DLZ lets you store zone data in an LDAP directory (Figure 9.3). The driver supplies a schema that you can use, or you can design your own. The LDAP driver is flexible in that it allows the systems administrator to adapt the queries used by the driver to make it work with any available schema as long as it contains an attribute type for the TTL of a DNS record. If your DNS schema doesn't contain one, you must alter your existing schema and/or re-provision the directory to accommodate the driver's requirements: each and every LDAP entry that represents a DNS record requires an attribute containing the TTL. (Unlike SQL, where you could simply `SELECT` a constant in your SQL query, LDAP URLs don't have such a feature.)

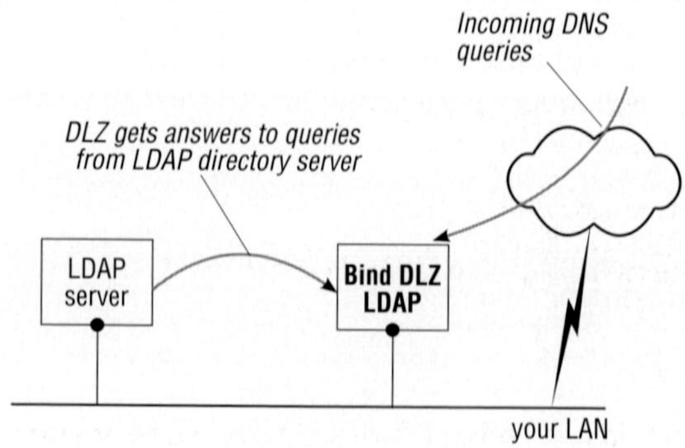

Figure 9.3: Bind DLZ LDAP driver

To get you started with DLZ's LDAP driver:

1. We begin by showing you how to configure the LDAP driver in `named.conf`.
2. We then discuss a minimal schema we designed for this book.
3. Finally, we give a brief overview over the LDAP schema provided by the Bind DLZ project.

9.8.1 Configuring the LDAP driver

Instead of imposing a specific schema, Bind DLZ requires you configure it with LDAP URLs that contain the queries and the attribute types that should be returned by the directory server. These URLs have the tokens embedded in them as explained in Section 9.6.3. Remember, when searching for a wild card host, Bind DLZ replaces the * in the wild card by a tilde (~) because the asterisk would be translated in an LDAP search to mean "any value".

Activate the LDAP driver in `named.conf` via a `database` command contained within a `dlz` clause in `named.conf`:

```
dlz "descriptive name" {
    database "ldap...
        ...
      ";
};
```

The *descriptive name* is any string you like to identify this DLZ driver. The `database` statement describes the DLZ driver; This is the hardest part to get right in the configuration: all other Bind DLZ configuration parameters are contained *within the double quotes*. The LDAP driver's `database` statement consists of seven lines (including the `database` line), and even if LDAP URLs are shown wrapped to accommodate the width of these pages, they *must each be written on a single line* in the file. To help you further, when complete, the beginnings of the lines in the `dlz` clause will look like this, all neatly beneath one another:

```
1 dlz "descriptive name" {
2     database "ldap 2
3     v3 method {binddn} {bindpass} {ip-addresses}
4     ldap:///... definition of findzone() ...
5     ldap:///... definition of lookup() ...
6     ldap:///... definition of authority() ...
7     ldap:///... definition of allnodes() ...
8     ldap:///... definition of allowzonexfr() ... ";
9 };
```

The function of each line is:

1. Introduces the `dlz` clause, giving it a descriptive name of your choice (something like `Our Domains`) contained within double quotes. The content of the `dlz` clause starts at the opening brace ({).

2. This line configures the LDAP driver. The `database` statement is mandatory and it takes a single value enclosed in double quotes. The opening quote is on this line, but note that its closing counterpart is on line 8!

   The ldap keyword is mandatory for the LDAP driver, and the decimal number following it specifies the number of simultaneous connections that Bind DLZ should open to the back-end directory server. Match this number to the number of threads used by named.

   Upon startup, Bind DLZ creates the specified number of connections to the directory server and keeps these open throughout its lifetime.

3. The authentication method with which to bind to the LDAP server, the credentials, and a list of IP addresses of LDAP servers to attempt to connect to (see below).

4. URL used by `findzone()` to determine if a zone exists (mandatory).

5. URL used by `lookup()` to find a domain (mandatory).

6. URL used by `authority()` to return SOA and NS records if the `lookup()` query (line 5) doesn't (optional).

7. URL used by the `allnodes()` function (optional).

8. URL used by `allowzonexfr()` (optional). Note the terminating double-quotes and semicolon; these close the `database` statement that started on line 2.

9. Ends the `dlz` clause. Note the terminating semicolon, which is part of BIND syntax.

All lines must be specified and must not be empty. For optional URLs, if you don't want to specify a value, use an empty pair of braces ({}) without whitespace. If any of the queries contains a space (such as in an LDAP DN), the whole query must be enclosed in braces to protect the space.

Note that the LDAP URLs on lines 4–8 have an empty *host:port* portion (see also Section A.3.11); you cannot specify alternate LDAP servers in the URLs: DLZ uses a single connection, and we describe how you configure that, now.

Describing the LDAP directory connection

Line 3 of the `dlz` clause configures the LDAP connections to the back-end directory servers:

```
v3 method {binddn} {bindpass} {ip-addresses}
```

The string `v3` specifies the LDAP protocol version to use and may be changed to `v2` if the target directory does not speak version 3. *method* is the authentication method the LDAP driver should use to authenticate with the back-end LDAP directory server. The supported methods are:

`simple`	Simple authentication using *binddn* and *bindpass*.
`krb41`	Kerberos 4.1.
`krb42`	Kerberos 4.2.

binddn is the distinguished name with which the LDAP driver should bind to the directory, *bindpass* is its password, and *ip-addresses* is a space-separated list of IP addresses of the LDAP directory servers this driver should contact. Each address is tried in order by `ldap_init()` until a connection is successfully established. The servers are always contacted in the same order, and the first available one is used.

For example, if you have an LDAP directory server running on 127.0.0.1 with a replica server running on 192.168.1.40 and DLZ should use an anonymous bind, you'd configure:

```
dlz "DEMO" {
 database "ldap 1
 v3 simple {} {} {127.0.0.1  192.168.1.40}
 ...
};
```

However, if DLZ should bind to the directory servers with a specific DN (*binddn*) and password (*bindpass*), you must supply these instead of the first two empty brace pairs:

```
dlz "DEMO" {
 database "ldap 1
 v3 simple {cn=fred,dc=qupps,dc=biz} {SuPERsecret} {127.0.0.1  192.168.1.40}
 ...
};
```

Minimal schema

We have developed a minimal schema for illustration purposes. You can download the schema definition from the book's Web site (☞ D093). The schema provides three attribute types `RRttl`, `RRtype`, and `RRdata`, that contain the *ttl*, *type* and *rdata* of the DNS record respectively. The full right-hand-side of the DNS record is contained in the `RRdata` attribute type. You must take care to populate this attribute correctly: for example, if you forget one of the SOA values in an entry for the Start of Authority (SOA) or the preference on a Mail Exchanger (MX) entry, Bind DLZ can crash.

To simplify the schema and avoid creating further object classes or attribute types, our minimal schema contains zones in organizational units (`ou`), and contains the host name portion of a domain name in the `cn` type. The following LDIF represents an entry for an A resource and a SRV resource for the host named @ (the zone apex):

```
dn: RRtype=A,cn=@,ou=qupps.biz,o=dns
cn: @
objectClass: RR
RRtype: A
RRdata: 192.168.1.131
RRttl: 3600

dn: RRtype=SRV,cn=@,ou=qupps.biz,o=dns
cn: @
objectClass: RR
RRtype: SRV
RRttl: 180
RRdata: 0 10 389 ldap.qupps.biz.
```

The attribute type `RRtype` becomes part of the entries' distinguished name (DN) to allow for more than one resource record type per host (Bind DLZ does not support multi-valued types), and the record type (`RRtype`) and its TTL (`RRttl`) are stored individually as required by the driver. Note how the right-hand side *rdata* is stored as a single string in `RRdata`, taking great care to separate the individual content values with single spaces.

The configuration of the driver in `named.conf` is shown below. Note how the two empty pairs of braces on line 3 are used to specify an empty *binddn* and *bindpass*:

```
1 dlz "DEMO" {
2  database "ldap 1
3  v3 simple {} {} {127.0.0.1}
4  ldap:///ou=$zone$,o=dns ?cn?sub?(objectclass=RR)
5  ldap:///cn=$record$,ou=$zone$,o=dns ?RRttl,RRtype,RRdata?sub?(objectclass=RR)";
6 };
```

Configured like this, Bind DLZ will not be able to offer outgoing zone transfers, as neither the `allnodes()` nor the `allowzonexfer()` queries have been defined, but apart from that, Bind DLZ will be fully functional as an authoritative content name server.

In the next section we look at the queries DLZ sends to the directory server, and after that we do enable zone transfers.

Observing queries

When Bind DLZ receives a DNS query, it uses `findzone()` to see whether it is authoritative for the domain. For a query of www.qupps.biz, Bind DLZ does not know what the zone's name is, so it first searches for www.qupps.biz (which could be a zone name), after which it removes a label from the name and looks for qupps.biz. In this minimal schema, the initial queries issued by DLZ for www.qupps.biz zone are:

```
ldap:///ou=www.qupps.biz ,o=dns?cn?sub?(objectclass=RR)
ldap:///ou=qupps.biz ,o=dns?cn?sub?(objectclass=RR)
```

Having ensured that it is authoritative for the requested zone, DLZ uses `lookup()` to find the resource records. An "A" DNS query for www.qupps.biz (which does not exist) results in the following LDAP searches by `lookup()`:

```
ldap:///cn=www,ou=qupps.biz,o=dns?RRttl,RRtype,RRdata?sub?(objectclass=RR)
ldap:///cn=~,ou=qupps.biz,o=dns?RRttl,RRtype,RRdata?sub?(objectclass=RR)
ldap:///cn=@,ou=qupps.biz,o=dns?RRttl,RRtype,RRdata?sub?(objectclass=RR)
```

In spite of appearances all these searches *are* necessary. Let's look at each of them:

1. DLZ looks for the A record for www.qupps.biz. This wasn't found, so now...

2. DLZ looks for a wild card record instead. (Remember that this DLZ driver translates the asterisk (`*`) in a DNS wild card to a tilde (`~`) for the LDAP searches.)

3. DLZ finally looks at the zone apex (hostname is `@`) in order to find the SOA for the zone.

The schema we have presented is minimal but functional. As it stands, it does not allow outgoing zone transfers, as there are two types of query missing. We'll fix that now, in the next section.

Enabling zone transfers in the minimal schema

It is easy to add outgoing zone transfer capabilities: we just have to specify the LDAP search URLs to be used for the `allowzonexfr()` and `allnodes()` functions. `allowzonexfr()` determines whether a zone transfer is permitted for the client requesting it, and `allnodes()` produces all the DNS resource records which make up the zone. The Bind DLZ configuration in `named.conf` then becomes:

```
dlz "DEMO with axfr" {
 database "ldap 1
 v3 simple {} {} {127.0.0.1}
 {ldap:///ou=$zone$, o=dns?cn?sub?(objectclass=RR)}
 {ldap:///cn=$record$,ou=$zone$,o=dns?RRttl,RRtype,RRdata?sub?(objectclass=RR)}
 {}
 {ldap:///ou=$zone$,o=dns?RRttl,RRtype,cn,RRdata?sub?(objectclass=RR   )}
 {ldap:///cn=@,ou=$zone$,o=dns?description=$client$?sub?(objectclass   =RR)}";
};
```

There are several points to note in this configuration:

1. The LDAP driver binds anonymously to our directory, meaning that both *binddn* and *bindpass* are empty strings (which we enclose in braces {} to avoid 127.0.0.1 being interpreted as a *binddn*).

2. We have surrounded each of the LDAP queries by braces because one of the search bases contains a space (which we inserted purely for illustration purposes). Otherwise, we could have omitted the braces, but using them is good practice, to ensure that no runaway space causes problems.

3. The `authority()` query is not specified because our `lookup()` query also returns SOA and NS records (if our LDAP entries provide them). Nevertheless, we have to mark the query as empty, with the empty pair of braces on the 6th line, because otherwise line 7 would be incorrectly interpreted as the `authority()` URL.

4. Lines 7 and 8 contain the URLs for the `allnodes()` and `allowzonexfer()` queries. Note how the `allnodes()` query returns the hostname in `cn`, unlike the `lookup()` query which doesn't. (We discussed this in Section 9.5.)

5. The `allowzonexfr()` query demonstrates the flexibility of the LDAP driver. We use an existing `description` attribute type to store IP addresses of clients allowed to perform zone transfers. (This is an example only; we recommend that in real life your schema should use a dedicated attribute type.)

The queries that DLZ sends to the LDAP back-end upon receipt of an outgoing zone transfer request are:

```
ldap:///ou=qupps.biz,o=dns?cn?sub?(objectclass=RR)
ldap:///cn=@,ou=qupps.biz,o=dns?description =127.0.0.1?sub?(objectclass=RR)
ldap:///cn=@,ou=qupps.biz,o=dns?RRttl,RRtype,RRdata?sub?(objectclass=RR)
ldap:///ou=qupps.biz,o=dns?RRttl,RRtype,cn,RRdata?sub?(objectclass=RR)
```

which perform the following:

1. Use `findzone()` to check whether Bind DLZ is authoritative for the zone.

2. Is the client at IP address 127.0.0.1 allowed to transfer this zone?

3. Find the Start of Authority (SOA) for the zone using a `lookup()` query.

4. Use the `allnodes()` query to enumerate all the DNS records returned in the zone transfer.

That completes a configuration for an authoritative DNS server retrieving a zone in an LDAP directory. In the next section we cover the LDAP schema provided by the Bind DLZ project.

9.8.2 LDAP schema suggested by the Bind DLZ project

The Bind DLZ project has published a schema which you can use with the LDAP driver. It represents DNS resource records in LDAP objects in a much more structured way than the minimal schema we designed above, with a number of object classes that inherit from one another. (Download the schema definition file from (☞ D094).)

A sample LDIF that describes three DNS resource records using this schema is:

```
dn: dlzZoneName=qupps.biz,ou=dlz,o=dns
objectclass: dlzZone
dlzZoneName: qupps.biz

dn: dlzHostName=@,dlzZoneName=qupps.biz,ou=dlz,o=dns
objectclass: dlzHost
dlzHostName: @

dn: dlzRecordID=1,dlzHostName=@,dlzZoneName=qupps.biz,ou=dlz,o=dns
objectclass: dlzSOARecord
dlzRecordID: 1
dlzHostName: @
dlzType: soa
dlzSerial: 196205280
dlzRefresh: 10800
dlzRetry: 900
dlzExpire: 604800
dlzMinimum: 3600
dlzAdminEmail: hostmaster.mens.de.
dlzPrimaryns: ns1.qupps.biz.
dlzTTL: 86400

dn: dlzRecordID=2,dlzHostName=@,dlzZoneName=qupps.biz,ou=dlz,o=dns
objectClass: dlzNSRecord
dlzRecordID: 2
dlzHostName: @
dlzType: ns
dlzTTL: 3600
dlzData: ns1.qupps.biz.

dn: dlzRecordID=3,dlzHostName=@,dlzZoneName=qupps.biz,ou=dlz,o=dns
objectClass: dlzARecord
dlzRecordID: 4
dlzHostName: @
dlzType: a
dlzTTL: 3600
dlzIPAddr: 192.168.1.20
```

DNS resources can be stored in `dlzZoneName` containers (but need not be), and most record types have their own object class (`dlzSOARecord`, `dlzNSRecord`, `dlzPTRRecord`, ...) that inherit types from the structural classes `dlzGenericRecord` and `dlzAbstractRecord`.

The great advantage of this schema is that attribute types are enforced by the schema; it is therefore difficult to forget, say, the preference value on an MX record, as the LDAP directory server would refuse to add such an incomplete object. The schema furthermore includes an object class `dlzXFR` with a `dlzIPAddr` type to control zone transfers in the `allowzonexfer()` query, making it feature-complete.

You will find the required configuration for this schema on the DLZ Web site.

The comfort offered by the this schema comes at a price. We tested this schema, and our own minimal schema, on identical hardware, with the same LDAP server configuration. Our minimal schema gave twice the throughput. (See Chapter 23 for testing details.)

That completes our discussion of the DLZ's LDAP driver and how you configure and use it. Now we discuss DLZ's so-called BDBHPT driver.

9.9 The Berkeley DB High Performance Text (BDBHPT) driver

DLZ's BDBHPT driver is quite different to the SQL and LDAP drivers; the latter are non-trivial to configure with their long queries, whereas BDBHPT is easy to configure but quite difficult to implement due to lack of data management tools for its databases. In this section we describe the BDBHPT driver, how its databases are organized, and how best to implement it.

BDBHPT is layered on Berkeley DB (BDB), an embedded non-relational database for applications that require persistent storage and fast access to data.

- BDB offers programmers a high performance embedded database library, with a number of language bindings, providing functions for data manipulation.

- SQL databases typically offer a query language with which to access their data; BDB doesn't have a query language.

- BDB stores arbitrary key/data pairs in an index. In SQL databases the index is typically an additional data set, but in BDB it *is* the database.

- BDB offers indexed and sequential access methods to data stored in it via the Btree, Queue, Recno, and Hash methods. (See the BDB documentation for details.)

- BDB supports replication over multiple systems by having a single master which receives and distributes updates.

- BDB stores data reliably and ensures data integrity by allowing a group of database modifications to be grouped together into a transaction. Note that if you want to have Berkeley DB support replication for a database, the application you use to write to the database must explicitly use the Berkeley DB replication API. Berkeley DB replication does not come "out of the box": you have to program it. To make this quite clear: Bind DLZ does *not* include support for Berkeley DB database replication, as it simply reads from the Berkeley DB databases.

- A BDB database is represented as a file on a file system. BDB also supports multi-database files, i.e. a collection of one or more databases contained in a single file. These are what DLZ's BDBHPT driver use.

- What are called tables in relational databases, are called databases in Berkeley DB, and a relational database is called an *environment*. Berkeley DB's environment contains the databases, together with an optional configuration file, and file-based backing stores for the shared memory that Berkeley DB uses to coordinate concurrent access to, and locking of, its databases. An environment is needed in *transactional* and *concurrent* modes, but not in *private* modes (see below).

Bind DLZ with the BDBHPT driver has excellent performance. This is achieved by not having to contact an external data repository (perhaps even on a remote host), thus eliminating all TCP/IP and UNIX socket communications overhead. As the BDB database API is

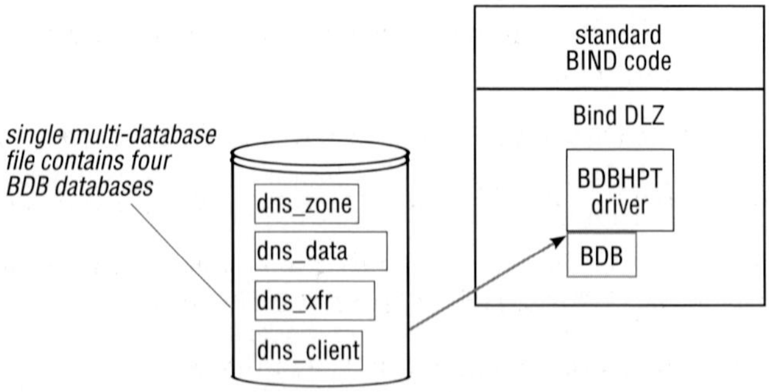

Figure 9.4: Bind DLZ BDBHPT driver

part of Bind DLZ's address space (Figure 9.4), the BDBHPT driver offers the highest possible performance without sacrificing the advantages of a transactional database.

Bind DLZ's BDBHPT driver is fast, but it is difficult to implement – you will need some programming experience. Before you start implementing it, you have to consider whether it will be worth your while:

- The first question that often arises is: why would *anyone* implement BDBHPT if they have to write code to do so?

  The answer is, that DLZ's BDBHPT driver is fast, and due to its BDB layer, dispenses with any communications overhead between the DNS server (Bind DLZ) and the backend database (Berkeley DB). Large organizations may have the human resources required to implement BDBHPT, but if you are a small organization, we cannot recommend you use it: it is simply too complex, and you'll be much happier using one of DLZ's other drivers.

- BDBHPT's use of Berkeley DB also leverages BDB's replication framework onto DLZ's databases, but this means writing even more (complex) code to implement such functionality. Here again, you will do this only if you have lots of experience and plenty of time at hand.

If you like programming, BDBHPT will whet your appetite, and we show you how to get started, now.

9.9.1 Configuring a BDBHPT zone

Bind DLZ's BDBHPT driver is easier to configure than most others: there is so little to configure. You create a BDBHPT zone using a `dlz` clause such as this, in your `named.conf` file:

```
dlz "our DNS data" {
    database "bdbhpt C /usr/local/dlz DLZ.db";
};
```

The `database` statement expects a single string surrounded by quotes and terminated with a semicolon, containing four parameters:

1. The keyword `bdbhpt` telling Bind DLZ to use the BDBHPT driver.
2. The operating mode of the BDBHPT driver, which we explain in a moment.
3. The name of the directory on disk containing the database environment, i.e. the directory in which Berkeley DB stores the files on the file system.
4. The name of the database as it is stored in the file system.

9.9.2 BDBHPT operating modes

A BDBHPT database has an *operating mode* which defines whether it should support transactions, whether file locking is to be used, etc. With a non-embedded database, you specify this sort of thing in a configuration file. However, as BDBHPT is embedded, you have to specify the mode in your program when you call the BDB function that creates the database. You do this by passing one or more flags to the create function. Once you've created the database, you have to tell BDBHPT which mode it should use when using the database you created. You do this by giving BDBHPT a single letter code in its `database` directive.

There are three modes of operation:

T Mode `T` is transactional and supports full transactional operation, including logging, locking and multiple simultaneous database writers. This functionality adds overhead, so this is the slowest of the three modes. The flags passed to Berkeley DB are:

```
DB_INIT_TXN | DB_INIT_MPOOL | DB_INIT_LOCK | DB_INIT_LOG | DB_CREATE
```

C Mode `C` is the concurrent mode, which allows multiple processes to simultaneously read and write to the database, but it does not support the commit or rollback features of transactional mode. This mode uses the flags:

```
DB_INIT_CDB | DB_INIT_MPOOL | DB_CREATE
```

P Mode `P` is the "private" mode. In private mode, only a single process may access the database, as there is no locking or transactional support. This mode offers the best performance for the BDBHPT driver, and it uses these flags:

```
DB_PRIVATE  | DB_INIT_MPOOL | DB_CREATE
```

When running in private mode, you cannot update the Berkeley DB file while Bind DLZ is using it. A good way around this is to make a copy of the Berkeley DB file to another location, update it, and then rename it atomically, replacing the original file. If you then restart named, it will open the new file: since Bind DLZ starts quickly, using private mode like this is reasonable if:

- You want to use Bind DLZ.
- You need the utmost in performance using a database back-end.
- You don't modify your zone data very often.

The Berkeley DB flags described above are Or-ed together by the BDBHPT driver, and you must pass the same combination of flags to the BDB functions you use in your custom programs when you create or update your database. In other words, when configuring DLZ you specify only the mode character (one of `T`, `C`, or `P`), and BDBHPT uses the corresponding flags when it invokes the appropriate Berkeley DB functions. So, for example, when you configure Bind DLZ with:

```
dlz "our DNS data" {
    database "bdbhpt C /usr/local/dlz DLZ.db";
};
```

DLZ's BDBHPT driver will open the file `DLZ.db` with the Berkeley DB flags set to:

```
DB_INIT_CDB | DB_INIT_MPOOL | DB_CREATE
```

9.9.3 Layout of the BDBHPT databases

The Berkeley DB database used by Bind DLZ with the BDBHPT driver is a single file on the file system, containing four internal databases called `dns_zone`, `dns_data`, `dns_xfr`, and `dns_client` (Figure 9.4, page 242).

The four internal databases contain carefully crafted keys and values, that consist of strings of text. As Berkeley DB does not offer a high-level query language such as SQL to access data in its databases, programs accessing them (in our case, it is DLZ with its BDBHPT driver) resort to direct keyed access using BDB functions. Now, let's look at each of these four databases in turn.

1. The `dns_zone` database.

   This Btree database contains the list of zones for the DNS data. The key is a reversed zone name (`zib.sppuq`) and the data is an empty string. In Perl, the appropriate hash[3] can be populated with:

   ```
   $DNSzone{'zib.sppuq' } = "";
   ```

   BDBHPT looks up this database in the same way that `findzone()` is used by the LDAP and MySQL drivers.

   When BIND calls DLZ, it must first determine which portion of the query is the zone name and which the host. A query received for a domain www.qupps.biz, could be for a zone qupps.biz or for biz, but it could also be for a zone called www.qupps.biz. As the initial portions of these strings are alphabetically quite different, looking up each of these keys would cause Berkeley DB to "move around" a lot in the database (seek from one disk block to a different one), which would reduce its effectiveness. BDBHPT avoids this by searching for reversed zone names: zib.sppuq, zib and zib.sppuq.www respectively.

   Done this way, the BDBHPT driver preserves "database locality" because these names sort almost identically, and are likely to occur within a single disk block within the database.

[3] A Perl hash creates one-to-one associations between a variable (key) and its value. Hash elements can be accessed only via their keys, and keys within a hash must be unique.

2. The `dns_data` database.

   The `dns_data` database contains all the resource records for a zone. It is used for lookup operations and outgoing zone transfers. For best performance, the underlying Berkeley DB database should be a Hash database with duplicates allowed on it.

   The key on this database is the name of the zone (not reversed this time) followed by a single space (" ") and the host name. The value is a textual representation of the DNS resource record. The exact format of the record is as follows (Table 9.3):

Order	Item	Description
1	*replication_id*	Unique alphanumeric ID for the record
2	*host*	DNS hostname
3	*ttl*	Time to live (must be a number)
4	*type*	DNS record type (A, SOA, NS)
5	*data*	Content of data

Table 9.3: Format of DNS records in BDBHPT

   (a) *replication_id* is a sequence of non-whitespace characters which uniquely identifies a record within the database. Although each record can have any value you desire for the *replication_id*, using non-unique values would make it impossible to identify a single record during update operations, so we could never change an existing record – we could only add new records. For example, if you have two A records in the database for host www, and both have the same *replication_id*, it is impossible to specify the one you want to update.

   For this reason, we recommend you have a unique *replication_id* on each record in order to allow a database management utility to identify a record. This value is mandatory, i.e. the BDBHPT driver expects something to be there, even if it isn't unique.

   (b) *host* is the domain name as described above. Use `@` for the name of the zone's apex.

   (c) *ttl* is the Time to Live in seconds. It must be a numeric string.

   (d) *type* is a string containing the DNS resource record type.

   (e) *data* contains the *rdata* of the DNS record, i.e. the right-hand side in a zone master file. For an MX resource, it includes a numeric priority and a host, for an A RR the IP address, for a CNAME just a domain name, etc.

For example, the data for qupps.biz can be set with a Perl hash as follows:

```
$DNSdata{"qupps.biz @"}    = "91 @ 10 SOA ns1.qupps.biz. jp.mens.de. 17 ↩
        18000 3600 64800 3 600";
$DNSdata{"qupps.biz @"}    = "92 @ 86400 NS ns1.qupps.biz.";
$DNSdata{"qupps.biz www"}  = "90 www 3600 A 192.168.1.164";
$DNSdata{"qupps.biz www"}  = "17 www 3600 MX 10 mail.isp.net.";
$DNSdata{"qupps.biz ldap"} = "99 ldap 3600 A 192.168.1.20";
```

BDBHPT looks up this database in the same way that the MySQL and LDAP drivers use the `lookup()` query.

3. The `dns_xfr` database.

   When performing an outgoing zone transfer for a particular zone, qupps.biz say, Bind DLZ has to retrieve all DNS records for that zone, i.e. search for records with key beginning "`qupps.biz`*space*". However, Berkeley DB does not support searching by sub-strings like this, so therefore the `dns_data` database, which contains keys like "`qupps.biz www`"cannot be used for zone transfers. BDBHPT solves this problem by adding another database, `dns_xfr`. This uses the zone name as key and the host name as value. Note that, here again, the host name of the zone apex is symbolized by an "at" character (`@`).

   ```
   $DNSaxfr{'qupps.biz'} = '@';
   $DNSaxfr{'qupps.biz'} = "www";
   $DNSaxfr{'qupps.biz'} = "ldap";
   ```

   An outgoing zone transfer works as follows: the BDBHPT driver searches the queried zone name in the `dns_xfr` database and enumerates all unique host names. Then, for each host found, the driver queries the `dns_data` database for the actual data which it returns in the zone transfer.

   It is quite possible (deliberately or by mistake) to provide a zone transfer with DNS records missing, by not including the respective zone/host pair in `dns_xfr` for a specific DNS resource.

   The `dns_data` and `dns_xfr` databases together implement the equivalent of what the `allnodes()` function does for the LDAP and SQL drivers.

4. The `dns_client` database.

   This database specifies which clients may transfer which zones. The database key is the zone name, and the record values are string representations of IP addresses; a zone/IP combination must be unique.

   ```
   $DNSclient{'qupps.biz'} = '127.0.0.1';
   $DNSclient{'qupps.biz'} = '192.168.1.20';
   $DNSclient{'example.net'} = '127.0.0.1';
   ```

   BDBHPT looks up this database in the same way that the MySQL and LDAP drivers use the `allowzonexfr()` query.

That completes our discussion of the Berkeley DB databases used by DLZ's BDBHPT driver, and you might want to take a breather before we continue with a discussion of how you actually enter data into these databases.

9.9.4 Creating your BDBHPT database

There is no special utility that you use to create your BDBHPT databases, because that is part of the Berkeley DB API. So the programs you use to manipulate data in your BDBHPT databases (see next section) will create the necessary files for you.

9.9.5 Manipulating data in the BDBHPT databases: dlzdb-util

How do you get the data into the database? Good question. Bind DLZ doesn't provide a utility for doing that, so we have to roll our own or use one created by somebody else.

- In Section 9.9.6 we give you some pointers on how to manage your DNS data in an SQL database, and how you could provision your Berkeley DB databases from an SQL database.

  People who use BDBHPT are usually willing to spend the necessary time creating utilities adapted to their specific environment. We have done a bit of that work for you, and have created a small example, with a program that reads and dumps the content of an SQL database into a Berkeley DB database ready to be used by DLZ's BDBHPT driver. We discuss the program in Appendix D.

- In the remainder of this section we cover dlzdb-util, which is a good starting point if you're developing your own tools to update BDB databases.

dlzdb-util is a Perl script, written by Jorgen Lundman. After downloading it, configure the database filename and path at the top of the script. You can add a new zone (by adding the necessary SOA, NS and A records) from the command line by invoking the script to create appropriate SOA, NS and A records in the database. (See the program's documentation for a description of its options.)

```
$ dlzdb-util -a -z example.net -t SOA -S 1 -F 10800 -R 900 \
          -E 608400 -T 86400 -H hostmaster.example.net. -N ns1.example.net.
Creating SOA for example.net...

$ dlzdb-util  -a -z example.net -t NS -n '@' -v ns1.example.net.
add [example.net @] [2 @ 86400 NS ns1.example.net.]

$ dlzdb-util -a -z example.net -t A -n ns1 -v 192.168.1.20
add [example.net ns1] [1 ns1 86400 A 192.168.1.20]

$ dlzdb-util -a -z example.net -t A -n www -v 192.168.1.164
add [example.net www] [1 www 86400 A 192.168.1.164]
```

To see what the database contains for a zone, use:

```
$ dlzdb-util  -s -z example.net
status for domain example.net
dns_zone: [ten.elpmaxe]
dns_client: [example.net] [127.0.0.1]
dns_xfr: [example.net] [ns1]
dns_data: [example.net ns1] [1 ns1 86400 A 192.168.1.20]
dns_xfr: [example.net] [www]
dns_data: [example.net www] [1 www 86400 A 192.168.1.164]
dns_data: [example.net @] [1 @ 86400 SOA ns1.example.net. ↩
            hostmaster.example.net. 1 10800 900 608400 86400]
dns_data: [example.net @] [2 @ 86400 NS ns1.example.net.]
```

dlzdb-util is available at `http://www.lundman.net/wiki/index.php/DLZUtil` and it uses BDBHPT in concurrent (C) mode by default, but you can change the Berkeley DB flags in the program to suit your needs.

9.9.6 Pushing DNS records into a BDBHPT database

Instead of fiddling around with inserting individual records into Berkeley DB databases, you can take a different route: store your DNS data in a stand-alone SQL database or in an LDAP directory (the provisioning server), write a program to read the zone data from SQL/LDAP, and then automatically generate the necessary database files for Berkeley DB. This means you don't have to write a user interface to maintain the data in Berkeley DB, and it's a good approach especially if you already have a Web-based GUI or other management utilities with which you add DNS records to the SQL/LDAP database. The downside to provisioning of back-end databases with such a technology is of course the delay that occurs between updating a DNS record and its availability on the satellite servers. Most users of DLZ's BDBHPT driver do it as above; unfortunately, we are not aware of "ready to use" programs you can download and start using.

With a bit of programming skill, you can stack a layer of code on top of the the programs you use to provision your database, ensuring that updates are written to a BDBHPT database used by Bind DLZ. There are two implementation techniques you can choose from:

pull Have DLZ's BDBHPT server *poll* the provisioning server periodically, to determine whether any updates to the database have been made, and if so, read the modifications, and update the Berkeley DB databases accordingly.

The disadvantages of this approach are:

- If you poll frequently, you consume resources on both the Bind DLZ machines and the provisioning system, even if there are no changes.
- If you poll only at long intervals, you lose much of the benefit of DLZ's dynamic nature, because it will be a long time before updates reach Bind DLZ.

push Modify the software that you use to add, modify and delete the zone data on your SQL/LDAP system, so that when it makes a modification, it automatically triggers a *push* to the satellite Bind DLZ machines and causes appropriate updates to the Berkeley DB databases. This approach is the most dynamic – your live server data is updated almost instantly. The downside is that if one or more of the Bind DLZ satellites is unreachable, you have to queue updates and distribute them at a later time.

9.9.7 Replication with Berkeley DB

If you have several peer Bind DLZ servers on separate machines, all using the BDBHPT driver, how do you replicate the same data to each server? You can use two different methods:

1. BDB databases are files on a file system. As long as no process has the database open for writing, the file can be transported to a remote location by your preferred means of file synchronization (rsync, etc.). This method is suitable where changes to the database are infrequent.

2. BDB supports a "single master" replication strategy. You update the data only on a single, master, database. Then, using code you've written, you instruct the master to

replicate the updated data to multiple read-only replicas (Figure 9.5). Berkeley DB transmits transactional log records to its replicas, so the application must be transactional in nature (i.e. BDBHPT `T` mode). Note again, that Bind DLZ is not responsible for Berkeley DB replication, as it just *reads* the database. If you want replication in your BDB databases, you must provide replication support in the programs that you write to manipulate the data in the databases.

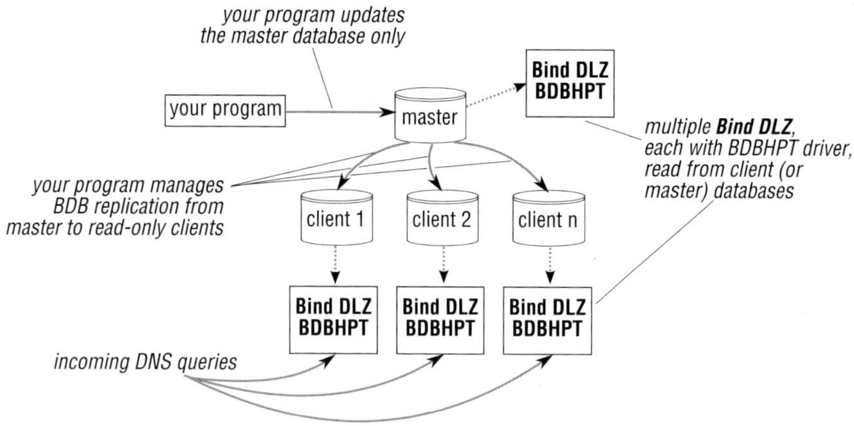

Figure 9.5: Using BDB's single-master replication in your program

9.9.8 Zoned: the BDBHPT replicator

Zoned, by William Ahern, is a package that provides replication for a BDBHPT zone in Bind DLZ (Figure 9.6). Zoned manages the Berkeley DB database and uses the Berkeley DB Replication Base API to provide high availability and load distribution. Zoned basically builds a cluster of nodes (i.e. machines) on which you provide Bind DLZ servers that use the Berkeley DB databases. Zoned includes the Zoned replication manager, the zonectl utility for managing server nodes and editing DNS resource records, and a Perl module called Zoned.

Zoned and Berkeley DB manage the cluster autonomously, handling the necessary messaging and the routing of zone updates to the master node (updates are contained in messages and they have to be directed to individual nodes). Replication is managed by Zoned and the underlying Berkeley DB API. Nodes are "found" with the help of Service (SRV) records.

You manage all changes to DNS zone data through one of the nodes controlled by Zoned. To add or modify a resource record, you either use the zonectl utility, or you write an application which uses the supplied Perl module. You can also build your own tools for interacting with Zoned; the *ASN.1* message schema definition is provided, defining the communications protocol for interacting with the nodes in a cluster.

Zoned is an interesting set of tools and you should look closely at it if you intend to deploy Bind DLZ with BDBHPT (see `http://25thandclement.com/~william/projects/`

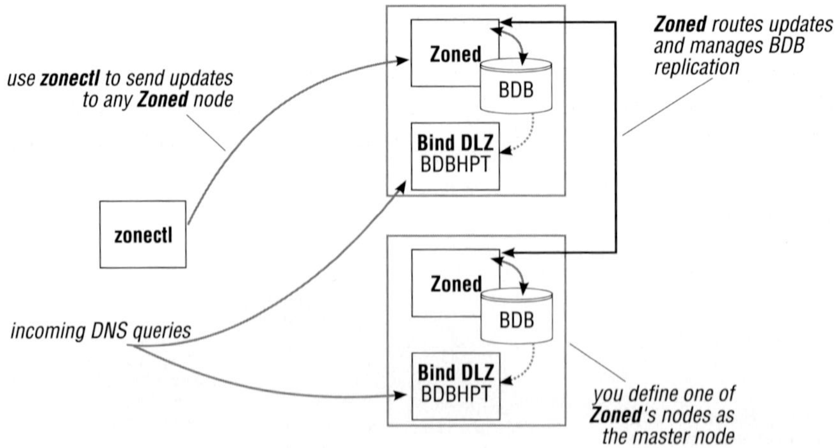

Figure 9.6: Zoned architecture

zoned.html).

That concludes our explanation of the individual Bind DLZ back-end drivers. In the next section we cover common Bind DLZ deployment scenarios.

9.10 Implementing Bind DLZ

9.10.1 Split-horizon DNS with views in Bind DLZ

In Chapter 7 we discussed how you can create "views" in BIND to give you different perspectives on a zone's content, based on the network location of the querying client. You can also use BIND views with Bind DLZ.

You implement views in Bind DLZ the same way as in a vanilla BIND configuration; the difference lies in the source of your zones. Whereas in BIND you load zones from master files and include a `zone` clause in a view definition, Bind DLZ finds zones in one of its back-end databases, so you include a `dlz` clause in a view definition. The general syntax for defining views in your `named.conf` for Bind DLZ is thus:

```
view "name1" {
    dlz "driver-a" { ... };
};
view "name2" {
    dlz "driver-b" { ... };
};
```

An example: two views with different Bind DLZ drivers

In the example that follows, we implement Bind DLZ with two views:

- A view called `inside` which uses the LDAP driver. This view is used when the address of the querying client is in the `trusted` ACL.

- A view called `outside` which uses the MySQL driver.

(You do not have to use two different drivers when implementing views in Bind DLZ; we simply illustrate that it is possible. And in the next section we show how you can use the same driver in both views.) In your `named.conf` define the views with their respective `dlz` clauses:

```
acl "trusted" {
   127.0.0.1;
   192.168.1.20/32;
};
options {
        directory ".";
        listen-on { 127.0.0.1; 192.168.1.164; };
};

view "inside" IN {
   match-clients { "trusted"; };
   dlz "ldap-minimal" {
     database "ldap 1
     v3 simple {} {} {127.0.0.1}
     {ldap:///ou=$zone$,ou=dlz-demo,o=dns?cn?sub?(objectclass=RR)}
     {ldap:///cn=$record$,ou=$zone$,ou=dlz-demo,o=dns?RRttl,↩
                        RRtype,RRdata?sub?(objectclass=RR)}
     {}
     {ldap:///ou=$zone$,ou=dlz-demo,o=dns?RRttl,RRtype,cn,RRdata↩
                        ?sub?(objectclass=RR)}
     {ldap:///cn=@,ou=$zone$,ou=dlz-demo,o=dns?description=$client$?↩
                        sub?↩(objectclass=RR)}";
   };
};

view "outside" IN {
   match-clients { any; };
   dlz "mysqlzone" {
     database "mysql
     {host=localhost dbname=dlz ssl=false}
     {SELECT zone FROM dns_records WHERE zone = '$zone$'}
     {SELECT ttl, type, mx_priority, CASE WHEN lower(type)='txt'↩
                         THEN concat('"', data, '"')
        WHEN lower(type) = 'soa' THEN concat_ws(' ', data, resp_person,↩
            serial,refresh, retry, expire, minimum)
        ELSE data END FROM dns_records WHERE zone = '$zone$' ↩
            AND host = '$record$'}
     {}
     {SELECT ttl, type, host, mx_priority, case when lower(type)='txt' THEN
         concat('"', data, '"') ELSE data END, resp_person, serial,↩
            refresh, retry,↩
                          expire, minimum FROM dns_records WHERE zone = '$zone$'}
     {SELECT zone FROM xfr_table WHERE zone = '$zone$' AND client = '$client$'}
     {INSERT INTO hits (zone) VALUES ('$zone$') ON DUPLICATE KEY UPDATE↩
                     nr = nr + 1}";
   };
};
```

Note:

- The `database` statements within the `dlz` clause *must* be on a single line. (They are shown wrapped here to fit on the page.)

- The configuration provides two views:

inside This uses the LDAP driver to provide answers to DNS queries. A client that matches the `trusted` ACL sees the following:

```
$ dig @192.168.1.164 www.qupps.net
;; ANSWER SECTION:
www.qupps.net.          3600    IN A        127.0.0.1

;; AUTHORITY SECTION:
qupps.net.              3600    IN NS       ns.qupps.net.
```

outside The `outside` view uses the MySQL driver to provide answers to DNS queries from "any other" clients. These clients see the following, when querying the *same* name server:

```
$ dig @192.168.1.164 www.qupps.net
;; ANSWER SECTION:
www.qupps.net.          86400   IN A        192.168.1.20

;; AUTHORITY SECTION:
qupps.net.              86400   IN NS       dns.qupps.net.
qupps.net.              86400   IN NS       ns.qupps.net.
```

- We recommend you initially launch named with debugging enabled (see Notes) in order to watch the queries being performed by the Bind DLZ drivers.

Using similar Bind DLZ drivers in views

You can configure split horizon with BIND views with identical DLZ drivers. To implement this, the drivers in your `dlz` sections must access separate resources:

- For the LDAP driver, you can use different search bases, or expand your filters to include an additional attribute type. So, on the `outside` view, specify a search base `ou=public-dns,o=qupps.biz`, but on the `inside` view, specify a different search base: `ou=private-dlz,o=qupps.biz`.

  Another way to implement this, if want to avoid different search bases, is to extend your schema with a multi-valued type that indicates whether a specific entry is "private" and/or "public". You then add the attribute type to the LDAP query filters, to select only the entries for a particular view. For example, the filter for the private view might be:

```
ldap:///ou=$zone$,o=dns?cn?sub?(&(view=private)(objectclass=RR))
```

  with, of course, a different filter on the `public` view, for its DLZ LDAP driver. (Don't forget to add an index to the attribute type you use on the LDAP server, for performance reasons.)

- For the SQL drivers, you can use separate databases, different tables, or even expand the SQL queries, by adding conditions:

```
... WHERE ... AND view = 'public';
```

- If you use the BDBHPT driver, you specify different databases to use.

9.10.2 Don't create a single point of failure

If you have two Bind DLZ installations (i.e. two distinct name servers) that use a single back-end database server, then you have a single point of failure, which is risky. If your database server goes down, both your name servers stop answering queries, and die. You also halve the possible throughput of the name servers, as the single back-end database has to share the load of two name servers hitting it with queries.

Never *ever* do that; one Bind DLZ name server gets exactly one back-end database server. (There is no point in giving one Bind DLZ two back-end servers, because Bind DLZ does not have fail over capabilities built in to it.) The back-end server should preferably be on the same machine as DLZ, to minimize both the communications overhead and latency incurred by talking to a remote host. If the back-end database goes away temporarily, Bind DLZ will attempt to reconnect to it (as long as it's using the PostgreSQL, MySQL or LDAP driver; this doesn't apply to the BDBHPT driver).

However, what *is* of course possible, is to have a couple of back-end database servers – either behind a load balancer or carefully managed with heartbeat (see Notes) – ensuring that the cluster always represents a "single" instance. The whole cluster appears to Bind DLZ as a single back-end database, but you have added resilience.

9.10.3 High-availability through heterogeneous replication

The highest availability is probably attained by using heterogeneous database replication to replicate data from an LDAP directory server or an SQL database directly to an BDBHPT database which is local to the Bind DLZ name servers (Figure 9.7). It also performs well, because it saves on the communications overhead between Bind DLZ and its database. This setup offers the highest level of resilience as it allows the SQL database or the LDAP directory server to be unavailable for maintenance, for example, without affecting your Bind DLZ name servers. Note that you would have to implement such a system yourself, and that it involves a lot of programming.

9.10.4 Automatically creating PTR records

No matter which back-end you use with Bind DLZ, you will probably be providing both forward (name-to-address) and reverse (address-to-name) lookups for your clients. If so, automatically creating reverse (PTR) resource records whenever you create an A record is very convenient. Below we show you how you can do this using the MySQL driver as an example. This requires a few custom MySQL functions and a database trigger. We have tested this with MySQL version 5.0.45.

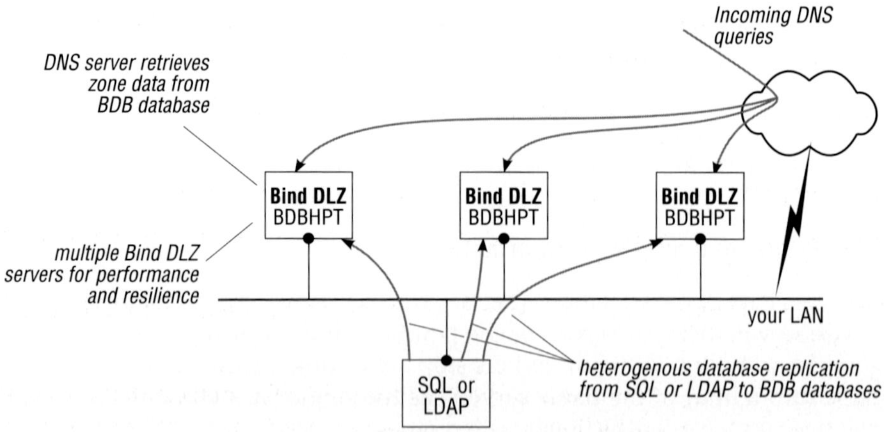

Figure 9.7: Heterogeneous replication for Bind DLZ

We want to detect when an Address record (A) is inserted into the database table, and trigger another `INSERT` to enter the corresponding PTR record. There are two problems:

- MySQL doesn't permit an `INSERT` to trigger another `INSERT` on the same table.
- We have to write a lot of MySQL functions to implement our automatic PTR records.

Our solution uses two database tables and a database view:

1. The database table provided by Bind DLZ is called `dns_records`. We continue to use this table in unmodified form, and it is into this table that we enter DNS resource records (SOA, NS, A, etc.). When an A record is inserted, the insertion triggers the insertion of a PTR record into the second table.
2. The second database table is called `dns_ptrrecords` and is created with the same schema as the `dns_records` table.
3. A database view in the MySQL database, which is a union of both tables above:

   ```
   CREATE VIEW vdns AS
     SELECT * from dns_records
     UNION
     SELECT * from dns_ptrrecords;
   ```

   It is via this view that Bind DLZ reads records with its `SELECT` statements. The `UNION` causes the two database tables to appear as one, when selecting records from the view. In the `dlz` clause of `named.conf` you configure Bind DLZ to query this view:

   ```
   dlz "our dns data" {
    database "mysql
    {host=127.0.0.1 dbname=dlzdns ssl=false}
    {SELECT zone FROM vdns WHERE zone = '$zone$'}
    ...
    ...
   ```

Configured like this, Bind DLZ reads data from the `vdns` view and so it sees whatever is in the `dns_records` and in the `dns_ptrrecords` tables.

4. You then create three helper functions (the code for these MySQL functions is in Section D.2 on page 619):
   (a) `revip4()` takes a dotted-decimal IPv4 address and reverses it.
   (b) `ip4octet()` uses MySQL's `inet_aton()` function to return the rightmost octet of an IPv4 address.
   (c) `inarpa4()` uses `revip4()` to return the in-addr.arpa zone for a dotted-decimal IPv4 address.
5. The trigger on the `dns_records` table fires when MySQL detects that an `INSERT` has succeeded. It uses the functions defined above to insert a new record of type PTR into the `dns_ptrrecords` table.

Listing 9.1: MySQL trigger copies records in Bind DLZ

```
-- automatic insert of 'PTR' when an 'A' is inserted (JPM)

DELIMITER $$
CREATE TRIGGER dlz_dns_ptrrecords AFTER INSERT ON dns_records
FOR EACH ROW BEGIN
  IF (NEW.type = 'A') THEN
     -- data *must* contain an IPv4 Address
     INSERT INTO dns_ptrrecords (zone, host, ttl, type, data)
        VALUES (
           inarpa4(NEW.data),         -- 1.168.192.in-addr.arpa
           ip4octet(NEW.data),        -- 4
           NEW.ttl,                   -- copy ttl
           'PTR',                     -- PTR
           CONCAT_WS('.', NEW.host, CONCAT(NEW.zone, '.'))
         );
  END IF;
END $$
DELIMITER ;
```

That completes the preparations on the database tables and the data dictionary. Now we show you what happens when we use this.

If we start off with empty database tables, when we list all A and PTR records:

```
mysql> SELECT zone,host,ttl,type,data FROM vdns WHERE type IN ('A', 'PTR');
```

we get nothing, as expected. If we insert a new Address record:

```
mysql> INSERT INTO dns_records (zone,host,ttl,type,data)
             VALUES ('qupps.biz', 'w4', 60, 'A', '192.168.1.4');
Query OK, 1 row affected (0.00 sec)
```

what does the view now show?

```
mysql> SELECT zone,host,ttl,type,data FROM vdns WHERE type IN ('A', 'PTR');
+-----------------------+------+------+------+---------------+
| zone                  | host | ttl  | type | data          |
+-----------------------+------+------+------+---------------+
| qupps.biz             | w4   |   60 | A    | 192.168.1.4   |
| 1.168.192.in-addr.arpa | 4   |   60 | PTR  | w4.qupps.biz. |
+-----------------------+------+------+------+---------------+
2 rows in set (0.01 sec)
```

The database contains one A record and one PTR, as expected. A DNS query for the inverse of the record we just added shows:

```
$ dig @127.0.0.1 -x 192.168.1.4

;; ANSWER SECTION:
4.1.168.192.in-addr.arpa. 60    IN    PTR w4.qupps.biz.
```

This is a very useful addition to the database schema and a great time-saver.

9.11 How you can process Dynamic DNS Updates

While BIND supports Dynamic DNS Updates, you cannot have a Bind DLZ-managed zone receive updates, because the APIs support only reading *from* the back-end databases, and don't include any functions to allow DLZ to write *to* the back-end. There are, however, certain things you *can* implement:

- While DLZ zones can't process Dynamic DNS Updates, any other zone master files in the same BIND instance can, of course.
- If you want to have the updated DNS records in a database, you can write a program to periodically parse the zone master files and update Bind DLZ's back-end database, performing additions, modifications and deletions as required.
- You can set up a MyDNS (Chapter 5) name server that receives the dynamic DNS updates into its own PostgreSQL or MySQL database, and trigger updates into tables you use with Bind DLZ. For this to work, specify the MyDNS server as your primary name server. (The MNAME field in the SOA must point to the MyDNS name server for it to receive the updates.)

Summary

- The DLZ add-on enables BIND to maintain zones in databases – SQL databases, LDAP directory servers, Berkeley DB databases, ODBC connections and even from file systems.
- Bind DLZ does not restrict BIND's functionality; it augments it. You can have zone master files and DLZ zones in a single instance of named.
- DLZ is dynamic – it serves new zones and resource records without you having to reconfigure BIND.
- DLZ allows you to provide all sorts of zones, even from different databases, in a single instance of BIND.
- Some of the Bind DLZ drivers allow you to configure the schema used, enabling you to adapt Bind DLZ to your existing data infrastructure.
- BDBHPT is very fast, but non-trivial to implement.

Related topics

- BIND SDB (Chapter 8) will interest you if you need to create a back-end that answers queries from any data source you want. (Don't forget however, that Bind DLZ has an API you can use as well.)
- If you need a name server that can act as a slave server and provision its back-end database via zone transfers, consider PowerDNS (Chapter 6).

Notes and further reading

Downloading Bind DLZ

Bind DLZ's home and documentation are at `http://bind-dlz.sourceforge.net/`, but you download Bind DLZ itself from the Internet Software Consortium (ISC), as it has been incorporated into the BIND distribution (see `http://www.isc.org/sw/bind/`).

Building DLZ

Broadly, you build Bind DLZ the same way as you build BIND, but you supply options to its configure program to link in the necessary Bind DLZ drivers. A typical build will look like this:

```
$ wget ftp://ftp.isc.org/isc/bind9/cur/9.4/bind-9.4.2.tar.gz
$ tar xvzf bind-9.4.2.tar.gz
$ cd bind-9.4.2
$ ./configure --prefix=/usr/local ...
```

and the extra configure options you need for the various drivers are as follows:

MySQL To build MySQL support into Bind DLZ:

```
$ export CFLAGS='-I/usr/include/mysql'
$ export LDFLAGS='-L/usr/lib64/mysql'
$ ./configure ... --enable-threads=no --with-dlz-mysql
```

Note that Bind DLZ must run with only a single thread when using the MySQL driver, due to a limitation in the MySQL API.

LDAP Before building the LDAP driver into Bind DLZ, apply our small patch which modifies the token names used in LDAP URLs (see below):

```
$ patch -p1 < bind-dlz-patch-ldap-url.patch
```

If you want to add the LDAP driver to Bind DLZ, use the additional flags:

```
$ ./configure ... --enable-threads=yes \
      --with-dlz-ldap=/opt/symas \
      --with-openssl=/opt/symas
```

BDBHPT To build the BDBHPT driver, add the following switches to configure:

```
$ ./configure ... --enable-threads=yes --with-dlz-bdb
```

Launching named

After you build Bind DLZ and configure one or more of its back-ends, we recommend you initially launch named as we do below. This tells it to remain in the foreground (i.e. not run as a background daemon), force all logging to standard error, create a single thread, and set its debug level to 1.

```
# /usr/local/sbin/named -g -n 1 -d 1 -c named.conf

starting BIND 9.4.2 -n 1 -g -d 1 -c named.conf
found 2 CPUs, using 1 worker thread
loading configuration from '/usr/local/etc/named/named.conf'
listening on IPv4 interface lo, 127.0.0.1#53
Loading 'ldapzones' using driver ldap
LDAP driver running multithreaded
command channel listening on 127.0.0.1#953
ignoring config file logging statement due to -g option
load_configuration: success
...
```

Run like this, Bind DLZ prints (to stderr) the queries it sends to the back-end database servers, so you can observe what it is doing.

Patching token names in the drivers

The Bind DLZ drivers use the percent sign (`%`) in the tokens of the `dlz` clause (e.g. `%zone%`). The percent sign collides with its use as a hex prefix in LDAP URLs in newer versions of OpenLDAP (e.g. `%20` specifies a space). We propose a two-line change to `sdlz_helper.c` to solve the problem; it changes the token notation (`%zone%` et.al.) to `$zone$` which ought to be safe enough for the time being. Note that this modifies the tokens for all drivers that use them. (Download the patch from the Web site (☞ D096).)

Listing 9.2: Patch to Bind DLZ changes tokens

```
--- bind-9.4.2/contrib/dlz/drivers/sdlz_helper.c.orig
+++ bind-9.4.2/contrib/dlz/drivers/sdlz_helper.c
@@ -166,12 +166,12 @@
                ISC_LIST_APPEND(*tql, tseg, link);

                /*
-                * split string at the first "%". set query segment to
+                * split string at the first "$". set query segment to
                 * left portion
                 */
                tseg->sql = isc_mem_strdup(mctx,
                                isc_string_separate(&right_str,
-                                                       "%"));
+                                                       "$"));
                if (tseg->sql == NULL) {
                        /* no memory, clean everything up. */
                        result = ISC_R_NOMEMORY;
```

Berkeley DB

- The Berkeley DB (BDB) project started at the University of California in Berkeley and has since been integrated into Oracle's product suite. (See `http://www.oracle.com/technology/products/berkeley-db/index.html`)
- We recommend *The Berkeley DB Book*, by Himanshu Yadava, published by Apress. It is a practical guide to the intricacies and programming of Berkeley DB, and it discusses its fault tolerant and high-availability frameworks.

Heartbeat

The heartbeat program is one of the core components of the Linux High Availability project. It provides sophisticated high-availability (fail-over) capabilities to machines you define. It provides monitoring of cluster nodes and applications. When a fault occurs – for example a machine becomes unreachable – your user-supplied rules are followed to provide the desired resource placement in the cluster. heartbeat lives at `http://linux-ha.org/`.

sheerdns

sheerdns, written by Paul Sheer, is a simple DNS server that stores resource records in the file system, similar to Bind DLZ's File System driver. It keeps each resource record in a separate file (e.g. `/var/sheerdns/`*XX*`/www.qupps.biz/`*query-type*), where *XX* is the hashed domain name. Consequently, updates are immediate: the program doesn't have to be restarted or reloaded. When sheerdns receives a query, it checks whether the file exists and serves up its content. To speed up processing, sheerdns hashes domain names into subdirectories. sheerdns is well suited for embedding into specialized applications; for example, if you want to implement a Web site that serves dynamic DNS, as we discuss in Section 19.8, then sheerdns is a good solution. The project's home is at `threading.2038bug.com/sheerdns/`.

Related projects

- Cisco Sytems has incorporated Bind DLZ into at least one of its products (see `http://tinyurl.com/2zg6yg`).

Chapter

10 Name Server Daemon (NSD)

The Domain Name Server (DNS) is the Achilles heel of the Web. The important thing is that it's managed responsibly.

Tim Berners-Lee

Introduction

The Name Server Daemon is a very fast authoritative-only name server. It can act as a master, slave, or root name server.

NSD is the Name Server Daemon. It was developed in cooperation with the RIPE NCC by NLnet Labs of Amsterdam[1]. NSD uses master zone files (the same files as those used by BIND). You compile these into a binary database using NSD's zone compiler. Pre-compiling zone data lets NSD start up very quickly. NSD evolved out of a server designed to power the K.ROOT-SERVERS.NET installation. The H-ROOT-SERVERS.NET, K-ROOT-SERVERS.NET L-ROOT-SERVERS.NET backbones, and several top-level domains (e.g. Sweden) use NSD.

Pros	•	Very fast authoritative-only name server
	•	Supports DNS security (TSIG and DNSSEC)
	•	Produces BIND-compatible statistics for monitoring usage
	•	Zone compiler catches errors before daemon starts
	•	Good documentation in manual pages
Cons	○	No RFC 2136 Dynamic DNS
Scenarios		Very large environments that need maximum performance.

Table 10.1: NSD at a glance

NSD is authoritative only, i.e. it will not answer queries for which it isn't responsible. It cannot act as a caching or recursive server. NSD can be set up as a master name server and as a slave name server. We discuss version 3 of NSD.

10.1 Overview of NSD

10.1.1 NSD's architecture

The name server nsd serves DNS records from an intermediate database, not directly from its zone master files. The database, usually called `nsd.db`, is created from the zone master files by the zone compiler zonec (Figure 10.1) – all zone files must be "compiled" before nsd can serve them. This has the following advantages:

- Errors in zone files are caught by the zone compiler (zonec). Syntax errors in zone master files cannot cause the main daemon (nsd) to fail upon startup.

- The main server (nsd) does not have to check syntax of the zone files on startup; this greatly reduces NSD's startup time.

- Large portions of the database are in "wire format". This speeds up NSD's operation, as it doesn't have to perform these conversions at run-time.

NSD stores incoming zone transfers (AXFR or IXFR) into a temporary journal file from which it also serves the modified zone data – if the "newer" data is in the journal file, NSD serves it from that, otherwise from its database. You periodically invoke a program (via cron) to

[1] NLnet Labs promotes open source and open standards and is an expertise centre in the area of DNS and DNSSEC (see `http://www.nlnetlabs.nl/`).

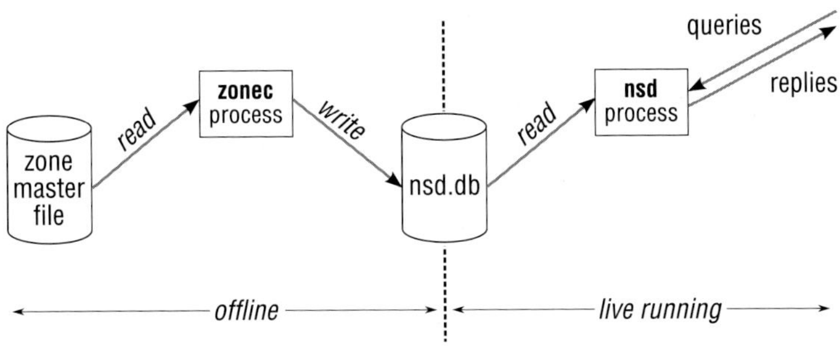

Figure 10.1: NSD's database: offline and live-running

"patch" (i.e. merge) the records from the journal file (called `ixfr.db`) into the respective zone master files, and when the patch completes, the journal file is removed (until it is re-created on the next incoming zone transfer) (Figure 10.2). In other words, NSD always serves the correct data: the data is retrieved either from the `nsd.db` database or, if it is newer, from the journal file. After merging the journal file back into the zone master files, the journal file no longer exists.

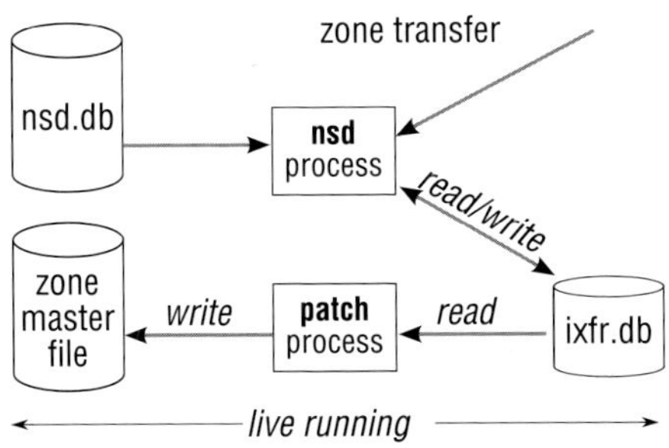

Figure 10.2: How NSD processes incoming zone transfers

10.1.2 Setting up NSD

Setting up the Name Server Daemon is straightforward:

- Install the software (see Notes).
- Create NSD's configuration file, `nsd.conf`. An easy way to do this is to adapt the sample configuration that is installed as part of the installation procedure.
- If you are setting up a master name server, create your zone files.
- Launch NSD.

10.1.3 A minimal configuration file

The file `nsd.conf` contains configuration directives for the server and lists the zones you intend to serve. A very small `nsd.conf` might contain:

```
server:
  ip-address: 192.168.1.164

zone:
  name: "qupps.biz"
  zonefile: "qupps.biz"
```

We discuss the configuration file in detail in Section 10.2. The file `qupps.biz` containing the resource records for the zone qupps.biz in this example, is in zone master file syntax (Section 2.4).

10.1.4 Compile your zones

You have to compile zone master files for NSD. The zone compiler (zonec) performs syntax checks on the zone master files and, if the file is valid, adds a compiled form of the zone to NSD's database (`nsd.db`). What the zone compiler effectively does is:

- Reads the entire zone into main memory.
- Checks the syntax of resource records, verifies that CNAME are used legitimately, etc.
- Compiles the records into sets of resource records (RRsets).
- Prepares answers to CNAME queries.
- Stores everything in a database on the file system.

All compiled zones are in a single database, for which the domain name and the resource record type are the key.

Instead of invoking zonec manually, we recommend you use the nsdc script to rebuild the zones that need compiling, because it processes all zones configured in `nsd.conf`, without you having to remember which zones need compiling. For example:

```
$ nsdc rebuild
zonec: reading zone "qupps.biz".
zonec: processed 30 RRs in "qupps.biz".

zonec: done with 0 errors.
```

10.1.5 Launch NSD

You start NSD by launching the nsd daemon. We recommend you do this via the the nsdc program, as it performs sanity checks on your `nsd.conf`:

```
# nsdc start
```

Even with many thousands of zones, NSD is up and available to answer queries after just a few seconds.

That completes our overview of NSD and its architecture. In the next two sections, we describe the configuration in detail.

10.2 Configuring NSD with its `nsd.conf` file

`nsd.conf` is NSD's configuration file. Empty lines in the file are ignored, as is whitespace at the beginning of a line. A comment starts with a hash (#) symbol and extends to the end of the line. The file is split into three clauses or sections:

a. Server options which define global options for the NSD server.

b. Zone options.

c. Key declarations.

Each of these sections consist of *attribute / value* pairs. You configure an attribute and its value by separating them with a colon and whitespace. You can include the content of additional files at any point within `nsd.conf` with the include directive, which takes a single filename as argument. Note that the filename can be in double quotes.

```
include: "my-zones.inc"
```

After you modify `nsd.conf`, we recommend you use nsd-checkconf to ensure the file is free from syntax errors (Section 10.3).

a. Server options

The syntax for this clause is:

```
server:
    attrib-1: value-1
    attrib-2: value-2
    ...
```

This clause defines global options for the NSD server. Some of these may be overridden by command-line options when launching nsd. The more interesting options are:

ip-address — The IP address (IPv4 or IPv6) that nsd should listen on. You can specify this option more than once, to have nsd listen on more than one address. If you don't specify this option, nsd binds to all the machine's interfaces.

database — The database that nsd should use for serving zone data. The default is `/var/db/nsd/nsd.db`.

logfile — nsd should log messages to this file. The default is to log to both syslog and to standard error output (stderr).

server-count — The number of copies of the NSD server to start. This defaults to 1. We recommend you start one NSD server for each CPU on the host.

statistics — If NSD was built with the `--enable-bind8-stats` switch, it can log statistics. This option determines how often it should do so. If the option is not present, no statistics will be logged; otherwise, this specifies the frequency as a number of seconds (see Section 10.4).

chroot — If this option is specified, the server should `chroot()` into this directory on startup.

username — If this option is specified, NSD should switch to the specified username on startup, so it no longer runs with root privileges.

zonesdir — Change the working directory to the specified directory before accessing zone files. Also, nsd will access its *pid* file, database file and log files relative to this path. Set the value of zonesdir to the empty string ("") to disable a change of working directory.

difffile — When NSD receives updates via incoming zone transfers, it should store them in this journal file. It contains the differences between the compiled `nsd.db` database and the latest zone version. The default filename is `/var/db/nsd/ixfr.db`. You use the `patch` command of the nsdc program to convert the journal file to zone files (Section 10.3).

identity — Sets the *string* to be returned when the server is queried for id.server in the Chaosnet class. (Default is the machine's hostname.) For example, setting:

```
identity: "go.away"
```

results in the following answer:

```
$ dig @192.168.1.20  +short id.server ch txt
"go.away"
```

hide-version — Prevents NSD from replying with the version string on Chaosnet class queries. (Default: no.) If you don't hide the version, anybody can query NSD's version number using version.bind or version.server:

```
$ dig @192.168.1.20 +short version.server ch txt
"NSD 3.1.0"
```

b. Zone options

Every zone served by NSD must have its own zone clause. The syntax for zone clauses is:

```
zone:
      attrib-1: value-1
      attrib-2: value-2
      ...
```

The more interesting attributes available in zone clauses are:

name — This attribute is mandatory. It defines the name or origin of the zone. Whether you qualify it with a trailing period or not doesn't matter:

```
name: "qupps.biz"
```

zonefile — This mandatory attribute specifies the file containing zone information. Its value is a filename which is relative to zonesdir; if you specify a full path name, it must be available from within the chroot jail. If you have many thousands of zones, we recommend you split up the files into many sub-directories – perhaps organized by initial letter:

```
zonefile: "q/qupps.biz"
```

allow-notify You use this option on a slave server to specify which master server is allowed to send NOTIFYs to it. The syntax is:

```
allow-notify: ip-spec {<key-name | NOKEY | BLOCKED>}
```

The *ip-spec* address is allowed to send NOTIFYs to *this* slave server. Notifies from unlisted or explicitly `BLOCKED` addresses are discarded. If you specify `NOKEY`, no TSIG signature is required. (You must specify one of *key-name*, `NOKEY` or `BLOCKED`.)

```
allow-notify: 192.168.1.20 NOKEY
```

The *ip-spec* can be a plain IP address (either IPv4 or IPv6), or a subnet of the form *a.b.c.d*/24 or masked as *a.b.c.d*&255.255.255.0 or a range of the form *a.b.c.d*–*w.x.y.z*.

request-xfr You use this option to specify from which master server *this* slave server should obtain a zone transfer for the zone. The syntax of this option is:

```
request-xfr: [AXFR] ip-address { <key-name | NOKEY> }
```

The *ip-address* you list is for a master server (to *this* slave). This slave server queries the master for AXFR/IXFR using either the specified key *key-name* or no TSIG key if you specify `NOKEY`.

```
request-xfr: 192.168.1.20 NOKEY
```

If you specify AXFR, the server will query its master only with AXFR requests and not with IXFR. Note that NSD does not support incremental zone transfers (IXFR) when acting as a master name server. If you have an NSD slave to an NSD master, ensure you use the `AXFR` keyword in this option on the NSD slave.

notify You use this option on a master server to tell it which slave(s) it should NOTIFY. The syntax of this option is:

```
notify: ip-address { <key-name | NOKEY> }
```

The IP address of the slave server on the single *ip-address* is notified of updates to this zone.

```
notify: 192.168.1.20 NOKEY
```

When NSD reloads changed zones, it notifies slave servers.

If you are migrating from BIND, be aware that BIND automatically sends notifications to the servers you specify in a zone's Start of Authority (SOA) and Name Server (NS) records, whereas NSD doesn't. If you want to notify those servers, you have to enumerate them in `nsd.conf` with multiple notify options.

provide-xfr You use this option on a master server to tell it which slave servers may request zone transfers from it. The syntax of this option is:

```
provide-xfr: ip-spec { <key-name | NOKEY | BLOCKED> }
```

Slave servers at the specified address(es) are allowed (or explicitly forbidden if BLOCKED) to request a zone transfer via AXFR from this server.

```
provide-xfr : 192.0.0.0/8 NOKEY
```

AXFR requests from addresses not contained in *ip-spec*, or from BLOCKED addresses, are discarded.

The attributes allow-notify, request-xfr, notify, provide-xfr are access controls (ACLs). You can add multiple ACLs per zone if you need them. For example, if you have two slave servers for a zone, you would configure:

```
zone:
    name: "qupps.biz."
    ...
    provide-xfr: 192.168.1.20 NOKEY
    provide-xfr: 10.0.12.10 NOKEY
    ...
```

c. Key declarations

The key clause defines a key for use in access control lists (ACLs). The syntax for the key declaration clauses is:

```
key:
    attrib-1: value-1
    attrib-2: value-2
    ...
```

It has the following attributes, all of which are mandatory:

name — The key name. You use this to refer to this key in an ACL.

algorithm — The authentication algorithm for this key. For TSIG keys, you set this to hmac-md5. Other algorithms and uses are beyond the scope of this book.

secret — The base64-encoded shared secret. You can put the secret and its base64 blob into a separate file which you include into nsd.conf to make it more readable.

We discuss how you use TSIG for securing NSD in Section 10.6.1.

10.3 Controlling NSD's behavior with its utilities

The NSD *control script,* nsdc

nsdc is a shell script for controlling both the Name Server Daemon (nsd) and the zone compiler (zonec). Every time you invoke nsdc, the first thing it does is check the syntax of your nsd.conf configuration file for errors and reports them:

```
# nsdc
/usr/local/etc/nsd/nsd.conf:1: error: syntax error
read /usr/local/etc/nsd/nsd.conf failed: 1 errors in configuration file
Usage: nsdc [-c configfile] {start|stop|reload|rebuild|restart|
                        running|update|notify|patch}
```

nsdc supports the following commands:

start
: Starts nsd.

stop
: Stops nsd by sending it a SIGTERM signal.

reload
: Initiates a reload of nsd, causing it to reopen its database, by sending it a SIGHUP signal.

rebuild
: Rebuilds the NSD database by invoking the zone compiler (zonec) with appropriate arguments. It rebuilds the database into a temporary database in the directory containing `nsd.db`. The temporary database is then atomically renamed if the build is successful. After a rebuild you must reload to have nsd reload its database.

restart
: Restarts nsd. A restart is exactly equivalent to a stop followed by a start.

running
: Check whether nsd is running. If it is not, nsdc issues a diagnostic message and exits with a non-zero code.

```
# nsdc running || nsdc start
nsd is not running
# nsdc running || nsdc start
# nsdc running && echo "NSD is running"
NSD is running
```

update
: Updates all slave zones that have an allow-notify from this host. This command is deprecated as it is not really required: the server notifies its slaves automatically.

notify
: Sends DNS NOTIFY messages to all the zones that have a notify keyword in `nsd.conf`. This command is deprecated as it is not really required: the server notifies its slaves automatically.

patch
: NSD stores incoming zone transfers in a journal file, which you specify as the difffile in `nsd.conf`. The patch command cleans up the journal file:

1. It checks if there is a journal file. If so, it temporarily moves it aside.
2. It merges modifications to zones into the respective files (i.e. the file you specified as zonefile in each zone clause).
3. It rebuilds the `nsd.db` database if any zones have changed and issues a reload command.
4. The temporary journal file from step 1 above is discarded.

You run this regularly (e.g. from cron) to ensure that the difffile does not grow indefinitely.

Check and parse the `nsd.conf` file with nsd-checkconf

nsdc uses the nsd-checkconf program to check the syntax of `nsd.conf`, every time you invoke nsdc. nsd-checkconf is useful in itself: when you use its `-o` option, it parses `nsd.conf` and prints out a specified attribute from it; you can use this in shell scripts.

- To print an attribute (e.g. zonesdir) from the global server clause of the configuration file:

```
$ nsd-checkconf -o zonesdir nsd.conf
/usr/local/etc/nsd/zones
```

- To print out an attribute from a zone, you have to specify the zone, with option `-z`, in addition to the attribute:

```
$ nsd-checkconf -z example.net -o notify nsd.conf
192.168.1.20 NOKEY
```

Manually perform a zone transfer with nsd-xfer

You initiate a manual incoming zone transfer with the nsd-xfer utility on the slave server. The initial query for the Start of Authority record is sent via TCP instead of via UDP, so the master server you are transferring from from must support DNS over TCP, not just AXFR over TCP. To perform a zone transfer for the specified zone into a file `q.tmp` you invoke:

```
$ nsd-xfer -z qupps.biz -f q.tmp 192.168.1.20
info: send AXFR query to 192.168.1.20 for qupps.biz.
```

Note that this command is deprecated as the server performs zone transfers automatically; the command may be removed in a future release.

Unlike nsd-xfer, zone transfers initiated by the built-in transfer process of nsd do not use an initial SOA query; the SOA serial number is determined from the first packet in the AXFR result.

10.4 Monitoring NSD

If you include NSD's optional BIND-style statistics when you compile it, NSD will periodically log statistics about the number of queries it receives, and their types. You typically use this information to keep an eye on the health and the performance of NSD.

```
NSTATS 1204922160 1204912050 A=40891 CNAME=2 MX=31326 TXT=13208 TYPE252=1
XSTATS 1204922160 1204912050 RR=0 RNXD=0 RFwdR=0 RDupR=0 RFail=0 RFErr=0 RErr=0↩
                             RAXFR=0 RLame=0 ROpts=0 SSysQ=0 SAns=85427 SFwdQ=0↩
                             SDupQ=0 SErr=0 RQ=85428 RIQ=0 RFwdQ=0 RDupQ=0 RTCP=1↩
                             SFwdR=0 SFail=44534 SFErr=0 SNaAns=0 SNXD=0 RUQ=0↩
                             RURQ=0 RUXFR=0 RUUpd=0
```

- The `NSTATS` line contains totals for the query types received.
- The two large numbers following the `NSTATS` and `XSTATS` keywords respectively are the current time and boot time (i.e. NSD startup time), in UNIX time format.

- The `XSTATS` line contains additional statistics on the server's operation. The codes are defined in the BIND8 distribution (file `ns_stats.c`). We list them in Table 10.2 for completeness but don't otherwise discuss them:

`RR`	sent us an answer.
`RNXD`	sent us a negative response.
`RFwdR`	sent us a response we had to forward.
`RDupR`	sent us an extra answer.
`RFail`	sent us a SERVFAIL.
`RFErr`	sent us a FORMERR.
`RErr`	sent us some other error.
`RAXFR`	sent us an AXFR.
`RLame`	sent us a lame delegation.
`ROpts`	sent us some IP options.
`SSysQ`	sent them a sysquery.
`SAns`	sent them an answer.
`SFwdQ`	forwarded a query to them.
`SDupQ`	sent them a retry.
`SErr`	sent failed (in `sendto()`).
`RQ`	sent us a query.
`RIQ`	sent us an inverse query.
`RFwdQ`	sent us a query we had to forward.
`RDupQ`	sent us a retry.
`RTCP`	sent us a query using TCP.
`SFwdR`	forwarded a response to them.
`SFail`	sent them a SERVFAIL.
`SFErr`	sent them a FORMERR.
`SNaAns`	sent them a non autoritative answer.
`SNXD`	sent them a negative response.
`RUQ`	sent us an unapproved query.
`RURQ`	sent us an unapproved recursive query.
`RUXFR`	sent us an unapproved AXFR or IXFR.
`RUUpd`	sent us an unapproved update.

Table 10.2: NSD statistic codes

10.5 The different NSD server roles

NSD can fulfill the following authoritative roles:

- Master server.
- Slave server.
- Root server.

In the following examples (pages 272–280), our master server has the address 192.168.1.164, and the slave's address is 192.168.1.20.

10.5.1 Running NSD as a master server

NSD is a full master and therefore fully supports outgoing zone transfers via AXFR (Figure 10.3). You initiate slave notifications with nsdc's `notify` command, to send out notifications to all slave servers, but as a master, NSD automatically notifies slaves for which you've specified a notify (Section 10.2).

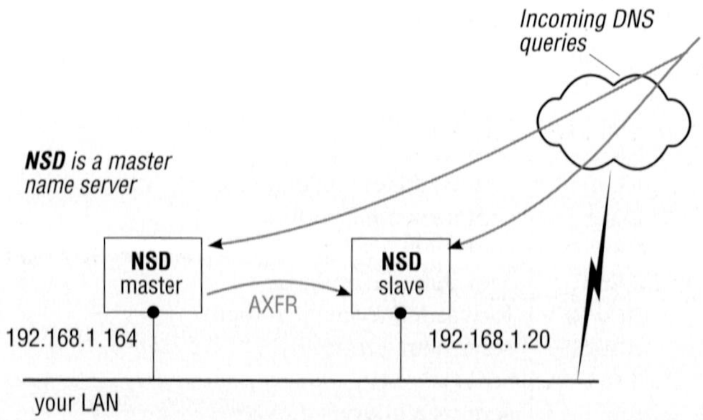

Figure 10.3: NSD as a master server

Adding a new master zone

To add a new master zone:

1. Create and populate the zone master file.
2. Add the zone to `nsd.conf`:

```
zone:
  name: "example.net"
  zonefile: "example.net"
  notify: 192.168.1.20 NOKEY
  provide-xfr: 192.168.1.20 NOKEY
```

   Note how there is no keyword that says "I am a master zone": the behavior is inferred from the attribute that specifies that this instance of NSD *provides* zone transfers (i.e. is a master).

3. Rebuild `nsd.db` by compiling the zone:

```
$ nsdc rebuild
```

4. Restart nsd.
5. Add the zone to your slave name server (Section 10.5.2).

Changes in your master zone

To modify or add resource records in your master zone:

1. Edit the zone file and modify the record(s) you need. Make sure to update the serial number in the zone's Start of Authority (SOA).

2. Compile the zone:

```
# nsdc rebuild
```

3. Instruct NSD to reload the changes:

```
# nsdc reload
```

   NSD reloads the changes, and sends a DNS NOTIFY to the slave servers for the zones you configured with the notify parameter.

10.5.2 Running NSD as a slave server

On an NSD slave (Figure 10.4), NSD writes incoming zone transfer data temporarily to the the `ixfr.db` file, from which it is immediately served for new DNS queries. The data is merged back into a zone file with an invocation of nsdc with the `patch` command, which creates the zone file if necessary (i.e. if the zone master file didn't yet exist). You can set up cron to periodically perform the `patch`ing for you.

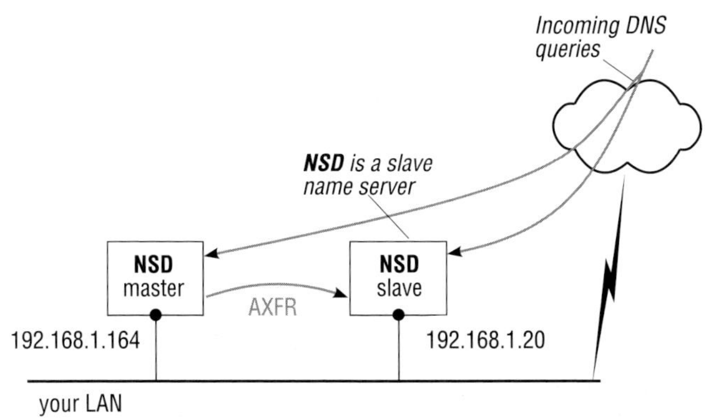

Figure 10.4: NSD as a slave server

Adding a new slave zone

To add a new slave zone to your NSD, you perform the following tasks:

1. Configure the slave zone in `nsd.conf`:

```
zone:
  name: "example.net"
  zonefile: "example.net"
  request-xfr: 192.168.1.164 NOKEY
  allow-notify: 192.168.1.164 NOKEY
```

You specify the masters for this slave zone with the request-xfr option in the zone, and if you want NSD to react to incoming NOTIFY requests, you specify allow-notify options for each of the servers that will send DNS NOTIFY to *this* NSD.

Note how there is no keyword that says "I am a slave zone": the behavior is inferred from the attribute that specifies that this instance of NSD *requests* zone transfers from a master, and as such, it is a slave.

2. Optionally create an empty file for the zone's zonefile, making sure that nsd is allowed to write to the file:

```
$ touch example.net
$ chown nsd example.net
```

This step is optional because nsdc creates the zone file for you (permissions on the file system provided), when you `patch` the zone.

3. Restart NSD with:

```
# nsdc restart
```

4. The new incoming zone is automatically temporarily written to the difffile `ixfr.db`, from where it is immediately available for DNS queries on the zone.

5. At your convenience, you patch the zone transfer changes back into the zone files. We like to perform the `patch` frequently (e.g. every 10 minutes), but you may want to do it only once a day:

```
# nsdc patch
reading database
reading updates to database
writing changed zones
writing zone example.net to file example.net
zone qupps.biz had not changed.
done
zonec: reading zone "qupps.biz".
zonec: processed 30 RRs in "qupps.biz".
zonec: reading zone "example.net".
zonec: processed 29 RRs in "example.net".

zonec: done with 0 errors.
```

This program reads the NSD database (`nsd.db`) and the difffile (`ixfr.db`), and updates the zone master files if there were any changes. Note how nsdc automatically invoked the zone compiler (zonec) to re-compile the zone back into `nsd.db`.

After `patch`ing, the slave's resource records for the zone are in the zonefile file.

10.5.3 Running NSD as a private root server

NSD can operate as a root server (which is, after all, what it was originally written for!). We discuss root servers in Chapter 18, but we show you here how to enable NSD to act as a private root server in your environment (Figure 10.5). To use NSD as a root server, you have to enable that functionality at build time with an option to configure; otherwise NSD refuses to serve the "." zone:

```
$ ./configure ... --enable-root-server
```

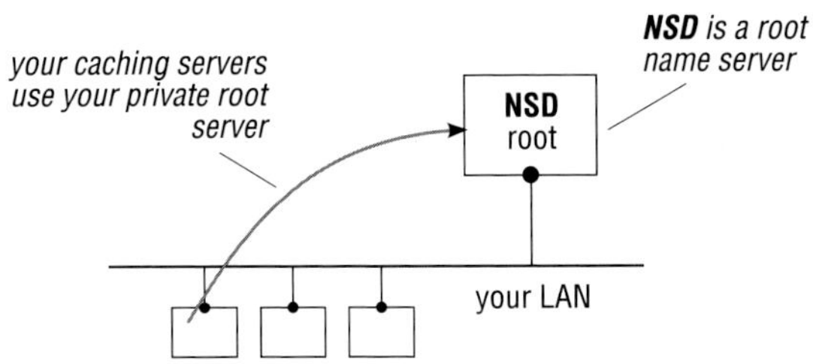

Figure 10.5: NSD as a root server

Thus enabled, NSD functions as a root name server (in addition to a master and slave server) and can serve your private root. You configure the root zone in `nsd.conf` with a zone clause like this:

```
zone:
  name: "."
  zonefile: "my-root.zone"
```

and you configure your root zone resource records in the file `my-root.zone` located in zonesdir. There is no keyword specifying "I am a root name server", because it isn't necessary. NSD serves the content of the root zone as it serves any other zone. If you set up an NSD server as a master or a slave for your root zone, you add attributes specifying the addresses of master or slave servers respectively, as discussed in Section 10.5.1 and Section 10.5.2.

10.6 Securing NSD

NSD has no built-in mechanism to restrict which clients are allowed to send queries to it. Instead of bloating the NSD server with access controls to DNS queries, NSD expects that you protect your installation with a suitably configured and managed firewall. We consider this a good approach because it makes the NSD server code much easier to maintain, resulting in better-quality code, and configuring the NSD server is much simpler. Finally, you have a firewall protecting your network anyway, so why not use that? There are, however, two aspects of security that are implemented in NSD itself:

- NSD fully support the DNS Security Extensions (DNSSEC). We discuss DNSSEC in Chapter 22 and show you examples of how to configure NSD for DNSSEC there.

- You protect zone transfers to and from NSD with Transaction Signatures (TSIG), which we discuss next.

10.6.1 Transaction signatures (TSIG)

RFC 2845, *Secret Key Transaction Authentication for DNS*, defines TSIG (Transaction SIGnature), a protocol used for authenticating two things:

- DNS queries, most commonly zone transfers.
- Dynamic DNS Updates (RFC 2136).

TSIG uses a shared secret key, a time-stamp, and one-way hashing to provide a cryptographically secure means of identifying the endpoints of a connection. The use of a time-stamp means that all clients and servers that participate in TSIG transactions must have synchronized clocks. (Time synchronization of machines is beyond the scope of this book, but you typically use NTP, the Network Time Protocol for keeping the clocks of machines in your network synchronized to a time source. This is not a limitation of NSD, but rather a requirement of the TSIG protocol.)

NSD supports TSIG for protecting zone transfers (incoming and outgoing) and for sending or receiving DNS NOTIFY notifications. The shared secrets on which TSIG keys are based must be defined in the configuration file (`nsd.conf`) or in files you include therein. You define keys in the key clause of the configuration file.

To implement TSIG to protect zone transfers in NSD you:

A. Generate TSIG keys and include them in `nsd.conf`.

B. Set up ACLs for your zones.

C. Test a zone transfer.

A – Generate TSIG *keys for inclusion in* `nsd.conf`

You generate the keys for NSD in one of two ways:

- With the ldns-keygen utility from the ldns package of NLnet Labs (see Notes). You invoke ldns-keygen with the `-H` option to create the keys in the "HMAC-MD5" format required by TSIG. The domain – qupps.biz in this example – is not used in the key, but the program requires it so it can name its output files correctly.

  ```
  $ ldns-keygen -H -b 128 qupps.biz
  ```

  The command creates two files named:

  ```
  Kdomain+algorithm+id.key
  Kdomain+algorithm+id.private
  ```

  with:

  – *domain* set to the domain you specify when invoking ldns-keygen.

- *algorithm* specified as the numeric signing algorithm (157 for HMAC-MD5 keys).
- *id* to a random number, usually the process ID.

The keys in both files are identical because HMAC-MD5 encrypts symmetrically. The file you need for the TSIG key is the file with the `.private` extension. It will have a content like this:

```
Private-key-format: v1.2
Algorithm: 157 (HMAC_MD5)
Key: HHRNUcikVl9Be3x9rImfBA==
```

The value of the key is the base64-encoded "blob" which you set in the secret option of your key.

- With the dnssec-keygen of the BIND distribution. To create a key for use with TSIG you run it like this:

```
$ dnssec-keygen -H HMAC-MD5 -b 256 -n HOST qupps.biz
```

Then, in the NSD configuration file (`nsd.conf`), define a key clause with a key name, algorithm and the base64-blob that you just generated:

```
key:
  name: quppskey
  algorithm: hmac-md5
  secret: "HHRNUcikVl9Be3x9rImfBA=="
```

Both the key's name and the base64-blob are important, and you will need both on the "other" name server.

B – Set up ACLs for your zones

Now add the key to the ACL that protects your zone. To avoid (even known) clients performing zone transfers for a zone if they don't have the correct key, add the ACL to the zone definition in `nsd.conf`:

```
zone:
  name: qupps.biz
  zonefile: q/qupps.biz
  provide-xfr: 192.168.1.20 quppskey
```

Now DNS client 192.168.1.20 will only be able to transfer the zone if it has the correct key. Without the TSIG key, the client will be refused the zone transfer. Other clients aren't allowed zone transfer at all.

C – Test a zone transfer

You can test with dig whether a transfer would be successful:

```
$ dig -y 'quppskey:HHRNUcikVl9Be3x9rImfBA==' @192.168.1.164 qupps.biz axfr
quppskey.     0  ANY TSIG hmac-md5.sig-alg.reg.int.  1200925504 300 0  ↩
         9434 BADTIME 6 AABH1L1S
```

Make sure your clocks are synchronized! If you use the wrong key, the server reports *BADTIME*. If the clocks had been in sync we'd have seen the result of the zone transfer performed by dig.

In the preceding steps (A) through (C) we set up an NSD master server to provide zone transfers for the zone qupps.biz to a client at 192.168.1.20 only if the client has the corresponding TSIG key. We show you in Section 10.6.2 and Section 10.6.3 how you configure NSD and BIND servers to transfer zones from eachother using TSIG keys.

10.6.2 Using NSD as a master and BIND as slave

To set up NSD as master, and a BIND server as a slave (Figure 10.6), proceed as follows:

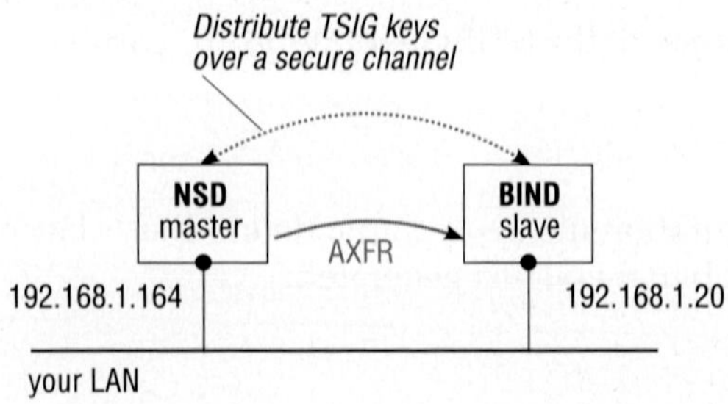

Figure 10.6: NSD as a master, BIND as a slave

- First configure your NSD master server:

  1. Create an HMAC-MD5 key.
  2. Distribute that key over a secure channel to the other server. A secure channel can be an ssh connection in which you copy the file with scp, or it might be a telephone call in which you literally dictate the key to a colleague who types it in.
  3. In `nsd.conf`, define a key clause, giving it a name and a secret consisting of the base64-blob you created in step 1.

     ```
     key:
       name: samplekey1
       algorithm: hmac-md5
       secret: "DD69fLqJe4uycMqQvq/gNqZj6WfxpH70IT15fkH+7AQ="
     ```

  4. As NSD is the master server, you will be *providing* zone transfers, so you specify a provide-xfr ACL, and add the key's name to this. If you want to DNS NOTIFY the slave server, you specify notify so that NSD sends notifications to the BIND slave server.

     ```
     zone:
       name: beispiel.de
       zonefile: beispiel.de
       provide-xfr: 192.168.1.20 samplekey1
       notify:  192.168.1.20 samplekey1
     ```

- Now configure the BIND slave server:

    1. Add the key you generated, to a `key` clause in `named.conf`. The key's name must be the same as you used in NSD above:

    ```
    key "samplekey1 " {
      algorithm hmac-md5;
      secret "DD69fLqJe4uycMqQvq/gNqZj6WfxpH70IT15fkH+7AQ=";
    };
    ```

    2. Ensure BIND will use that key when communicating with the NSD name server, by adding a `server` clause to `named.conf`. BIND's `server` clause allows certain characteristics to be defined when *this* server is interacting with remote server 192.168.1.164. In this case, we want BIND to use the specified TSIG key when communicating with the NSD master server:

    ```
    server 192.168.1.164 {
      keys { samplekey1 ; };
    };
    ```

    3. Create the slave zone in `named.conf`:

    ```
    zone "beispiel.de" IN {
      type slave;
      file "beispiel.de";
      masters { 192.168.1.164; };
    };
    ```

10.6.3 Using BIND as a master and NSD as slave

To set up NSD as a slave to a BIND name server (Figure 10.7) you proceed as follows:

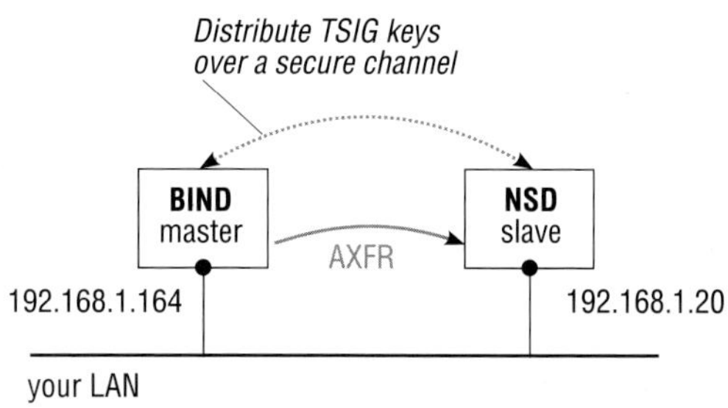

Figure 10.7: BIND as a master, NSD as a slave

- First configure your BIND server:

    1. Create an HMAC-MD5 key.
    2. Distribute that key over a secure channel to the other server.
    3. Add the key you generated, to a `key` clause in `named.conf`:

```
key "llave2" {
  algorithm hmac-md5;
  secret "OtTcknKkyKByCURfU95Ifdnl5++lmf7Z2N6KhSh9haI=";
};
```

4. Ensure BIND will use that key when communicating with the NSD name server, by adding a `server` clause to `named.conf`:

   ```
   server 192.168.1.20 {
     keys { "llave2"; };
   };
   ```

5. Optionally, create an access control list to protect zone transfers, by allowing only certain IP addresses to transfer the zone. You would add that to the `zone` clause with an `allow-transfer` statement.
6. Create the master zone in `named.conf`:

   ```
   zone "ejemplo.es" IN {
     type master;
     file "ejemplo.es";
   };
   ```

- Now configure NSD:

1. In `nsd.conf`, define a key clause, giving it a name and a secret consisting of the base64-blob you created in step 1 above. The key's name must match that used by BIND:

   ```
   key:
     name: llave2
     algorithm: hmac-md5
     secret: "OtTcknKkyKByCURfU95Ifdnl5++lmf7Z2N6KhSh9haI="
   ```

2. As NSD is the slave server, you will be *requesting* zone transfers, so you specify a request-xfr ACL, and you add the key's name to the zone ACL, optionally setting up allow-notify for notifications arriving from the BIND slave server:

   ```
   zone:
     name: ejemplo.es
     zonefile: ejemplo.es
     request-xfr: 192.168.1.164 llave2
     allow-notify: 192.168.1.164 llave2
   ```

Remember, incoming zone transfers on NSD are stored in the difffile, and you have to use nscd's `patch` command to have the zone(s) written to their zone files. (We mention this again because you might be looking for the incoming data and not seeing it.)

Summary

- NSD is an exceptionally fast authoritative-only name server.
- NSD serves answers to DNS queries out of its in-built static database which contains compiled zone files.
- You use the single control script, nsdc, for most maintenance tasks.
- NSD supports TSIG and DNSSEC.

Related topics

- NLnet Labs, the creators of NSD have released Unbound, which is a caching name server. We discuss Unbound in Chapter 17.
- We discuss delegation and private DNS roots in Chapter 18.
- We discuss how you can provision (i.e. generate) zone files from databases in Chapter 19.
- We show you how to configure NSD to serve DNSSEC signed zones in Chapter 22.
- In Appendix B we discuss a method for automatically increasing serial numbers in SOA records when you modify a zone file with resource records. You can apply that method to NSD as well.

Notes and further reading

NSD *home*

The main distribution site for NSD is `http://www.nlnetlabs.nl/nsd/`.

If you want to get an idea of the amount of system memory you will require to run NSD, NLnet Labs has an on-line estimation tool at `http://www.nlnetlabs.nl/nsd/nsd-memsize.html`.

Building NSD

NSD uses GNU autoconf and you build it with the usual magic incantation. For example:

```
$ wget http://www.nlnetlabs.nl/downloads/nsd/nsd-3.1.0.tar.gz
$ tar xvzf nsd-3.1.0.tar.gz
$ cd nsd-3.1.0
$ ./configure --prefix=/usr/local --enable-bind8-stats
$ make
# make install
```

The installation creates a sample file in `/usr/local/etc/nsd/nsd.conf.sample`. You can use this as the basis for your own configuration.

The ldns *package*

NLnet Labs.nl supplies libraries and tools for creating and manipulating TSIG keys. The package is available at `http://www.nlnetlabs.nl/ldns/`. To build the ldns-keygen tool, follow these steps:

```
$ wget http://www.nlnetlabs.nl/downloads/ldns-1.2.2.tar.gz
$ tar xvzf ldns-1.2.2
$ cd ldns-1.2.2
$ ./configure --prefix=/usr/local
$ make
$ make install
$ cd examples
$ ./configure --prefix=/usr/local
$ make
$ make install
```

A basic requirement

The file `REQUIREMENTS` in the NSD source distribution contains a number of basic requirements that NSD was designed to fulfill. One of these requirements is given verbatim here, because it ought to be a requirement for all DNS name server operators:

> *"NSD operators are considered to have basic Unix and networking knowledge and are also considered to be able to read and understand reasonably written user documentation."*

Chapter

11 tinydns

From a security perspective, if you're connected, you're screwed.

Daniel J. Bernstein

Introduction

djbdns is a modular set of tools that lets you provide only the DNS services you really want to use. The djbdns package consists of: tinydns, the authoritative name server; dnscache, the caching recursive name server; and a number of related support tools.

11.1 An overview of djbdns and its component parts

Daniel J. Bernstein wrote the djbdns package. He applied the UNIX philosophy, and instead of creating a large multi-purpose binary program, he built djbdns as a modular system. It is a collection of small special-purpose components, each designed to fulfill a specific task, reliably and fast. You run only the components you need, to offer only those DNS services you require. For example, if you want to offer authoritative DNS you use tinydns. If you want to provide a DNS caching server for a set of machines on a LAN, for an office or home network (Small Office / Home Office), you use dnscache. tinydns and dnscache run independently of one another.

Although by no means as feature-rich as BIND, djbdns was the second most popular name server software on the Internet as of the year 2004, according to a survey[1] performed by Dan Moore, the author of MyDNS.

Pros	•	Very modular standalone programs
	•	Separate DNS caching server
	•	Fast
Cons	○	Lacks human-readable representation for many DNS records
	○	Terse documentation
	○	No RFC 2136 Dynamic DNS
Scenarios		Small to medium DNS servers.

Table 11.1: djbdns at a glance

As illustrated in Figure 11.1, the component programs of djbdns and their specific roles are:

tinydns: an authoritative name server which answers over UDP only.

axfrdns: answers queries received via TCP (as opposed to UDP) and answers those via TCP authoritatively, as well as providing support for outgoing zone transfers. (axfrdns is autonomous – you don't have to deploy it with tinydns – if you want queries answered via TCP only.)

dnscache: a recursive, caching name server that is very careful about what it caches.

rbldns: a server designed for implementing a DNS blacklist[2].

walldns: accepts queries for in-addr.arpa domains from hosts and supplies generic responses to them. (We don't further cover walldns.)

axfr-get: a utility to perform an incoming zone transfer.

djbdns also includes many client tools, used for querying DNS servers, some of which we cover later in this chapter.

---

[1] `http://mydns.bboy.net/survey/`

[2] See rbldnsd (not to be confused with rbldns) in Chapter 16 for a more flexible implementation.

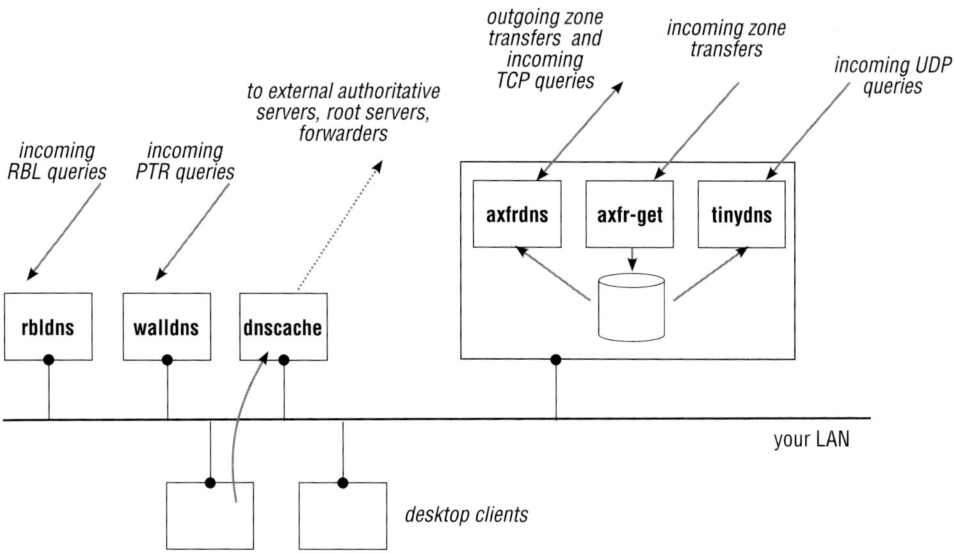

Figure 11.1: djbdns overview

11.2 The tinydns authoritative server

tinydns is the authoritative name server component of djbdns. It answers DNS queries over UDP, only. If you want to answer queries over TCP, you must implement axfrdns. If you want to allow queries over both TCP and UDP, you must set up and run both tinydns and axfrdns. tinydns runs off a very small and efficient file-system based database.

tinydns serves only authoritative data; if tinydns receives a query that it can't answer from its own database, it will not answer at all, and the client that sent the query will time out. Only if tinydns knows from its database (by the presence of a Start of Authority record) that it is authoritative for a queried domain, will it return an NXDOMAIN reply to indicate that the queried domain definitely does not exist. For example, if your tinydns is authoritative for qupps.biz only and it receives a query for cnn.com it will not answer that query at all.

11.2.1 Setting up tinydns

Configuration files and environment variables – overview

Apart from the file containing resource records, tinydns is configured by way of environment variables. You must set these before the tinydns process starts. There are two ways to set them:

1. Explicitly, "by hand", on the command line.

2. By entering the values of the environment variables in files (Figure 11.2), and using the envdir utility from the daemontools package to define the variables from these files.

The filename is the name of the environment variable, and the content of the file is the value the variable is to be set to. For example, exporting `IP=127.0.0.1` from a shell before starting tinydns, and creating a file named `env/IP` containing `127.0.0.1` are equivalent.

Creating your configuration files, directories, and startup scripts

The package provides a special configuration program, tinydns-conf, which sets up tinydns's runtime environment as a set of files and directories. For example:

```
# tinydns-conf nobody nolog /usr/local/tinydns 192.168.1.20
```

creates a new directory structure at `/usr/local/tinydns` as shown in Figure 11.2, for an authoritative name server which listens only on IP address 192.168.1.20. The two system usernames `nobody` and `nolog` must exist and should not have login privileges. tinydns-conf also creates the program run, which is a shell script to launch tinydns.

```
/usr/local/tinydns
├─env
│  ├── IP     192.168.1.20
│  └── ROOT   /usr/local/tinydns/root
├─log
│  ├── main
│  ├── run
│  └── status
├─root
│  ├── add-alias
│  ├── add-childns
│  ├── add-host
│  ├── add-mx
│  ├── add-ns
│  ├── data
│  ├── data.cdb
│  └── Makefile
└─run
```

Figure 11.2: The tinydns directory structure

11.2.2 Where tinydns stores its zone data

You enter your DNS resource records in the flat text file called `data` in the `root` directory of the installation; as configured above, it would be the file `/usr/local/tinydns/root/data`. The contents of this file are then converted into a CDB database file called `data.cdb` by the tinydns-data program. tinydns reads its information from `data.cdb` (Figure 11.3); tinydns itself never reads the `data` text file. CDB is an efficient file format for read-only databases (see Notes for details), and consists of key/value pairs, where the the DNS queries are the keys and the DNS replies are the values. This scheme minimizes the work that tinydns has to do at runtime.

tinydns-data writes its output to a temporary CDB file which is then renamed to `data.cdb`. As the rename is atomic, the conversion may take place while tinydns is running. tinydns will recognize that the file `data.cdb` has changed, reopen it, and immediately use the new answers, without requiring you to to restart or otherwise signal the tinydns server to reload its data file.

As tinydns needs the CDB file when starting, an initial conversion by tinydns-data must be performed before tinydns is started the first time.

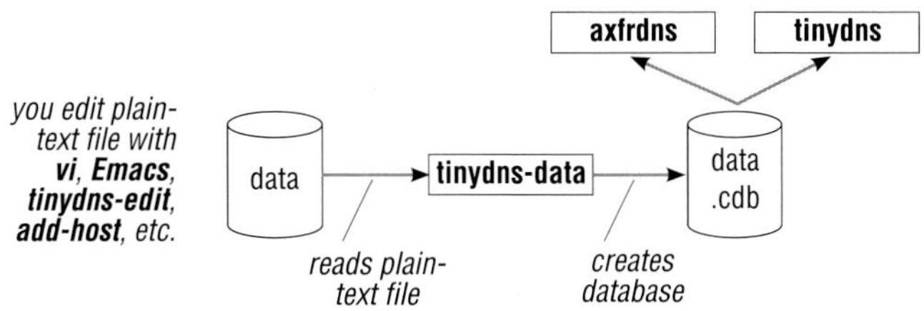

Figure 11.3: tinydns and axfrdns relationship to tinydns-data

The `root` directory created during a tinydns-conf contains a `Makefile` with a recipe to convert the single `data` file to the `data.cdb` database by invoking tinydns-data. You edit your resource records in the `data` file and use make to convert it to `data.cdb`:

```
# cd /usr/local/tinydns/root
# edit data
# make
/usr/local/bin/tinydns-data
```

As the `data` file can become large and unwieldy it may of course be split up into multiple files to ease maintenance. There is probably no best practice here, but maintaining individual files named *domain*`.z` and concatenating these to form a single `data` file, before running tinydns-data works well [3].

Alternatively, the jumbo patch to djbdns (see Notes) gives tinydns-data the capability to read multiple filenames on the command line. In addition to allowing each zone to have its own default SOA serial number gleaned from the file's modification time, separation of zones into individual files allows you to handle zone files as individual entities and possibly delegate their management to distinct administrators.

11.2.3 Format of information in the `data` file

We said above that you enter your DNS information into the `data` file. You can do this in several ways:

- Manually, using any text editor.
- Manually, using the tinydns-edit program (only for additions to the database, not for changes or deletions).

[3] Dan Peterson's zcat.pl does a nice job of this (see `http://danp.net/djbdns/patches.html`).

- Manually, using the add-* scripts created by tinydns-conf in `root`. These simply invoke tinydns-edit.
- By a provisioning system, which we discuss in Section 11.2.7 on page 297.

Apart from the generic record type which can be used to represent any DNS resource record type, tinydns-data has only a few built-in record types. There are patches that add support for additional records such as SRV, but these must be obtained separately.

The content of the `data` file is a series of lines:

- Empty lines, and lines starting with a hash (#) symbol, are comments and are ignored.
- Every other line starts with a "magic" character (shown in bold in Table 11.2) that determines the line's function.

1	2	3	4	5	6	7	8	9	10	11	12	Makes
#	comment											;
%	lo	ipprefix										
.	fqdn	ip	x	ttl	ts	lo						SOA,NS,A
&	fqdn	ip	x	ttl	ts	lo						NS,A
=	fqdn	ip	ttl	ts	lo							A, PTR
+	fqdn	ip	ttl	ts	lo							A
@	fqdn	ip	x	dist	ttl	ts	lo					MX,A
^	fqdn	p	ttl	ts	lo							PTR
Z	fqdn	mname	rname	ser	ref	ret	exp	min	ttl	ts	lo	SOA
-	fqdn	ip	ttl	ts	lo							
'	fqdn	string	ttl	ts	lo							TXT
C	fqdn	p	ttl	ts	lo							CNAME
:	fqdn	n	rdata	ttl	ts	lo						other

Table 11.2: tinydns-data record syntax

- Lines that are not comments or empty represent DNS resource records.
- A line contains a number of colon-separated fields or properties (Table 11.2). These are specific to the line's function, and must be entered in the order shown for each line-type. Some fields are optional and may be empty, or omitted completely (i.e. you don't even have to enter their terminating colon) if they occur at the end of the line.
- Each data line may contain a TTL that specifies the number of seconds a DNS resource record may be cached. The TTL defaults to 86 400 seconds (24 hours).
- Each data line may contain an optional time stamp field in TAI64 format (see Notes, page 313):
  - If the TTL field in the line is omitted or non-zero, the time stamp is a starting time for the related data (i.e. the line will be ignored before that time).

```
+jp.qupps.biz:1.2.1.7::40000000483d4242
```

means that the Address for jp.qupps.biz will come into operation on Wed May 28 2008 at 13:30:00.

- If TTL is zero, the time stamp specifies an "end of validity" time of the related data.

```
+jp.qupps.biz:1.2.1.4:0:40000000483d4242
```

means that the Address for jp.qupps.biz will be invalidated on Wed May 28th 2008 at 13:30:00

The two lines above effectively cause the IP address for jp.qupps.biz to switch from 1.2.1.4 to 1.2.1.7 on the specified date. You can use this to automatically change a server's configuration at a specific time in the future. For example, you might want to change the IP address that your Web server listens on in the middle of the night, and instead of being present to do so at the exact time, you would prepare two data lines like those above.

In the following sections we look at the line types, their syntax and how to use them.

Line type % (percent) – create a "location"

%*lo* : *ipprefix*

Use a line of type % to define a *location name*, which you can use to implement split-horizon DNS (or views as they are called in BIND). The location name consists of one or two ASCII letters. It is followed by an IP prefix that denotes the range of IP address that will *see* the record. For example:

```
%IN:192.168.1
%LO:127
```

creates two locations: INternal and LOcal. We can use these in the `data` file to serve different replies for a particular query, depending on the address of the client. For example, if `data` also contains the following:

```
.qupps.biz:192.168.1.20:ns.qupps.biz:3600::IN
.qupps.biz:127.0.0.2:ns.qupps.biz:3600::LO
```

a client on the 192.168.1 network will get the reply 192.168.1.20 when it queries the name ns.qupps.biz, whereas a client on the local machine querying over a loop-back interface will get 127.0.0.2.

We do not recommend the use of locations to implement split-horizon DNS, preferring to implement two separate tinydns content servers with two completely separate `data` files.

Line type . (period) – create a "complete name server"

.*fqdn* : *ip* : *servername* : *ttl* : *timestamp* : *lo*

This line type causes tinydns-data to create a Start of Authority resource record, with an optional Name Server resource record, and its associated Address record, creating three resource records in all.

fqdn is a domain name, *ip* an IP address. The time to live for the resulting DNS resource record is specified in *ttl* and *timestamp* and *lo* are the time stamp for the line and its *location* respectively, as described above. These meanings are valid for all other line types as well; we won't mention them again.
If *servername* contains a period, then tinydns-data will use *servername* as the name server's name; otherwise it will construct a name *servername*.ns.*fqdn*. If *servername* is empty, the name server will be called ns.*fqdn*. Instead of relying on tinydns-data to make names of name servers for you, always fully qualify *servername*. For example:

```
.qupps.biz:192.168.1.20:
```

produces:

```
;; ANSWER SECTION:
qupps.biz.          2560     IN   SOA   ns.qupps.biz.  hostmaster.qupps.biz.↩
                                        1193737192 16384 2048 1048576 2560
qupps.biz.          259200   IN   NS    ns.qupps.biz.

;; ADDITIONAL SECTION:
ns.qupps.biz.       259200   IN   A     192.168.1.20
```

as answer to an ANY query, whereas

```
.qupps.biz:192.168.1.20:dns:3600::
```

changes the answer to be:

```
;; ANSWER SECTION:
qupps.biz.          2560    IN   SOA   dns.ns.qupps.biz.  hostmaster.qupps.biz.↩
                                       1193737352 16384 2048 1048576 2560
qupps.biz.          3600    IN   NS    dns.ns.qupps.biz .

;; ADDITIONAL SECTION:
dns.ns.qupps.biz.   3600    IN   A     192.168.1.20
```

In the first example, the name server created is called ns.qupps.biz because *servername* is empty. In the second example, the name server's name becomes dns.ns.qupps.biz because the word "dns" doesn't contain a period.

If you don't like the default values used by this tinydns-data record type, use can use the Z, & and = line types instead, to create SOA records with the particular values you want.

Line type Z – create "start of authority"

Z*fqdn* : *mname* : *rname* : *ser* : *ref* : *ret* : *exp* : *min* : *ttl* : *timestamp* : *lo*

With this line type you create only a Start of Authority (SOA) for a domain; unlike the & type, it doesn't create any NS records.
mname is the primary server, *rname* is the e-mail address of a responsible person with the @ replaced by a period. *ser* is the serial number, *ref* the refresh time, *ret* the retry time, *exp* the expire time, and *min* the minimum time. All of *ser*, *ref*, *ret*, *exp*, and *min* may be omitted, in which case they default to the modification time of the data file, 16 384 seconds, 2 048 seconds, 1 048 576 seconds, and 2 560 seconds respectively.

An SOA resource record specified with Z is not sufficient to create a domain; you will also need at least one name server entry, as shown in this example:

```
Zqupps.biz:ns.qupps.biz:dns.foo.bar:2007102800:86400:7200:3600000:172800
&qupps.biz:192.168.1.21:

;; ANSWER SECTION:
qupps.biz.           2560    IN  SOA ns.qupps.biz.  dns.foo.bar.↩
                                  2007102800 86400 7200 3600000 172800
qupps.biz.           259200  IN  NS  ns.qupps.biz.

;; ADDITIONAL SECTION:
ns.qupps.biz.        259200  IN  A   192.168.1.21
```

You can use a Z line with an & line if you want more precise control over the resource records created than you get when you use a . line.

Line type & (ampersand) – create a "name server"

&*fqdn* : *ip* : *servername* : *ttl* : *timestamp* : *lo*

The & line type creates two resource records: a Name Server record for a domain, and an associated Address record for the Name Server. It you want to have more than one Name Server record (always recommended), use this together with the Z data line.

You use this line type for domains that are delegated *from* this server, whereas you would use the . data line for domains that are delegated *to* this server. *servername* is handled as with the . line above. In order to add a second name server to the zone created with the . record, we specify:

```
.qupps.biz:192.168.1.20:dns:3600::
&qupps.biz:192.168.1.21:foobar:
```

which results in a host foobar.ns.qupps.biz because foobar does not contain a period in it.

```
;; ANSWER SECTION:
qupps.biz.           2560    IN SOA  dns.ns.qupps.biz.  hostmaster.qupps.biz.↩
                                           1193740884 16384 2048 1048576 2560
qupps.biz.           3600    IN NS   dns.ns.qupps.biz.
qupps.biz.           259200  IN NS   foobar.ns.qupps.biz.

;; ADDITIONAL SECTION:
dns.ns.qupps.biz.    3600    IN A    192.168.1.20
foobar.ns.qupps.biz. 259200  IN A    192.168.1.21
```

Line type = (equals) – create a "host"

=*fqdn* : *ip* : *ttl* : *timestamp* : *lo*

You use this line type to create two resource records: an Address record for the domain *fqdn* with the IP address specified in *ip*, as well as a PTR resource record in the in-addr.arpa domain pointing to *fqdn*.
For example, to create an A record for host mail.qupps.biz, we use:

```
=mail.qupps.biz:192.168.1.20
```

which results in:

```
;; ANSWER SECTION:
mail.qupps.biz.          86400   IN      A       192.168.1.20
```

We will also get the associated PTR record:

```
;; ANSWER SECTION:
20.1.168.192.in-addr.arpa. 86400 IN     PTR     mail.qupps.biz.
```

if, and only if, this server is authoritative for the domain 1.168.192.in-addr.arpa, that is, only if the `data` file contains a line like:

```
.1.168.192.in-addr.arpa:192.168.1.20:dns:3600::
```

Neither an Address record nor its associated PTR record will be served by tinydns if it is not authoritative for the zones containing them. If you add

```
=www.ibm.de:21.3.40.62
```

to your `data` file, tinydns will never serve them, because it is neither authoritative for ibm.de nor for 3.21.in-addr.arpa.

(This = line type is similar to the FQDN4 type in MaraDNS.)

Line type + (plus) – create an "alias"

+*fqdn* : *ip* : *ttl* : *timestamp* : *lo*

This record type is identical in syntax to the = record above. However, it does *not* create a reverse PTR resource, so this is what you should use to create A resource records for IP addresses that are in in-addr.arpa zones not delegated to our servers.

Line type @ (at) – create a "mail exchanger"

@*fqdn* : *ip* : *mailhost* : *prio* : *ttl* : *timestamp* : *lo*

As the at sign (@) is reminiscent of an e-mail address, this line type is easy to remember: it creates a mail exchanger (MX). In effect, this line type creates two resource records:

1. An MX record, pointing at host name *mailhost*, for domain *fqdn*. The MX priority is set to *prio*, with a default of zero. (The djbdns documentation refers to this preference number as a *distance*.)

2. An A record, specifying IP address *ip* for host name *mailhost*

If *mailhost* does not contain a period, it defaults to *x*.mx.*fqdn*, which may not be what you want, so we recommend you always qualify it. For example, the lines:

```
@qupps.biz:192.3.4.4:post.qupps.biz:80
@qupps.biz:192.3.4.9:exim.qupps.biz:40
```

create the resource records:

```
;; ANSWER SECTION:
qupps.biz.              86400   IN      MX      80 post.qupps.biz.
qupps.biz.              86400   IN      MX      40 exim.qupps.biz.

;; ADDITIONAL SECTION:
post.qupps.biz.         86400   IN      A       192.3.4.4
exim.qupps.biz.         86400   IN      A       192.3.4.9
```

Quite obviously, you should specify an MX resource record only if the target machine (*mailhost*) is a mail server willing to accept mail for domain *fqdn*; make a point of clarifying this with the maintainers of *mailhost*.

Line type - (dash) – disable a line

This record type is a pseudo type: it disables a record, and is like a comment.

Line type ' (single-quote) – create a "text"

'*fqdn* : *string* : *ttl* : *timestamp* : *lo*

This creates a TXT DNS resource record, containing the text *string* for the domain *fqdn*. You can have multiple ' lines for the same *fqdn*; each line creates a separate TXT record. Take care to quote colons with an octal \072. You may include arbitrary characters in the string with an octal \nnn, where *nnn* is a three-digit octal number.

```
'whatmon.qupps.biz:version=3.0.4
'whatmon.qupps.biz:author\072\040Jan-Piet Mens
'whatmon.qupps.biz:http\072//fupps.com/extensions

;; ANSWER SECTION:
whatmon.qupps.biz.      86400   IN      TXT     "version=3.0.4"
whatmon.qupps.biz.      86400   IN      TXT     "author: Jan-Piet Mens"
whatmon.qupps.biz.      86400   IN      TXT     "http://fupps.com/extensions"
```

Line type ^ (circumflex) – create a "pointer"

^*fqdn* : *ptr* : *ttl* : *timestamp* : *lo*

Use this line to create a PTR record, with *fqdn* pointing to domain *ptr*. *fqdn* is a fully qualified in-addr.arpa domain name. For example:

```
^164.1.168.192.in-addr.arpa:www.qupps.biz
```

creates the PTR:

```
;; ANSWER SECTION:
164.1.168.192.in-addr.arpa. 86400 IN    PTR     www.qupps.biz.
```

Note that if you use the = line to create an A record, it automatically creates the PTR record too, so you don't need to create the PTR explicitly with an ^ line. The ^ line type is used for setting up PTR resource records for which you do not create the Address record.

Line type C – create a "canonical name"

C*fqdn* : *cname* : *ttl* : *timestamp* : *lo*

You create a canonical name resource with the C line type, setting up *fqdn* to point to the domain *cname*.

```
Cwww.qupps.biz:mail.qupps.biz
```

creates the record:

```
;; ANSWER SECTION:
www.qupps.biz.          86400    IN       CNAME    mail.qupps.biz.
```

The DNS specification mandates that CNAME records for a given domain *fqdn* must not be used if there are any other records for the domain *fqdn* (Section 2.3.3). If you do mix them, the result of their use is undefined and other name servers (BIND is an example) performing zone transfers might choke on the results.

Line type : (colon) – create "generic record"

.*fqdn* : *type* : *rdata* : *ttl* : *timestamp* : *lo*

You can create almost any type of valid DNS resource record with a : line.

- *type* is a DNS record type specified as a positive integer between 1 and 65 535, but not 2 (NS), 5 (CNAME), 6 (SOA), 12 (PTR), 15 (MX), or 252 (AXFR). The list of DNS resource record types is maintained by the IANA (see http://www.iana.org/assignments/dns-parameters).
- *rdata* is the data for the record. This can contain arbitrary bytes encoded as octal *nnn*.

```
:_ldap._tcp.qupps.biz:33:\000\012\000\036\001\205\↩
004ldap\005qupps\003biz\000:86400

;; ANSWER SECTION:
_ldap._tcp.qupps.biz.   86400    IN       SRV      10 30 389 ldap.qupps.biz.
```

This is the how you can create DNS resource record types for which tinydns-data doesn't have built-in support[4].

Notes on data syntax

When editing the data file, you must ensure that the syntax is correct, as tinydns-data doesn't do full syntax checking on the input. The following are common mistakes:

- If you forget the second field (*ip*) of a + or = line, tinydns-data silently ignores the entire line.

[4] An on-line tinydns record builder that simplifies this task greatly can be found at http://www.anders.com/projects/sysadmin/djbdnsRecordBuilder/

- If the second field of an `&`, `.` or `@` record does not contain an IP address, tinydns-data simply ignores the whole line and skips it silently.
- Location codes (`%` lines) are silently truncated to two characters, which may cause "internal" records to be published to the outside world. The intention in:

```
%sa:127
%sales:192.168.1
.qupps.biz:192.168.1.20:ns.qupps.biz:3600::sa
```

  is to protect the qupps.biz domain, serving it to internal hosts only, but it "slips" out because the location "sales" is silently truncated to two characters.
- Non decimal digit characters in TTL cause the subsequent portion of the TTL field to be ignored (although subsequent fields are still correctly recognized).

Using tinydns-edit *to add records to the* `data` *file*

tinydns-edit is a program to add records to the `data` file. (A better name would have been tiny-add, as it can neither modify nor delete records.) You run the program as:

```
tinydns-edit datafile tempfile add type name address
```

tinydns-edit reads in *datafile* (usually the tinydns `data` file), `add`s the specified record, writes the result to a temporary file, *tempfile*, and if all is successful, atomically renames *tempfile* to *datafile* (so both files must reside on the same file system). *type* is the type of record to be added, *name* the domain name and *address* the IP address of *name*. (The `add` verb is required, even though that is the only action supported.)

tinydns-edit supports the following *types*:

ns: This creates a `.` record for a name server.

childns: creates a `&` record for a name server to which we delegate.

mx: creates a `@` record.

host: creates an = record for a host.

alias: creates a + record.

Instead of invoking tinydns-edit directly, you can use the utility scripts add-ns, add-childns, etc. which were created in the tinydns `root` directory when you ran tinydns-conf. They invoke tinydns-edit with the first four arguments appropriately set.

Randomizing RR

If a client queries a domain name that has more than eight address resource records (A records), tinydns chooses eight of them at random, and returns only these eight in the reply. All A records will be used in the course of time, but a single client's query will never see more than 8 of them. This random selection of no more than eight A records was originally contained in the djbdns pickdns program but has since been rolled in to tinydns.

Wild-cards

tinydns supports wild cards. Lines in the `data` file that have `*`.*fqdn* provide resource records for any domain ending in *fqdn* except those that you have explicitly qualified in `data` and those that are covered by more specific wild cards (*.*subdomain.fqdn*).

For example, if you enter the lines:

```
+qupps.biz:192.168.1.21
C*.qupps.biz:qupps.biz
+*.eu.qupps.biz:192.168.2.40
```

then a query for qupps.biz will return the Address record 192.168.1.21 whereas a query for foo.qupps.biz will return the CNAME qupps.biz. If the domain foo.bar.qupps.biz is queried, the CNAME qupps.biz is also returned, but queries for www.eu.qupps.biz return the Address record 192.168.2.40.

11.2.4 Starting tinydns

There are two ways to launch tinydns, one for normal running, and the other for when you need to run it with non-standard configuration.

1. The run script that tinydns-conf created (Section 11.2.1) is the easiest way to start tinydns. Assuming you created your config files in `/usr/local/tinydns`, to launch tinydns, you invoke:

   ```
   # cd /usr/local/tinydns
   # ./run
   ```

2. As a systems administrator you may want to launch tinydns manually, exercising full control over what is happening. Assuming tinydns' `data` file is stored in the directory `/usr/local/tinydns/root`, you could launch tinydns with:

   ```
   # env - \
       UID=99 \
       GID=99 \
       IP=192.168.1.20 \
       ROOT=/usr/local/tinydns/root \
       /usr/local/bin/tinydns
   ```

explicitly passing environment variables to tinydns as you need them. We now describe these environment variables in detail.

11.2.5 Controlling tinydns with environment variables

As described in Section 11.2.1, there are some variables you can set to modify tinydns' behavior:

`$IP` tinydns listens on the IP address defined in `$IP`, and if you need it to listen on more than one interface, you can start more than one instance of tinydns, each with its own directory, ideally having `$ROOT` pointing to the same directory so that every instance of tinydns reads the same database. Alternatively, the jumbo patch (see Notes) adds a feature that allows `$IP` to contain multiple IP addresses, separated by slashes.

$UID On startup, tinydns will switch to the *uid* of the username specified in `$UID`.

$GID On startup, tinydns will switch to the *gid* of the group name specified in `$GID`.

$ROOT On startup, tinydns will `chroot()` to this directory. It is in this directory that tinydns expects to find its `data.cdb`.

11.2.6 IPv6

Neither tinydns nor any of the other djbdns tools has in-built support for IPv6. You can use the generic record type ":" to produce IPv6 answers for AAAA requests, but if you use them a lot, the data file can get a bit messy.

Instead, you can use a patch (developed by Felix von Leitner) to add support for AAAA resource records, as well as another that adds IPv6 functionality to axfrdns. The patch adds two record types to tinydns-data:

- Line type "6" creates an IPv6 AAAA record and its associated PTR records.
- Line type "3" creates only the AAAA record (and not the matching PTR).

IPv6 addresses must be fully qualified and may not be abbreviated with colons ("::") (see `http://www.fefe.de/dns/`).

11.2.7 Provisioning DNS information for tinydns' `data` file

Whether or not you maintain tinydns' data file manually, hand-crafting entries with a text editor, is a matter of taste and your existing infrastructure. For a small number of zones, it is easy to maintain the file manually, interspersing it with blank lines and comments as documentation. Placing the data file under a revision control system is also a good idea.

The alternative is to maintain DNS information in a relational database, or in an LDAP directory. You then generate the `data` file from those, and use tinydns-data to convert the resulting `data` into CDB format, as `data.cdb`. Automating this is straightforward, as we'll illustrate in the following example.

A medium-sized ISP has a relational database, in which they track customers, invoices etc. All the customers have identical hosting packages, so generating the DNS data is easy. Part of their database looks like this:

```
mysql> SELECT id,cust,name,ns1,ns2,modif,UNIX_TIMESTAMP(modif) AS secs
              FROM zones WHERE name IN ('qupps.biz', 'example.com');
+-----+-------+-------------+-----+-----+---------------------+------------+
| id  | cust  | name        | ns1 | ns2 | modif               | secs       |
+-----+-------+-------------+-----+-----+---------------------+------------+
| 145 | 24101 | qupps.biz   |   0 |   2 | 2007-11-01 05:00:06 | 1193889606 |
| 146 | 24102 | example.com |   3 |   1 | 2007-11-04 22:50:42 | 1194213042 |
+-----+-------+-------------+-----+-----+---------------------+------------+
2 rows in set (0.00 sec)
```

The `ns` columns indicate on which name server pool (i.e. group of name servers) the DNS entries are to be distributed. The small Perl program below connects to the database, extracts the DNS-related information from it using a query like that shown above, and writes a `data` file to standard output.

Listing 11.1: isp2tiny.pl creates a tinydns data file from a MySQL database at an ISP

```
#!/usr/bin/perl
# isp2tiny.pl (C)2008 Jan-Piet Mens

use strict;
use DBI;

my %NSERV = (
        0    => '192.168.100.1',
        1    => '192.168.100.32',
        2    => '192.168.100.42',
        3    => '192.168.100.44',
    );

my $dbdsn = 'DBI:mysql:tiny:localhost';
my $dbh = DBI->connect($dbdsn, 'dnsadmin', 'hah!')
    or die "Can't connect to $dbdsn";

$dbh->{RaiseError} = 1;

my $q = "SELECT id,cust,name,ns1,ns2,UNIX_TIMESTAMP(modif) AS secs \
        FROM zones ORDER BY cust";
my $sth = $dbh->prepare($q);

$sth->execute() or die $dbh->errmsg;

# Bind Perl variables to columns:
my ($id, $cust, $name, $ns1, $ns2, $modif);
$sth->bind_columns(\($id, $cust, $name, $ns1, $ns2, $modif));

while ($sth->fetch) {
    print "# cust=$cust. Modified " . localtime($modif) . "\n";

    my $mname = "dns${ns1}.isp.net";
    my $dns2  = "dns${ns2}.isp2.net";
    my $ser = $modif;
    print "Z${name}:${mname}:hostmaster.isp.net:${ser}:10800:900:604800:3600\n";
    print ".${name}:" . $NSERV{$ns1} . ":$mname:\n";
    print ".${name}:" . $NSERV{$ns2} . ":$dns2:\n";
    print "+${name}:192.168.1.20:\n";
    print "Cwww.${name}:${name}:\n";
    print "\@${name}:192.168.9.20:mail.${name}:10:\n";
    print "\n";
}

$sth->finish;
$dbh->disconnect;
exit 0;
```

This program produces output in `data` file format, suitable for tinydns-data to convert into a `data.cdb` file.

```
# cust=24101. Modified Thu Nov  1 05:00:06 2007
Zqupps.biz:dns0.isp.net:hostmaster.isp.net:1193889606:10800:900:604800:3600
.qupps.biz:192.168.100.1:dns0.isp.net:
.qupps.biz:192.168.100.42:dns2.isp2.net:
+qupps.biz:192.168.1.20:
Cwww.qupps.biz:qupps.biz:
@qupps.biz:192.168.9.20:mail.qupps.biz:10:

# cust=24102. Modified Sun Nov  4 22:50:42 2007
Zexample.com:dns3.isp.net:hostmaster.isp.net:1194213042:10800:900:604800:3600
.example.com:192.168.100.44:dns3.isp.net:
.example.com:192.168.100.32:dns1.isp2.net:
+example.com:192.168.1.20:
Cwww.example.com:example.com:
@example.com:192.168.9.20:mail.example.com:10:
```

We have kept the example simple to illustrate the concepts, so keep the following in mind if you implement something similar:

- The sample database uses the notion of a DNS server "pool" because that is what many ISPs use; you can just as easily maintain the names of the servers if you prefer.
- Use any programming language you are comfortable with.
- Either make sure that the data contained in the database is strictly checked when entering it, or ensure that your conversion program does error-checking; errors in the `data` file are hard to spot.

11.2.8 Replication to other tinydns servers

The `data.cdb` file contains everything that tinydns needs to serve DNS information. Therefore, if we copy or replicate this file in its entirety to other tinydns server(s), they will act as as "identical masters" of this server.

In the case of `data.cdb` being created from a provisioning system such as from an SQL database or from an LDAP directory, there are two different methods we can use to ensure that name servers contain the same data.

1. On each machine on which tinydns runs, create a new `data.cdb` from the (common) provisioning system.
2. Create a new `data.cdb` on a single machine and then copy the result to all the other machines running tinydns.

You can use these methods irrespective of whether you have two or more tinydns servers providing authoritative name services.

1. **Create `data.cdb` on every machine**

   Each machine running tinydns requires an up-to-date copy of the `data.cdb` file. This file can be created on each of the tinydns servers from a single source, such as an SQL database (Figure 11.4).

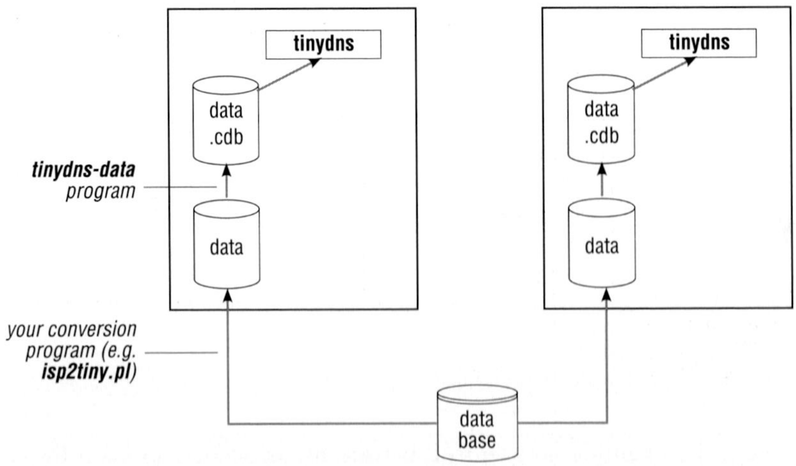

Figure 11.4: tinydns provisioning from database

It might sound as though `data.cdb` re-creation is very time consuming, but on a modern Intel machine, running tinydns-data on a 60 MB `data` file with over a million records takes only four or five seconds, and a 410MB `data` file with 11 million records is converted to CDB format in under a minute.

2. **Create a single `data.cdb` and distribute to every machine**

   A more common scenario is to create the `data.cdb` on a single machine and then copy it to all servers running tinydns (Figure 11.5).

   There are some variations to the process you could consider deploying:

   (a) Replicate the original back-end `data` file, and have the individual servers re-create the `data.cdb` file.

   (b) Replicate only the differences in `data` and re-create the `data.cdb` file.

   (c) Replicate the binary `data.cdb` file using programs such as rsync or CVsup.

   Methods for copying files safely from one machine to another abound and include tools such as the excellent rsync, and CVsup, which is a software package for distributing and updating collections of files across a network. CVsup can efficiently and accurately mirror all types of files, including sources, binaries, hard links, symbolic links, and even device nodes.

Whichever method you choose, we strongly recommend you:

- Create a checksum on the source `data` or `data.cdb` file, send that too to the remote machine, and verify the checksum there, before you put the zone data into production.
- Use your monitoring system (Chapter 24) to detect inconsistencies between your authoritative tinydns servers.

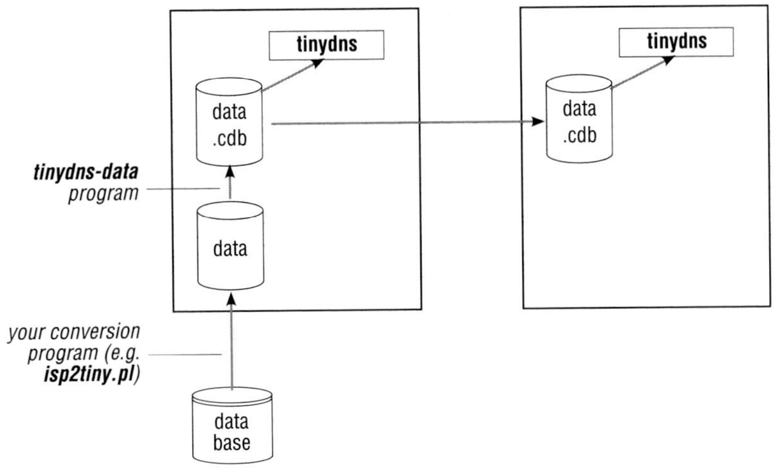

Figure 11.5: Replicating tinydns's `data.cdb`

11.2.9 Using AXFR zone transfers

In the previous section we discussed how to replicate data between two or more cooperating tinydns servers. You might want to have tinydns cooperate with non-tinydns servers, in which case you will have to use standard zone transfers via AXFR. Scenarios using AXFR to or from tinydns include:

1. A tinydns master has a BIND slave name server.
2. A non-tinydns master, such as a PowerDNS or Bind DLZ server, has a tinydns slave.

Let's look at these two cases in more detail.

1. **From tinydns to another server (outgoing AXFR)**

   If tinydns is to be a primary name server for secondary or slave servers that can be provisioned only via zone transfers, you can use the axfrdns utility. axfrdns uses TCP on port 53 to provide outgoing zone transfers. It is designed to run alongside tinydns and in fact uses the same data file (Figure 11.3). It requires the tcpserver program from the ucspi-tcp package (see Notes).

   axfrdns runs under control of tcpserver, which accepts an incoming TCP connection and applies a set of rules to the connection to decide whether to allow or deny it. tcpserver uses a separate CDB database compiled with the tcprules program. The file contains `allow` and `deny` rules that specify whether a connection is permitted.

   Here's an example:

   ```
   :allow,AXFR=""
   1.2.3.4:allow,AXFR="qupps.biz/aa01.net"
   9.1.0.8:deny
   ```

You store these 3 lines into a file called `tcp.rules`, say, and run:

```
$ tcprules tcp.cdb tcp.tmp < tcp.rules
```

to create the `tcp.cdb` database. If you launch tcpserver as:

```
# tcpserver -x tcp.cdb -- 192.168.1.20 53 /usr/local/bin/axfrdns
```

it will listen on TCP port 53 on the specified IP address for an incoming connection. If tcpserver permits the connection, it launches axfrdns, passing it an environment variable named `$AXFR` in which you determine which clients are allowed to request which zones. The restrictions imposed by axfrdns are thus atop those enforced by tcpserver.

The three rules specified above mean:

(a) Any host is allowed to connect (the IP address to the left of the colon (`:`) is empty). When a host connects, axfrdns will be launched with the `$AXFR` variable set to the empty string.

(b) A host with a source IP address of 1.2.3.4 is allowed to connect, and when it does, axfrdns will be invoked with `$AXFR` set to the slash-separated list of two zone names. So, a host with this source address may AXFR the two specified zones.

(c) The host with IP address 9.1.0.8 is not allowed to connect.

Effectively, the above sample permits anyone except 9.1.0.8 to connect to axfrdns for simple DNS queries over TCP (typically used for large replies), but only the host at 1.2.3.4 is allowed to request a zone transfer for domains qupps.biz and aa01.net.

Since axfrdns exports tinydns data in zone transfer format it is in effect a conversion tool from tinydns-data into master zone file format. We mention this in case you want to migrate to a DNS server that understands only zone master files.

Neither tinydns nor axfrdns have support for NOTIFY messages to inform slave servers of modifications to zone data. This means that either slave servers will have to await expiry of the SOA refresh timer before they check for updates on the djbdns system, or that notifications have to be sent out manually. Fortunately there is a small program, dnsnotify, to do that. (see `http://www.tinydns.org/dnsnotify`).

2. **From another server to tinydns (incoming AXFR)**

   If you are setting up tinydns as a slave to a master name server that supports outgoing zone transfers (AXFR), you can use the axfr-get tool, in conjunction with tcpclient of the ucspi-tcp package, to perform an incoming zone transfer, in which resource records are converted to tinydns-data format. For example, the following command grabs a zone from a BIND name server (on mens.de) and stores it in the file `/tmp/data.mens`; this file is in the tinydns `data` file format, so you can use it directly as input to tinydns-data:

```
$ tcpclient 192.168.1.40 53 axfr-get mens.de /tmp/data.mens /tmp/m.t
```

   As its name suggests, tcpclient tries to connect over TCP to the specified host and port. If successful, it runs the specified program (here axfr-get) on that connection, with file descriptor 6 reading from the network, and file descriptor 7 writing to the network. In the example above, axfr-get is then actually talking to a DNS server which it asks for the specified zone, storing that in `/tmp/data.mens` and using `/tmp/m.t` as a temporary file. Here is the result of this transfer:

```
#200705537 auto axfr-get
Zmens.de:mens.de.:jp.mens.de.:200705537:10800:900:604800:86400:86400
&mens.de::home.mens.de.:86400
+dom.mens.de:192.168.1.51:86400
Cpr.mens.de:printer.mens.de.:86400
...
```

When the incoming zone data has been transferred, you append it to the `data` file and then convert that to `data.cdb`, but you have to do that manually. We recommend you create a controlling script to automate the task.

11.2.10 Private root name server

If you have an isolated network – for example, in a corporate environment with private IP addresses — you will want to provide full DNS infrastructure for services running on those networks, including a functioning root name server. As the official ICANN root servers are not available (and you obviously don't want them to be available if you need the isolation from the Internet) you can provide your own, an easy task with tinydns.

You use the add-ns script in the `root` directory, to add one or more such root servers. For example, the commands:

```
$ ./add-ns . 192.168.1.20 ; ./add-ns . 192.168.4.20
```

add the following lines to the `data` file: (The first "." is the line type, meaning create a complete name server, and the second "." is the fully qualified domain name of the DNS root zone.)

```
..:192.168.1.20:a:259200
..:192.168.4.20:b:259200
```

Making your name server authoritative for the root zone in this way is only the first step. After that, you have to delegate your actual zones to other servers (or possibly the same servers) that will serve these zones.

Having checked that the delegation works by running:

```
$ dig @IP-of-tinydns-server . NS
```

you then configure your caching name servers on your network to use your private root server(s). For dnscache (Section 17.4 on page 402) you just add the IP addresses of your root name servers to the file `@` in `root/servers`, removing any existing ICANN servers from the `@` file.

We discuss private roots servers in Chapter 18.

11.2.11 Useful utilities that assist in handling tinydns `data` files

A pre-processor for the `data` file

Ward Vandewege has a pre-processor to create a whole zone using a simple one-line syntax. This is useful if you have a lot of zones which, apart from the name, are otherwise identical. By adding a record of type **newfqdn:fqdn* somewhere in the data file, the script creates data for the domain *newfqdn* with all resources of the existing *fqdn*, but with the domain names suitably modified. The pre-processor only handles lines that begin with the asterisk (*). As an example, consider the following input file:

```
Zqupps.biz:ns1.qupps.biz.:hostmaster.mens.de.:196205281:10800:900:604800:3600
.qupps.biz:192.168.1.173:ns1.qupps.biz:
@qupps.biz::mail.qupps.biz.:10:
#
# now the "duplicates"
#
*foo.net:qupps.biz
*example.com:qupps.biz
*example.net:qupps.biz
*aa01.net:qupps.biz
```

If we dig an MX for aa01.net we find:

```
$ dig aa01.net mx
;; ANSWER SECTION:
aa01.net.                86400   IN      MX      10 mail.aa01.net.

;; AUTHORITY SECTION:
aa01.net.                259200  IN      NS      ns1.aa01.net.

;; ADDITIONAL SECTION:
ns1.aa01.net.            259200  IN      A       192.168.1.173
```

illustrating that everything we need for the aa01.net domain has been created correctly. (See `http://patch.be/djbdns/tinydns-predata.html`.)

Creating the `data` file from BIND zone files

Daniel Erat has a small C program that converts BIND zone master files to tinydns-data format. This is useful if you have to periodically do such a conversion and/or you aren't able to use axfr-get to pull in a zone transfer (see `http://www.erat.org/`).

Perl program to create SRV lines in the `data` file

If you require an elegant way to create DNS SRV resource records for tinydns-data, Rob Mayoff has a Perl program with built-in documentation with which you can do that.

```
$ make-srv -service _ldap._tcp.qupps.biz -weight 10 -target ldap.qupps.biz -port 389
:_ldap._tcp.qupps.biz:33:\000\000\000\000\001\205\004ldap\005qupps\003biz\000
```

11.3 Logging and statistics

tinydns outputs log information when it is queried. The program outputs the log on standard output; if you want to save the log, standard output has to be redirected to a file or piped through a program. The log looks like this:

```
7f000001:8000:f87b + 0001 qupps.biz
7f000001:8000:33a8 + 0001 www.qupps.biz
7f000001:8000:9ad4 + 0001 ww.qupps.biz
7f000001:8000:6934 + 000f qupps.biz
7f000001:8000:b548 + 000f mail.qupps.biz
7f000001:8000:76ad + 0021 _ldap._tcp.qupps.biz
7f000001:8000:2445 C 0010 version.bind
7f000001:8000:762d - 0001 www.cnn.com
```

Each line corresponds to a single query and contains:

ip The IP address from which the request was received. The IP is logged as as a hexadecimal string.

port The port number from which the request was received.

id The request id of the DNS query. This is chosen by the client and the server includes it in its response.

code An indicator of how the query was processed: This can be

- **+** tinydns answered the request
- **-** tinydns dropped this request. It is not authoritative for the requested domain. Hint: tinydns has no Start of Authority record for the domain.
- **I** A request received by tinydns cannot be answered because it is not implemented. This includes invalid bits in the DNS request header.
- **C** tinydns received a query for a class other than `IN` (Internet), such as a version.bind query in the `Chaos` class.

type The type of request received, represented as a hexadecimal number (see `http://www.iana.org/assignments/dns-parameters`).

name The domain name for which records were requested.

11.3.1 tinystats

Luca Morettoni wrote tinystats, a filter that reads tinydns logs and stores data about your authoritative DNS (see `http://morettoni.net/tinystats.en.html`). A full discussion of its installation is beyond the scope of this book, but you can get started by downloading and installing the software with:

```
$ wget http://morettoni.net/bsd/tinystats-1.1.tar.gz
$ tar xvzf tinystats-1.1.tar.gz
$ cd tinystats
$ make
# make install
$ more README
```

and reading the program's documentation contained in the `README` file. Apart from creating human-readable logs from tinydns output like:

```
starting tinydns
127.0.0.1  32768 [21614] + A    qupps.biz
127.0.0.1  32768 [61899] + A    www.qupps.biz
127.0.0.1  32768 [16604] + A    ww.qupps.biz
127.0.0.1  32768 [36613] + MX   qupps.biz
127.0.0.1  32768 [08583] + MX   mail.qupps.biz
127.0.0.1  32768 [28825] + 0021 _ldap._tcp.qupps.biz
127.0.0.1  32768 [48016] C TXT  version.bind
127.0.0.1  32768 [41586] - A    www.cnn.com
```

the tinystats program has support for creating nice usage graphs with RRD (Figure 11.6).

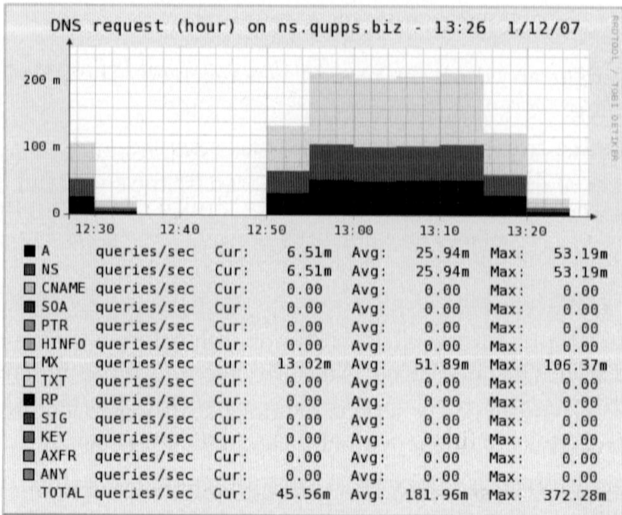

Figure 11.6: Graphing tinydns queries with tinystats and RRD

11.4 Utilities

In this section we give an overview of some of the query tools included with djbdns. (We don't cover in detail tools from other packages required by djbdns, namely daemontools and ucspi-tcp.)

Even though most of what these individual programs do can also be done with dig, these tools are useful because they are ideal for use in scripts to provide just the desired information, without requiring extensive grepping, cutting and awking.

11.4.1 Query domain names with dnsip

dnsip uses `/etc/resolv.conf` to resolve the fully qualified domain names specified on the command line, and prints their IP addresses line by line on the output. If a name cannot be resolved, dnsip prints an empty line; if a name resolves to multiple A resource records, dnsip prints them all on a single line, separated by spaces. For example:

```
$ dnsip qupps.biz amazon.de cnn.com
192.168.1.20
87.238.81.130 87.238.85.130
64.236.29.120 64.236.16.20 64.236.16.52 64.236.24.12
```

Note how dnsip found multiple addresses for the domains amazon.de and cnn.com.

11.4.2 Qualify and query names with dnsipq

dnsipq is similar to dnsip, but before trying to resolve the name it first attempts to *fully qualify* (see `http://cr.yp.to/djbdns/qualify.html`) it, as follows:

1. If the file `/etc/dnsrewrite` exists, dnsipq applies the rules in it.
2. If `/etc/dnsrewrite` doesn't exist or is empty, the qualification process looks for domains in the following places and appends them to the the name you pass to the program.
   (a) The `$LOCALDOMAIN` environment variable, if it is set, or ...
   (b) The first domain or search line in `/etc/resolv.conf`, if the file exists and has such a line; or ...
   (c) Everything after the first period in the system's hostname.

This procedure is called *djbdns qualification*. Having qualified the name, dnsipq attempts to resolve it in exactly the same was as dnsip does. For example:

```
$ hostname
master.qupps.biz
$ dnsipq www
www.qupps.biz 192.168.1.20
$  LOCALDOMAIN=amazon.de dnsipq www
www.amazon.de 87.238.85.130
```

The first dnsipq invocation shows how the name www is qualified by appending the domain name found after the first period of the value determined by hostname, and the second invocation shows how the qualification is altered by setting `$LOCALDOMAIN` to amazon.de, whereupon dnsipq then searches for www.amazon.de.

11.4.3 Lookup reverse names with dnsname

dnsname does a reverse lookup for the specified IP address(es) and prints their names on standard output, one per line with a blank line where a reverse lookup cannot be completed for an address. For example:

```
$ dnsname 192.168.1.20 127.0.0.1
qupps.biz
localhost
```

11.4.4 Query TXT records with dnstxt

dnstxt is like dnsip but instead of querying for A records, it queries for, and prints, DNS TXT resource records. If a name resolves to multiple TXT records, dnstxt unfortunately concatenates them onto a single line without otherwise separating them, as illustrated in this example:

```
$ dnstxt qupps.biz whatmon.qupps.biz
v=spf1 a:mail.qupps.biz a:mail.uit.co.uk mx:qupps.biz ~all
author: Jan-Piet Menshttp://fupps.com/extensionsversion=3.0.4
```

11.4.5 Query MX records with dnsmx

dnsmx prints the MX resource records of the domain names given on the command line, one per line. If a domain name cannot be found, dnsmx prints a priority of zero (0) followed by the given domain name.

```
$ dnsmx nosuchname.de qupps.biz
0 nosuchname.de
80 mail.uit.co.uk
10 mail.qupps.biz
```

11.4.6 Resolve addresses from a file with dnsfilter

dnsfilter reads lines of text from standard input and performs reverse lookups on the IP address at the beginning of each line. For each address resolved successfully, dnsfilter prints the address and its name separated by an equals sign (=); addresses that cannot be resolved are printed as is.

```
$ cat /tmp/ip
192.168.1.20 this is mine
127.0.0.1
192.168.1.173
64.233.167.99 should be google
192.168.1.27

$ dnsfilter < /tmp/ip
192.168.1.20=qupps.biz this is mine
127.0.0.1=localhost
192.168.1.173=jp830w.mens.de
64.233.167.99=py-in-f99.google.com should be google
192.168.1.27
```

While dnsfilter is looking up an address in DNS, it reads ahead in the input and parallelizes lookups, doing a default of 10 simultaneous queries. dnsfilter is useful in expanding IP addresses found at the start of lines in log files, such as those produced by the Apache Web server.

11.4.7 Query a name and type with dnsqr

dnsqr is invoked with a *type* and a fully qualified name. It asks the DNS for resources of *type* for the name and prints its results in a human-readable form that is more compact than the dig output, but not necessarily clearer.

type may be a name or number. Currently recognized names are: ANY, A, NS, MX, PTR, TXT, CNAME, SOA, HINFO, RP, SIG, KEY, AAAA, and AXFR, specified as either upper or lowercase.

```
$ dnsqr a www.qupps.biz
1 www.qupps.biz:
129 bytes, 1+2+2+2 records, response, authoritative, noerror
query: 1 www.qupps.biz
answer: www.qupps.biz 86400 CNAME qupps.biz
answer: qupps.biz 86400 A 192.168.1.20
authority: qupps.biz 86400 NS ns2.qupps.biz
authority: qupps.biz 86400 NS ns1.qupps.biz
additional: ns1.qupps.biz 86400 A 192.168.1.20
additional: ns2.qupps.biz 86400 A 192.168.1.173
```

dnsqr should not and cannot be used for performing zone transfers; use axfr-get for that.

11.4.8 Tracing queries with dnstrace

dnstrace uses the standard DNS resolution algorithm and searches for all DNS servers that can affect the resolution of records of type *t* under the domain name *fqdn*, starting from the root server *r*. You can list more than one root server.

It prints all the responses it receives from DNS servers; it also prints warnings about slow servers, dead servers, misdelegated ("lame") servers, and misformatted packets.

```
$ dnstrace any www.amazon.de k.root-servers.net
0:.:.:start:NS:.:.
0:.:.:start:A:.:198.41.0.4
255:www.amazon.de:.:198.41.0.4:tx
255:www.amazon.de:.:198.41.0.4:NS:de:a.nic.de
255:www.amazon.de:.:198.41.0.4:A:a.nic.de:194.0.0.53
255:www.amazon.de:.:198.41.0.4:A:l.de.net:89.213.253.189
...
```

(We've truncated the listing because the full output is 1.2 megabytes!) A good way to view dnstrace output is with the dnstracesort utility of djbdns (which outputs underlining codes) piping the result to the less pager.

11.5 Caching DNS

The recursive caching DNS name server of the djbdns package is a standalone program called dnscache. We cover dnscache fully in Chapter 17, Recursion (Section 17.4).

Summary

- djbdns is a package of tools that provides authoritative as well as caching DNS services, and a number of useful utilities for querying DNS servers.
- tinydns is the authoritative name server. It is configured via environment variables which are set up through files in a directory, and it reads authoritative DNS data from a CDB file produced from a text source file.
- axfrdns and axfr-get can be used to provide outgoing and incoming zone transfers (AXFR) for inter-operating with non-tinydns name servers.

Related topics

- The caching name server of djbdns is called dnscache, and we cover that in Chapter 17.
- Web based management of tinydns data in Chapter 19.
- Performance in Chapter 23.

Notes and further reading

Building djbdns

You install djbdns in a different way to most of the other tools in this book. djbdns had very specific licensing restrictions which prohibited the distribution of modified versions. These restrictions made it difficult to find ready-to-run packages of djbdns, requiring users to build it themselves. At the time of this writing, Dan. J. Bernstein placed all his code in the public domain[5], opening the path to binary packages.

We recommend you proceed to build djbdns in the following order:

1. Prepare and install the programs in the daemontools package, even if you are not going to use the supervise mechanism (see below).

   After downloading the source of the daemontools package you have to fix the command with which the programs are compiled (on GNU/Linux), and launch compilation. The fix adds the required inclusion of the `errno.h` file on newer GNU/Linux platforms.

   ```
   $ wget http://cr.yp.to/daemontools/daemontools-0.76.tar.gz
   $ tar xvzf daemontools-0.76.tar.gz
   $ cd admin/daemontools-0.76
   $ echo "gcc -O2 -include /usr/include/errno.h" > src/conf-cc
   $ package/compile
   ```

   If the compilation was successful, the resulting binaries are in the `command` subdirectory. Copy them to a directory of your choice:

[5] http://cr.yp.to/distributors.html

```
$ ls -l command/
-rwxr-xr-x 1 root root 17216 Nov 11 14:50 envdir
-rwxr-xr-x 1 root root 16376 Nov 11 14:50 envuidgid
-rwxr-xr-x 1 root root 16264 Nov 11 14:50 fghack
-rwxr-xr-x 1 root root 27744 Nov 11 14:50 multilog
-rwxr-xr-x 1 root root 16152 Nov 11 14:50 pgrphack
-rwxr-xr-x 1 root root  4816 Nov 11 14:50 readproctitle
-rwxr-xr-x 1 root root 16384 Nov 11 14:50 setlock
-rwxr-xr-x 1 root root 16232 Nov 11 14:50 setuidgid
-rwxr-xr-x 1 root root 16336 Nov 11 14:50 softlimit
-rwxr-xr-x 1 root root 18832 Nov 11 14:50 supervise
-rwxr-xr-x 1 root root 13456 Nov 11 14:50 svc
-rwxr-xr-x 1 root root 11584 Nov 11 14:50 svok
-rwxr-xr-x 1 root root 17032 Nov 11 14:50 svscan
-r-xr-xr-x 1 root root   740 Nov 11 14:50 svscanboot
-rwxr-xr-x 1 root root 13232 Nov 11 14:50 svstat
-rwxr-xr-x 1 root root 11680 Nov 11 14:50 tai64n
-rwxr-xr-x 1 root root  9328 Nov 11 14:50 tai64nlocal

$ cp command/* /usr/local/bin/
```

A typical way of running djbdns is via a supervise daemon, which is a program that supervises execution of long-running daemons. This program is part of the daemontools package. If you wish to run the supervise daemon, which was built as part of daemontools, see `http://cr.yp.to/daemontools.html`. (We don't discuss this method further.)

2. If you require incoming or outgoing zone transfers for tinydns, prepare and install the programs in the ucspi-tcp package. Otherwise, skip this step.

   Download the ucspi-tcp package and fix its compilation command as above if you are running on GNU/Linux:

```
$ wget http://cr.yp.to/ucspi-tcp/ucspi-tcp-0.88.tar.gz
$ tar xvzf ucspi-tcp-0.88.tar.gz
$ cd ucspi-tcp-0.88
$ echo "gcc -O2 -include /usr/include/errno.h" > conf-cc
$ make
```

   The included `Makefile` will install the programs into the directory contained in the file `conf-home` (default: `/usr/local/bin`). Then copy the binaries to the destination, using:

```
$ make setup
```

   (Note the "setup" as opposed to "install".)

3. Prepare and install the programs in the djbdns package.

```
$ wget http://cr.yp.to/djbdns/djbdns-1.05.tar.gz
$ tar xvzf djbdns-1.05.tar.gz
```

   At this point you may optionally decide to install the jumbo patch:

```
$ wget http://www.ro.kde.org/djbdns/mywork/jumbo/jumbo-p13.patch.gz
$ gunzip jumbo-p13.patch.gz
$ patch -p0 < jumbo-p13.patch
$ cd djbdns-1.05
$ echo "gcc -O2 -DDUMPCACHE -include /usr/include/errno.h" > conf-cc
$ make
```

and if you don't, then use these steps:

```
$ cd djbdns-1.05
$ echo "gcc -O2 -include /usr/include/errno.h" > conf-cc
$ make
```

As with ucspi-tcp, install thedjbdns binaries in their final destination with:

```
$ make setup
```

This also puts a slightly outdated list of root servers into the `/etc/dnsroots.global` file.

4. Before continuing, it may be useful to check the list of ICANN's root servers in `/etc/dnsroots.global` (and also in any existing `$ROOT/servers/@` of dnscache configurations). Retrieve a new list of root server names with dnsqr:

   ```
   $ dnsqr ns . | awk '/answer/ {print $5;}'
   a.root-servers.net
   h.root-servers.net
   ...
   ```

   You can then use dnsip to query their addresses, producing a list of IP addresses of the root name servers.

   ```
   $ dnsip `dnsqr ns . | awk '/answer/ {print $5;}'`
   198.41.0.4
   128.63.2.53
   ...
   ```

   Copy this list into the file `/etc/dnsroots.global`, which dnscache-conf uses to prime the `$ROOT/servers/@` file.

5. Select the djbdns components you will be running on your machines and use the "*-conf" program(s) to set them up.

You are now ready to configure, for live running, tinydns (Section 11.2.1) and/or dnscache (17.4) as you require.

CDB databases

CDB is the *constant database*, and it refers to both the data format and a library of access routines created by Daniel J. Bernstein. The database is "constant" because it allows only two operations: creation and reading; once created, you can't write to it, and updates are not possible. However, reads are very efficient. Since the database does not change while in use, multiple processes can access it simultaneously without requiring any locking. (See `http://cr.yp.to/cdb.html`)

Michael Tokarev created an alternative library to access CDB databases (see `http://www.corpit.ru/mjt/tinycdb.html`), and you'll find a benchmark comparison of the various database formats at `http://qdbm.sourceforge.net/benchmark.pdf`.

Patches and djbdns related software

Claudiu Costin put together what he calls the "Jumbo Patch", a collection of 13 individual patches that he collected from various places. The collection adds several interesting features to djbdns:

- Support for SRV in tinydns-data and axfr-get.
- "D" line type for tinydns-data for SOA contact address.
- tinydns-data accepts multiple filenames on command line.
- `$OKCLIENT` makes dnscache accept queries from everywhere.
- `$IP` may contain multiple IP addresses for dnscache.
- dnscache can dump and load the cache.
- dnsfilter uses names in lieu of IP addresses.
- tinydns listens on multiple IP addresses.
- dnscache reloads configuration on SIGHUP.
- dnscache returns custom IP for NXDOMAIN.
- tinydns logs NXDOMAIN with 'X'.
- tinydns logs 'N' when NOTIFY is received.
- dnscache serves round-robin A RR.

TAI64

Temps Atomique International (*TAI*) is the international real-time standard. It is used by djbdns and daemontools as it overcomes the limitation of the original UNIX time stamp format stored as a 32-bit signed integer, which will expire in 2038. If you need to process djbdns TAI64 timestamps as produced in logs, you might be interested in the Time::TAI64 Perl module available on CPAN; it makes handling of these times easy, as the following sample shows:

Listing 11.2: Example of Perl's Time::TAI64

```
#!/usr/bin/perl

use strict;
use Time::TAI64 qw/:tai64/;
use POSIX qw(mktime);

my $clock = POSIX::mktime( 0, 30, 12, 28, 4, 62 );
print "Date = ", POSIX::ctime($clock);

my $tai = unixtai64($clock);
print "$tai\n";

print tai2strftime($tai, '%Y-%m-%d %H:%M:%S') . "\n";
```

When the program is run it produces the following output:

```
Date = Mon May 28 12:30:00 1962
@40000000f1b62f42
1962-05-28 12:30:00
```

For more information on TAI as it is used by djbdns, see `http://pobox.com/~djb/libtai/tai64.html`, and for information on TAI in general, consult `http://en.wikipedia.org/wiki/International_Atomic_Time`.

Man pages

The daemontools, ucspi-tcp and djbdns packages don't include manual pages, but Gerrit Pape has created manual pages for the three packages; we recommend you download them and copy them to your `man` directory. (See `http://smarden.org/pape/djb/`)

Recommended reading

- Henning Bauer's *Life with djbdns* has a lot of interesting information and insight into the workings of djbdns; it is located at `http://www.lifewithdjbdns.com/`
- Felix von Leitner's unofficial FAQ is also a good starting point `http://www.fefe.de/djbdns/`

Chapter

12 ldapdns

Simple Updates and true replication... This is the future.

A Brenk

Introduction

ldapdns is a lean and mean program that retrieves its zone data from an LDAP directory. Although its documentation is sparse, ldapdns is worth more than just a cursory glance.

ldapdns is a small DNS server that authoritatively answers DNS queries directly from an LDAP directory. The author, who prefers to be called "Mrs. Brisby", appears to have stopped development, but ldapdns still does its job well and reliably.

Pros	• Authoritative-only DNS server • LDAP back-end • Choice of schema
Cons	◦ Lacks representation for many DNS records ◦ Minimal documentation ◦ Further development uncertain
Scenarios	Small DNS servers in an LDAP directory server environment.

Table 12.1: ldapdns at a glance

The similarities between ldapdns and some of the tools of the djbdns package (Chapter 11) are not coincidental: the author of ldapdns originally implemented ldapdns as an extension to tinydns. Today, it is a standalone program that shares only some ideology with tinydns.

Several years ago we successfully deployed ldapdns onto a dozen lightly loaded Mail Transfer Agents (MTA, or mail servers); these systems have most of their configuration data stored in an OpenLDAP directory server. We wanted a lightweight and resilient DNS name server on the machines that stored its zone data in LDAP, giving us a uniform method of managing all configuration of these hosts. ldapdns was ideal and continues to serve us well.

12.1 Choosing your LDAP schema

ldapdns looks up answers to DNS queries in an LDAP directory server. It walks up and down the LDAP tree to search for domains. (For example, if you query for www.qupps.biz, if ldapdns finds SOA and NS records for the domain, it uses them.) If it finds www.qupps.biz without SOA or NS records, it walks back up and searches qupps.biz for them. Domains can exist with NS records only: if ldapdns doesn't find a SOA, it creates it synthetically for you. Domain names must be fully qualified, but you can omit the trailing period in a domain name.

You can configure ldapdns to use an LDAP schema depending on your requirements. It supports one of several approaches for finding LDAP entries. We describe them by using samples for a query of www.qupps.biz:

cosine This is the default, and the method used in our examples. ldapdns performs base-level searches for the attribute types defined in the Cosine schema. The searches are:

```
base="dc=www,dc=qupps,dc=biz,ou=zones,ou=LDAPdns,ou=dns,o=qupps.biz"
base="dc=qupps,dc=biz,ou=zones,ou=LDAPdns,ou=dns,o=qupps.biz"
base="dc=*,dc=biz,ou=zones,ou=LDAPdns,ou=dns,o=qupps.biz"
```

rfc1279 Identical to `cosine`.

msdns ldapdns performs base-level searches on `dNSRecord` attribute types:

```
base="dc=@,dc=quppsbiz,ou=zones,ou=LDAPdns,ou=dns,o=qupps.biz"
base="dc=@,dc=,ou=zones,ou=LDAPdns,ou=dns,o=qupps.biz"
base="dc=@,dc=,ou=zones,ou=LDAPdns,ou=dns,o=qupps.biz"
```

There is evidently something wrong in that, because the second `dc` attribute in the distinguished names is incorrect, so we can't use this schema.

ldapdns ldapdns performs subtree searches of your LDAP directory starting at the base you configure it to use. A DNS query for qupps.biz is translated to a search filter for

```
(|(associatedDomain=qupps.biz)(associatedDomain=biz))
```

You choose which schema to use depending on how you organize and manage your LDAP entries. We've had good experience with the Cosine schema, and we discuss that.

In the Cosine schema, domains and zones are split into a sequence of `domainComponent` (`dc`) objects (Figure 12.1). ldapdns uses attribute types of the LDAP entries of `dNSDomain` objects from which it constructs replies.

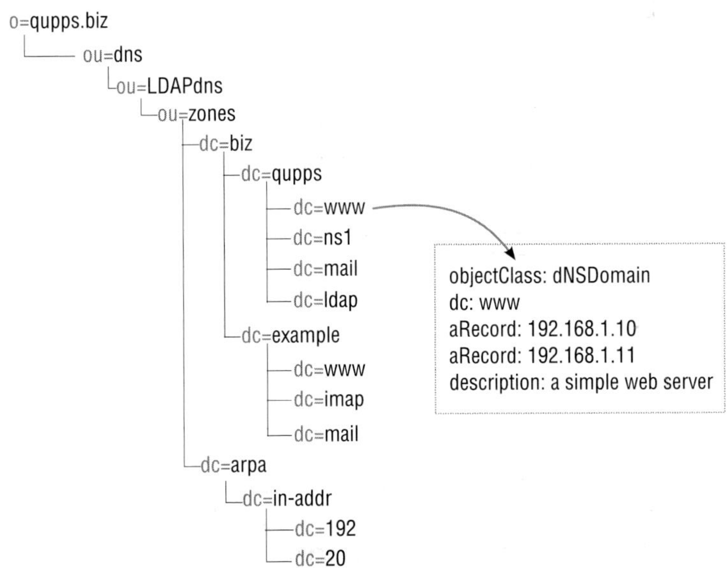

Figure 12.1: ldapdns maps DNS queries to domainComponents

12.2 Setting up ldapdns with ldapdns-conf

Install the binary programs (see Notes). The program inherits ideas from the djbdns package, so it uses a ldapdns-conf program for setup. Its syntax is:

ldapdns-conf *acct logacct /path yourip ldaphost binddn* [*suffix*]

Where the arguments are:

acct ldapdns should run as this user.

logacct ldapdns should create log files as this user.

path ldapdns `chroot()`s into this directory on startup. It is populated by ldapdns-conf with three directories and a shell script:

`env` As with djbdns, the files in this directory are used to load environment variables. For each file envdir (from the daemontools package) creates an environment variable with the same name, and with the file's contents as the variable's value. The files that ldapdns-conf creates in this directory are:

- `HOSTMASTER`
- `IP`
- `LDAP_AUTH_NAME`
- `LDAP_HOSTS`
- `LDAP_SUFFIX` if *suffix* was specified on the command line.
- `ROOT`

We discuss these in Section 12.3 below.

`log` This directory contains a script with which you can run multilog, just as you would do with djbdns. We don't discuss this further here; for details, see Section 17.4.8.

`root` This directory contains the file `passwd`, which should contain the password that ldapdns is to use to bind to the LDAP directory. The file's permissions must be set read-only to `root`.

```
# echo TerriblySecret > root/password
# chmod 400 root/password
```

`run` You use this script to launch ldapdns. It has a small bug that causes ldapdns to fault upon startup. We recommend you change the script to read:

```
#!/bin/sh
exec 2>&1
exec envuidgid nobody envdir ./env /usr/local/bin/ldapdns
```

yourip The IP address of the interface on this machine, that ldapdns is to listen on, for incoming DNS queries. This address is written to the file `IP` in the `env` directory. Set this to 0.0.0.0 to have ldapdns listen on all the machine's interfaces.

ldaphost The IP address or URI (for example, `ldap://192.168.1.164/`) at which your LDAP directory server is reachable. This address is written to the `LDAP_HOSTS` file in the `env` directory. When running with OpenLDAP, the URI may also be an `ldapi` (note the final "i") URI, in which case ldapdns will communicate with your OpenLDAP server over a UNIX domain socket:

```
ldapi://%2fvar%2frun%2fsldapd.sock
```

For this to work, your slapd needs to be started with something similar to this:

```
# slapd ... -h "ldap:/// ldapi://%2fvar%2frun%2fsldapd.sock " ...
```

binddn The DN with which ldapdns binds to your LDAP directory. The value of this variable is written to the LDAP_AUTH_NAME file in the env directory.

suffix The optional search base of your LDAP directory tree. This value is written into the file LDAP_SUFFIX in the env directory.

As an example, to configure ldapdns to run in the directory /usr/local/ldapdns, listen on IP address 192.168.1.164, contact your LDAP server on IP address 127.0.0.1, and bind as manager, you could use:

```
# ldapdns-conf nobody nobody /usr/local/ldapdns \
        192.168.1.164 127.0.0.1 cn=manager,o=qupps.biz
Don't forget to set $ROOT/root/password
```

Note that the program warns that you still have to set the password with which ldapdns will bind to your LDAP directory.

12.3 Environment variables for controlling ldapdns

Like tinydns, when ldapdns starts, it uses the values of several environment variables that you set earlier in one of two ways:

1. Using the ldapdns-conf program to populate a directory structure (discussed in Section 12.2 above). The name of each file in the env directory is used as a variable name, and the file's content as variable's value.
2. By creating a script that sets the variables explicitly, and then launching ldapdns from that script. For example:

Listing 12.1: ldapdnsrun: a script to start ldapdns

```
$ cat /etc/ldapdnsrun
#!/bin/bash
export IP="192.168.1.164"
export HOSTMASTER="jp@xyz.de"
export LDAP_HOST="192.168.1.20"
export ROOT=/usr/local/ldapdns   # for the password file
export LDAP_SUFFIX="dc=qupps.biz"
export SCHEMA=cosine
env UID=90 GID=90 /usr/local/sbin/ldapdns
```

Some of the environment variables that ldapdns uses are:

$AXFR Determines how ldapdns-axfr should handle TCP requests. See Section 12.6. $LDAP_AXFR is synonymous with $AXFR.

$DEFAULT_EXPIRE The value to use as the SOA expire time if it is zero in the entry.

$DEFAULT_MINIMUM The value to use as the SOA minimum time if it is zero in the entry.

$DEFAULT_REFRESH The value to use as the SOA refresh time if it is zero in the entry.

$DEFAULT_RETRY The value to use as the SOA retry time if it is zero in the entry.

$DNS_THREADS The number of threads used for handling DNS queries (default: 1).

$LDAP_THREADS ldapdns uses this number of threads to talk to the LDAP directory server (default: 1). Increasing this number increases concurrency.

$HANDLERS ldapdns uses a default of 128 "handlers" (internal queues) to handle DNS requests. It sets `$HANDLERS` to be twice the sum of `$LDAP_THREADS` and `$DNS_THREADS` (if set), but you can override this by setting `$HANDLERS`.

$HELPER_NOTIFY The path to a program that should be `fork()`ed whenever a DNS NOTIFY is detected. ldapdns expects you to create such a program if you need it.

$HOSTMASTER contains an email address (with an `@` character). This address is used as the *rname* field in the Start of Authority (SOA) records.

$IP The single IP address that ldapdns should listen on for incoming DNS requests. If this variable is set to `0.0.0.0`, ldapdns listens on all the machine's interfaces.

$LDAP_AUTH The value of this variable must be one of:

- **simple** Use simple LDAP authentication. The password is taken from the `password` file in `$ROOT`.
- **sasl** Use SASL authentication. The authentication name is taken from `$LDAP_SASL`. ldapdns first attempts Kerberos V2, and if that doesn't work, it tries Kerberos V1.

$LDAP_AUTH_NAME The distinguished name (DN) with which ldapdns attempts to bind to the directory. If this value is not set, it tries to find the DN in `$LDAP_BINDDN`.

$LDAP_HOSTS You use either `$LDAP_HOSTS` or `$LDAP_HOST` (synonymous) to specify the IP addresses at which your LDAP directory server is located. The value of this variable is either a space-separated list of IP addresses or a space-separated list of LDAP URIs; they are tried in order until the first one succeeds.

$LDAP_SUFFIX The search base under which ldapdns will perform searches.

$LOG Specifies how ldapdns should perform logging. You can:

- Log to stderr, by either not setting the variable at all, or setting it to an empty value.
- Avoid all logging, by setting:

```
LOG=quiet
```

- Use syslog with a facility of DAEMON, by setting:

  ```
  LOG="syslog"
  ```

- Log to a file, by setting the value of `$LOG` to a path name beginning with a slash, or to a URI beginning with `file://`

  ```
  LOG=/var/log/ldapdns
  ```

- Log to a program or pipe, by setting `$LOG` to a string beginning either with a vertical bar (|), or to a URI beginning with `pipe:/`, `exec:/`, `prog:/` or `program:/`.

  ```
  LOG=pipe://usr/sbin/mylogger
  ```

Queries are printed to the log like they are with tinydns:

```
c0a801a4:0000:a0a6 + 0001 qupps.biz
c0a801a4:0000:58cc - 0001 www.qupps.biz
c0a801a4:0000:def2 + 000f qupps.biz
```

$PORT The UDP port number (default: 53) on which ldapdns should listen, and the TCP port number on which ldapaxfr should listen.

$ROOT The directory containing the `root` directory, which in turn contains the `password` file.

$SCHEMA Modifies how ldapdns searches your LDAP directory tree. The value may take on one of the values `rfc1279`, `msdns`, `cosine`, or `ldapdns` (Section 12.1).

$SUPERVISE If you set this variable to any value, ldapdns forks and backgrounds itself upon start. Use this when running ldapdns under the supervision of daemontools (see Notes).

$THREADS The number of threads to use (default: 1). If you set this variable, ldapdns sets `$LDAP_THREADS` to this number, and it sets `$DNS_THREADS` to half this.

We obtained the best performance with these settings:

```
HANDLERS=128
THREADS=2
```

With these values, we obtained 1120 queries per second instead of 90 qps.

$UID / $GID `$UID` and `$GID` are the numeric user id and group id to which ldapdns will `setuid()` and `setgid()` respectively. ldapdns refuses to run as root unless you set:

```
$I_AM_STUPID_LET_ME_RUN_LDAPDNS_AS_ROOT
```

12.4 Configuring zones and resource records

As soon as you launch ldapdns, it is ready to answer queries, assuming you have entries in your LDAP directory that satisfy the queries. You launch ldapdns with:

```
# cd /usr/local/ldapdns
# ./run
```

We recommend you keep an eye on the logs of your LDAP directory server. OpenLDAP in particular, can show you what searches are being performed by ldapdns, and this can be helpful when troubleshooting. (We discuss OpenLDAP logging in Section A.3.10.)

12.4.1 DNS resources supported by ldapdns

The Cosine schema used by ldapdns is straightforward to implement. ldapdns uses the attribute types provided in the schema to represent a number of DNS resource records:

SOA A Start of Authority (SOA) is mapped onto the `sOARecord` attribute type. The attribute value must contain five space-separated numbers:

1. *serial number*. You can specify three different values for the serial number:
   - If you specify a numeric value, that value is used as the serial number.
     `sOARecord: 17 ...`
   - If you specify a zero (`0`), the current time (in UNIX time format), when the SOA is read, is used as the serial number.
     `sOARecord: 0 ...`
   - If you specify a literal `nnn`, ldapdns uses the value of `modifyTimestamp` of the LDAP entry as the serial number.
     `sOARecord: nnn ...`

   If the serial number portion of the attribute's value begins with an asterisk (`*`) the entire zone is disabled. You can use this to disable a zone if your customer hasn't paid their bill, without having to delete and later re-create the zone.
2. *refresh time*. If this value is zero, it defaults to 10 800 seconds or to `$DEFAULT_REFRESH` if set.
3. *retry time*. If this value is zero, it defaults to 7 200 seconds or to `$DEFAULT_RETRY` if set.
4. *expire time*. If this value is zero, it defaults to 604 800 seconds or to `$DEFAULT_EXPIRE` if set.
5. *minimum* TTL. If this value is zero, it defaults to 86 400 seconds or to `$DEFAULT_MINIMUM` if set.

ldapdns does not require Start of Authority records, as it can synthetically create them. You do that by omitting the SOA altogether, adding a Name Server (NS) record.

ldapdns automatically constructs the *rname* value of the SOA record by appending the domain name of the host ldapdns is running on to the word "hostmaster". You can change this on a zone-by-zone basis if you want to, by adding a `mail` attribute type to the LDAP entry containing the SOA record (`sOARecord`). The last attribute value of `mail` will be used as *rname* (with any `@` character replaced by a period).

NS The Name Server (NS) resource is mapped onto the `nSRecord` attribute type. The value is a domain name (i.e. a fully qualified host name).

```
nSRecord: ns.qupps.biz
```

A An Address record (A) is mapped by ldapdns onto the LDAP `aRecord` attribute type. Its value is a dotted decimal IP address.

```
aRecord: 1.2.3.4
```

ldapdns can also provide split-horizon in this attribute type, but we don't recommend you do that. To enable split-horizon, you append a slash and a network mask to the IP address. Consult the documentation on how to do that.

MX A Mail Exchanger (MX) is mapped onto an LDAP `mXRecord` attribute type. Its value must contain a numeric preference followed by a single space, followed by the domain name of the mail server.

```
mXRecord: 19 mail.qupps.biz
```

CNAME ldapdns retrieves a Canonical name (CNAME) from the LDAP `cNAMERecord` attribute type. The value is a domain name.

```
cNAMERecord: www.google.com
```

TXT A DNS query for a Text record (TXT) is served from the LDAP `description` attribute type. Its content is an arbitrary string.

```
description: expensive colour laser printer
```

If you have more than one value for the `description` attribute type, then more than one TXT RR will be served.

PTR Pointer resource records (PTR) are created in the in-addr.arpa domain by setting the `cNAMERecord` attribute type to a domain name.

```
dc=10,dc=3,dc=2,dc=1,dc=in-addr,dc=arpa,...
cNAMERecord: home.mens.de
```

12.4.2 Adding a zone to ldapdns

Adding a minimal zone

Adding a zone to ldapdns involves adding an object to your LDAP directory server. The following LDIF provides all that is necessary to add a zone:

```
dn: dc=qupps,dc=biz,ou=zones,ou=LDAPdns,ou=dns,o=qupps.biz
dc: qupps
objectClass: dNSDomain
objectClass: dcObject
objectClass: extensibleObject
mail: jp@xyz.de
nSRecord: ns.qupps.biz
```

If we now query ldapdns we get the following:

```
$ dig @192.168.1.164 qupps.biz
;; ->>HEADER<<- opcode: QUERY, status: NOERROR, id: 19751
;; flags: qr aa rd; QUERY: 1, ANSWER: 1, AUTHORITY: 1, ADDITIONAL: 0

;; ANSWER SECTION:
qupps.biz.              86400    IN       SOA      ns.qupps.biz.  jp.xyz.de. ↩
                                  1199309678 10800 7200 604800 86400

;; AUTHORITY SECTION:
qupps.biz.              86400    IN       NS       ns.qupps.biz.
```

Note the following:

- The "aa" bit is set in the "flags" line. ldapdns is authoritative for the zone.
- We didn't include an `sOARecord` in the LDAP entry for the zone, so ldapdns used its defaults, using the `modifyTimestamp` for the serial number.
- The object we added to the directory has a class `extensibleObject`. That allows us to add an attribute type `mail` which is used by ldapdns to construct the *rname* for the SOA record. This is just for illustration: you do not have to do this; if you omit an e-mail address, ldapdns uses the value of `$HOSTMASTER` instead.
- The `nSRecord` attribute type is mandatory.

Adding a zone with more records

The following LDIF shows a zone with two name servers, two Mail Exchangers and a host with four IP Address records:

```
dn: dc=qupps,dc=biz,ou=zones,ou=LDAPdns,ou=dns,o=qupps.biz
dc: qupps
objectClass: dNSDomain
objectClass: dcObject
sOARecord: 17 180 90 180 180
nSRecord: ns.qupps.biz
nSRecord: ns2.qupps.biz
mXRecord: 10 mail.qupps.biz
mXRecord: 25 mail.uit.co.uk
description: This zone belongs to me
description: contact me

dn: dc=mail,dc=qupps,dc=biz,ou=zones,ou=LDAPdns,ou=dns,o=qupps.biz
objectClass: dcObject
objectClass: dNSDomain
dc: mail
aRecord: 192.168.1.20
aRecord: 192.168.1.21
aRecord: 192.168.1.22
aRecord: 192.168.1.23
```

```
$ dig @192.168.1.164 qupps.biz  any
;; ANSWER SECTION:
qupps.biz.       86400  IN  MX   25 mail.uit.co.uk.
qupps.biz.       86400  IN  MX   10 mail.qupps.biz.
qupps.biz.       180    IN  SOA  ns.qupps.biz.  hostmaster.qupps.biz. 17 180 90 180 180
qupps.biz.       86400  IN  NS   ns.qupps.biz.
qupps.biz.       86400  IN  NS   ns2.qupps.biz.

;; AUTHORITY SECTION:
qupps.biz.       86400  IN  NS   ns.qupps.biz.
qupps.biz.       86400  IN  NS   ns2.qupps.biz.

;; ADDITIONAL SECTION:
mail.qupps.biz. 86400  IN  A    192.168.1.23
mail.qupps.biz. 86400  IN  A    192.168.1.22
mail.qupps.biz. 86400  IN  A    192.168.1.21
mail.qupps.biz. 86400  IN  A    192.168.1.20
```

12.4.3 Adding an in-addr.arpa zone to ldapdns

Create the zone

To add a reverse Pointer (PTR) to an in-addr.arpa zone, you reverse the dotted decimal numbers of an IP Address and use each of the decimal numbers in the relative distinguished name (RDN) of an LDAP entry. An example LDIF for creating the containers for a zone is:

```
dn: dc=arpa,ou=zones,ou=LDAPdns,ou=dns,o=qupps.biz
dc: arpa
objectClass: dcObject
objectClass: dNSDomain

dn: dc=in-addr,dc=arpa,ou=zones,ou=LDAPdns,ou=dns,o=qupps.biz
dc: in-addr
objectClass: dcObject
objectClass: dNSDomain

dn: dc=192,dc=in-addr,dc=arpa,ou=zones,ou=LDAPdns,ou=dns,o=qupps.biz
dc: 192
objectClass: dcObject
objectClass: dNSDomain

dn: dc=168,dc=192,dc=in-addr,dc=arpa,ou=zones,ou=LDAPdns,ou=dns,o=qupps.biz
dc: 168
objectClass: dcObject
objectClass: dNSDomain

dn: dc=1,dc=168,dc=192,dc=in-addr,dc=arpa,ou=zones,ou=LDAPdns,ou=dns,o=qupps.biz
dc: 1
objectClass: dcObject
objectClass: dNSDomain
nSRecord: ns.qupps.biz
```

The zone now exists, because the last entry in the example above contains the required `nSRecord` attribute type for the NS resource record.

Create the PTR *resource record*

The LDIF for the PTR record for an IP address 192.168.1.10 looks like this:

```
dn: dc=10,dc=1,dc=168,dc=192,dc=in-addr,dc=arpa,ou=zones,ou=LDAPdns,ou=dns,
 o=qupps.biz
dc: 10
objectClass: dcObject
objectClass: dNSDomain
cNAMERecord: www.qupps.biz
```

Note how the `cNAMERecord` attribute type is used to create a pointer resource record (PTR). Querying the ldapdns server, we get a correct answer:

```
$ dig @192.168.1.164 -x 192.168.1.10
;; ->>HEADER<<- opcode: QUERY, status: NOERROR, id: 23060
;; flags: qr aa rd; QUERY: 1, ANSWER: 1, AUTHORITY: 1,

;; ANSWER SECTION:
10.1.168.192.in-addr.arpa. 86400 IN     PTR     www.qupps.biz.

;; AUTHORITY SECTION:
1.168.192.in-addr.arpa. 86400    IN     NS      ns.qupps.biz.

;; ADDITIONAL SECTION:
ns.qupps.biz.            86400    IN     A       192.168.1.164
```

12.5 Managing zone data

You will probably not want to create long LDIF files for adding a DNS resource record to your LDAP directory server, and we certainly don't. There are a number of different ways you can manipulate LDAP entries on your directory server:

- Use an LDAP browser (Section 2.5.4) to edit your LDAP entries.
- We like creating small specialized scripts or programs for the job. You can use a simple shell script that utilizes ldapadd or ldapmodify, or you can invest a bit more time and use Perl's Net::LDAP (or any other programming language with LDAP support) to create custom tools to add DNS zones and resource records to your LDAP directory.
- You can use some of the scripts provided in the `admin` directory of the ldapdns source distribution.

We discuss some further methods in Chapter 19.

12.6 Providing DNS over TCP with ldapdns

Like tinydns, ldapdns only answers DNS queries over UDP. If you want to provide DNS over TCP with ldapdns, you have to deploy the zone transfer program, ldapaxfr, which also uses your LDAP directory server. You set up ldapaxfr with the ldapaxfr-conf program:

```
# ldapaxfr-conf nobody nobody /usr/local/ldapaxfr /usr/local/ldapdns 192.168.1.164
```

ldapaxfr uses the same `env` directory (that you specified when you configured ldapdns with the ldapdns-conf utility), to find the variables pertaining to the LDAP directory. In addition to other variables used by ldapdns, ldapaxfr uses the variable `$AXFR` to control what it will serve over TCP. You have two possibilities:

1. If `$AXFR` is unset or it is set to an empty string (`""`), ldapaxfr will not provide outgoing zone transfers, limiting its operation to supplying answers to DNS queries over TCP.
2. If the variable `$AXFR` is set to a single period (`.`) it provides zone transfers for all zones. If you set `$AXFR` to a domain name (e.g. biz) it provides transfers to all sub-domains of the one specified, as well as normal answers over TCP.

12.7 Integrate ldapdns with BIND

We said in the introduction to this chapter that we use ldapdns as authoritative DNS server on a group of e-mail servers within an organization, and we said that we've had good experience with it, which is quite true. In fact, we set this system up as shown in Figure 12.2: the machines have a BIND name server configured as a caching name server, providing DNS services to the local LAN. The same BIND server is also configured to forward queries for the special domain email.qupps.biz to ldapdns.

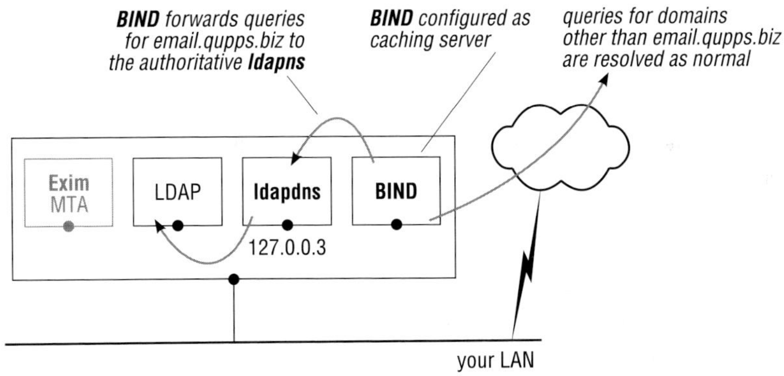

Figure 12.2: Forwarding BIND queries to ldapdns

The forwarding in BIND is configured as:

```
zone "email.qupps.biz" {
    type forward;
    forward only;
    forwarders {
        127.0.0.3 port 53;
    };
};
```

Note the use of the loop-back address 127.0.0.3 to which ldapdns is bound.

Summary

- ldapdns is an authoritative DNS server that retrieves its zone data from an LDAP directory.
- Its organization and administration are similar to tinydns.
- ldapaxfr provides DNS replies and outgoing zone transfers over TCP.
- Development of ldapdns appears to have come to a standstill.

Related topics

- Other authoritative DNS servers that can retrieve DNS data from an LDAP directory are PowerDNS (Chapter 6), BIND SDB (Chapter 8), and Bind DLZ (Chapter 9).
- You can use dnsproxy (Section 17.5) if you want to operate a cache and ldapdns on the same host.
- If ldapdns is causing a large load on your LDAP servers, you might want to consider placing a cache in front of it. dnscache (Section 17.4) is up to snuff.

Notes and further reading

Building and installing ldapdns

Download ldapdns from `http://www.nimh.org/code/ldapdns/`. The configure script supplied is just a small wrapper that supports the `--prefix` option only.

```
$ wget http://www.nimh.org/dl/ldapdns.tgz
$ tar xvzf ldapdns.tgz
$ cd ldapdns-2.06
```

On our system we had to patch ldapdns slightly, because it uses a function called `log()` which conflicts with a routine of the same name from the standard C library. We have made the patch available at the URL shown here and on the book's Web site (☞ D121):

```
$ wget http://fupps.com/code/sundry/ldapdns/ldapdns-2.06.patch
$ patch -p0 < ldapdns-2.06.patch
patching file ldapdns.c
patching file error.h
patching file engine.c
patching file error.c

$ ./configure --prefix=/usr/local
$ make
$ PREFIX=/usr/local make install
```

To use the facilities provided by ldapdns-conf you must install the daemontools package, a collection of tools for managing UNIX services. We recommend you do so at this point. (See Notes on page 310.)

Are you a developer?

- ldapdns could do with a new breath of life. If you are a developer, many people would be pleased to see development continue on ldapdns.
- Version 2 of ldapdns (the version we have discussed in this chapter) has not been modified for some time. There are some "features" that could do with a bit of polish.
- A newer code base of ldapdns is named LDAPDNS3. There hasn't been development on it since early 2004, but you may nevertheless be interested in taking it for a test drive. It could use a good developer to get it going again (see `http://ldapdns.sourceforge.net/`).

Chapter

13 dnsmasq

Why is it drug addicts and computer aficionados are both called users?

Clifford Stoll

Introduction

For Small Office / Home Office or branch-office networks, using one of the "big" name servers is overkill and requires too much effort. dnsmasq is a gem of a program: it uses the simple `/etc/hosts` file for its zone data, has support for ad-blocking and has a built-in DHCP server as well.

Many small home or office networks don't use DNS, because it appears to be too difficult to set up. Consequently, either their users have to refer to local machines by numeric IP address, or the "administrator" has to maintain and distribute `/etc/hosts` files to all machines on the LAN, which is tedious and error-prone. dnsmasq, written by Simon Kelley, is a gem. It comes to the rescue for these environments, combining a very lightweight DNS server, an optional DHCP server with DNS integration, and a caching resolver which talks to the outside world.

dnsmasq accepts DNS queries and either answers them from your `/etc/hosts` file, or forwards them to a "real" DNS server for resolving; dnsmasq can't act as a full recursive resolver itself because it wasn't made to do so. It uses the content of a local `/etc/hosts` or similar file to create resource records and serves them under any domain name you specify. dnsmasq's built-in DHCP server supports static and dynamic address assignments, can be configured to send any desired set of DHCP options, supports BOOTP, and includes a TFTP server.

Pros	• Trivial to set up and maintain • Built-in DHCP server with some DNS integration • Lightweight • Used in router boxes and distributions • Advanced options for complex scenarios
Cons	○ No IPv6 for DHCP
Scenarios	Small networks (Small Office / Home Office or branch office) without a dedicated systems administrator.

Table 13.1: dnsmasq at a glance

In some countries, Germany for example, it is common to have an ISDN or ADSL connection to the Internet. It is often the case that a small router is used to provide DHCP service to the LAN and act as a gateway to the Internet. The router sets itself up as a non-caching DNS proxy and provides DHCP service to clients, giving them its address as DNS server. When users surf the Internet or use an e-mail client, all DNS requests are passed to the router which forwards them to the ISP's DNS servers for resolution. This works well enough for qualified domain names but it's not ideal:

- If the Internet connection is down, the query from the router to the Internet has to time out before errors are reported to a user.
- If your local network has a server of any kind – for example a network printer, a file server, or media server – it too needs to be addressed. The only way to make it addressable by hostname across the whole network is to enter it manually in the `/etc/hosts` files (`\windows\system32\drivers\etc\hosts` on Microsoft Windows) on each of the workstations.

Putting dnsmasq on a small machine in your network addresses all these issues (Figure 13.1).

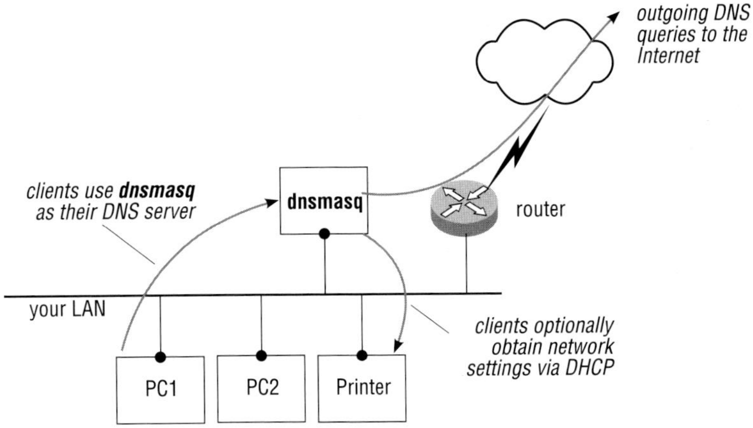

Figure 13.1: Placing dnsmasq on your network

Workstations on the local network set up their resolver to point to the dnsmasq host or get this set up automatically via dnsmasq's built-in DHCP server (in which case you should *disable* any other DHCP server on your network[1]). If you have a single host on your network, you can use dnsmasq as a caching name server for that machine.

If your operating system vendor has not already packaged dnsmasq for you, you will have to build and install it yourself, but that is not difficult (see Notes). dnsmasq is supported on FreeBSD, GNU/Linux, Mac OS X, and Solaris.

13.1 Preliminary explorations

With dnsmasq installed, you can immediately run it to provide seamless DNS to your network, before you explore its more advanced configuration options which we discuss in the next sections. There is no danger at all in setting up a test DNS server on your LAN because your clients will only "see" it when you explicitly configure them to use it.

First add an exotic host name to the `/etc/hosts` file of the machine you will be launching dnsmasq on, to test the DNS server:

```
# echo "192.168.1.17  foozy.local foozy" >> /etc/hosts
```

Now launch dnsmasq in the foreground and make it log queries to the console, so that you can see things as they happen:

```
# dnsmasq --no-daemon --log-queries
dnsmasq: started, version 2.43 cachesize 150
dnsmasq: compile time options: IPv6 GNU-getopt no-ISC-leasefile no-DBus no-I18N
dnsmasq: reading /etc/resolv.conf
dnsmasq: using nameserver 192.168.13.2#53
dnsmasq: read /etc/hosts - 3 addresses
```

[1] Is it just us or do you also get feeling that every device on the market today has a built-in DHCP server? At the time of this writing, we purchased a NAS device, and guess what? Yes.

If you query dnsmasq for the host name you previously added to `/etc/hosts` (foozy.local) you should get an authoritative answer (i.e. with "aa" bit set in dig's "flags" line):

```
$ dig @127.0.0.1 foozy.local
;; ->>HEADER<<- opcode: QUERY, status: NOERROR, id: 47776
;; flags: qr aa rd ra; QUERY: 1, ANSWER: 1, AUTHORITY: 0, ADDITIONAL: 0

;; ANSWER SECTION:
foozy.local.            0       IN      A       192.168.1.17
```

and the debugging output of dnsmasq shows the received query:

```
dnsmasq: reading /etc/resolv.conf
dnsmasq: using nameserver 192.168.13.2#53
dnsmasq: read /etc/hosts - 3 addresses
dnsmasq: query[A] foozy.local from 127.0.0.1
dnsmasq: /etc/hosts foozy.local is 192.168.1.17
```

If that does not work as expected, check the following:

- Did you launch dnsmasq as the root user? You must. (dnsmasq can drop privileges after it starts; Section 13.3.1 shows you how to configure this.)
- Did you see any error messages when you started dnsmasq? If so, try and get them cleared away.
- Your machine may already have a DNS server running on it. (If you installed dnsmasq from a binary package, your package manager may have already launched dnsmasq for you.). Two DNS servers can't listen on the same port 53 and on the same IP addresses, so the second one you try to start will fail. Ensure that no other program is "grabbing" your DNS traffic. To see which programs are listening on which addresses:

  ```
  # netstat -anp | grep 53
  tcp 0  0 127.0.0.1:53        0.0.0.0:* LISTEN     15338/named
  udp 0  0 192.168.1.20:53     0.0.0.0:*            15338/named
  udp 0  0 127.0.0.1:53        0.0.0.0:*            15338/named
  ```

  If you see a program such as named, you are already running a version of BIND. Either stop it, or get it to listen on a different IP address, or read on to see how to configure dnsmasq to do so.

- If you are testing the query logging from a Windows machine and don't see any entries being made in the log, your PC might be using the Windows DNS cache and not passing the query to dnsmasq at all. Either flush it with:

  ```
  C:\> ipconfig /flushdns
  ```

  or try a query for a different name, that you know you haven't accessed recently.

By default dnsmasq uses its local `/etc/resolv.conf` to find addresses of DNS caches and will forward queries to them. So if your Internet connection is active, you should be able to direct queries for public hosts to dnsmasq and receive answers for them.

13.2 Live running

To put dnsmasq into production on your LAN, you:

1. Edit `/etc/hosts` and enter all the hosts you want to name. (You don't have to fully qualify their names.)
2. Make sure the `/etc/resolv.conf` file on the host running dnsmasq has at least one correct `nameserver` entry, so that dnsmasq can forward DNS queries for the public DNS to upstream name servers.
3. Configure `/etc/resolv.conf` on the other clients of your network to point to your dnsmasq host. Below, we show how you can use dnsmasq's built-in DHCP server to accomplish that if you like.
4. Configure your system to launch dnsmasq at system startup. (Consult your documentation for how to do that.)

If you don't intend to use the DHCP features of dnsmasq or if you don't need to adapt the sensible defaults it uses, you can stop right here.

13.3 Advanced dnsmasq configuration

dnsmasq uses very sensible default options. In many environments you won't need to adjust them in any way. Nevertheless, to get more out of dnsmasq, such as setting up DHCP to enable other machines on your network to automatically obtain network parameters, you will have to create a custom configuration.

You configure dnsmasq either by invoking it with options or by letting it read its default `/etc/dnsmasq.conf` (or the file specified with `--conf-file=`). Most options have both a short one-character name, and a long name, that is the same as the option-name used in the configuration file. You must restart dnsmasq for changes to take effect (because a SIGHUP does not cause it to re-read its configuration).

The following sections group the more interesting options by task, not alphabetically; other options are documented in the dnsmasq manual page.

13.3.1 Interfaces and addresses

With these options, you configure dnsmasq to listen only on specific interfaces or addresses with these options. The default of listening on all interfaces is fine for many installations.

port
: Listen on the specified port instead of the default DNS port (53). If you set the port number to 0, the DNS server is disabled.

```
port=53
```

interface
: Listen only on the specified interface(s). dnsmasq can be made to listen on any number of the system's real (not aliased) interfaces. The loop-back interface is included automatically, but may be excluded with the interface-except option.

```
interface=eth0
interface=eth1
```

interface-except
: Listen on all interfaces except those listed.

```
interface-except=lo
```

listen-address
: Use this option to get dnsmasq to listen on aliased interfaces by providing their addresses. If no interface option is given but listen-address is, dnsmasq will not automatically listen on the loop-back interface; if you want it to, you must explicitly add 127.0.0.1 to this option.

```
listen-address=192.168.1.164
listen-address=127.0.0.1
```

no-dhcp-interface
: Provide only DNS on the specified interface (i.e. no DHCP or TFTP service).

```
no-dhcp-interface=eth0
```

user
: Specify the userid to which dnsmasq will change after startup. dnsmasq must normally be started as `root`, but it drops root privileges after startup by changing userid to another user. (Default: `nobody`.)

13.3.2 Hosts and domains

A few options tell dnsmasq how it should handle host names and from which files it should create local DNS resource records. As a small reminder, hosts files on *nix and Microsoft Windows are formatted as a list of IP addresses and hostnames, one on each line:

```
127.0.0.1        localhost.localdomain localhost
192.168.1.20     home
192.168.1.179    ls1
192.168.1.185    pc2
192.168.1.17     foozy.local foozy
```

no-hosts
: Don't process the default `/etc/hosts`. Often used with addn-hosts, next.

addn-hosts
: ("additional hosts") Specify a file in `/etc/hosts` format that dnsmasq should also read in addition to the system's `/etc/hosts` file. If no-hosts is also set, only this file will be used.

```
addn-hosts=/etc/my.hosts
```

expand-hosts
: Append our domain, specified in domain, below, to unqualified host names read from `/etc/hosts`, i.e. to names that do not contain a period.

```
expand-hosts
```

domain

This option sets "ourdomain" – the domain that is appended to unqualified names. For example, if you set:

```
domain=foo.bar
```

the name www in `/etc/hosts` will be expanded to www.foo.bar.

This setting also sets the DHCP `domain` option, thereby providing all DHCP clients with a DNS domain name, and it ensures that DHCP clients that provide their own names must do so with names that end with this value. For example:

```
domain=office
```

causes DHCP clients that supply their host name as alex or alternatively as alex.office (qualified) to be called alex.office. However, dnsmasq will not register – in the local DNS cache – any clients that announce their names as alex.fupps.com. This ensures that a client on the network cannot announce itself as being www.cnn.com and have HTTP requests for the news agency falsely directed to its IP.

We recommend you do not use `.local` as your domain name because it may interfere with mDNS on Mac OS X systems.

domain-needed

This option instructs dnsmasq to never forward queries to upstream DNS name servers, for names that are unqualified (i.e. do not contain a period). You should enable this option.

13.3.3 DNS resolution

A number of options affect the way dnsmasq resolves names; some are given here, but see also Section 13.3.2.

alias

This option can be used to alter IP addresses that are returned from upstream DNS servers. For example:

```
alias=10.0.0.1,192.168.1.20
```

makes dnsmasq return 192.168.1.20 instead of the "real" address 10.0.0.1.

bogus-priv

All reverse lookups for private IP ranges (i.e. 192.168.x.y, 10.x.y.z, etc.) that are not found in `/etc/hosts` or the DHCP leases file are answered with "no such domain" (NXDOMAIN) rather than being forwarded upstream. We recommend you generally set this, because private IP addresses (RFC 1918) aren't routed on the Internet, so you'd never get an answer anyway.

filterwin2k

Filter out SOA, SRV and type ANY queries where the requested name contains underscores. These queries are frequently sent by later versions of Microsoft Windows. Do note however, that this option blocks *all* queries of type SRV as well.

resolv-file

dnsmasq uses the `resolv.conf` file to find upstream name servers. This means, however, that other programs on this host also use the same `resolv.conf` for query resolution and therefore bypass dnsmasq.

To work around this, the resolv-file option allows you to specify an alternative file that dnsmasq uses to find upstream name servers. dnsmasq reads the IP addresses of the upstream name servers from the specified file *instead* of `/etc/resolv.conf`. The format of the file is the same as `/etc/resolv.conf`, but dnsmasq uses only the `nameserver` lines. Here's an example of how you'd set this up:

1. Enter your ISP's name server addresses in `nameserver` lines in `/etc/resolv.dm`, say, and set the option:

   ```
   resolv-file =/etc/resolv.dm
   ```

2. Make sure the only `nameserver` line in `/etc/resolv.conf` is:

   ```
   nameserver 127.0.0.1
   ```

Now your local stub resolver will send its queries to 127.0.0.1, i.e. to dnsmasq, which will forward them to your ISPs servers.

no-poll

By default, dnsmasq checks whether the modification time stamp of `/etc/resolv.conf` (or the file specified as resolv-file) has changed, and reloads it if it has, on receiving a DNS query. This allows dnsmasq to work in environments that have their DNS servers set dynamically with PPP or DHCP, since both protocols generally modify the local resolver file. To avoid this behavior, set no-poll.

Even if no-poll is set, sending dnsmasq a SIGHUP will cause it to re-read `/etc/resolv.conf`.

clear-on-reload

Whenever dnsmasq re-reads `resolv.conf` because it has changed, it should clear the content of its cache. Although this means loosing cached entries, it is probably wise, as different upstream name servers may have differing DNS data to that which is in the cache.

local
server

The options server and local are synonymous; use whichever seems more logical to you. They specify the addresses of upstream DNS servers directly.

If one or more optional domains are given, that server is used only for those domains and they are queried only using the specified server. The setting

```
server=/fupps.com/qupps.biz/192.168.13.129
```

causes dnsmasq to forward all queries for domains fupps.com and qupps.biz to the DNS server at 192.168.13.129; all other queries are sent to the upstream DNS servers read from `/etc/resolv.conf` if they cannot be answered from `/etc/hosts` or DHCP.

Specifying just a domain, without a DNS-server address, has a different meaning. It tells dnsmasq that the domain is local; it might answer from `/etc/hosts` or DHCP but it should never forward queries for the domain to upstream name servers. For example, the setting:

```
local=/my.home/
```

has dnsmasq answer a query for pc27.my.home from `/etc/hosts` (if it contains an IP for pc27 or pc27.my.home), but it will never forward queries for *anything*.my.home to other name servers.

address

This option is useful for home networks. With it, you specify a domain, and the single IP address to be returned for *any* host in that domain. Queries for these domains are never forwarded, although they can be overridden by `/etc/hosts` or DHCP entries. This is often used to redirect HTTP traffic for specific unwanted sites to a local HTTP server (think advertisement blocking). For example:

```
address=/foo.bar/foo.de/1.2.3.4
address=/singleclick.com/127.0.0.1
```

returns the address 1.2.3.4 for all queries to the two domains foo.bar and foo.de and queries for singleclick.com are answered with an Address (A) record of 127.0.0.1. As shown, you can specify this option multiple times. Now, the DNS directs any Web browser connecting to `http://www.singleclick.com` to IP address 127.0.0.1 instead of to the domain's real address.

txt-record

This option causes dnsmasq to add a TXT resource record to the built-in DNS server. The value is given a host name (which is not automatically qualified with the name of our domain), and a comma-separated list of strings. The example adds two TXT records for the same name:

```
txt-record=what,This is my server,Contact JP
txt-record=what,at 555-1001
```

and a query for a TXT record produces:

```
$ dig @127.0.0.1 what. TXT
;; ANSWER SECTION:
what.   0   IN   TXT   "at 555-1001"
what.   0   IN   TXT   "This is my server" "Contact JP"
```

Note that two records are returned, one of which contains two strings.

cache-size

The compiled-in limit of dnsmasq's internal cache is 10 000 entries, which is more than sufficient for the intended deployment scenarios. The default cache size is defined in `config.h` to be 150 entries, which is a bit small. This variable sets the size of the cache to the desired number of entries; more consumes more memory and a value of 0 (zero) disables the cache entirely. We don't recommend you disable it.

Just like all other caching servers, when dnsmasq is shut down, it does not store the cache's content for reloading later, and it cannot be made to do so. (Due to the nature of DNS and the sometimes quite short TTL on DNS records, there is little point in saving a cache that contains mostly records that will have expired when it comes to be reloaded.)

13.3.4 DHCP

By default, dnsmasq does not offer DHCP services on the network, but you can easily configure it to do so. dnsmasq's DHCP service is quite complete and includes supplying options to its clients, IP address pools from which clients are assigned a dynamic address, multiple subnets, and static host assignments for devices to which you want to give a permanent address.

dhcp-range

This option enables the DHCP server. It allows dnsmasq to give out addresses from the range *start-addr* to *end-addr* inclusive, and from statically defined addresses given in the dhcp-host option, below.

```
dhcp-range=start-addr,end-addr[,netmask,bcast][,lease-time]
dhcp-range=192.168.1.50,192.168.1.150,3d
```

If the lease time is given, then leases will be given for that length of time (default: 1h). Lease times are specified in seconds, minutes, hours or days by appending the character `s` (default), `m`, `h` or `d` respectively, and may be infinite with the literal `infinite`. This option may be repeated with different addresses to enable DHCP service to more than one network.

dhcp-host

This option specifies per-host parameters for the DHCP server. It allows a machine with a particular hardware address to be always allocated the same host name, IP address and lease time. A host name specified like this overrides any supplied by the DHCP client software on the client machine. You can omit the hardware address and include the host name; then, the IP address and lease times will apply to any machine claiming that name.

```
dhcp-host=hardware-addr,name,IP addr,lease
dhcp-host=00:0F:1F:C5:0B:65,jp510m,192.168.1.60,48h
```

dhcp-hostsfile

This variable causes dnsmasq to read DHCP host information from the specified file. The file contains information about one host per line. The format of a line is the same as text to the right of the "=" in dhcp-host. The advantage of storing DHCP host information in this file is that it can be changed without restarting dnsmasq: the file is re-read when dnsmasq receives a SIGHUP signal.

```
dhcp-hostsfile=/etc/dhcp.machines
```

dhcp-option

This setting allows you to override the default DHCP options sent to clients by dnsmasq. Options may be specified as decimal numbers or as option names (Table 13.2).

```
dhcp-option = option:netmask, 255.255.255.0
dhcp-option = option:router, 192.168.1.1
dhcp-option = 3, 192.168.1.1
```

The last two lines are synonymous; the last line specifies the option's decimal number (3) whereas the second-last line specifies it as an option name with a leading "`option:`". (We prefer the textual representation as they document themselves better.)

1	netmask	37	tcp-ttl
2	time-offset	38	tcp-keepalive
3	router	40	nis-domain
6	dns-server	41	nis-server
7	log-server	42	ntp-server
9	lpr-server	44	netbios-ns
13	boot-file-size	45	netbios-dd
15	domain-name	46	netbios-nodetype
16	swap-server	47	netbios-scope
17	root-path	48	x-windows-fs
18	extension-path	49	x-windows-dm
19	ip-forward-enable	60	vendor-class
20	non-local-source-routing	64	nis-domain
21	policy-filter	65	nis-server
22	max-datagram-reassembly	68	mobile-ip-home
23	default-ttl	69	smtp-server
26	mtu	70	pop3-server
27	all-subnets-local	71	nntp-server
31	router-discovery	74	irc-server
32	router-solicitation	77	user-class
33	static-route	119	domain-search
34	trailer-encapsulation	120	sip-server
35	arp-timeout	121	classless-static-route
36	ethernet-encap		

Table 13.2: DHCP options supported by dnsmasq's DHCP server

dhcp-authoritative

Use this when dnsmasq is definitely the only DHCP server on a network. It changes the behavior from strict RFC compliance, so that

DHCP requests for unknown leases (even renew requests) from unknown hosts are not ignored. This allows new hosts to get a lease without a tedious timeout under all circumstances. It also allows dnsmasq to rebuild its lease database without each client needing to reacquire a lease, if the database is lost.

```
dhcp-authoritative
```

dhcp-leasefile
dnsmasq should record the leases it has granted, in the specified file (default is `/var/db/dnsmasq.leases`). This file is re-used when dnsmasq starts up, if it exists.

dhcp-script
dnsmasq can be instructed to run a program or a script when a lease is obtained or released. The option:

```
dhcp-script=/bin/myprog
```

defines the path to the program that should be executed, which can be an executable script or program. This program can do anything it desires: a simple example follows, to show the arguments and the environment that the program receives:

```
#!/bin/sh

exec > /tmp/myprog.out
echo "ARGS: " $*
env|grep '^DNSMASQ'
```

In our example, the following would be saved in the `myprog.out` file.

```
ARGS:  add 00:0f:1f:c5:0b:65 192.168.1.60 jp510m
DNSMASQ_TIME_REMAINING=2700
DNSMASQ_LEASE_EXPIRES=1196471835
```

The first argument passed to the program is one of the following three keywords:

add Indicates that a new lease has been created.

old Indicates that an existing lease is being renewed.

del Indicates that an existing lease is being destroyed.

For very small small environments the dhcp-script option is probably overkill, unless you want to experiment with writing a script that notifies you whenever a new client has been connected to the network. Larger environments might want to do something useful with the data, such as performing usage analysis.

13.3.5 Debugging

The following options are normally disabled, but are useful for debugging.

keep-in-foreground Do not `fork()` and do not run in background. This is useful on Mac OSX when running under launchd control.

no-daemon dnsmasq should run in the foreground, in debugging mode. It will not change user and won't write a PID file. Sending this process a SIGUSR1 will cause it to create a full cache dump, which is logged with syslogd or into a file, depending on your setting of log-facility.

log-facility The "facility" with which dnsmasq should send entries to the system's syslog daemon. The default is DAEMON or LOCAL0 when you run it as no-daemon, which runs it in debugging mode. Setting this variable to a path, which must contain a forward slash (/), causes dnsmasq to write to the specified file instead of using syslog. When logging to a file, dnsmasq closes and reopens the file when it receives SIGUSR2. This allows the log file to be rotated without stopping dnsmasq.

log-dhcp Log additional information about DHCP requests sent to clients. We recommend you use this when you first start using DHCP, as it shows you what the clients are sending and what dnsmasq is replying with.

log-queries Log the result of DNS queries. Here are three sample log entries:

```
query[A] kiki.office from 192.168.1.60
DHCP kiki.office is 192.168.1.53

query[A] myserver.office from 192.168.1.60
/etc/hosts myserver.office is 192.168.1.21

query[A] cnn.com from 192.168.1.60
forwarded cnn.com to 192.168.1.20
reply cnn.com is 64.236.29.120
reply cnn.com is 64.236.16.20
reply cnn.com is 64.236.16.52
reply cnn.com is 64.236.24.12
```

dnsmasq shows the query type in square brackets. (A is a query for an A record, ...). On the second line of each entry it shows where the query was answered from. In the first case, the answer came from a DHCP registration, the second came from the `/etc/hosts` file on the machine dnsmasq is running on, and the third was forwarded to a recursive name server running on 192.168.1.20.

Setting this option also enables a full cache dump to the log-facility on receipt of SIGUSR1.

```
time 196386581, cache size 150, 0/4 cache insertions ...
Host             Address       Flags   Expires
localhost6       ::1           6FRI  H
foozy.local      192.168.1.17 4FRI  H
foozy            192.168.1.17 4F I  H
mail.qupps.biz   192.168.1.20 4F       Sat Dec  1 18:15
x.qupps.biz      qupps.biz     CF      Sat Dec  1 18:15
```

```
qupps.biz        192.168.1.20 4F       Sat Dec  1 18:15
localhost        127.0.0.1    4F I  H
```

dnsmasq recognizes other options, as well as more advanced forms of some of the options described. We encourage you to read the dnsmasq manual for details.

13.4 A complete example

Here we show you a configuration suitable for a number of scenarios. We've used only a small subset of dnsmasq's facilities, but we can boot FreeBSD, GNU/Linux and even Microsoft Windows XP PCs from this and that is good enough for us.

Listing 13.1: dnsmasq configuration

```
# Logging.
#   1. Use file instead of syslog
#   2. Log DNS queries
#   3. Log DHCP details
log-facility=/var/log/dnsmasq
log-queries
log-dhcp# disable if too noisy

# DNS things
#   1. Set domain to .office
#   2. Never forward anything.office
#   3. Don't forward unknown PTR for private addrs
#   4. Drop Win2K stuff
#   5. Must have period in name to forward
#   6. Add domain (.office) to simple names

domain=office
local=/office/
bogus-priv
filterwin2k
domain-needed
expand-hosts

# more DNS
#   1. Add explicit forwarder for qupps.biz
server=/qupps.biz/192.168.1.20

# DHCP
#   1. I am *the* DHCP server
#   2. Write leases to this file
dhcp-authoritative
dhcp-leasefile=/var/lib/dnsmasq.leases

# DHCP Options ('dnsmasq --help dhcp')
#   1. Netmask
#   2. Gateway (router)
#   (3. optional: DNS server; default is dnsmasq host)
#   4. Tell MS client to RELEASE on shutdown

dhcp-option = option:netmask, 255.255.255.0
```

```
dhcp-option = option:router, 192.168.1.1
# dhcp-option = option:dns-server, 192.168.1.164
dhcp-option = vendor:MSFT,2,1i

# Dynamic DHCP
#  1. range with 3 day lease (lowers traffic)
dhcp-range=192.168.1.50,192.168.1.150,3d

# A few static DHCP hosts
dhcp-host=00:0F:1F:C5:0B:65,jp510m,192.168.1.60,45m
dhcp-host=00:80:77:B1:0E:38,printer,192.168.1.60,72h
```

Here's a summary of what this configuration does for you:

Logging

1. Log to the specified file instead via syslogd.
2. DNS queries will be logged.
3. Details about DHCP requests received and answered will also be logged. This is very useful for debugging.

DNS settings

1. Our local DNS domain is set to .office.
2. The local option specifies that dnsmasq will not forward any query containing the domain .office to an upstream name server.
3. Forbidding dnsmasq to forward requests for PTR resource to private IP addresses records to upstream name servers is always a good idea unless you are deploying dnsmasq in an environment in which the upstream name servers use private IP addresses.
4. Newer unwanted Microsoft Windows DNS queries are filtered out with filterwin2k.
5. Forward queries to upstream servers only if the query contains a domain name.
6. Furthermore dnsmasq should add our domain name (.office) to unqualified names read from `/etc/hosts`.

More DNS As an example, we set up a forwarder for the domain qupps.biz to a name server at 192.168.1.20. You may need several server lines if you have several private domains you want to serve.

DHCP

1. DHCP is set to be authoritative.
2. Set the location of the leases file.

DHCP options

1. Netmask.
2. Gateway or router.
3. DNS server. This option is commented out, because dnsmasq defaults to supplying its own address as the DNS server.
4. A vendor setting that causes Microsoft Windows clients to relinquish their lease upon shutdown.

Dynamic Define a range of IP addresses (an address pool) from which dnsmasq assigns IP addresses to clients. The lease is given for three days.

Static Static DHCP assignments can also be specified.

1. A special laptop is given a fixed IP address.
2. The office printer is also assigned a static address. It will be available to office users as the host name printer.office.

13.4.1 Booting a PC and watching it happen

Starting a Microsoft Windows PC or renewing a lease with the ipconfig.exe utility produces the following debug output if DHCP debugging is enabled on dnsmasq:

```
DHCP packet: transaction-id is 1331026398
Available DHCP range: 192.168.1.50 -- 192.168.1.150
DHCPRELEASE(eth0) 192.168.1.53 00:0c:f1:71:67:ca
DHCP packet: transaction-id is 2846010516
Available DHCP range: 192.168.1.50 -- 192.168.1.150
Vendor class: MSFT 5.0
DHCPDISCOVER(eth0) 192.168.1.53 00:0c:f1:71:67:ca
DHCPOFFER(eth0) 192.168.1.53 00:0c:f1:71:67:ca
requested options: 1:netmask, 15:domain-name, 3:router, 6:dns-server,
requested options: 44:netbios-ns, 46:netbios-nodetype, 47:netbios-scop
requested options: 31:router-discovery, 33:static-route, 249,
requested options: 43:vendor-encap
sent size:  1 option: 53:message-type  02
sent size:  4 option: 54:server-identifier  c0:a8:01:a4
sent size:  4 option: 51:lease-time  00:00:2a:30
sent size:  4 option: 58:T1  00:00:15:18
sent size:  4 option: 59:T2  00:00:24:ea
sent size:  4 option: 28:broadcast  c0:a8:01:ff
sent size:  4 option:  6:dns-server  c0:a8:01:a4
sent size:  3 option: 15:domain-name  6c:61:6e
sent size:  4 option:  3:router  c0:a8:01:01
sent size:  4 option:  1:netmask  ff:ff:ff:00
sent size:  7 option: 43:vendor-encap  02:04:00:00:00:01:ff
DHCP packet: transaction-id is 2846010516
Available DHCP range: 192.168.1.50 -- 192.168.1.150
Vendor class: MSFT 5.0
DHCPREQUEST(eth0) 192.168.1.53 00:0c:f1:71:67:ca
DHCPACK(eth0) 192.168.1.53 00:0c:f1:71:67:ca kiki
...
```

You can view the configuration retrieved via DHCP on Microsoft Windows clients, with the ipconfig.exe tool from the command line. An XP client that booted via dnsmasq shows the following information:

```
C:\> ipconfig /all
Windows IP Configuration

 Host Name . . . . . . . . . . . . : kiki
 Primary Dns Suffix  . . . . . . . :
 Node Type . . . . . . . . . . . . : Unknown
 IP Routing Enabled. . . . . . . . : No
 WINS Proxy Enabled. . . . . . . . : No
 DNS Suffix Search List. . . . . . : office
```

```
Ethernet adapter Local Area Connection:

  Connection-specific DNS Suffix : office
  Description . . . . . . . . . : Intel(R) PRO/100 VE Network Connection
  Physical Address. . . . . . . : 00-0C-F1-71-67-CA
  Dhcp Enabled. . . . . . . . . : Yes
  Autoconfiguration Enabled . . : Yes
  IP Address. . . . . . . . . . : 192.168.1.53
  Subnet Mask . . . . . . . . . : 255.255.255.0
  Default Gateway . . . . . . . : 192.168.1.1
  DHCP Server . . . . . . . . . : 192.168.1.164
  DNS Servers . . . . . . . . . : 192.168.1.164
  Lease Obtained. . . . . . . . : Freitag, 30. November 2007 23:15:00
  Lease Expires . . . . . . . . : Samstag, 1. Dezember 2007 02:15:00
```

The leases file on the dnsmasq host contains the DHCP leases that dnsmasq issued:

```
1196475348 00:0c:f1:71:67:ca 192.168.1.53 kiki 01:00:0c:f1:71:67:ca
1196467231 00:0f:1f:c5:0b:65 192.168.1.60 jp510m 01:00:0f:1f:c5:0b:65
```

Summary

- dnsmasq provides an easy solution for all DNS and DHCP requirements in small to medium branch-office networks or Small Office / Home Office environments.
- dnsmasq can provide services for more complex networks, with additional configuration.
- dnsmasq is also useful on single-machine networks because of its caching DNS proxy.

Related topics

- dnscache (Chapter 17).
- Chapter 19 expands on the DHCP topics.

Notes and further reading

Building dnsmasq

Building dnsmasq yourself might not be necessary, as many GNU/Linux distributions have ready-made packages of dnsmasq which can be installed from your usual package manager; do check whether your distribution comes with dnsmasq. For Mac OS X, ports are available from `http://dnsmasq.darwinports.com/` and from the Fink project `http://finkproject.org/`.

If you do want to build it yourself, download the latest version of dnsmasq from `http://www.thekelleys.org.uk/dnsmasq/`, extract the archive, and make the binary:

```
$ wget http://www.thekelleys.org.uk/dnsmasq/.....
$ tar xvzf dnsmasq-2.43.tar.gz
$ cd dnsmasq-2.43
$ make clean
# make install
```

The file `src/config.h` contains path names which you might want to tweak before building the program. By default the program is installed in `/usr/local/sbin/dnsmasq`. To install a commented configuration file, which is useful for getting started:

```
# cp dnsmasq.conf.example /etc/dnsmasq.conf
```

Router distributions

dnsmasq is used in a number of router boxes, and in some software distributions that can be used to flash supported routers. Some of the known packages that contain dnsmasq are DD-WRT, OpenWRT, La Fonera, Tomato, and Meraki.

Chapter

14 DNS on Microsoft Windows

Why would you want to do that?

JP Mens

Introduction

There are several options for running DNS on Microsoft Windows. Some of the programs discussed in the preceding chapters are available as native Windows executables, and there is of course the Microsoft Windows DNS Server, which can be Active-Directory-enabled.

It is widely recognized that the Domain Name System is a domain[1] of *nix systems: you would be hard pressed to find a notable ISP that uses a Microsoft Windows system to provide DNS services to its customers[2]. Be that as it may, valid reasons for running DNS services on Microsoft Windows are:

- Microsoft Windows is the only operating system allowed in your organization.
- You want Active Directory integration.
- You want to run Microsoft Windows DNS Server because of the automatic DNS updates performed by your client workstations. You may still have your main DNS servers on a UNIX platform, and you can define your Microsoft domain controllers as subdomains of your primary UNIX-served DNS domain, and have them perform zone transfers if required.

If you are obliged to offer DNS services on Microsoft Windows you have several options:

1. Use Microsoft Windows DNS Server.
2. Use one of the open source DNS servers that has a native Microsoft Windows port.
3. Use the Cygwin environment (Section 14.2.2) on which to run a name server.
4. Consider using virtualization software on Windows, such as VMware server, on which you install a *nix operating system. Within that environment, you install and operate one of the *nix DNS servers.

We cover only options 1, 2 and 3 in the following sections.

14.1 An overview of Microsoft Windows DNS Server

In Windows 2003, DNS has become the primary method of name resolution for a Microsoft Windows environment. If you use Active Directory (AD) you must run DNS, and it must support dynamic updates. (Dynamic updates are supported in MyDNS and BIND, so you can use those name servers instead, if you prefer.) The Windows 2003 DNS can either be AD-integrated or non-AD integrated (which is then called "normal DNS"). The benefits of having integrated DNS are:

- DNS data is stored in AD.
- AD automatically replicates DNS data, which removes the need to configure AXFR zone transfers.
- AD-integrated DNS still supports outgoing zone transfers to non-AD integrated Microsoft DNS servers or *nix DNS servers.

[1] Pun intended...

[2] According to the October 2007 survey at `http://dns.measurement-factory.com/surveys/200710.html`, only 2.74% of the world's public DNS servers run on Microsoft Windows.

You specify at installation time whether DNS is to be integrated in AD or not:

- If Microsoft Windows DNS Server is not AD-integrated, its zones are stored as individual files, named *zone*.dns, in the directory (folder):

  ```
  %systemroot%\system32\dns
  ```

  Whenever you change a zone, the system automatically keeps a single backup copy (of the version before the change), in the `backup` directory.

- For AD-integrated DNS, it is good practice to manually create a backup of zones with the dnscmd.exe utility before changing them:

  ```
  C:\> dnscmd servername /ZoneExport qupps.biz qupps.biz.dns
  ```

  Unless otherwise specified, the file is created in:

  ```
  %systemroot%\system32\dns
  ```

14.1.1 Zone types

Whether AD-integrated or not Microsoft Windows DNS Server can host the following types of zones:

- Primary zones. They can be AD-stored or not. They can zone transfer to secondary or slave servers if required.

- Secondary zones containing read-only copies of DNS records that were obtained via incoming zone transfers (AXFR). Microsoft Windows DNS Server can offer zone transfers for secondary zones to other secondaries (i.e. secondary of a secondary).

- BIND-style stub zones containing only pointers to another zone.

14.1.2 Forwarders

In Windows 2003 you configure forwarders on the General tab of the DNS server's property sheet in the DNS console. You can also configure so-called conditional forwarders, which handle name resolution only for specific domains. This can be useful to get name resolution between two different companies coupled. For example, if your company merges with QUPPS, you create a conditional forwarder for QUPPS' domains so that queries for *anything*.qupps.biz are forwarded to QUPPS's name servers for resolution. This is like the `forward` zone in a BIND configuration.

When querying a Windows DNS server with a conditional forwarder, we noticed that all replies from that forwarder are returned as authoritative (the replies have the "aa" bit set on them) even if they are not authoritative.

14.1.3 DNS on the command-line

The Microsoft Windows 2003 DNS server has good support for management via a command line, using a program called dnscmd.exe which ships with the support tools on the Windows 2003 Server media. Navigate to the `Support\Tools` folder and right-click on the `SUPPORT.CAB` file to choose Explore from the context menu. Locate dnscmd.exe, right-click it and choose Extract from the context menu, saving it in a suitable path.

Microsoft Windows DNS Server does not support DNSSEC, although it will transfer DNSSEC-enabled zones. Support for DNSSEC was slated for the release of Microsoft Windows 2008, but the first release does not contain DNSSEC.

14.2 Using Open Source DNS servers on Windows

You have a number of options for deploying an Open Source DNS server on Microsoft Windows:

- BIND, BIND SDB, Bind DLZ, MaraDNS, PowerDNS can be built for running on native Microsoft Windows, and some of them already exist as pre-built packages or binaries.
- Run a virtual machine on VMware, and run your chosen DNS server brand on this *nix virtual machine.
- Use the Cygwin environment, which is a set of utilities that implements a GNU/Linux-like environment on Microsoft Windows.

14.2.1 DNS servers with native Win32 support

Running BIND *on Win32*

It is pleasantly easy to install BIND on Microsoft Windows using ISC's binary installer. The installation includes the dig program, which is essential in all things DNS. After downloading the binary package from ISC's Web site, you:

1. Extract the content of the ZIP archive to a temporary location.
2. Install BIND on Microsoft Windows by running BINDInstall.exe. The installer creates an account called `named` under which the service will run.
3. Before starting the service, you have to create a `named.conf` file in:

   ```
   %SYSTEMROOT%\system32\dns\etc\named.conf
   ```

   A small example that you use to serve a single master zone is:

   ```
   options {
       directory "c:\windows\system32\dns";
       pid-file "c:\temp\named.pid";
       dump-file "cache_dump.db";
       statistics-file "named_stats.txt";
       allow-query { any; };
   ```

```
        recursion no;
    };

    zone "qupps.biz" IN {
        type master;
        file "qupps.biz";
    };
```

4. If you install BIND as a service (recommended), you can start and stop the service from the usual Services dialog or using the net command:

   ```
   C:\> net start|stop named
   ```

5. Any errors or warnings issued by named on Microsoft Windows are logged via the Microsoft Windows event log.

6. The utilities (not the name server, but the tools such as dig) supplied with the Microsoft Windows version of BIND look for the addresses of your name servers by consulting the registry for the typical resolver settings used by Microsoft Windows. However, if you want to, you can override their settings by creating a `resolv.conf` file, and installing it as:

   ```
   C:\> type %SYSTEMROOT%\system32\drivers\etc\resolv.conf
   nameserver 127.0.0.1
   ```

The supplied tools include dig, dnssec-keygen, dnssec-signzone, host, nslookup, nsupdate, rndc, and rndc-confgen.

The great thing about BIND on Microsoft Windows is that it has the same features that you get running BIND on *nix.

Running Bind DLZ *on Windows*

Although there are no pre-built binary packages of Bind DLZ, you can build it for Microsoft Windows. You will need the appropriate tool chains to do so, but that is documented on the Bind DLZ Web site.

Running MaraDNS *on Win32*

You install MaraDNS from the pre-built binary package available on the MaraDNS download site (see `http://www.maradns.org/download.html`). The binary is compiled with mingw32. After downloading the file, you unpack the zip file:

```
C:\> unzip maradns-1-3-10-win32.zip
C:\> cd maradns-1-3-10
```

A startup script is provided as run_maradns.bat, which is just a wrapper for:

```
C:\> start maradns -f mararc
```

You can also run MaraDNS as a service on your Windows workstation with these steps:

1. We recommend you create a special directory for MaraDNS and its supporting files. In the following examples, we use:

```
C:\> mkdir c:\mara
C:\> cd c:\mara
```

2. Download and install the srvany.exe and instsrv.exe executable programs from the Microsoft resource kit, and copy both into your newly created directory:

```
C:\> copy "\Program Files\Windows Resource Kits\Tools\srvany.exe" c:\mara
C:\> copy "\Program Files\Windows Resource Kits\Tools\instsrv.exe" c:\mara
```

3. Run the instsrv.exe program to set up srvany.exe as a service. After that, you can safely delete the instsrv.exe program file:

```
C:\> cd \mara
C:\> instsrv MaraDNS c:\mara\srvany.exe
C:\> del instsrv.exe
```

4. Use the registry editor (regedit) to edit the registry. You will have to create a new key and three values (Figure 14.1). Consult MaraDNS's documentation in `service.html` on how to do this.

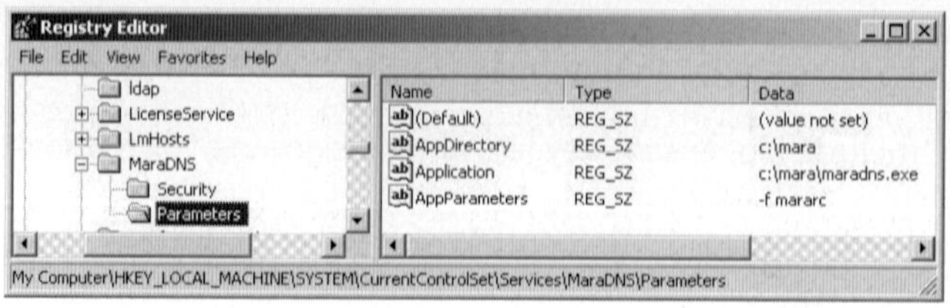

Figure 14.1: Adding registry entries for MaraDNS

5. You can then start the service from the Services control panel (Figure 14.2) or directly from the command-line:

```
C:\> net start maradns
```

Running PowerDNS *on Win32*

PowerDNS can be built for a Microsoft Windows platform. There are currently no up-to-date pre-built packages available from the download site.

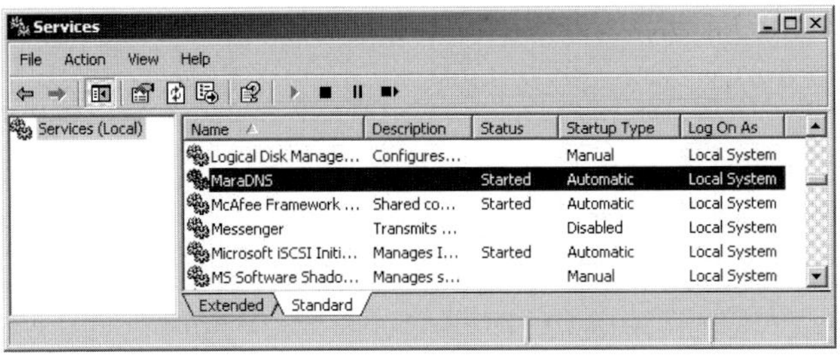

Figure 14.2: Starting or stopping the MaraDNS service

14.2.2 Cygwin

Cygwin is a GNU/Linux-like environment for Microsoft Windows. It consists of a set of dynamic link libraries (DLL) and a huge number of prepackaged utilities from which you choose whatever parts you are interested in. After you install Cygwin on Microsoft Windows you have an environment at your fingertips that allows you to compile and run most *nix programs as though you are on *nix.

The Cygwin distribution contains the GCC compiler suite and many other utilities (bash, xterm, make, grep, sed, ldapsearch, vi[3], etc.), so if you don't have ready access to a UNIX or GNU/Linux workstation, you can at least experiment with the programs we have discussed in this book.

If you have a choice, don't deploy a production name server on Cygwin because a real *nix platform is faster (on the same hardware) and more stable, but Cygwin is a valuable platform for experimentation[4].

After you install Cygwin and launch a bash shell, you can download and install *nix source code and compile it, following the instructions for a typical *nix system. This usually includes running a series of commands and/or compiler invocations, all of which are available from within Cygwin, as long as you install the required packages in Cygwin:

```
$ tar xvzf ...
$ ./configure ...
$ make ...
```

Although the resulting binary programs have an `.exe` extension to them, they are *not* "normal" Microsoft Windows programs (i.e. not WIN32). In order to run, these programs require the Cygwin environment, which consists of a number of DLLs.

[3] Some might say "yuk", but there are also other text editors to choose from.

[4] In fact the samples we wrote for BIND SDB were initially created and tested on a Cygwin environment in a hotel room.

Summary

- Microsoft Windows DNS Server is little used on the public Internet, although it is widely used within organizations.
- Microsoft Windows DNS Server is either Active Directory-enabled or not; you choose at install time.
- For a seamless UNIX / Microsoft Windows DNS integration, you typically deploy BIND on both platforms.

Notes and further reading

Obtaining Cygwin

Cygwin's home is at `http://cygwin.com/`. You typically download a small executable installer (Figure 14.3). It prompts you to specify the packages you want, and then it downloads and installs them. Whenever you wish to install further packages, you run the installer again. Installation is very simple and it is well documented.

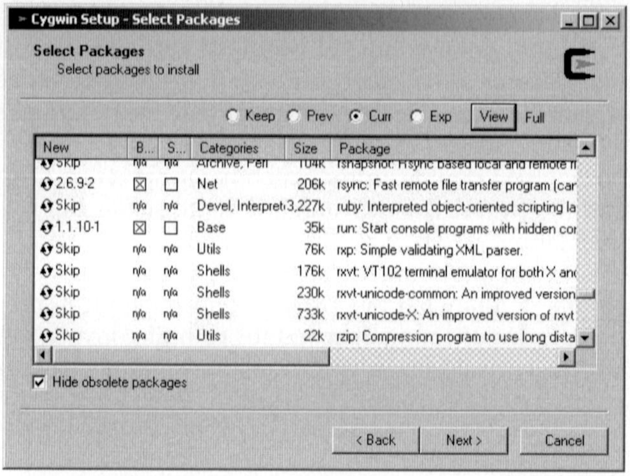

Figure 14.3: Selecting packages in Cygwin's installer

Further reading

- The book *DNS on Windows Server 2003* by Cricket Liu, Matt Larson, and Robbie Allen is a special Windows-oriented edition of the classic *DNS and BIND*, updated to document the many changes to DNS, large and small, found in Windows Server 2003. `http://www.oreilly.com/catalog/dnswinsvr/`
- *How to Integrate Windows 2003 Server DNS with an Existing DNS Infrastructure* `http://support.microsoft.com/kb/323417`.

Chapter

15 DNS and Perl

Unix is simple. It just takes a genius to understand its simplicity.

Dennis Ritchie

Introduction

Sometimes a regular DNS server will not provide what you need, but a small bit of coding will. The Perl modules we present in this chapter allow you to create specialized DNS servers that provide answers to DNS queries directly from code you write in Perl. We also show you how you can query the DNS from Perl.

The name servers we have discussed so far store their zone data in text files or in an SQL or LDAP back end; some of these are even "dynamic", in that they can serve new zones as soon as they are added to the back end, without any reconfiguration of the name server. However, you may want something even more dynamic than that. For example, in Section 8.5.1 we described a dynamic load balancing server: the answer to a query for an A record for www.qupps.biz is calculated dynamically each time and the value returned is the A record for the least-loaded of three different Web server hosts.

PowerDNS (Chapter 6) with its "Pipe" back-end, and BIND SDB (Chapter 8), let you program an interface to return whatever you want, based on a query received. While the former may not be performing enough, the latter means programming in the C language. A name server in Perl may not perform as fast as BIND SDB, but it is easier to learn, is quicker than programming in C, and is great for prototyping.

This happy medium is provided by Perl modules that you can use to implement a fully functional DNS server in Perl. The nitty-gritty of the communications protocol is handled automatically by the modules, so you have to provide only the functions or subroutines that handle answers to the DNS queries.

Pros	• Completely programmable and customizable • Access whatever back-end you want to, however you want to • Support for zone transfers (AXFR) and TCP • Three different implementations
Cons	○ Difficult to learn
Scenarios	Small to medium environments that need maximum customization.

Table 15.1: Perl name servers at a glance

Before we discuss how you implement your own name server in Perl, we show you how to query the DNS using Perl.

15.1 Querying the DNS from Perl

When you want to translate a hostname to an IP address in Perl, you typically use the `gethostbyname()` or `gethostbyaddr()` subroutines (provided by the `Socket` module, which is included in the standard Perl installation). These routines are just Perl wrappers for the resolver functions of the same name from the standard C library (Section 20.1). If you want to do more than name-to-address (or address-to-name) translation, such as querying the DNS for a Text (TXT) resource record, you use the Net::DNS Perl module, which we describe in the rest of this section.

- Net::DNS contains functions for all facets of DNS: performing queries, dissecting DNS packets, changing name servers, performing DNS updates, using different resolvers, etc.

- Net::DNS allows you to add DNSSEC support to your programs with its Net::DNS::SEC modules.

With Net::DNS you typically use a "resolver object" to query the DNS. To create the resolver object, you use methods provided by the package to specify whether you want recursion, debugging, DNSSEC, etc. You can also specify which name server(s) to use; if you don't, the system's configuration (i.e. `/etc/resolv.conf`) is consulted to find addresses of caching name servers. Once you've obtained a resolver object, you use its `search` method to perform queries. The `search` method returns either an array of answers obtained from name servers, or an error on failure.

Here is a very small example, using Net::DNS to resolve a domain name:

Listing 15.1: Query a hostname with Net::DNS

```
#!/usr/bin/perl

use strict;
use Net::DNS;

my $domain = "qupps.biz";

my $res   = Net::DNS::Resolver->new;   # create resolver object
my $query = $res->search($domain);     # perform query

if ($query) {
    foreach my $rr ($query->answer) {
        next unless $rr->type eq "A";
        print "${domain}'s address is: ", $rr->address, "\n";
    }
} else {
    warn "query failed: ", $res->errorstring, "\n";
}
```

We show you more examples of Net::DNS in different chapters:

- Update your DNS with Net::DNS (Chapter 19).
- Initiate an incoming zone transfer (Chapter 23).
- Monitor DNS notifications sent out by name servers, which you integrate into your monitoring environment (Chapter 24).
- Resolve Service (SRV) records (page 365).
- Query a DNS server for TXT records (Section G.1.1).

15.2 Create your own dynamic name server in Perl

Have you ever worked at a help desk? As a system administrator you know the drill when a user needs help: (a) User reports a problem, and you decide to connect to user's workstation with VNC (see Notes). (b) You ask the person for a username. (c) You ask them for the workstation's IP address. (d) User doesn't know it (obviously), so you explain how to determine it (very long explanation omitted here...). (e) You connect to user's workstation, and tell the user you'll call back in a minute to give your ear a rest. (f) You ask user for a telephone number, and you jot it down.

We hate all that. When a user calls us, we ask them for their unique username – `alexi`, for example – and run:

```
$ dig   alexi.info.qupps.biz  any
;; ANSWER SECTION:
alexi.info.qupps.biz.   3600   IN    A     192.168.2.96
alexi.info.qupps.biz.   3600   IN    TXT   "name: Ilexa Snem"
alexi.info.qupps.biz.   3600   IN    TXT   "phone: +34 71 10019345"
```

A single DNS query to our special domain info.qupps.biz returns all the information we need:

- The user's IP address – we didn't have to ask the user to try and find it.
- The user's full name – we didn't have to ask the user and write it down incorrectly.
- The user's telephone number – we didn't have to jot it down.

Is that magic? Well, perhaps; but we implemented this with a name server in Perl, integrated into our DNS environment. We show you exactly how we did it, on page 365. Before that, let's look at Perl name servers more generally.

15.2.1 Why would I want to create my own name server?

Perl lets you do almost anything you want with the name server modules. Here are some ideas:

- Using some sort of geographical data (see Notes), implement a GEO-capable name server: when you query it for www.example.com, it returns an answer that depends on the geographical location of the DNS client. E.g. a query for www.example.com might return the Address (A) of www.de.example.com to a client in Germany, but return the Address of www.uk.example.com to a client in England – you get the idea. (Note that PowerDNS (Chapter 6) already has a ready-built GEO back-end you can use if you don't want to make your own.)
- For one of our clients we implemented an internal "pseudo-Geo" name server, that again returns an A value depending on the geographical location of the querying client. The internal network uses private 10.*.*.* addresses; obviously, no real geographical data is available for these. Instead, we have a table that maps ranges of IP addresses, specified by Perl regular expressions, to countries. We used Stanford::DNSserver (Section 15.3) to implement this system, with Perl's Net::IP::Match::Regexp module performing the network-to-country mapping.
- Load balancing. You can implement a DNS server that answers a query for a specific domain name with the address of the machine with the lowest load (Figure 15.1). This is similar to our own load balancing example in Section 8.5.1, and also similar to lbnamed (see Notes).

A name server implemented in Perl can use almost any kind of monitoring software that keeps track of the availability or current performance of hosts. The monitoring software regularly updates a database or file with this information, and then your Perl code in your DNS server uses the information to determine which address (A) to return as answer to the query.

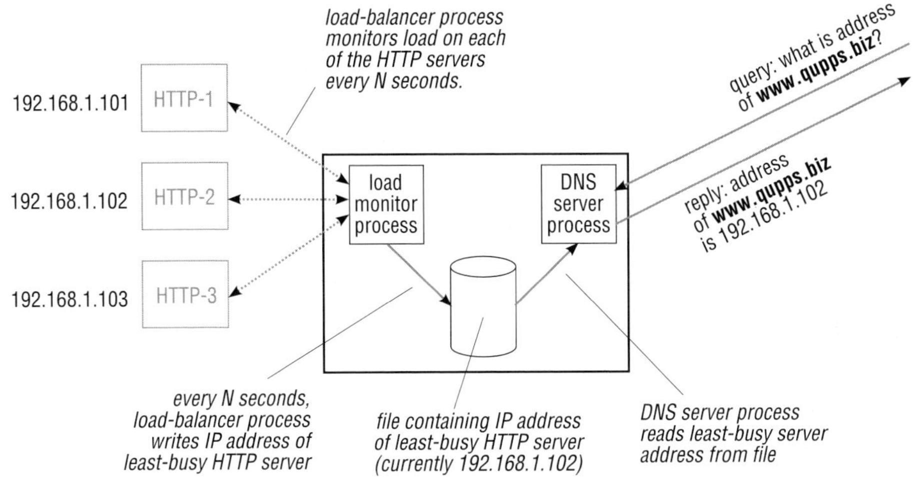

Figure 15.1: An idea for a SNMP-controlled load-balancing DNS server in Perl

15.2.2 Perl tools for creating name servers

There are three different Perl modules you can use to implement a fully dynamic name server:

1. Stanford::DNSserver

   The Perl module Stanford::DNSserver was assembled by Rob Riepel, and it is based on lbnamed by Roland Schemers (see Notes). We describe Stanford::DNSserver in detail in Section 15.3, and use it to develop our own example DNS server.

2. Net::DNS::Nameserver

   The Perl module Net::DNS::Nameserver implements a DNS server class. We show you a simple example in Appendix E. At our request, the module's maintainer, Olaf Kolkman, added a handler to detect DNS NOTIFY requests. We use these in an unusual way to detect if our name servers are sending out notifications (Chapter 24).

3. Net::DNS::Server

   Net::DNS::Server, developed by Luis E. Muñoz, is a set of Perl modules. You use methods to provide answers to specific query types. We show a simple example of how to use it in Appendix E.

Each of these three modules has its own, specific, API. Look at the examples here and in the Appendixes to see which you prefer, or which is closest to your needs.

15.3 Example – Implementing a custom dynamic server using Stanford::DNSserver

Stanford::DNSserver is an extensible name server written in Perl. The Perl code you write determines the answers to the DNS queries it receives (Figure 15.2). The resource records it returns to the DNS client are constructed at runtime by code you supply.

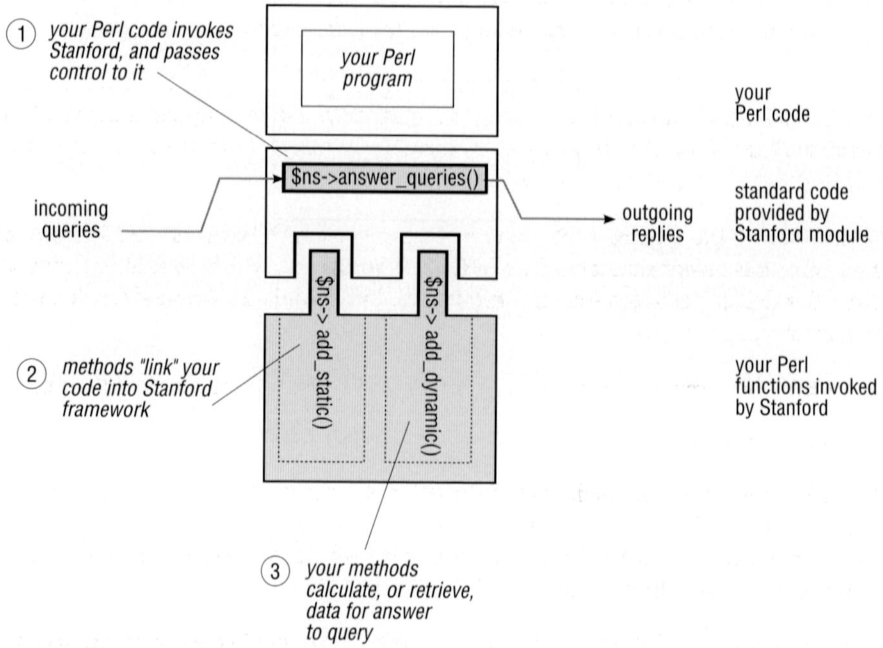

Figure 15.2: Architecture of Stanford::DNSserver

Installing Stanford::DNSserver

After downloading the code, apply the usual Perl incantation:

```
$ wget http://www.stanford.edu/~riepel/lbnamed/Stanford-DNSserver/↩
        Stanford-DNSserver.tar.gz
$ tar xvzf Stanford-DNSserver.tar.gz
$ cd Stanford-DNSserver-1.2.0
$ perl Makefile.PL
$ make
$ make test
$ make install
```

The package provides a sample name server in the file `example` that demonstrates the capabilities of the module. In the next section we show an example of our own using Stanford::DNSserver.

Using DNS to find a user's telephone number

The organization you work for may have an LDAP directory service that stores information about the users in your organization. And if your organization doesn't have an LDAP directory, now is the best time to start implementing one; grab a copy of OpenLDAP and go ahead: it is easier than you think (Appendix A), and your boss will raise your paycheck by 50 percent[1]. Don't skip this section if you don't have an LDAP directory; modifying the program to use an SQL database or even a plain-text file is trivial.

- Each user in our organization has a directory entry containing their name, telephone number, authentication information, etc. A lot of this data originates in the HR department, where it is added to the LDAP directory with custom made tools written in C and Perl.

- We know that the machine that user `alexi` sits at has IP address 192.168.2.96 because the address is assigned statically via DHCP. Our convention is that we give this machine the domain name alexi.users.qupps.biz. (We associate all users' workstations with the users.qupps.biz zone.)

- Using automatic tools, we create an address (A) record in our "normal" internal DNS:

  ```
  alexi.users.qupps.biz.  3600  IN   A    192.168.2.96
  ```

  Actually, addresses of users' workstations are entered into the DNS via our "poor man's dynamic DNS" (Chapter 19). Their addresses are in the DNS, but we could just as easily have obtained the addresses directly from the database used by the DNS server. Our code below retrieves them from the DNS.

That's how we create the information in the system. On page 359 we showed you an example of the result:

```
$ dig alexi.info.qupps.biz any
;; ANSWER SECTION:
alexi.info.qupps.biz.  3600  IN   A    192.168.2.96
alexi.info.qupps.biz.  3600  IN   TXT  "name: Ilexa Snem"
alexi.info.qupps.biz.  3600  IN   TXT  "phone: +34 71 10019345"
```

These are DNS resource records, but where did our Perl name server get the values from? We could have "copied" the information from the LDAP directory into our "normal" internal DNS with some batch program and created TXT records for each user, but we didn't. Doing so would have several disadvantages:

- We'd have to store data redundantly (in LDAP and in the DNS).

[1] Or she might cut your pay by the same amount if you fail.

- The DNS would contain hundreds (in large organizations, thousands) of TXT resource records, many of which would never be used.
- Data could get stale. Suppose the process of updating the TXT records from LDAP runs nightly: if a user's information is changed in LDAP early in the morning, the data would be updated in the DNS only at the next nightly run of the batch update.

That is why we want to retrieve the data "on-line". Now, let's see how the data is retrieved. Consider username `alexi` as an example; the numbered items below refer to the numbers in (Figure 15.3).

1. The syadmin is talking to user `alexi`. By definition, her "information" domain name is alexi.info.qupps.biz, so the sysadmin uses dig to query our normal (caching) DNS server for an ANY answer for this domain.

2. Our Perl server is authoritative for the info.qupps.biz zone, so we configure our caching name to forward any queries for this zone to our Perl server. (We show you in Chapter 18 how to set this up.)

   Now, when the query from the sysadmin arrives, the caching server forwards it for resolution to the Perl server.

3. The Perl server receives the query for alexi.info.qupps.biz, type ANY. This query is passed down within the server to the Perl code that we've written.

   Our convention is that user `alexi`'s host has the domain name alexi.users.qupps.biz. Therefore, our Perl code first queries the normal DNS for the (A) record for this domain. So now we have the first part of the answer to be returned to the sysadmin:

   ```
   alexi.info.qupps.biz.  3600  IN  A   192.168.2.96
   ```

4. We are still within our Perl code in the Perl server. We now have to retrieve the information (user's real name and phone number) to insert into Text (TXT) records. We retrieve this on the fly from the corporate LDAP directory server. Every user has a unique username, so we can find unambiguous directory information for a user. The LDAP entry (see Appendix A) describing a user contains:

   ```
   dn: uid=alexi,ou=usr,dc=qupps,dc=biz
   objectClass: inetOrgPerson
   objectClass: person
   telephoneNumber: +34 71 10019345
   uid: alexi
   cn: Ilexa Snem
   sn: Snem
   ...
   ```

   (We could have stored this data an SQL database if we had preferred. However, the scenario for this example assumed that the users' HR information was already in an LDAP directory.)

   We now take the information obtained via LDAP, and form it into TXT records:

```
alexi.info.qupps.biz.  3600  IN  TXT  "name: Ilexa Snem"
alexi.info.qupps.biz.  3600  IN  TXT  "phone: +34 71 10019345"
```

5. Our own Perl code has all the data it requires now. It passes it back to the main code of the Perl server, which returns the DNS reply to the sysadmin's dig (via the caching server).

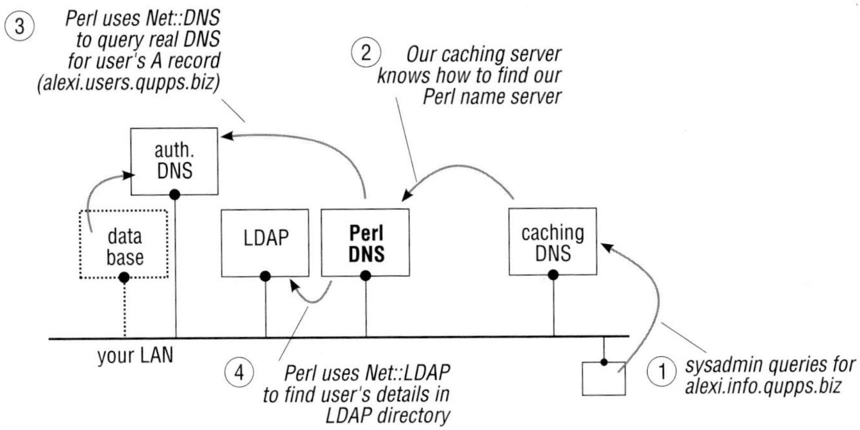

Figure 15.3: Stanford::DNSserver Perl server queries DNS and LDAP

The reason we use two distinct domains is that we used info.qupps.biz to get the authoritative "information" records, which is held on our Perl server (strictly, on the LDAP directory used by the Perl server). Then, we use the separate domain, users.qupps.biz, to get the authoritative A record for the user's machine.

Could we have consolidated the data into a single name server? Yes, but then we would have had to store the users' machine addresses – their A records – in our LDAP directory, instead of using a normal authoritative server as we did above.

The code

The name server we implement is a program is called clidnsd.pl. We go through the source ode explaining the most interesting portions here. The full code is in Appendix E.

1. We are going to use a "modern" DNS Service (SRV) record to find the LDAP directory server:

```
my $ldapsrv      = '_ldap._tcp.qupps.biz';
my $ldapbase     = 'ou=usr,dc=qupps,dc=biz';
```

2. Define defaults for our DNS server:

```
my $myname       = hostname();
my $tld          = 'info.qupps.biz';
my $atld         = 'users.qupps.biz';
my $ttl          = 3600;
```

`$myname` the host name of the machine this Perl DNS server will be running on. Our DNS server uses this name to publish its own NS record.

`$tld` The domain name you choose. We have to tell Stanford::DNSserver for what domains it will execute which code, and we associate our user-lookup code with this domain name.

`$atld` Another domain name you choose. We find A resource records for our users in this zone (i.e. user `alexi`'s workstation has a fully qualified name of alexi.users.qupps.biz).

`$ttl` The default Time to Live (TTL) for records served by the DNS server.

3. The program uses the `dnsSRV()` subroutine to query the DNS for a service record, resolves that into one or more IP addresses, and sorts them by priority. We then use these to attempt to connect to the LDAP directory server. The program then binds to the LDAP directory or dies if it cannot (this code is shown in Appendix E).

4. Stanford::DNSserver is instantiated next; we set the address(es) to listen on, the port number, TTL, and the optional flags that control whether it should `fork()` and become a daemon.

```
$ns = new Stanford::DNSserver (
        listen_on => ["127.0.0.1"],
        port      =>            53,
        defttl    =>            60,
        debug     =>             1,
        daemon    =>          "no",
        pidfile   => "/tmp/example.pid",
        logfunc   => sub { print shift; print "\n" },
        exitfunc  => sub {
                print "Bye!\n";
                $ld->disconnect;
                });
```

`logfunc()` and `exitfunc()` are subroutines (Perl subs) that are called for each received query and at the program's exit respectively.

5. Optionally add "static" answers to Stanford::DNSserver. This is how you "hard-code" answers to queries. We add static answers for queries of a Start of Authority (SOA), Name Server (NS) and Address (A) records:

```
$ns->add_static("$tld", T_SOA, rr_SOA($myname, "hostmaster.$tld",
        time, 3600, 3600, 86400, 0));
$ns->add_static("$tld", T_NS, rr_NS($myname));
...
```

6. Add a dynamic "handler" to Stanford::DNSserver. This handler, which we've called `userreq()`, is invoked for each DNS query received in the `$tld` domain. `userreq()` is the code that dynamically creates answers to queries apart from the "static" ones we hard-coded earlier:

```
$ns->add_dynamic("$tld" => \&userreq);
```

The add_dynamic method is how we "link" our own custom code, i.e. userreq(), into Stanford::DNSserver's DNS-query processing framework, which handles all the UDP communications, packet formatting, etc.

7. We have now finished our initialization. We call the answer_queries method to pass control to the main loop of Stanford::DNSserver. Control returns to our Perl program, to the statement after this, only when the DNS server ends.

```
$ns->answer_queries();
```

8. This is where the "hard" part begins, as we have to provide code for the handler userreq(). All queries received by Stanford::DNSserver for the domain $tld (except for the ones we defined as "static") are passed to the userreq() subroutine with arguments:

domain The zone for which Stanford::DNSserver is handling this request. In the example, it is info.qupps.biz.

host The domain name queried. For a query of alexi.info.qupps.biz, $host contains the string "alexi".

qtype The query type as an ASCII string: A, MX, NS, TXT, etc.

qclass The query class. Usually contains IN (Internet).

dm A pointer to the DNS message as defined by the Stanford::DNS module.

from The IP address of the client that issued the query. This will typically be the address of a name server.

(a) userreq() performs a sanity check on $host and returns a SERVFAIL if empty.

```
if (!$host) {
    $dm->rcode = SERVFAIL;          # No username specified
    return;
}
```

(b) Check the query type. For queries of type ANY or A, determine IP Address(es) of $host using dnsADDR() defined in dnssrv.pl (Appendix E), and pass answers back into Stanford::DNSserver.

```
if ($qtype == T_A || $qtype == T_ANY) {

    my @iplist = dnsADDR(9, "$host.$atld");

    for my $ip (@iplist) {
        $entry = unpack('N', inet_aton($ip));
        $dm->answer .= dns_answer(QPTR, T_A, C_IN, $ttl, rr_A($entry));
        $dm->ancount += 1;
    }
}
```

Note, that the original query is for alexi.info.qupps.biz, but we have to search the DNS (with dnsADDR()) for alexi.users.qupps.biz because that is the domain in which A records for users are stored.

(c) `userreq()` passes answers back to the main Stanford::DNSserver name server code by adding values to `$dm`. We modify this pointer to the DNS message by appending a resource record to `answer`, and by setting the number of records we return in `ancount`.

The subroutine `dns_answer()` is exported by Stanford::DNSserver and allows us to build a properly formatted DNS reply.

(d) If the query type is TXT or ANY, search the LDAP directory server for a user, and form the user details as TXT records back into Stanford::DNSserver, which will answer them when the `userreq()` subroutine returns.

```
if ($qtype == T_TXT || $qtype == T_ANY) {

    my $msg = $ld->search(base => $ldapbase,
            filter => "(&(objectclass=person)(userid=$host))",
            attrs => [ qw(cn telephonenumber) ]);
    if ($msg->code) {
        $dm->rcode = SERVFAIL;
        return;
    }
    my @entries = $msg->entries;

    foreach my $e (@entries) {
        my $cn = $e->get_value('cn') or 'unknown';
        my $tel = $e->get_value('telephonenumber') or 'unknown';

        $dm->answer .= dns_answer(QPTR, T_TXT, C_IN, $ttl,
         rr_TXT("name: $cn"));
        $dm->ancount += 1;
        $dm->answer .= dns_answer(QPTR, T_TXT, C_IN, $ttl,
                rr_TXT("phone: $tel"));
        $dm->ancount += 1;
    }
}
```

(e) If no DNS answers found, set the return code to NXDOMAIN.

```
if (! $dm->ancount ) {
    $dm->rcode = NXDOMAIN;
}
```

Integrate your Perl name server into your organization's DNS

The sub-domain served by our Perl name server (info.qupps.biz) has to be integrated into the organization's DNS so that a DNS query directed at our caching name servers finds it. The process by which this is done is called delegation, and we discuss that in detail in Chapter 18. Suffice it to mention at this point, that you would delegate info.qupps.biz from qupps.biz to the machine(s) on which your Perl name server is running.

A word of warning: we would recommend that you carefully consider whether you should offer this kind of service on a publicly accessible DNS server. Think of the potential implications of publishing details of your organization's users to the public Internet! (If in doubt, don't.)

Summary

- Using the Perl language, you can create your own DNS name server, which dynamically constructs answers to queries, using code that you write.
- There are three different Perl modules you can use to implement a fully dynamic name server; the choice is yours.

Related topics

- You like the idea of having DNS queries answered dynamically but you are wary of implementing your own DNS server? Have a look at PowerDNS (Chapter 6) with its Pipe back-end.
- Instead of implementing a separate name server to answer queries dynamically, you'd prefer embedding code into an existing program? With BIND SDB (Chapter 8) you can write an interface to the BIND name server in the C programming language.

Notes and further reading

The Net::DNS *package*

Net::DNS was written by Michael Fuhr; Chris Reinhardt maintained the package between 2002 and 2004 and now the package is maintained by Olaf Kolkman from NLnet Labs with active contributions by Dick Franks. Net::DNS' home is at `http://www.net-dns.org/`, where you will also find its excellent documentation with lots of examples.

VNC

Virtual Network Computing (VNC) is a graphical desktop sharing system to control another computer. Keyboard and mouse events are transmitted from your computer to the remote computer, and screen updates are relayed back from the remote to your computer. VNC is great because it is platform independent: you can use a VNC viewer on, say, GNU/Linux to control the screen of a Microsoft Windows PC or vice versa. There are clients and servers for many operating systems and even for Java. VNC was originally developed by the Olivetti & Oracle Research Lab, and today you'll find several different flavors of VNC. We like using TightVNC (see `http://www.tightvnc.com/`).

Geographical data

Maxmind have a database of geographical data which is free to use (see `www.maxmind.com/app/geoip_country`).

In Section G.2 we discuss a DNS blacklist you can use to determine the geographic location of an IP address.

lbnamed

lbnamed originated at Stanford. It is an extensible load-balancing DNS name server written in Perl. It serves either static or dynamic data. lbnamed reads a "poller" summary file produced by "poller" clients, and uses computed weights to determine which system to assign to a name request.

Chapter

16 DNS blacklists

I have no doubts that electronic mail will remain a powerful vector for propagation of viruses and other malware.

Wietse Venema

Introduction

Spam or Unsolicited Commercial E-mail (UCE) has long taken over the lion's portion of e-mail traffic on the Internet. DNS blacklists let you specify lists of IP addresses of servers or domain names from which you do *not* want to receive mail. You can use publicly available DNS blacklists and/or implement your own.

A DNS *blacklist* (*DNSBL*) or *blocklist*, is a list of hosts or TCP/IP addresses that are known to be senders of Unsolicited Commercial E-mail or Spam. Mail servers query these lists via the DNS to decide whether to accept a message from that host. DNS blacklists are useful, but controversial: your mail server relies on a third party to decide whether a particular message should be accepted. We discuss how you use a blacklist (i.e. your e-mail server queries the blacklist to fend off spammers), and we show you how you can implement your own blacklist (i.e. you publish your own data).

You can implement DNS blacklists with any DNS name server (and we show you how), but you will typically want to use a specialized program for implementing them because a specialized program consumes fewer resources. rbldnsd is one such specialized name server:

Pros	• Very fast, low memory usage • Supports several file formats • Good logging facilities
Cons	○ Individual addresses cannot be easily (or temporarily) removed from a blacklist
Scenarios	Medium to large environments with their own Mail Transfer Agents (mail servers).

Table 16.1: rbldnsd at a glance

Some DNS blacklist services (see Notes) are free, others charge for a subscription. Subscription rates are typically related to the volume of mail you receive, i.e. the number of DNS queries you submit to the blacklist. If you don't intend to "publish" your own blacklist you may want to use one of the publicly available ones, which gives you two options:

1. You configure your mail server to use one or more of the public DNS blacklists utilizing the public DNS to resolve the appropriate queries.
2. If you process large volumes of incoming e-mail, you will typically want to reduce the number of DNS queries over the Internet. You can usually obtain a copy of the DNS blacklist, which you then serve to your own mail servers with a specialized DNSBL name server (Section 16.4).

Before continuing, we need to define two terms:

1. A *Mail User Agent* (*MUA*) is your desktop e-mail client – a program such as Thunderbird, Outlook, Lotus Notes, Mutt, etc. As you probably know, there is more to e-mail than the Mail User Agent: there is ...
2. The *Mail Transport Agent* (*MTA*) or mail server. This is the program that receives an e-mail message from a User Agent (MUA) and tries to dispatch it to its destination. The Mail Transport Agent runs on a server machine. Typical implementations of Mail Transport Agents include Exim, Sendmail, Postfix, Lotus Domino, etc.

In the discussion that follows we concentrate on the Mail Transport Agent, i.e. the mail server side of things.

16.1 Why would I want to implement a DNS blacklist?

Reasons to implement a DNS blacklist on your own systems include:

- You are sick and tired of Spam. Your users already have a method in place with which they report Spam, and you want to use addresses gleaned from that "database" to populate a blacklist.
- You subscribe to (or otherwise use) a DNS blacklist service. Instead of using bandwidth over the Internet to query their DNS servers (which you mitigate with a caching name server), you want to become self-sufficient in case the DNSBL provider's name servers become unreachable.
- You maintain a "white list" of hosts that you *know* would never send spam, and wish to make that list available to friendly sites (or to the public at large) via DNS.

16.2 How to use an existing blacklist in your e-mail server

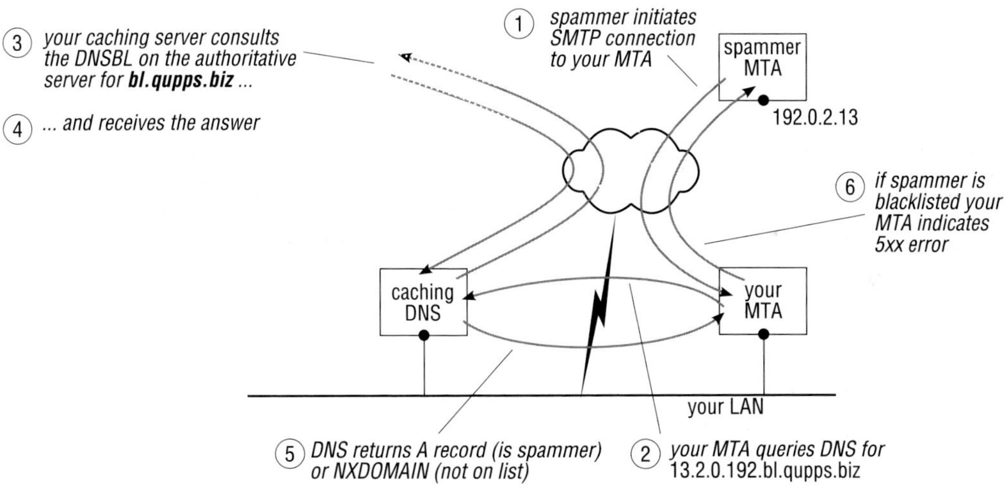

Figure 16.1: DNS blacklists attempt to combat spam

When your mail server receives a connection from a remote mail server (which acts as SMTP client, to your SMTP server) and wants to check that against a DNSBL, the process is more or less as follows: (Figure 16.1):

1. The (remote) sending server establishes a connection to your server. Your server examines the connection to find the IP address (192.0.2.13, say) of the sending server.
2. Your server creates a special "pseudo-domain name" by reversing the IP address and appending the domain name of the blacklist. For example, if the incoming address is

192.0.2.13 and the domain name of the blacklist is bl.example.com, the "pseudo-domain name" is 13.2.0.192.bl.example.com.

Your mail server performs a DNS lookup for an Address (A) record on this domain name. This is *not* an inverse query for a PTR (in an in-addr.arpa domain), but a forward query for an A record (in the bl.example.com domain).

3. Your caching name server queries the authoritative DNS servers for the blacklist domain. In our example, we use a domain name bl.example.com, so the authoritative name servers for the zone bl.example.com are queried.

4. If the DNS query resolves successfully (we discuss in a moment what it must resolve to), your mail server considers the sending server to be a spammer, indicates a fatal error condition, and closes the connection.

   If the lookup is successful, your MTA can query the DNS for a Text (TXT) record. The Text record typically contains a reason for communications denial (a short explanation or a URL pointing to a more verbose reason). MTAs include the value of the TXT record in the error message they return to the sending user.

   If the query does not resolve, your mail server has no reason (at this point in time) to consider the client offensive, and it continues processing the incoming message. In many installations, the receiving mail server next checks the *content* of the message (not just the sender's address) to decide whether it is spam, before finally accepting the message.

There are several things to note:

- Your mail server queries the DNS for an Address (A) record of any value:
  - Typically, if the DNS returns 127.0.0.4, the mail sender is to be blocked. The actual IP address returned is defined by the blacklist operator.

    If you use a publicly accessible blacklist you *must* check its documentation to find out what records are returned; failure to do so can make your Mail Transfer Agent (your mail server) incorrectly refuse mail, because it thinks that a successful query automatically means the client is black-listed, even though the DNSBL provider has perhaps actually white-listed it. In the examples that follow, we use 127.0.0.4 to indicate that a client is a spammer, and 127.0.0.10 for whitelisting the client. Our zone file contains both black-listed and white-listed clients.
  - If the A query resolves, an MTA can query query the DNS for a Text (TXT) record saying *why* the mail sender is on the blacklist (see below).
  - If the DNS query returns not found (i.e. NXDOMAIN), the address of the sending MTA is not on the blacklist, so your server continues processing this message.
- If you publish your DNS blacklist on the public Internet, you either use a separate zone name or you create a sub-domain of a publicly accessible Internet domain (e.g. bl.qupps.biz). If, on the other hand, you use your blacklist privately only, you can call the domain whatever you like (e.g. bad.guys).

- Some Mail Transfer Agents, such as Exim, allow you to use a DNS blacklist to query a sender's domain name (i.e. the part after the @ character in the sender's e-mail address), as opposed to the sender's IP address, to decide whether you want to accept or discard mail from a domain. This is very flexible because it catches many servers, including future ones.

- If you want to, and if your mail server supports the feature, you can use blacklist technology to implement a *whitelist*, i.e. a list of domain names or IP addresses that you know are good. By judiciously configuring your e-mail server, you can blindly allow incoming mail from hosts on your whitelist.

That's how you use a blacklist provided on the Internet, that someone else has set up, and we show you in Section 16.5 how you configure your e-mail servers to query the blacklist. Now we'll show you how to create your own blacklist; if that's not relevant to you, skip to Section 16.5.

16.3 Implementing a simple DNS blacklist

Mail servers query blacklists using the DNS, so you need a DNS server to implement one. You can implement a simple DNS blacklist on any DNS server you deploy. However, if you have a lot of entries in your DNS blacklist, or you want to use local copies of existing DNS blacklists, deploying a small, special-purpose DNS server reduces memory consumption on your main authoritative name servers and it can ease maintenance of blacklist entries. rbldnsd is great for this.

To implement a blacklist:

A. Choose a domain name in which you publish the blacklist entries.

B. Add Address (and optionally Text) records to this zone.

C. Configure your MTA to query your new DNS blacklist.

We cover each of these steps in the following sections.

16.3.1 A – Choose a domain to publish blacklist entries

Before implementing your DNS blacklist decide whether it will be publicly available or used only by your e-mail servers. If it is public, the DNS will have to "find" the blacklist, so you must use an officially-assigned (sub-)domain name for it. If it is private, you choose whatever name you want (see Notes on page 58 for help on choosing a name).

You configure the Mail Transfer Agent to query the DNS in the domain you choose for the blacklist. We'll implement a private blacklist, so we can choose what the name of that domain is. The domain we have chosen is bl.qupps.biz. An MTA might perform the following queries:

- If you configure the MTA to check IP addresses, when it wants to check address 192.168.1.181, it will submit a DNS query for an Address (A) record for the domain:

```
181.1.168.192.bl.qupps.biz.
```

Note that it is *not* a inverse query for a Pointer (PTR), but a forwards query for an Address (A). The Address record returned can have any value, but typically you give it a value in the loopback network (127.0.0.0/8). The exact address you want returned depends on how you configure your MTA, but conventionally the address 127.0.0.4 is used to indicate a spammer. When using some other organization's blacklist you have to find out from them which IP addresses they return.

- If you configure the MTA to check for good or bad sender domains (as opposed to numeric IP addresses), the DNS query submitted for a sending domain of example.com will also be for an Address (A) record, but this time for the domain:

```
example.com.bl.qupps.biz.
```

16.3.2 B – Add Address (and optionally Text) records to this zone

As the implementor of the DNS blacklist you decide what A resource record you will return for a query. Typical values are 127.0.0.2 or 127.0.0.4 to indicate a listed client, but that varies greatly. For example, the SORBS DNSBL[1] returns A records from 127.0.0.2 through 127.0.0.12 depending on the database the client is listed in. (They have different databases containing clients listed as being open proxies, spammers, badly configured e-mail servers, etc.)

Knowing how an MTA queries the DNS makes it easy to set up your DNS server with the blacklist. The zone file for bl.qupps.biz would thus look like this:

Listing 16.1: Zone file with a DNS blacklist

```
$ORIGIN .
$TTL 600          ; 10 minutes
bl.qupps.biz       IN SOA         ns1.qupps.biz. email.nospam.xa. (
                                  200801192   ; serial
                                  10800       ; refresh (3 hours)
                                  900         ; retry (15 minutes)
                                  604800      ; expire (1 week)
                                  600         ; minimum (1 hour)
                                  )
                    NS          ns.qupps.biz.
$ORIGIN bl.qupps.biz.

ns                  A          127.0.0.1

;-----------------------------------------------
; *** NO trailing periods from here on!!! ***
;-----------------------------------------------

; These guys are good
mens.de             A          127.0.0.10
qupps.biz           A          127.0.0.10

; Here come the spammers
```

[1] http://www.dnsbl.us.sorbs.net/

```
example.com         A        127.0.0.4
karok.info          A        127.0.0.4
                    TXT      "Go away!"

spammer.com         A        127.0.0.4
                    TXT      "Go pester somebody else"

*.kapit.info        A        127.0.0.4

; IP addresses
181.1.168.192       A        127.0.0.4
                    TXT      "Go to http://bl.qupps.biz/bad.cgi?q=192.168.1.181"
42.172.253.61       A        127.0.0.4
                    TXT      "Found by NiXSpam"
```

Notes:

- The domain names in our blacklist are not fully qualified, and they must not be: recall that they'll be qualified with the domain name of our blacklist.
- Some of the domains have a TXT record associated with them. For instance, the TXT record for the address 192.168.1.181 (reversed in the above example) contains a URL; this is common practice, and it is meant for consumption by a human who sees the mail server's error message. The user would hopefully point a Web browser at the URL to find details on the black-listing.

We have shown you a zone master file as you'd use for BIND or NSD, but you can consider other alternatives for serving DNSBL:

- Set up a MyDNS or PowerDNS server with a database back-end and provide a GUI for adding blacklist entries. If you provide your DNSBL as a public service (and receive a large volume of queries) you can place a caching name server in front of it, to lower the load on your back-end.
- Bind DLZ with a BDBHPT back-end (see Notes).
- Use a specialized server. We discuss rbldnsd in Section 16.4.

16.3.3 C – Configure your MTA to query your new DNS blacklist

If you want your Mail Transfer Agent to use a DNSBL:

- If you have integrated your DNS blacklist into the public DNS, you don't need any special DNS configuration, because your MTA sends queries to the DNSBL in exactly the same way as it sends any other, "normal", DNS query.
- If you have created a fictitious domain (bad.guys) for your DNSBL (which we recommend you do if you will not provide your blacklist to the public), you have to configure your caching name servers to specifically find that zone. In other words, since this is an internal list for your organization's use only, you have to configure your caching name server to "find" your blacklist zone. We discuss how you can set up forwarding for your caching name servers in Chapter 17, and give you an example, using BIND, in Section 16.4.3.

16.4 Serving DNSBL with rbldnsd

DNS blacklists are held in DNS zones, so these can be (and sometimes are) distributed via DNS zone transfers (AXFR). However some DNS blacklists are so big that this is no longer practical. Instead, a special condensed file format has been developed, which allows the database to be distributed efficiently. Special DNS servers, including rbldnsd, can directly retrieve all the information they need from these specially-formatted files, to serve the blacklist over the DNS.

DNS black-list files are often distributed via rsync. rsync is a remote file copy program, but where a file already exists, it's very efficient, because it transmits only the differences over the network (to minimize network load and transmission time), and then reconstitutes the new version of the file from the old version plus the differences. If a DNSBL is made available via rsync, you must configure its synchronization separately.

rbldnsd by Michael Tokarev is a DNS server specially made to serve DNS blacklist zones. It uses very little memory. By default, it answers only Address (A) and Text (TXT) queries, but it can answer Start of Authority (SOA) and Name Server (NS) if you configure it. Originally inspired by rbldns from the djbdns package, it has gained great popularity, and there is also a pre-built package available for Microsoft Windows-based systems (see Notes). The program serves both IP-address-based and name-based blacklists, and it supports ACLs, to control which hosts are allowed to query its database.

16.4.1 Running rbldnsd

You run rbldnsd either on a public IP address, if you intend to serve your own blacklist to the Internet, or on a local address, if it is for consumption within your organization only. rbldnsd automatically reloads its zone file(s) after a predetermined period of time, and all in all, requires little maintenance. If logging is enabled, the log files can get quite large on a busy MTA, so do remember to use some form of log rotation to handle these.

You typically launch rbldnsd at system startup with an invocation such as:

```
/usr/local/sbin/rbldnsd  \
     -u nobody \
     -b 127.0.0.3/53 \
     -4 \
     -c 60 \
     -l rbl.log \
     -s rbl.stats \
     -n \
     qupps.bl:combined:qupps-bl.in
```

The options specified here are:

- `u` Drop privileges to user `nobody` on startup. rbldnsd refuses to run as user `root`.
- `b` The address and port (separated by a forward slash) rbldnsd should bind to. You specify this option for each address you want the program to listen on. (Mandatory.)
- `4` Use IPv4 only and do not attempt to use IPv6.
- `c` rbldnsd checks the zone files' modification times periodically on the file system, to see if the files themselves have changed; this option specifies how long, in seconds, that

rbldnsd should wait between between checks. If rbldnsd detects that a file has changed, it reloads the zone from disk. If you set this value to zero, rbldnsd doesn't check for changes at all.

`l` rbldnsd logs all queries to this logfile. (No logging if not specified.)

`s` Specifies a file where rbldnsd will write a line with short statistic summary of queries made per zone, every check (`-c`) interval. (Default: no statistics.)

`n` Do not become a daemon. (Normally rbldnsd will `fork()` and go to the background; this option suppresses that.)

The first argument to rbldnsd is made up of three parts: (a) The zone name of the blacklist. (b) The data set type. (c) The file containing the data set. The data set type (in the example above, `combined`) specifies that rbldnsd accepts different kinds of data in a single file, and we discuss that file format now.

16.4.2 Zone file formats in rbldnsd

rbldnsd supports a number of different zone file formats, making it very flexible: you can specify default entries that can be returned to queries, and include entries describing CIDR network blocks, individual IP addresses, and domain names. rbldnsd's manual page has full details of these; here we give only a small sample:

Listing 16.2: An example input for rbldnsd

```
1 $DATASET ip4set @
2 :127.0.0.2:Bad guy (http://bl.qupps.biz/q?ip=$)
3 192.168.1.1
4 10/8
5 $DATASET dnset @
6 $TTL 172800
7 :127.0.0.10:added by HR
8 example.com
9 .example.org
```

The lines in the above example have the following meanings:

1. Defines the format of the data (the data set) as being of type `ip4set`. An `ip4set` is a set of addresses or CIDR address ranges, together with A and TXT records.

2. The default answer to queries is the A record 127.0.0.2, with a TXT record containing `Bad guy...`

3. This IP address 192.168.1.1 is blocked...

4. As is the whole block of addresses 10.0.0.1 through 10.255.255.255.

5. A new data set, `dnset`, is defined. This new dataset has a different format to that of an `ip4set`. A `dnset` is a set of possibly wildcarded domain names with associated A and TXT records. Instead of the IP addresses used in an `ip4set`, a `dnset` contains domain names.

6. The TTL for subsequent lines is set to 2 days.

7. Sets the default answer for subsequent lines to an A resource record 127.0.0.10 with the corresponding TXT record containing `added by HR`.

8. The domain example.com is added; as it follows a 127.0.0.10 line, we are whitelisting it.

9. Similarly, we whitelist *anything*.example.com.

We store the above example into a file called `qupps-bl.in`. Recall, that this is the file we specified as argument to rbldnsd earlier.

We'll now send off a number of queries, remembering to append our imaginative domain name to the query:

```
$ dig @127.0.0.3 example.com.qupps.bl  any
;; flags: qr aa rd; QUERY: 1, ANSWER: 2, AUTHORITY: 0,

example.com.qupps.bl. 172800  IN      A       127.0.0.10
example.com.qupps.bl. 172800  IN      TXT     "added by HR"


$ dig @127.0.0.3   1.1.2.10.qupps.bl  any
1.1.2.10.qupps.bl.   2100   IN  A    127.0.0.2
1.1.2.10.qupps.bl.   2100   IN  TXT "Bad guy (http://bl.qupps.biz/q?ip=10.2.1.1)"

$ dig @127.0.0.3   10.9.2.72.qupps.bl  any
;; ->>HEADER<<- opcode: QUERY, status: NXDOMAIN , id: 37844
;; flags: qr aa rd; QUERY: 1, ANSWER: 0, AUTHORITY: 0, ADDITIONAL: 0
```

16.4.3 Running rbldnsd and a caching name server on the same system

You can run rbldnsd and a caching name server on the same system, and yes, even on the same TCP/IP address (as long as you use a different port number, of course). rbldnsd's `-b` option specifies the address and slash-separated port number to listen on. So, for instance, with `-b 127.0.0.3/54` rbldnsd listens only to a loopback interface on port 54. Or, if you want BIND to forward queries for qupps.bl to your rbldnsd, set up forwarding for that zone with a `forward` statement in `named.conf`:

Listing 16.3: Adding a forwarder to BIND for rbldnsd

```
zone "qupps.bl" {
    type forward;
    forward only;
    forwarders {
        127.0.0.3 port 54;
    };
};
```

16.5 Integrate DNS blacklists into your e-mail infrastructure

DNS blacklists work only if your MTA is set up as a Mail Exchanger (MX) for your domain. (If your MTA receives its mail via a third party application or a specialized appliance, it can't use IP-based DNS blacklists, as it doesn't have access to the sender's IP Address during the SMTP session.) How you integrate your DNSBL into your Mail Transfer Agent's infrastructure is MTA-specific. We show you examples for several systems in the following sections.

16.5.1 Exim

The Exim documentation describes exactly how to integrate a DNS blacklist, but we show you a configuration snippet here.

Telling Exim *to use the blacklist*

Telling Exim to use a DNSBL is a two-stage process:

1. Create an Exim ACL.

   The ACL we've chosen is checked when Exim reads the recipients of the message. (It's called `acl_check_receipt` in the sample configuration supplied with Exim.) It allows local hosts, and perhaps authenticated remote hosts (such as your traveling users in hotel rooms) to deliver mail without checking them against the blacklist, but we don't show that here. After that, we check the blacklist:

   ```
   my_acl_check_rcpt:
     ...
     deny  message = rejected because $sender_host_address is on a ↩
                     black list at $dnslist_domain\n$dnslist_text
          dnslists = bl.qupps.biz
     ...
   ```

   The ACL above uses three Exim variables:

   - `$sender_host_address` is the address of the sending host.
   - `$dnslist_domain` is the name of the blacklist. In our example, the name of the blacklist is bl.qupps.biz. This variable is interpolated into the message returned during the SMTP transaction (see below for an example).
   - `$dnslist_text` is the value of the Text (TXT) record returned for the DNS query.

2. Tell Exim when/where to use this ACL.

   You specify the ACL in Exim's configuration:

   ```
   ...
   acl_smtp_rcpt = my_acl_check_rcpt
   ...
   ```

A sample SMTP dialog

Thus configured, your Exim Mail Transfer Agent will perform an inverse DNS query for the IP address in `$sender_host_address` when it reaches the ACL. The following example shows the SMTP dialog:

```
220 qupps.biz ESMTP Exim 4.43 Sat, 12 Jan 2008 13:44:18 +0100
helo x
250 qupps.biz Hello p192-168-001-181.somewhere [192.168.1.181]
mail from:<joe@somewhere.uk>
250 OK
rcpt to:<manager@qupps.biz>
550-rejected because 192.168.1.181 is in a black list at bl.qupps.biz
550 Bad guy (http://bl.qupps.biz/q?ip=192.168.1.181)
quit
221 qupps.biz closing connection
```

Note the "rejected" message: it contains the name of the blacklist (from `$dnslist_domain`) as well as the content of the TXT resource record, interpolated from `$dnslist_text`.

Black-lists and white-lists

Exim can use both white and black lists. You may want to have specific sender domains white-listed, but do note that the sender's domain can easily be forged, so you might be forced to whitelist IP addresses instead. The following shows how we implement it:

```
1 accept  dnslists     = bl.qupps.biz=127.0.0.10/$sender_address_domain : \
2                        bl.qupps.biz=127.0.0.10
3         log_message  = WHITELISTED found in $dnslist_domain
4
5 deny    message      = rejected because $sender_host_address is in a black list \
6                                    at $dnslist_domain\n$dnslist_text
7         dnslists     = bl.qupps.biz!=127.0.0.10 : \
8                        bl.qupps.biz!=127.0.0.10/$sender_address_domain : \
9                        bl.qupps.biz
```

- Lines 1–3 white-list an SMTP client. If the Address (A) record returned from a query on the sender's domain (`$sender_address_domain`) returns `127.0.0.10`, or a query on the sender's IP address returns the same value, accept the sender, and the `deny` clause isn't checked.

- Lines 5–9 implement the blacklist. (This clause is reached only if the sending host isn't in the whitelist.) Here we check whether a lookup for the host in the white/back-list returns a value other than 127.0.0.10 (i.e. is in the list, but isn't a whitelist entry) by negating the checks used in lines 1–3.

16.5.2 Sendmail

Sendmail's configuration file, `sendmail.cf`, is generated from M4 macros in an `.mc` file. To add a DNSBL to Sendmail, add one or more `dnsbl` feature lines to the `.mc` file. You can also customize the message that sendmail returns when a DNS blacklist matches a host:

```
FEATURE('dnsbl','bl.qupps.biz')dnl
FEATURE('dnsbl','bl.qupps.biz','"554 Rejected " $&{client_addr} ↩
         " blacklisted in bl.qupps.biz"')dnl
```

Sendmail also supports *enhanced* DNS blacklist support, in which you specify the result that a DNS query to a blacklist should return:

```
FEATURE('enhdnsbl','bl.qupps.biz', , , '127.0.0.9')dnl
```

16.5.3 Postfix

Adding support for a DNSBL in Postfix is also easy. You configure the DNSBL domain(s) you wish Postfix to handle, and it checks the IP address of the sending server against these blacklists. If the IP address is registered at any of the DNSBL domains, then the message is rejected. (The names `reject_maps_rbl` and `maps_rbl_domains` are Postfix keywords.)

```
stmpd_client_restrictions = ...,reject_maps_rbl,...
         maps_rbl_domains = bl.qupps.biz
```

You can query more than one DNSBL, by adding multiple names to the `maps_rbl_domains` parameter.

16.5.4 IBM Lotus Domino

IBM Lotus Domino has supported DNS-based blacklists since version 6. It is easy to set up: open your server's configuration document and locate the tab Router/SMTP, Restrictions and Controls, SMTP Inbound Controls. The settings you need are on the section headed DNS Blacklist Filters (Figure 16.2).

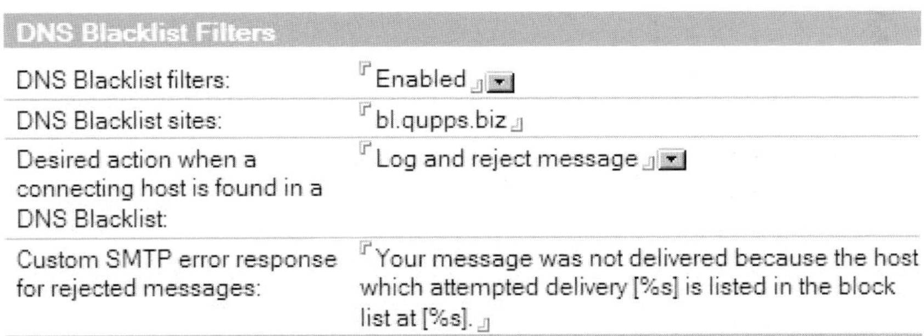

Figure 16.2: Lotus Domino has support for DNS blacklists

Here's the result of an attempt by an SMTP client to deliver a message to a suitably configured Lotus Domino server:

```
220 domi.fupps.com ESMTP Service (Lotus Domino Release 6.5.4) ready at ...
helo x
250 domi.fupps.com Hello x ([192.168.1.181]), pleased to meet you
mail from:<joe@someplace.com>
554 Your message was not delivered because the host which attempted delivery↩
            [192.168.1.181] is listed in the block list at [bl.qupps.biz].
quit
221 domi.fupps.com SMTP Service closing transmission channel
```

and the attempt is also logged on the Domino console and log.

Summary

- DNS blacklists help combat Spam. You can either use an existing blacklist or implement your own.
- DNS blacklists can be used to blacklist or whitelist senders.
- The implementor of the DNSBL defines what address is returned to a DNS query to indicate that the entry is blacklisted (or whitelisted).
- The rbldnsd program is a specialized DNS server for publishing IP addresses for your DNS blacklist.
- When a mail server (MTA) receives a message it can query one or more DNS blacklists during the SMTP dialog to determine whether it should accept the message.

Related topics

- You can use Bind DLZ with the BDBHPT driver (Chapter 9) to implement a DNS blacklist. Implementing a DNS blacklist with Bind DLZ might sound far fetched, as we've just shown you how you can do it much more easily with rbldnsd, but Jorgen Lundman has implemented an RBL with Bind DLZ and the BDBHPT driver for a reason: so that he can add and remove IP addresses from it very quickly – which is very difficult to do with rbldnsd (see `http://www.lundman.net/wiki/index.php/Rbl-add-ip`).
- rbldns (without the trailing "d") is a part of djbdns. However, we haven't covered it (there or here) because rbldnsd is more flexible (with its support for different data sets), and it is used more widely.
- We discuss how you create and use a DNSBL for determining the geographic location of an IP address in Section G.2. That blacklist is also served by rbldnsd.

Notes and further reading

Installing rbldnsd

rbldnsd does not use autoconf; its configure script is minimal, but sufficient.

```
$ wget http://www.corpit.ru/mjt/rbldnsd/rbldnsd_0.996a.tar.gz
$ tar xvzf rbldnsd_0.996a.tar.gz
$ cd rbldnsd-0.996a
$ ./configure --enable-stats --enable-zlib
$ make
```

After completing the build, you install the program (rbldnsd) and its associated manual page (`rbldnsd.8`) to directories of your choice.

```
$ install -m 755 rbldnsd /usr/local/sbin
$ install rbldnsd.8 /usr/local/man/man8
```

DNS Blacklists

- Wikipedia has a good article on DNS blacklists at `http://en.wikipedia.org/wiki/DNSBL`, as well as a comparison of the available DNSBL at `http://en.wikipedia.org/wiki/Comparison_of_DNS_blacklists`.
- The SpamHaus Project provides DNS-based blacklist queries free of charge for small sites, and provides an rsync-based subscription that you can use on your own hosts with rbldnsd. The documentation you receive when you purchase their subscription service is excellent (see `http://www.spamhaus.org/`).
- For a huge list of DNSBL providers see `http://www.moensted.dk/spam/`

A packaged rbldnsd for Microsoft Windows

ITeF!x Consulting have combined rbldnsd, rsync, ssh, and Cygwin into a package, Wrbldnsd, for Microsoft Windows. It comes with an installer to ease the pain of installing the individual components (see `http://tinyurl.com/yrxdmr`).

Further reading

We recommend these books be on the bookshelf of any self-respecting e-mail admin:

- *The Exim SMTP mail server*, 2nd edition, by Philip Hazel (UIT Cambridge Ltd.).
- *The Book of Postfix*, by Ralf Hildebrandt and Patrick Koetter (No Starch Press).
- *sendmail*, 4th edition, by Bryan Costales, Claus Assmann, George Jansen, and Gregory Shapiro. This is the so-called "bat book" (O'Reilly).

Combatting spam with Lotus Domino

If you have Lotus Domino, you may be familiar with Chris Linfoot's *IBM Lotus Notes/Domino spam bible*. It is an excellent source for all things Spam and Lotus Domino (see `http://chris-linfoot.net/`).

Chapter

17 Caching name servers

caching: the act of recording response to resolver queries for future reference.

definition

Introduction

Caching name servers are the front-line DNS servers that clients use when accessing services on the Internet or on private networks. This Chapter initially explains the the factors to consider when deploying any caching server. Then we describe several caching servers, each in what is almost a mini-chapter of its own, explaining how to configure it, with common deployment scenarios.

We discussed in Chapter 1 that a caching name server is the first line of name server that you configure your clients to use. Caching name servers talk directly to authoritative name servers, performing the hard work of query resolution. In order to do that, they follow a chain of referrals starting at the root servers, and following those referrals from one authoritative server to the next, until they find the required answer, as illustrated in Figure 17.1.

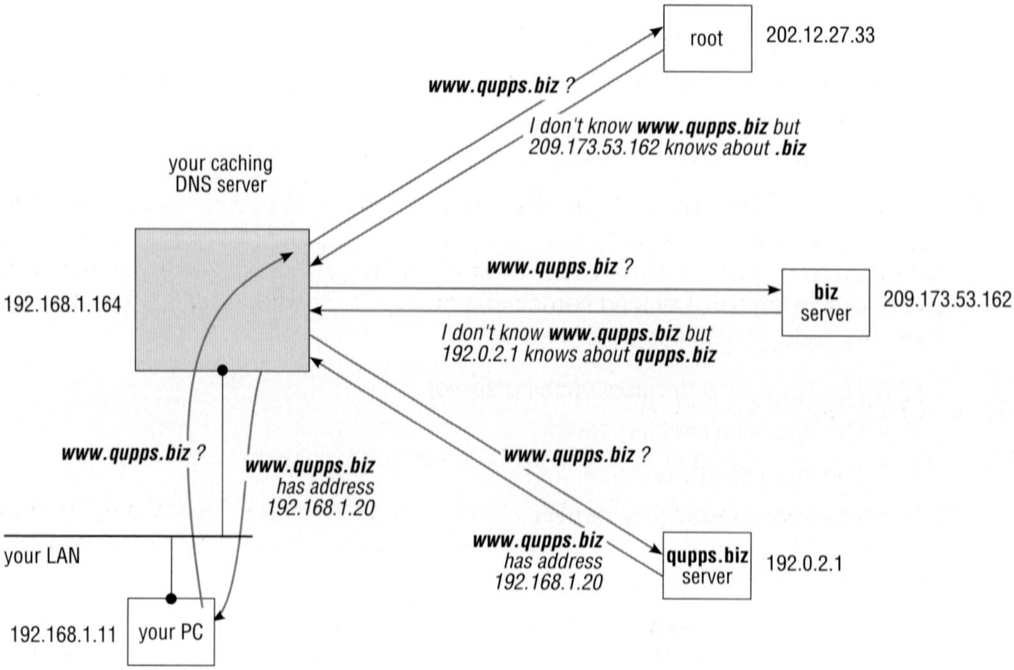

Figure 17.1: The different steps in resolving the name www.qupps.biz

17.1 Deploying your caching name servers

17.1.1 Where you place your caching name server

In the sections that follow, we discuss examples of where you place a caching name server:

- Directly on a workstation or e.g. a mail server, if it makes heavy use of the DNS. If the workstation has no access to the public Internet, you must set up the name server to forward to a more central DNS cache such as the main caching server in your organization.

- In a Small Office / Home Office, you typically run a single caching name server, on your main workstation (or server), to be used by all devices on your network. Your caching name server will use the public Internet DNS or forward to your ISP's forwarder.

- A branch office, often connected over a Virtual Private Network to a central network, typically has a caching name server directly on the LAN. It will often be configured to forward all queries to the main DNS caches at your organization's head office.
- On a corporate network you place a caching server at strategic places on your network, of which there are typically many:
  - Close to large groups of users' workstations.
  - Close to (or even better, on) machines that make heavy use of DNS (mail servers, proxies, etc.).
  - In branch offices, as described above.
- To ease the workload on authoritative name servers, you might even place a DNS cache in front of them. Do note however, that in doing so you deny your clients the "aa" bit on the authoritative answers. Some DNS registries check your authoritative servers to see whether they are answering correctly; if the answers don't have the "aa" bit set, the registry can refuse delegation.

17.1.2 Checklist for deployment

When deploying your caching name servers, here are some points to keep in mind:

- We strongly recommend you deploy at least two DNS caches. Always observe the motto "two of everything", because you don't want a failure on one of the caches to cripple your network services.
- Carefully consider where you place the caches on your network. We recommend you do not have caches on publicly accessible IP addresses, as that would allow Tom, Dick and Harry to use your DNS cache, and opens it to attack. You don't want those guys to use your e-mail server either, do you?
- On machines such as e-mail servers (Mail Transfer Agents and relays) or Web proxy servers (e.g. squid) that make heavy use of DNS, we recommend you install a local caching DNS server. You configure the caching name server to listen on a loop-back interface (IP 127.0.0.1) and you set up the system's `/etc/resolv.conf` to use that as well as at least one more cache on another machine.
- You can install a small caching name server on workstations if you want to. We recommend either dnscache or dnsmasq (Chapter 13) for this.

17.1.3 Don't forget the stub resolver

In Chapter 1 we introduced the resolver – the client-side software on a host that uses the DNS:

- On UNIX and GNU/Linux systems it is the so-called stub resolver which is configured via the Name Service Switch (Chapter 20) and `/etc/resolv.conf`.

- On Microsoft Windows it is the DNS Client service.

Resolvers are frequently overlooked although they can be a major point of failure:

- You configure the resolvers of each of the workstations, servers and devices on your network to use the network addresses of both (or more, if you deploy more than two) of your DNS caches. (We were called from dinner one evening because services on a client's mainframe computer were not responding. One of the site's caching DNS servers had conked out, but why was the mainframe reacting so? Its resolver had two `nameserver` entries, but both pointed to the *same* crashed name server!)

- Ensure resolvers on your hosts do not contain entries for name servers that you take out of service. Wherever possible, use DHCP to provide hosts and devices with an up-to-date list of your caches. Even so, there will almost always be machines that are not configured via DHCP; for these you have to update their resolver configuration by other means.

17.1.4 Special-case resolution requirements

Unless you are on a private network disconnected from the public Internet (in which case you have to configure your caching name server specially), caching name servers usually do "the right thing" automatically. They prime themselves with a list of (compiled-in) root name server addresses, and start at these roots when they receive a query. From the root servers, they successively find their way to authoritative name servers in the attempt to resolve the query as illustrated in Figure 17.1. However, there may be situations in which you will want to change the behavior of your cache:

- You want a specific domain name to be resolved to another address. For example, you might want to avoid images from the domain singleclick.biz to be loaded in your Web browser. If you configure your caching server to resolve singleclick.biz to the address 127.0.0.1 you bypass the domain entirely.

- You want to have queries for a domain directed at (i.e. forwarded to) a specific name server. If, for example, you host a copy of a DNS blacklist, say spamhaus.org, on your own servers, you will want queries for that domain to be handed off to your own authoritative servers for the blacklist instead of directing them at Spamhaus' public servers on the Internet.

- You want to add "a bit of authority" to your caching server by configuring it to serve some data from a file on disk instead of having it recurse. As a developer, for example, you want to test applications even when you are on the road. Although you are disconnected when sitting in your hotel room, the caching name server you run on your laptop can resolve *myserver.mydomain*.

Many of the servers we discuss in this chapter have the capability of being tweaked in this manner, and we show you how to do so. If you are on a disconnected network (i.e. a network without connectivity to the public Internet), you will have to modify the list of root name servers the caches use. We show you how to do this as well.

17.1.5 The recursive caching name servers

The caching name servers we cover are:

- BIND is a versatile server, and it can be configured to perform recursion; we show you how to do so in the next section.
- PowerDNS Recursor (Section 17.3) is a standalone recursive resolver, from the makers of PowerDNS.
- dnscache (Section 17.4) that is part of djbdns, is a standalone recursive resolver.
- dnsproxy is a special kind of recursor. We discuss dnsproxy in Section 17.5
- Unbound (Section 17.6) is a standalone recursive caching name server with optional support for DNSSEC validation. (We discuss DNSSEC in Chapter 22.)
- dnsmasq is a recursive resolver with a twist. The program is ideally suited for a Small Office / Home Office environment as it provides an optional DHCP server. We covered dnsmasq fully in (Chapter 13).

17.2 The BIND caching server

As BIND is supplied by most operating system vendors (and GNU/Linux distributions) you probably already have it on the machines you want to set up a cache on. In this section we provide you with a boilerplate configuration you can use to set up BIND as a caching server.

Pros	•	Very good documentation available
	•	Access Control Lists
	•	Can serve authoritative zones
	•	Can forward queries for selected or all zones
Cons	○	Memory hungry
Scenarios		Medium to large environments with BIND knowhow.

Table 17.1: BIND caching name server at a glance

We discussed how you build and install BIND in Chapter 7. For a caching name server, you must provide:

A. BIND's main configuration file, `named.conf`, which is probably located in `/etc`.

B. Keys to allow the control program (rndc) to communicate with to BIND.

C. Optionally, a hints file to override BIND's compiled-in default root name servers. You have to provide this if you are setting up a caching name server in an environment that has private roots.

D. You typically configure BIND to provide DNS answers for the domain localhost and the domain 0.0.127.in-addr.arpa in order to answer queries about the local loop-back interface. This is not strictly necessary, but it is a good practice, even if you already have the necessary information in your `/etc/hosts` file.

We discuss each of these steps in the following sections.

17.2.1 Setting up a BIND caching name server

A – Create `named.conf`

The `named.conf` for your caching name server will typically contain the following clauses:

Listing 17.1: `named.conf` for a BIND caching name server

```
options {
    directory        "/var/named";
    pid-file         "/var/named/named.pid";
    allow-query      { 127.0.0.1; };
    allow-transfer   { none; };
    listen-on        {
                         127.0.0.1;
                         192.168.1.164;
                     };
};

zone "." IN {
    type hint;
    file "root.zones";
};

zone "localhost" IN {
    type master;
    file "localhost.zone";
};

zone "0.0.127.in-addr.arpa" IN {
    type master;
    file "127.zone";
};
```

B – Create an rndc *key*

The program rndc-confgen generates configuration files for rndc. It is a convenient alternative to manually setting up an `rndc.conf` file and creating the `controls` and `key` statements in your `named.conf`. You typically have it create the files for you, by running:

```
# rndc-confgen -a
wrote key file "/usr/local/etc/rndc.key"
```

(You can specify a different output file with option `-c`.) rndc-confgen chooses the file name based on how BIND was built, and its defaults are usually sensible.

C – Hints file for the root servers

You create the hints file containing the root name servers by one of two methods:

1. Download the file via FTP:

```
$ wget -O root.zones ftp://ftp.internic.net/domain/named.root
```

2. By performing a DNS query to one of the root name servers:

```
$ dig @m.root-servers.net . ns | tee root.zones
;; flags: qr aa rd; QUERY: 1, ANSWER: 13, AUTHORITY: 0, ADDITIONAL: 13

;; ANSWER SECTION:
.                         518400   IN      NS      A.ROOT-SERVERS.NET.

...

;; ADDITIONAL SECTION:
A.ROOT-SERVERS.NET.       3600000 IN      A       198.41.0.4
...
```

D – Master zones for localhost

You will typically provide zones for the localhost as well as for the 0.0.127.in-addr.arpa domains.

Listing 17.2: Master zone file for the domain localhost

```
$TTL     86400
$ORIGIN localhost.
@        IN      SOA    localhost. root.localhost. (
                               1          ; Serial
                               28800      ; Refresh
                               14400      ; Retry
                               3600000    ; Expire
                               86400 )    ; Minimum
         IN      NS      localhost.
         IN      A       127.0.0.1
```

Listing 17.3: Master zone file for the domain 0.0.127.in-addr.arpa

```
$TTL     86400
@        IN      SOA    localhost. root.localhost. (
                               1          ; Serial
                               28800      ; Refresh
                               14400      ; Retry
                               3600000    ; Expire
                               86400 )    ; Minimum
         IN      NS      localhost.

1        IN      PTR     localhost.
```

17.2.2 Adding features

The caching BIND name server as configured above fulfills most requirements of a cache, but there are some features you might want to add:

- Private roots.

  If you are in an environment that has its own root servers without Internet connectivity, you have to set up your cache so that it can find those root servers. We discuss private roots in Chapter 18, but suffice it to say at this point that you normally just replace the `root.zones` file with one containing the Name Server (NS) and Address (A) records for your private root servers.

- Forwarding.

  If you want BIND to resolve specific domains via specialized servers, you set up forwarding. In a forward zone you define the zone's name and a list of one or more upstream name servers that are willing to do recursion on your behalf.

  ```
  zone "myzone.internal" IN {
      type forward;

      forward only;
      forwarders {
          192.168.1.20;
          192.168.1.118 port 5300;
      };
  };
  ```

  - Queries for the zone myzone.internal are forwarded for resolution to the server(s) defined in the `forwarders` statement.
  - You can optionally specify a non-standard port number on a server-by-server basis, with the `port` statement.
  - The `forward` statement controls how BIND should handle forwarding:
    * With the `only` setting, BIND attempts to resolve the query only by forwarding it to the target name servers. If it receives no reply, it sends no reply at all, and clients time out.
    * Without the `only` setting, BIND first attempts to forward to the specified forwarders. If it receives no reply, it reverts to normal resolution and starts searching for an answer on the public Internet.

  A typical use for forwarding is to get access to a zone which is not otherwise delegated to. For example, if you have an internal zone on an authoritative name server, and you want your BIND caching server to "find" it, you set up forwarding for that zone as in the example above, and then you don't have to worry about setting up private root servers.

- Some authority.

  If you also need your BIND cache to provide authoritative answers for a zone, you can of course add a `master` zone to it, as discussed in Chapter 7.

Reloading named

After you change BIND's configuration in `named.conf`, you activate the changes by telling named to re-read its configuration:

```
# rndc reload
```

That concludes our discussion of the BIND caching name server.

17.3 The PowerDNS Recursor caching server

The PowerDNS Recursor is a powerful and fast recursive caching name server. It used to be an integral portion of PowerDNS but was split out to become a standalone program beginning with version 3 of the PowerDNS Recursor.

Pros	• Authoritative local zones • Good monitoring built-in • Very flexible • Integration with Lua provides scriptable answers (Section H.2)
Cons	○ No DNSSEC validation
Scenarios	Caching name service for medium to large environments.

Table 17.2: PowerDNS Recursor at a glance

PowerDNS Recursor (Figure 17.2) can be configured to:

- Serve the content of the local `/etc/hosts` file. This is useful on e.g. developer workstations for testing programs when you are working away from your usual environment (i.e. you are working disconnected). Recall that dnsmasq (Chapter 13) has a similar feature.
- Forward queries for specific domains to other caching name servers. For example, if your organization uses PowerDNS Recursor and joins up with QUPPS, you could configure your PowerDNS Recursor to forward queries for qupps.biz to QUPPS' internal DNS servers, which contain more information than QUPPS' public name servers.
- Serve local zones authoritatively from locally configured master zone files. This is useful if you want to add a few authoritative internal zones to a PowerDNS Recursor without deploying a separate full-blown authoritative name server.
- Use a list of root name servers you configure. Modify this list if your organization uses its own private root name servers. We discuss how you do this in Chapter 18.

PowerDNS Recursor and its sister program, PowerDNS, are similar in several ways (a) They use similar configuration files (b) They both have separate controlling programs – PowerDNS has pdns_control and PowerDNS Recursor has rec_control (c) They both have facilities for graphing operations statistics with RRDtool.

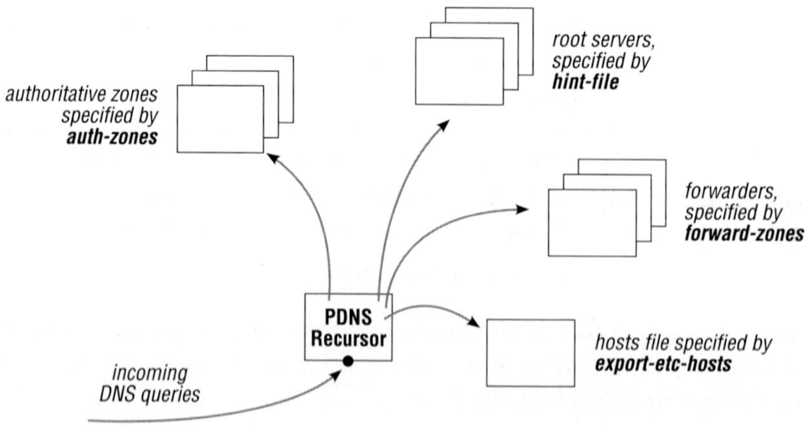

Figure 17.2: PowerDNS Recursor overview

17.3.1 Configuration

On startup PowerDNS Recursor reads its `recursor.conf` file from the directory configured as `CONFIGDIR` during the build. Each of the following settings can appear either in the configuration file, separated from its value with an "=" sign, or as a command-line switch prefixed by "--". A typical configuration file for a workstation or central cache running PowerDNS Recursor could be as simple as:

```
local-address=192.168.1.202
```

which will have PowerDNS Recursor listen on 192.168.1.202 on port 53 (default) of the specified IP address for TCP and UDP connections from clients, and using the default access control, i.e. allowing only clients from private IP networks (RFC 1918) to submit queries.

Other interesting configuration directives include:

allow-from
: A comma-separated list of network/mask addresses of clients allowed to use this server. The default permits access only from clients on private IP networks as specified by RFC 1918 (i.e. 10/8, 172.16/12 and 192.168/16). Queries from addresses not listed here will be ignored.

```
allow-from=192.168.2.0/24 ,19.4.0.0/16
```

auth-zones
: PowerDNS Recursor can serve zones locally from files in master zone file format[1]. Each zone and its file are separated by an "=" sign, and multiple pairs are separated by commas. For example, to serve qupps.biz and example.net from this PowerDNS Recursor:

```
auth-zones=qupps.biz=/etc/powerdns/quppszone ,\
    example.net=/etc/powerdns/ex.zone
```

[1]Note that `$ORIGIN` parsing is not implemented.

Note that PowerDNS Recursor currently does not set the "aa" bit on responses for its authoritative zones.

chroot

Name of a directory into which the program should `chroot()` at startup. Any files referred to must be accessible from the new root directory. In particular, care must be taken to ensure that rec_control and PowerDNS Recursor can access the control socket they use to communicate with (see socket-dir).

```
chroot=/var/dns/pdns
```

daemon

Whether PowerDNS Recursor should `fork()` and operate as a daemon. Default is yes.

```
daemon=yes
```

export-etc-hosts

If this flag is set, IPv4 addresses from the local `/etc/hosts` file are made available in the DNS. For example, setting this flag:

```
export-etc-hosts=yes
```

with an `/etc/hosts` containing:

```
192.168.1.20 mypc
192.168.1.21 myserver
192.168.1.51 dom.jp dom
```

causes PowerDNS Recursor to print the following upon startup:

```
Inserting forward zone 'mypc.' based on hosts file
Inserting reverse zone '20.1.168.192.in-addr.arpa.'...
Inserting forward zone 'myserver.' based on hosts file
Inserting reverse zone '21.1.168.192.in-addr.arpa.'...
Inserting forward zone 'dom.jp.' based on hosts file
Inserting forward zone 'dom.' based on hosts file
Inserting reverse zone '51.1.168.192.in-addr.arpa.'...
```

and a lookup on mypc returns:

```
$ dig @localhost mypc
;; ANSWER SECTION:
mypc.        86400    IN    A    192.168.1.20
```

forward-zones

Queries for specific zones can be forwarded by PowerDNS Recursor to other caching name servers by listing the zone names and their forwarders in the forward-zones setting[2]. For example:

```
forward-zones=qupps.biz=192.168.1.20,\
      jp.com=192.168.1.20,\
      mens.de=127.0.0.1
      qupps.bl=127.0.0.3
```

[2]At the time of this writing, only a single forwarder can be set up for a zone, but the code for enabling multiple forwarders per zone is ready, and it will be available in the next release.

The above configuration causes PowerDNS Recursor to (a) Direct queries for qupps.biz and jp.com to 192.168.1.20 (b) Send queries for mens.de to a caching server on the local machine (c) Forward queries for the DNS blacklist configured as qupps.bl to an rbldnsd listening on 127.0.0.3.

If you have to forward many zones, you can enter *zonename=IP address* tuples, one per line, in a file, and you then specify this file's name in the forward-zones-file setting.

hint-file

On startup, PowerDNS Recursor uses either built-in hints or the content of the hint-file to determine the addresses of the root name servers. The format of this file is as in a master zone file.

You need to change this setting only if you are setting up a private DNS system with private roots, in which case you create a hints file looking like this:

```
$ cat /etc/powerdns/hints
.                    608400 IN NS root1.qupps.biz.
.                    608400 IN NS root2.qupps.biz.
root1.qupps.biz.     608400 IN A 192.168.1.80
root2.qupps.biz.     608400 IN A 192.168.9.65
```

and enable that for PowerDNS Recursor with a :

```
hint-file=/etc/powerdns/hints
```

local-address

By default PowerDNS Recursor binds to port 53 on the machine's local loop-back interface. You will want to change this behavior for a caching name server on your network, so that all your clients can query it. Set the interfaces on which PowerDNS Recursor listens to:

```
local-address=192.168.1.20 ,127.0.0.2:530
```

You can add more than one interface by separating them by commas (" , "), and you specify an alternate port number by appending it after a colon.

Note that for security reasons, you will probably not want to have a public PowerDNS Recursor listening on an Internet-facing interface.

max-cache-entries

The number of cache entries that PowerDNS Recursor should hold.

remotes-ringbuffer-entries

If you change this value is from its default of 0, PowerDNS Recursor keeps statistics on the clients that query the recursor. It stores client statistics in a ring buffer; this variable defines how many entries should be held in the buffer.

```
remotes-ringbuffer-entries=100
```

After changing this and restarting PowerDNS Recursor, use the rec_control program to display the content of the ringbuffer.

```
# rec_control top-remotes
Over last 100 queries:
66.00%  192.168.1.18
34.00%  127.0.0.1
```

serve-rfc1918 — This setting (on by default) causes PowerDNS Recursor to not forward queries for private IP addresses (RFC 1918) to the Internet, because they wouldn't be answered anyway. The setting makes the server authoritatively aware of 10.in-addr.arpa, 168.192.in-addr.arpa and 16-31.172.in-addr.arpa, which saves load on the AS112 servers. Individual parts of these zones can still be loaded or forwarded.

server-id — By default, the PowerDNS Recursor replies to a query for id.server with its host name. This option changes the reply value to the specified string. For example, if we set:

```
server-id=fool
```

then a query gives:

```
$ dig @192.168.1.164 CH id.server TXT
;; ANSWER SECTION:
id.server.              86400   CH      TXT      "fool"
```

setuid / setgid — In addition to chrooting, PowerDNS Recursor can switch to a different user and/or group after binding to its socket (which must be done as a privileged user). These settings define the user and/or group to switch to:

```
setuid=nobody
```

Note that files required by the PowerDNS Recursor must be accessible by the user or group, and cache dump files created with rec_control are owned by this user.

socket-dir — PowerDNS Recursor and its rec_control utility "talk" to each-other via a control socket. This defines where the control socket and the file containing the process-id (PID) of the daemon should be stored. It defaults to `LOCALSTATEDIR` defined during build (`/var/run`) but can be modified at run-time.

```
socket-dir=/tmp
```

This option also affects the rec_control controller (Section 17.3.2).

trace — If turned on, the PowerDNS Recursor prints impressive heaps of logging information. This option should be disabled for any production system, as it ruins performance.

```
trace=on
```

A single query will start printing DNS trace information:

```
question for 'fupps.com.|A' from 127.0.0.1
Looking for CNAME cache hit of 'fupps.com.|CNAME'
No CNAME cache hit of 'fupps.com.|CNAME' found
No cache hit for 'fupps.com.|A', trying to find an NS
Checking if we have NS in cache for 'fupps.com.'
no valid/useful NS in cache for 'fupps.com.'
Checking if we have NS in cache for 'com.'
no valid/useful NS in cache for 'com.'
Checking if we have NS in cache for '.'
NS (with ip, or non-glue) in cache '.' -> 'a.root ...
within bailiwick: 1, in cache, ttl=1209571
...
```

version-string — By default, PowerDNS Recursor replies to the version.bind query with its version number. Security conscious users may wish to override the reply that the recursor issues (although you cannot disable the reply completely). For example:

```
version-string=Foo server
```

causes PowerDNS Recursor to issue the following answer to the query:

```
$ dig @192.168.1.164 CH version.bind TXT
;; ANSWER SECTION:
version.bind.   86400   CH   TXT "Foo server"
```

17.3.2 Controlling PowerDNS Recursor

You control and influence a running PowerDNS Recursor process with the rec_control utility. The program talks to PowerDNS Recursor via a UNIX socket stored in the directory specified with option socket-dir. rec_control understands the following commands:

ping — Checks if PowerDNS Recursor is alive.

```
# rec_control ping
pong
```

quit — Requests a shutdown of the PowerDNS Recursor.

```
# rec_control quit
bye
```

reload-zones — Tells PowerDNS Recursor to reload all external zone data from authoritative zone files (i.e. from the zones you specify with auth-zones). It also checks the configuration file to determine if the export-etc-hosts statement has changed and possibly incorporates the changes if required.

```
# rec_control reload-zones
ok
```

top-remotes — Shows the list of top clients (see remotes-ringbuffer-entries).

wipe-cache — Clears the cache for a specified domain. This is useful if you know that a server's IP has changed, but the TTL hasn't yet expired.

```
# rec_control wipe-cache example.com
wiped 2 records
```

get — Retrieves one or more variables from the running PowerDNS Recursor. Some of the variables currently defined are listed in Table 17.3; the whole list is at `http://doc.powerdns.com/recursor-stats.html`

```
# rec_control get all-outqueries questions
2404
1504
```

`all-outqueries`	counts the number of outgoing UDP queries since starting
`answers0-1`	counts the number of queries answered within 1 millisecond
`answers100-1000`	counts the number of queries answered within 1 second
`answers10-100`	counts the number of queries answered within 100 milliseconds
`answers1-10`	counts the number of queries answered within 10 milliseconds
`cache-entries`	shows the number of entries in the cache
`cache-hits`	counts the number of cache hits since starting
`cache-misses`	counts the number of cache misses since starting
`questions`	counts all End-user initiated queries with the RD bit set
`uptime`	number of seconds process has been running (version 3.1.5+)

Table 17.3: A selection of rec_control variables

17.3.3 PowerDNS Recursor statistics

Approximately every half hour, PowerDNS Recursor outputs a few lines of statistics which can be used to create MRTG graphs:

```
stats: 1461 questions, 1177 cache entries, 0 negative entries, 7% cache hits
stats: throttle map: 0, ns speeds: 2
stats: outpacket/query ratio 159%, 0% throttled, 0 no-delegation drops
stats: 0 outgoing tcp connections, 1 queries running, 21 outgoing timeouts
```

You can dump a readable representation of the current cache of a running PowerDNS Recursor to a file:

```
# rec_control dump-cache /tmp/newfile
# head /tmp/newfile
googlemail.l.google.com. 153 IN A 209.85.137.18
googlemail.l.google.com. 153 IN A 209.85.137.19
googlemail.l.google.com. 153 IN A 209.85.137.83
www.modsecurity.org. 8819 IN A 82.165.78.202
netherlabs.nl. 1617 IN NS ahu.casema.net.
netherlabs.nl. 1617 IN NS ns1.pine.nl.
netherlabs.nl. 1617 IN NS ns2.pine.nl.
www.connexitor.com. 5224 IN A 208.97.143.153
www.nsftools.com. 1677 IN CNAME nsftools.com.
ns1.technorati.com. 59254 IN A 208.66.64.37
```

17.3.4 Graphing PowerDNS Recursor

The `rrd` directory of the PowerDNS Recursor source distribution includes tools for plotting RRD graphs of the numbers provided by rec_control. The create script creates the necessary RRD databases for the numbers, update must be invoked every five minutes (by cron) and makegraphs generates the image files which are served up by `index.html` on a Web server of your choice. Figure 17.3 shows just one of the images produced.

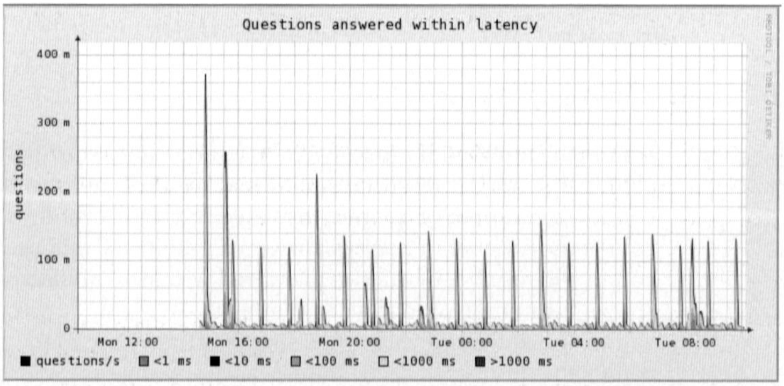

Figure 17.3: Statistics graphed by PowerDNS Recursor and RRD

17.4 The dnscache caching server

The caching DNS server of the djbdns package is a standalone program called dnscache. It performs recursive hostname-to-address, or address-to-hostname, queries, to service requests from DNS clients.

Pros	•	Low memory usage
	•	Flexible configuration
	•	Easy to set up
Cons	◦	Too many choices for installing
Scenarios		Anything from a workstation cache to a large DNS cache.

Table 17.4: dnscache at a glance

By default, dnscache contacts authoritative name servers on the Internet, but you can easily configure it to contact your own private root name servers instead.

For efficiency, dnscache stores all responses it receives in a local in-memory cache, so that future identical queries can be answered quickly. However, dnscache is very careful about what it caches:

- It caches records for at most one week, even if their TTLs request longer times.

- It does *not* cache SOA records, although it does use SOA TTLS to determine cache times for NXDOMAIN answers.

- It does not cache, or pass back in a reply, any records outside an authoritative server's authority, as they could be poisoned (i.e. they could have been forged). For example, records for qupps.biz are accepted only from the root servers, the .biz servers and the qupps.biz servers.

- As a cache, dnscache never sets the "aa" bit (except in NXDOMAIN responses).

17.4.1 Installing and setting up dnscache

We covered the installation of the dnscache binary in Chapter 11, and we recommend you read about tinydns-conf inSection 11.2.1. Like the related tinydns authoritative content server, you set up dnscache with an invocation of dnscache-conf:

```
# dnscache-conf nobody nolog /usr/local/dnscache 192.168.1.164
```

This prepares a new directory `/usr/local/dnscache` and populates it with the necessary directories and files (Figure 17.4). It adds a run script you can use to launch dnscache. When you run dnscache it will listen on IP address 192.168.1.164, will drop privileges to the user `nobody`, and it will `chroot()` to `/usr/local/dnscache`. The second username (`nolog`) is used to create the logging directory (Section 17.4.8).

```
/usr/local/dnscache
├─env
│   ├── CACHESIZE                 1000000
│   ├── DATALIMIT                 3000000
│   ├── IPSEND                    0.0.0.0
│   ├── IP                    192.168.1.164
│   └── ROOT  /usr/local/dnscache/root
├─log
│   ├── main
│   ├── run
│   └── status
├─root
│   ├──ip
│   │   ├── 127.0.0.1
│   │   └── 192.168
│   └──servers
│       ├── @
│       └── qupps.biz          192.168.1.20
└─run
```

Figure 17.4: dnscache directory structure

Like tinydns, dnscache is primed from a set of environment variables. It also requires the `root` directory (which we defined in our example as `/usr/local/dnscache/root`): dnscache uses the files in `root/ip` for client access control, and files in `root/servers` to determine which forwarders or root servers it should direct its queries to.

There are three methods of starting dnscache:

1. Via the supervise method of daemontools (which is beyond the scope of this book – see `http://cr.yp.to/daemontools.html`).

2. By setting, on the command line, all the environment variables dnscache needs upon start. You can use this if you want to start dnscache from your own scripts. In this case, you use something like:

```
# env - \
    UID=99 \
    GID=501 \
    IP=192.168.1.164 \
    CACHESIZE=1000000 \
    DATALIMIT=3000000 \
    IPSEND=0.0.0.0 \
    ROOT=/usr/local/dnscache/root \
    /usr/local/bin/dnscache  < /dev/random
```

3. By invoking the run script (Section 17.4.3).

Upon startup, dnscache reads up to 128 bytes of random data from standard input which it uses to seed itself[3].

17.4.2 Scenarios for dnscache deployment

dnscache is frequently used as an efficient recursive cache; its small memory footprint makes it ideal for installation on workstations or other machines on a LAN, to speed up and cache their DNS queries. The authors of both MyDNS[4] and PowerDNS[5] recommend it.

Centralized cache on your local network

All the machines on your network use a central dnscache, which provides a large DNS cache for the whole network (Figure 17.5).
You configure the resolvers of your network's machines to point to the IP address of the central dnscache. You must also ensure that dnscache allows them to query the cache, by adding appropriate prefixes to the `servers/ip` directory. For example:

```
# touch /usr/local/dnscache/root/ip/192.168
```

permits all machines on the 192.168/16 network to query the cache.

Caching DNS server on a Workstation

*nix workstations generally do not cache DNS requests by default; the stub resolver used by programs requesting name-to-address (or address-to-name) resolution will query the DNS

[3] A process reading `/dev/random` has to wait until the system has generated sufficient entropy for the amount of bytes requested, which is why dnscache reads from standard input and doesn't use `/dev/random` by default.

[4] `http://mydns.bboy.net/faq/`

[5] `http://doc.powerdns.com/recursion.html`

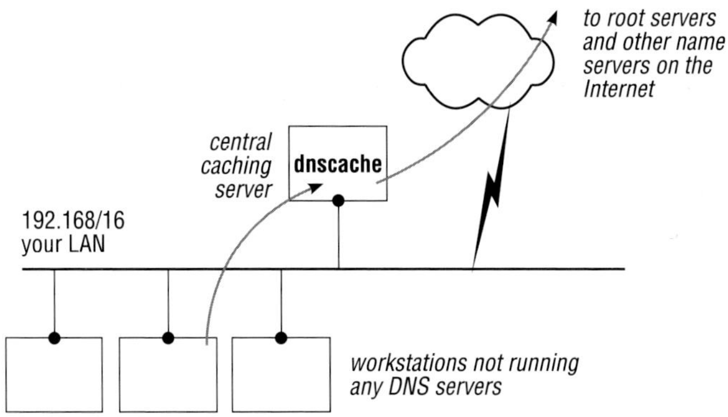

Figure 17.5: Central dnscache

servers contained in `/etc/resolv.conf`, return the answer and forget about it. If the program requesting an answer does not explicitly "remember" (i.e. cache) the answer itself, it is lost and has to be repeated for subsequent identical queries. Users of Microsoft Windows 2000 and above are used to the workstation caching answers; this is handled explicitly by the DNS Client service. In essence, setting up a dnscache on a UNIX or GNU/Linux workstation emulates that feature of Microsoft Windows. On a workstation or computer with Internet connectivity, if you set up dnscache with a default configuration, it contacts the root servers specified in its `$ROOT/servers/@` file and caches results of queries (see Figure 17.6). In this configuration, each workstation's `/etc/resolv.conf` points to the local dnscache IP address at 127.0.0.1.

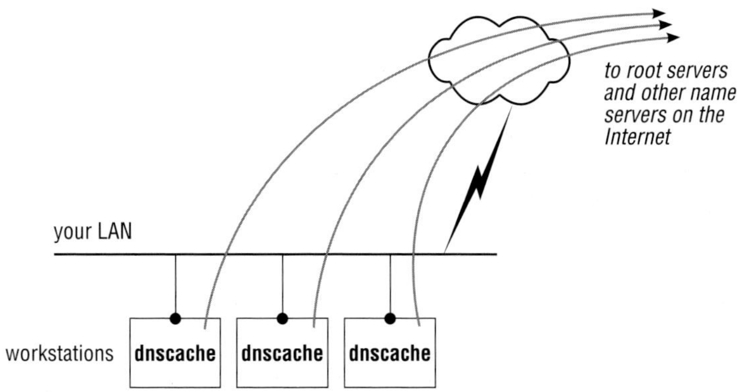

Figure 17.6: dnscache on a workstation

The difference between this and the scenario in Figure 17.5, is that in Figure 17.5 one dnscache services all the machines on the local network, and not just the machine that dnscache is running on.

Workstation as forwarder

The large central cache (Figure 17.5) may also be used as a forwarder for workstations: dnscache runs on each workstation and forwards queries to this central dnscache. You might have a large DNS cache on a central machine in your network, (Figure 17.7, left), or at your ISP (Figure 17.7, right), in which case your workstations can profit from the work it has already done in caching queries. In this case, you set up a local dnscache on a workstation, which forwards its requests to the upstream cache.

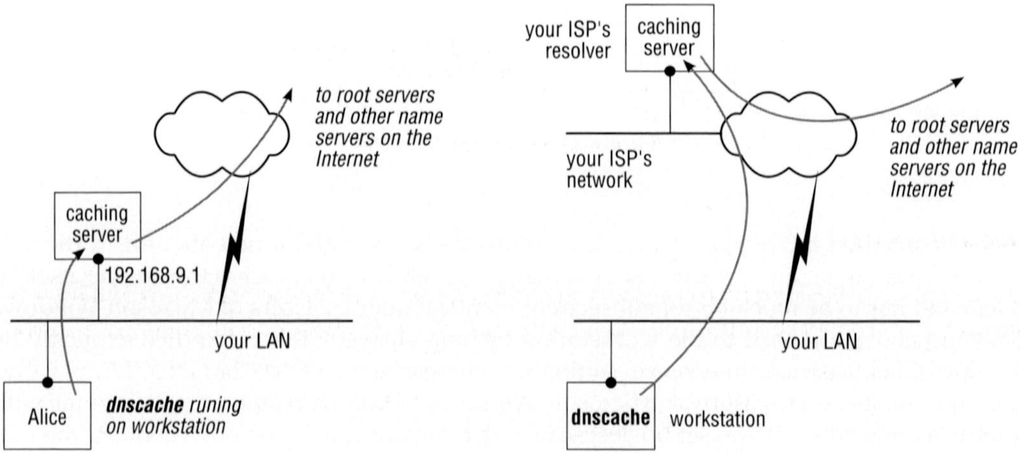

Figure 17.7: dnscache as a forwarder

In Figure 17.7, left, Alice's stub resolver points to her own local dnscache IP address on 127.0.0.1. (Alice's dnscache listens on 127.0.0.1 only, because it doesn't have to handle queries from any other host.) To enable forwarding, edit Alice's `$ROOT/servers/@` file, adding the IP address(es) of the upstream cache(s), and set `$FORWARDONLY`. For example, if the upstream cache has IP address 192.168.9.1, you configure Alice as follows, and then restart dnscache:

```
alice# echo 192.168.9.1 > /usr/local/dnscache/root/servers/@
alice# echo 1 > /usr/local/dnscache/env/FORWARDONLY
```

Central cache with forwarding

This is an extension of the previous scenario. Suppose you have a tinydns (or other authoritative) server that serves a few zones. You add forwarding for those zones to dnscache so that it directs queries for those zones directly to your authoritative name server, without using the root servers (Figure 17.8). You configure your workstations' resolvers to query dnscache; they don't query tinydns directly. Adding a forwarder for a zone is easy enough:

```
# echo 192.168.1.20 > /usr/local/dnscache/root/servers/qupps.biz
```

After restarting dnscache, queries for qupps.biz are directed to 192.168.1.20, whereas all other queries are resolved via the root servers (specified in the file `$ROOT/servers/@`).

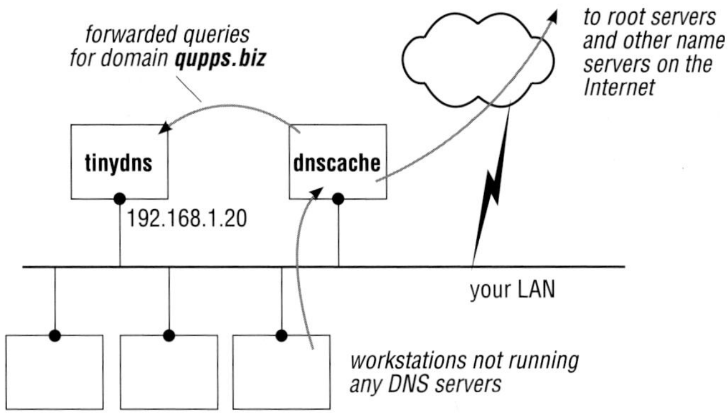

Figure 17.8: Central dnscache with forwarders

Inbound cache

Authoritative DNS content servers that make heavy use of database back-ends and offer no caching of their own can profit from a front-end dnscache as shown in Figure 17.9. Here,

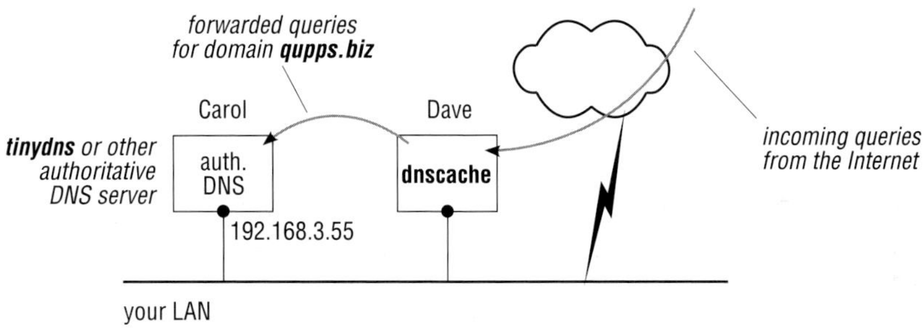

Figure 17.9: Inbound dnscache for content servers

dnscache is accessible on an external IP address (the address to which zones have been delegated to in the worldwide DNS). dnscache forwards all queries to an internal authoritative DNS server. If the authoritative server is on Carol (192.168.3.55), you configure dnscache on Dave with:

```
dave# echo 192.168.3.55 > /usr/local/dnscache/root/servers/@
dave# echo 1 > /usr/local/dnscache/env/FORWARDONLY
```

This configuration provides good caching for your content servers. However, a side effect is that dnscache will never return answers for your zones with the "aa" authority bit set in the replies (because it is the tinydns server that is authoritative, and it's not the one replying). Some DNS registries complain when they check that zones for which your servers are authoritative, aren't answered with the "aa" bit set.

17.4.3 Detailed dnscache configuration options

dnscache uses a handful of environment variables and some files in `$ROOT` (Figure 17.10). When you use the default run script, the environment is primed from files in the `env` directory: as we saw with tinydns, the filename is used as the environment variable name, and the file content becomes the variable's value. If you want to have dnscache start with `$ROOT` set to `/dns` you would:

```
# echo /dns > /usr/local/dnscache/env/ROOT
```

After modifying a variable's value you must restart dnscache for the change to take effect.

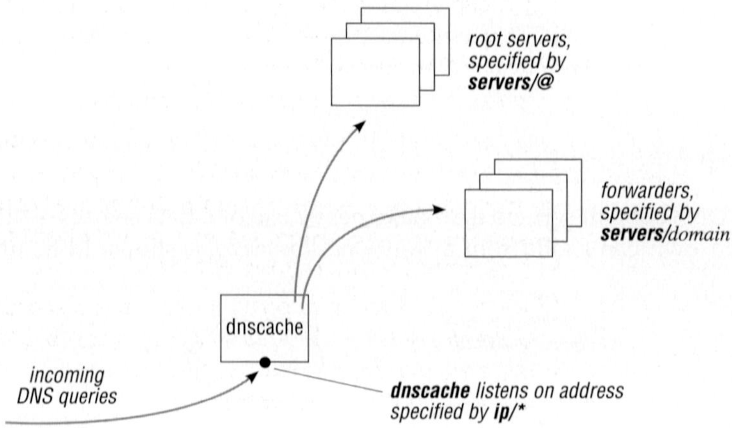

Figure 17.10: Files used by dnscache

Here are the variables and filenames used by dnscache:

$CACHESIZE
: The size of dnscache's in-memory cache. Default: one million bytes.

$DATALIMIT
: The run script sets the limit on the maximum size of the process's data segment to `$DATALIMIT`, using the `setrlimit()` system call, effectively limiting the maximum size of the dnscache process. The default is three million bytes.

$FORWARDONLY
: If this variable is set to any value, dnscache treats the addresses in `$ROOT/servers/@` as a list of forwarders (i.e. addresses of other caching name servers), not root servers. Any domain in the `servers` directory will be contacted directly while all other queries go to the back-end caching name server(s) that you specify in the `$ROOT/servers/@` file.

If you do set this variable, ensure that your `@` file does *not* contain addresses of root servers; the addresses listed must be of name servers willing to handle recursive queries.

$IP
The single IP address on which dnscache listens for incoming UDP queries and TCP connections, on port 53. If you have applied the jumbo patch to djbdns (see Notes on page 310), this variable can contain a slash-separated list of addresses (for example `192.168.1.164/127.0.0.1`).

Note that to run dnscache and tinydns on the same machine the programs must listen on separate IP addresses, so either the machine must be multi-homed, or you start dnscache on a loopback interface (127.0.0.1) and tinydns on the external IP, or you run dnsproxy (Section 17.5) to front tinydns and dnscache.

$IPSEND
dnscache sends outgoing packets from the address `$IPSEND`. You usually set `$IPSEND` to `0.0.0.0`, meaning the machine's primary IP address, but in the case of a multi-homed host, you can set this to any valid interface address.

$ROOT, $UID, $GID
dnscache runs chrooted in the directory specified by `$ROOT`, under the uid and gid specified by `$UID` and `$GID` respectively. Files in the `ip` and `servers` directories are relative to `$ROOT`, and they must be accessible by uid `$UID`. Both `$UID` and `$GID` may contain names or numeric ids.

$ROOT/ip
Files in this directory control client access to dnscache. For example, dnscache will accept a query from IP address 1.2.3.4 if there exists a file named `ip/1.2.3.4`, `ip/1.2.3`, `ip/1.2`, or `ip/1`. (The files can be empty.)

For example, to allow queries from a network 192.168/16 and from network 127/8 as well as from 10.0.12/24, create the following files:

```
# touch /usr/local/dnscache/root/ip/192.168
# touch /usr/local/dnscache/root/ip/127
# touch /usr/local/dnscache/root/ip/10.0.12
```

$ROOT/servers/@
dnscache reads a list of dotted-decimal root server IP addresses (one per line) from `$ROOT/servers/@`. When you initially set up dnscache with dnscache-conf, it copied the list of root name servers from `/etc/dnsroots.global` to the `@` file. However, if you are using private root servers, you have to configure the list manually by editing the `@` file; you add one IP address per line. (See Notes on page 312 regarding updating the list of root servers.)

$ROOT/servers/*dom.ain*
dnscache scans the `servers` directory for a list of domains. For example, if there are addresses listed (one per line) in a file `servers/qupps.biz`, then dnscache will send queries for *anything*.qupps.biz to those servers, and it will not cache records for *anything*.qupps.biz from any server other that those listed, in order to avoid cache pollution.

If you also run tinydns (or another brand of authoritative name server), it's a good idea to create a file pointing to your authoritative server(s) for each domain you create, as we have just done above for qupps.biz. Then dnscache doesn't have to recurse from the root servers for queries to your own zones.

The run *script*

One of the actions performed by dnscache-conf is to create a shell script that starts dnscache; this script is called `run`. The script must be executed within the directory specified, so in our example above, to start dnscache we should:

```
# cd /usr/local/dnscache
# ./run
```

There will be a copious amount of diagnostic log messages sent to standard output, which we cover in Section 17.4.8.

17.4.4 Testing dnscache

As shown in the following example, you test dnscache by pointing dig at it, and issuing some queries. After the five second pause, query again; note that the total query time is drastically reduced – that is, after all, the purpose of using a cache – and the TTL of the queried records has correctly been modified to reflect the time they have been in the cache.

```
$ dig @192.168.1.164 fupps.com
;; ANSWER SECTION:
fupps.com.    10800 IN A  82.165.102.119

;; Query time: 250 msec
;; SERVER: 192.168.1.164#53(192.168.1.164)
;; WHEN: Mon Nov  5 23:49:03 2007
;; MSG SIZE  rcvd: 43

$ sleep 5
$ dig @192.168.1.164 fupps.com
;; ANSWER SECTION:
fupps.com.    10795 IN A 82.165.102.119

;; Query time: 0 msec
;; SERVER: 192.168.1.164#53(192.168.1.164)
;; WHEN: Mon Nov  5 23:49:08 2007
;; MSG SIZE  rcvd: 43
```

If dnscache doesn't answer, ensure that:

- A firewall is not blocking your requests
- dnscache is the *only* program running on the machine which is listening to the the IP address and port number you assigned to it. (Hint: is there a BIND name server already running by default on your host?)

17.4.5 Implicit answers returned by dnscache

dnscache handles a number of queries internally without querying other name servers or data in files:

- It answers a query for localhost with 127.0.0.1
- It answers a query for 1.0.0.127.in-addr.arpa with a PTR record of localhost.
- It answers A record queries for hostnames consisting of dotted-decimal IP addresses with an A reply consisting of that IP address. For example, if you query dnscache for the address of 192.0.2.14 it will answer with 192.0.2.14. (This is quite useless, but there are people who ask a name server for the IP address of an IP address...)

17.4.6 Adding a forwarder for one or more domains

Adding a forwarder to dnscache for a specific domain, *domainname*, is trivial, as we saw on page 406. Create a file in the `servers` directory with name *domainname*, containing the IP address(es) of the name servers to which we should forward the requests for the specific domain. For example:

```
# echo 192.168.1.20 > /usr/local/dnscache/servers/qupps.biz
```

tells dnscache to forward queries for qupps.biz to the server at 192.168.1.20 instead of trying to resolve them recursively itself. When you change files in the `servers` directory you must restart dnscache to force it to re-read the contents of `servers`.

17.4.7 Configuring client machines to use dnscache

After successfully installing dnscache you must configure the resolvers of the hosts that will use it. Modify `/etc/resolv.conf` on each client host, to contain the IP addresses of your new dnscache servers. For example, if you have a single dnscache running on 192.168.1.20:

```
# echo "nameserver 192.168.1.20" > /etc/resolv.conf
```

On Microsoft Windows you enter the IP address of the host running dnscache in the properties of the TCP/IP settings for the PC.

17.4.8 Logging dnscache statistics

dnscache prints statistical messages on standard output. If you want to save the statistics, you either redirect standard output to a file, or you pipe it through a program. You typically pipe the output of dnscache through multilog, a component of the daemontools package (see Notes on page 310). multilog is a filter with the following features:

1. It reads lines of text from standard input.
2. It can select, or alternatively deselect, any number of lines of the input with a *pattern* which, unfortunately, is *not* a regular expression. Initially all lines are selected.

3. It writes selected lines to any number of logfiles, optionally prepending lines with a TAI64 timestamp (see Notes on page 313).

4. It can perform log rotation.

A full discussion of multilog (see `http://cr.yp.to/daemontools/multilog.html`) is beyond the scope of this book, but we will show you a sample recipe we use on production systems:

```
1 multilog \
2   t \
3   s1000000 n20 '-* cached *' '-* rr *' '-* tx *' '-* stats' /var/log/dnscache \
4   '+*' s1000000 n20 /var/log/dnscache/details \
5   '-*' s1000000 '+* stats *' /var/log/dnscache/stats
```

The lines mean the following:

1. Run multilog. The arguments to multilog are called a *script* which is made up of *selectors*, *actions* and files. A *selector* consists of a *+pattern* or *–pattern*, indicating whether lines matching *pattern* should be included (+) or excluded (–). For example, the pattern "`-* cached *`" means multilog should exclude lines containing "*space*`cached`*space*".

2. Timestamps. Action `t` means prepend a TAI64 timestamp to lines printed.

3. Minimum. dnscache is quite verbose in its logging. The arguments on this line cause logging to `/var/log/dnscache` and *excludes* lines with the "`-`" patterns. The result is written to a maximum of 20 files, none of which will exceed a size of 1 000 000 bytes. When a file exceeds the size it is renamed from `current` to a name like `@400000047628222252a8c9c.s` which is the time (in TAI64-format) when the file was last written to.

4. Details. All lines read by multilog are written to files in `/var/log/dnscache/details` and are also rotated, with a maximum of 20 such files being produced. Some log file entries you might see:

   ```
   stats 1 1334 1 0
   cached 1 ns2.dnspartner.de.
   tx 0 1 www.qupps.biz. qupps.biz. 5413b06e 5bb82022
   rr 5413b06e 86400 1 www.qupps.biz. c0a80101
   ```

5. Statistics. Lines containing the *pattern* `"* stats *"` are written to the directory `/var/log/dnscache/stats`.

Analyzing dnscache *logs with* dlog

Rasmus Skaarup has written dlog, a program to analyze log files produced by dnscache, tinydns and others. A complete discussion is beyond the scope of this book (see `http://dlog.gal.dk/`) but we will show you the kind of graphs it can produce for dnscache when used with RRD. Figure 17.11 shows the types of answers dnscache has returned.
That concludes our discussion of the dnscache caching name server.

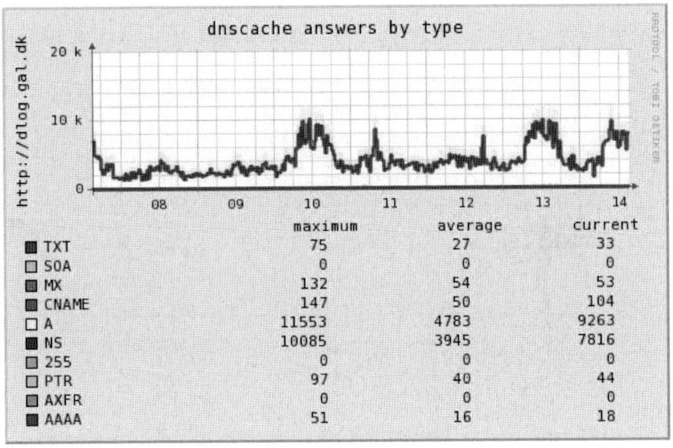

Figure 17.11: Graphing dnscache answers with dlog and RRD

17.5 The dnsproxy proxying server

dnsproxy, by Armin Wolfermann, is an unusual, special purpose DNS server. It proxies DNS queries by forwarding them to two previously configured name servers: one for authoritative queries, and the second for recursive queries (Figure 17.12). dnsproxy receives the answers from the "real" servers, and sends them, unchanged and uncached, to the requesting client.

Pros	•	Preserves "aa" bit for answers from authoritative server
	•	Concise configuration file
Cons	○	Easy to confuse the two forwarders in the configuration file
Scenarios		Environments that need authoritative and caching name services behind a single IP address.

Table 17.5: dnsproxy at a glance

According to the documentation, the primary motivation for this project was to enable djbdns to run in an ISP environment, where a single target server listening on UDP port 53 was to answer authoritative queries by clients and recursive queries at the same IP address. djbdns cannot be set up to do that because the authoritative server (tinydns) and the caching server (dnscache) would compete for the same IP address. dnsproxy solves the problem by listening for UDP requests on a single IP address and forwarding the requests either to tinydns or to dnscache.

dnsproxy runs chrooted and doesn't require root privileges. It is easy to set up: a single configuration file which is read at program startup defines how dnsproxy should handle requests.

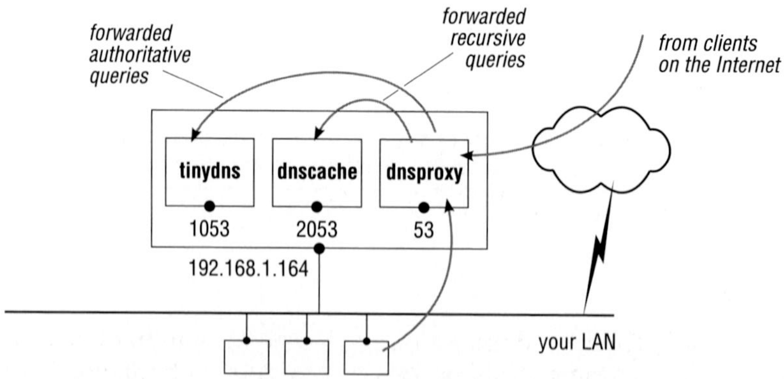

Figure 17.12: dnsproxy

17.5.1 Installing dnsproxy

You install dnsproxy in the usual way:

```
$ wget http://www.wolfermann.org/dnsproxy-1.15.tar.gz
$ tar xvzf dnsproxy-1.15.tar.gz
$ cd dnsproxy-1.15
$ ./configure --prefix=/usr/local
$ make
# make install
```

The package has its own manual page, a good tradition for tools on *nix. (We sorely miss "man pages" on a number of other programs...)

17.5.2 Configuring dnsproxy with `/etc/dnsproxy.conf`

You configure dnsproxy with the file `dnsproxy.conf` located in `/etc`. The configuration illustrated in Figure 17.12 is shown in the following Listing:

Listing 17.4: `dnsproxy.conf`

```
# Authoritative server (e.g. tinydns, bind, powerdns, ...)
authoritative           127.0.0.1
authoritative-port      1053
authoritative-timeout   10

# Recursive resolver (e.g. dnscache, powerdns-recursor)
recursive               127.0.0.1
recursive-port          2053
recursive-timeout       90

# Local address and port of dnsproxy
listen 192.168.1.164
port 53
statistics 1800
```

```
# Security features
chroot /var/empty
user nobody

# Internal networks (allowed to do recursive queries)
#
internal 192.168.1.0/24     # Our LAN
internal 192.168.6.0/24     # Friends
internal 127.0.0.1
```

The keywords are:

authoritative
: The IP address on which the separate authoritative DNS server is listening. This can be any brand of authoritative DNS server you want to use.

authoritative-port
: The port number on which the authoritative DNS server is listening.

authoritative-timeout
: The time (in seconds) that dnsproxy should wait until the authoritative server has answered. If this time is exceeded, the client's query fails.

recursive
: The IP address of the separate recursive server. This can be any brand of server you want to use.

recursive-port
: The port number on which the recursive server is listening. The default is 53.

recursive-timeout
: The time (in seconds) that dnsproxy should wait for the recursive server to answer, before causing the query to fail.

listen
: The IP address dnsproxy should listen on for incoming DNS queries.

port
: The port number at which dnsproxy should listen. (Default: 53)

chroot
: If you use this option, dnsproxy `chroot()`s to the specified directory on startup.

user
: The username to which dnsproxy switches to on startup. Use this, together with `chroot()` to lower dnsproxy's privileges.

statistics
: dnsproxy periodically produces statistics about the number of recursive and authoritative queries it has processed. This option specifies the length of the interval, in seconds, between statistics outputs. Set this to zero to disable statistics.

  If dnsproxy is running as a daemon, it logs its statistics via syslog; otherwise it prints them to standard output.

internal
: You can specify this option multiple times. It defines the addresses of internal or friendly hosts and networks; these source addresses are allowed to perform recursive queries via dnsproxy. You can specify either individual IP addresses or CIDR-formatted network numbers.

  Note that you will certainly *not* want to allow all public users query your dnsproxy (and thus allow them to use your dnsproxy for performing recursive queries). Instead, allow only internal hosts, and select remote clients on the Internet (e.g. customers or your own employees) to access the proxy.

17.5.3 Sending DNS queries to dnsproxy from "external" hosts

dnsproxy acts like a DNS server, and it may be used by clients as a recursive (albeit non-caching) DNS server. Therefore clients can use the address of the dnsproxy server in a `nameserver` line in their `/etc/resolv.conf`.

Queries sent to dnsproxy by hosts that are not allowed to perform recursion (i.e. are *not* listed on the internal option in `dnsproxy.conf`) are forwarded to the authoritative server even if the query has the "rd" (recursion desired) bit set.

```
$ dig @192.168.1.164 qupps.biz
;; ->>HEADER<<- opcode: QUERY, status: NOERROR, id: 28035
;; flags: qr aa rd; QUERY: 1, ANSWER: 1, AUTHORITY: 2, ADDITIONAL: 2

;; ANSWER SECTION:
qupps.biz.          86400    IN       A        192.168.1.20
```

Note that the query is returned with the authoritative answer ("aa") bit set, even though it passed via dnsproxy.

17.5.4 Sending DNS queries to dnsproxy from "internal" hosts

Queries sent to dnsproxy by hosts that are considered "internal" are forwarded to the caching name server *only*. Queries are not passed to the authoritative server. So, if you want "internal" hosts to be able to query zones held on the authoritative DNS content server (which will almost always be the case), you must ensure that the caching name server behind dnsproxy knows how to find them.

dnsproxy is a useful utility if you are short on IP addresses; it can consolidate two DNS servers (a content server, and a recursive cache) into one. dnsproxy lives at `http://www.wolfermann.org/dnsproxy.html`

17.6 The Unbound caching server

Unbound is a caching name server developed at NLnet Labs[6] by Wouter Wijngaards. It is based on a prototype developed in the Java programming language by Verisign labs, Nominet, Kirei and EP.NET. The current Unbound implementation is written in the C programming language.

Pros	• Sensible defaults in its default configuration file • DNSSEC validation • Access control • Local data and stub zones • libunbound provides embeddable Unbound in your own programs • Very informative logging • Fast
Cons	○ No DNSSEC look-aside validation
Scenarios	Medium to large environments that need a fast, flexible and validating caching name server.

Table 17.6: Unbound at a glance

Unbound was designed as a validating recursive DNS resolver with DNSSEC support and full RFC compliance. It is very fast, and you can use it as:

- A stub resolver.
- A caching name server.
- From within a program, by using Unbound's libunbound library (Section 17.6.6). This lets you launch an Unbound server within your application, rather than creating a separate Unbound process.

Unbound has three main components. These components are modular: you enable or disable some of them according to your requirements:

- The "Iterator" is in charge of sending iterative queries to the DNS servers. Don't disable this module, or Unbound will not be able to fetch answers to DNS queries from other servers.
- The "Cache" stores data received from other DNS servers and doles it out on request. This module is built-in to Unbound and cannot be disabled.
- The "Validator" validates the security fingerprints on data sets received by the name server. We discuss how you configure portions of this module in Chapter 22, when we discuss DNSSEC.

[6] We are grateful to *NLnet Labs* for having provided us with the code to Unbound before its release.

17.6.1 Installing Unbound

We recommend you proceed in the following order when deploying Unbound:

1. Download and install the prerequisite libraries for building Unbound. These are ldns and libevent.

   - ldns is a library that simplifies programming with DNS. It supports DNSSEC and it is also used by NSD (Chapter 10). If you don't have ldns installed, Unbound uses a version of ldns packaged with it. The developers recommend, however, that you install ldns prior to building Unbound, as it will then use the shared libraries of ldns, reducing Unbound's memory footprint.
   - libevent provides an API for executing a callback function when a specific event occurs on a file descriptor, or after a timeout has been reached. The libevent library was created by Niels Provos. libevent also contains the evdns API by Adam Langley, with asynchronous functions for DNS name resolution, but this part of the library isn't used by Unbound.

2. Download the source code to Unbound and build and install it. We chose to build from the subversion repository, but by the time you read this, pre-built packaged versions will be available (see `http://unbound.net`).

```
$ mkdir /tmp/unbound && cd /tmp/unbound
$ svn co http://unbound.nlnetlabs.nl/svn/trunk
A    trunk/Makefile.in
A    trunk/LICENSE
...
A    trunk/install-sh
 U   trunk
Checked out revision 1144.
$ cd trunk
$ ./configure --prefix=/usr/local
$ make
# make install
```

3. Configure Unbound with its `unbound.conf` file (Section 17.6.3). This is similar in form to the `nsd.conf` file we discussed in Chapter 10.

17.6.2 Setting up Unbound as a caching server

It is easy to set up Unbound as a caching name server: it provides very sensible defaults, so you typically will not have to provide a complex configuration file. We suggest you start with a small configuration, as shown below, and then add features as you need them:

```
server:
    verbosity:     1
    pidfile:       "/run/unbound.pid"
    use-syslog:    yes
    chroot:        "/usr/local/etc/unbound"
    username:      "unbound"
    directory:     "/usr/local/etc/unbound"
    module-config: "validator iterator"
```

Save this as `unbound.conf`. (You can use unbound-checkconf (Section 17.6.5) to check the configuration for errors.) This example configures caching server that accepts queries on the loop-back interface only (default); it cannot be accessed by other clients on the network. Note that because of the `chroot()` system call, all paths are anchored to the new root, so the pidfile is actually located in `/usr/local/etc/unbound/run/unbound.pid`.

Launching Unbound

Unbound starts up and daemonizes itself when you run:

```
# unbound
```

Unbound writes its process id into the file you specify as pidfile. You can force it to remain in the foreground (i.e. not to `fork()`) with option `-d`, and you can increase its verbosity by specifying one or more `-v` options, one for each level of verbosity you want.

Signaling and stopping Unbound

To stop Unbound, send it a SIGTERM signal:

```
# kill 'cat /usr/local/etc/unbound/run/unbound.pid'
```

To reload Unbound, send it a SIGHUP signal: it performs the following actions:

- If run with verbosity of at least 1, Unbound writes some statistics to its log. The statistics show the number of queries processed by the cache, the number that required recursion, and the number answered from the cache, which helps you determine if your cache is large enough. The output also includes a numerical histogram that tells you how your service to clients is performing. The `requestlist` tells you how many recursive queries Unbound was servicing at the same time on average.

```
info: sent 3657 replies, with average wait of 2.745577 sec
info: histogram of reply wait times
info: [25%]=0.00800497 median[50%]=0.0348871 [75%]=0.129392
info: lower(secs) upper(secs) replycount
info:    0.000032    0.000064 21
info:    0.000064    0.000128 138
info:    0.000128    0.000256 1
...
info:  128.000000  256.000000 28
info:  256.000000  512.000000 2
info: server stats for thread 0: 49035 queries, 45378 from cache
info: server stats for thread 0: requestlist max 17 avg 3.96609 exceeded 0
```

- Unbound clears its cache, reopens its configuration file, attempts to reconfigure itself, and then gets ready to answer queries again.

- During this reconfiguration process, Unbound keeps the sockets open. This means that, although Unbound cannot answer queries during this short period of time, the underlying operating system will queue up the UDP queries, and Unbound will answer them as soon as it is ready. Although the operating system's queue can fill up, it is rather unlikely to happen in most situations.

- If you have changed the Unbound configuration by setting new ports or interfaces, Unbound closes its sockets while it reconfigures itself. In this case, it is "deaf" to queries while it is restarting.

- Unbound also reopens the log file, so you can do log-rotation with popular tools like logrotate and have them send SIGHUP when they rotate the log files.

17.6.3 Configuring Unbound with `unbound.conf`

Unbound uses the configuration file `unbound.conf`. The file contains attributes and values separated by a colon. Values may be unquoted, or enclosed in double quotes (`"..."`) or single quotes (`'...'`); values containing whitespace must be quoted. (Use single quotes in local-data statements with long TXT records that require double quotes.) You can include the content of further files with the `include` directive, which can appear anywhere. Comments can appear anywhere; they are introduced with a hash symbol (`#`) and continue until the end of a line. Some of the options you can define in `unbound.conf` are:

verbosity
: An integer number that controls how verbose Unbound's logging should be i.e. how much information it should produce. Set to 0 to disable all messages. The default value of 1 gives operational information. Set this value to 2 for query-level information, and to 3 for algorithm-level information.

num-threads
: The number of threads Unbound should create to serve clients. Set to 1 to disable threading.

port
: The port number on which Unbound will listen for incoming queries. The default value is 53.

interface
: The IP address (either IPv4 or IPv6) on which Unbound should listen to queries from clients. You specify this option as often as needed. If you don't specify any interface, Unbound uses the loop-back interface by default.

outgoing-interface
: The IP address you specify for this attribute is used to send queries to authoritative content servers and receive their replies. You may specify this attribute multiple times. If you omit it entirely, the default of `all` is used. If you specify more than one address, Unbound chooses outgoing addresses depending on the interface it uses.

  Note that you may specify the same address in the interface and outgoing-interface attributes. This causes Unbound to use it both for incoming and outgoing requests.

outgoing-port
: Unbound requires a port number allocated from a pre-defined range to provide the client side of the communication. Specify the starting port number of this *ephemeral* port. Default is 1053. The range starts at this number and extends to outgoing-range.

outgoing-range The number of ports to open per thread for every interface. It must be at least 1, and defaults to 16. Larger numbers require more resources from the underlying operating system.

num-queries-per-thread The number of queries that each thread will service simultaneously. If more queries arrive they are dropped, which will force a client to resend the query after a timeout. Default is 1024.

rrset-cache-size Size of the RRset cache in bytes. Default is 4 megabytes. A plain number is in bytes; append `k`, `m` or `g` for kilobytes, megabytes or gigabytes respectively.

cache-max-ttl Maximum time to live in seconds for resource record sets and replies in the cache. The default is 86400. You can use this to force low TTL on records. For example, if you want to force Unbound to discard items from its cache after 600 seconds (ignoring any higher TTL on DNS records), you set cache-max-ttl to 600.

do-ip4 / do-ip6 Enable (`yes`) or disable (`no`) queries on IPv4 or IPv6. The default value for both attributes is `yes`. If you don't use IPv6, we recommend you disable it in Unbound to conserve memory.

do-udp / do-tcp Enable (`yes`) or disable (`no`) handling queries over UDP or TCP. The default value for both attributes is `yes`.

access-control Which clients are allowed to use your Unbound cache. The syntax of this attribute is:

`access-control:` *IP-netblock action*

You specify *IP-netblock* as an IPv4 or IPv6 address with */size* appended for a CIDR network block. The *action* defines how the *IP-netblock* is handled by the cache:

`deny` Stops queries from the specified network. Unbound silently drops the query, and the client times out.

```
access-control: 192.168.0.0/24 deny
```

`refuse` Stops the queries like `deny`, but sends a REFUSED error-message back to the client, which is friendlier than `drop`.

```
access-control: 10.0.0.0/8 refuse
```

`allow` Enables clients to use the cache.

```
access-control: 127.0.0.0/8 allow
access-control: 192.168.1.0/24 allow
```

The default Unbound configuration allows only localhost to use the cache, and *refuses* all other clients.

You can allow a netblock of addresses to use the cache, but prohibit single hosts or sub-blocks within that block, by specifying them in order:

```
access-control: 192.0.0.0/8 allow
access-control: 192.168.1.20 deny
```

chroot

If you specify chroot, which we recommend, Unbound `chroot()`s to the specified directory name on startup. If you specify an empty value:

```
chroot: ""
```

no `chroot()` is performed. The default setting is `/etc/unbound`. Note that Unbound changes to its configured directory (see next item) before it `chroot()`s.

directory

Sets the working directory for the program. (C.f. chroot above.)

```
directory: "/usr/local/etc/unbound"
```

username

If you specify a username, Unbound drops its privileges to the named user after binding to the port. If you specify an empty value (`""`) for this attribute, Unbound doesn't change user. The default user is unbound.

```
username: "nobody"
```

pidfile

The name of the file into which Unbound writes its process id when it starts. The file is relative to chroot and must be writable by username. Default `/var/run/unbound.pid`.

```
pidfile: "/run/unbound.pid"
```

logfile

The name of the file to which Unbound writes its log messages. Setting this to an empty string ("") turns off logging if Unbound is running as a daemon, or causes Unbound to log to standard error (stderr) if running in the foreground.

use-syslog

Messages are sent to syslog with a log facility of LOG_DAEMON. Setting use-syslog to `yes` overrides the logfile setting.

If you use chroot, you have to ensure that Unbound can access resources required by syslog within the `chroot()` environment. In our environment we have to:

- Create a `dev` directory below our chroot directory.
- Ensure syslogd is started with an alternate UNIX socket in that path:

```
# syslogd -m 0 -p /usr/local/etc/unbound/dev/log
```

root-hints

The name of a file specifying the root servers Unbound should use. The file must be in zone file format, and contain only root name server and addresses. We recommend you do set this option, and keep your root hints file up to date. You obtain a list of current root servers with:

```
$ dig @k.root-servers.net . ns > root-servers.zone
```

and configure unbound to use this list with:

```
root-hints: "root-servers.zone"
```

By default Unbound uses a compiled-in list of root servers. (We discuss how you create your own private root name servers in Chapter 18.)

identity / version

Set the values Unbound reports when queried for TXT records in the Chaosnet class. identity contains the string returned for id.server (defaults to the hostname) and version is the string returned for version.server (defaults to Unbound's version). If you want to disable these queries, set hide-identity and/or hide-version respectively.

```
$ dig @127.0.0.1 ch id.server txt
;; ANSWER SECTION:
id.server.          0    CH       TXT "ns.qupps.biz"

$ dig @127.0.0.1 ch version.server txt
;; ANSWER SECTION:
version.server.    0    CH       TXT      "unbound 0.9"
```

do-not-query-address

You can prohibit Unbound from querying specific servers by using this attribute one or more times. You specify the addresses as IPv4 or IPv6 addresses, and you can add */size* to indicate a CIDR netblock.

```
do-not-query-address: 10.14.0.0/16
do-not-query-address: 192.168.1.13
```

For example, you can use this as a method of preventing users from resolving names of sites with dubious content. Use this with care, as you can stop Unbound serving queries for specific domains if you inadvertently add addresses of the domain's name servers.

module-config

The list of modules that Unbound should load. The modules currently provided are:

- `validator`. This enables DNSSEC support.
- `iterator`. This was implemented as a module to better fit in with the code, but you cannot disable it because it would render the program unusable.
- `cache`. This module is built-in and cannot be disabled. You can however, effectively disable the cache by setting its size to 100 bytes, which fits at most one item.

You specify the modules, separating their names with spaces within a quoted string. The two valid settings are:

- `"validator iterator"`:

  Unbound becomes a validating server, i.e. it enables DNSSEC validation. The validator module verifies the security fingerprints on data sets, and clients are shielded from data with bad fingerprints – Unbound will not serve them, and will just not answer. You must configure public keys for the validator to start checking. With no keys, the validator does nothing.

  ```
  module-config: "validator iterator"
  ```

- `"iterator"`:

  Unbound becomes a non-validating server, i.e. doesn't use DNSSEC validation, and if there are any security fingerprints on data sets, Unbound ignores them.

  ```
  module-config: iterator
  ```

The default value for this attribute is `iterator`.

local-zone / local-data These options allow you to have Unbound answer queries in special ways. We discuss this in depth in Section 17.6.4.

statistics-interval Unbound periodically logs statistics. This option specifies the length of the interval, in seconds, between log dumps. Set to 0 or to an empty string to disable statistics logging.

This completes our discussion of some of Unbound's configuration settings. Consult Unbound's documentation for some others.

You can configure Unbound to answer queries in special ways (Figure 17.13), and we discuss that now.

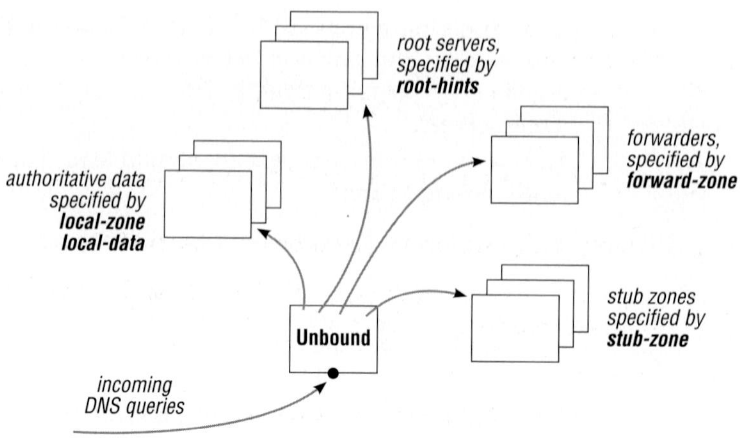

Figure 17.13: Unbound overview

17.6.4 Intercepting domains: serving data locally

You can configure Unbound to serve DNS answers from data you specify in its configuration file. It can also hand-off queries for specific zones to name servers you define.

A. Using the local-zone and local-data directives, Unbound can serve DNS data directly from its configuration file.

B. Using the stub-zone directive, you can have Unbound hand off all queries for specified zones to a specific list of name servers.

C. Using the forward-zone directive, you can set up forwarding to other recursive caching name servers.

We cover these in the following three sections.

A – Serving data authoritatively from a local file

You can configure Unbound to serve answers to certain DNS queries from data you specify in its `unbound.conf` configuration file (Figure 17.14). You use this to have Unbound provide answers for a few hosts on your network without having to set up a separate, authoritative, name server.

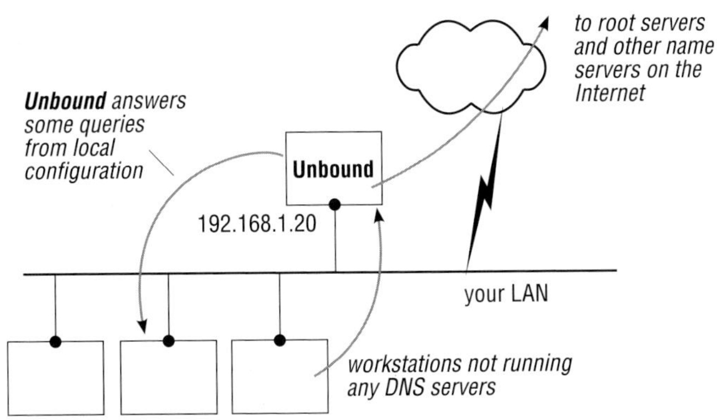

Figure 17.14: Unbound can serve local data authoritatively

You use local-zone, and optionally local-data, to handle zones specially:

local-zone — This configures a zone that is handled locally and is answered authoritatively. The syntax of this option is:

```
local-zone: zone type
```

zone is the name of the zone (e.g. example.com) and *type* is one of:

`deny`	Drop the query unless there is a match from local-data.
`refuse`	Answer the query if there is a match from local-data, and reply with code REFUSED if not.

`static` Answer the query if there is a match from local-data, otherwise answer with NXDOMAIN. If you have defined a Start of Authority (SOA) in local-data, it is included in the answer.

`redirect` Answer the query from local-data for the zone name. This answers all queries for the zone and all sub domains of the zone with local data for the zone. The difference between `redirect` and `static` is that the former includes sub-domains of the zone name.

You typically use this to redirect a domain to a different address. Note that the zone specified in local-zone must match the domain you specify in local-data.

`transparent` Answer the query if there is a match from local-data, otherwise resolve the query normally, by querying other name servers.

If you have only local-data for a zone and no corresponding local-zone configured for it, the zone is transparent by default. This means you can either have:

```
local-data: "www.example.com A 10.0.0.1"
```

by itself, or you define

```
local-zone: example.com transparent
local-data: "www.example.com A 10.0.0.1"
```

We recommend you use the second form, as it documents itself.

`nodefault` The default for AS112 zones (the in-addr.arpa zones for RFC 1918 private addresses) is to return NXDOMAIN answers to queries for them. Set `nodefault` to enable Unbound to process queries for AS112 zones. See below for an example, and consult the Unbound manual for an exact description of the AS112 zones.

local-data This is where you set up the DNS data that will be used to serve up replies to queries in the zones you defined with local-zone.

The value of the local-data attribute is a double quoted string containing the resource record in zone file format that you wish to provide as answer. If the data is unparseable, Unbound and unbound-check exit with a diagnostic message. A typical setting is:

```
local-data: "www.example.com 120 IN A 127.0.2.3"
local-data: "www.example.com A 127.0.2.3"
```

The first example contains a full answer including Time to Live (TTL) and class (`IN`). In the second example, the TTL is unspecified, so it defaults (to 3 600 seconds). You typically have quite a few local-data lines, one per resource record.

B – Stub zones

You define one or more stub zones for zones that cannot be found using the public DNS, or zones that have no delegation to them or that are otherwise private (Figure 17.15). For example, you might have internal private zones (myzone.private) or an internal DNS blacklist (bad.guys) and you want your internal clients to find those.

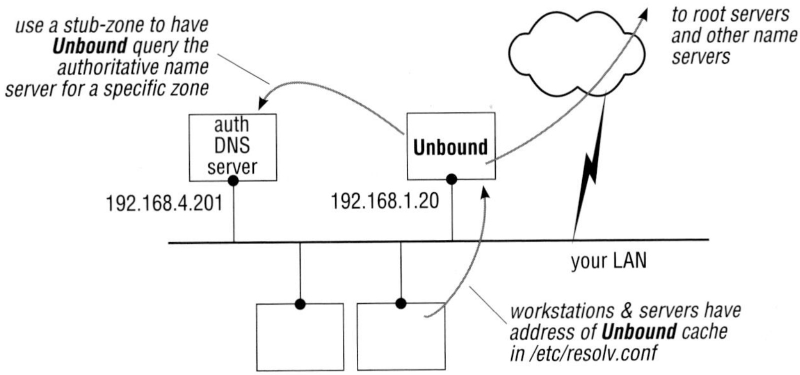

Figure 17.15: A stub zone points Unbound to a content server

You have such zones running on separate authoritative servers. Here's the stub zone definition for the example in Figure 17.15:

```
stub-zone:
  name: qupps.private
  stub-addr: 192.168.4.201
  stub-addr: 192.168.4.202
```

You use stub-addr to specify the name server by IP address, or stub-host to specify it by (resolvable) name. Append an @ and the port number to the hostname (stub-host only) to use a non-standard port number.

C – Forwarding

You define one or more forward zones for which you want to have queries forwarded to an upstream caching name server (e.g. another Unbound server in your DMZ perhaps). The server you forward to must be able (and willing) to handle recursion.

Here's the configuration for the example in Figure 17.16:

```
forward-zone:
  name: qupps.bl
  forward-addr: 192.168.1.20
  forward-addr: 192.168.2.20
```

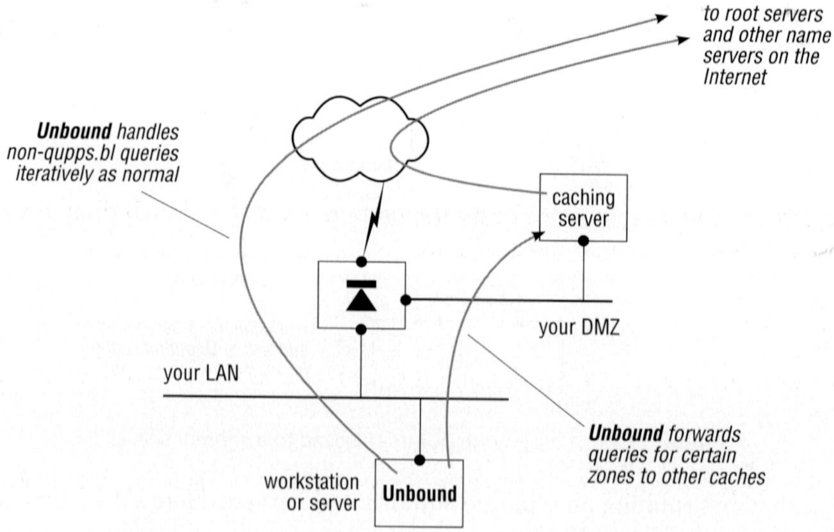

Figure 17.16: A forward zone points Unbound to another cache

You use forward-addr to specify the name server by IP address, or forward-host to specify it by (resolvable) name. Append an @ and the port number to the hostname (forward-host only) to use a non-standard port number.

Scenarios for using local zones and forwarding

The functionality provided by local-zone and local-data, and the forward-zone and stub-zone directives is very powerful. Some scenarios demonstrate the flexibility provided by Unbound:

- You want to intercept queries for specific hosts in a domain, but you want most queries to be answered from their origin servers. This is useful if you want to redirect certain domain names to hosts you manage. For example, you can intercept the host images.singleclick.biz and point that to your own Web server, transparently having the DNS answer all other queries for the domain singleclick.biz.

  Lets look at an example for the yahoo.com domain. If you configure:

  ```
  local-zone: yahoo.com transparent
  local-data: "www.yahoo.com A 192.168.1.11"
  ```

  Queries to the domain will be answered as follows (recall that `transparent` answers queries from local-data if there is a match, otherwise queries are resolved normally):

```
$ dig @127.0.0.1 www.yahoo.com
;; flags: qr aa rd ra; QUERY: 1, ANSWER: 1, AUTHORITY: 0, ADDITIONAL: 0

;; ANSWER SECTION:
www.yahoo.com.          3600    IN   A 192.168.1.11


$ dig @127.0.0.1 weather.yahoo.com
;; flags: qr rd ra; QUERY: 1, ANSWER: 2, AUTHORITY: 0, ADDITIONAL: 0

;; ANSWER SECTION:
weather.yahoo.com.      300     IN   CNAME weather.yahoo6.akadns.net.
weather.yahoo6.akadns.net. 300  IN   A 69.147.78.254
```

- You wish to catch all queries for a whole domain and all its sub domains and direct those to a single address. You configure:

  ```
  local-zone: clickme.com redirect
  local-data: "clickme.com A 192.168.1.11"
  ```

  Note how all queries for the domain are answered authoritatively with a single address:

  ```
  $ dig @127.0.0.1 clickme.com
  ;; flags: qr aa rd ra; QUERY: 1, ANSWER: 1, AUTHORITY: 0, ADDITIONAL: 0

  ;; ANSWER SECTION:
  clickme.com.            3600    IN  A 192.168.1.11

  $ dig @127.0.0.1 www.usa.clickme.com
  ;; flags: qr aa rd ra; QUERY: 1, ANSWER: 1, AUTHORITY: 0, ADDITIONAL: 0

  ;; ANSWER SECTION:
  clickme.com.            3600    IN  A 192.168.1.11
  ```

- By default Unbound blocks reverse in-addr.arpa queries to the AS112 addresses for the private IP addresses defined in RFC 1918. If you are on such a network (e.g. 10.0.0.0/8) you will have to disable Unbound's default handling so that it doesn't return NXDOMAIN for any 10.in-addr.arpa query. As an example, consider the inverse query for:

  ```
  $ dig @127.0.0.1 -x 10.0.12.1
  ;; ->>HEADER<<- opcode: QUERY, status: NXDOMAIN, id: 20261
  ;; flags: qr aa rd ra; QUERY: 1, ANSWER: 0, AUTHORITY: 1, ADDITIONAL: 0

  ;; AUTHORITY SECTION:
  10.in-addr.arpa.    10800   IN  SOA localhost. nobody.invalid. 1↩
                                      3600 1200 604800 10800
  ```

  Note how it returns NXDOMAIN without having passed the query to any upstream name server (i.e. Unbound just says "this doesn't exist"). Now change `unbound.conf`, and configure:

  ```
  local-zone: 10.in-addr.arpa nodefault
  ```

If you now submit the same query, you obtain a different answer:

```
$ dig @127.0.0.1 -x 10.0.12.1
;; ->>HEADER<<- opcode: QUERY, status: NXDOMAIN, id: 22361
;; flags: qr rd ra; QUERY: 1, ANSWER: 0, AUTHORITY: 1, ADDITIONAL: 0

;; AUTHORITY SECTION:
10.in-addr.arpa.          604800   IN      SOA prisoner.iana.org. ↩
          hostmaster.root-servers.org.  2002040800 1800 900 604800 604800
```

Where did that answer come from? From the Internet: the Start of Authority (SOA) indicates the source of the answer.

You should only change the default handling of AS112 addresses if you have authoritative name servers for your private addresses (as in our example, for the zone 10.in-addr.arpa). On an Internet-connected Unbound cache, you would cause unnecessary traffic (which is why Unbound catches queries for the AS112 zones by default).

- You have Unbound set up as a caching name server in a DMZ, and you need an authoritative zone for addressing an LDAP server or two, for example. Instead of installing a full-blown authoritative name server, you want Unbound to serve that content for you. Create the following entries in `unbound.conf` to define a zone called foo.xa:

```
local-zone: foo.xa static
local-data: "foo.xa SOA foo.xa. jp.foo.xa. 1 60 60 60 60 60"
local-data: "foo.xa NS foo.xa."
local-data: "foo.xa A 192.168.1.164"
local-data: "foo.xa TXT This is local"
local-data: "ldap.foo.xa A 192.168.1.183"
local-data: "_ldap._tcp.foo.xa SRV 0 0 389 ldap.foo.xa."
```

Because you define the local-zone as being static, queries for non-existent hosts are correctly answered with NXDOMAIN.

- You have created a DNS blacklist using rbldnsd (Chapter 16) and you want Unbound to forward queries received for your DNS blacklist to rbldnsd running on 127.0.0.3. You configure a forward-zone:

```
forward-zone:
  name: qupps.bl
  forward-addr: 127.0.0.3
```

Note that this is not the same as setting up a local-zone of type "redirect". The configuration:

```
local-zone: qupps.bl redirect
local-data: "qupps.bl A 127.0.0.3"
```

would have Unbound itself immediately answer all queries for *anything*.qupps.bl with 127.0.0.3, which is not at all the same thing.

17.6.5 Utilities

Unbound comes with some useful utilities:

unbound-checkconf
: This program checks your configuration file for syntax errors. We recommend you use this after updating your `unbound.conf` to ensure it contains no mistakes.

```
# unbound-checkconf
unbound-checkconf: no errors in ↩
                          /usr/local/etc/unbound/unbound.conf
```

unbound-host
: This is a DNS lookup utility similar to host. It uses the Unbound resolver code to query the DNS for a host name, and then displays results.

By default, unbound-host uses the servers defined in your local resolver (i.e. `/etc/resolv.conf`). You can force it to react differently, by setting up a separate `unbound.conf` file for it and invoking it as:

```
$ unbound-host -C my-unbound.conf ...
```

17.6.6 libunbound

Unbound comes with the libunbound library. This provides functions you use in your own programs for controlling the resolution (both synchronously and asynchronously) of host names and addresses. libunbound gives you access to the power of the Unbound caching name server inside your own application. You would typically implement this in programs that make extensive use of DNS queries, such as a Web browser. By using libunbound in your (multi-threaded) program, your application contains its own caching name server, without requiring the system it is running on to have one. The sample program below queries the DNS for an Address (A) record for a given host name. Commented-out portions show you how you can:

- Specify your own `unbound.conf` configuration file for libunbound, so you can easily provide more detailed configuration options.
- Use `ub_resolve()` to launch an Unbound server to perform your resolutions, but without creating an additional process. If you use `ub_resolve()` from multiple threads, your program becomes a multi-threaded Unbound cache during the lifetime of your process. If you use `ub_resolve_async()`, then a process or thread (your choice) is created to handle it. If you call `ub_resolve_async()` multiple times, the function will re-use that process or thread as a caching resolver.
- Specify a forwarder that the program should use, with the `ub_ctx_set_fwd()` function. You can set up as many as you wish.
- You can also use the function `ub_ctx_resolvconf()` to parse a `/etc/resolv.conf` file you specify and extract the `nameserver` lines to set up forwarders as above.

Listing 17.5: unboundq.c: a sample program for libunbound

```
/* unboundq.c (C)2008 by Jan-Piet Mens. Portions by NLnet Labs
 * Use libunbound to query an A RR. */
#include <stdlib.h>
#include <unistd.h>
#include <stdio.h>
#include <unbound.h>

#include <sys/socket.h>
#include <sys/uio.h>
#include <netinet/in.h>
#include <arpa/inet.h>
#include <openssl/err.h>
#include <openssl/rand.h>
#include <ldns/ldns.h>

static void print_rd(int t, char* data, size_t len);
#define CLASS_IN (1)

int lookup(char *name)
{
   struct ub_ctx *ub;
   struct ub_result *res;
   int rc;

   if ((ub = ub_ctx_create()) == NULL) {
      fprintf(stderr, "Can't create Unbound context\n");
      return (-1);
   }

   /* Use this to provide your own unbound.conf*/ /*
   if ((rc = ub_ctx_config(ub, "/home/jpm/unbound/unbound-my.conf")) != 0) {
      fprintf(stderr, "config error: %s\n", ub_strerror(rc));
      return (-1);
   }
   */

   /* Use this to manually set up a forwarder */ /*
   if ((rc = ub_ctx_set_fwd(ub, "192.168.1.164")) != 0) {
      fprintf(stderr, "config error: %s\n", ub_strerror(rc));
      return (-1);
   }
   */

   /* Use this to provide your own resolv.conf */ /*
   if ((rc = ub_ctx_resolvconf(ub, "my-resolv.conf")) != 0) {
      fprintf(stderr, "config error: %s\n", ub_strerror(rc));
      return (-1);
   }
   */

   if ((rc = ub_resolve(ub, name, LDNS_RR_TYPE_A, CLASS_IN, &res))) {
      fprintf(stderr, "lookup error: %s\n", ub_strerror(rc));
      return (-1);
```

```
    }

    if (!res->havedata && res->rcode) {
        printf("Host not found\n");
    } else {
        int n;

        for (n = 0; res->data[n]; n++) {
            printf("qname: %s: ", res->qname);
            print_rd(LDNS_RR_TYPE_A, res->data[n], res->len[n]);
            printf("\n");
        }
    }

    ub_resolve_free(res);
    ub_ctx_delete(ub);
    return 0;
}

int main(int argc, char **argv)
{
    return lookup(argv[1]);
}


/** convert and print rdata; Swiped from smallapp/unbound-host.c */
static void print_rd(int t, char* data, size_t len)
{
    size_t i, pos = 0;
    uint8_t* rd = (uint8_t*)malloc(len+2);
    ldns_rr* rr = ldns_rr_new();
    ldns_status status;
    if(!rd || !rr) {
        fprintf(stderr, "out of memory");
        exit(1);
    }
    ldns_rr_set_type(rr, t);
    ldns_write_uint16(rd, len);
    memmove(rd+2, data, len);
    ldns_rr_set_owner(rr, NULL);
    status = ldns_wire2rdf(rr, rd, len+2, &pos);
    if(status != LDNS_STATUS_OK) {
        free(rd);
        printf("error_printing_data");
    }
    for(i=0; i<ldns_rr_rd_count(rr); i++) {
        printf(" ");
        ldns_rdf_print(stdout, ldns_rr_rdf(rr, i));
    }
    ldns_rr_free(rr);
    free(rd);
}
```

Summary

- BIND is a very versatile name server. You can configure it as a caching server, with or without authoritative zones.
- PowerDNS Recursor is the recursive resolver complementary to PowerDNS. You can use it stand-alone or together with PowerDNS. PowerDNS Recursor can serve zones directly from a master zone file.
- dnscache is the recursive resolver from the djbdns package. It is ideally suited for installation on single workstations or as a corporate recursor.
- dnsproxy is a special-purpose program that allows you to run separate authoritative and caching servers behind a single public IP address.
- Unbound is a fast caching name server. You use it as a standalone cache. It is highly configurable.

Related topics

- If you want to set up a recursive resolver with some DNS and optional DHCP features, consider dnsmasq (Chapter 13).
- PowerDNS (Chapter 6) is the powerful DNS server complementary to PowerDNS Recursor.
- The djbdns package (Chapter 11) contains an authoritative name server called tinydns.
- We show you how to configure Unbound and BIND to validate DNSSEC signed zones, in Chapter 22.
- NSD (Chapter 10) is the very fast authoritative name server complementary to Unbound.

Chapter

18 Delegation and private DNS roots

Surround yourself with the best people you can find, delegate authority, and don't interfere.

Ronald Reagan

Introduction

Delegation is the process by which the authority for a zone is given to one or more DNS name servers, in order to distribute the management of sub-domains. We explain delegation and how to do it, with several examples using different brands of name server. We also discuss why and how you set up private root name servers.

The Domain Name System is a hierarchy made up of nodes, each of which is assigned to an authority. The authority is the entity responsible for the management of the node or zone. By default, the authority for a node applies to all nodes below it, as well. However, the entity in charge of a zone may split up the the hierarchy of its domain into subordinate nodes or zones, each of which becomes authoritative in its own right. This authority is delegated from parent domain to sub-domain. In the early days there were no delegations, so everything was in the root. The first delegations, therefore, had to be from the root. Without delegation there would be no hierarchy in the DNS.

18.1 The root of the Domain Name System

The authority for the root domain (which is generally written as a single period "`.`") lies with ICANN, the Internet Corporation for Assigned Names and Numbers. ICANN is also responsible for the root servers, although diverse organizations operate the physical servers. While the root server installations might be a bit larger and will probably receive more queries than servers that you set up, they have the same ingredients as your DNS:

- One or more DNS name servers.
- Zone data. The root name servers cater for the single zone called "`.`".

18.1.1 The root zone file

The root zone file contains the names and addresses of all authoritative DNS servers for all top-level domains (TLDs). These include the *generic top-level domains* (*gTLDs*) such as COM, NET, ORG as well as the *country-coded top-level domains* (*ccTLDs*), which include DE, UK and ES[1]. The first few lines of the 2 681-line root zone file dated early July 2008 were:

```
. IN    SOA     A.ROOT-SERVERS.NET. NSTLD.VERISIGN-GRS.COM. (
                                   2008071200 ;serial
                                   1800 ;refresh every 30 min
                                   900 ;retry every 15 min
                                   604800 ;expire after a week
                                   86400 ;minimum of a day
                                   )
$TTL 518400
. NS A.ROOT-SERVERS.NET.
. NS H.ROOT-SERVERS.NET.
...
A.ROOT-SERVERS.NET. A 198.41.0.4
H.ROOT-SERVERS.NET. A 128.63.2.53
...
$TTL 172800
ZM. NS HIPPO.RU.AC.ZA.
ZM. NS NS1.ZAMNET.ZM.
...
HIPPO.RU.AC.ZA. A 146.231.128.1
NS1.ZAMNET.ZM. A 196.46.192.26
```

The root zone file is published at `ftp://ftp.internic.net/`.

[1]For a list of ccTLDs see `http://www.iana.org/root-whois/index.html`

18.1.2 Querying the root servers

Assuming you have Internet connectivity and a working recursive name server, you can enumerate the current list of root name servers by querying the DNS. The domain you query is the root domain:

```
$ dig . ns
;; ->>HEADER<<- opcode: QUERY, status: NOERROR, id: 30269
;; flags: qr rd ra; QUERY: 1, ANSWER: 13, AUTHORITY: 0, ADDITIONAL: 13

;; QUESTION SECTION:
;.                              IN      NS

;; ANSWER SECTION:
.               518400  IN      NS      a.root-servers.net.
.               518400  IN      NS      b.root-servers.net.
...

;; ADDITIONAL SECTION:
a.root-servers.net.     518400  IN      A       198.41.0.4
b.root-servers.net.     518400  IN      A       192.228.79.201
...
```

When you query a root server for a specific top-level domain, it answers with referrals to the authoritative servers that the TLD has been delegated to, or with an error if that the TLD does not exist:

```
$ dig biz. ns
;; ->>HEADER<<- opcode: QUERY, status: NOERROR, id: 22765
;; flags: qr rd ra; QUERY: 1, ANSWER: 8, AUTHORITY: 0, ADDITIONAL: 0

;; QUESTION SECTION:
;biz.                           IN      NS

;; ANSWER SECTION:
biz.                    518398  IN      NS      a.gtld.biz.
biz.                    518398  IN      NS      b.gtld.biz.
biz.                    518398  IN      NS      c.gtld.biz.
biz.                    518398  IN      NS      d.gtld.biz.
biz.                    518398  IN      NS      e.gtld.biz.
biz.                    518398  IN      NS      f.gtld.biz.
biz.                    518398  IN      NS      g.gtld.biz.
biz.                    518398  IN      NS      h.gtld.biz.

$ dig foo. ns
;; ->>HEADER<<- opcode: QUERY, status: NXDOMAIN, id: 30622
;; flags: qr rd ra; QUERY: 1, ANSWER: 0, AUTHORITY: 1, ADDITIONAL: 0

;; QUESTION SECTION:
;foo.                           IN      NS

;; AUTHORITY SECTION:
.  10800   IN   SOA  A.ROOT-SERVERS.NET.   NSTLD.VERISIGN-GRS.COM. 2008010701↩
                                    1800 900 604800 86400
```

18.2 Delegating a sub-domain to a name server

A parent domain delegates responsibility for a domain to a different name server just like your spouse might delegate to you the task of taking the rubbish out. The decentralized administration of the DNS works through delegation: name servers delegate the task of managing sub-domains to other name servers; the delegating name servers keep and publish pointers to the name server(s) the administrative responsibility has been given to. A name server given the responsibility for such a sub-domain becomes authoritative for that zone's data.

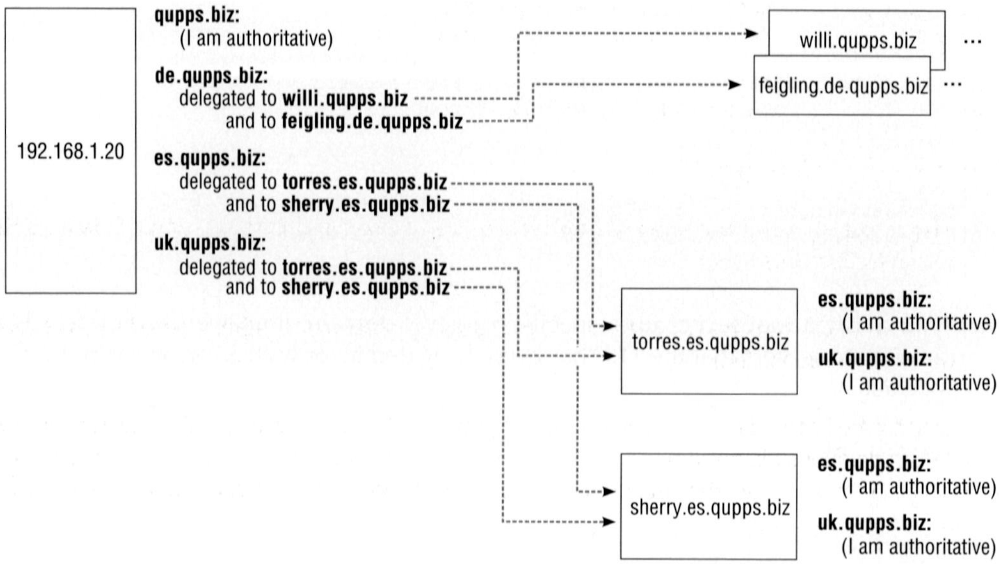

Figure 18.1: Delegating sub-domains to Name Servers

Figure 18.1 shows how domain qupps.biz has been split up into more manageable chunks:

- The zone qupps.biz is managed centrally. This zone contains domain names (i.e. hosts) in the qupps.biz domain, such as www.qupps.biz and imap.qupps.biz, as well as delegation records for the sub-domains.

- Domain de.qupps.biz is managed in Germany.

- Domain es.qupps.biz is managed in Spain, and domain uk.qupps.biz is also managed on servers in Spain because there are no qualified system administrators in the UK portion of the QUPPS organization (and because the food is much better in Spain).

In the following sections we explain how we carried out the above delegations.

18.2.1 Name Server (NS) records are used for delegation

Responsibility for a sub-domain is delegated from a parent domain by using Name Server (NS) records in the parent zone. It is important to note that NS records contain domain names and *not* IP addresses. In master zone file format, the delegation to our three sub-domains is contained in the zone master file for the qupps.biz zone:

```
$ORIGIN qupps.biz.
de              86400 NS willi.qupps.biz.
de              86400 NS feigling.de.qupps.biz.

uk.qupps.biz.   86400 NS torres.es.qupps.biz.
uk.qupps.biz.   86400 NS sherry.es.qupps.biz.

es              86400 NS torres.es.qupps.biz.
es              86400 NS sherry.es.qupps.biz.
```

There are a few points to note:

- The origin of the zone file is qupps.biz, so the unqualified domain named de actually refers to de.qupps.biz.

- You can of course always write domain names qualified if you prefer (just like we have done for uk.qupps.biz).

- One of the Name Servers, willi, for de.qupps.biz is a host in the qupps.biz zone rather than in the de.qupps.biz zone itself. This is perfectly legal and demonstrates good practice, because you spread the risk over a wide geographical area, minimizing the likelihood of a total blackout.

- All of the Name Servers for uk.qupps.biz and es.qupps.biz are in their respective zones, which is how delegation is most frequently done. For example, if you have been delegated example.com, your servers, not .com's servers, will be authoritative for the domain.

- Seen from "the top" (i.e. seen from the domain qupps.biz), qupps.biz does not know how how to resolve the domain sherry.es.qupps.biz, as it would have to contact the name server running on that host to determine the Address (A) record of sherry.es.qupps.biz. But without an IP address, it cannot contact the server[2]...

  This is where *glue* comes to the rescue. Servers that delegate a sub-domain to a Name Server in that sub-domain must provide Address records for that name server. So, in qupps.biz zone data, we add:

  ```
  sherry.es       86400 A  192.168.2.164
  es              86400 NS sherry.es.qupps.biz.
  ```

[2]Have you read *Catch 22* already?

18.2.2 Delegation in the in-addr.arpa domain

We discussed in Section 2.3.3 that address-to-name lookups are performed via so-called reverse queries in the in-addr.arpa domain. There are, however, two different cases:

A. Delegating a full Class A, B or C in-addr.arpa network.

B. Delegating a classless in-addr.arpa network.

18.2.3 A – Normal in-addr.arpa delegation

Delegation in the in-addr.arpa domain is straightforward, if your address-range is a full class A, B or C. For example, if your network is 192.168.4.0/24 a delegation to your servers in the in-addr.arpa domain would contain:

```
4.168.192.in-addr.arpa.            86400 NS willi.qupps.biz.
4.168.192.in-addr.arpa.            86400 NS feigling.de.qupps.biz.
```

This is the simplest form of reverse in-addr.arpa delegation.

18.2.4 B – Classless in-addr.arpa delegation

The delegation of reverse DNS (address-to-name) was for a time only possible on network-class boundaries, with the longest prefix being 24 bits. If you were assigned, say, a network 192.0.2.0/28, reverse delegation had to be managed by your ISP, requiring you to wait until the ISP modified its DNS for the changes you sent them to become active.

RFC 2317, *Classless in-addr.arpa delegation*, defines a best practice for delegation of classless in-addr.arpa networks. Classless in-addr.arpa delegation allows administrators to provide authoritative reverse DNS on subnets that don't fall on octet boundaries. It is specially useful for subnets with less than eight bits in the host portion (i.e. smaller than a class C).

Using this method, the master name server retains authority over the in-addr.arpa zone. It uses "dummy" entries to identify the classless subnets, and pseudo-delegates these using Canonical Name (CNAME) records.

For example, let's assume that an ISP has two customers (First Customer with domain example.org, and Second Customer with domain example.net). Let's further assume, the network 192.0.2.0/24 is split equally between them – First Customer has been assigned 192.0.2.0/28 (IP addresses 192.0.2.0 – 192.0.2.15) and Second Customer has been assigned 192.0.2.16/28.

The authoritative name server (i.e. the ISP's name server) is configured as authoritative for the entire /24 netblock, i.e. for the zone 2.0.192.in-addr.arpa. For each of its customers it contains "pseudo-hosts" pointing to the delegated name server(s). (We show you one name server, but each customer of course has two.)

This is the zone file at the ISP:

```
$ORIGIN .
$TTL 86400      ; 1 day
2.0.192.in-addr.arpa.   IN SOA  nsa.ISP.net. jp.ISP.net.  200804132 ↩
                                       28800 14400 3600000 86400
                        IN NS   nsa.ISP.net.
                        IN NS   nsb.ISP.net.
                        IN NS   nsc.ISP.net.

$ORIGIN 2.0.192.in-addr.arpa.
; First customer
0-28                    IN NS ns1.example.net.
1                       IN CNAME 1.0-28
2                       IN CNAME 2.0-28
3                       IN CNAME 3.0-28
4                       IN CNAME 4.0-28
...
15                      IN CNAME 15.0-28

; Second customer
16-28                   IN NS ns1.example.org.
16                      IN CNAME 16.16-28
17                      IN CNAME 17.16-28
...
31                      IN CNAME 31.16-28
```

Domain 0-28 (fully qualified it is 0-28.2.0.192.in-addr.arpa.) represents the 28-bit block starting at 0, and domain 16-28 represents the 28-bit block starting at 16. Each of these is delegated to one or more servers at the customers' sites. (We use dashes ("–") in the domain names; you will frequently see a slash ("/") used instead, but we prefer the former because it is a valid character in a domain name.)

First Customer configures their server to be authoritative for the zone 0-28.2.0.192.in-addr.arpa. In BIND's `named.conf`, for example, they would configure:

```
zone "0-28.2.0.192.in-addr.arpa" IN {
    type master;
    file "my-subnet.zone";
};
```

The zone master file contained in `my-subnet.zone` would be:

```
$TTL 3600;
0-28.2.0.192.in-addr.arpa.   IN SOA   ns1.example.net. master.mens.de. ↩
                                      19 10800 900 604800 3600
                                 NS   ns1.example.net.

$ORIGIN 0-28.2.0.192.in-addr.arpa.

1                           IN   PTR mail.example.net.
;2                          IN   PTR reserved.example.net.    ; not allocated yet
;3                          IN   PTR reserved.example.net.    ; not allocated yet
;4                          IN   PTR reserved.example.net.    ; not allocated yet
5                           IN   PTR imap.example.net.
...
;15                         IN   PTR reserved.example.net.    ; not allocated yet
```

Configured this way, a reverse query for, say, 192.0.2.5 translates initially to 5.2.0.192.in-addr.arpa as usual, which is answered by your ISP's name server. Your ISP's server resolves it to a CNAME, 5.0-28.2.0.192.in-addr.arpa, for which they have delegated authority to the NS at ns1.example.net. The First Customer's name server receives a query for 5.0-28.2.0.192.in-addr.arpa and returns the final PTR record as reply:

```
$ dig -x 192.0.2.5
;; flags: qr aa rd ra; QUERY: 1, ANSWER: 2, AUTHORITY: 1, ADDITIONAL: 1

;; ANSWER SECTION:
5.2.0.192.in-addr.arpa. 86400    IN   CNAME 5.0-28.2.0.192.in-addr.arpa.
5.0-28.2.0.192.in-addr.arpa. 3600 IN PTR    imap.example.net.

;; AUTHORITY SECTION:
0-28.2.0.192.in-addr.arpa. 3600 IN    NS     ns1.example.net.
```

This method has the advantage that the actual authority for the zone remains on the Customer's name servers. The downside is that the actual resolution of an address-to-name lookup by the resolver requires two indirections via a CNAME: the first to obtain the "pseudo-hostname" contained in the alias, and the second to obtain the actual PTR record for the "pseudo-hostname".

18.2.5 Examples of delegation by different brands of name server

All the following sections show the same delegation – that illustrated in Figure 18.1 – but for different brands of name server.

Delegation in NSD *or* BIND

The example in Section 18.2.1 shows how you set up delegation for NSD and BIND (because the example is in zone master file format, which is what these two name servers use.) We omitted the uk and de delegations to save space.

Delegation in MaraDNS

The csv2 file for MaraDNS contains the following entries:

```
es.%   +86400 NS torres.es.%
es.%   +86400 NS sherry.es.%

torres.es.%  A 192.168.1.22
sherry.es.%  A 192.168.1.20
```

The first two lines set up delegation of the es.qupps.biz sub-domain to the two name servers, and the last two lines create the glue for them.

Delegation in PowerDNS

For PowerDNS the delegation records depend on the back-end used:

- Using the LDAP back-end.

  PowerDNS uses `dNSDomain2` objects to store zone data. The following entries in LDIF format show you how you add the Name Servers and the appropriate glue:

```
dn: dc=es.qupps.biz,ou=pdns,ou=dns,o=qupps.biz
dc: es.qupps.biz
nSRecord: sherry.es.qupps.biz
nSRecord: torres.es.qupps.biz
dNSTTL: 86400
associatedDomain: es.qupps.biz
objectClass: dNSDomain
objectClass: dNSDomain2
objectClass: dcObject
objectClass: domainRelatedObject

dn: dc=sherry,dc=es.qupps.biz,ou=pdns,ou=dns,o=qupps.biz
associatedDomain: sherry.es.qupps.biz
dNSTTL: 86400
aRecord: 192.168.1.20
dc: sherry
objectClass: dNSDomain2
objectClass: domainRelatedObject
objectClass: top

dn: dc=torres,dc=es.qupps.biz,ou=pdns,ou=dns,o=qupps.biz
associatedDomain: torres.es.qupps.biz
dNSTTL: 86400
aRecord: 192.168.1.22
dc: torres
objectClass: dNSDomain2
objectClass: domainRelatedObject
objectClass: top
```

  Note that the delegation via the LDAP back-end does not work on the release version; we had to install build 1123 from the Subversion repository (see Notes in Chapter 6).

- Using the OpenDBX back-end.

  For the OpenDBX back-end you first define the Name Server entries:

```
INSERT INTO records (domain_id, name, type, ttl, content)
   VALUES (1, 'es.qupps.biz', 'NS', 86400, 'sherry.es.qupps.biz');
INSERT INTO records (domain_id, name, type, ttl, content)
   VALUES (1, 'es.qupps.biz', 'NS', 86400, 'torres.es.qupps.biz');
```

  and the necessary glue:

```
INSERT INTO records (domain_id, name, type, ttl, content)
   VALUES (1, 'sherry.es.qupps.biz', 'A', 86400, '192.168.1.20');
INSERT INTO records (domain_id, name, type, ttl, content)
   VALUES (1, 'torres.es.qupps.biz', 'A', 86400, '192.168.1.22');
```

Delegation in MyDNS

In the MySQL or PostgreSQL database for the MyDNS server, you create Name Server records like this:

```
INSERT INTO rr (zone, name, type, data)
   VALUES (1, 'es', 'NS', 'torres.es.qupps.biz.');
INSERT INTO rr (zone, name, type, data)
   VALUES (1, 'es', 'NS', 'sherry.es.qupps.biz.');
```

and create the glue with:

```
INSERT INTO rr (zone, name, type, data)
   VALUES (1, 'sherry.es', 'A', '192.168.1.20');
INSERT INTO rr (zone, name, type, data)
   VALUES (1, 'torres.es', 'A', '192.168.1.22');
```

Delegation in tinydns

In tinydns's `data`, to specify a name server that this zone is delegating to, you use the `&` (ampersand) line-type. In the following `data` file, the first line defines the qupps.biz zone, and the two following lines create the glue for the servers you're delegating es.qupps.biz to:

```
.qupps.biz:192.168.1.164:dns.qupps.biz:
&es.qupps.biz:192.168.1.22:torres.es.qupps.biz:
&es.qupps.biz:192.168.1.20:sherry.es.qupps.biz:
```

Delegation in ldapdns

ldapdns uses `dNSDomain` objects to store zone data. The following entries in LDIF format show you how you add the Name Servers and the appropriate glue:

```
dn: dc=es,dc=qupps,dc=biz,ou=zones,ou=LDAPdns,ou=dns,o=qupps.biz
dc: es
objectClass: dNSDomain
objectClass: dcObject
nSRecord: torres.es.qupps.biz
nSRecord: sherry.es.qupps.biz

dn: dc=torres,dc=es,dc=qupps,dc=biz,ou=zones,ou=LDAPdns,ou=dns,o=qupps.biz
dc: torres
objectClass: dNSDomain
objectClass: dcObject
aRecord: 192.168.1.22

dn: dc=sherry,dc=es,dc=qupps,dc=biz,ou=zones,ou=LDAPdns,ou=dns,o=qupps.biz
dc: sherry
objectClass: dNSDomain
objectClass: dcObject
aRecord: 192.168.1.20
```

That concludes our discussion of delegation. In the next section, we discuss how you create a private root name server, and why you might need to.

18.3 Creating your own private root name servers

Do you need your own private root name server? That depends on what you are trying to accomplish:

- If you are in a Small Office / Home Office or small organization with a caching name server and Internet connectivity, the answer will most probably be: "no".
- If you need your own authoritative zone (e.g. *you*.example) and the brand of caching name server you deploy can serve such a zone for you, then the answer is also: "no". For example, our publisher runs a BIND name server that performs caching (for when their users want to query the public DNS), and it serves a zone uit.private in which they maintain their servers, printers and other devices they want to make addressable by hostname. They do not need a private root server.
- If, however, you are deploying DNS in a large organization that has private IP addresses and wants to set up name resolution for various domains within that network, then the answer will likely be: "yes". (See Figure 1.15 for an example.)

  These organizations can simply set up authoritative name servers, of course, and point their caching name servers at them. However, the caching servers will always attempt to query the public root servers, because they contain a built-in list of root servers. To fully override that, such organizations frequently set up private root name servers.

Organizations that want to create a disconnected DNS environment (i.e. one which has no connectivity to the public DNS) can create private root servers as the entry point into the DNS (Figure 18.2).

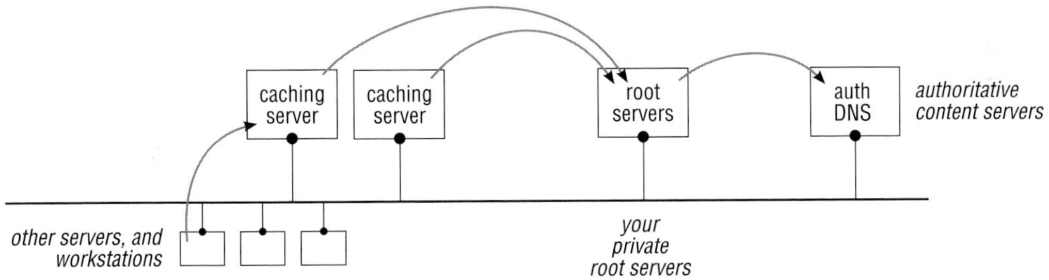

Figure 18.2: Private root servers on your network

To create private root servers:

A. Install two or more servers as your private root name servers. These do not have to be dedicated machines; you typically implement your root servers and a portion of your content servers on the same machine. You can of course use separate machines, and many organizations do so.

B. Configure the name servers to serve the root zone, which you define yourself. Most authoritative content servers we have discussed are able to provide root service, and we show you how to do that in Section 18.3.2.

The root zone consists of delegations to your authoritative content servers. For each of your zones, you provide Name Server (NS) resource records, as well as glue in the form of Address (A) records.

This completes your root name server setup.

C. Now set up (or modify) the configuration of your caching name servers:

 (a) These typically attempt to contact the public DNS root servers when performing recursion, and you must "teach" them not to do so.

 (b) The "lesson" typically consists of configuring your caches with a different list of the addresses of the name servers (often called a *hints file*). A hints file typically consists of a Name Server (NS) and an Address (A) resource record for each of your root name servers.

We illustrate how you create your own root environment with three different name servers, NSD, MyDNS, and BIND SDB, in the following sections. Do note, however, that you can use any of the authoritative content servers discussed earlier, applying the same principles.

18.3.1 A – Install your root name servers

We covered the installation of authoritative name servers in Part II of the book. You can chose any brand of name server to serve the root zone, however, you may have to build the server binary with special options (see the description of the individual brands of name server).

18.3.2 B – Configuring name servers to serve the root zone

B1 – Using NSD *as a root server*

NSD (Chapter 10) was designed to operate as a root name server, and it is easy to set up as one. To set up NSD as a root name server we recommend you proceed as follows:

1. Create your root zone, with a Start of Authority (SOA), Name Server (NS) and its Address (A) records:

Listing 18.1: Private root zone

```
$TTL 604800
$ORIGIN .
.                    604800 IN SOA  ROOT1.MYROOT.NET. jp.MYROOT.NET. (
                                    2008020301 1800 900 604800 86400 )
.                    604800 IN NS   ROOT1.MYROOT.NET.
.                    604800 IN NS   ROOT2.MYROOT.NET.

ROOT1.MYROOT.NET.  604800 IN A    192.168.1.20
ROOT2.MYROOT.NET.  604800 IN A    192.168.1.164
```

It doesn't matter what domain names you allocate to your root server machines. For clarity it's best if you use names that are not registered in the public DNS, but you don't have to (see Notes in Chapter 2). To emphasize this, in the example above we have used names *not* in the real qupps.biz domain – root1.myroot.net, ...

2. Add delegation to the qupps.biz name servers to the root zone file.

```
; Delegations and Glue
$ORIGIN .
qupps.biz.          604800 IN NS    ns1.qupps.biz.
qupps.biz.          604800 IN NS    ns2.qupps.biz.
ns1.qupps.biz.      604800 IN A     192.168.1.20
ns2.qupps.biz.      604800 IN A     192.168.1.164
```

3. Configure NSD to serve your root zone by adding the zone to `nsd.conf`. Our root zone is contained in the file `my-root.zone`:

```
zone:
  name: "."
  zonefile: "my-root.zone"
```

4. Rebuild the zone database and reload or restart NSD:

```
# nsdc rebuild
# nsdc restart
```

We discuss in Section 18.3.3 how you set up your DNS caching servers (e.g. Unbound) to access your new root server.

B2 – Using MyDNS as a root server

To use MyDNS as a root server, add the following to your database:

1. The Start of Authority (SOA) for the root zone, which is called " . ". Whereas we demonstrated in the example for NSD above that you can use fictitious names in root zones, here we use names in our own name space:

```
INSERT INTO soa (origin, ns, mbox)
  VALUES ('.', 'root.qupps.biz.', 'jp.qupps.biz.');
```

2. The Name Server (NS) records describing at least one name server, but preferably more than one:

```
INSERT INTO rr (zone, name, type, data)
   SELECT id, '.', 'NS', 'root.qupps.biz.' FROM soa WHERE origin = '.';

INSERT INTO rr (zone, name, type, data)
   SELECT id, '.', 'NS', 'root2.qupps.biz.' FROM soa WHERE origin = '.';
```

3. The glue:

```
INSERT INTO rr (zone, name, type, data)
   SELECT id, 'root.qupps.biz.', 'A', '192.168.1.164.' FROM soa ↩
         WHERE origin = '.';
INSERT INTO rr (zone, name, type, data)
   SELECT id, 'root2.qupps.biz.', 'A', '192.168.1.20.' FROM soa ↩
         WHERE origin = '.';
```

Then add delegations from the root name space to your domains, as shown above for NSD.

B3 – Using BIND-sdb-LDAP *as a root server*

Create the master "." zone in `named.conf`

Define a master `zone` clause for the zone "." (a single period). For example, using the LDAP driver in BIND SDB, create the following entry in `named.conf`:

```
zone "." {
  type master;
  database "ldap ldap://127.0.0.1/ou=ROOT,ou=sdb,o=dns 172800";
};
```

LDIF *for the root zone*

Your LDAP directory server needs an entry for the root zone itself, as well as an entry for each zone it delegates to:

1. The LDAP entry for the root zone must contain Name Server (NS) records pointing to your root name servers.

   ```
   dn: relativeDomainName=@,ou=ROOT,ou=sdb,o=dns
   objectClass: top
   objectClass: dNSZone
   relativeDomainName: @
   zoneName: .
   dNSTTL: 86400
   dNSClass: IN
   nSRecord: ns1.qupps.biz.
   nSRecord: ns2.qupps.biz.
   sOARecord: ns1.qupps.biz. ROOT-MASTER.qupps.biz. 1 10800 900 604800 3600
   ```

   Note that the `zoneName` attribute type in these examples contains a single period: the name of the root zone.

   At this point, as we haven't delegated any zones, your BIND SDB root servers answer queries with NXDOMAIN, but do return the Start of Authority (SOA) of the root zone:

   ```
   $ dig @127.0.0.1 qupps.biz
   ;; ->>HEADER<<- opcode: QUERY, status: NXDOMAIN, id: 20633
   ;; flags: qr aa rd; QUERY: 1, ANSWER: 0, AUTHORITY: 1, ADDITIONAL: 0

   ;; AUTHORITY SECTION:
   .  3600 IN SOA  ns1.qupps.biz. ROOT-MASTER.qupps.biz. 1 10800 900 604...
   ```

2. Add an LDAP directory entry for the delegation to the qupps.biz name servers:

   ```
   dn: relativeDomainName=qupps.biz,ou=ROOT,ou=sdb,o=dns
   objectClass: top
   objectClass: dNSZone
   relativeDomainName: qupps.biz
   zoneName: .
   dNSTTL: 7200
   dNSClass: IN
   nSRecord: dns1.qupps.biz.
   nSRecord: dns2.qupps.biz.
   ```

If you now query your name server for qupps.biz you get:

```
$ dig @127.0.0.1 qupps.biz

;; AUTHORITY SECTION:
qupps.biz.              7200    IN NS       dns1.qupps.biz.
qupps.biz.              7200    IN NS       dns2.qupps.biz.
```

The authority section is correct, and the delegation is successful, but there is something missing: the glue records.

3. The glue records are searched for at the LDAP search base of the root zone, by performing subtree searches for:

   ```
   (&(zoneName=.)(relativeDomainName=dns1.qupps.biz))
   (&(zoneName=.)(relativeDomainName=dns2.qupps.biz))
   ```

   Add the glue records with the following LDIF:

   ```
   dn: relativeDomainName=dns1.qupps.biz,ou=ROOT,ou=sdb,o=dns
   objectClass: top
   objectClass: dNSZone
   relativeDomainName: dns1.qupps.biz
   zoneName: .
   dNSTTL: 86400
   dNSClass: IN
   aRecord: 192.168.1.20

   dn: relativeDomainName=dns2.qupps.biz,ou=ROOT,ou=sdb,o=dns
   objectClass: top
   objectClass: dNSZone
   relativeDomainName: dns2.qupps.biz
   zoneName: .
   dNSTTL: 86400
   dNSClass: IN
   aRecord: 192.168.1.164
   ```

   Now when you query your BIND SDB name server for qupps.biz you get the glue in the `ADDITIONAL SECTION`:

   ```
   $ dig @127.0.0.1 qupps.biz
   ;; ->>HEADER<<- opcode: QUERY, status: NOERROR, id: 20
   ;; flags: qr rd; QUERY: 1, ANSWER: 0, AUTHORITY: 2, ADDITIONAL: 2

   ;; QUESTION SECTION:
   ;qupps.biz.                  IN    A

   ;; AUTHORITY SECTION:
   qupps.biz.          7200    IN    NS dns1.qupps.biz.
   qupps.biz.          7200    IN    NS dns2.qupps.biz.

   ;; ADDITIONAL SECTION:
   dns1.qupps.biz.     86400 IN    A     192.168.1.20
   dns2.qupps.biz.     86400 IN    A     192.168.1.164
   ```

How clients query the root zone

To better understand how BIND-sdb-LDAP handles queries, we show you the LDAP searches it performs. If your BIND SDB name server is asked about a domain qupps.biz, the LDAP back-end will have these queries directed at it:

```
(&(zoneName=.)(relativeDomainName=biz))
(&(zoneName=.)(relativeDomainName=qupps.biz))
(&(zoneName=.)(relativeDomainName=@))
```

The first query is for the generic Top-Level domain (gTLD) .biz, the second for the name servers of the domain qupps.biz and the last for the Start of Authority (SOA) of the root domain proper. The LDAP search base for these filters is the base you specify in the `database` statement of the `zone` clause.

18.3.3 C – Configure your caching servers

All the caching name servers on your network have to be configured to know about and locate your new root zone. We show you three examples of how to do this with Unbound, BIND, and dnscache in the following two sections.

Configuring Unbound and BIND to access your root servers

Both Unbound and BIND, which we discussed in Chapter 17, are easy to set up; they use the same form of hints file.

- Create a "hints" file for you new root name servers. The hints file contains only Name Server (NS) and Address (A) resource records. Notice that the hints file is a copy of a portion of the `my-root.zone` we created on page 446 for NSD – the NS and A records for our root servers.

```
$ cat my-root.hints
.                    604800 IN NS    ROOT1.MYROOT.NET.
.                    604800 IN NS    ROOT2.MYROOT.NET.

ROOT1.MYROOT.NET.    604800 IN A     192.168.1.20
ROOT2.MYROOT.NET.    604800 IN A     192.168.1.164
```

- You configure Unbound to load the root hints file by adding a root-hints option to `unbound.conf`:

```
server:
  interface: ...
  ...
  root-hints : "my-root.hints"
  ...
```

- For BIND, you define a hint zone:

```
zone "." IN {
    type hint;
    file "my-root.hints";
};
```

Configuring dnscache *to access your root servers*

The file `@` in the dnscache's `$ROOT` directory contains a list of IP addresses of the root name servers, one per line. Modify this file to contain only the addresses of your new root servers:

```
$ cd /usr/local/dnscache
$ cat root/servers/@
192.168.1.164
192.168.1.20
```

Don't forget to restart dnscache after this modification.

It isn't difficult to set up and configure a private root server environment, and unless you are in a large organization, you probably won't have to do it at all.

This completes Part II of the book, in which we discussed the individual brands of server you can use to set up DNS services, as well as delegation and private root servers.

Summary

- Delegation is the process by which the authority or manager of a name server devolves responsibility for a sub-domain to another authority or manager. This allows the management of domains to be distributed. Typically a sub-domain or zone is managed by the organization or department most connected with it.
- To delegate authority over a zone, you set up Name Server (NS) records in the zone that is delegating.
- Name servers can only find subordinate name servers (i.e. name servers "below" them in the hierarchy) if they have the glue – the Address records – that point to the subordinate servers.
- Private root name servers are used in organizations that are not connected to the public DNS.

Related topics

- We discuss the process of recursion and the caching name servers that recurse in Chapter 17.

Notes and further reading

The thirteen root servers

Currently there are thirteen root servers (see `http://www.root-servers.org/`). A root server is not usually a single machine, but rather a cluster of machines available at a single address. It is worth noting that the IP address of a root server occasionally changes; for example, the address of the l.root-servers.net installation underwent a scheduled change in November 2007.

Alternative root servers

In addition to the "official" (i.e. ICANN-operated) root name servers, there are alternative root servers with their own top-level domains (TLDs) (see `http://en.wikipedia.org/wiki/Alternative_DNS_root`).

Online CIDR calculator

If you need a program to calculate CIDR networks, there is a good one at `http://www.subnet-calculator.com/cidr.php`

Part

III

Operational Issues

This Part of the book covers topics common to all brands of name server:

- Chapter 19 covers tools and methods for updating your DNS data.
- Chapter 20 covers the Name Service Switch.
- Chapter 21 explains Internationalized Domain Names and how to use them.
- Chapter 22 introduces DNSSEC – secure DNS.
- Chapter 23 shows how we measured the performance of the various name servers, and the results we obtained.
- Chapter 24 discusses how to secure your name servers, and how to monitor them.

Chapter

19 Updating DNS zones and their associated records

A lot of hacking is playing with other people, you know, getting them to do strange things.

Steve Wozniak

Introduction

This chapter explains the procedures for day-to-day updating of your DNS data. Larger organizations should consider a registry group or department for managing all aspect of DNS operations. We discuss "manual" updating – where you decide on and perform changes to the data yourself. Finally, we cover Dynamic DNS Updates, which can be linked in to your DHCP service, so that your DNS is automatically updated as client PCs join and leave the network.

Information in the DNS changes continually. In the worldwide DNS, domains are constantly being added and deleted; the architecture of the DNS ensures that you always receive the latest, correct, values automatically.

However, you have to treat your own zones – the ones that you are authoritative for, whether internal (private) or external (public) – differently. You have to explicitly update your zone data when you add a new domain, for example, or add or remove a mail server, or even when a desktop workstation joins the network. You have to consider how best to perform these changes.

This chapter explains how you update your DNS data, and the standard protocols and APIs for performing the updates dynamically, i.e. triggered by a program, rather than manually. But first, you should decide whether your organization should have a dedicated a registry group or department for managing all aspect of DNS operations, which we discuss in the next section.

19.1 Using a registry to manage your DNS operations

A *registry* (also called a *Network Information Center*) is an organization that coordinates how domain names are issued, and runs the technical infrastructure required for operating the name servers for those domains (Figure 19.1). A registry typically maintains or manages the following:

- A list of all domains (not individual host names) used, now and in the past. You can store this list in any suitable format – text file, XML file, SQL database, etc. Larger organizations will probably integrate this with their provisioning systems.
- The contact details associated with the domains. Owners' names and addresses, the name servers a domain has been delegated to, contact data, administrative and technical contacts, billing, etc.
- Procedures for creating and removing zones. A Small Office / Home Office environment might simply remove the zone, whereas a larger organization might have an automated process, coupled into their customer or department billing system.
- The name server hardware and software that host the zones and serve DNS data.
- Provisioning and monitoring the organization's DNS servers, using specialized tools created for doing that.
- A system to back up the DNS and also your registry data (which is separate from the DNS data), and disaster-recovery procedures for hardware, software and data.

19.1.1 Do you need a registry?

Yes, you do. We strongly recommend you create an infrastructure for managing the information associated with issuing and managing domains. Getting the infrastructure running is not difficult, and it will help you streamline your work.

Your registry requirements will differ according to your organization:

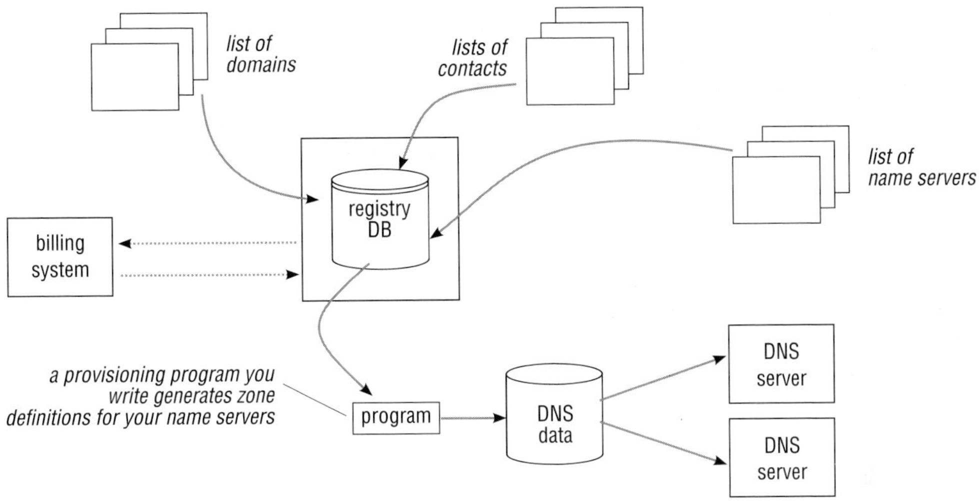

Figure 19.1: A typical registry

- Small Office / Home Office: you will probably organize yourself on a sheet of paper, or note changes in comments in a zone file. You are your own registry.
- Large organization: you will want a registry to identify and track which department "owns" your various domains, when they expire, whether they have to be renewed, who the contacts for the domains are, etc.
- An Internet Service Provider needs a registry, ideally with automated tools to handle the hundreds or thousands of clients.

19.1.2 How to set up a registry

Setting up a registry is not necessarily a difficult task, and there are plenty of Open Source tools which will help you to get started. Here are two implementations:

- Stephane Bortzmeyer of the French AFNIC registry has a writeup on how to implement a simple registry using basic tools and data contained in an XML file (see `www.generic-nic.net/sheets/practical/xml-registry-en`). He proposes using the XML file as the database containing technical and social data, and using XSLT to produce the zone file. While this might be a little simplistic, the ideas are interesting.
- The Internet Systems Consortium (ISC) has an implementation of a domain registry that top-level domain operators might use to manage the delegation of domains. The package is called OpenReg, and its source code is available at `http://www.isc.org/sw/openreg/`.

Many large organizations have a dedicated group of people who manage the organization's DNS registry; others out-source the task to specialized firms.

19.2 How you update your DNS data

How your server stores its zone data – in text files, or LDAP or SQL databases – obviously affects your choice of updating tool. There is no all-round tool that will satisfy your requirements for the simple reason that most people's requirements are quite different. Just as your registry requirements (Section 19.1) depend on your organization and the number of DNS domains you maintain, so your requirements for maintaining the data in your DNS will be quite different to the next organization's.

Your attitude towards tools will also depend on your workload. An awkward tool is tolerable if you modify DNS data only occasionally, but not if you are adding new zones and lots of resource records every day.

In the next section we discuss how you maintain your DNS data in text files, and in Section 19.4 we discuss how you update data stored in non-text back-end databases.

19.3 Managing DNS data in text files

Four of our name server implementations store their zone data in text files on a file system: BIND and NSD use zone master file format and MaraDNS and tinydns use their own proprietary formats. Broadly, you can maintain the DNS data in these files in two ways:

A. Manually, with a text editor.

B. Generate their content from a database.

Let's look at these two methods in turn.

19.3.1 A – Editing by hand with a text editor

You typically edit zone files with a text editor of your choice, but there are some points you should note:

- Place zone files and configuration files under some sort of revision control system. This allows you to easily back out of a change when something goes wrong, and gives you a full history of your configurations.

- If you work in a team, set up some form of file-locking system so that you don't clobber changes made by a colleague, or vice versa. A small script that uses the lockfile command (from the procmail package) before invoking your editor is easy to create and is an effective solution. (Unless you start your text editor every few months only, in which case there is no easy solution.)

- Use tools to make your life easier. *nix systems have a large number of excellent tools that you can put to good use for maintaining your DNS. For example:

  subversion — A version control system. It allows you to create so-called hooks – scripts that subversion executes when a particular action occurs. It is easy to write a little script that notifies others whenever a zone or configuration file has changed.

You can go a step further still, and create a script that reloads your name server when a zone change has been committed by subversion, so you don't have to remember to do it manually.

make

make is an indispensable tool for a systems administrator, and you probably know it. Although it was created for building code, we use it in all areas of system administration. In Appendix B we show you how you can use make to automatically track changes to zone master files and "fix" the serial number of your zones when you modify resource records.

19.3.2 B – Generating file content from an external data source

Even though your server needs its zones in text files, why not generate them from data contained in an SQL database or in an LDAP directory instead of editing zone files by hand? (Figure 19.2)

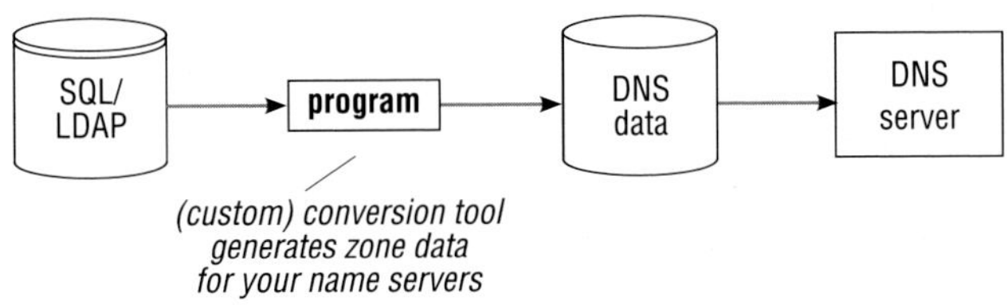

Figure 19.2: Generating zone data from SQL/LDAP

While this adds complexity at the outset, it gives you all the benefits of data management in databases and directories.

- Section 11.2.7 showed how to generate text files for tinydns from an SQL database.
- Another interesting program is ldap2dns by Jacob Rief and Ben Klang. This creates a `data` file suitable for tinydns, or zone files suitable for NSD or BIND, directly from entries stored in an LDAP directory (see `http://projects.alkaloid.net/`).
- For NSD or BIND, with LDAP, you can use ldap2zone by Stig Venaas instead. It reads LDAP directory entries from your LDAP directory and produces a zone master file on standard output. Saved in a file, this output is ready to feed to either NSD or BIND[1]. If you have organized your LDAP directory with entries as discussed in Chapter 8, running ldap2zone will search all entries and produce a zone master file:

[1]The program does not take into account the use of a tilde as a wild-card character in the LDAP directory (see Notes on page 212).

```
$ ldap2zone qupps.biz ldap://localhost/o=qupps.biz 3600
$TTL 3600
@       86400   IN      SOA     ns1.qupps.biz. hostmaster.mens.de. (
                        196205281 ; Serialnumber
                        10800     ; Refresh
                        900       ; Retry
                        604800    ; Expire
                        3600 )    ; Minimum TTL
        86400   NS      ns1.qupps.biz.
        86400   NS      ns2.qupps.biz.
        86400   A       192.168.1.20
...
...
```

- The Time To Live specified on the command-line (3600) is used to create the `$TTL` directive in the zone.
- You can give ldap2zone a serial number as an optional last parameter. It compares this with the serial number in the the LDAP directory: if the numbers match, the program prints:

  ```
  $ ldap2zone qupps.biz ldap://localhost/o=qupps.biz 3600 196205281
  ldap2zone: serial numbers match
  ```

  and exits with an error-code indicating the zone has not changed. You can use this to check whether a zone has changed in your LDAP directory: if it has, you create the zone master file, reload your master and notify your slaves and record the new serial number for use in the next check; if no change has occurred you do nothing.

That completes our coverage of maintaining zone text files. Next we look at good practice for maintaining zone data in database back-ends.

19.4 Updating name server back-end data stores

One of the main reasons for deploying a DNS server with an external database back-end is flexibility in maintenance of your DNS zone data. As soon as you add or modify a database entry, the DNS server "picks" it up and uses it automatically. MyDNS, PowerDNS, BIND SDB, Bind DLZ, and ldapdns can all be configured to utilize an external SQL database or LDAP directory, and you can update those databases on the fly.

While you may be able to use one of the Web-based utilities (Section 19.5) to update your back-end databases, most organizations that maintain a large number of domains bite the bullet and create their own tools for maintaining zones and zone data. Whether you do so depends on your programming skills, how much time (and money) you are willing to invest and the volume of DNS updates you'll be handling.

Updating DNS data can be a tedious task if you don't have the proper tools. For example, Section 2.5.5 explained how you can use basic command-line utilities to manage your SQL database or your LDAP directory, but if you have lots of updates to do, that's unsatisfactory. You have to remember the exact format of the data used by the back-end, and the names of database tables, and to change the PTR when you change its associated A record, and so on.

If you have a lot of DNS work to do, automating your task will save you time and reduce the number of errors in your data.

What sort of programs should you create? Here are some ideas to get you started:

- You frequently add a new zone that needs a Web server, two Mail Exchangers and some Service records. Create a program that adds the zone and its associated records to your back-end database. So, for example, to add, say, a complete example.net to your DNS, you execute:

```
$ add-zone example.net
```

  Your program should allow you to specify the zone name with or without a trailing period to reduce the possibility of a common error.

- You constantly deploy new workstations and assign them static IP addresses. Create a utility for yourself to add the A record (and its associated PTR) to the DNS. For example, when you "deliver" Alice her new workstation, you use:

```
$ new-pc alice
```

The investment in creating custom utilities for DNS maintenance is generally quickly recouped in time savings on these (usually tedious) tasks. A small shell script wrapper around command-line tools may be sufficient, or, if you need a bit more logic in your utility, use a programming language you are comfortable with:

- Updating SQL databases is not difficult to do, and there are language bindings for most databases. Many programming languages and scripting languages have in-built SQL database tools: Perl with its DBI, PHP, and C. We show you a small PHP example in Section 19.8.2.

- Libraries are available for manipulating LDAP directories, too. These client libraries usually offer both an synchronous and an asynchronous interface. A typical update procedure will look something like this:

  1. Create a session handle with `ldap_initialize()` (or `ldap_open()`, which is deprecated).
  2. Use `ldap_set_option()` to set parameters for communication with the LDAP directory server.
  3. Establish a session by invoking `ldap_bind()`, possibly passing credentials.
  4. Perform other operations such as `ldap_search()`, `ldap_add()`, etc. depending on what the application needs to do, and then...
  5. Terminate the LDAP association and underlying connection with `ldap_unbind()`.

  The exact details depend on the API you choose; for example, some APIs provide additional functionality (such as `START TLS`). Most programming languages today including Perl with the Net::LDAP module, PHP, C, have support for LDAP.

If you have a heavy DNS maintenance load, it will almost certainly be worth your while creating custom tools for updating your zones and resource records. On the other hand, some people are satisfied with Web-based management tools, which we discuss next.

19.5 Web-based management

Web-based management of zones and zone data might well be one of the most sought-after tools when you set up your DNS infrastructure, because they can ease your way into the sometimes daunting task of creating records in SQL databases or entries in LDAP directory servers. There is a large amount of programs written to satisfy their authors' needs, and you may well find that some of these programs satisfy your DNS requirements.

Unfortunately, many Web-based tools are far from perfect. Common problems include:

- Difficult installation requiring a specific version of PHP, for example, can mean you can't install this tool without breaking some other component on your machine.
- Some of the interfaces we tested assume just a handful of zones. As soon as you try to use thousands of zones the tools fall to pieces or take ages to do anything.
- Most of the programs support just a handful of DNS resource record types (probably because the authors didn't have the need for more).

However, the programmers went to a lot of work, and we are grateful that they made their work available for everyone to use. We have selected a handful of programs you might consider adding to your DNS infrastructure:

Web-based tools for PowerDNS

PowerAdmin
: for PowerDNS with a MySQL or PostgreSQL back-end. The original PowerAdmin project was abandoned and has been replaced by a "complete(r) PowerAdmin" with support for all zone types (master, slave, native), support for Superslaves, DNS RR validation, multiple languages, custom skins and a new user and permission management system (see `www.poweradmin.org`).

ZoneAdmin
: for a PowerDNS with a MySQL back-end (see `http://open.megabit.net/index.php?section=pro_home&project=ZoneAdmin`).

PDNS-Admin
: for PowerDNS with a MySQL back-end. It can create and restore your database, it has a skinnable interface, and support for multiple languages (see `http://pdnsadmin.iguanadons.net/`).

Web-based tools for BIND

NicTool
: NicTool calls itself a "management solution for DNS". It implements some very interesting concepts, providing "provisioning agents" that communicate via XML-RPC or SOAP with a mod_perl module to populate a MySQL database. It then generates output for tinydns and BIND zone files from the database (see `http://www.nictool.com/`).

ProBIND
: This PHP-based tool manages zones in a MySQL database and generates zone files for BIND on demand (see `http://probind.org/`).

Web-based tools for Bind DLZ

dnsEditor — This program (Figure 19.3) by Lokkju Brennr makes some use of AJAX but unfortunately loads all zones from the MySQL database tables on startup, which makes it very slow if you have many zones. It is available via subversion at `https://svn.lokkju.com/svn/dnsEditor`.

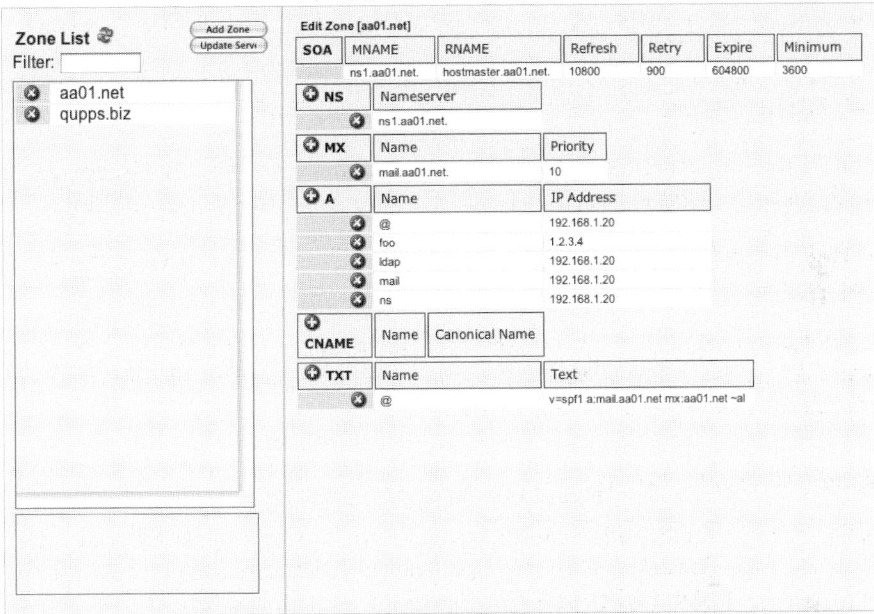

Figure 19.3: dnsEditor for Bind DLZ

Ant — This program, by Kris Nielander, is for the PostgreSQL back-end to Bind DLZ (see `http://antdns.sourceforge.net/`).

Web-based tools for tinydns

NicTool — See above.

VegaDNS — This stores DNS zones and records in a MySQL database from which a `data` file is created on the fly for tinydns (Figure 19.4). A very useful feature is that you can specify a set of records that are automatically added to new domains you create via the Web interface; for example, if most of the zones you create have 4 MX records and 2 Web servers, you can have VegaDNS add these when you create new zones (see `http://www.vegadns.org`).

That completes our overview of some of the Web-based management tools for DNS data. In the next section we discuss how you manage Dynamic DNS Updates.

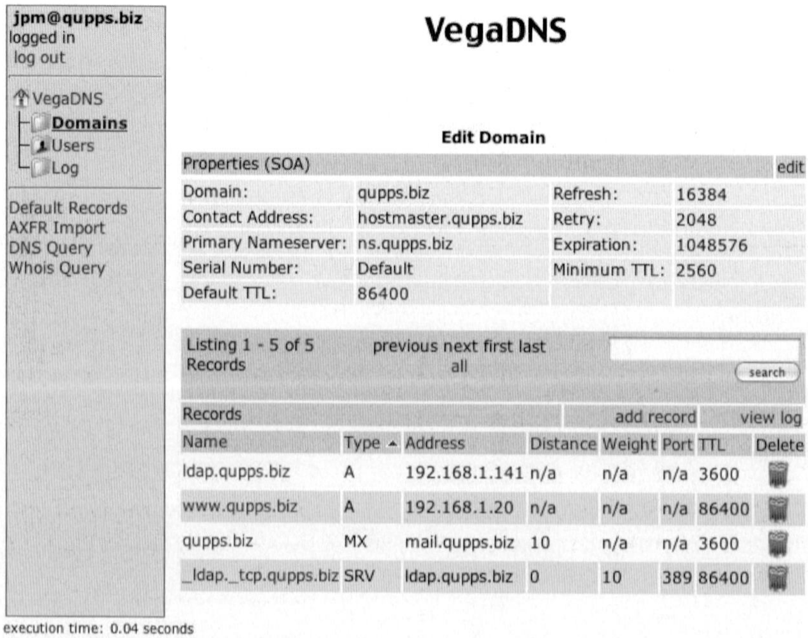

Figure 19.4: VegaDNS in action

19.6 Dynamic DNS Updates (RFC 2136)

Dynamic DNS Updates as defined in RFC 2136 allow the data of a DNS server to be updated in real time (Figure 19.5). When a user's workstation starts up, you can ensure its IP address is registered in the DNS, allowing it to be addressed within your domain. Dynamic DNS allows an updater to add, modify or delete individual resource records and RRsets. (However, neither the Start of Authority (SOA) nor the Name Server (NS) records may be added or modified: the standard thus prohibits the creation or deletion of zones.)

Of the name servers discussed in this book, only two support RFC 2136 Dynamic DNS Updates:

- MyDNS (Chapter 5). Dynamic updates can be written directly to its back-end database. As discussed, it has a simple IP-based access control to prevent unauthorized hosts from performing updates.

- BIND (Chapter 7). For each master zone, you can specify whether dynamic updates are allowed. You limit which clients can perform updates, with IP-based access control, or you create and deploy TSIG keys that authorize select clients to perform updates. Note that BIND SDB back-ends do not support RFC 2136, nor does Bind DLZ. BIND can also update DNSSEC-signed zones (Chapter 22).

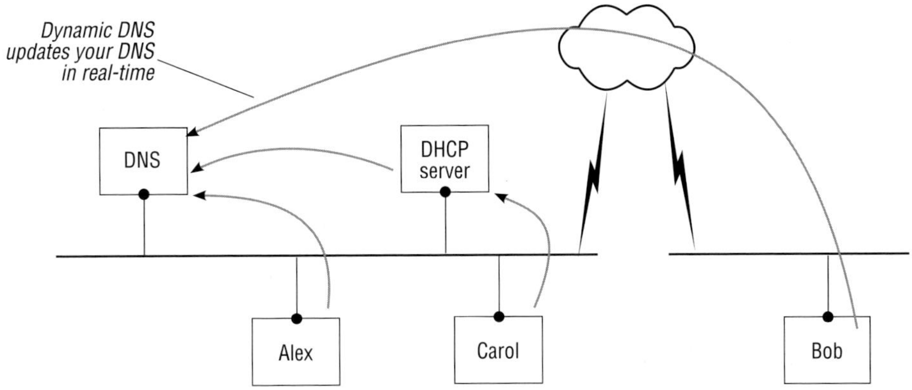

Figure 19.5: Dynamic DNS Updates

We show you how you submit dynamic updates to a suitably configured name server, from the command-line with the nsupdate utility in the next section, and with Perl's Net::DNS package in Section 19.6.3.

19.6.1 Dynamic updates from the command-line with nsupdate

nsupdate submits Dynamic DNS update requests to a name server. nsupdate reads commands from a file (or from standard input) and processes these in order. Each command must be on exactly one line of input. An update request consists of zero or more *prerequisites* and zero or more updates; a prerequisite allows you to ensure nsupdate performs an update only if certain resource records are present or absent. For example, you may wish to add an Address record for a host only if that host does not yet exist. Here's a simple example, adding a TXT record for the domain i5.qupps.biz:

```
$ nsupdate
> server 192.168.1.20
> zone qupps.biz.
> update add i5.qupps.biz 3600 TXT "Hello World"
> send
> quit

$ dig @192.168.1.20 i5.qupps.biz any
;; ANSWER SECTION:
i5.qupps.biz.      3600   IN TXT    "Hello World"
```

Commands understood by nsupdate

server — The address of the server to be updated. If the server command is omitted, nsupdate determines the address it from the MNAME field (primary name server field) of the Start of Authority (SOA) of the zone it is operating on.

```
server 192.168.1.20
```

zone — All updates are to be made to the specified zone name. If omitted, nsupdate determines the zone from the rest of the input.

```
zone qupps.biz.
```

prereq nxdomain — Requires that *no* resource records of any type exist with the *domain-name*.

```
prereq nxdomain www.qupps.biz.
```

prereq yxdomain — Requires that *domain-name* does exist, with at least one resource record of any type.

```
prereq yxdomain www.qupps.biz.
```

prereq nxrrset — Requires that *no* resource records of the specified *domain-name*, *class* and *type* exist.

```
prereq nxrrset imap.qupps.biz. IN A
```

update delete — Deletes any resource records named *domain-name*. If *type* or *type* and *data* are specified, only matching resource records will be removed.

```
update delete imap2.qupps.biz. A
update delete imap4.qupps.biz. A 192.168.4.39
```

update add — Adds a new resource record with the specified *domain-name*, *ttl*, *type* and *data*.

```
update add imap.qupps.biz. 3600 A 192.168.1.201
```

send — Sends the current update request. (Entering a blank line does the same.)

quit — Exits nsupdate.

So, that is the nsupdate's syntax, and now, we show you an example of using it to update a record in the MyDNS name server.

19.6.2 Using nsupdate to add a host to MyDNS

We mentioned above that dynamic updates can add, modify or delete domain names in a zone only, if the name server is authoritative for that zone. For MyDNS that means the database must contain a record for the zone in the soa table. You can't add new zones to the server via dynamic DNS; if you attempt to do so anyway, MyDNS logs an error:

```
... REFUSED Zone_not_found 1 0 0 0 LOG N QUERY ""
```

Let's see how MyDNS processes a dynamic update, next:

1. Before we begin, let's prove that the host we want to add (pc.qupps.biz) does not exist:

```
mysql> SELECT origin, name, type, r.ttl, data FROM soa s, rr r
    ->   WHERE s.id = r.zone AND name LIKE 'pc%';
mysql>
```

2. Use the nsupdate program to send a set of updates to a name server. Here is the simple script we use:

```
$ nsupdate
> server 127.0.0.1
> update add pc.qupps.biz. 3600 A 192.168.1.178
> send
> quit
$
```

If you watch the MyDNS log in verbose mode, you will see two queries:

(a) The first query is for the Start of Authority (SOA) of the domain we are adding. If the server is not authoritative for the domain, it will refuse any updates on it:

```
IN SOA pc.qupps.biz. NOERROR - 1 0 1 0 LOG N QUERY ""
```

(b) The second query is the update proper:

```
IN SOA qupps.biz. NOERROR - 1 0 0 0 LOG N UPDATE↩
  "ADD pc.qupps.biz. 3600 IN A 0 192.168.1.178"
```

3. Check that MyDNS has created the domain in the `rr` table; yes, it has:

```
mysql> SELECT origin, name, type, r.ttl, data FROM soa s, rr r
    ->   WHERE s.id = r.zone AND name LIKE 'pc%';
+------------+---------------+------+------+---------------+
| origin     | name          | type | ttl  | data          |
+------------+---------------+------+------+---------------+
| qupps.biz. | pc.qupps.biz. | A    | 3600 | 192.168.1.178 |
+------------+---------------+------+------+---------------+
```

4. Check that we can query MyDNS for the resource record, by sending a DNS query:

```
$ dig @127.0.0.1 pc.qupps.biz
;; ANSWER SECTION:
pc.qupps.biz.        3600    IN      A 192.168.1.178
```

The domain name has been created and we can query it via DNS.

Using nsupdate *with* TSIG

In Chapter 5 we discussed how you set up IP-based ACLs to authorize dynamic updates to MyDNS. If you have a BIND server, you can also use IP-based ACLs, but a more secure approach is to use TSIG authorization to protect your server. Then you can invoke nsupdate with the TSIG key. nsupdate reads the key either from an option on the command-line (not recommended), or from a file:

```
$ nsupdate -k key-file
...
```

Note:

- You can pass the key on the command line, but this is dangerous, as any user on your system can see the key by running a ps command at the right moment.
- When you invoke nsupdate with:

```
$ nsupdate -y keyname:hash
```

you specify a colon-separated *keyname* and the key as *hash*. If the key name does not match the server's key name, the update fails with a `NOTAUTH(BADKEY)` error.

- The clocks on the client machine and the DNS name server must be synchronized for TSIG to work, so we recommend you use the Network Time Protocol (NTP) for that. If your clocks are not synchronized, updates fail with `NOTAUTH(BADTIME)`.

19.6.3 Net::DNS

We introduced you to Net::DNS in Chapter 15. Net::DNS::Update implements Perl modules for sending dynamic updates. The two examples presented here are just small variations on the excellent samples in the Net::DNS distribution.

1. This example works with suitably configured MyDNS and BIND servers. It first checks that the domain mypc.qupps.biz doesn't exist, by specifying a prerequisite, and then adds the domain and an associated Address (A) record.

Listing 19.1: Perform an RFC 2136 Dynamic DNS Update with Net::DNS

```
#!/usr/bin/perl

use Net::DNS;
use strict;

my $zone = 'qupps.biz';

# Create the update packet.
my $update = Net::DNS::Update->new($zone);

# Prerequisite is that no A records exist for the name.
$update->push(pre => nxrrset("mypc.$zone. A"));


# Add an A record for the name.
$update->push(update => rr_add("mypc.$zone. 86400 A 192.168.1.189"));

# Send the update to the zone's primary master; specify
# it either as a domain name that will be resolved via
# your system's resolver, or as an IP address.
my $res = Net::DNS::Resolver->new;
$res->nameservers("127.0.0.1");

my $reply = $res->send($update);
if ($reply) {
     if ($reply->header->rcode eq 'NOERROR') {
          print "Update succeeded\n";
     } else {
          print 'Update failed: ', $reply->header->rcode, "\n";
     }
} else {
     print 'Update failed: ', $res->errorstring, "\n";
}
```

2. This example uses TSIG to authorize itself with the DNS server and then adds a TXT record. Currently this example will work only against a suitably configured BIND name server that has a TSIG key defined as described in Section 7.4.

Listing 19.2: Perform an RFC 2136 Dynamic DNS Update with Net::DNS and TSIG

```
#!/usr/bin/perl

use Net::DNS;
use strict;

my $zone = 'qupps.biz';
my $keyname = 'ma-clef';
my $keyblob = 't3Q+wdd6Nzt0VnKslPuHk5JkE931QqPyntA33Z1AjEo=';

# Create the update packet.
my $update = Net::DNS::Update->new($zone);

# Add a TXT  record for the name.
my $txt = "Hello " . time;
$update->push(update => rr_add("mypc.$zone. 3600 TXT \"$txt\""));

# Sign the update
$update->sign_tsig($keyname, $keyblob);

# Send the update to the zone's primary master.
my $res = Net::DNS::Resolver->new;
$res->nameservers("127.0.0.1");

my $reply = $res->send($update);

# Did it work?
if ($reply) {
     if ($reply->header->rcode eq 'NOERROR') {
         print "Update succeeded\n";
     } else {
         print 'Update failed: ', $reply->header->rcode, "\n";
     }
} else {
     print 'Update failed: ', $res->errorstring, "\n";
}
```

19.7 Dynamic DNS updates performed by DHCP client or server

DHCP, the *Dynamic Host Configuration Protocol*, can automatically configure new and existing hosts on your network. The aspect of DHCP that most concerns us here is IP address allocation. When a DHCP client machine starts up, it requests an IP Address from a DHCP server. The server, which has been configured by its administrator with a pool of available addresses, chooses an available address, and assigns it to the client. The client then configures itself to use the server-assigned address. The client doesn't own the address forever, but is only given a time-limited *lease* on the address; the server specifies how long the lease is valid; before the lease expires, the client should ask the server to renew it.

A DHCP client can obtain other settings, in addition to its IP address: addresses of DNS servers and routers, routing information, addresses of mail and time servers, etc.

From the DNS point of view that doesn't really help very much; you have a whole bunch of hosts that have addresses assigned, but how do you access services on these hosts by name (rather than by IP address)? In the next sections we look at how you configure DHCP, how it operates on a client host, and how it can dynamically update the DNS.

19.7.1 ISC DHCP

A widely-used DHCP server is the distribution from ISC, who also make BIND (see `http://www.isc.org/products/DHCP/`). The package contains a DHCP server (dhcpd), a DHCP client (dhclient) and a DHCP relay agent. You configure dhcpd with the file `dhcpd.conf`. While a full discussion of the `dhcpd.conf` and dhcpd is beyond the scope of this book (see Notes) we show you a sample `dhcpd.conf` below, which we will refer to in the following sections.

Listing 19.3: A `dhcpd.conf` file

```
server-identifier home.mens.de;
authoritative;

ddns-update-style interim;
ddns-updates on;

include "/etc/our.key";

zone mens.de. {
        primary 192.168.1.20;
        key our;
}
zone 1.168.192.in-addr.arpa. {
        primary 192.168.1.20;
        key our;
}

subnet 192.168.1.0 netmask 255.255.255.0 {
        range  192.168.1.101 192.168.1.200;
        option subnet-mask 255.255.255.0;
        option broadcast-address 192.168.1.255;

        option domain-name "mens.de";
        option time-offset -18000;

        option routers 192.168.1.1;
        option domain-name-servers 192.168.1.20, 192.168.1.164;
}
```

The format is similar to `named.conf`'s, but do note that clauses such as `subnet` or `zone` are *not* terminated by a semi-colon outside the closing brace.

19.7.2 ISC's dhclient

When a GNU/Linux workstation boots up, it typically launches dhclient. dhclient reads the file `dhclient.conf` for configuration instructions, and gets a list of all network interfaces installed on the system. For each interface, dhclient contacts the DHCP server and retrieves a list of options and values with which it configures that interface. The actual configuration is often performed by a shell script called dhclient-script. The list of DHCP variables that dhclient requests from the server is controlled by options given to dhclient when it's invoked, but there is a sensible list of defaults.

dhclient invokes dhclient-script and passes to it (by means of exported environment variables) the option values that dhclient received from the DHCP server. A set of options and values will contain something like this:

```
interface=eth0
reason=REBOOT
new_broadcast_address=192.168.1.255
new_dhcp_lease_time=14400
new_dhcp_message_type=5
new_dhcp_server_identifier=192.168.1.40
new_domain_name=mens.de
new_domain_name_servers=192.168.1.20 192.168.1.164
new_expiry=1200112399
new_ip_address=192.168.1.202
new_network_number=192.168.1.0
new_ntp_servers=192.168.1.20
new_routers=192.168.1.1
new_subnet_mask=255.255.255.0
new_time_offset=-18000
```

Note that the dhclient-script script may be invoked more than once with differing `$reason` depending on the state of the DHCP initialization. The reasons currently defined are described in full in the program's documentation and include: MEDIUM, PREINIT, BOUND, RENEW, REBIND, REBOOT, EXPIRE, FAIL and TIMEOUT.

19.7.3 How an IP address is registered in the DNS

When a client obtains an IP address from a DHCP server, there are several ways to register the client address in your DNS (Figure 19.6):

A. The DHCP server updates the DNS using RFC 2136 dynamic updates.

B. The DHCP client (i.e. the workstation) updates the DNS using RFC 2136 from dhclient.

C. dhclient-script can run "hooks" – scripts that you write to perform special processing, perhaps because you want to secure your communication between client and the DNS server. Depending on your environment, your hook scripts may or may not use RFC 2136.

The following two methods don't use RFC 2136:

D. If the DNS server doesn't support RFC 2136: the DHCP server writes leases (i.e. IP address allocations) to the file `dhcpd.leases`, and a program can automatically scan the file for modifications and update your DNS from that.

E. The "poor man's" way. We discuss this in Section 19.8 below.

We cover each of these in later sections. But first, if we are going to use method A, B, or C, we must configure the DNS server so it will accept dynamic update requests.

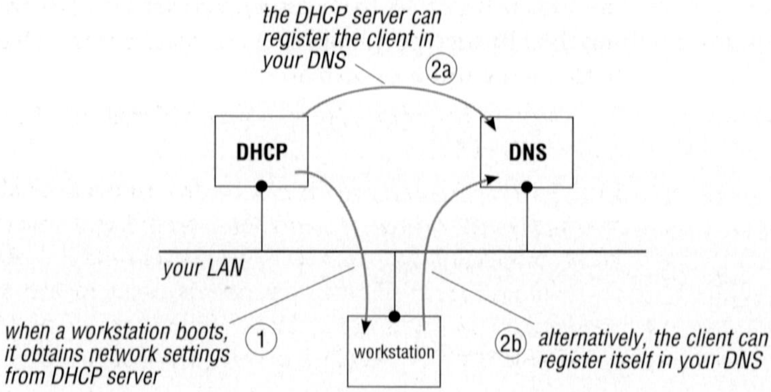

Figure 19.6: DHCP and dynamic DNS updates

To have your DHCP server perform dynamic DNS updates:

Configure your DNS server

Set up your name server to allow incoming RFC 2136 updates:

BIND For BIND, create one or more keys using rndc-keygen, and include an allow-update statement in each of the zones that is to be dynamically updatable:

```
zone "mens.de" IN {
  type master;
  file "mens.zone";
  allow-update { key our; };
};
```

MyDNS For MyDNS, add the update_acl column to the `soa` database table, populate it with the address of the DHCP server, and set allow-update in `mydns.conf`:

```
allow-update = yes
```

A – The DHCP server updates the DNS

1. Configure your DHCP server to perform RFC 2136 updates. We assume you're using the ISC DHCP server; as both DHCP and BIND are ISC products, their configuration syntaxes are similar, and it's easy to get confused: the following statements are for the DHCP server:

   ddns-update-style
   : The update style of dynamic DNS. The only style that works is the `interim` style.

   ddns-updates
   : Controls whether the DHCP server will attempt to submit DNS updates when a DHCP lease is confirmed. Set this to `on` if the server will submit the updates, or to `off` if the DHCP client will perform the updates instead.

   ddns-ttl
   : The Time to Live (TTL) for resource records that the DHCP server adds to the DNS.

   key
   : If you want dhcpd to update a BIND name server that uses TSIG, you need a key that you share between dhcpd and named. Ideally you store the key in a file and include that file in both `named.conf` and `dhcpd.conf`. The key name is used in the `allow-update` statement of BIND's `zone` clause. If you are using MyDNS you do not require keys, as MyDNS does not support TSIG.

   zone
   : The `zone` clauses specify which zones dhcpd will attempt to send updates for. The clauses specify the name of the zone (which should be qualified with a period), the address of the primary name server (which must correspond to the MNAME of the Start of Authority (SOA) record) and an optional key with which updates are authenticated.

   For example, we set the following:

   ```
   ddns-update-style interim;
   ddns-updates on;
   ```

   in `dhcpd.conf` and define the zones and optional keys (for BIND) that are used to authorize updates (see example in Section 19.7.1 above).

2. When the DHCP client (dhclient) is invoked, it contacts the DHCP server and requests that the server perform an update to DNS, which it does upon successful allocation of a lease to the client.

   You might set up your `dhclient.conf` to contain

   ```
   $ cat /etc/dhclient.conf
   send fqdn.fqdn "joey.mens.de.";
   send fqdn.server-update on;
   ```

   in which case dhclient will request that the DHCP server perform the DNS updates on its behalf. The DHCP server logs show:

```
Added new forward map from joey.mens.de to 192.168.1.202
added reverse map from 202.1.168.192.in-addr.arpa. to joey.mens.de
```

This confirms that the DHCP server has been able to "convince" the name server to do the updates. The logs of the target name server confirm the update was successful:

```
client: updating zone 'mens.de/IN': adding an RR
journal file mens.zone.jnl does not exist, creating it
zone mens.de/IN: sending notifies (serial 200712224)
client: updating zone '1.168.192.in-addr.arpa/IN': deleting an rrset
client: updating zone '1.168.192.in-addr.arpa/IN': adding an RR
zone 1.168.192.in-addr.arpa/IN: sending notifies (serial 200612686)
```

B – dhclient *updates the DNS*

In the preceding section we discussed how you set up the DHCP *server* to perform the updates on behalf of the client. If you want to, you can have the client itself update the DNS. If you enable this functionality it means of course, that the RFC 2136-conforming name server has to allow the *client* to do the dynamic DNS update, something you probably *don't* want to allow, because you would have to open up dynamic updates on your name server to *all* possible clients.

To configure dhclient to perform updates:

1. Edit `dhclient.conf`:

```
$ cat /etc/dhclient.conf
send fqdn.fqdn "alex2.mens.de.";
send fqdn.server-update off;

zone mens.de. {
    primary 192.168.1.164;      # primary name server
}
```

2. Configure the target DNS server to allow updates. For example, if you are using MyDNS, set up the update_acl column to allow the machine on which dhclient will perform the update to do so. Now, when the machine boots, we see the following MyDNS logs:

```
UDP 192.168.1.202 IN SOA mens.de. NOERROR - 1 0 0 0 LOG N UPDATE↩
     "ADD alexi.mens.de. 7113 IN A 0 192.168.1.202"
UDP 192.168.1.202 IN SOA mens.de. NOERROR - 1 0 0 0 LOG N UPDATE↩
     "ADD alexi.mens.de. 7113 IN TXT 0 00b9c4d2c00fa90e5cc1c9638055ab565a"
```

and if you follow dhclient's progress, you will see the following messages logged via syslog:

```
bound to 192.168.1.202 -- renewal in 7114 seconds.
Added new forward map from alexi.mens.de. to 192.168.1.202
```

The IP address of the *client* in both logs proves that dhclient and not the DHCP server performed the dynamic DNS update.

> To complicate the issue, if your DHCP server allows ddns (the server has ddns-updates enabled), you would see the *server* updating DNS with the pointer (PTR) and the *client* (dhclient) perform the update for the A and TXT records. The reason is that the client doesn't update PTR records.

If you forget to configure dhclient on your workstation, or if you are using a Microsoft Windows PC (and thus no dhclient), nothing happens. Literally: no DNS update will be performed.

C – Use dhclient-script *to update the DNS*

We have discussed how either the DHCP server or client can initiate the DNS updates. However, if you have high security requirements (e.g. if you need SIG(0) – see Notes) you can't use the methods discussed so far. However, you *can* still perform dynamic DNS registration from dhclient-script, rather than dhclient itself. First, disable updates by dhclient itself by unsetting:

```
# send fqdn.fqdn ... ;
# send fqdn.server-update ... ;
```

in `dhclient.conf`. When dhclient runs dhclient-script, the script receives a number of values passed to it as environment variables. For example:

```
interface=eth0
reason=REBOOT
new_dhcp_lease_time=14400
new_domain_name=mens.de
new_domain_name_servers=192.168.1.20 192.168.1.164
new_ip_address=192.168.1.202
```

dhclient-script sources a script called dhclient-exit-hooks, typically from `/etc`, and it is in this script that you add your extra functionality. For example, you can:

- Use the environment variables as arguments to an nsupdate command, to perform the dynamic DNS update.
- Create a custom script or program that issues SQL statements or LDAP modification requests to the back-end DNS store to reflect the new DNS resource.

Note that dhclient-script is invoked as user `root`.

Only MyDNS and BIND support Dynamic DNS Updates. The next two methods don't use RFC 2136, so you can use them even if your name server doesn't support the standard.

D – Processing the `dhcpd.leases` *file*

If you cannot use RFC 2136 updates from the DHCP server or the DHCP client, you can process the lease file that the DHCP server creates when it grants a lease, and from there update your DNS data back-end. The lease file is called `dhcpd.leases`. It is usually located in `/var/lib/dhcpd`. A typical entry is:

```
lease 192.168.1.133 {
  starts 6 2008/01/12 11:54:18;
  ends 6 2008/01/12 15:54:18;
  binding state active;
  next binding state free;
  hardware ethernet 00:0c:29:6b:19:1f;
  uid "\001\000\014)k\031\037";
  set ddns-rev-name = "133.1.168.192.in-addr.arpa.";
  set ddns-txt = "31f80d4b48e282fd6c0fbebcbe8ba0b0df";
  set ddns-fwd-name = "domi6.mens.de";
  client-hostname "domi6";
}
```

Michael Stella has created a small Perl program that parses the `dhcpd.leases` file and creates output suitable for tinydns-data and tinydns (not for zone master files). For the above lease, the program generates:

```
=domi6.mens.de:192.168.1.133:300
```

The program lives at `www.thismetalsky.org/magic/projects/dhcp_dns.html`.

E – Updating your DNS the "poor man's" way

If none of the above methods are satisfactory, you can use what we call the "poor man's" way. We discuss this next.

19.8 Poor man's dynamic updates

At a customer site that has a large PowerDNS installation, we designed a mechanism so a client machine can register itself with a DNS server, irrespective of whether RFC 2136 support is available or not. The DNS name for a workstation is based on the name of the user who last logged on to it. There were a number of prerequisites and issues:

- The solution had to work on Microsoft Windows PCs, Mac OS X, and *nix workstations, and work with both DHCP and non-DHCP workstations.
- When a user logs on to a workstation, the login (user) name is to be used as the host name and entered in a special DNS zone. So, if user `alexi` logs on to a PC, a DNS record of alexi.*domain-name* has to be created. System administrators use this to determine the IP address of a user without having to ask the user, by querying the domain users.qupps.biz for an A record based on the user's name:

  ```
  $ dig alexi.users.qupps.biz
  ...
  ```

- If a user logs on to two different workstations, the last one wins. For example, if our user `alexi` has a laptop and a desktop, her DNS entry will point to the last machine she logged on to.
- We remove DNS records created for users from the DNS servers during non-working hours, by an automatic process. In the current PowerDNS solution, an SQL `DELETE FROM ...` does the job satisfactorily.

We wrote a single executable client program, pmc, that can be compiled on multiple platforms, and distributed it to the workstations. The implementation ensures that the complexity is centralized on the server, not on the clients. This approach has the following benefits:

- Because the program distributed to user's workstations is so simple, it requires no maintenance or updates.
- Authentication and authorization are performed by the server. The server decides if the DNS entry is allowed, and if so, how to add it.
- The back-end DNS servers can be replaced if necessary, without requiring the client program to be altered.

To limit the complexity of the client program, we determine the client's IP address address *on the server*, not on the client. At this point, you must be asking yourself, whether we've gone off our rocker. Hang on.

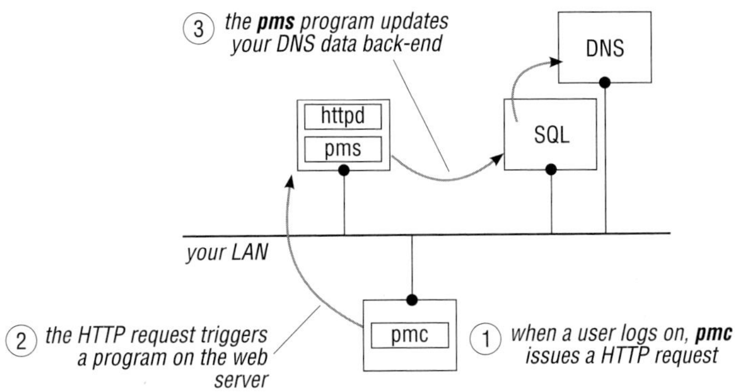

Figure 19.7: poor man's Dynamic DNS

The server program, pms, runs under the control of a Web server. The client contacts the server via HTTP, and in the HTTP request, gives the username of the user currently logged on (Figure 19.7). The server, pms, then determines the client's IP address: it is passed to the HTTP server in the `$REMOTE_ADDR` variable, which is generally made available to a Common Gateway Interface (CGI) program or to a PHP script. pms then creates a DNS resource record or two (an Address (A) and a PTR) for the client.

The service provided by our "poor man's dynamic DNS" is comparable to that offered by dyndns.org (see Notes) and similar providers. We developed this idea for a closed corporate environment. Consider using it if Dynamic DNS Updates a la RFC 2136 aren't possible or are too cumbersome.

19.8.1 pmc: the poor man's dynamic DNS client

We wrote the pmc client program in the C programming language because it is very portable. We use libcurl from the cURL project (see Notes). You can compile the program on any UNIX platform, as well as on Mac OS X or Microsoft Windows (with the Visual C or the MingW compilers, or GCC for Cygwin). The program performs the following steps (Figure 19.8):

1. pmc initializes the cURL environment and sets options for the connection to the HTTP server. It builds a POST request containing the username and submits the HTTP request to the Web server.
2. The Web server invokes the PHP or CGI program and passes it standard variables, such as the IP address of the requestor (i.e. the client workstation), and also the variables set by pmc (i.e. the username).
3. The pms server, on the Web server host, updates the corresponding database, LDAP directory, or file, to record the workstation's address in the DNS.
4. The DNS server now has access to the record, and it can start answering queries for it.
5. pms answers the client request with a "thank you" (or an error-message) to indicate success or failure. This is passed back to the Web server, which transforms it to an HTTP response and returns it to the client.
6. The client displays (or ignores) the response and cleans up the cURL environment.

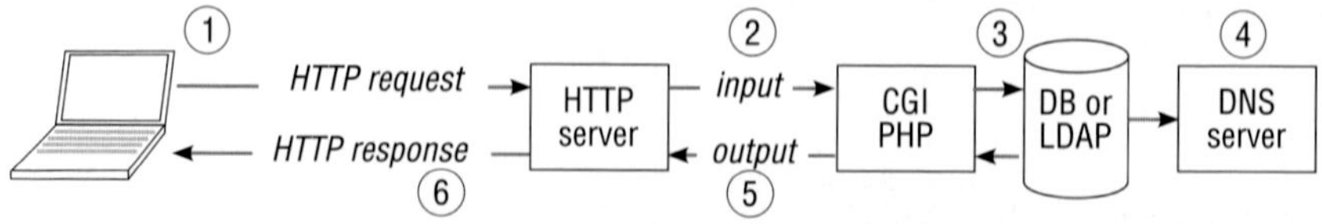

Figure 19.8: pms data flow

Listing 19.4: pmc.c: the poor man's dynamic DNS client (☞ D191)

```
#include <stdio.h>
#ifdef WIN32
# include <windows.h>
# include <wininet.h>
#else
# include <unistd.h>
# include <pwd.h>
#endif
#include <curl/curl.h>
#include <curl/easy.h>
#define Cso(opt, val)   curl_easy_setopt(con, (opt), (val))

#define URL "http://webbin.qupps.biz/pms.php"
```

```
static char *userid(void);

int main(int argc, char **argv)
{
    CURL *con;
    CURLcode rc;
    struct curl_httppost *post = NULL, *last = NULL;

    curl_global_init(CURL_GLOBAL_DEFAULT);
    con = curl_easy_init();

    Cso( CURLOPT_URL, URL );
    Cso( CURLOPT_VERBOSE, 0 );
    Cso( CURLOPT_USERAGENT, "pmc 3.1" );

    curl_formadd(&post, &last,
        CURLFORM_COPYNAME, "username",
        CURLFORM_COPYCONTENTS, userid(), CURLFORM_END);

    Cso( CURLOPT_POST, 1);
    Cso( CURLOPT_HTTPPOST, post );

    rc = curl_easy_perform(con);
    if (rc != CURLE_OK) {
        fprintf(stderr, "Can't GET %s: easy-error: 0x%X", URL, rc);
    }

    curl_formfree(post);
    curl_easy_cleanup(con);
    curl_global_cleanup();
    return (0);
}

static char *userid()
{
    char *username = "unknown";

#ifdef WIN32
    static char lpName[128] = "unknown";
    long rc, dlen = sizeof(lpName);

    rc = WNetGetUser(NULL, lpName, &dlen);
    if (rc == NOERROR) {
        username = lpName;
    }
#else
    struct passwd *pw;

    if ((pw = getpwuid(getuid())) != NULL) {
        username = pw->pw_name;
    }
#endif

    return (username);
}
```

Hardcoding the URL to the pms service into the client is a Bad Thing™, because whenever the URL to the service changes (e.g. because you relocate the server, change the path to the pms server, switch from using PHP to CGI, etc.) you have to rollout a new version of pmc to all workstations. We show you, in Appendix G, how you can use DNS TXT records to "configure" applications from "outside", using the DNS as a configuration database.

Invoking pmc *on *nix*

On a *nix host, there are a several places where you can invoke the pmc client program:

- From `/etc/profile` when a user logs on.
- From a user's `.profile` (or `.bashrc`) initialization file, allowing finer control over which users get their DNS registered.
- You might think we could run pmc from the dhclient-exit-hooks script (Section 19.7.3) which is sourced by the dhclient-script invoked by dhclient. However, because the program is invoked as the `root` user, you don't have access to the "real" username of the user who will be utilizing the workstation, so you can't really use this in our context.

Invoking pmc *on Microsoft Windows*

On Microsoft Windows you can launch pmc:

- From a login script that your users execute when they log in to your domain; this avoids the need for software distribution, as the program is launched from the network.
- From the "Run" tree of the registry. (The commands listed in this tree are launched when a user logs in to a workstation.)
- From the "Startup" folder of the Microsoft Windows start menu.

pmc is usually compiled to not show a console, so your users will not see pmc while it executes.

19.8.2 pms: a server for pmc

The server component for the poor man's dynamic DNS is implemented as a program, pms, under the control of a Web server. We use PHP running on an Apache Web server, but you could implement it in any language. Our sample implementation assumes the Bind DLZ name server (Chapter 9), but adapting it to work with any of the other SQL-database or LDAP schemas is trivial. The program does the following:

1. It retrieves the IP address of the pmc client, as well as the username sent by pmc in the HTTP request.
2. It constructs the name of the client by concatenating the username with our special zone name (users.qupps.biz). This is the host name by which the client will be known.

3. It connects to the database using a Pear module (which allows you to easily adapt the program to a different SQL database back-end).

4. If the entry for this host does not exist, it is created and inserted into the `dns_records` table with an Address (A).

5. If the entry for the host name exists, the IP address of its Address (A) record is updated.

6. The program issues a small message. You can disable this in a production environment, as your users will not usually see it.

Listing 19.5: pms.php: the poor man's dynamic DNS server component (☞ D192)

```
<?php
    # pms.php (C)2008 by Jan-Piet Mens
    # Server for poor man's dynamic DNS

    require_once "DB.php";

    $zone = 'users.qupps.biz';

    $driver = "mysql";              # driver name
    $user = "dnsadmin";
    $password = "hah!";
    $host = "192.168.1.164";
    $db = "perfdlz";                  # database name
    # build DSN (data set name)
    $dsn = "$driver://$user:$password@$host/$db";

    $conn =& DB::connect ($dsn);
    if (DB::isError ($conn))
        die ("Cannot connect: " . $conn->getMessage () . "\n");

    $ip = $_SERVER['REMOTE_ADDR'];
    $host = $_POST['username'];

    $sql = "SELECT zone FROM dns_records
                WHERE zone = '$zone' AND host = '$host' AND type = 'A'";
    $result =& $conn->query($sql);
    if (DB::isError ($result))
            die ("SELECT failed: " . $result->getMessage () . "\n");

    if ($result->numRows() == 0) {
        $sql = "INSERT INTO dns_records (zone,host,ttl,type,data)
                    VALUES ('$zone', '$host', 3600, 'A', '$ip')";
        $result =& $conn->query ($sql);
        if (DB::isError ($result))
            die ("INSERT failed: " . $result->getMessage () . "\n");

        $message = "INSERTED $host.$zone with IP=$ip";
    } else {
        $sql = "UPDATE dns_records SET data = '$ip'
                    WHERE zone = '$zone' AND host = '$host' AND type = 'A'";
        $result =& $conn->query ($sql);
        if (DB::isError ($result))
```

```
            die ("UPDATE failed: " . $result->getMessage () . "\n");

        $message = "UPDATED $host.$zone with IP=$ip";
    }
    $conn->disconnect();
    echo "Thanks: $message\n";
?>
```

When pmc runs, it contacts the Web server via HTTP, and the Web server invokes the pms PHP script. The "echo" on the last line of the program causes pmc to print out the server's summary of what it did:

```
$ pmc
Thanks: INSERTED alexi.users.qupps.biz with IP=192.168.2.22
```

Running it from a workstation with a different IP address would produce:

```
$ pmc
Thanks: UPDATED alexi.users.qupps.biz with IP=192.168.2.83
```

Our sample pms server inserts or updates a record in an SQL database table, but you could do things differently:

- If you use tinydns, your pms could just create a line in a tinydns-data file, which is periodically transformed to a CDB database (e.g. via cron, or inotify – see Notes)
- If you use a DNS server with an LDAP directory back-end, you change pms to add or modify LDAP directory entries accordingly.

The source code for pmc and pms is available from this book's Web site (☞ D190).

Summary

- We recommend you set up a DNS registry in your organization if you manage more than a handful of domains.

- How you update and manage DNS data depends on the name server you're using. It can involve editing zone master files, adding a record to a database with an SQL `INSERT`, or adding an entry to an LDAP directory server.

- Make your life easier and use existing tools, or fashion new ones, to administer and quickly modify DNS resource records.

- Dynamic DNS Updates are specified in RFC 2136. However, only MyDNS and BIND support it.

- Combining dynamic updates with DHCP lets you automatically register new clients in the DNS. The DHCP client program (dhclient) can be configured to suit your infrastructure.

- If you can't use RFC 2136 Dynamic DNS, you can use our "poor man's" DNS instead, within your organization, or you can process the `dhcpd.leases` file and update your DNS from that.

Related topics

- MyDNS Chapter 5.

- BIND Chapter 7

- dnsmasq Chapter 13

- In Chapter 15 we show you how we use the DNS data entered via our Poor man's dynamic DNS together with user's details taken from an LDAP directory, to provide an information system you query via the DNS, using a custom-made Perl name server.

Notes and further reading

SIG(0)

SIG(0) is defined in RFC 2931, *DNS Request and Transaction Signatures.* It provides protection for DNS transactions. SIG(0) is beyond the scope of this book, but you can learn about it at `http://www.ietf.org/rfc/rfc2931.txt`, and you can use it with dynamic updates as described in the *Secure dynamic DNS howto* at `http://ops.ietf.org/dns/dynupd/secure-ddns-howto.html`

inotify

inotify is a GNU/Linux kernel subsystem that provides file system event notification (think trigger for file system operations). It allows applications to request the monitoring of a set of files against a list of events; when the event occurs, the application is notified. The inotify API is available in a number of programming languages.

DHCP information

- *The DHCP Handbook* (2nd edition) by Ralph Droms and Ted Lemon (Sams) is a complete reference for DHCP clients and servers. Chapters on configuration, Microsoft Windows, DHCPv6, and DNS-interaction address problems that network administrators are bound to encounter. Ted Lemon is one of the main authors of ISC DHCP, and the book covers that program extensively (see `http://www.dhcp-handbook.com/`).
- For a more concise coverage of DHCP, read the companion book in this series, *Practical TCP/IP* by Niall Mansfield.

Storing DHCP configuration data in LDAP

If you store DNS information in LDAP, why not store DHCP data in an LDAP directory as well? The ISC DHCP server can be made to store its configuration in an LDAP directory server, in the same data store as the DNS data:

```
dn: cn=192.168.1.0, ou=DHCP, ou=dev, o=qupps.biz
cn: 192.168.1.0
objectClass: top
objectClass: dhcpSubnet
objectClass: dhcpOptions
dhcpOption: domain-name-servers 192.168.1.20
dhcpOption: routers 192.168.1.1
dhcpOption: subnet-mask 255.255.255.0
dhcpOption: broadcast-address 192.168.1.255
dhcpNetMask: 24
```

In large environments, this can make distribution and maintenance of DHCP's configuration as easy to manage as the DNS resources that we also keep in the same directory. Brian Masney created a patch to version 3.0.5 of the ISC DHCPD server to add LDAP functionality to dhcpd. You will find the patch at `http://home.ntelos.net/~masneyb/dhcp-3.0.5-ldap-patch`; the file README.ldap contains information on how the patch works and how you apply it.

The cURL program and libcurl library

cURL, created by Daniel Stenberg, is a command line tool for transferring files with URL syntax, supporting FTP, FTPS, HTTP, HTTPS and many other protocols. libcurl is a well documented library which allows you to embed cURL's capabilities into a program (see `http://curl.haxx.se/`).

The DynDNS Update Specifications

Dynamic Network Services, Inc. is well known for its free DynDNS services at `www.dyndns.com`. Computers that have non-fixed IP addresses can register a domain name which points to that IP address and can update the DNS details whenever the IP address changes. This lets you run publicly accessible servers on the Internet without having to get a fixed IP address. Their DynDNS system has a published API, the DNS Update API (see `https://www.dyndns.com/developers/specs/`).

tinyddns

If you use tinydns (Chapter 11), you may be interested in tinyddns, a simple dynamic-DNS client and server. The client uses a secret to authenticate with the server and sends that with a configurable hostname to the server over UDP. The server determines the client's IP from the UDP socket, decrypts the secret and, if it validates, adds or replaces the client's address in the `data` file for tinydns-data to process. tinyddns lives at `http://sourceforge.net/projects/tinyddns/`

Chapter

20 The Name Service Switch

A box of crayons and a big sheet of paper provides a more expressive medium for kids than computerized paint programs.

Clifford Stoll

Introduction

On a DNS client machine, hostname and IP-address resolution begins with a stub resolver. On modern UNIX and GNU/Linux systems this is handled by a library of functions called the Name Service Switch (NSS). We discuss NSS and how you modify it to query an LDAP directory server directly.

20.1 How the resolver operates

We discussed in Section 1.1.5 that the first step in a possibly long chain of events that leads to a client program getting the answer to a query of "what is the address of www.qupps.biz please?" is a resolver. A resolver is the component of a system that performs queries on behalf of a client program, to translate a hostname to an IP address or vice versa. The resolver isn't a separate program, but just a set of library functions and system calls. In the simplest case, a resolver receives a request for name translation via a function call (i.e. `gethostbyname()`), contacts a name server to obtain the desired information and returns it to the calling application. For example, a Web browser calls `gethostbyname()` with code similar to this Perl example, when you click on a hyperlink:

```
#!/usr/bin/perl

use strict;
use Socket;

my $packed_ip = gethostbyname("www.qupps.biz");
if (defined $packed_ip) {
    # Convert bytes to printable representation
    my $ip_address = inet_ntoa($packed_ip);
    print "IP Address: $ip_address\n";
}
```

20.1.1 Unix stub resolver

On *nix, the resolver is a set of functions contained in a library linked to the program. Originally, these functions used a static file named `/etc/hosts`. When the DNS was introduced, the file `/etc/host.conf` let you control in which order the resolution procedure tried the `/etc/hosts` file and the DNS; on modern GNU/Linux systems the file still exists, but it is no longer used. The flexibility of the name lookup system was greatly enhanced by the introduction of the Name Service Switch (NSS) (Section 20.2) which adds a level of both complexity and flexibility to the resolution process. NSS is used on most *nix systems today.

Configuring the resolver

You configure how a *nix system uses the DNS with the file `/etc/resolv.conf`. You typically specify a number of DNS caching servers that this host's stub resolver should send its DNS queries to. The file contains a sequence of lines of the form *keyword value*(s), with whitespace separating the entries on a line. Two of the keywords supported are:

search This is optional. It specifies a list of up to six domains[1]. The values are used only if the queried name isn't an FQDN (i.e. if it doesn't *end with* a dot).

If the queried name contains a dot somewhere in the middle, the resolver first queries it "as is"; if that doesn't succeed, or if the name doesn't contain a dot, the resolver appends the first element of the search list, and tries to

[1] Defined as MAXDNSRCH in `resolv.h`.

resolve that; if that doesn't succeed, it appends the next element instead, and so on, until a match is found or the resolution fails. E.g. if you set:

```
search  dev.es.qupps.biz  qupps.biz
```

`ping foo` can generate queries foo.dev.es.qupps.biz followed by foo.qupps.biz, whereas `ping foo.bar` might generate foo.bar, foo.bar.dev.es.qupps.biz and foo.bar.es.qupps.biz.

nameserver Specify an address of a DNS server to use. You may use multiple nameserver[2]. The resolver attempts to contact name servers in the order you specify to find one that answers, so if you have a local DNS caching server on the machine, you should specify the local address first.

A typical `resolv.conf` will specify a search and two or three nameserver entries:

```
search qupps.biz.
nameserver 127.0.0.1
nameserver 192.168.1.20
nameserver 192.168.1.164
```

Note that you might not have to manually maintain this configuration if your networking software is configured via DHCP.

20.1.2 The lightweight resolver

We discuss in Section 20.2, that NSS can use the lightweight resolver daemon (lwresd) to query the DNS. lwresd is essentially a stripped-down version of a BIND caching-only name server that answers queries (on UDP port 921) using the lightweight resolver protocols instead of using the DNS protocol. lwresd can be used only by processes running on the local machine, due to its hard-coded use of the 127.0.0.1 address. If you use lwresd, note that it uses the `nameserver` entries of `resolv.conf` to find addresses of upstream "normal" caching DNS servers. If it cannot find any `nameserver` entries, it resolves queries starting at a built-in list of root name servers.

20.1.3 Microsoft Windows DNS Client

On windows, applications perform DNS lookups by calling functions contained in a dynamic link library (DLL), which also supports legacy NetBIOS name lookup functionality. These functions handle all communications with the DNS servers and return DNS answers back to the application. Modern Microsoft Windows systems include a caching resolver service called the *DNS Client* which clients "talk to" via local IPC. The DNS Client service itself communicates with DNS servers, and caches the results that it receives. Upon startup, the DNS client service loads an `/etc/hosts`-type file from `%SYSTEMROOT%\system32\drivers\etc\hosts`, and it reloads it periodically whenever it detects a modification to the file.

[2]The maximum number of entries is defined as MAXNS when the resolver code is built. On our system, MAXNS is defined as 3.

The process of resolving a name on a modern Microsoft Windows system is as follows. As soon as a step succeeds, the requested value is returned and the procedure terminates.

1. If the name is the local host name, the library returns the local address.
2. Search the cache of the DNS Client service. If the name is not in the cache, the DNS Client service contacts DNS servers to attempt to resolve the name. If the query can be satisfied, the reply is cached and returned to the client.
3. If the name contains a period or is 16 characters or longer, jump to step 4, below.

   Otherwise, convert the name to a 15-character NetBIOS name by converting to uppercase and appending spaces as required, and check the local NetBIOS cache for this name.
4. If the name isn't in the NetBIOS cache, Microsoft Windows contacts its configured WINS server(s) for resolution.
5. If there is no reply to the NetBIOS name query request, Microsoft Windows searches its local `LMHOSTS` and `hosts` files.

Due to the interaction with NetBIOS (if configured), we strongly recommend you do not test your DNS with a ping on Microsoft Windows, to ensure you don't run into the NetBIOS trap – a ping on a simple name can be resolved via NetBIOS instead of using the DNS, and you can't see the difference. Use dig instead (Chapter 14 tells you how to get dig for Microsoft Windows).

20.2 NSS – the Name Service Switch

Many aspects of a *nix host require configuration files containing lists of "things" – users and passwords, user groups, host names and addresses, network service names and ports, etc. Originally these were stored in static files, and each host had to have its own copy of each file. This obviously caused maintenance and distribution problems. To get over these, several systems have been developed that allow the information to be stored centrally on the network and queried from the separate hosts. Other systems have been developed that still require local storage, but perform well even with very large numbers of items.

The Name Service Switch (NSS), introduced by Sun, lets you control which databases and other data sources are used for which configuration information. The NSS has been adopted by most *nix implementations.

The functions that use the NSS include: `gethostbyname()` and `gethostbyaddr()` for resolving host names and addresses, and `getpwnam()` and `getpwuid()` for retrieving username and password information.

NSS provides a common interface for simple system database lookup operations (Figure 20.1). This interface lets the system administrator configure which data sources the lookup functions use, and in which order.

In this book, we limit the discussion of NSS to the routines needed to perform name-to-address resolution, although much of what we discuss applies in a similar form to the other library function groups.

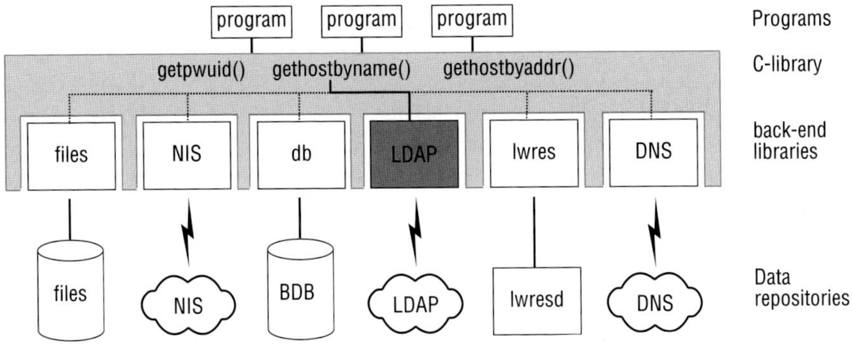

Figure 20.1: Name Service Switch architecture

20.2.1 How NSS determines where to look for information

The Name Service Switch typically offers the following services for name-to-address and address-to-name mapping:

files Use files (i.e. `/etc/hosts`) on the machine's file system for linear lookup of host names and addresses.

nis Use NIS, the Network Information System. NIS is an RPC (Remote Procedure-Call)-based client/server system that allows a group of machines to share a set of configuration files, typically `passwd`, `group`, `hosts` and others. It is an industry standard. (Many organizations are now moving their user data from NIS to LDAP because NIS is quite dated and doesn't scale well.)

db Use Berkeley DB files. NSS on GNU/Linux supports different versions of Berkeley DB files (2.4, 2.7 and 3.0). `db` is great because it uses indexed rather than linear searching, so on huge files it still performs very well. Berkeley DB's key/value databases are typically used on systems with large `passwd` files because they are very effective. Look at the `Makefile` in `/var/db` for information on how to build the Berkeley DB files with makedb.

ldap Use an LDAP directory server (Section 20.3).

lwres provides (`gethostby`() functions only) support for the lightweight resolver on systems that use the GNU C library. The lightweight resolver can replace the DNS module in NSS for name server lookups. To use this module, you have to ensure that the lightweight resolver daemon (lwresd) is running.

dns Use the DNS. The stub resolver needs the `/etc/resolv.conf` file to determine the address(es) of the name server(s) to contact for query resolution.

NSS uses the services in the order you specify. On a typical *nix system, the file controlling the Name Service Switch (`/etc/nsswitch.conf`) contains the following line for host name resolution:

```
hosts:    files dns
```

indicating that the system should consult `/etc/hosts` before attempting to resolve via DNS.

20.3 Using LDAP (RFC 2307) with the Name Service Switch

The Name Service Switch lets you to configure the system lookup functions to retrieve their information from an LDAP directory server. RFC 2307, *An Approach for Using LDAP as a Network Information Service*, defines mechanisms for outsourcing to an LDAP directory server the information usually contained in static system files. The reference implementation of RFC 2307 is NSS LDAP (see `http://www.padl.com/OSS/nss_ldap.html`). A newer implementation that attempts to address some of the limitations of the reference implementation is nss-ldapd (see `http://ch.tudelft.nl/~arthur/nss-ldapd/`).

Most modern GNU/Linux systems already contain NSS LDAP, so you will not have to install it from source. Before you use it, you will have to configure it:

A. Configure the NSS LDAP module to use your LDAP directory server.

B. Prepare your LDAP directory server.

C. Load your LDAP directory server with entries containing hosts and their IP addresses.

D. Configure `nsswitch.conf`.

E. Test your NSS LDAP setup.

20.3.1 A – Configure NSS LDAP with /etc/ldap.conf

NSS LDAP uses the file `/etc/ldap.conf` to determine the addresses of your LDAP directory server(s) and where it can find the required LDAP entries. (Do not mistake this file for OpenLDAP's client configuration file which is called `/etc/openldap/ldap.conf`.) A minimal `ldap.conf` that you can use to enable NSS LDAP to look up host information is:

Listing 20.1: `ldap.conf` for NSS LDAP

```
uri                 ldap://192.168.1.20/
base                ou=dev,o=qupps.biz
ldap_version        3
scope               sub
nss_base_hosts      ou=Hosts,ou=dev,o=qupps.biz?sub
```

A typical `ldap.conf` contains a large number of additional options, many of which also enable the system's Pluggable Authentication Modules (PAM) to work hand in hand with NSS LDAP.

20.3.2 B – Prepare your LDAP directory server

Your LDAP directory server must accommodate the object classes used by NSS LDAP. For host information, the auxiliary object class is called `ipHost`.

- OpenLDAP supplies the required object classes in a file called `nis.schema`. To activate this include the schema file in your server's `slapd.conf`:

  ```
  include path/schema/nis.schema
  ```

- If you use Microsoft Active Directory, you typically extend its schema by installing *Services for Unix* (*SFU*).

20.3.3 C – Migrating /etc/hosts to NSS LDAP

The Migrationtools (see http://www.padl.com/OSS/MigrationTools.html) contain scripts that facilitate the migration from existing static system files to NSS LDAP. For example, the migrate_hosts.pl program converts an existing /etc/hosts file to LDIF format. It uses $LDAP_BASEDN to form the distinguished name of the entries.

Listing 20.2: Migrating /etc/hosts to NSS LDAP

```
$ cat /etc/hosts
127.0.0.1        localhost
192.168.1.20     home mail server
192.168.1.179    ls1 storage
192.168.1.185    pc2

$ export LDAP_BASEDN='ou=dev,o=qupps.biz'
$ migrate_hosts.pl  /etc/hosts
dn: cn=localhost,ou=Hosts,ou=dev,o=qupps.biz
objectClass: top
objectClass: ipHost
objectClass: device
ipHostNumber: 127.0.0.1
cn: localhost

dn: cn=home,ou=Hosts,ou=dev,o=qupps.biz
objectClass: top
objectClass: ipHost
objectClass: device
ipHostNumber: 192.168.1.20
cn: home
cn: mail
cn: server

dn: cn=ls1,ou=Hosts,ou=dev,o=qupps.biz
objectClass: top
objectClass: ipHost
objectClass: device
ipHostNumber: 192.168.1.179
cn: ls1
cn: storage

dn: cn=pc2,ou=Hosts,ou=dev,o=qupps.biz
objectClass: top
objectClass: ipHost
objectClass: device
ipHostNumber: 192.168.1.185
cn: pc2
```

You can feed the LDIF directly to ldapadd to add the entries to your LDAP directory server.

20.3.4 D – Configure `nsswitch.conf`

Ensure that you modify `nsswitch.conf` to include LDAP:

```
hosts:     files ldap dns
```

NSS will use the order you specify when processing a query it receives (Figure 20.2).

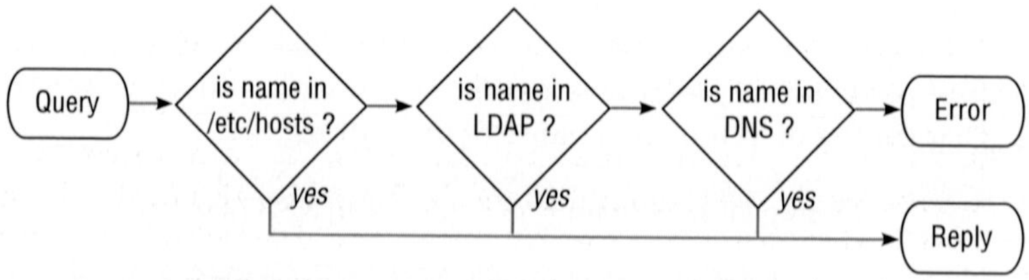

Figure 20.2: How NSS processes a name request

20.3.5 E – Testing your NSS LDAP

At this point you you have configured the Name Service Switch to access your LDAP directory server and have created some host entries in the directory server, so you can start putting it to use. Use the getent utility to test your lookups. (Make sure you don't accidentally lookup a host name contained in your local `/etc/hosts` file.)

```
$ getent hosts storage
192.168.1.179    ls1 storage
```

From now on, any program that uses the system's `gethostbyname()` and related routines, will use your LDAP directory server to find results. (You can't use dig to test, because dig doesn't use `gethostbyname()`, and doesn't use the NSS functions.)

```
$ ping -c 1 storage
PING ls1 (192.168.1.179) 56(84) bytes of data.
64 bytes from ls1 (192.168.1.179): icmp_seq=1 ttl=128 time=0.184 ms
```

Note how NSS LDAP returns the "official" host name (ls1) for the IP address when the name we query is an alias, just like when using the `hosts` file.

Your LDAP directory server receives a query for each lookup. E.g. if a user uses lynx:

```
$ lynx http://www.yahoo.de
```

you might see the following search on your LDAP directory server:

```
SRCH filter="(&(objectClass=ipHost)(cn=www.yahoo.de))"
```

Why is this happening? Any name-to-address query by `gethostbyname()` or address-to-name query by `gethostbyaddr()` uses NSS. As we have configured NSS to use LDAP before it uses DNS, it is forced to query LDAP in order to determine whether or not the requested name (or address) exists, before continuing on to ask the Domain Name System. This can and will impose a load on your LDAP directory servers.

Theoretically you could deploy an LDAP directory server and configure all your *nix workstations with NSS LDAP and not worry about DNS. However, that isn't a real solution because (a) you still need DNS for Microsoft Windows and devices that don't support NSS LDAP, and (b) NSS LDAP is much more "heavyweight" than DNS.

20.3.6 Points to note when you implement RFC 2307 LDAP in NSS

Implementing the Name Service Switch over LDAP with RFC 2307 is not a panacea; there are several points we recommend you keep in mind:

- NSS LDAP will impose an additional load on your LDAP directory servers, as already mentioned. You might wish to implement the Name Service Cache Daemon (nscd), a program designed to cache lookups. Although nscd dramatically reduces the load on your directory servers, older implementations did cause problems, so we recommend you test it carefully.
- If your LDAP servers are unreachable, NSS LDAP will cause delays for all lookups. This will be visible when a user attempts to log in to a system configured to use NSS LDAP; the login "hangs" for a while.
- Just as resolution via DNS requires that you configure every machine by modifying its `/etc/resolv.conf`[3], NSS LDAP also requires local configuration. You can simplify the configuration because NSS LDAP can use Service (SRV) records to find its LDAP servers. This allows NSS LDAP to be self-configuring from information stored in the DNS. To enable this support, comment out the `host` and `uri` entries in the `ldap.conf` file; this forces the NSS library to search the DNS for a domain name like _ldap._tcp.qupps.biz.
- NSS LDAP can "override" answers that would otherwise be returned by the DNS, if you configure NSS to use LDAP before DNS. For example, if you create a host entry for www.singleclick.com, a query for this will be answered by NSS LDAP instead of being answered by the DNS.

[3]This is usually automated for workstations by the use of DHCP.

Summary

- The Name Service Switch is used by the stub resolvers on *nix systems. It determines which data sources are used to find host information, and in which order.
- If NSS is incorrectly configured, users will experience delays when programs perform name lookups.
- You can implement NSS LDAP to lookup host information in an LDAP directory.

Notes and further reading

- When writing programs that make heavy use of hostname resolution, you do not typically use `gethostbyname()` because it "blocks", and your program can't do anything else while it is waiting for the answer. Instead, you can:
  - Use the routines from the resolver library (`-lresolv`) to query the DNS directly (`res_query()`, etc.).
  - We discussed in Chapter 17 that the Unbound caching name server builds on libunbound, a library of functions you use to control name resolution, both synchronous and asynchronously. These give you the functionality of Unbound directly in your application but don't require a caching name server, because libunbound implements one itself.
  - adns is an alternative asynchronous stub resolver by Ian Jackson and Tony Finch. (see `http://www.chiark.greenend.org.uk/~ian/adns/`).

  Note however, that these three methods all bypass NSS.

- Section 20.1.3 explained that a Microsoft Windows workstation has a caching DNS Client resolver service which is normally enabled. This is useful because it lowers the load on your caching name servers. Nevertheless, because of the way it has been implemented, it also impedes DNS round robin from functioning (because an answer to the query is already cached). If you want to disable the cache you can do so permanently by disabling the service, but you can also tune the service (see `http://support.microsoft.com/kb/318803`).

Chapter

21 Internationalized Domain Names

It's been a long time coming.

anonymous

Introduction

An internationalized domain name is a domain that contains non-ASCII characters. Because the DNS does not allow eight-bit-characters, a standard was developed to support international domain names. We discuss IDNA, Internationalizing Domain Names in Applications, which is the current standard. This allows a client application to use a non-ASCII domain name, while the DNS server represents the same name in a special way, using ASCII characters only.

The DNS does not allow eight-bit/non-ASCII characters. Instead of changing the DNS to allow such characters, RFC 3490 the IDNA (*Internationalizing Domain Names in Applications*) standard lets client-side applications use international domain names (containing non-ASCII characters – see Notes); the application converts an international domain name to a special ASCII format before passing it to the DNS, and converts it back again when it receives it from the DNS. The internationalized name remains displayed in the user program. IDNA has security problems – it is vulnerable to "homograph spoof attacks", which we cover in Section 21.1.

The benefit of the IDNA approach is that resolvers and DNS servers remain unchanged – the whole DNS infrastructure doesn't have to be changed at all. The downside is that IDNA puts the burden of translation on the applications (Web browsers, e-mail clients, etc.) that need to support internationalized domain names.

An IDNA-conforming application takes the internationalized (i.e. non-ASCII) domain name entered by the user, translates it to its ASCII representation, and queries the DNS for this; the internationalized name remains displayed in the user program.

In the rest of this chapter we discuss how internationalized domain names are converted, and how you enter those into your DNS. As our example internationalized domain name, we use théâtre.qupps.biz; as you've probably guessed, théâtre is the French word for theatre.

21.1 Converting internationalized domain names to ASCII

An application uses the algorithm called ToASCII to convert from a domain name in *IDN* (Internationalized Domain Name) format, and the algorithm ToUnicode to convert from the ASCII representation to IDN.

The application applies these algorithms to each label of a domain name, not to the name as a whole. For example, for domain théâtre.qupps.biz, théâtre is translated first, then qupps, and finally biz. Here's how ToASCII works (Figure 21.1):

1. Transform each label using the Nameprep algorithm (RFC 3491). Broadly speaking, Nameprep converts the label to lowercase and removes code points (i.e. characters) that are invisible.

2. Transform each resulting lower-cased label to ASCII using Punycode (RFC 3492). A full discussion is beyond our scope, but broadly, in a first pass over a label, Punycode groups together all ASCII characters, and then all Unicode code points (i.e. characters). The process first outputs the ASCII characters; if any Unicode characters were found, it outputs these, separated from the first group by a single dash.

3. Prepend to the result the four-character string constant `"xn--"`, called the *ASCII Compatible Encoding* (*ACE*) prefix (see Notes). This distinguishes Punycode-encoded labels from ordinary ASCII labels.

The reverse procedure, ToUnicode, is applied when converting a domain name back to its internationalized form, for example to display the result in an application.

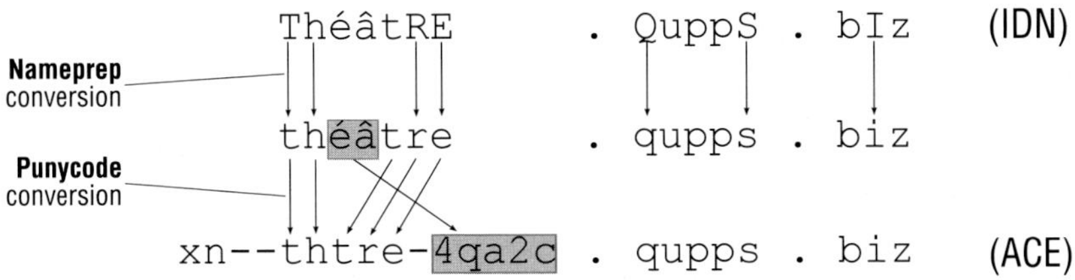

Figure 21.1: How ToASCII converts from IDN format to ACE

Homograph attacks on internationalized domain names

Unfortunately, international domain names are vulnerable to so-called "homograph" spoofing attacks. (A *homograph* is a word that shares the same spelling as another, but has a different meaning – e.g. wind as in weather and wind as in clock.) In the case of internationalized domain names, homograph spoofing comes about because there are many different characters that have indistinguishable glyphs (graphical representations in a particular typeface).

Homograph attacks consist of choosing and registering a suitable domain, sending so-called phishing e-mail to users and waiting for them to react, for example, by clicking on a link in the e-mail. That click takes them to a Web page that appears to be that of a known organization, but is in fact a fake.

A well-known example[1] used in a paper on homograph attacks is Paypal: the first "a" in the word should be the English lowercase "a", represented with a decimal 91 – hexadecimal 0x61. However, if you replace that first letter with the Cyrillic lowercase "a" (which has a decimal value of 1072 – hex 0x430), it *looks* exactly like an English "a", but it is in fact a completely different character. So, instead of sending the victim to `www.paypal.com`, the attacker was able to send the victim to `www.paypal.com` (remember, they look the same, right?), resulting in the victim actually reaching the site `www.xn--pypal-4ve.com`!

Unfortunately, there is little that you can do to protect your users (see Notes).

21.2 Adding internationalized domains to your DNS server

Adding an internationalized domain name to your DNS server is not terribly much more difficult than adding an ASCII domain name. Ensure that your shell is set up to utilize a correct character set. You must be sure that when you enter a non-ASCII character, you get the Unicode character, and not one of a different code set (such as ISO-8859-1). If you aren't sure of how to do that, you may prefer to use a Web interface (see Notes).

If, in the next step, you're using idn and it gives an error message saying that it cannot convert your domain name, then `$CHARSET` if defined, or `$LANG`, is incorrectly set.

1. Use one of the tools (e.g. idn, see Section 21.3.3 for others) to translate a non-ASCII name to Punycode format:

```
$ idn --quiet --idna-to-ascii théâtre.qupps.biz
idn: Could not convert from ANSI_X3.4-1968 to UTF-8.
```

[1] See `http://www.shmoo.com/idn/`

```
$ export CHARSET=UTF-8
$ idn --quiet --idna-to-ascii théâtre.qupps.biz
xn--thtre-4qa2c.qupps.biz
```

The character set UTF-8 is the 8-bit Universal Character Set/Unicode Transformation Format – a variable-length character encoding for Unicode. The IDN we need for the domain théâtre.qupps.biz is `xn--thtre-4qa2c.qupps.biz`. We add that domain name to our name server.

In this second example, the encoding appears to work, but it produces incorrect results. After you set the character set to ISO-8859-1, and feed idn not with an ISO-8859-1 string containing accents but with UTF-8 encoded accents, the program appears to do its job correctly but in actual fact it produces an IDN which is useless.

```
$ export CHARSET=ISO-8859-1
$ idn --quiet --idna-to-ascii théâtre.qupps.biz
xn--thtre-5fa2c35ab.qupps.biz
```

To double-check the result, try converting back to Unicode. When we do that on our terminal, we get something resembling this:

```
$ idn --quiet --idna-to-unicode xn--thtre-5fa2c35ab.qupps.biz
th■■tre.qupps.biz
```

That is a very visible example that we did something wrong. (Unfortunately not all conversions will be so obviously incorrect.)

2. Query the server to check whether it answers correctly. dig doesn't know about IDNA, so you have to give it a domain name that has already been converted using idn:

```
$ export CHARSET=UTF-8
$ dig `idn --quiet -a théâtre.qupps.biz`
; <<>> DiG 9.2.4 <<>> xn--thtre-4qa2c.qupps.biz
;; ->>HEADER<<- opcode: QUERY, status: NOERROR, id: 30000
;; flags: qr aa rd ra; QUERY: 1, ANSWER: 1, AUTHORITY: 2, ADDITIONAL: 2

;; QUESTION SECTION:
;xn--thtre-4qa2c.qupps.biz.      IN      A

;; ANSWER SECTION:
xn--thtre-4qa2c.qupps.biz . 60   IN      A        192.168.1.20
```

Look at what happens when you query the DNS for a domain name containing UTF-8 characters without first converting them with idn:

```
$ dig théâtre.qupps.biz
;; ->>HEADER<<- opcode: QUERY, status: NXDOMAIN, id: 54411

;; QUESTION SECTION:
;th\195\169\195\162tre.qupps.biz. IN    A
```

The result is garbage, because the DNS doesn't handle 8-bit characters. As a rule of thumb, whenever you see strange escaped characters in domain names of DNS replies, you are dealing with an illegal non-ASCII character, and something is going wrong.

21.3 Using IDNA in applications

21.3.1 Using IDNA in Web browsers

Web browsers should support internationalized domain names when the user types them into the address bar, or when used in a link on a Web page. Current versions of Mac OS X Safari, Mozilla's Firefox and the Netscape offerings are IDNA-aware. Here's an example of how you can verify this. Enter a URL such as `http://théâtre.qupps.biz` in your Web browser's URL bar, and assuming you're using a BIND server, look at its query log to see the query the server received:

```
client 192.168.1.181#2591: query: xn--thtre-4qa2c.qupps.biz IN A
```

which is correct – the IDN has been converted as expected.

However, Microsoft Windows Internet Explorer versions prior to version IE7 are not IDNA-capable. In this case the query you see in the log is:

```
client 192.168.1.181#3582: query: th\195\169\195\162tre.qupps.biz IN A
```

Figure 21.2 illustrates how IDNs are handled, emphasizing that the application displays IDNs but converts them ToASCII before looking them up in the DNS. The page we're connecting to in this example uses PHP's `phpinfo()` to show details about the server it's running on. You can see that our Mozilla Firefox browser, which supports IDNA, displays the internationalized domain name in the URL bar, whereas the server's real name is xn–thtre-4qa2c.qupps.biz – the ASCII conversion of the IDN.

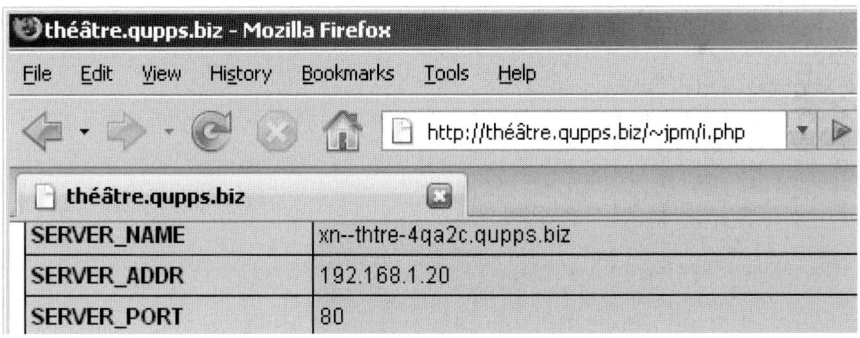

Figure 21.2: Mozilla Firefox supports IDN

The ISC has an open source plug-in for Internet Explorer versions 5 and 6 on Windows (see `http://idn.isc.org/`). Setting it up is trivial as it has a nice installer. Upon starting the plug-in, it appears in the Windows task bar and intercepts IDN URLs, converting them before giving them to the Windows DNS Client for resolution (Figure 21.3).

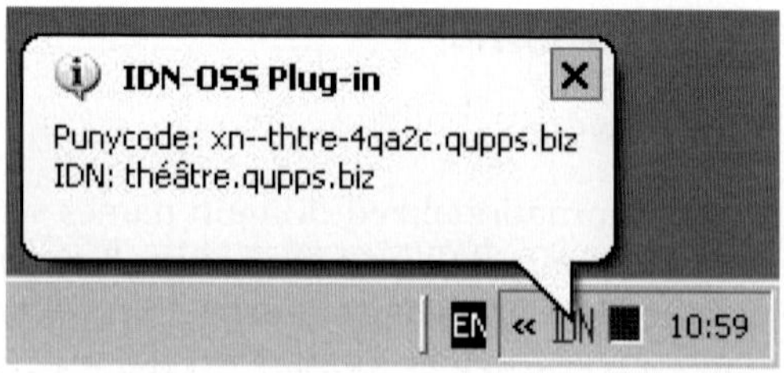

Figure 21.3: IDN OSS Plug-in on Microsoft Windows

21.3.2 Using IDNA in e-mail clients

On UNIX and GNU/Linux systems, the Mutt Mail User Agent (MUA) supports IDN, translating the domain names and submitting correct ACE domain names to the mail server for processing. Here is an example of a message which we received, that was sent with a Mutt e-mail client:

```
Envelope-to: alexi@xn--thtre-4qa2c.qupps.biz
Delivery-date: Sat, 08 Mar 2008 21:44:26 +0100
Received: from jpm by home.mens.de (Exim 4.43)
   with local (:userid=jpm) id 1JY5u6-0000sN-DA;
   for alexi@xn--thtre-4qa2c.qupps.biz; Sat, 08 Mar 2008 21:44:26 +0100
Date: Sat, 8 Mar 2008 21:44:26 +0100
From: Jan-Piet Mens <jp@home.mens.de>
To: Alexandra <alexi@théâtre.qupps.biz >
Subject: Connaissez vous IDNA?
Message-ID: <20080308204426.GB3237@home.mens.de>
MIME-Version: 1.0
Content-Type: text/plain; charset=us-ascii
Content-Disposition: inline
User-Agent: Mutt/1.5.16 (2007-06-09)

This is a test sent to an internationalized e-mail address.

        -JP
```

Neither Mozilla Thunderbird nor Microsoft Outlook Express support internationalized domain names; both programs warn the user, when setting up new accounts, that host names containing non-ASCII characters in them are illegal. When submitting a message for an internationalized e-mail address, both programs attempt to submit the non-ASCII characters in the domain name directly to the Mail Transfer Agent (MTA), which is illegal.

We didn't detect support for IDNA in any other popular e-mail clients, not even the commercial offerings. This would indicate that the market hasn't yet requested the feature.

21.3.3 Programming IDNA applications

If you are interested in adding IDNA capabilities to your own programs, check the following sources for the respective languages:

C

- The GNU IDN Library (libidn) implements an API for C, C# and Java (see `http://www.gnu.org/software/libidn/`).
- idnkit included in the `contrib` directory of the BIND source distribution.

Perl

- Net::LibIDN by Thomas Jacob. This module links against libidn.
- The Internet Mail Consortium has an IDNA test tool with Perl code at `http://www.imc.org/idna/`.
- Net::IDN::Encode from the Net-IDN-tools distribution on CPAN.

PHP

- The PHP API for the GNU LibIDN implementation. This was written by Turbo Fredriksson (see `http://php-idn.bayour.com/`).
- An online tool that allows translation of Unicode to Punycode names and links to a downloadable PHP class (see `http://idnaconv.phlymail.de/index.php`)

Python The `contrib` directory of the GNU libidn package contains a Python interface.

Summary

- DNS clients have to translate Internationalized Domain Names to ASCII before querying the DNS, because DNS servers *don't understand* non-ASCII domain names.
- Not all Web browsers and applications natively support IDNA.
- Two toolkits and a number of Application Programming Interfaces exist adding Internationalized Domain Name support to your own programs.

Notes and further reading

- Character sets and encoding are difficult topics, but you have to learn a bit about them to work with Unicode. We suggest you start your journey at `http://en.wikipedia.org/wiki/Character_encoding`
- The selection of the two-character ACE code ("xn") was performed with an interesting "protocol", described in (`http://www.atm.tut.fi/list-archive/ietf-announce/msg13572.html`).

Web interface to the libidn *toolkit*

A Web interface to the libidn toolkit is available at `http://josefsson.org/idn`

Preventing homograph spoofing attacks

There is little you and your users can do to protect yourselves against homograph spoofing attacks, although if you use Mozilla's Firefox Web browser or Thunderbird e-mail client, there are a few options available:

- Disable IDN support entirely by setting the preference `network.enableIDN` to false; the browser will neither parse nor attempt to resolve internationalized domain names (Figure 21.4).
- Whitelist individual TLDs by setting or clearing `network.IDN.whitelist.`*tld*.
- Force Firefox to show the Punycode URL instead of the IDN in the URL bar, by setting `network.IDN_show_punycode` (default is false).

Preference Name	Status	Type	Value
network.IDN_show_punycode	default	boolean	false
network.enableIDN	default	boolean	true
network.IDN.whitelist.dk	default	boolean	true

Figure 21.4: Firefox IDN settings in about:config

Chapter

22 Introducing DNSSEC

To give real service you must add something which cannot be bought or measured with money, and that is sincerity and integrity.

Douglas Adams

Introduction

The DNS was originally designed when security on the Internet was not a big issue so security wasn't built in. Attackers can compromise the DNS, and tamper with answers, causing users to connect to wrong, usually fraudulent, servers. DNSSEC – Secure DNS – overcomes this, by letting you verify that the DNS answers you receive are genuine. Even so, there are many other security issues that DNSSEC does *not* address.

22.1 The problem

If you receive an e-mail message from a national lottery saying you have won a million dollars, would you send off your bank details as requested, or would you check the message headers to see if the message is a forgery, because you know that e-mail messages can easily be forged? Something similar can happen with the DNS. If you visit your favorite daily news Web page, only to find a horrible site in your browser, do you think you clicked the wrong page, even though your browser is apparently displaying the correct address? In fact, the DNS answer your browser received when about to connect to the site may not have been genuine: DNS – just like SMTP – was not designed to withstand forgery. However, most people trust the DNS implicitly, and this can lead to clients contacting bad servers, which can cause financial losses or damage to your organization. (At a personal level, think what would happen if you thought you'd paid for something with Payfriend, but the DNS had been compromised, so that instead of giving your browser the IP address of the real payfriend.com, it gave the IP address of a criminal site instead.)

In the DNS, replies from authoritative servers can be replaced by spoofed data, somewhere on the path between the authoritative server and your caching servers that sent the request. DNSSEC attempts to solve this problem by adding a "transparent envelope" around DNS replies:

- This envelope is sealed (i.e. licked closed and stamped) by the authoritative server. The recipient can verify that the content – the DNS answer – has not been altered. The server "seals" the envelope with cryptographic functions that we describe in Section 22.2.

- The envelope is transparent: anybody can see its content – which is the DNS answer. This is important, for two reasons:

  1. The system is "backwards compatible". DNS clients that do not support DNSSEC can still use the reply as normal, but DNSSEC-aware clients get the benefits of the extra security.

  2. DNSSEC does not make your DNS queries and replies confidential. (It was not designed to do so.)

The next section is a short introduction to cryptography, which we need because DNSSEC uses standard cryptographic techniques, and because DNSSEC solves some management problems in a way similar to some other cryptographic systems. After that we explain:

- If you run your own authoritative servers: how you can use DNSSEC so that clients (within your own organization, or on the public Internet) can verify they are receiving genuine answers for your domains (Section 22.4.3).

- If you administer caching name servers: how to use configure your caching servers to use DNSSEC to validate DNS replies (Section 22.5).

22.2 A very brief introduction to cryptography

You can keep information confidential, even when transmitted in public, by encrypting it – transforming it in some way, so that (ideally) only the recipient can un-transform it and view the original content. Broadly, there are two general forms of encryption: *symmetric* (*secret key*) encryption, and *asymmetric* (*public key*) encryption, which we now describe.

22.2.1 Symmetric encryption

Symmetric or Secret key encryption has been used for thousands of years. It includes any form of encryption in which the same key is used to both encrypt and decrypt the information (Figure 22.1).

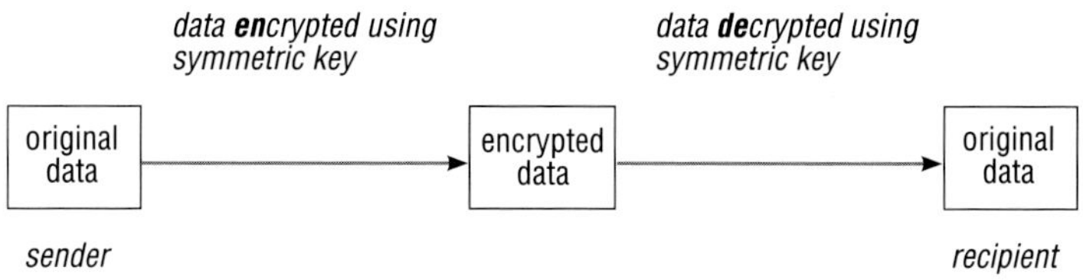

Figure 22.1: Symmetric encryption

As an example, suppose your encryption algorithm consists of "rotating" the letters in your message, and the key specifies how many positions to rotate by. For example, a key of 2 means A rotates to C, B to D, C to E, etc. The algorithm is public, but the key is secret, although susceptible to brute-force attacks (start off with key = 1, key = 2, ...). You use the same key to encrypt (rotate forward by 2 positions) and to decrypt (rotate back by 2 positions). A very popular example is the ROT13 substitution cipher (popular with Usenet postings), that uses key = 13. For example, if you apply ROT13 to the very secret message "`Nygreangvir QAF Freiref`" you get the title of the book you hold in your hands, and when you apply ROT13 to the title of this book, you get the secret message above.

Symmetric cryptography is fast, but it has a number of problems:

- The key has to be known to all parties that communicate with each other. If Alice and Bob want to exchange messages, both need the key, and they must exchange that key securely, e.g. by Alice visiting Bob and giving him a printout or a USB drive containing the key.

- The more parties involved in communication, the more have to know the key. If Alice and Bob want to exchange messages with Charlie, Charlie needs to know Alice's and Bob's key, and he can then also decrypt messages that Alice had intended for Bob's eyes only.

- Symmetric keys usually don't expire, so there is no method by which you can conveniently stop somebody who knows your key decrypting your messages. If Alice and Bob decide they don't like Charlie any longer, they have to create a new key and use that instead. (Charlie knows the first key.)

22.2.2 Asymmetric encryption

Public key (asymmetric) encryption solves the problems of symmetric encryption by using two different keys:

1. A private key, which you keep secret.
2. A public key, which you make public. Public keys are typically published in directory systems, or on a Web page. They can also be transported via insecure mechanisms such as via an e-mail.

The two keys are called a *key pair*, and they are mathematically related (see Notes).

Consider Figure 22.2: the sender has a copy of the recipient's public key, and he uses that to encrypt a message with the recipient's public key before transmitting it. A message encrypted to a public key can only be decrypted by the corresponding private key; the sender is sure that only the owner of the private key can see the sender's message. So even though both Alice and Bob have used the same key to encrypt their messages, neither can read the other's message; everyone can use the same public key to send to Carol, without any loss of security.

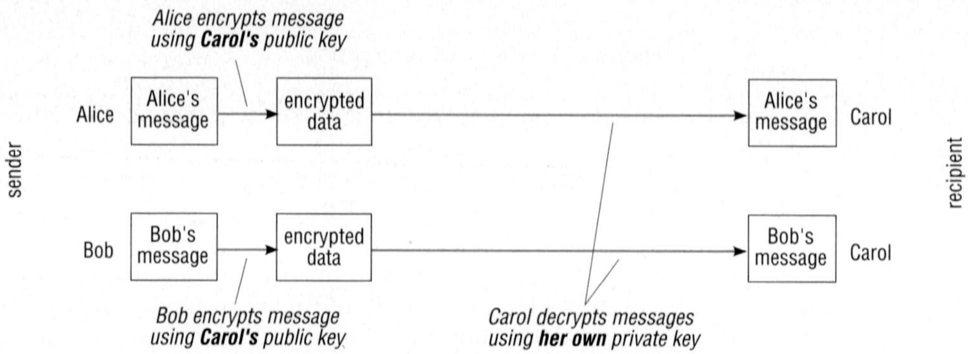

Figure 22.2: Asymmetric encryption

Because public keys are, well, *public*, they are readily available and don't have to be protected. This deals with the problem of key distribution: the public key can be transmitted by any means, even insecurely over e-mail for example, without endangering confidentiality.

Asymmetric cryptography is slow because of the very large computations involved. Because of this, it is often combined with symmetric cryptography, which is much faster: asymmetric encryption is used for an initial brief conversation, e.g. to agree on a shared secret, and then the shared secret is used with symmetric encryption for the real task of exchanging larger quantities of data securely.

You are already using public key encryption if you use PGP or S/MIME for your e-mail, and you have certainly used public key encryption when you visited an online shopping site with your Web browser. The Transport Layer Security (TLS) protocol (formerly Secure Socket Layer (SSL) protocol) uses public key encryption to encrypt the communication between your Web browser and a TLS-enabled Web server. When your browser first connects to the server, the server sends its public key to the browser. Your browser then encrypts a random number with the public key of the server (which it now has) and sends that encrypted number back to the server. Only the server can decrypt that number, as only it holds the corresponding private key. Based on that initial encrypted exchange, the client Web browser and Web server then generate new, symmetric, keys that are used for encryption of the rest of the communication.

So far we've only shown how you can use public key cryptography to preserve the confidentiality of data, by encrypting it. In the next Section we show you how a sender can use public key cryptography to "sign" data: anybody who has the sender's public key can verify that it really was the sender who sent the message, and that the message was not altered in transit.

22.2.3 Using public key encryption

Signatures, hashes and digests – verifying the sender of a message

An important feature of public key cryptography is that a message encrypted with a private key can be decrypted by its corresponding public key, and not just the other way round. If our bank sends us something encrypted with their private key, we can decrypt it with *their* public key (Figure 22.3). While that doesn't keep the contents of the message confidential, it *does* give us a way of proving that it was the bank and not some intruder that sent us the message. Later on, we'll see that this functionality is crucial to DNSSEC: we will want to be sure that the server sending us DNS answers really is the authoritative server.

As we said, asymmetric encryption is slow, so to save time, instead of encrypting a whole message, we send the message in clear text, and attach a public key *digital signature*. This is the computing equivalent of a handwritten signature: both prove that the sender is who we think he is. Here's how digital signatures work.

Loosely, what we do is "summarize" the message, and then encrypt the summary with our private key. The recipient decrypts the encrypted summary, using our *public* key, so they now have a copy of our summary. They make their own summary of the clear-text message: if their summary is the same as ours, they know we genuinely sent the message, because nobody else could have encrypted with our private key, and the decryption wouldn't have worked if any other key had been used to encrypt it.

Formally, to summarize the message we use a *hash* function; this takes a message of any length as input, and produces a fixed-length output called a *message digest* (which is our "summary"). The output of hash functions is short – between about 20 and 64 bytes – irrespective of the size of the input message. Popular hash functions include: MD4, MD5, SHA-1, and SHA-256.

A hash function is considered secure if it's "one-way" (given the output, it's computationally infeasible to find what the input message was) and if it's computationally infeasible to find two different messages that produce the same message digest as output.

As an example, the MD5 hash value of the file containing the text of this chapter[1] is `ce5eca7d2ee7044782eae8c3b301ad99`. If we change the first lowercase "d" in the chapter

[1] At the time it was written; the book's editor is sure to ~~mess up~~ alter the MD5 hash of the chapter before you get to see it...

to the letter "e", and apply the same MD5 hash algorithm, it gives us a completely different hash value: `c3b8dad3fd116b85a0219a44102a36fa`.

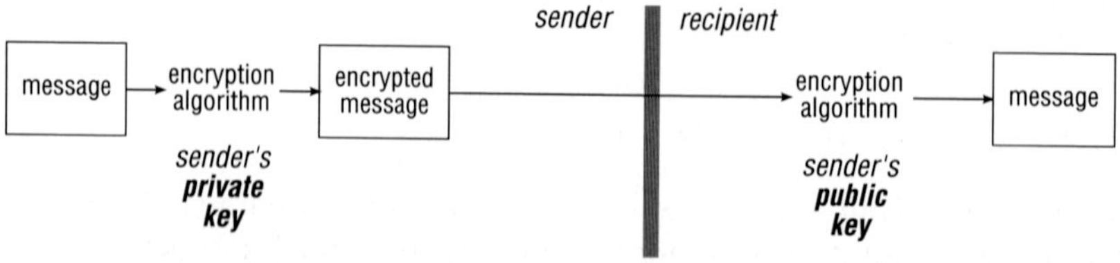

Figure 22.3: Verifying the contents of a message – simple but slow method

Figure 22.4 shows how a hash function (i.e. a message digest algorithm) is used to create a digital signature, which is then attached to the clear-text messages to prove it is authentic. (We use the term "message", which suggests an electronic mail message, but the term is not limited to e-mail. It refers to an arbitrary set of data, such as DNS queries and replies transmitted between DNS clients and name servers.)

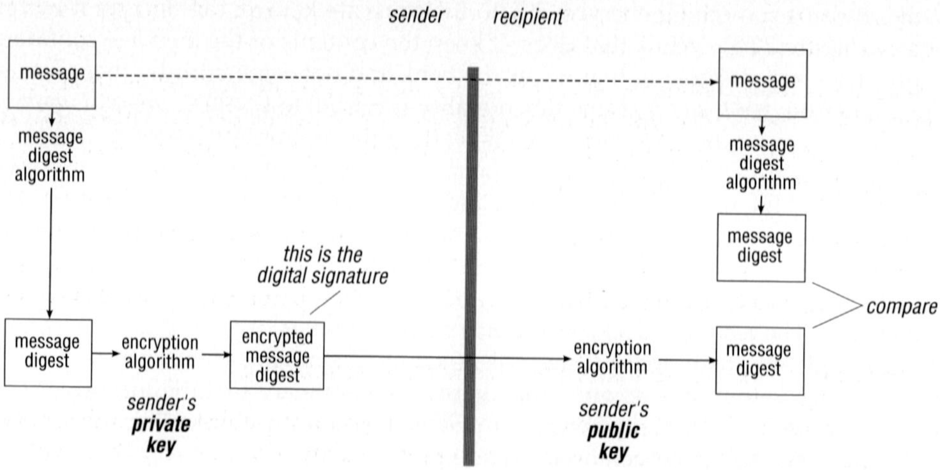

Figure 22.4: Using a digital signature to verify the contents of a message

1. The sender runs the message through a one-way hash function (message digest algorithm) to create a message digest. He encrypts this message digest using his own private key to produce a digital signature, which he attaches to the message.

2. To authenticate the message, the recipient detaches the digital signature and decrypts it with the sender's public key, to obtain the original message digest. He runs the clear-text message through the same hash function, to produce a second message digest; if this is identical to the original message digest, the recipient knows the message is authentic.

Note that in the steps above, the sender wanted to prove that he sent the message; he wasn't concerned about the confidentiality of the message, and sent it in clear. To have made the message confidential as well as verifiable, he could have *additionally* encrypted the message with the recipient's public key.

Typical applications of public key cryptography

Once Alice and Bob have their own separate key pairs, and have exchanged public keys, they can use public key cryptography to perform many different, useful, tasks:

- When Alice wants to send Bob a secret message she encrypts it with Bob's public key. By doing that, she well knows that only Bob will be able to decrypt the message[2]. When Bob receives Alice's message, he uses his private key to decrypt the message.

  Note that the message Bob has successfully been able to decrypt could have been sent by anybody with access to his public key. There is no way to determine from the encrypted message sent by Alice, that it was Alice who actually sent it. To solve that problem...

- Alice owes Bob some money and he wants her to send him an IOU, but he wants to be quite sure that it is from Alice, so he asks her to sign it.

  Alice signs the message by encrypting it with her private key. When Bob gets the message, if he can decrypt the message with Alice's public key, he knows that Alice sent it. Note once again that the security of the private key remains a very important aspect of public key cryptography.

- Both Alice and Bob can encrypt and digitally sign a message they send to one another. By doing so, they ensure that no third party can read the message (because it is encrypted), and that the recipient can verify who the sender is (because it is signed).

Ensuring public keys are genuine: certificates and authorities

We said in Section 22.2.2 that a public key is public: you can publish it in a directory, on the Internet, for example, without compromising the security of your encryption. But when Bob retrieves Alice's public key from the directory, how does he know that it really is Alice's public key and not a key introduced by Eve? (If Eve can trick Bob into mistaking her public key for Alice's, then Eve can pretend to be Alice when communicating with Bob.)

This problem is solved by having trusted organizations called *Certification Authorities* (*CA*s). A CA generates a *certificate* for Alice. Alice's certificate is a message containing Alice's name and her public key (and perhaps additional information, such as her e-mail address, locality, country of residence, etc.), signed with the CA's private key.

The Certification Authority also has public keys which everyone trusts (because they have been distributed to computers with the software that uses them – e-mail clients and Web browsers). Bob imports the CA's keys into his computer system via an out-of-band mechanism (software distribution, magnetic data carriers, etc.). Once Bob trusts the CA's

[2]Unless Bob has been very stupid and has shared his private key with somebody...

public key (called the CA's *root certificate*) and the CA's integrity, he can trust certificates that the CA has issued. Therefore he can now trust Alice's certificate, and can use that to verify that her public key is genuine. Because Bob trusts the CA, he trusts certificates issued by the CA; this process results in a *chain of trust*.

Certificates can be, and are, published in directories. While an intruder might be able to create or modify a certificate in the directory, the affected certificate won't be valid: the intruder can't produce a valid certificate, because only the CA can generate the correct signature on it.

Certificates generally contain an expiration date, after which they should not be trusted any longer. (You have probably seen warning messages in your Web browser when visiting sites with expired certificates.) Certification Authorities also publish *Certificate Revocation Lists* (*CRLs*) containing lists of certificates that have been revoked. These are used, for example, when a private key has been reported lost or stolen.

You can create your own CA within your organization, and there are several tools for this: Lotus Domino has a CA database, Microsoft Windows provides the functionality in its server component, and the OpenSSL tool chain lets you create your own CA. However, creating your own CA creates an isolated *island of trust*: certificates issued by your own CA are trusted only within your own organization, and not by third parties. To set up trust with third parties, you must explicitly exchange the root certificate(s) of your CA with them out of band, and have them explicitly recognize your certificates as trustworthy.

As we shall see in Section 22.5.1, key distribution is a major issue in DNSSEC, because name servers must exchange keys in order to validate DNS replies. We will be using public and private keys later in the chapter, but we won't be using certification authorities at all – we discussed them only as an analogy for the DNS' own system for key distribution, which is DLV (Section 22.7).

That completes our introduction to general cryptography, and we discuss DNSSEC now.

22.3 An overview of DNSSEC

DNSSEC is complex, and it is difficult to deploy. Quoting Paul Vixie (of DNS fame)[3]:

> DNSSEC is the worst design-by-committee effort I've ever seen, both in terms of how late it is, how fuzzy the goals have been, how often the goals have changed, and how complicated and heavy it is now that it is trying to be all-things-to-all-people.

DNSSEC ensures the *integrity* of the DNS data. It is specifically *not* intended to keep your DNS data confidential (which would be quite stupid, as nobody would be able to connect to your services), nor does it improve the availability of your DNS data. (It might even degrade it as we'll see in Section 22.9.)

DNSSEC uses asymmetric public key encryption. If a caching name server receives an answer from an authoritative server and DNSSEC validates the answer successfully, then you know that:

[3] `http://psg.com/lists/namedroppers/namedroppers.2006/msg01514.html`

- The reply came from an authoritative source for that data.
- The reply has not been altered between the authoritative name server and your caching name server.
- If the authoritative name server says that a host does not exist (NXDOMAIN), you can believe it.

22.3.1 The scope of DNS data integrity in DNSSEC

DNSSEC ensures the integrity of the data only between name servers that implement DNSSEC, but not beyond: it is not end-to-end. For example, in Figure 22.5, the caching name server and the authoritative name server exchange DNSSEC messages, but the workstation clients that use the caching name server don't.

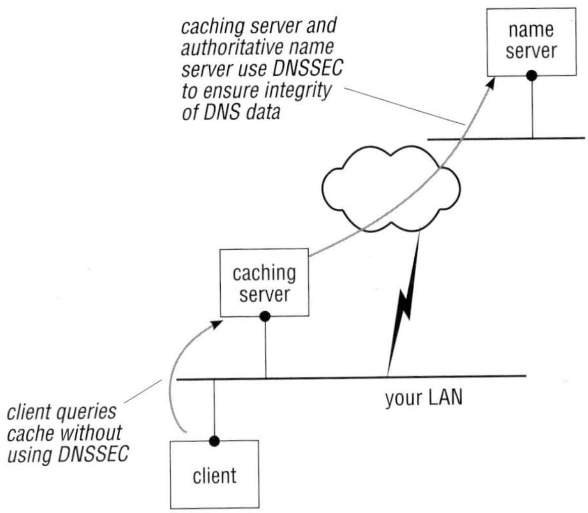

Figure 22.5: DNSSEC is not an end-to-end encryption of DNS

To understand the difference between an end-to-end encryption and one that only encrypts a portion of the path, consider this analogy with electronic mail:

1. When you send an e-mail, your Mail User Agent might securely connect to your e-mail provider via SSL or TLS to deliver the message. Your provider then typically passes your message on to its final destination (possibly via other hosts) unencrypted. Similarly, when you use a Web browser to "securely" access your on-line e-mail account, the interaction between your Web browser and the HTTP server that shows your messages, is secured, but any mail you send is not. In both cases, only a portion of the path uses encryption.
2. If, on the other hand, you use S/MIME or PGP to encrypt your messages, they are encrypted by your e-mail client and are transported encrypted to their final destination mail box. This is end-to-end encryption.

DNSSEC is more like the first example: it secures traffic from the authoritative name server to your local caching server, and it will typically not secure DNS traffic all the way to your workstation[4]. Note however, that it is typically acceptable to "stop" at the caching name server because from there on the traffic is within your organization and you trust its network.

22.3.2 How a zone file is signed for DNSSEC

DNSSEC protects clients from forged DNS data by adding additional information to DNS replies. The information allows clients to check that the response is authentic and complete. To achieve this, DNSSEC uses public/private keys to sign zone data, and it adds the signatures and other DNSSEC information to the zone file, in the form of several additional DNS resource records.

Now let's look at how you sign a zone file, and what the resulting signed zone file looks like. The numbers in the list below refer to items in the Figure on page 515 (which you can also print from our Web site (☞ D221), for ease of reference). This overview emphasizes the broad principles of operation; for precise details of the new resource record types see the Notes.

0. The starting point is the (small) zone for es.qupps.biz which we're going to sign. The original zone file contains four resource records, and three RRsets or resource record sets, because the two A records make up a single RRset. (Remember, an RRset is a collection of resource records that share a common domain name, class and type.)

1. We generate two key pairs for this zone, using the dnssec-keygen program. One key pair is the *Key Signing Key* (*KSK*) and the other is the *Zone Signing Key* (*ZSK*). We explain why we use two keys in Section 22.4.1. We will use the notation X_{priv} to mean "the private key of key pair X" (and X_{pub} to mean the corresponding public key).

   We manually insert the KSK_{pub} and ZSK_{pub} into the zone file, in the form of DNSKEY resource records. For clarity, in the figure we show newly-inserted records with their record type in bold. Later on, clients will use these keys when verifying answers from this zone's server.

```
es.qupps.biz.      86400   DNSKEY  257 3 5 (
                                   uuNP35sG1rfIWH0ZM64mSEs7vxv8+2kRNEUX
                                   +Q0=
                                   ) ; key id = 29062
es.qupps.biz.      86400   DNSKEY  256 3 5 (
                                   nKA+tqy11Mex0JpfsIc8HuXWaeoq1/9w5Pzq
                                   ) ; key id = 56172
```

2. We run the dnssec-signzone program on the zone file containing the DNSKEY resource records. We discuss this utility in detail in Section 22.4.2: it does all the hard work, and signs the contents of the zone file with the *private* keys of the key pairs we generated in step 1, above. The rest of this section explains in detail what dnssec-signzone has done,

[4] To achieve end-to-end security, you'd have to install and run a caching name server that supports DNSSEC, such as Unbound, on each of your workstations.

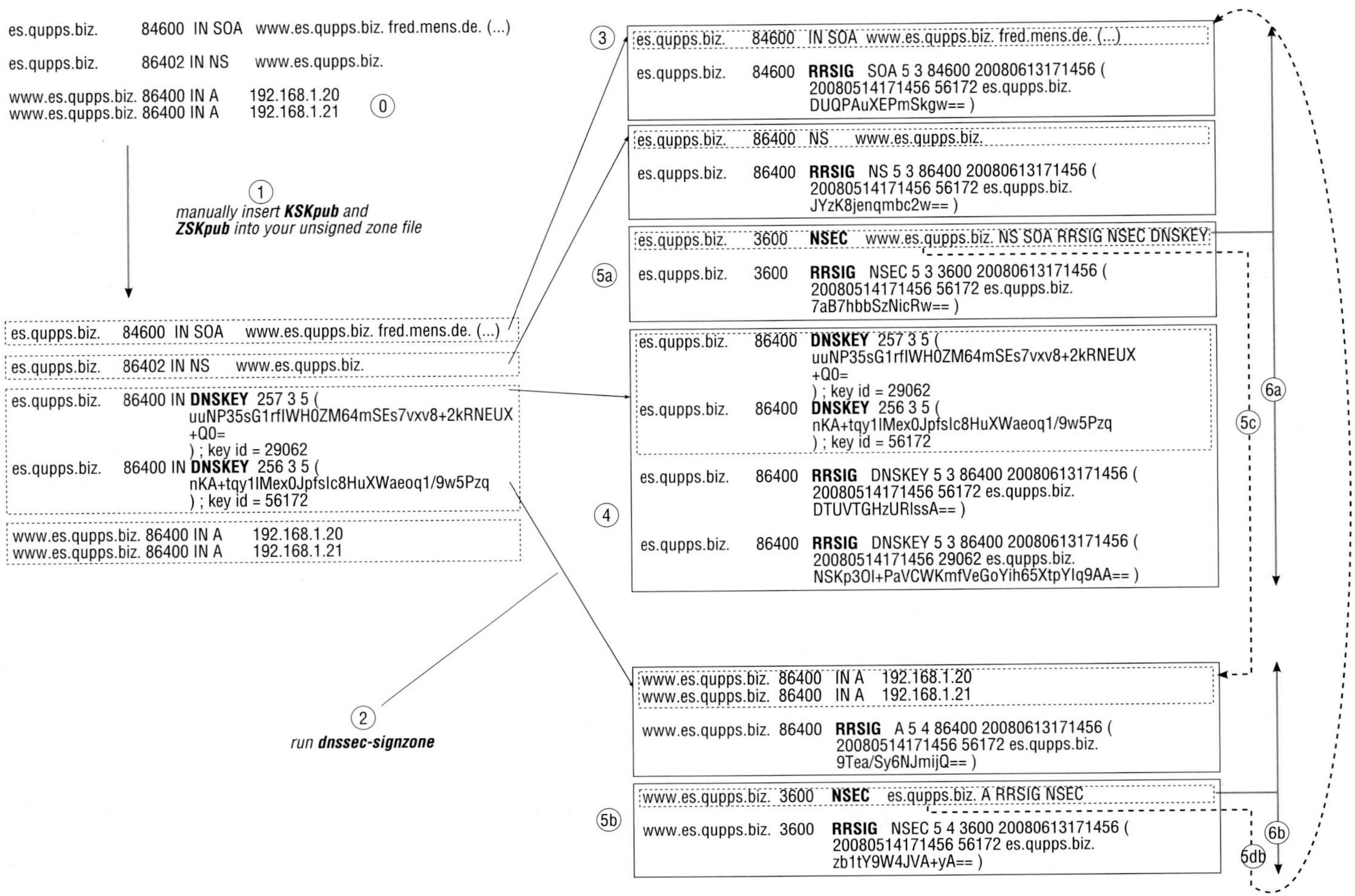
es.qupps.biz. 84600 IN SOA www.es.qupps.biz. fred.mens.de. (...)
es.qupps.biz. 86402 IN NS www.es.qupps.biz.
www.es.qupps.biz. 86400 IN A 192.168.1.20
www.es.qupps.biz. 86400 IN A 192.168.1.21
0
1
manually insert KSKpub and ZSKpub into your unsigned zone file
es.qupps.biz. 84600 IN SOA www.es.qupps.biz. fred.mens.de. (...)
es.qupps.biz. 86402 IN NS www.es.qupps.biz.
es.qupps.biz. 86400 IN DNSKEY 257 3 5 (
uuNP35sG1rfIWH0ZM64mSEs7vxv8+2kRNEUX
+Q0=
) ; key id = 29062
es.qupps.biz. 86400 IN DNSKEY 256 3 5 (
nKA+tqy1IMex0JpfsIc8HuXWaeoq1/9w5Pzq
) ; key id = 56172
www.es.qupps.biz. 86400 IN A 192.168.1.20
www.es.qupps.biz. 86400 IN A 192.168.1.21
2
run dnssec-signzone
3
es.qupps.biz. 84600 IN SOA www.es.qupps.biz. fred.mens.de. (...)
es.qupps.biz. 84600 RRSIG SOA 5 3 84600 20080613171456 (
20080514171456 56172 es.qupps.biz.
DUQPAuXEPmSkgw==)
es.qupps.biz. 86400 NS www.es.qupps.biz.
es.qupps.biz. 86400 RRSIG NS 5 3 86400 20080613171456 (
20080514171456 56172 es.qupps.biz.
JYzK8jenqmbc2w==)
5a
es.qupps.biz. 3600 NSEC www.es.qupps.biz. NS SOA RRSIG NSEC DNSKEY
es.qupps.biz. 3600 RRSIG NSEC 5 3 3600 20080613171456 (
20080514171456 56172 es.qupps.biz.
7aB7hbbSzNicRw==)
4
es.qupps.biz. 86400 DNSKEY 257 3 5 (
uuNP35sG1rfIWH0ZM64mSEs7vxv8+2kRNEUX
+Q0=
) ; key id = 29062
es.qupps.biz. 86400 DNSKEY 256 3 5 (
nKA+tqy1IMex0JpfsIc8HuXWaeoq1/9w5Pzq
) ; key id = 56172
es.qupps.biz. 86400 RRSIG DNSKEY 5 3 86400 20080613171456 (
20080514171456 56172 es.qupps.biz.
DTUVTGHzURIssA==)
es.qupps.biz. 86400 RRSIG DNSKEY 5 3 86400 20080613171456 (
20080514171456 29062 es.qupps.biz.
NSKp3OI+PaVCWKmfVeGoYih65XtpYIq9AA==)
www.es.qupps.biz. 86400 IN A 192.168.1.20
www.es.qupps.biz. 86400 IN A 192.168.1.21
www.es.qupps.biz. 86400 RRSIG A 5 4 86400 20080613171456 (
20080514171456 56172 es.qupps.biz.
9Tea/Sy6NJmijQ==)
5b
www.es.qupps.biz. 3600 NSEC es.qupps.biz. A RRSIG NSEC
www.es.qupps.biz. 3600 RRSIG NSEC 5 4 3600 20080613171456 (
20080514171456 56172 es.qupps.biz.
zb1tY9W4JVA+yA==)
6a
5c
6b
5db

and how this can secure a zone. But bear in mind that all this resulted from a single command: the amount of work *we* had to do was very small.

3. For each RRset, dnssec-signzone generates a digital signature, and inserts it immediately after the RRset, in the form of an RRSIG record. To help us keep track of what's happening, the RRSIG contains the original RRtype of the record that the RRSIG refers to. (The example RRSIG record below relates to an SOA RRset.) Later on, clients will use the RRSIG to verify that the contents of this RRset are unchanged, and that they were sent by the genuine authoritative server.

```
es.qupps.biz.        84600    RRSIG    SOA 5 3 84600 20080613171456 (
                                       20080514171456 56172 es.qupps.biz.
                                       DUQPAuXEPmSkgw== )
```

Our small zone started off with three RRsets, so dnssec-signzone inserts three RRSIGs – one for each.

The reason why DNSSEC signs RRsets and not the individual resource records, and not the zone file as a whole, is that a name server replies to a query with the RRset and not individual RRs.

4. Back in step 1 we manually added another RRset – the two DNSKEYS – so dnssec-signzone has to sign this RRset too. In fact, dnssec-signzone signs this RRset twice: once with KSK_{priv} and once with ZSK_{priv}, so it inserts *two* RRSIGS for this RRset (and only this one – all other RRsets get just a single RRSIG).

```
es.qupps.biz.        86400    DNSKEY   257 3 5 (
                                       uuNP35sG1rfIWH0ZM64mSEs7vxv8+2kRNEUX
                                       +Q0=
                                       ) ; key id = 29062
es.qupps.biz.        86400    DNSKEY   256 3 5 (
                                       nKA+tqy11Mex0JpfsIc8HuXWaeoq1/9w5Pzq
                                       ) ; key id = 56172

es.qupps.biz.        86400    RRSIG    DNSKEY 5 3 86400 20080613171456 (
                                       20080514171456 56172 es.qupps.biz.
                                       DTUVTGHzURlssA== )

es.qupps.biz.        86400    RRSIG    DNSKEY 5 3 86400 20080613171456 (
                                       20080514171456 29062 es.qupps.biz.
                                       NSKp3Ol+PaVCWKmfVeGoYih65XtpYIq9AA== )
```

5a,b,c,d The RRSIG records let a client verify that RRsets returned in DNS answers are genuine. However, DNSSEC has to protect against one more risk: that an intruder might spoof a reply, stating incorrectly that a requested domain doesn't exist. How do you verify that a negative answer (NXDOMAIN) is genuine? Digital signing doesn't help, because by definition, there is no RRset to return.

DNSSEC solves this using *Next Secure* (NSEC) resource records. DNSSEC sorts the domain names in the signed zone in a particular order, and for each distinct domain name (as opposed to each RRset) inserts an NSEC (5a, 5b) that points from this name to the next one. Let's say mail and www are successive domain names in our signed zone file. If a client queries for smtp (which, if it existed, would sort between mail and www) the server will reply with an NXDOMAIN. The way DNSSEC protects this is by returning mail's NSEC record in the NXDOMAIN answer. The NSEC points to www as the next domain name in the file: in other words, there are no domains between mail and www, so the client knows the NXDOMAIN for smtp is genuine. 5c in the figure shows how the NSEC for es.qupps.biz points to www.es.qupps.biz, and then the NSEC for www.es.qupps.biz (5d) points back to the beginning of the zone file, to show that this is the last domain name in the zone.

Of course, the client must be able to verify that the NSEC itself is genuine, so DNSSEC signs all the NSEC RRsets, as usual. (DNSSEC has inserted seven RRSIGs in total.)

```
es.qupps.biz.       3600     NSEC     www.es.qupps.biz. NS SOA RRSIG NSEC DNSKEY

es.qupps.biz.       3600     RRSIG    NSEC 5 3 3600 20080613171456 (
                                      20080514171456 56172 es.qupps.biz.
                                      7aB7hbbSzNicRw== )
```

6a,b The last thing DNSSEC has to protect is another aspect of NXDOMAIN operation: how to verify a reply that says an existing domain doesn't contain a record of the requested type. For example, how do you verify an NXDOMAIN for an MX for www.es.qupps.biz? The NSEC as described above doesn't help, because domain www.es.qupps.biz does exist and contains several resource records – it just doesn't have an MX.

DNSSEC solves this by including in each NSEC record a list of the record types that *do* exist for this domain. For example, www.es.qupps.biz's NSEC says www has A, RRSIG and NSEC records. If the server returns this NSEC with the NXDOMAIN for the MX, we know the NXDOMAIN is genuine.

That's how DNSSEC signs a zone, and how the information in the signed zone lets a DNSSEC client verify the answers it receives from the DNSSEC-enabled server. Now we have to explain how you implement this – first of all on the authoritative servers for the DNSSEC signed zones, and after that on caching servers that want to use DNSSEC to verify answers from authoritative servers.

22.4 Implementing DNSSEC on an authoritative server

Figure 22.6 shows the steps involved in implementing DNSSEC on your authoritative servers:

A. Create the necessary keys for signing your zones.

B. Sign your zones with these keys.

C. Configure your authoritative name servers to provide the signed zones via DNS. Currently the only servers you can use for this are NSD and BIND.

D. Provide the necessary information (public keys) about your signed zones to the administrators of caching servers that want to validate answers from your authoritative servers.

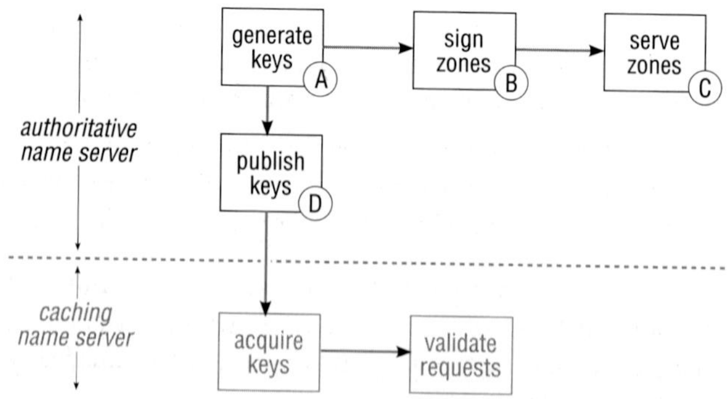

Figure 22.6: Steps for signing and publishing zones

22.4.1 A – Generating your keys

When signing a zone file, you use two different types of key pairs:

- The Zone Signing Key (ZSK_{priv}) is used to sign every RRset within the zone; the corresponding ZSK_{pub} is inserted in the zone file as a DNSKEY record at the zone's apex. For example, when you sign a zone called es.qupps.biz, the public key ZSK_{pub} is in a DNSKEY record for domain name es.qupps.biz.

- The Key Signing Key (KSK_{priv}) is used to sign only the keys at the apex of a zone, i.e. the DNSKEY RRset; the corresponding KSK_{pub} is inserted in the zone file as a DNSKEY record at the zone's apex. (So, at the apex of every DNSSEC zone, you expect to see two DNSKEYs – one the KSK and the other the ZSK.)

  Later on (Section 22.5.1) you will give a copy of your KSK_{pub} to caching server owners that want to DNSSEC-validate answers from your zone.

Note that the DNSKEYs themselves form an RRset, which – like every other RRset – is signed with ZSK_{priv}. It is this RRset, not just the ZSK_{pub} DNSKEY, that is signed with the KSK_{priv}, adding another RRSIG. Therefore, at the apex of every DNSSEC zone, you expect to see two RRSIGs as well as two DNSKEYs.

DNSKEY records (Figure 22.9 on page 540) contain a "flags" field, indicating what type of key this is:

256 This value indicates that the key is a ZSK.

257 This value indicates that the key is a KSK.

Why two separate keys?

The DNSSEC protocol does not distinguish between ZSK and KSK keys (so you could make do with a single key pair). We recommend you *do* use two different keys because:

- You can update (i.e. renew) your ZSK without having to inform anybody else. This lets you manage your signed zones, and change keys ("roll over" keys, see Notes) frequently, which is good security practice, with minimum effort.

  (By contrast, administrators of caching servers that use DNSSEC to validate data from your server have to have a copy of your KSK_{pub}. Therefore, when you change your KSK, a lot have people have to be informed, or else something will break.)

- You can afford to create a stronger KSK (a key with more bits), as you use it to sign only a small amount of zone data. And you want a stronger KSK, because you are likely not to change it as frequently as your ZSK – because of the need to inform other people, as we explained above.

There are two widely-available tools you can use to create keys and sign zones. In our examples we use dnssec-keygen from the BIND distribution, because it's more widespread, but you could use the tools from the ldns package (see Notes).

Creating your Zone Signing Key (ZSK) :

Create the Zone Signing Key (ZSK) for the zone using the command below. Option `-r` specifies the source of random data (see Notes), `-a` the key algorithm, `-b` the key length in bits and `-n` that we are signing a zone. The last argument is the name of the zone file we are signing.

```
$ dnssec-keygen -r /dev/random -a RSASHA1 -b 512 -n ZONE es.qupps.biz.zone
Kes.qupps.biz.+005+56172
```

This command creates two files in the current directory. The file names begin with the string that dnssec-keygen prints to standard output:

`.key` Contains the public key (i.e. ZSK_{pub}) in the form of a DNSKEY resource record.

```
es.qupps.biz. IN DNSKEY 256 3 5 AwEAAaRYLrJ6+tDtTDfnKA+↩
                            tqy1lMex0JpfsIc8 HuXWaqFlGMHFttlDA8=
```

In Section 22.4.2 you will include this file without change in your zone master file. The key's flag value of 256 indicates it should be used as a Zone Signing Key, and not as a Key Signing Key.

`.private` Contains the private key (i.e. ZSK_{priv}), that you keep securely, and *never* publish.

```
Private-key-format: v1.2
Algorithm: 5 (RSASHA1)
Modulus: pFgd6BrqHtZKGBfouYNLusO1MN+cHQml+whzwe5dZp...
PublicExponent: AQAB
PrivateExponent: QGbPgW9ao67x5jDr5Lw658mSwyf9d7C...
Prime1: z3qdb+Pw42QnoF3qaF68jx1AOdEPuvyVykyzSyc=
Prime2: yscaXIQNMJrGbAeHCO+bknlj+baqrE+jnaeZ6Nk=
Exponent1: nyvsOHjgxzKBDBDA0o1LP5shfjmbHdLFf8vUCSU=
Exponent2: Uac3EEYEYawRdnLZh1mk/y12/pj1xQkUo2lX6pE=
Coefficient: XzbHBHsv5ODiiBO5NszG6SSTx8x/IQHtVhTiNKM=
```

Creating your Key Signing Key (KSK) :

To create a Key Signing Key (KSK), use dnssec-keygen's `-f` option, to indicate that the program should generate a KSK:

```
$ dnssec-keygen -a RSASHA1 -b 1280 -n ZONE -f KSK es.qupps.biz.zone
Kes.qupps.biz.+005+29062
```

The program prints the so-called *key tag* as the last number in its output (29062 here); this is in effect a numeric name or ID for the key, and lets you refer conveniently to a particular key. As for the ZSK, this command creates two files: the `.key` file (KSK_{pub}) and the `.private` file (KSK_{priv}). The key's flags are set to 257, indicating it is a KSK:

```
es.qupps.biz. IN DNSKEY 257 3 5 AwEAAbyaEjQit0Evpo6C9qgh7maTf+ThQkB8Y58↩
                                TZN/bWuJOSxNpHYkMhjhuC3Pmc68nEf3AYgxCee↩
                                OD0pzTCryG2aXruy8MGVee9A3pobw0FA3A8e0HX↩
                                Qwf2J8p8XYIk5SBI4U2xEtXZtUkH1efBxSbzDk9↩
                                hXLjRY92qVOUNTbJs1ONNjY7uuNP35sG1rfIWH0↩
                                ZM64mSEs7vxv8+2kRNEUX+Q0=
```

We store the key files for a zone with that zone's zone file, but in a subdirectory appropriately called `keys`.

Here are a few points to keep in mind regarding your keys:

- Don't rename the files that are produced by the key generation tools.
- Use `$INCLUDE` statements to embed key files in your zone files, instead of cutting and pasting the file contents. That way, it's easier to see where a particular key came from and what it refers to.
- Key sizes: as we said in Section 22.4.1, your KSK can be larger than your ZSK, because it is used less frequently. The larger the key size, the more resistant your keys will be to brute-force attacks, but the larger your signed zones will be, too. In the sections that follow, we use short key lengths so that our listings are readable, but in real life you will normally use key lengths of 1 024 bits or longer: perhaps 1 024 bits for the ZSK, and 1 280 bits for the KSK. (dnssec-keygen can generate keys of up to 4 096 bits.)

22.4.2 B – Sign the zone with your keys

1. Include the public keys of both key pairs in your zone file, either copying and pasting, or with the `$INCLUDE` directive which both BIND and NSD support, as in:

```
$INCLUDE keys/Kes.qupps.biz.+005+56172.key;    Zone Signing Key
$INCLUDE keys/Kes.qupps.biz.+005+29062.key;    Key Signing Key
```

2. Increment your zone's SOA serial number.
3. Sign the zone with dnssec-signzone:

```
$ dnssec-signzone \
            -k keys/Kes.qupps.biz.+005+29062 \          KSK
            es.qupps.biz.zone \                         zone file
es.qupps.biz.zone.signed
```

Option `-k` specifies the filename prefix of the KSK's `.key` and `.private` files. The first non-option argument is the name of the zone file that is to be signed. To sign the resource records, dnssec-signzone uses the ZSK_{priv} that corresponds to the ZSK_{pub} that's in the zone file.

Run as above, the dnssec-signzone program produces three files:

`.signed` This is the most important: it contains the result of the signing of your zone. By default the name of the file is created by appending `.signed` to the input zone filename. (Look at the file: you will be happy that you didn't have to calculate and enter the information manually.)

This is the zone file you use when configuring your authoritative name server (Section 22.4.3).

`.keyset` The *key set* is a small file (with the same syntax as a zone file) that contains one or more key-signing keys. You provide this file to administrators of caching name servers (Section 22.5.3).

`.dsset` The *ds-set* is a small file (with the same syntax as a zone file) that contains the DS resource records to be included in the parent zone. (We explain DS records in Section 22.6; ignore them for now.)

At the end of this procedure, your signed zone file contains two DNSKEY records forming a single RRset, and that RRset has been signed twice, once with ZSK_{priv} and once with KSK_{priv}. Your signed zone file is ready to be served. In the next section we show you how to set up your authoritative name server to serve your newly signed DNSSEC zone.

22.4.3 C – Configure your authoritative servers

Your DNSSEC zones are served by an authoritative name server, so you have to set that up, and test it:

1. Configure your authoritative name server to load the *signed* zone file – the one with the `.signed` extension. Warning: a common mistake is to use the unsigned file, out of forgetfulness; if you load that, no DNSSEC answers will be returned to queries.

   We show you how to configure NSD and BIND:

   NSD Edit the `zone` clause in your `nsd.conf` to include the *signed* version of the zone file:

   ```
   zone:
       name: "es.qupps.biz"
       zonefile: "es.qupps.biz.zone.signed"
   ```

   Rebuild the `nsd.db` database, reload NSD, and your zone is ready; there is nothing else you have to do, as NSD has DNSSEC support built in and enabled by default.

BIND Configure your BIND name server similarly, by setting your master zone to load the *signed* zone file. To enable named to respond appropriately to DNS requests from DNSSEC-aware clients, the `dnssec-enable` option must be set to `yes`. We recommend you set up BIND to log DNSSEC queries to a dedicated file, so that you can follow what it is doing.

```
options {
    ...
    dnssec-enable yes;
};

zone "es.qupps.biz" IN {
    type master;
    file "es.qupps.biz.zone.signed";
};

logging {
    channel dnssec_log {
        file "/tmp/dnssec" size 20m;
        severity debug 9;
        print-time yes;
        print-category yes;
        print-severity yes;
    } ;
    category dnssec { dnssec_log; };
};
```

Reload your name server, and your zone is ready.

2. Two utilities (and two options to dig) are worth mentioning, as they provide useful information and they can help you in debugging your setup:

   - unbound-host from the Unbound caching server (Chapter 17) provides an easy interface to test whether queries are being returned securely:

```
$ unbound-host -v www.es.qupps.biz
www.es.qupps.biz has address 192.168.1.20 (secure)
www.es.qupps.biz has address 192.168.1.21 (secure)
www.es.qupps.biz has no IPv6 address (secure)
www.es.qupps.biz has no mail handler record (secure)

$ unbound-host -v mail.es.qupps.biz
Host mail.es.qupps.biz not found: 3(NXDOMAIN).  (secure)

$ unbound-host -v www.yahoo.de
www.yahoo.de is an alias for www.euro.yahoo-eu1.akadns.net. (insecure)
www.euro.yahoo-eu1.akadns.net has address 217.12.3.11 (insecure)
www.euro.yahoo-eu1.akadns.net has no IPv6 address (insecure)
www.euro.yahoo-eu1.akadns.net has no mail handler record (insecure)
```

- drill (the name is a pun on dig) is a dig-like program specifically designed to be used with DNSSEC. It has many options, but one interesting one is shown here:

```
$ drill -S @192.168.1.164 www.es.qupps.biz
;; flags: qr aa rd ; QUERY: 1, ANSWER: 3, AUTHORITY: 2, ADDITIONAL: 0

;; ANSWER SECTION:
www.es.qupps.biz.          83972   IN      A        192.168.1.20
www.es.qupps.biz.          83972   IN      A        192.168.1.21
www.es.qupps.biz.          83972   IN      RRSIG    A 5 4 84600 200803...

...
---
[XX] VERIFY RRSET:
www.es.qupps.biz.          83972   IN      A        192.168.1.20
www.es.qupps.biz.          83972   IN      A        192.168.1.21
[XX] RESULT: All OK


DNSSEC Trust tree:
www.es.qupps.biz. (A)
|---es.qupps.biz. (DNSKEY keytag: 56172)
    |---es.qupps.biz. (DNSKEY keytag: 29062)
You have not provided any trusted keys.
;; Chase successful
```

  Note how drill displays the key tags of the keys used to sign the zone.

- When using dig, use the +dnssec option for DNSSEC queries, and the +multiline option makes the output easier to read.

That completes the (simple) task of configuring your authoritative name server to serve signed zones.

22.4.4 D – Provide your public keys to caching server administrators

To validate replies returned by your DNSSEC authoritative servers, administrators of caching servers need a copy of your KSK_{pub}. They will use that to verify your ZSK_{pub}, and then they are able to use that and the RRSIG digital signatures to verify the "real" records – A, SOA, MX, etc. ("Verifying" the KSK_{pub} is trivial: the copy in the zone file must be identical to the copy retrieved by the system administrator.)

Cache administrators could just retrieve your KSK_{pub} directly via the DNS:

```
$ dig +multiline es.qupps.biz dnskey
;; ANSWER SECTION:
es.qupps.biz.           86400 IN DNSKEY 257 3 5 (
                        AwEAAbyaEjQit0Evpo6C9qgh7maTf+ThQkB8Y58TZN/b
                        ...
                        NjY7uuNP35sG1rfIWH0ZM64mSEs7vxv8+2kRNEUX+Q0=
                        ) ; key id = 29062
es.qupps.biz.           86400 IN DNSKEY 256 3 5 (
                        AwEAAaRYHega6h7WShgX6LmDS7rJ6+tDtTDfnKA+tqy1
                        1Mex0JpfsIc8HuXWaeoq1/9w5PzqFl2FhG4WfaMHFttl
                        DA8=
                        ) ; key id = 56172
```

There you are, those are the zone's keys (go ahead: compare the base 64-encoded key of the first one to the KSK we generated on page 520; you'll see they are identical).

The question however, is: are those *really* the keys that es.qupps.biz's administrator, Fred, created, or are these keys in a spoofed reply sent by an intruder? (We've shown you that they are identical, but in real life you can't look up other people's KSK keys on page 520 of this book.)

To solve this problem, you have to provide your KSK_{pub} key *securely* via an out-of-band method to any cache administrator who wants to DNSSEC-validate answers from your zone. The relevant key is in the `.keyset` file that dnssec-signzone produced when you signed your zone. To distribute this you can:

- Place the key on a secure (and trusted) Web site, for anybody to retrieve. Ensure you let people know when your key expires and how and when you plan to publish a new key.
- Assuming you have a secure (S/MIME or PGP) mail system, send the key in a signed e-mail to anybody who asks.

  You should also create a mailing list or RSS feed that cache administrators can subscribe to, in order to receive notifications of new keys, key expiry etc.

  That completes the DNSSEC installation on your authoritative server. Unfortunately, to fully test out your configuration you have to wait until you have finished installing a DNSSEC-enabled caching server (Section 22.5.5).

Managing your key distribution can involve a lot of work. We discuss this further in Section 22.8. Later on in this chapter we'll show how you can automate key distribution slightly for a chain of delegated zones (parent, child, grand-child, ...), and then how you can use the DNSSEC equivalent of a certification authority to automate key management as fully as is currently possible.

However, for now we stay with the simplest case, and in the next section we change hats, and show how to implement DNSSEC on a caching name server, to verify answers from a DNSSEC-enabled authoritative server.

22.5 Implementing DNSSEC on a caching name server

The two caching servers that support DNSSEC are Unbound and BIND. We first explain why using DNSSEC does require a configuration change on your your caching servers. Then we show you how to make the necessary changes, first for Unbound (in Section 22.5.3), and then for BIND (in Section 22.5.4).

Up to now we've been explaining how you sign your zone files and configure your authoritative servers to serve those zones. Here we cover the opposite side of the coin: how you as a caching server administrator use DNSSEC to validate replies for a zone on someone else's authoritative servers. (A special case is where you've set up DNSSEC on your own authoritative servers, and you want to use DNSSEC between your own caching and authoritative servers. This is exactly the same as working with another site, except that you use data about your own servers instead of theirs.)

One important point may not be obvious: given that all the keys, etc. are in the signed zone on the authoritative server, why does a caching server need any extra configuration at all (other than a "use DNSSEC" directive, perhaps)? The reason is that *anyone*, including an intruder, can generate a signed zone file for any zone. The signed zone file will be internally consistent – because the intruder can use exactly the same tools for zone signing as you do. So how can you determine whether the data you're receiving is from the correct zone file? To solve this problem you must somehow create a degree of trust between your caching server and the authoritative server, and that's what the caching server configuration is all about.

There are several ways of creating this trust, depending on what you want to do. Here we cover only the simplest case: configuring your server to DNSSEC-validate one zone from one authoritative server. (A master server for a zone, and all its slaves count as "one server" here.) If you want to be able to validate many different zones, you repeat the configuration process we describe, once for each extra zone. Later on in this chapter we explain how to handle the more complex scenarios.

22.5.1 How a caching server validates a DNSSEC-signed answer

Let's assume you want to use DNSSEC when you query our es.qupps.biz domain names, and you know that es.qupps.biz's authoritative server is DNSSEC-enabled, because you phoned our administrator, Fred, and asked him. You want to query for the A record for the domain www.es.qupps.biz.

To do this, your caching server needs to know es.qupps.biz's KSK_{pub}. Fred reads this out to you over the phone, or sends it by e-mail, or you retrieve it from a trusted Web site, and you store it in your caching server configuration files. Then you proceed as follows. (It will soon become obvious why you had to get the KSK_{pub} from Fred.)

1. You query our server for es.qupps.biz's DNSKEY records. This gives you our KSK_{pub} and ZSK_{pub} keys.

2. You compare that KSK_{pub} with the copy that Fred sent you previously. You now know you have the genuine KSK_{pub}.

3. Using the KSK_{pub}, you verify the digital signature (the RRSIG) on the DNSKEY RRset. If this is valid, you now know that the ZSK_{pub} you've just retrieved is valid. (That's why the KSK is so-called: it's a key used to sign the zone signing *key*.)

4. You query our server for www.es.qupps.biz's A record.

5. Our DNSSEC server returns the corresponding RRset for the A record with its RRSIG (which is the second-last block in the Figure on page 515):

```
;; ANSWER SECTION:
www.es.qupps.biz. 86400 IN A 192.168.1.20
www.es.qupps.biz. 86400 IN A 192.168.1.21
www.es.qupps.biz. 86400 IN RRSIG A 5 4 86400 20080613171456 (
                              20080514171456 56172 es.qupps.biz.
                              f4+w1GftLNloqGQhgCpe1phRoSyz0fwdozkx5ICqIaE+
                              EPhGZp6SA9xg99XndhpvC4VC6uqv9Tea/Sy6NJmijQ==)
```

6. You extract the digital signature from the RRSIG.

7. You verify this signature using the method shown in Figure 22.4 on page 510.

8. If all these checks succeed, you know that the DNS response is complete and authentic.

Step 3 is why you had to phone Fred for es.qupps.biz's KSK_{pub}. If you haven't received a "trustworthy" copy of it by some out-of-band method, all the checks above (except 3, of course) would succeed, even on a bogus signed zone file. Obtaining the KSK_{pub} through some other (trusted) means is a non-DNSSEC way to establish trust between you and us. (This is a bit like your bank sending you the PIN for your ATM card by post. It would be very difficult for an intruder to hijack your mailman or your mailbox to steal the letter containing the PIN, *as well as* burgling your house to get your physical ATM card.)

In practice, many of the steps above can happen simultaneously: the authoritative server can send DNSKEY and RRSIG records in the Additional Information section of the same packet it sends the A record in.

That explains in principle how your caching server DNSSEC-validates an answer. Now we'll show you how to configure your server so it can do that.

22.5.2 Trust anchors, and islands of trust

The KSK_{pub} that you obtain from a zone's administrator (Fred, in our example), and that you add to your caching server's configuration, is called a *trust anchor*: it's a definite point (an anchor) within the domain tree where you can trust the KSK_{pub} that you have.

The trust anchor is the starting point of a *chain of authority* (or chain of trust). You can trust the anchor, so things that are derived or validated from there – the ZSK_{pub}, for example – can also be trusted, and using the now-trusted ZSK_{pub} you can verify and trust the RRSIG, and using that you can trust the related A records. The trust anchor is said to be an *entry point* or *secure entry point* (*SEP*) into the chain of trust. (See the Notes, and Section 22.6, for a more formal definition of SEP.)

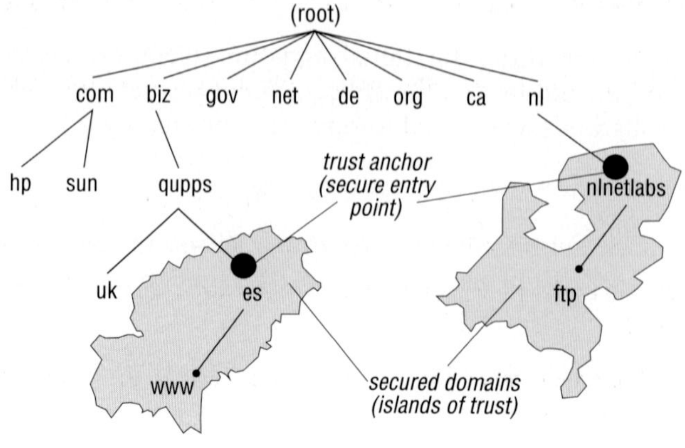

Figure 22.7: Trust anchors and islands of trust

Figure 22.7 illustrates this. Zones es.qupps.biz and nlnetlabs.nl use DNSSEC, but most of the DNS tree doesn't, so these two are isolated "islands of trust" in a sea of untrusted zones. You can enter the chains of authority in these secured zones at the trust anchors (secure entry points), i.e. where you have obtained trustworthy KSK_{pub}s.

Ideally, you'd need only a single entry point – the public key of the root zone – for the whole DNS: the root zone would be signed and it would contain chains of trust through all top-level domains to the second-level domains and further down into your own domains. In that case, validating DNSSEC-aware caching name servers would need only the single trust anchor into the root zone. However, the root isn't signed (yet), and therefore you have to set up trust anchors for all DNSSEC zones you want your caching name servers to validate.

22.5.3 Configuring trust anchors in your caching server – Unbound

To configure your caching server for a secured zone, you first obtain the KSK_{pub} – the trust anchor – of the signed zone from the zone's administrator (Section 22.4.4). In this section we show you how you configure the trust anchor for Unbound, and in the next section for BIND.

To configure Unbound to validate replies from your DNSSEC-signed zone(s):

1. Unbound's "`validator`" module is responsible for validating DNSSEC replies from secured DNS name servers. This module is enabled by default, but ensure that you haven't disabled it in your `unbound.conf`:

   ```
   module-config: "validator iterator"
   ```

2. Set up trust anchors for the zones you want to validate. You can use either or both of the following options in the `unbound.conf` file:

   - The trust-anchor attribute specifies the trust anchor for a single zone. You copy the whole key into the value of the trust-anchor attribute and surround it in quotes. Remember, you can take the key from the `keyset-`*zone* file:

     ```
     trust-anchor: "es.qupps.biz. IN DNSKEY 257 3 5 AwEAAb ... +2kEUX+Q0="
     ```

     Use multiple instances of trust-anchor to include the trust anchors for multiple zones.

   - The trust-anchor-file option specifies a filename containing the DNSKEY resource records.

     ```
     trust-anchor-file: "/etc/unbound/my.anchors"
     ```

     You copy the content of your trust-anchor-file directly from your key file(s):

     ```
     # cat keys/Kes.qupps.biz.+005+29062.key >> my.anchors
     ```

     We prefer this method as it can be automated, and avoids the error-prone copying of chunks of text needed above.

3. Reload your unbound server by signaling it with a SIGHUP signal, after checking that the configuration is correct.

If you run unbound with a verbosity setting of 2, and you query your caching name server, you should see messages like these:

```
info: finishing processing for <es.qupps.biz. DNSKEY IN>
info: validator operate: query <es.qupps.biz. DNSKEY IN>
info: validator: inform_super, sub is <es.qupps.biz. DNSKEY IN>
info: super is <www.es.qupps.biz. A IN>
info: verify rrset <es.qupps.biz. DNSKEY IN>
info: validate keys with anchor(DNSKEY): sec_status_secure
info: Successfully primed trust anchor <es.qupps.biz. DNSKEY IN>
info: validator operate: query <www.es.qupps.biz. A IN>
info: validator: FindKey <www.es.qupps.biz. A IN>
info: verify rrset <www.es.qupps.biz. A IN>
info: verify rrset <es.qupps.biz. NS IN>
info: verify rrset <torres.es.qupps.biz. A IN>
info: verify rrset <sherry.es.qupps.biz. A IN>
info: validate(positive): sec_status_secure
info: validation success <www.es.qupps.biz. A IN>
```

If you have configured your trust anchor(s) incorrectly, Unbound will show you:

```
info: verify rrset <es.qupps.biz. DNSKEY IN>
info: validate keys with anchor(DNSKEY): sec_status_bogus
info: failed to prime trust anchor -- could not fetch secure DNSKEY ↩
                rrset <es.qupps.biz.  DNSKEY IN>
info: validator operate: query <www.es.qupps.biz. A IN>
info: Could not establish a chain of trust to keys for <es.qupps.biz. DNSKEY IN>
```

A clear indication of failure is returned to the client. Since the caching name server cannot trust the data it received from the authoritative name server, it drops it entirely, and dig shows:

```
$ dig +dnssec +multiline @192.168.1.164  www.es.qupps.biz
;; ->>HEADER<<- opcode: QUERY, status: SERVFAIL, id: 46972
;; flags: qr rd ra; QUERY: 1, ANSWER: 0, AUTHORITY: 0, ADDITIONAL: 1
```

If you want to force Unbound to supply the response, even if it is bogus, set val-permissive-mode in `unbound.conf`:

```
val-permissive-mode: yes
```

The value of this attribute defaults to "no" and we recommend you use the default.

22.5.4 Configuring trust anchors in your caching server – BIND

For BIND to validate answers from other servers, you must set both `dnssec-enable` and `dnssec-validation`, and configure some `trusted-keys` in your `named.conf`:

```
options {
    ...
    dnssec-enable yes;
    dnssec-validation yes;

};
```

You configure trust anchors in your BIND caching server in a `trusted-keys` clause. Copy the data from your Key Signing Key (the `.key` file with the 257 on it) into a trusted key:

```
trusted-keys {
  "es.qupps.biz" 257 3 5 "AwEAAbyaEjQit0Evpo6C9qgh7maTf+↩
                          ThQkB8Y58TZN/bWuJOSxNpHYkMhjhu↩
                          C3Pmc68nEf3AYgxCeeOD0pzTCryG2a↩
                          Xruy8MGVee9A3pobw0FA3A8e0HXQwf↩
                          2J8p8XYIk5SBI4U2xEtXZtUkH1efBx↩
                          SbzDk9hXLjRY92qVOUNTbJs1ONNjY7↩
                          uuNP35sG1rfIWH0ZM64mSEs7vxv8+2↩
                          kRNEUX+Q0=";
};
```

Note how the domain name of the key is optionally enclosed in double quotes, whereas the base64-blob of the key (all on a single line) *must* be quoted.

If you've enabled logging (as shown in Section 22.4.3), BIND logs details to the file you specify:

```
debug 3: validating: www.es.qupps.biz A: starting
debug 3: validating: www.es.qupps.biz A: attempting positive response validation
debug 9: validating: www.es.qupps.biz A: get_key: creating fetch for es.qupps.biz DNSKEY
debug 3: validating: es.qupps.biz DNSKEY: starting
debug 3: validating: es.qupps.biz DNSKEY: attempting positive response validation
debug 3: validating: es.qupps.biz DNSKEY: verify rdataset (keyid=29062): success
debug 3: validating: es.qupps.biz DNSKEY: signed by trusted key; marking as secure
debug 3: validator : dns_validator_destroy
debug 3: validating: www.es.qupps.biz A: in fetch_callback_validator
debug 3: validating: www.es.qupps.biz A: keyset with trust 7
debug 3: validating: www.es.qupps.biz A: resuming validate
debug 3: validating: www.es.qupps.biz A: verify rdataset (keyid=56172): success
debug 3: validating: www.es.qupps.biz A: marking as secure
debug 3: validator : dns_validator_destroy
```

That concludes the simple way of configuring caching servers to use DNSSEC.

22.5.5 Example of a DNSSEC validation

At last you are in a position to test your caching server setup with dig; we recommend you use the `+multiline` switch to make output easier to read:

```
$ dig +dnssec +multiline @192.168.1.20  www.es.qupps.biz
;; ->>HEADER<<- opcode: QUERY, status: NOERROR, id: 41792
;; flags: qr aa rd; QUERY: 1, ANSWER: 3, AUTHORITY: 2, ADDITIONAL: 1
;; ANSWER SECTION:
www.es.qupps.biz. 86400 IN A 192.168.1.20
www.es.qupps.biz. 86400 IN A 192.168.1.21
www.es.qupps.biz. 86400 IN RRSIG A 5 4 86400 20080613171456 (
                           20080514171456 56172 es.qupps.biz.
                           f4+w1GftLNloqGQhgCpe1phRoSyz0fwdozkx5ICqIaE+
                           EPhGZp6SA9xg99XndhpvC4VC6uqv9Tea/Sy6NJmijQ==
)

;; AUTHORITY SECTION:
es.qupps.biz.     86400 IN NS www.es.qupps.biz.
es.qupps.biz.     86400 IN RRSIG NS 5 3 86400 20080613171456 (
                            20080514171456 56172 es.qupps.biz.
                            Mth2xiu4yyNArX4t45oFZZmlAgck8qBopIMvZ48imZla
                            jrr1DrEC8BNdujI6yJ4pWdB6GpGNJYzK8jenqmbc2w==
)
```

The above command was sent to an authoritative name server for the es.qupps.biz zone, so dig's flags don't give us any DNSSEC-specific information, because dig doesn't validate DNSSEC responses. If, however, we ask a caching name server for the same information, we see the Authenticated Data (see Notes) flag in the response: the caching server *has* DNSSEC validated the reply, and set the flag (and dig has just passed it on to us as it received it).

```
$ dig +dnssec +multiline www.es.qupps.biz
;; ->>HEADER<<- opcode: QUERY, status: NOERROR, id: 13668
;; flags: qr rd ra ad; QUERY: 1, ANSWER: 3, AUTHORITY: 2, ADDITIONAL: 1
...
```

In both cases, the respective RRSIG is returned with the A RRset.

22.6 The chain of trust for delegated zones; DS records

In Section 22.5.3 we explained how you must obtain a trust anchor (a zone's KSK_{pub}) via an out-of-band method, to establish a level of trust in that anchor. You then configure this trust anchor into your caching server. If there is a tree of delegation – zone to sub-zone (to sub-sub-zone ...) – you can treat each zone individually with respect to DNSSEC, and configure each separately, as described in Section 22.5.

However, DNSSEC has a special mechanism for handling delegated zones, to reduce the admin load on owners of caching servers. DNSSEC lets you build, on the authoritative servers handling the zones, a *chain of trust* – a mechanism that lets a client trust suitably-configured child zones automatically, as long as it trusts the parent zone. On the caching server you don't have to do anything extra at all – it works automatically, as long as you've configured the trust anchor of the topmost DNSSEC zone in the delegation tree into your caching server as normal.

The starting point of the chain of trust is called an *entry point*. Consider a parent zone with a child zone that in turn has a grand-child zone. A caching server can "enter" this chain at any level, as long as it has the trust anchor (i.e. the KSK_{pub}) for the zone at that level: the KSK_{pub} is the "entry point" into the chain of trust. Once a caching server has securely obtained a public key high in your DNS hierarchy, it can automatically follow the chain to validate DNS replies given by name servers that host your child zones.

To create the necessary chain of trust on authoritative servers, you use a new type of resource record, the *Delegation Signer* (DS). You insert the DS record into the parent zone. No change is required to the child zone. The DS resource record contains the child zone's name (so the DS points to the child zone) and a digest of the child zone's KSK_{pub}. Figure 22.8 shows how the DS record in the parent qupps.biz points to es.qupps.biz.

To validate a child zone's DNSKEY record, presumably when following a referral from qupps.biz to es.qupps.biz, a client proceeds as follows:

1. The client retrieves the DS from the parent zone, and validates it just like any other RRset in a trusted zone. (Remember, the parent zone is trusted, because that's where the trust anchor/entry point is.)

2. The client queries for the DNSKEY records of the child, es.qupps.biz, and looks for a key that matches the key tag listed in the DS record. This is the child's KSK_{pub}.

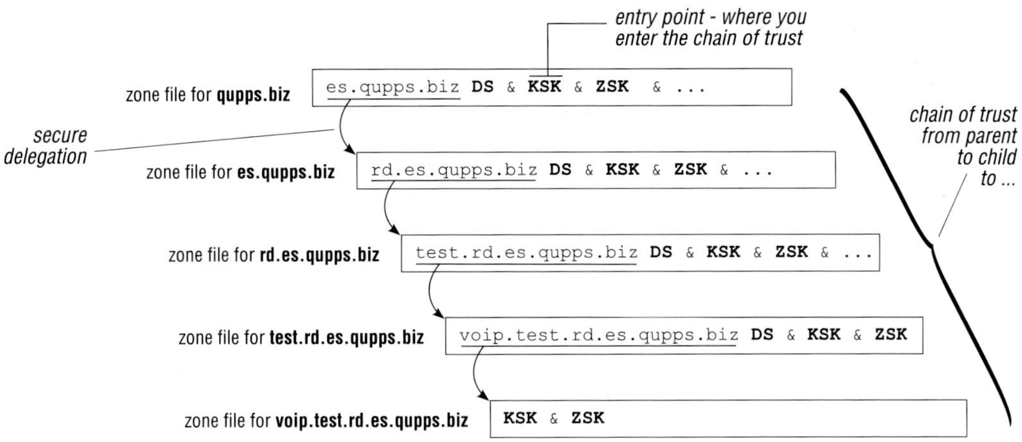

Figure 22.8: Chain of trust formed with DS secure delegations

3. Having found the the child's KSK_{pub}, the client creates a digest of that, using the correct hash algorithm specified in the DS record. If this calculated digest is the same as the digest in the DS resource record, we know the child's KSK_{pub} is genuine, and we can proceed as before (Section 22.5.1), but this time we haven't had to configure the child zone's trust anchor manually,

22.6.1 To configure the chain of trust from parent to child zone

1. When we signed our (child) zone es.qupps.biz (Section 22.4.2) dnssec-signzone automatically created a file called `dsset-`*`domain`* (`dsset-es.qupps.biz` in this case). The file is a so-called *ds-set* – a small file (in zone master file syntax) containing one or more digests of a child zone's KSK_{pub}.

   The child's administrator, Fred, sends the child's `dsset` to the parent zone administrator, Tim – by secure e-mail, or by publishing it on a secure web site, etc. The `dsset` for es.qupps.biz currently contains:

```
$ cat dsset-es.qupps.biz
es.qupps.biz. IN DS 29062 5 1 5BE64B2CC32616B419C2ED5C332D9E223F40127E
es.qupps.biz. IN DS 29062 5 2 02B80FB9EA40C2A9286C6C7BF8AAF4240F5880C6↩
                              DBF0655BC234C217 2145665F
```

   Note how there are two DS records (see Notes).

2. Tim, the parent zone administrator, includes the `dsset` file into the parent zone. So, the qupps.biz zone file now contains the KSK and ZSK for qupps.biz as well as the DS records from its child zone es.qupps.biz:

```
qupps.biz. 84600  IN SOA  ns1.qupps.biz.  tim.mens.de. (18 10800 900 604...
                  IN NS   ns1.qupps.biz.

ns1               IN A    192.168.1.164

$ORIGIN es.qupps.biz.

@                 IN NS   www.es.qupps.biz.
www.es.qupps.biz. IN A    192.168.1.20  ;      Glue RR

$INCLUDE qkeys/Kqupps.biz.+005+03507.key;      ZSK
$INCLUDE qkeys/Kqupps.biz.+005+02329.key;      KSK
$INCLUDE keysets/dsset-es.qupps.biz;           DS of child
```

3. Tim, the parent's administrator, signs the parent zone, using dnssec-signzone, but with a new option, `-d`, specifying the directory containing the children's `dsset` file(s). So he runs:

```
$ dnssec-signzone \
      -o qupps.biz \                              zone origin
      -d keysets \                                directory
      -k qkeys/Kqupps.biz.+005+02329 \            KSK
      qupps.biz.zone \                            zone file
      qkeys/Kqupps.biz.+005+03507                 ZSK
```

   If you have several signed child zones, you use the same command – all the child `dsset`s are in the directory you specify with the `-d` option, and you are signing the *single* parent zone.

   Warning: it is a bit confusing that the parent's own `keyset` and `dsset` files land in the directory specified with the `-d` option. You can ignore the files, or even delete them, unless you want your own parent (.biz in this example) to set up a chain of trust to you, in which case you'll have to send your own `keyset` to .biz's administrator.

4. The resulting signed zone file for qupps.biz contains (signatures truncated for brevity):

```
qupps.biz.          84600    IN SOA  ns1.qupps.biz. tim.mens.de. ( ... )
                    84600    RRSIG   SOA 5 2 84600 20080624120443 (
                                     20080525120443 3507 qupps.biz. ...
                    84600    NS      ns1.qupps.biz.
                    84600    RRSIG   NS 5 2 84600 20080624120443 (
                                     20080525120443 3507 qupps.biz. ...
                    3600     NSEC    es.qupps.biz. NS SOA RRSIG NSEC DNSKEY
                    3600     RRSIG   NSEC 5 2 3600 20080624120443 (
                                     20080525120443 3507 qupps.biz. ...
                    84600    DNSKEY  256 3 5 (
                                     AwEAAaEW+zydEhqpwH3iSBF/ihaZYdyZNmSN
                                     /QKlW//Q9M8YB1jHl8eo7LVrUeUrvmOeyDp8
                                     jos=
                                     ) ; key id = 3507
                    84600    DNSKEY  257 3 5 (
                                     AwEAAedjD68wxmNp6slv7IF5OfRhKd29btKF
                                     H/hbpn0kVASwXVFybzdwgma6adWl31KkQZYQ
                                     aP8=
                                     ) ; key id = 2329
```

```
                    84600   RRSIG   DNSKEY 5 2 84600 20080624120443 (
                                    20080525120443 3507 qupps.biz. ...
                    84600   RRSIG   DNSKEY 5 2 84600 20080624120443 (
                                    20080525120443 2329 qupps.biz. ...
es.qupps.biz.       84600   IN NS   www.es.qupps.biz.
                    84600   DS      29062 5 1 (
                                    5BE64B2CC32616B419C2ED5C332D9E223F40
                                    127E )
                    84600   DS      29062 5 2 (
                                    02B80FB9EA40C2A9286C6C7BF8AAF4240F58
                                    80C6DBF0655BC234C2172145665F )
                    84600   RRSIG   DS 5 3 84600 20080624120443 (
                                    20080525120443 3507 qupps.biz. ...
                    3600    NSEC    ns1.qupps.biz. NS DS RRSIG NSEC
                    3600    RRSIG   NSEC 5 3 3600 20080624120443 (
                                    20080525120443 3507 qupps.biz. ...
www.es.qupps.biz.   84600   IN A    192.168.1.20
ns1.qupps.biz.      84600   IN A    192.168.1.164
                    84600   RRSIG   A 5 3 84600 20080624120443 (
                                    20080525120443 3507 qupps.biz. ...
                    3600    NSEC    qupps.biz. A RRSIG NSEC
                    3600    RRSIG   NSEC 5 3 3600 20080624120443 (
                                    20080525120443 3507 qupps.biz. ...
```

At this point the parent zone is signed, so any caching servers that want to query it will have to be configured as normal (Section 22.5.1). What's important, though, is that no caching servers need to be configured now for the delegated sub-zones in the chain of trust.

Note that the only thing the child zone administrator, Fred, had to do was send the `dsset` file to Tim.

22.7 Using DNSSEC automatically – DLV, look-aside validation

So far, we covered setting up DNSSEC for an individual zone, or for a delegated tree of zones. In both cases we end up with an island of trust, and a trust anchor for it must be set up in every caching server that wants to DNSSEC-validate the zone's records. The more zones there are, and the more clients there are, the more work has to be done: this system does not scale well.

An extension to the DNSSEC protocol called *DLV* (DNSSEC *Look-aside Validation*), RFC 5074, gets over this. In the same way that trusted organizations become Certification Authorities (CAs) in the public-key infrastructure (Section 22.2.3), trusted organizations set up *DLV registries* for the DNS. The administrator of an authoritative server for a zone, example.com say, registers the zone's KSK_{pub} with the registry. The administrator of a caching server configures their server to use the DLV registry. When the caching server wants to check the authenticity of replies from example.com's server, the caching server obtains example.com's KSK_{pub} – the trust anchor – it requires from the DLV registry. Here, unlike the previous two scenarios, the caching server's administrator has no direct contact with example.com's administrator at all. (A different way of looking at this is that a DLV registry provides an additional, higher, entry point at which you can enter the chain of trust.)

If you explicitly set up trust to a DLV registry, you subsequently trust the keys that that registry returns to your name servers (in the same way that if you trust a Certification Authority, you also trust certificates that the CA issues).

One of the better known DLV registries is run by the Internet Systems Consortium (ISC) at `http://www.isc.org/ops/dlv`.

In the next two sections we show how the administrator of an authoritative server, and the administrator of a caching server, respectively, configure their servers to use a DLV registry.

22.7.1 Authoritative server: create records to include in a DLV registry

Assume that Fred, es.qupps.biz's administrator, wants to register es.qupps.biz with the ISC DLV registry. He submits es.qupps.biz's KSK_{pub} (trust anchor) to the ISC, who include it in their dlv.isc.org zone. DLV-aware servers retrieve the KSK from the DLV.

The easiest way to submit the KSK_{pub} is by using the `-l` option when you sign the zone with dnssec-signzone. This option generates a *DLV-set* (similar to a `keyset` or `dsset`) – a small file (in zone file format) containing the keys to be inserted at the DLV registry.

```
$ dnssec-signzone \
        -o es.qupps.biz \                    zone origin
        -l dlv.isc.org \                     DLV domain
        -k keys/Kes.qupps.biz.+005+29062 \   KSK
        es.qupps.biz.zone \                  zone file
        keys/Kes.qupps.biz.+005+56172        ZSK
es.qupps.biz.zone.signed
```

This generates a DLV set for the DLV registry operator's domain (dlv.isc.org), in addition to the DNSKEY and DS sets. In our example, the resulting file contains:

```
$ cat dlvset-es.qupps.biz.
es.qupps.biz.dlv.isc.org. IN DLV 29062 5 1 5BE64B2CC3261...C3E223F40127E
es.qupps.biz.dlv.isc.org. IN DLV 29062 5 2 02B80FB9EA40C...BF4240F5880C6↩
                                           DBF0655BC234C217 2145665F
```

For how to submit this DLV set to the ISC, see Notes.

Now we discuss what you have to do to configure your caching name server to use a DLV registry.

22.7.2 Caching server: configure to use a DLV registry

As the administrator of a caching server, you have to configure your caching name servers to consult a DLV registry, and to enable look-aside validation. Currently, only BIND 9.3.3 and 9.4.0 or later have support for DLV.

To implement the ISC DLV registry in your caching BIND name server:

1. Obtain dlv.isc.org's KSK_{pub} key from the ISC Web site (see Notes) and verify its PGP signature.

2. Enable DNSSEC in the `options` clause in `named.conf` and instruct BIND to use DLV in addition to normal DNSSEC validation with the `dnssec-lookaside` statement:

```
options {
    ...
    dnssec-enable yes;
    dnssec-validation yes;
    dnssec-lookaside "." trust-anchor "dlv.isc.org";

};
```

3. Add the key you downloaded in Step 1 to a `trusted-keys` statement in `named.conf`:

```
trusted-keys {
    rd.qupps.biz 257 3 5 "BbaEa ... ";
    dlv.isc.org  257 3 5 "BEAAA ... ";
};
```

   Note how in the example above, we have configured a trust anchor for our own zone rd.qupps.biz (e.g. an internal zone we don't want to submit to ISC's DLV registry) as well as for ISC's DLV zone.

If you have set everything up correctly, you should be able to query any DLV-registered domain via your caching server, and for those zones that are signed, get validated responses.

Testing DLV: off to Brazil

We know that the zone maintainers for Brazil's .BR ccTLD zone have DNSSEC enabled, so we'll query that:

```
$ drill -S a.dns.br
;; ->>HEADER<<- opcode: QUERY, rcode: NOERROR, id: 47853
;; flags: qr rd cd ra ; QUERY: 1, ANSWER: 2, AUTHORITY: 6, ADDITIONAL: 0

;; ANSWER SECTION:
a.dns.br.       172800  IN      A       200.160.0.10

...
...

[XX] VERIFY RRSET:
a.dns.br.       172800  IN      A       200.160.0.10
[XX] RESULT: All OK

[XX] VERIFY RRSET:
dns.br. 86400   IN      DS      943 5 1
1880e0a19bdd1187747214b84a2f50f63ae539dc
[XX] RESULT: All OK

DNSSEC Trust tree:
a.dns.br. (A)
|---dns.br. (DNSKEY keytag: 943)
    |---dns.br. (DS keytag: 943)
        |---br. (DNSKEY keytag: 23238)
            |---br. (DNSKEY keytag: 61207)
```

If you look at the trust tree at the bottom of the above example, you see the signing hierarchy, shown bottom first.

Look at BIND's log to see what is happening; here is a short excerpt from it:

```
debug 3: validating: . NS: starting
debug 3: validating: . NS: looking for DLV
debug 3: validating: . NS: plain DNSSEC returns unsecure (.): looking for DLV
debug 3: validating: . NS: looking for DLV dlv.isc.org
debug 9: validating: . NS: finddlvsep: creating fetch for dlv.isc.org DLV
debug 3: validating: . NS: DLV lookup: wait
debug 3: validating: dlv.isc.org DLV: starting
debug 3: validating: dlv.isc.org DLV: attempting negative response validation
debug 9: validating: dlv.isc.org DLV: nsecvalidate: creating validator for dlv.isc.org SOA
debug 3:   validating: dlv.isc.org SOA: starting
debug 3:   validating: dlv.isc.org SOA: attempting positive response validation
debug 9:   validating: dlv.isc.org SOA: get_key: creating fetch for dlv.isc.org DNSKEY
debug 3: validating: dlv.isc.org DNSKEY: starting
debug 3: validating: dlv.isc.org DNSKEY: attempting positive response validation
debug 3: validating: dlv.isc.org DNSKEY: verify rdataset (keyid=14383): success
debug 3: validating: dlv.isc.org DNSKEY: signed by trusted key; marking as secure
debug 3: validator : dns_validator_destroy
...
```

Points to note about DLV

- If you enable DLV in your caching name servers, you must keep an eye out for key-rollovers (see Notes) performed by your DLV registry. If the registry has a mailing list or an RSS feed, be sure to subscribe to that in order to be forewarned of any changes they make to their keys.

- Unbound currently does not support DLV, so with Unbound you have to maintain trust anchors manually.

- BIND currently does not support DLV for non-root zones, so you cannot implement look-aside validation for your hierarchy and for a public DLV registry simultaneously. In other words, if you implement DLV for your own internal zones, you cannot simultaneously use a public DLV registry with BIND.

- Although DLV eases the administrative effort required to deploy DNSSEC, it does not scale well. A different scheme – the signing of the root zone (currently under consideration by ICANN) – would scale. If the root zone gets signed, DLV will diminish in importance, although it might remain useful for private use within large organizations.

22.8 Housekeeping and DNSSEC key management

We've discussed how you get started with DNSSEC, and you've seen that there is quite a lot of housekeeping and management you have to perform. We've collected the most important points here, for reference.

22.8.1 Organizing your keys to avoid confusion

If you use two keys as recommended, and if you have to manage keys for more than one zone (which you probably will), organize your keys as follows:

- Create a dedicated directory for your key files. Carefully protect the private keys by setting file system permissions and file ownership appropriately.
- The names of the key files generated by dnssec-keygen are not obvious (the first four lines below). Create symbolic links to make the names clearer. We specially recommend you clearly mark which keys are KSK and which are ZSK (last two lines below).

```
$ ls -l keys
-r--r--r-- 1 dns mens  256 Feb 16 21:41 Kes.qupps.biz.+005+29062.key
-r-------- 1 dns mens 1125 Feb 16 21:41 Kes.qupps.biz.+005+29062.private
-r--r--r-- 1 dns mens  126 Feb 16 21:37 Kes.qupps.biz.+005+56172.key
-r-------- 1 dns mens  549 Feb 16 21:37 Kes.qupps.biz.+005+56172.private
lrwxrwxrwx 1 dns mens   28 Feb 16 21:42 KSK -> Kes.qupps.biz.+005+29062.key
lrwxrwxrwx 1 dns mens   28 Feb 16 21:40 ZSK -> Kes.qupps.biz.+005+56172.key
```

- Create a registry of keys for yourself. Use a database table, a spreadsheet or even a plain text file to record which keys you used for what, and which keys you sent to whom.

22.8.2 Administering your keys

Before launching your own DNSSEC zones, there are several points regarding key management that you should consider:

- How will administrators of caching name servers obtain your public keys, and how will they be able to verify them? You can:
  - Place the key on a secure (and trusted) Web site, for anybody to retrieve. Ensure you inform potential takers of when your key expires and how and when you plan to publish a new key.
  - Assuming you have a secure (S/MIME or PGP) mail system, send the key in a signed mail to anybody who asks.

    Additionally create a mailing list that cache administrators can subscribe to, in order to receive notifications of new keys, key expiry etc.
- How often your keys will roll over, i.e. how often you will re-issue them (see Notes).
- How will you signal a key rollover, or how can you ensure that all interested parties are aware of your key rollover? If you deploy DNSSEC within your own organization only, then you will typically know when that happens, but if you have distributed your keys to third parties, they must be informed when your keys roll over, or they won't be able to validate your DNS replies any more.

22.9 Points to note when you deploy DNSSEC

- When sent over UDP, DNS messages are limited to 512 octets in size, but that is too small to handle some of the large records that DNSSEC requires. RFC 2671 defines *EDNS0*, the *Extension Mechanisms for DNS*, which allows clients and server to negotiate a maximum packet size. Name servers that implement DNSSEC must implement EDNS0 as well. This might be affected by firewalls, which might block UDP DNS traffic which is larger than 512 octets. If your authoritative name servers are behind a firewall, keep that in mind when implementing DNSSEC.

- DNSSEC does not prevent unauthorized access to name servers. To do that you use TSIG (Chapter 7). You can use both TSIG and DNSSEC on the same server.

- DNSSEC increases the load on your authoritative name servers. The cryptographic calculations involved require CPU, and your servers will be queried for more resource records than with unsecured DNS.

  Caching servers will spend additional CPU time validating responses.

  The size of zone files increases. For example, in 2003 a test signing was performed on the .nl ccTLD, containing approximately 800 000 delegations. The zone file increased from about 40 MB to over 350 MB when signed, and signing took around 1.5 hours, with an additional 15 minutes to load the zone.

- If you implement strict DNSSEC validation on your caching servers, and validation fails (e.g. because a key has become invalid), your DNS clients will not see *any* replies. This might be termed a degradation of service. Apart from monitoring that your caching servers have valid trust anchors, there is little you can do about this.

- When using non-DNSSEC DNS, you always disable zone transfers to non-authorized clients, so that unauthorized people can't get get a full listing of your zone, because zone data can reveal information about your network that you don't want published.

  However, DNSSEC-enabling your zones makes their content fully visible, even with zone transfers disabled. This is because a NSEC resource record points to the next domain in a zone, and by judiciously walking the list of NSEC records, you can enumerate a zone's content. Note however, that NSEC3 (defined in RFC 5155) mitigates this zone walking. DNSSEC servers can choose to send an NSEC3 record instead of an NSEC record to indicate that a specific record is not found (i.e. NXDOMAIN). The NSEC3 record is signed, but instead of including the domain name (which enables zone walking), the NSEC3 record includes a hashed value of the name. NSEC3 is implemented in the Unbound and NSD servers, and in the ldns package which you can use instead of dnssec-signzone to sign zones (see Notes),

- RFC 5011, *Automated Updates of DNS Security (DNSSEC) Trust Anchors*, proposes mechanisms for renewing trust anchors automatically. In theory, you could implement something similar with a clever shell script. NLnet Labs is working on a tool for it, and you can look at trustman (see `http://www.dnssec-tools.org/`) for something similar.

- We have not discussed how and when you perform key rollovers. Consult the excellent *DNSSEC Howto* (see Notes) on what to watch out for when rolling over your keys.

Summary

- DNSSEC provides security by guaranteeing that the DNS replies you get are authentic. It does not make your DNS queries and their replies confidential.
- DNSSEC adds additional data to the DNS protocol that provides information to allow clients to authenticate responses.
- Only BIND, NSD and Unbound support DNSSEC.
- DNSSEC is complex to manage because you have to create keys, secure the private keys, distribute public keys and manage key rollover.
- DLV is a mechanism for publishing DNSSEC trust anchors; it allows caching name servers (resolvers) to validate DNSSEC-signed data from zones that don't publish Delegation Signer (DS) records. DLV greatly eases the migration to DNSSEC. Only BIND has support for DLV.

Related topics

- Two of the authoritative name servers we discuss have support for DNSSEC-signed zones: BIND (Chapter 7) and NSD (Chapter 10).
- Unbound (Chapter 17) is a validating DNSSEC-aware caching name server.

Notes and further reading

DNSKEY records

Every secured DNS zone has at least one public/private key pair associated with it, generated by the zone's administrator. The administrator keeps the private key secure and secret, but publishes the public key in the zone file in the form of a DNSKEY resource record (Figure 22.9).

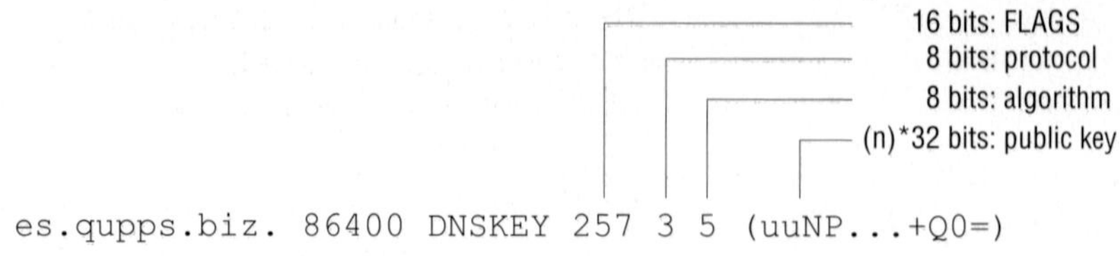

Figure 22.9: The DNSKEY resource record

As explained in Section 22.4.1, you usually use two different key pairs, a Zone Signing Key (ZSK) pair and a Key Signing Key (KSK) pair. The DNSKEY record contains a "flags" field (Figure 22.9) which indicates the type of key:

256 The key is a ZSK.

257 This value indicates that the key additionally has the Secure Entry Point (SEP) bit set. This is used as the Key Signing Key (KSK), and the public portion of the KSK is what you use to configure trust anchors.

Because zones can contain more than a single DNSKEY resource record (ZSK and KSK, as we have used them), RFC 3757 defines a Secure Entry Point (SEP) as a key that is either used to generate DS resource records (Section 22.6) or that is distributed to caching name servers (resolvers) as the root of a trusted subtree. The SEP is the key with an odd flags value – 257.

RRSIG records

DNSSEC generates the digital signature for an RRset by creating an SHA-1 digest of the RRset, and encrypting the digest with the zone administrator's private key, ZSK_{priv}. Signing the DNSKEY RRset is a special case: DNSSEC signs this twice, once with ZSK_{priv} and once with KSK_{priv}.

Comparing the *key tag* in the RRSIG record (56172 in Figure 22.10) with the *key id* comments, if present, in the DNSKEY records lets you work out which is the KSK and which the ZSK.

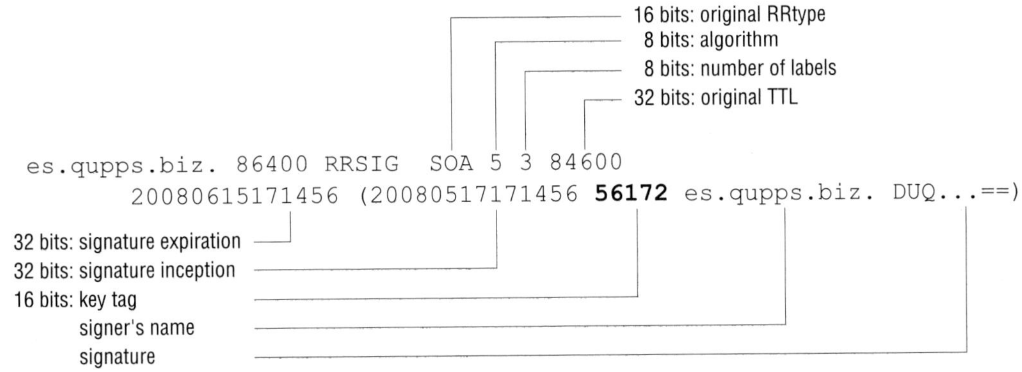

Figure 22.10: The RRSIG resource record

NSEC records

The *Next Secure* (NSEC) resource records (Figure 22.11), defined in RFC 3845, are created by dnssec-signzone, after it has sorted the entire zone into "canonical order" (see below). The NSEC record for one domain name points to the next domain in order, in the zone, which allows clients to verify that NXDOMAIN replies are genuine.
The NSEC for a domain name (note – not for an RRset) lists which resource record types the name has. For example, www.es.qupps.biz has A, RRSIG and NSEC records.

A different way of looking at NSEC is: the "next name" part defines the gap between this domain name and the next. The "RRs for this domain" defines the extent of the non-gap, so the sums of all the NSEC records defines all the gaps and all non-gaps, i.e. they define the full extent of the zone.

Figure 22.11: The NSEC resource record

Here's an example of how NSEC works. If a DNSSEC-aware client queries mail.es.qupps.biz, it receives the following response:

```
$ dig +dnssec mail.es.qupps.biz
;; ->>HEADER<<- opcode: QUERY, status: NXDOMAIN, id: 4122
;; flags: qr aa rd; QUERY: 1, ANSWER: 0, AUTHORITY: 4, ADDITIONAL: 1

;; AUTHORITY SECTION:
es.qupps.biz. 3600 IN NSEC www.es.qupps.biz. NS SOA RRSIG NSEC DNSKEY
```

The status remains NXDOMAIN as in a non-DNSSEC query, but the NSEC resource record securely announces to the client that the requested name doesn't exist, and that the "next available" name is www.es.qupps.biz.

Canonical order is defined in RFC 4034. Roughly, here's how it works: sort the names according to their most significant (rightmost) labels (.com, .biz, etc.). Within that, sort the next most significant label (e.g. example, qupps, ...) alphabetically, and so on. See section 6.1 of RFC 4034 for examples of canonical ordering.

DS records

DS resource records (Figure 22.12) have different digest types: type 1 uses the SHA-1 hash algorithm, and predates type 2 (RFC 4509), which uses the SHA-256 algorithm, and which is considered to be more resilient to attack than SHA-1.

The digest is calculated by concatenating the domain name and the *rdata* portion of the zone's DNSKEY record (*flags, protocol, algorithm,* and *public key*), and hashing the result with the algorithm.

A caching server can choose which DS record to use, according to which of the listed algorithms it knows about. This is so that new algorithms ("4" say) can be added without suddenly breaking older implementations that don't know about "4" algorithm. In this case, the "older" implementation would use algorithm type 1 or 2 if those DS records are still provided.

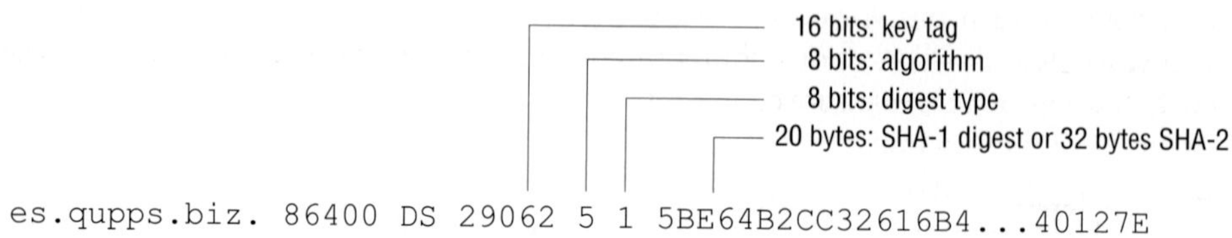

Figure 22.12: The DS resource record

Mathematical relationship between keys

The RSA algorithm is the most widely used in public/private encryption. It defines the mathematical relationship between the private and public keys used in asymmetric encryption. It was published by Ron Rivest, Adi Shamir, and Leonard Adleman at MIT (see `http://en.wikipedia.org/wiki/RSA`).

The ldns package

The ldns package we introduced in Chapter 10 also provides tools for generating keys and signing zones. They are called ldns-keygen and ldns-signzone respectively.

Random numbers

When you create keys, you require a lot of random data. UNIX and GNU/Linux systems provide `/dev/random` as a source of entropy, but it typically blocks until enough "noise" is created to fill the pool with random numbers, so on a quiet system it can take five minutes to create a single 1 280 bit key.

Furthermore, the random numbers produced by these pseudo-devices may not be strong enough for your needs, and you might want to consider using an external device to provide reliable random numbers or a different implementation of a pseudo-number generator. See `http://openfortress.org/cryptodoc/random/` or `http://random.org/`.

Header bits

DNSSEC introduces three new DNS message header bits:

- *Authenticated Data* ("`ad`") is set by DNSSEC-enabled caching name servers in replies if *they* have verified all the DNSSEC-related resource records before returning an answer to the client. If any records fail to verify, the caching name server clears the flag, and you won't see it in dig's `flags` line.

- *Checking Disabled* ("`cd`") is used by resolvers (e.g. libunbound) to indicate that they are able to do DNSSEC verification on their own. By setting this flag, the resolver instructs upstream caching name servers *not* to bother verifying DNSSEC records, because it can handle the task itself.

- *DNSSEC OK* ("`do`") specifies that the client supports DNSSEC and wants DNSSEC-related records in the response.

ISC's DLV registry

The Internet Systems Consortium (ISC) runs a DLV (DNSSEC look-aside validation) service. It defines a set of procedures for submitting your data to be included in their DLV zone. (See `http://www.isc.org/ops/dlv`)

Key management

- The RIPE NCC has a suite of tools (created by Olaf Kolkman) designed to ease the management of keys in DNSSEC: maintkeydb is a shell for creating and maintaining keys, and dnssigner signs zones (see `https://www.ripe.net/projects/disi/dnssec_maint_tool/`).
- You'll find some more tools for managing authoritative DNSSEC zones and settings for caching name servers at `http://www.dnssec-tools.org/`

Key rollover

Signed RRSIGs created when you sign a zone for DNSSEC have a default lifetime of 30 days, starting 1 hour prior to the current time. You can specify different start and end validity times for keys when running dnssec-signzone with the `-s` and `-e` options respectively; specify the option's value as either +*N*, where *N* is a number of seconds, or as an absolute time in *YYYYMMDDHHMMSS* notation.

Because DNSSEC keys – technically, the RRSIGs – have a limited lifetime (i.e. they expire), you have to replace them occasionally, taking great care to not break existing chains of trust during this so-called *key rollover*.

Here's what happens when the keys used to sign a zone have expired:

```
$ unbound-host -v www.es.qupps.biz
www.es.qupps.biz has address 192.168.1.20 (BOGUS (security failure))
www.es.qupps.biz has address 192.168.1.21 (BOGUS (security failure))
www.es.qupps.biz has no IPv6 address (BOGUS (security failure))
www.es.qupps.biz has no mail handler record (BOGUS (security failure))

$ dig www.es.qupps.biz
;; ->>HEADER<<- opcode: QUERY, status: SERVFAIL, id: 49100
;; flags: qr rd ra; QUERY: 1, ANSWER: 0, AUTHORITY: 0, ADDITIONAL: 0
```

If you compare this with unbound-host's output on page 522, you get an inkling of the problems that DNSSEC can cause: programs start failing because their addresses cannot be resolved.

We don't discuss key rollover further; read the *DNSSEC HOWTO* (see below) for information on how to go about this.

Signing metrics

A report on the signing of a large TLD zone (.CA) discusses methods and signing characteristics (see `http://www.nlnetlabs.nl/downloads/ca-reg.pdf`).

Further reading

- Olaf Kolkman's *DNSSEC HOWTO*, is a must-read. It contains tips on key rollover, troubleshooting etc. (see `http://www.nlnetlabs.nl/dnssec_howto/`).
- `http://www.dnssec.net/` is a gateway to a huge selection of documents, articles and presentations about DNSSEC.

Chapter

23 Performance

If your experiment needs statistics, you ought to have done a better experiment.

Ernest Rutherford

Introduction

So, you are going to set up your preferred DNS server, but how much can it actually deliver? Is performance important for you? (Surprisingly perhaps, for many sites it won't be a major concern.) In this chapter we discuss how we tested both the authoritative and the caching servers, the results we obtained, and what you should observe when measuring performance.

Benchmarks are difficult to conduct and even more difficult to trust, as they reflect only the requirements of the people who conducted the benchmarks. (As the saying goes, "Never believe a statistic unless you have forged it yourself".) We have not conducted the ultimate benchmark – we don't have the means to do so. We have not measured network latency, just as we haven't measured the impact a firewall imposes on serving DNS.

Our intention is to gather information on the possible throughput that the authoritative and caching name servers can deliver, and what the memory requirements are. How fast these program run depends on many factors including, but not limited to: hardware (CPU, disks, memory), software (operating system, swapping behavior), network throughput and latency, and the SQL or LDAP back-end used, if any.

23.1 How we carried out the performance tests

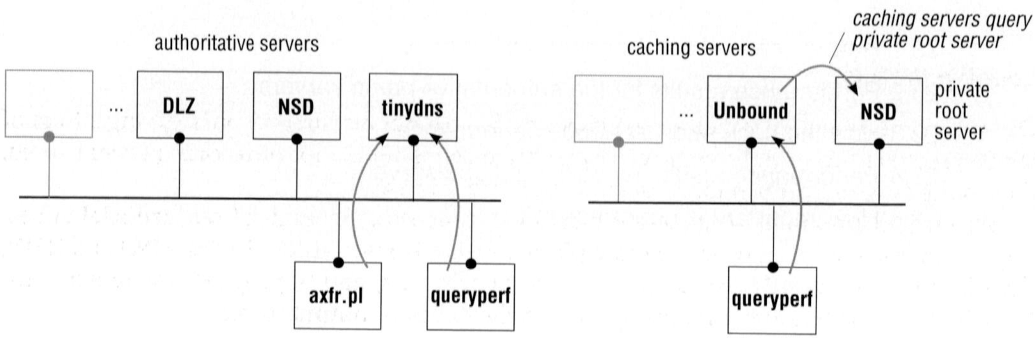

Figure 23.1: Lab environment for performance tests

23.1.1 Test environment

We used the following hardware and software environment:

- A dual core Intel T7300 CPU running at 2.0 GHZ with 32K of L1 and 4MB of L2 cache enabled, 2GB RAM, a single ST9120823AS hard disk, and an Ethernet NIC (PCI Express) running at 100Mb/s.
- Centos 5 release (x86_64 Final) operating system running a GNU/Linux kernel version 2.6.18-8.1.14.el5 SMP, with 3993.77 BogoMIPS.
- OpenLDAP version 2.3.38 provided as *Symas OpenLDAP Gold* by Symas Corp.
- MySQL version 5.0.22 (in tests that required an SQL database).
- Wherever possible we used the latest versions of the name servers, and we compiled them ourselves from their respective source distributions.

We set up the lab shown in Figure 23.1 to conduct the performance tests. The following sections explain how we configured the servers, and the results we obtained.

23.1.2 Creating thousands of zone names

We created 100 001 zones (qupps.biz and another artificial 100 000 zones) as follows:

- We obtained a list of words (see Notes), chose the first 100 000, and appended "01" to each. (Our test setup should not contact the public DNS at all, but just in case we make a mistake, we used zone names that are unlikely to exist in the real world.)
- We randomly appended one of net, org and com to each name:

```
#!/usr/bin/perl
srand (time ^ $$ ^ unpack "%L*", `ps axww | gzip`);
@tld = qw(net org com);
while (<>) {
    chomp;
    $n = rand(3) % 3;
    print "$_" . "01." . $tld[$n] . "\n";
}
```

Loading the zones

Our zones are small. All zones except qupps.biz have eight resource records, giving a total of 800 036 records. You might very well have huge zones with a lot of records in them. If so, the results of your performance tests may vary from ours.

We created programs to generate consistent zone data for each of our artificial zones. The programs have options to generate plain text files (for MaraDNS, tinydns, BIND and NSD), LDIF files for the OpenLDAP directory server back-ends, and SQL `INSERT` statements for MySQL. Note the following points specific to the different output formats:

file system — Performance of UNIX file systems degrades when you have very large numbers of files in a directory. For this reason, we stored the zone files for MaraDNS, BIND and NSD in a series of subdirectories, named after the first two characters in the zone name, in order to limit the directory sizes. This gave us 176 subdirectories, each containing 1–5 954 zone files; most directories contained 100–1 000 files.

LDAP — We reconfigured the OpenLDAP directory server, and repopulated it with zone data, before each server test. (I.e. each test had its own directory server configuration and database.) When populating the database with slapadd, we were able to use the quick load option (`-q`) because we knew that the data we were loading was valid.

- If you use OpenLDAP, you know that it uses Berkeley DB databases as its back-end storage. We ran all tests of name servers with an LDAP directory back-end, with BDB's environment containing a `DB_CONFIG` file with these settings:

```
set_cachesize  0    26214400    0
set_lg_max          10485760
set_lg_bsize        2097152
```

This gives Berkeley DB a $\frac{1}{4}$GB of cache.

- The size of slapd's cache for entries has a big effect on OpenLDAP's performance. We used the following settings in all tests:

  ```
  cachesize    50000
  idlcachesize 50000
  ```

  You will typically configure the cache settings for slapd according to the data you load into your directory and the amount of memory you have available. (Consult the OpenLDAP documentation for more information on tuning.)
- We didn't use any access control lists on the OpenLDAP server.
- We always used the `bdb` back-end in OpenLDAP, but you might well achieve better results with the hierarchical `hdb` back-end.

MySQL

- One of the main reasons for using an SQL database is to use transactions. In particular, PowerDNS with the SQL back-ends *requires* transactions, to be able to handle incoming AXFR zone transfers safely.
- We configured our MySQL 5.0.22 server to use the InnoDB storage engine, and to separate tables into distinct files, with the following directives in `my.cnf`:

  ```
  [mysqld]
  datadir=/var/lib/mysql
  socket=/var/lib/mysql/mysql.sock
  default_storage_engine  = InnoDB
  innodb_file_per_table
  old_passwords=1
  ```
- We didn't tune the MySQL server in any other way.

23.1.3 How we ran the tests

1. We generated a file of test queries (Section 23.1.4).

Then, for each name server, we did the following, always in the same order:

2. We started the name server.
3. To ensure that the server was serving the correct data, we ran a small preliminary test suite that performed ten queries with the "short" option of dig. This prints only an answer, and we compared that answer (automatically of course) to the answer we expected to see.

   ```
   $ dig +short foo.qupps.biz cname
   qupps.biz.
   ```

   We ran this preliminary test with logging enabled on the name server to check that the server was actually receiving and processing the queries correctly. We then disabled logging and restarted the name server (and the MySQL or OpenLDAP server, if used).

4. We ran the queryperf benchmark.

   For this test, we ran queryperf on the loop-back interface, to ensure that the results are independent of the network. (We perform the same test, but over a network, in the next step, so we can compare the two.) The downside is that, in this step, queryperf's use of the CPU reduces the CPU time available to the name server. We ran the benchmark three times, and took the average result, which we label "Queries /sec" in the results tables below.

5. We ran the same test over a 100Mb switched network from a GNU/Linux client. We conducted this test three times and took the average. (The result is labeled "Queries /sec (LAN)".)

6. We ran the queryperf benchmark from the same client machine, starting it ten times simultaneously. The result is labeled "Queries /sec (10 clients)".

7. We then ran the zone transfer test. The elapsed time is labeled "AXFR test".

8. We stopped the name server.

23.1.4 Queries per second

queryperf is a program created by Stephen Jacob of Nominum[1]. It is primarily intended for measuring the performance of authoritative DNS servers, but we also use it for measuring caching server performance. The documentation accompanying queryperf explicitly warns *against* running queryperf and the name server on the same machine, as the CPU usage of queryperf may adversely affect the name server process(es). We ignore this advice so as to isolate the network effects.

We generated an input file, `queryperf.input`, for queryperf from the list of zones we created above. We used the same `queryperf.input` to drive each of the tests 4—6 above. To create `queryperf.input`:

- We fed our list of zones from Section 23.1.2 through the following filter to randomize (un-sort) them:

  ```
  $ rev < zonenames | sort | rev > zonenames.new
  ```

- We fed this new list through the following Perl program:

Listing 23.1: Generating `queryperf.input`

```
#!/usr/bin/perl

use strict;

my @qtypes = qw(A MX TXT);

srand (time);
```

[1]You will find queryperf in the directory `contrib/queryperf` of the BIND source distribution.

```
my $nzone = 0;
while (<>) {
    chomp;
    my $n = rand( 5 ) % 5;

    next if (++$nzone % 9 == 0);
    if ($nzone % 20 == 0) {
        do {
            my $q = rand( $#qtypes ) %  $#qtypes  + 1;
            print "$_ " . $qtypes[$q] . "\n";
        } while ($n--);
    } elsif ($nzone % 8 == 0) {
        print "qupps.biz A\n";
        print "qupps.biz MX\n";
        print "$_ A\n";
    } elsif ($nzone % 25 == 0) {
        print "www.qupps.biz A\n";
    }
}
```

- The resulting file contains queries such as the following:

```
qupps.biz A
qupps.biz MX
cayubaba01.org A
qupps.biz A
qupps.biz MX
calaba01.net A
araba01.org TXT
qupps.biz A
qupps.biz MX
artaba01.net A
www.qupps.biz A
...
```

  The list contains:

  – 13 335 unique zones chosen randomly from the total set of zones.
  – 42 712 total queries in the data set, which are distributed as:
    * 20 445 queries for records of type A.
    * 15 663 queries for records of type MX.
    * 6 604 queries for records of type TXT.

- This distribution of query types closely resembles a sample that we took on live DNS servers at an ISP. Depending on the type of service you provide, the distribution of query types may vary in your environment. For example, a lot of CNAME records can alter the throughput of your name server, because CNAME records cause additional overhead.

- All queries are for zones from our list. While this isn't true in real life, we had to do this or the results for the tinydns server would have plummeted, because tinydns drops queries on zones it is not authoritative for. These queries then result in timeouts on the queryperf client, which drastically reduces throughput.

23.1.5 Testing the performance of zone transfers

If you run slave name servers, zone transfer performance may be important to you.

To measure the performance of outgoing zone transfers from our name servers, we wrote a small Perl program that uses the Net::DNS module to transfer zones. We did this, rather than use a script that invokes a dig command for each transfer, so that we don't have to worry about process execution overheads, etc.

Listing 23.2: Zone transfers (AXFR) with Net::DNS

```
#!/usr/bin/perl

use Net::DNS;
use Time::HiRes qw( gettimeofday tv_interval );
use strict;

my @zones = qw(qupps.biz aa01.net mazdaist01.net);

my $tstart = [gettimeofday];

my $reso = Net::DNS::Resolver->new(
    nameservers    => [ qw(127.0.0.1) ],
    recurse        => 0,
    debug         => 0,
    port         => 53,
    );

for (my $n = 0; $n < 100; $n++) {
    foreach my $z (@zones) {
        my @zone = $reso->axfr($z) or
            warn "Can't transfer: ". $reso->errorstring;

        #foreach my $rr (@zone) {
        #    $rr->print;
        #}
    }
}

my $tend = [gettimeofday];

printf "Elapsed %.2lf\n", tv_interval($tstart, $tend);
exit 0;
```

23.1.6 Process sizes

The ps program displays information about a process's resource utilization. Outputs RSS (resident set size) and VSZ (virtual set size) show how much memory the process is consuming. As we can't gather an exact representation of how much memory a program is consuming, we use ps to show us the information, using:

```
$ ps -eo pid,rss,vsize,cmd -ww
```

The numbers obtained for the "resident set size" and "virtual set size" are labeled "RSS size" and "VSZ size" respectively in the result tables below.

23.2 Performance results for the authoritative name servers

23.2.1 Performance results for MaraDNS

To determine the time required for MaraDNS to start up and load all its zones, we invoked MaraDNS as an authoritative-only daemon via duende (which spawns MaraDNS and logs its output to syslog). While MaraDNS offers very respectable throughput, it takes a long time – nearly 20 minutes – before it is ready to answer queries. The performance results for MaraDNS are in Table 23.1.

Name server	**MaraDNS**
Version	1.3.07.08
Startup time	00:19:41
RSS size	691 668
VSZ size	694 904
Queries /sec	33 572
Queries /sec (LAN)	33 054
Queries /sec (10 clients)	5 439
AXFR test	00:02:50
KB disk usage	409 248

Table 23.1: Performance results of MaraDNS

23.2.2 Performance results for tinydns

As mentioned in Section 23.1.4, because tinydns drops queries on zones for which tinydns is not authoritative, we had to construct the queries for zones for which tinydns *was* authoritative. Failure to do so would have caused queryperf to wait for a timeout before continuing, which would have distorted the results.

Name server	**tinydns**
Version	1.05
Startup time	minimal
RSS size	716
VSZ size	8 404
Queries /sec	14 354
Queries /sec (LAN)	15 054
Queries /sec (10 clients)	1 515
AXFR test	132.25
KB disk usage	123 960 [a]

Table 23.2: Performance results of tinydns

[a] Size includes `data` and `data.cdb`.

23.2.3 Performance results for MyDNS

Startup time for MyDNS is very low; there is no messing about on the back-end initially, because MyDNS just waits for the first query before searching the database. In our tests, MyDNS and its MySQL database ran on the same machine. We ran the MyDNS tests with caching disabled and enabled. The different settings are:

- With zone cache disabled we had the following settings active:

```
zone-cache-size = 0
zone-cache-expire = 0
reply-cache-size = 0
reply-cache-expire = 0
```

- We then re-ran the test with the zone cache enabled:

```
zone-cache-size = 65536
zone-cache-expire = 240
reply-cache-size = 65535
reply-cache-expire = 240
```

The results we obtained for the MyDNS test are in Table 23.3.

Name server	**MyDNS**	**MyDNS**
Special settings	no caching	with zone cache
Version	1.1.0	1.1.0
Startup time	minimal	minimal
RSS size	1 698	182 028
VSZ size	94 010	280 418
Queries /sec	1 288	5 964
Queries /sec (LAN)	1 332	26 141
Queries /sec (10 clients)	141	6 657
AXFR test	00:00:03	00:00:06
Loading time[a]	00:08:31	00:08:31
KB disk usage[b]	627 340	627 340

Table 23.3: Performance results of MyDNS

[a] MySQL bulk-load time.
[b] MySQL size on disk.

During the local queryperf tests with caching disabled, the MySQL database server was handling upwards of an average of 4 800 SQL queries per second, running on the same machine as the MyDNS server.

23.2.4 Performance results for BIND

As with NSD later on, we stored the 100 000 zone files for BIND into sub directories keyed on the first two characters of the zone name. named logs to syslog, from which we can determine how long the program needed to start. named initially loads zone files at a rate of about

1 000/sec, slowing down to about 150/sec at the end of the load. Only when named logs that it is "running" is it ready to answer queries; until that time, it is "deaf". The results are in Table 23.4.

Name server	**BIND**
Version	9.5.0b1
Startup time	00:11:34
RSS size	899 536
VSZ size	992 260
Queries /sec	21 378
Queries /sec (LAN)	26 375
Queries /sec (10 clients)	2 939
AXFR test	00:01:35
KB disk usage[a]	412 244

Table 23.4: Performance results of BIND

[a]File system space used by zone files.

Note, that stopping the BIND name server is also slow: it took 1 minute and 28 seconds for the named process to stop after being told to with rndc.

23.2.5 Performance results for PowerDNS

We ran tests for the PowerDNS with three back-ends: A) the LDAP back-end, B) the OpenDBX back-end with the MySQL driver, C) the bind back-end.

A – PowerDNS with the LDAP back-end

The schema used by the LDAP back-end of PowerDNS has an attribute type named `dNSTTL` which can store a string value containing the TTL of each individual DNS record which will be returned by the back-end. When an entry has the `dNSTTL` attribute type set, the LDAP back-end must convert that to an integer – a computation which might not be necessary. If all or most of your DNS records served by the LDAP back-end use the same TTL, it is preferable to set the PowerDNS global variable default-ttl, leaving the attribute type unset, than to set `dNSTTL` on every record. Nevertheless, individual LDAP entries that require a specific TTL can have the attribute type set to the required value. We ran our tests with only the default-ttl set.

The authors of the LDAP back-end suggest you design your LDAP tree with the "tree" method instead of using the default of "simple", because you gain an additional 7% increase in throughput. Our measurements indicate that there is indeed a small difference, and we would suggest using the "tree" design as well, which is why we did so.

Using indexes can make a huge difference to your LDAP directory's performance (Section A.3.12). OpenLDAP, at least, makes good use of an index when a search operation can utilize it.

We ran the tests for PowerDNS with the LDAP back-end twice: once with caching enabled and once with caching disabled.

B – PowerDNS with the OpenDBX *back-end*

We ran the tests for PowerDNS with the OpenDBX back-end twice: once with caching enabled and once with caching disabled.

C – PowerDNS with the BIND back-end

We ran the tests with the "bind" back-end several times, because we couldn't quite believe our eyes. The startup time of PowerDNS with the "bind" back-end is about 20 times less than that of the BIND name server. Note that we used exactly the same `named.conf` as a source for the BIND name server and for PowerDNS with the "bind" back-end.

Back-end	**OpenDBX**	**OpenDBX**	**bind**	**LDAP**	**LDAP**
Special settings	nocache	cache	nocache	nocache	cache
Version	3.0-svn	3.0-svn	3.0-svn	3.0-svn	3.0-svn
Startup time	minimal	minimal	00:00:36	minimal	minimal
RSS size	5 652	10 000	213 492	4 852	9 276
VSZ size	353 012	289 228	541 888	261 276	262 744
Queries /sec	4 153	23 441	23 943	2 133	24 591
Queries /sec (LAN)	4 308	31 983	28 363	3 289	34 235
Queries /sec (10 clients)	464	3 622	5 261	338	3 705
AXFR test	00:00:04	00:00:04	00:00:04	00:00:07	00:00:07
Loading time	00:09:39[a]	00:09:39	○	00:39:18 [b]	00:39:18
KB disk usage	191 844	191 844	412 244	1 002 464	1 002 464

Table 23.5: Performance results of PowerDNS

[a] MySQL loading time.
[b] slapadd bulk loading time.

23.2.6 Performance results for Bind DLZ

We tested Bind DLZ with: A) the LDAP driver, B) the MySQL driver, C) the BDBHPT driver.

A – LDAP driver

The schema you use for your Bind DLZ LDAP system can make a significant difference. We tested the DLZ-proposed schema, and the minimal schema we presented in Section 9.8.1, page 237, on identical hardware, with an otherwise identical configuration of OpenLDAP. The minimal schema was twice as fast as the DLZ schema in serving entries via Bind DLZ. We believe there are three reasons for this:

1. The LDIF file for our 100 000 zones is 121MB for the minimal schema, and 236 MB for the DLZ schema, so the DLZ schema produces objects that are about twice as large.
2. The DLZ schema recommends many indexes for attribute types, whereas the minimal schema has only two indexes (`objectClass` and `cn`).
3. The DLZ schema has a multitude (15) of attribute types, which require much more processing than the three attribute types of the minimal schema. With the DLZ schema, individual attribute types have to be retrieved from the directory server and then concatenated to form a string, whereas the minimal schema supplies a ready-made string.

For these reasons, we chose to test with our minimal schema, and the numbers below were obtained with that schema.

DLZ driver	LDAP	MySQL	BDBHPT
Version	9.5.01b	9.5.01b	9.5.01b
Startup time	minimal	minimal	minimal
RSS size	11 844	11 308	14 864
VSZ size	103 904	93 156	151 512
Queries /sec	535	1 185	6 715
Queries /sec (LAN)	573	1 116	6 790
Queries /sec (10 clients)	60	114	570
AXFR test	00:00:02.31	00:00:01.74	00:00:01.42
Loading time	00:02:58[a]	00:07:29[b]	00:21:04[c]
KB disk usage	1 037 808	151 964	195 588

Table 23.6: Performance results of Bind DLZ

[a] slapadd loading time.
[b] MySQL loading time.
[c] Berkeley DB loading time.

B – MySQL driver

As per instructions, the named built with MySQL support must be run single-threaded. (Use `-n 1` when launching named.)

How you formulate the queries when designing your database can have a huge effect on performance. As an example, when we ran the queryperf tests, MySQL registered on average 740 SQL queries per second. With the simple query (i.e. without using SQL functions) the SQL queries per second shot up to 3 700.

We ran the query tests without the `hits` table (the update query that you can specify in DLZ's `database` statement in `named.conf`).

C – Berkeley DB High Performance Text driver

The Berkeley DB High Performance Text driver is the fastest driver in Bind DLZ, although the time required to load its database fully is very long.

23.2.7 Performance results for BIND-sdb-LDAP

We had a problem with BIND version 9.5.01b: if we used more than about 15 000 zones it always crashed. We therefore conducted our tests with with version 9.4.1-P1, and we launched BIND with a single worker thread (`-n 1`): this version had no trouble with our large LDAP directory.

Name server	**SDB-LDAP**
Version	9.4.1-P1
Startup time	00:09:17
RSS size	534 988
VSZ size	588 016
Queries /sec	772
Queries /sec (LAN)	788
Queries /sec (10 clients)	95
AXFR test	00:00:02
Loading time	00:02:49 [a]
KB disk usage	884 240

Table 23.7: Performance results of BIND SDB LDAP

[a] slapadd bulk loading time.

23.2.8 Performance results for NSD

We stored the zone files for NSD into subdirectories as described in Section 23.2.4. A rebuild of a fresh `nsd.db` with NSD's zone compiler took just over two minutes of elapsed time, and NSD was ready to answer within a few seconds (Table 23.8). As you will see from the table, NSD is undoubtedly the server that offers the best performance in our environment.

Name server	**NSD**
Version	3.0.7
Startup time	minimal
RSS size	267 738
VSZ size	284 034
Queries /sec	78 757
Queries /sec (LAN)	38 806
Queries /sec (10 clients)	3 856
AXFR test	00:20:06
Loading time	00:02:17 [a]
KB disk usage	470 856 [b]

Table 23.8: Performance results of NSD

[a] Loading time is the time to compile all zones with nsdc rebuild.

[b] Size includes all zone files and `nsd.db`.

23.2.9 Servers not included in the performance tests

There are two servers we don't include values for, because we had problems with both.

ldapdns This server attained peaks of up to 2 920 queries/sec, but it froze after a while when flooded with queries.

Windows DNS This server took a very long time to load and we didn't obtain any figures.

23.3 How the back-ends influence performance

The performance tables show that the servers that use file system-based storage for zone data are an order of magnitude (or more) faster than the servers with a database or an LDAP directory back-end.

23.3.1 Databases and LDAP directories

We recommend you place your SQL database server or your LDAP directory server as close as possible, network-wise, to your name server. In fact, we recommend you run the back-end on the same machine as the name server. This eliminates network latency, and makes debugging your DNS more straightforward. The downside is a larger total load on the machine, but for many installations this will not be important.

LDAP

- You can improve performance by tuning Berkeley DB's `DB_CONFIG` file. Read the Berkeley DB documentation on how to do that.
- OpenLDAP profits tremendously by setting its cache sizes to the size of the database if possible. The values of `cachesize` and `idlcachesize` greatly influence slapd's performance, and you are well advised to experiment with your data set.
- Access Control Lists in slapd can reduce performance considerably. Try and determine exactly what ACLs you need and keep them to a minimum.

MySQL

- Which database engine you choose for MySQL affects performance. We chose the InnoDB engine because it supports transactions. This is important for slave servers loading a zone into your database tables; by treating the whole zone load as a single transaction, it can be safely rolled back to the pre-zone-load state if anything goes wrong. However, you might wish to deploy a different database engine to achieve better performance if zone transfers aren't a consideration at your site.
- Bind DLZ cannot make use of multi-threaded connections due to limitations in MySQL. You might be better off using PostgreSQL if you intend to deploy Bind DLZ and want to squeeze the last drop of performance out of it.

- Read the resources in the Notes section below for more information on MySQL performance.

23.3.2 Caching

The figures provided for MyDNS and PowerDNS show that enabling query and reply caching increases throughput, to the detriment of currency of the data. If a query (or its answer) is cached for a long time, a name server can quickly return a reply, but it takes a long time for an update to the back-end database to be refreshed by the name server. Nevertheless, we think you will probably want to enable packet caching, which also reduces the load on your back-end database servers.

23.4 Performance results for caching name servers

We were also interested in determining which of the caching name servers we discussed in Chapter 17 offered the best throughput. Since it is very difficult (if not impossible) to perform DNS queries over the public DNS with deterministic results, we proceeded as follows:

- We set up a private root server. To make sure that the root name server isn't the bottleneck, we chose the name server which performed best in the authoritative name server tests: NSD, the Name Server Daemon.
- On the same machine we ran the caching name server, which was set up to query its root name server on 127.0.0.1.
- We then ran the queryperf tests.

We did not tune the memory limits for the servers; we left them at their default settings. The values obtained for the caching name servers are in Table 23.9. Note also, that we have not measured how well these servers perform with DNSSEC queries.

	MaraDNS	**BIND**	**dnscache**	**Recursor**[a]	**Unbound**
Queries /sec[b]	13 846	16 066	14 957	10 796	25 072
Queries /sec (LAN)	13 308	26 656	13 114	21 218	30 569
Queries /sec (10 clients)	3 068	3 003	2 928	2 074	8 276
RSS size	1 336	40 916	1 712	14 336	16 828
VSZ size	168 408	195 380	6 044	26 500	180 648

Table 23.9: How the caching name servers performed

[a] PowerDNS Recursor
[b] Includes first run which is generally slow.

23.5 How important is performance?

The question "is performance important?" is a difficult one to answer generally. The answer will usually be "yes, but...". The "but" is important.

- If you operate a root name server installation or you are a huge ISP, performance might be important to you. (On the other hand, for an ISP, functionality, manageability, etc. might be more important than the performance offered by a particular name server brand.)
- At the other end of the scale, performance is the very least of your worries in a Small Office / Home Office environment; ease of use is much more important.
- Performance requirements depend on the query load on your name servers. We have discussed that it is difficult to predict the load, but we recommend you keep an eye on the load of your name servers so that you can react quickly if need be.
- One of our customers has several companies and a few thousand DNS zones in its portfolio. Their four Internet-facing name servers have to serve a total of about 400 queries per minute (i.e. about 7 queries per second). To them, performance is very low on the list of requirements, so their choice of name server depends not on throughput but on manageability.

Summary

- Performance depends on a number of factors, some of which you can influence directly, such as hardware.
- The performance data we obtained relate to our environment, with our test methods, on our hardware. The data you obtain may be quite different.
- For some installations, performance may be crucial. For others, ease of maintenance, or the ability of a specific brand of name server to integrate with existing infrastructure, will be more important than straight performance.

Notes and further reading

Tuning MySQL

Tuning can improve the performance of MySQL. We recommend the following for more information:

- *High Performance MySQL* by Jeremy Zawodny (O'Reilly).
- The tuning-primer program on `http://day32.com/MySQL/` prints suggestions on adapting MySQL's configuration to your running system.
- `http://tinyurl.com/ovmzq`

Tuning OpenLDAP

Two good sources of documentation for setting up your OpenLDAP directory server are:

- The *OpenLDAP Admin Guide* (see `http://www.openldap.org/doc/admin/`)
- The *OpenLDAP Faq-O-Matic* (see `http://www.openldap.org/faq/`)

Getting words

The list of words we used to synthetically create names of zones were taken from resources on the Web, including:

- `http://wordlist.sourceforge.net/`
- `http://www.net-comber.com/wordurls.html`
- `http://www.outpost9.com/files/WordLists.html`

Further reading

- Nonimum Inc. has a very interesting paper on *How to Measure the Performance of a Caching DNS Server* (see `http://www.nominum.com/info_center/dns_dhcp/`).

Chapter

24 Securing and monitoring your DNS servers

As soon as the boss decides he wants his workers to do something, he has two problems: making them do it and monitoring what they do.

Robert Krulwich

Introduction

Because the DNS is such an important service, both on the Internet as well as within your organization, you need to make sure it is secure, and you should monitor it to ensure it is always available and performing adequately. Set up a monitoring system (if you don't yet have one) to monitor the health of your DNS service.

A very embarrassing, and frequently encountered, situation is where a prospective customer tries to contact a company's Web site, but gets a "can't find the server at www.qupps.biz" error message, instead of the very expensive corporate-branded Web site. While an error message like "can't establish a connection to the server" clearly indicates a temporary problem in some unspecified place, the first message is a no-no and you should *never* let it happen. "Domain name does not exist" (NXDOMAIN) answers are often cached, sometimes for long periods, so even if the client retries a few minutes later, they are likely to get the same error, and to give up for good. Bye bye prospective client.

24.1 Securing your DNS name servers

The DNS requires[1] every zone to have at least two authoritative servers, to maintain a high level of availability: if one server cannot be reached, the remaining server(s) can answer the queries. Here are some points to keep in mind:

- DNS is important, not just for "computer systems". You might be using VOIP telephony, which relies on DNS. If your telephone system cannot get DNS replies, it may prevent you from using your phone system in an emergency.
- Have two or more servers serving your DNS data, whether you are offering authoritative zones on the public Internet, or whether you are hosting DNS within your organization.
- If disaster strikes, you don't want your complete DNS infrastructure to go down with you. Place the servers as far apart, geographically, as possible. If you can, place your servers in different countries, or within your organization, in different buildings. If you have different data centers, use them for your DNS servers as well.
- If you cannot spread your servers to different locations because you don't have offices there, you might be able to find some friendly organization who is willing to host servers for you. In this case, the hoster must allow you to monitor your infrastructure at their site.
- Within your organization, or within a single building, place your servers as far apart as possible from a network point of view. Ensure that if a single switch or router fails, it doesn't make your DNS infrastructure inaccessible.
- DNS servers do not typically require a tremendous amount of processing power, as we saw in Chapter 23, so the cost of providing a hot (or cold) standby-system that takes over in an emergency can be low. If your data is relatively static, a VMware system or other virtual machine image that you can boot up in case of emergency might even satisfy your needs in terms of serving DNS when disaster strikes.

[1] RFC 1034, section 4.1

- You will want to secure the systems on which you provide DNS services, and permit only authorized personnel to access them. Securing *nix systems is beyond the scope of this book, but there is a lot of good literature on the topic (see Notes), and we recommend you protect your machines.

- Use TSIG wherever possible to secure zone transfers to or from your DNS servers.

- Use DNSSEC to secure your zone data if you can, i.e. if you're using BIND or NSD.

- Always deploy more than one caching name server. Place a caching name server on each machine (such as mail servers, proxy servers, etc.) that makes heavy use of the DNS.

- Carefully consider where you place your caching servers on your network. You almost certainly don't want a caching server open to the public Internet, for the following reasons:

  - Resources.

    Your network and system resources are consumed.

  - Cache poisoning attacks.

    Attackers can generate spoofed traffic to caching DNS servers in so-called *cache poisoning* attacks, causing caching name servers to return bogus (forged) results to queries.

  - DDoS attacks.

    Name servers can be used as distributed denial of service (DDoS) attack amplifiers. The attacker sends a small spoofed UDP name service query to an open name server, forging the victim's IP address; the open name server then returns a large answer, such as a TXT record, to the forged IP address. If this is done on an ongoing basis with a large number of open name servers, it can flood the victim's IP address with responses from thousands (or tens of thousands) of name servers, exhausting the victim's available network bandwidth.

- If you use a DNS server with a database back-end, such as PowerDNS, MyDNS or Bind DLZ, secure the SQL database or LDAP directory servers as carefully as you secure the DNS servers. Place the back-end as close as possible, network wise, to the DNS server. Use Access Control Lists (ACL) to protect data from unauthorized clients, and disable network access to the services from all but your DNS servers and management stations.

- Most sites use firewalls to protect their DNS servers and networks. While a firewall will increase DNS query-reply round trip time, the increase will not typically be a problem unless you want the last drop of performance.

- Use secure mechanisms to replicate your SQL database or LDAP directory data. Setting up SSL/TLS is not difficult and it ensures confidentiality.

- Use ssh, scp, and rsync securely, by creating and using SSH keys to access your systems. Not only is this more secure than passwords, you can even dispense with passwords altogether if you take the time to set up your SSH environment appropriately.

  If you use an LDAP directory server for authentication purposes, consider the patch to OpenSSH that allows it to look up public keys in an LDAP directory[2]. We use this extensively, as it enables us to lock out accounts when an authorized user decides to leave the organization (so we don't have to mess around with `authorized_keys` files but just modify the departing user's LDAP entries).

- Place configuration files, zone files (if you use them), notes on what to do in a disaster scenario, etc. into a revision control system. Systems such as subversion are easy to set up, and allow you to back out of trouble if you misconfigure something.

- Back up your systems, your configuration files, and your zone data.

DNS is a vital network service, and as such it needs to be monitored. We discuss monitoring, what it does and what you should monitor, next.

24.2 Monitoring

You have set up your DNS infrastructure using one or other of the name server brands discussed, or you may already have a DNS infrastructure, but do you monitor it to ensure smooth and reliable service? As with all important IT services, it is vital to ensure continuous DNS operation with a minimum of unplanned downtime. Monitoring helps you do this and helps you detect when things go wrong. It is like Murphy says: "if anything can go wrong, it will", and you should be informed when your services fail.

24.2.1 What does the monitoring system do?

Broadly, monitoring a service can do three things for you:

1. Constantly check the state of services, and machines, and perhaps record this information for later analysis, if required.

2. Alert an administrator – or preferably a group of administrators – when an important service fails (e.g. a DNS server fails to answer a test query), or starts to degrade (e.g. a server answers a test query, but takes an abnormally long time to do so).

3. Attempt a recovery of the failed service (e.g. restart the server daemon if a DNS server fails to answer a test query).

   Unfortunately, automatic recovery is difficult to implement, as the reasons for failure can be sundry (Section 3.1.3).

[2]`http://dev.inversepath.com/trac/openssh-lpk`

By monitoring, you check that your vital DNS service is performing smoothly, that the machine on which the service is running isn't overloaded, and that it has enough spare capacity to handle any likely load growth in the near future. An increase in load can be due to normal growth (you have added a handful or a couple of hundred additional zones to your servers), or it could be due to a sudden high volume of queries being sent your way (imagine one of your Web sites gets "Slashdotted"[3]). Or it could be due to a Denial of Service attack.

Keeping an eye on your system is not always easy, but there are tool chains that help a lot. You might already have an enterprise monitoring system, but if you don't, look at mon (see `http://www.linux-ha.org/mon`) or Nagios, which we highly recommend (see Notes).

24.2.2 What should you monitor?

Deciding which components to monitor can be a daunting task, depending on the infrastructure you have set up. Here are some things we recommend you include in your monitoring. (If you use Nagios, it supplies ready-made plug-ins for many of them.)

- Hardware.

  Modern server hardware can detect and alert you about problems on components within the system. For example, a failure on a RAID system can be announced via SNMP or a defective NIC can trigger an alert on a management card. In all cases, we recommend you try and integrate hardware monitoring into your overall network monitoring system.

- System health.

  Monitor the overall health of the machine's operating system (c.f. plug-ins, item 1, page 576). This includes:

  - System availability. Has the machine recently rebooted? If so, why did that happen? Was it due to human intervention, power failure, or hardware failure?
  - Software updates. Are the versions of the software deployed on your systems up to date?
  - CPU utilization. Is your machine overloaded? Is it swapping too much?
  - RAID status. If you have RAID disks, is the RAID working? Is the software RAID mirroring your disks?

- Disk space.

  If your systems are low on free disk space, incoming zone transfers might fail because they can't be stored anywhere, and low disk space means log messages warning you of that can't be written either (c.f. plug-ins, item 2, page 576).

[3]The term stems from the huge amount of traffic produced by a link on the popular Slashdot news site, that can overwhelm underpowered sites.

- Processes.

  When you deploy a brand of name server, note how many instances of it are displayed in the process table. (Some programs are displayed more than once if they are multi-threaded). You can then monitor if the count of process-table entries changes, to detect whether the process(es) are running correctly (c.f. plug-ins, item 3, page 576).

- Connectivity.

  The DNS server host is network-connected on all its interfaces (c.f. plug-ins, item 4, page 576)

- Logs.

  Monitor your log files for unusual error-messages. Ensure that the system has enough free disk space to write messages to them (c.f. plug-ins, item 5, page 577)

You should monitor these components specific to the DNS:

- DNS replies: are your name servers replying to queries?

- Start of Authority (SOA) serial numbers: are your master and slave DNS servers up to date? Are zone transfers falling behind? (c.f. plug-ins, item 6, page 577)

- Are your slave servers performing incoming zone transfers correctly and in a timely fashion? Imagine you update your master server and your slaves fall behind. What happens when a client queries a domain name that exists only on the master server and not yet on the slaves? The reply depends on which of the servers the query was directed at – a Bad Thing.

  Are your BIND servers transferring zones from another name server with a database back-end to which you or a colleague have erroneously added an Address (A) record to a CNAME record[4]? BIND will fail to load the zone because of that.

- DNS notifications: are your servers sending out notifications? We discussed (Section 15.2.2) that Net::DNS::Nameserver has been modified at our request to add a handler for detecting DNS NOTIFY requests; you can use this in your monitoring software to detect whether DNS notifications are being received by your systems.

  The way we do this is with a small server written with Perl's Net::DNS::Nameserver module:

[4]No CNAME and other data...

Listing 24.1: NOTIFY handler with Perl's Net::DNS::Nameserver

```
#!/usr/bin/perl -w

use strict;
use Net::DNS::Nameserver;

sub notification {
    my ($qname, $qclass, $qtype, $peer, $packet) = @_;

    # We are being notified (NOTIFY) for domain $qname.

    print "WOW. Got NOTIFY for $qname!\n";

    # Submit this notification to your monitoring system. In
    # the case of Nagios, you could update a database table
    # from which it later reads the result, or you can
    # implement a passive notification, etc.

    return ('NOERROR', [], [], [],
                       { aa => 1, opcode => 'NS_NOTIFY_OP'});
}

sub handler {
    my ($qname, $qclass, $qtype, $peer) = @_;
    my (@ans, @auth, @add);

    return ('SERVFAIL', \@ans, \@auth, \@add);
}

my $ns = Net::DNS::Nameserver->new(
    LocalAddr     => '127.0.0.2',
    LocalPort     => 53,
    ReplyHandler => \&handler,       # Unused, but needs defining
    NotifyHandler => \&notification,
    Verbose       => 0,
    Debug     => 0,
) || die("Can't create nameserver object: $!");

$ns->main_loop;
```

With NSD for example, you set it up so that it sends an additional notification to your handler. In `nsd.conf` we configure:

```
zone:
   name: "qupps.biz"
   zonefile: qupps.biz.zone
   notify: 127.0.0.2 NOKEY
   notify: ...
```

That causes NSD to notify the host at address 127.0.0.2 (on the loop-back interface), thus contacting our notification handler.

- If you have a large group of DNS servers, you want ensure they are all running the same version number of the software. Use your monitoring infrastructure to check periodically whether your server versions differ. (Once a week should be enough).

If you haven't forbidden your name server answering to version.bind queries, you can check with a simple DNS query:

```
$ dig +short @192.168.1.20 version.bind ch txt
"9.2.4"

$ dig +short @192.168.1.164 version.bind ch txt
"NSD 3.0.7"
```

- Here's an example of a cheap form of load balancing that we implemented for a customer, which makes good use of the monitoring system. The site has two Web servers; one is a hot-standby for the other. By default, the DNS entry for www.*site* points to the primary Web server. We implemented a Nagios plug-in that determines whether the primary is responding correctly (Figure 24.1). As soon as the primary doesn't respond, Nagios updates the back-end database of the DNS server, and changes the www.*site* Address (A) record to point to the secondary Web server. The TTL of the DNS record is set to a very low value, so that the switch from primary to secondary happens quickly.

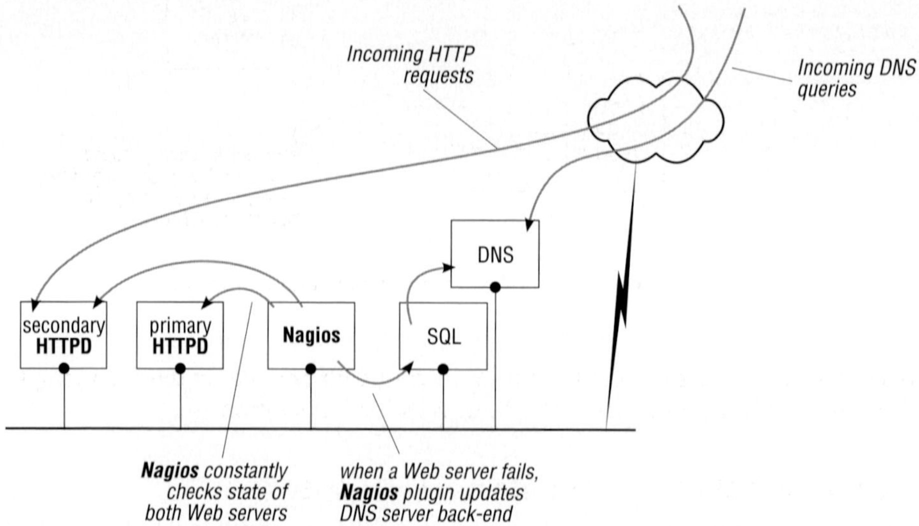

Figure 24.1: Nagios monitors Web servers and updates DNS

If your DNS servers make use of an SQL database or an LDAP directory server, you should also monitor these components:

- Connectivity between the DNS server and the external database or LDAP server, if these components are not both on the same physical machine (c.f. plug-ins, item 4, page 576)
- Replication between back-ends. Let's say you have two name servers, each with an LDAP back end. If the back-ends are not replicating correctly, a query to one DNS

server could obtain a different answer than from the other DNS server, but only while the back-ends are out of sync. These intermittent errors are hard to detect.

Here's an easy way to check your SQL or LDAP replication. Periodically, update a counter in the master back end; you can use cron or your monitoring system to do this regularly. Then use another tool to check the value of this counter in each instance of your back-end; if the counter is the same on all back-end instances, replication is working correctly Figure 24.2).

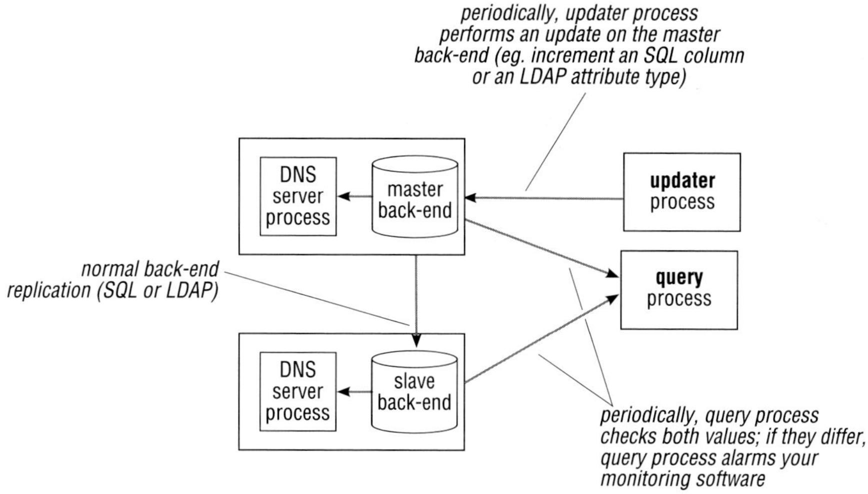

Figure 24.2: Using a "probe" to check back-end replication

That concludes our discussion on monitoring of your DNS service. In the following section we look at how you can gather statistics about your DNS operation.

24.3 Gathering statistics about your DNS operation

In the chapters about the individual brands of name servers, we discussed how (if at all) they produce their own statistics. Some don't produce the detailed statistics you might want, in which case you can use one or more of the tools below. These tools are name server agnostic: they sniff DNS packets on the wire, so they work with any name server implementation.

Even though some servers can produce their own statistics, if you are using more than one brand, or think you might change later, you might want to deploy a solution that caters for any brand of name server, as described in the next section.

24.3.1 DNS Statistics Collector: dsc

DNS Statistics Collector, dsc, is a program by The Measurement Factory, written by Duane Wessels and Ken Keys (see `http://dns.measurement-factory.com/tools/dsc/`). It is designed to collect and aggregate statistics from busy authoritative servers, such as those used by TLD and root server operators, but you can use it to collect statistics for any DNS servers you use. The program consists of two major components (Figure 24.3):

1. The collector process sniffs DNS messages received and sent on a network interface. You typically run it either on the machine on which your DNS server is located or on a system connected to a switch port configured with port mirroring, in which case you monitor the port that mirrors your DNS traffic. A configuration file specifies which datasets the collector should collect. The collector dumps the datasets to XML files every 60 seconds.

   Each machine on which DNS is monitored is called a "node", and nodes that have something in common (e.g. location) are called a "system" or "system cluster". For example, you could group the DNS servers for Spain (i.e. the hosts ns1.es.qupps.biz and ns2.es.qupps.biz) into a system you call "Spain".

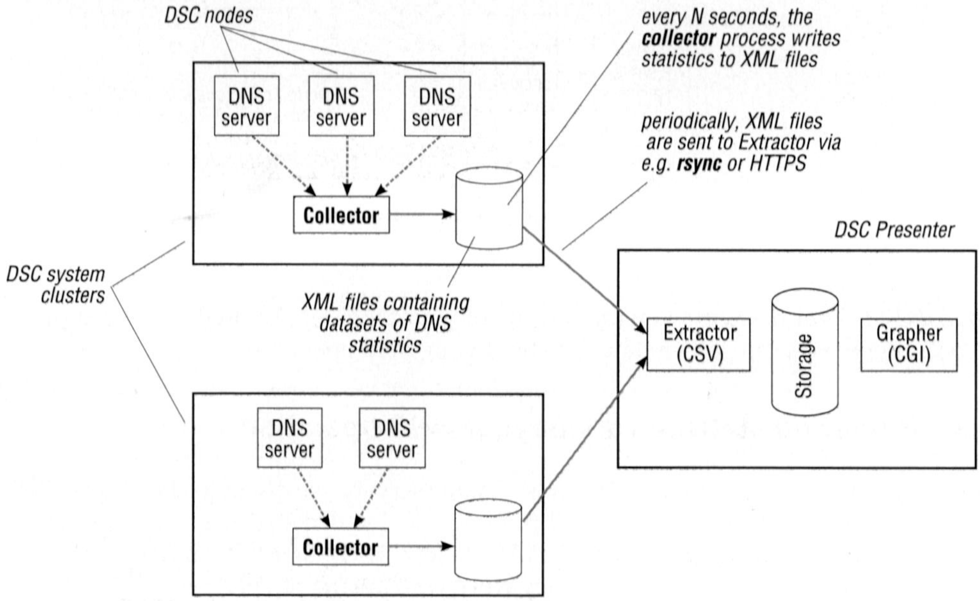

Figure 24.3: Architecture of the DNS Statistics Collector

2. The presenter component receives the XML files from collectors. It uses an extractor process to parse and convert them to a different text-based format. dsc provides scripts for "uploading" the XML files from your collectors to the presenter, but you are free to use any means at your disposal.

The presenter then uses a CGI script to display the data in a Web browser, where you select time scales or particular nodes within a server cluster you are interested in (Figure 24.4).

The presenter CGI lets you view your DNS traffic in many different ways, including: by node; by query type (including DNSSEC types); by client geography; by queried TLD; by IP version; by transport (UDP or TCP).

You can install the collector and the presenter on a single machine (i.e. they don't have to be on separate hosts). The documentation for dsc is excellent, and a guide gets you started quickly.

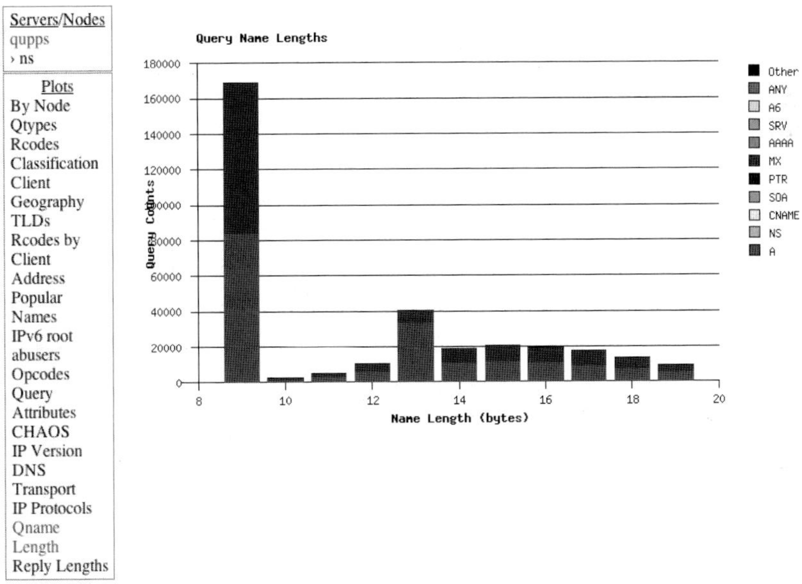

Figure 24.4: One of dsc's many views

24.3.2 Other interesting programs

collectd

If you are interested in collecting performance statistics about services on your machines – including DNS – we recommend collectd, a small daemon that periodically gathers data and stores it in RRD files. collectd doesn't draw the graphs itself, leaving that task to other programs (although the package does include a sample script to call some standard graphing tools). collectd includes numerous plug-ins that collect data, which you enable depending on the statistics you are interested in (see `http://collectd.org`).

dnstop

You're probably familiar with the *nix top program, which displays a list of processes in order of CPU consumption. The Measurement Factory's dnstop is to DNS queries what top is to processes (see `http://dns.measurement-factory.com/tools/dnstop/`). What are the top DNS queries arriving at my host's network interface? dnstop has the answer:

- First-level domains:

```
Query Name         Count       %
------------ --------- ------
com                  696   50.6
net                  228   16.6
de                    82    6.0
nl                    41    3.0
uk                    15    1.1
...
```

- Second level domains:

```
Query Name              Count       %
---------------- --------- ------
google.com                138   10.0
ntp.org                    53    3.9
mens.de                    24    1.7
dsbl.org                   14    1.0
sun.com                    11    0.8
co.uk                      11    0.8
...
```

- Query types and query sources:

```
Query Type      Count       %           Sources             Count       %
---------- --------- ------           ------------- --------- ------
A?               1024    74.6           192.168.1.20         1077    78.6
TXT?               54     3.9           192.168.1.179          23     1.7
MX?                 9     0.7           192.168.1.173          22     1.6
PTR?                8     0.6           192.168.1.203           1     0.1
NS?                 7     0.5
...
```

Summary

- Monitor the health of your DNS name servers and the services they depend on, to preserve business continuity.
- Monitoring should not be taken lightly; we recommend you invest time and effort to set up a reliable network operations monitoring.
- Use any combination of the many tools available to graph your name server utilization.

Where now?

There are hundreds of utilities and programs that involve the DNS, and we discussed only some of the more interesting ones. We recommend you take some time to peruse the offerings at:

- SourceForge (see `http://sourceforge.net/`).
- FreshMeat (see `http://freshmeat.net/`).

Notes and further reading

Nagios

Nagios (Figure 24.5) is a popular Open Source system monitoring tool developed and maintained by Ethan Galstad. It runs on *nix systems, but it can monitor all sorts of machines[5]. Nagios runs intermittent checks on hosts and services by spawning external "plug-ins" that perform the actual checking. Plug-ins can be quite simple: the following small example shows a tiny but functional Nagios plug in that checks for the existence of a file. If the file exists, an "`OK`" is returned to Nagios, otherwise a "`CRITICAL`" situation is announced by exiting with a status of 2:

```
#!/bin/sh

# define exit codes for Nagios
OK=0
WARNING=1
CRITICAL=2
UNKNOWN=3

# check for 'something' (eg. existence of file)
if [ -f "/path/to/some/file" ]; then
    echo "Ok, file exists"
    exit $OK
fi
echo "Critical: file not found"
exit $CRITICAL
```

[5]We deployed Nagios at a customer site and actually drove out a major-league commercial network monitoring system with it. At that site, Nagios today runs on 3 production servers, and monitors 2 800 hosts with 11 200 services on them.

The plug-in returns status information to Nagios, stating whether a service is operational or not (and a line of text that Nagios displays for human consumption). Based on those results, Nagios can send out alerts via e-mail or pagers, and you can configure Nagios to, say, restart a failed service, by hooking an appropriate script into it.

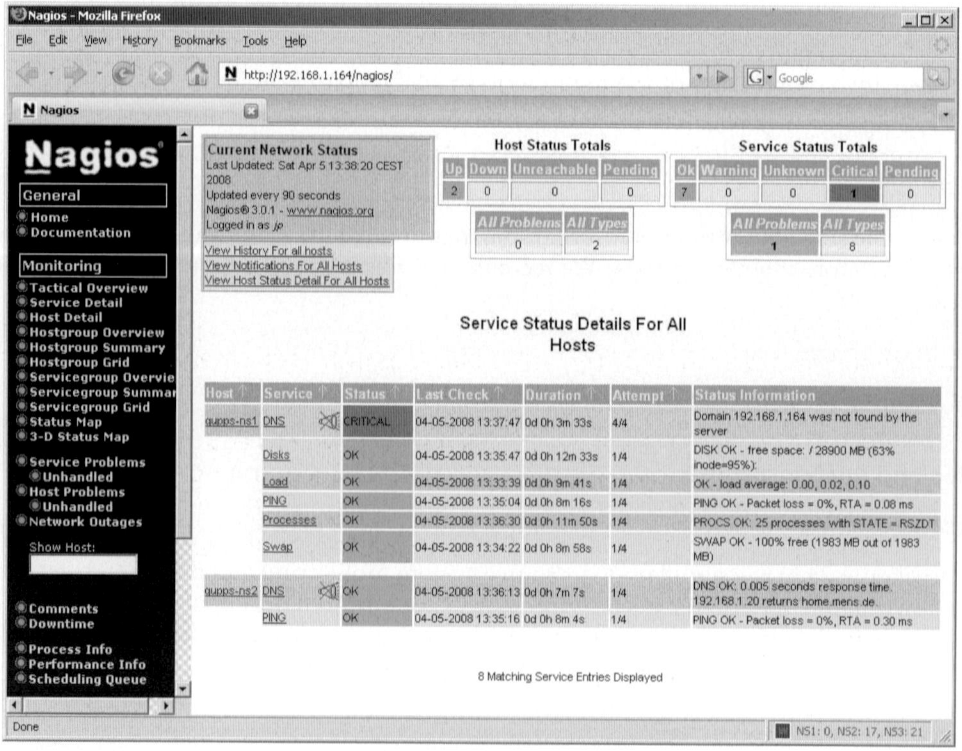

Figure 24.5: Nagios monitoring interface

Nagios delivers a whole array of plug-ins to check services, and you can quite easily create customized plug-ins (or download plug-ins written by others). Some of the available plug-ins include checks for:

1. System health: check_apt checks for software updates, and check_load warns when your machine's load rises above a pre-defined threshold.

2. Disk space: check_disk checks for available space on locally attached disks, check_swap does the same for swap space, and check_smb runs availability checks for remote SMB shares.

3. Processes: check_procs checks processes and warns if the number or names of processes you specify aren't running.

4. Connectivity: check_ftp , check_ldap , check_http , check_imap , check_mysql and check_pop warn you if FTP, LDAP, HTTP, IMAP, MySQL and POP-3 servers are behaving, and check_tcp and check_udp can query arbitrary TCP and UDP services.

5. Logs: check_log detects patterns in log files you specify.

6. DNS: check_dns and check_dig query the DNS with nslookup and dig respectively. The Measurement Factory has two interesting plug-ins which you can download and install: with check_zone_auth you ensure all authoritative name servers for a zone remain in sync, and check_zone_rrsig_expiration warns you when the DNSSEC signatures of your zones are about to expire (see `http://dns.measurement-factory.com/tools/nagios-plugins/`).

Nagios is available at `http://www.nagios.org/`.

whatmon

If you use Mozilla's Firefox browser or Mozilla's Thunderbird e-mail client, you may be interested in a tiny extension (add-on) we wrote called whatmon.

1. Your monitoring software creates an XML file that contains an integer code indicating a success, warning or critical condition, together with a string that whatmon displays on the client's status bar.

   For example, your XML file could contain the following text describing the status of 3 DNS servers:

   ```
   <whatmon>
     <code>0</code>
     <text>NS1: 23, NS2: 14, NS3: 21</text>
     <xhover>All is well.</xhover>
   </whatmon>
   ```

   The `code` 0 indicates success, and the string within the `text` element is what you want displayed. The content of the `xhover` element will be shown as tooltip text. You can display whatever you like – whatmon doesn't interpret the content.

2. whatmon periodically reads that XML from a URL and displays the result on the client's status bar (Figure 24.6). The integer `code` instructs whatmon to use a different colour (green, yellow, red) for the status bar.

Figure 24.6: whatmon at work

We typically create the XML on the fly, with a CGI program or PHP script, for example. whatmon is available from the Mozilla add-ons site, and the latest version and documentation are at `http://fupps.com/extensions/`.

Further reading

- *Building Internet Firewalls*, 2nd ed. by Elizabeth D. Zwicky, D. Brent Chapman, and Simon Cooper, (O'Reilly), is a step-by-step guide to building firewalls. The book covers UNIX, GNU/Linux and Microsoft Windows NT.
- *Real World Linux Security: Intrusion Prevention, Detection and Recovery*, 2nd ed. by Bob Toxen (Prentice Hall), is a guide to protecting GNU/Linux from security risks, including firewalls, break-in studies, and recovery from intrusions.
- We recommend two books for Nagios version 2:
  - *Pro Nagios 2.0*, by James Turnbull (Apress).
  - *Nagios System and Network Monitoring*, by Wolfgang Barth (O'Reilly).

Appendix

A Getting started with (Open)LDAP

LDAP directory servers are less well known than SQL databases, so here we give you a short introduction to LDAP, and show you how to get an OpenLDAP server running quickly and painlessly.

A.1 A brief introduction to directories

A *directory* is a collection of information that is generally read more frequently than it is written to. A prime example is an internal telephone directory, which you consult frequently (when you look up a telephone number), but which is seldom updated (only when someone relocates). Most people (even in the computing world) talk of a "database" when they actually mean a directory. For example, the file on *nix systems containing user entries (`/etc/passwd`) is called the "passwd database", but it is essentially a directory. Directories are used throughout the computing world; in particular, the DNS is a directory.

A.1.1 LDAP – the Lightweight Directory Access Protocol

Directories are frequently made available via *LDAP*, the *Lightweight Directory Access Protocol*. LDAP is a protocol for accessing directories. It is similar to SQL in that it is also a language for interacting with directories, but the similarity ends there: LDAP is *not* a relational database system, nor does it provide relational integrity, or transactions. LDAP is ideally suited to storing relatively small objects which are frequently read and seldom updated.

LDAP provides client-server access to directories over a network: it is a *directory service*. It offers an interface to search and read information from the directory, as well as an interface to add, modify and delete that information. LDAP lacks an SQL-like reporting and query interface, although there are programs that can guide you in obtaining the information you want. Generally LDAP is used with a set of programs that utilize it as a directory service. LDAP is very widely used for usernames (and their authentication information), e-mail addresses, telephone numbers, contacts, and e-mail routing information (for mail servers), but it can also be used as a data store for DNS zone data, as we have seen with the LDAP directory server back-ends to BIND SDB, Bind DLZ, ldapdns, and PowerDNS.

A.1.2 The Directory Information Tree

Data in an LDAP directory is organized hierarchically. Reasons for storing data hierarchically include:

- You may wish to grant permissions to a group of individuals (or an application) based on the directory structure. For example you will want to allow only the HR department to access employee payroll data, but allow anybody to see the DNS data in your directory.
- You can combine replication with individual branches of the tree. For example, you might replicate the branch containing data for a department to a dedicated distant server for that department.

LDAP data is stored hierarchically in a tree starting at a root (usual local to your LDAP server), and branching down into individual entries, just like the DNS or a computer's file system (Figure A.1). The top level entry, just below the root of the hierarchy, typically represents your organization. Under that in the hierarchy might be entries for smaller groupings, such as departments, etc. The hierarchy might end with entries for individual people or resources.

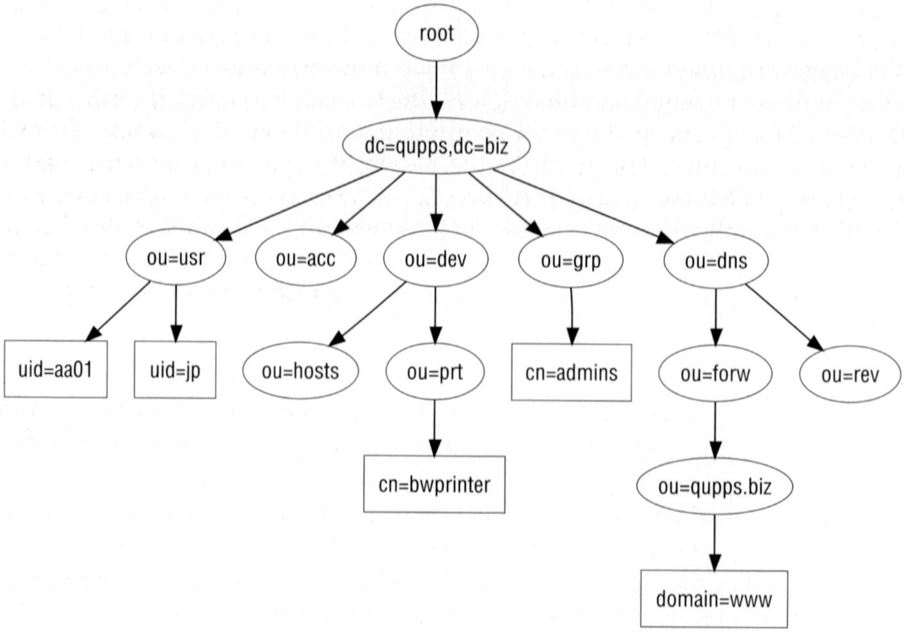

Figure A.1: LDAP tree

The tree structure is called the *Directory Information Tree* (*DIT*). Each entry in a directory is an *object*. Objects are of two types: containers and leaves. A *leaf* is an object at the end of a branch. A *container* is like a folder: it contains other containers or leaves. (In Figure A.1 we show containers as ovals and leaves as rectangles). Note that containers can be empty, and leaves can, at any time, be converted to containers by creating subordinate leaves. In other words, there is nothing really special about a container: you can create a container as a "person" object and later decide to change it to store "furniture" objects in it.

A.1.3 Entries in an LDAP directory

A directory consists of *entries*: each node in the directory information tree is an entry, that contains descriptive information. For example, entries might describe people or network resources such as printers or fax machines, or contain DNS data, which is what we want to do in this book. Each entry is *uniquely* identified in its hierarchical level by its *distinguished name* (*DN*) which is analogous to the full path of file in a file system. For example, the distinguished name for an entry for user `aa01` in Figure A.1 is:

```
uid=aa01, ou=usr, dc=qupps, dc=biz
```

To construct the DN take the name of the entry itself (called the *Relative Distinguished Name* or *RDN*) and concatenate the names of its ancestor entries, separating them with a comma and an optional space. In the example above, "`uid`" represents the user ID of the entry, "`ou`" represents the organizational unit in which the entry belongs (i.e. the container), and the rest (i.e. "`dc=qupps, dc=biz`") represents the the base DN. The RDN of an entry must be an attribute within the entry itself; for example, you cannot create an RDN of `uid=`*something* if the LDAP entry doesn't have an attribute called `uid` with a value of *something*.

RDNs can be multivalued (i.e. made up of more than one attribute-value pair), in which case the attribute-value pairs are separated by plus signs (`+`). This is typically used if it is difficult to ensure uniqueness of RDNs within a single container. For example, if you have a container called `ou=People`, and you have two Jane Smiths, you can use their e-mail address to construct unique RDNs; you'd specify `cn=Jane Smith+mail=jane.smith@example.net` as the RDN of one, and `cn=Jane Smith+mail=j.s@example.net` as the RDN of the second.

The top level of an LDAP directory tree is referred to as the *base DN*. The base DN (all objects in Figure A.1 are in `dc=qupps,dc=biz`) is a distinguished name which typically takes one of three forms:

`dc=``qupps,`**`dc=`**`biz` Here, the base DN is derived from the company's DNS domain. Each label of the domain name is a *domain component*. A domain component (`dc=`) is defined for each of the labels in the DNS domain name.

`o=``qupps.biz` Here, the base DN is derived from an organization's Internet presence. The `o=` stands for "organization".

`o=``qupps,`**`c=`**`DE` Here, the base DN is in what is sometimes called "organization/country" form. `o=` refers to the organization (QUPPS in this example) and `c=` to the country in which the organization has its headquarters.

You typically create containers under your base DN to logically separate your data. Historically, most LDAP directories create containers called `ou` (*Organizational Units*), but you can use a different naming convention if you prefer. (Microsoft Active Directory uses `cn`, for example.) The containers in Figure A.1 have short names ("`dev`" for devices, "`usr`" for users or people, etc.), but whether you use short container names or long ones is simply a matter of taste[1].

---

[1]We are lazy. We prefer short names because they are quicker to type.

A.1.4 Object classes and attribute types

Entries in an LDAP directory are made up of objects that contain similar attributes. An *object class* defines the set of *attributes* or *attribute types* (i.e. the descriptive information) that an object may contain:

- Each attribute describes a specific type of information. For example, attributes describing a person might include the person's name, telephone number, and e-mail address, whereas attributes describing a DNS domain name might contain an IP address and a Time to Live (TTL).

  Attributes can contain binary data – such as a person's photograph, or an SSL certificate – and not just textual information.

- For each attribute, the object class specifies whether it is:
  - Mandatory or optional.
  - *Single-valued* (i.e. may contain only one value), or *multi-valued*.

- While an object class specifies a set of attributes, it is itself also an attribute, and you can search for it. For example, you can search a directory for all objects of class `person`, or, expressed differently, for objects whose `objectclass` attribute is `person`.

- An object is part of an object class hierarchy, and it inherits all the properties of its parents. For example, the class `inetOrgPerson` is a child of `organizationalPerson`, which is a child of `person` which in turn is a child of `top`. (`top` is an abstract object class which is the common root of the object class hierarchy.)

- (This item may not be relevant to you unless you intend to define your own schema.)

  An object class can be of one of three types:

  structural — Every entry *must* belong to *exactly one* structural object class, which defines the contents of the entry. This object class usually represents a "real world" object. For example, you cannot define an object as being of type `inetOrgPerson` and `account`, as both of these object classes are structural.

  auxilliary — This type of object class indicates additional attributes that can be associated with an entry belonging to a particular structural object class. Although an entry belongs to a single structural object class only, it may belong to multiple auxiliary object classes. For example, the object class `pkiUser` is defined as an auxilliary class containing a single attribute called `userCertificate`. You can add this `pkiUser` object to any `person` for example, to contain an X.509 certificate for that person.

  abstract — This is used as a kind of "template" for defining other structural object classes and defines a set of attributes common to a number of structural object classes. Objects created from these classes inherit the attributes defined therein. For example, the class `inetOrgPerson` inherits from organizationalPerson which inherits from person (which inherits from top). So, the surname attribute (sn) defined in the person class is available in all these classes and need not be specifically defined in them.

Here's an example of a directory entry for a person object, with its attributes:

```
dn: uid=aa01, ou=usr, dc=qupps, dc=biz
cn: Anna Ackland
mail: aa01@example.net
mail: anna.ackland@example.net
telephoneNumber: +34 54891-3358
roomNumber: A5
```

A.1.5 LDAP schema

The definition of what object classes and attribute types are permitted in your LDAP directory is called an LDAP *schema*. You can have multiple schemas, to allow different classes of objects in your directory. For example, you might use the inetOrgPerson schema to define entries you'll use for people in your organization, and the songs schema to let you catalog your music. Schemas are contained in *schema files*, which you add to the configuration of your directory server. In this way, your directory schema is configurable, not fixed. For example, when you decide to use your directory for an additional purpose (such as storing DNS zone data) you can define new object classes in your LDAP server's schema, by adding an appropriate schema file, and the new classes then become available to LDAP client applications using that server. (E.g. in Figure A.1 we have entries for people, printers, groups and DNS data in a single tree). There are quite a few predefined schemas, including:

- The cosine schema defines Internet-related objects in X.500. (The ldapdns and BIND-sdb-LDAP name servers use this schema for storing DNS zone data.)
- The inetOrgPerson schema defines a very useful object that represents a person.
- The nis schema for Network Information Services.

If you do configure your LDAP directory server to support more than one schema in a single Directory Information Tree, we recommend you use different containers in which to do so (e.g. we have people in ou=usr,dc=qupps,dc=biz, devices in ou=dev,dc=qupps,dc=biz, DNS zone data in ou=dns,dc=qupps,dc=biz, etc.).

A.2 The OpenLDAP directory server

OpenLDAP is the LDAP directory server of choice: it is rock-solid, fast, Open Source, and standards-compliant. You might already have it installed as part of your GNU/Linux distribution. Some distributions, currently including Red Hat, provide outdated versions of the OpenLDAP directory server, which we recommend you do not use. Instead, do one of the following:

- Download and install OpenLDAP from source. It is not terribly difficult to do that, but there are a number of prerequisite software packages that you have to download and install as well. Exact details of how you do that are beyond the scope of this book; consult the official OpenLDAP documentation for further information.

- Use a ready made binary package. Symas Inc. provide binary packages of OpenLDAP for many distributions, including GNU/Linux (both i386 and x86_64), Solaris, HP/UX, and Microsoft Windows as a Silver edition, free to use, and a Gold edition with support and a few more features.

A.2.1 Symas OpenLDAP Silver

Symas has graciously made available a packaged version of OpenLDAP with all prerequisites, free of charge to our readers. It contains all you need to get started with OpenLDAP. If you require more functionality, you can later upgrade to Symas OpenLDAP Gold and purchase support for it.

The installation of Symas OpenLDAP is non-destructive; it will not modify existing libraries or binary programs on your machine, so even if, say, you already have an OpenLDAP package (which you don't want to or cannot use), you can install Symas OpenLDAP Silver without affecting existing components.

A – Download Symas OpenLDAP

To download Symas OpenLDAP:

1. Visit `http://www.symas.com/dns-silver.shtml`. Click on "Downloads", and then on "Get an account".

2. Create an account by registering your full name, and the e-mail address to which your account password will be sent.

   Read the Terms of Service, and press one of the buttons at the bottom of the page. If you agree to the Terms of Service, an account is created for you, and a password to the account is e-mailed to the address you specified above.

3. As soon as you receive the e-mail from Symas, you can login to your account with your e-mail address and the password you received; you will be taken to the "Symas Products" page.

4. From here, find your way to the download of "Symas OpenLDAP Silver Edition". (The site's navigation might change, so we can't give you exact instructions.) You require two packages:

   (a) The `cdssserver` package (note the three "s"s in the name), containing the OpenLDAP server and its associated files and utilities.

   (b) The `cdssclient` package, containing the OpenLDAP client utilities.

B – Install Symas OpenLDAP

After downloading the software, you install the packages. All libraries, programs, supporting files, and manuals are installed into `/opt/symas`.

- On Red Hat-based GNU/Linux you typically install these with the rpm program:

```
# rpm -i cdssserver-3.9-2.i686.rpm
# rpm -i cdssclient-3.9-2.i686.rpm
```

- On Debian-based systems we've had good results with alien for installing RPM packages:

```
# alien -i cdssserver-3.9-2.i686.rpm
# alien -i cdssclient-3.9-2.i686.rpm
```

You should configure your syslog daemon to store log messages issued by the OpenLDAP server into a file you specify; this will greatly help you detect problems, and we show you below how you can determine what queries your LDAP client programs are submitting. syslog is typically configured via the file `syslogd.conf`, and you add the following line of tab-separated fields to it:

```
local4.*                                   -/var/log/slapd
```

After creating the log-file, restart syslogd for these changes to take effect. We said above that OpenLDAP is installed into `/opt/symas`; from now on, you should add the `bin` directory to your `$PATH` environment variable:

```
$ export PATH=$PATH:/opt/symas/bin
```

(If you have older versions of the OpenLDAP tools installed, you might want to add the new path component to the *front* of `$PATH`.)

Note again, that the installation of Symas OpenLDAP is non-destructive (i.e. it doesn't modify any standard components of your machine), so you will want to tweak the installation:

- Add the Symas manuals directory to your `$MANPATH` variable.
- Copy the cdsserver startup script to `/etc/init.d`.

C – Configure the server with our silverinst.sh *script*

Instead of boring you with all the details you need to know about how to configure and set up an OpenLDAP server, we've written a program for use on *nix systems, to "magically" configure a basic OpenLDAP server tailored to your environment. Download the silverinst.sh program from the book's Web site (☞ D251), and run it as shown below. (You can run silverinst.sh over and over again if you make a mistake and want to start over.)

```
# cd /opt/symas/etc
# wget http://fupps.com/dnsbook/ldap/silverinst.sh
# bash silverinst.sh
```

After warning you that your current configuration (if you have one) will be destroyed, the program does the following:

1. Asks you for your DNS domain name (e.g. example.net); from this, the program determines the base DN of your directory (e.g. `dc=example,dc=net`). In the examples that follow, we used qupps.biz as our DNS name, so our base DN is `dc=qupps,dc=biz`.

2. Asks you to specify the manager-password which will be used to protect the directory. This password, which you re-enter to confirm, is hashed with the slappasswd utility in SSHA format. The hash is stored in the server's main configuration file (`slapd.conf`) as well as in the directory entry for the user `manager` (see below). You will need the password when you perform online modifications to the directory server (i.e. add or delete entries).

3. Kills any currently running slapd processes.

4. Creates three configuration files with sensible values for initial testing:

   `cds.conf` is specific to Symas OpenLDAP: it controls how the cdsserver startup script operates[2].

   `ldap.conf` is used by the OpenLDAP client utilities such as ldapsearch. It contains configuration variables that point to your directory server (on address 127.0.0.1) and contains the base DN of your installation.

   `slapd.conf` is the main configuration file for the directory server process (slapd). It specifies where the files containing the database reside, which ACLs should apply to the directory server, etc.

   Symas' original commented configuration files are left intact in `/opt/symas/etc` with names ending in `.default`; we recommend you study these later to learn of other features offered by OpenLDAP.

5. (Re)-creates a directory `/var/symas/openldap-data/dnsdemo` (called `$DATADIR` in silverinst.sh). In this directory, the program creates a `DB_CONFIG` file for the Berkeley DB database used by slapd, and it also creates an LDIF file called `demo.ldif` containing most of the hierarchy depicted in Figure A.1, plus a few dozen entries for fictitious people.

6. Bulk-loads slapd's database by invoking slapadd for you. During this procedure, the content of `demo.ldif` is loaded into the Berkeley DB database from which slapd later serves LDAP data.

7. When the silverinst.sh program finishes, it tells you how to start your OpenLDAP server:

   ```
   # cd /opt/symas/etc
   # ./cdsserver start
   ```

   This command launches slapd, the OpenLDAP directory server daemon. Run it now.

You are now ready to start manipulating your directory, and we discuss this next.

[2]CDS stands for Connexitor Directory Services, the former name of Symas OpenLDAP Directory Services.

A.3 Manipulating your LDAP directory

Your LDAP directory

At this point, you have started your directory server and can access the data loaded by silverinst.sh and can view or manipulate the directory's content, perhaps using one of the GUI clients (Section 2.5.4). A GUI such as Apache Directory Studio (Figure A.2) will typically ask you for the following configuration parameters:

hostname — The hostname or the IP address of the host running OpenLDAP.

bindDN — *bindDN* or *username* is the distinguished name of the user entry that is allowed to view and modify directory entries. We have configured the directory with a "user" called `cn=manager,dc=qupps,dc=biz`, so that is the DN you enter.

bindPW — The password that corresponds to the *bindDN* above. It is the password you entered in step 2 when you ran silverinst.sh.

search base — The *search base* is the distinguished name (DN) of the entry in your directory where you want to start searching. In our example, it is `dc=qupps,dc=biz`, but if you want to restrict searches to say, the container in which you store DNS entries, you specify `ou=dns,dc=qupps,dc=biz`. In other words, set the search base to the DN in the tree where you want the search to begin.

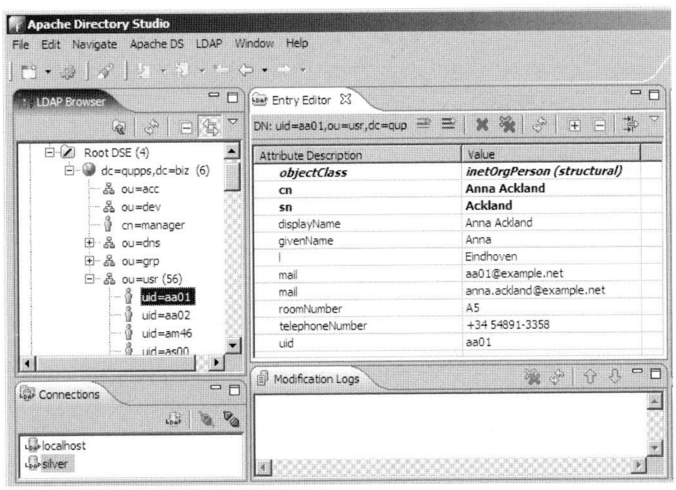

Figure A.2: Using Apache Directory Studio to browse your LDAP directory server

A.3.1 LDIF – LDAP Data Interchange Format

LDIF is the *LDAP Data Interchange Format*, an ASCII-based format both for representing entries in an LDAP directory, and for performing additions, modifications and deletions to it. As the internal representation of an LDAP directory is purely the business of the implementor, a standard was needed for representing entries in an LDAP directory; LDIF is the result. It is supported by all major vendors of directory servers, including OpenLDAP. LDIF, like LDAP itself, was designed to be as simple as possible. Conveniently, its pure ASCII-based representation also makes it human-readable.

An LDAP entry is represented in LDIF by a series of lines:

- The first line is the distinguished name (DN) of the entry.
- Next, there is one line for each object class in the entry, as well as one for each attribute type and attribute value pair.
- One entry is separated from the next with a blank line.

An LDIF representation of a person in a directory might look like this:

```
dn: uid=aa01,ou=usr,dc=qupps,dc=biz
objectclass: inetorgPerson
uid: aa01
givenname: Anna
sn: Ackland
cn: Anna Ackland
displayname: Anna Ackland
telephoneNumber: +34 54891-3358
roomnumber: A5
mail: aa01@example.net
mail: anna.ackland@example.net
description: Managing directory QUPPS Holland
l: Eindhoven
  ... blank line ...
dn: uid=alexi,ou=usr,dc=qupps,dc=biz
uid: alexi
givenName: Alexandra
...
```

Note: LDIF uses a single space at the start of a line to indicate continuation of the previous line. When editing LDIF files, ensure you don't introduce extraneous whitespace; most programs that parse LDIF don't like that and will produce errors if you try to use the LDIF. Many LDIF generators wrap text at 72 characters, although most parsers are happy to accept much longer lines.

A.3.2 Loading data into your OpenLDAP directory

For simplicity, you used the silverinst.sh program (Section A.2.1) to create an initial data set for your directory, and load that into your directory. When you ran silverinst.sh, it created a full LDIF file called `demo.ldif` in `$DATADIR` (which you can use as a starting point for creating your own LDIF files, later on, if you wish). silverinst.sh used the slapadd program to bulk-load your LDIF data into the server.

Figure A.3 shows the relationship between slapadd and typical LDAP clients:

- You typically use slapadd only once, when you bulk-load your directory. Even if the the "bulk" you are loading is only very small (because you will be adding more entries online later), you *never* run slapadd on a live directory.
- When your directory system is running live, you use LDAP clients to add new entries to your directory server. These clients (e.g. ldapadd, ldapmodify) connect to your directory server and perform LDAP additions and modifications to it.

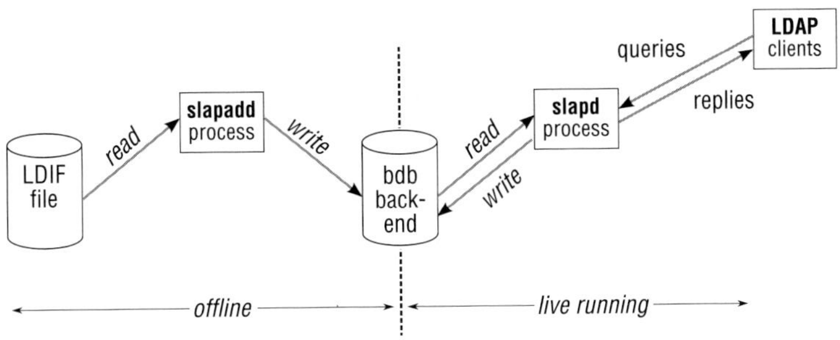

Figure A.3: slapd: bulk-load vs. LDAP clients

A.3.3 Access control

To make your life as easy as possible as you get started, silverinst.sh allowed anonymous access to the directory: everybody is able to see everything it contains, except passwords. You will typically protect a live LDAP directory server by adding a number of access control lists that:

- Force users of your LDAP directory to authenticate with valid credentials.
- Allow modifications to be performed by authorized users only.
- Allow users to "see" (i.e. search) only certain branches of your directory tree, and allow them to retrieve a limited number of entries only.
- Restrict access to certain attribute types to a specific subset of users.

Before bringing the server into production, you *must* fix this; consult the OpenLDAP documentation to see how.

A.3.4 Adding entries

To add entries to your OpenLDAP server, you use your favorite LDAP browser/editor, or the ldapadd command-line utility, which we show here:

1. Create an LDIF file representing the entry or entries you want to add to your directory. For example, to add a new user (i.e. an LDAP object of class `person`):

   ```
   $ cat john.ldif
   dn: cn=John Doe, ou=usr, dc=qupps, dc=biz
   objectclass: person
   cn: John Doe
   sn: Doe
   description: a test user
   ```

2. Use the ldapadd program. You specify options to "bind" (log on) as an authorized user (i.e. a user allowed to modify the directory):

   ```
   $ ldapadd -x -D cn=manager,dc=qupps,dc=biz  -W < john.ldif
   Enter LDAP Password: ... manager password here ...
   adding new entry "cn=John Doe, ou=usr, dc=qupps, dc=biz"
   ```

A.3.5 Introducing LDAP search filters

LDAP *search filters* (or just *filters*) are strings that you use to specify which data items you want to retrieve from an LDAP directory. An LDAP filter consists of one or more boolean expressions, optionally with logical operators ("`&`" for AND, "`|`" for OR) prefixed to the expression list. The boolean expressions have the following format:

attribute operator value

where *attribute* is the LDAP attribute-type name, and *value* is the the attribute value. These triplets are typically surrounded by parentheses. The *operators* include equality (`=`), negation (`!`), and substring match (`*`). The full syntax of LDAP filters is specified in RFC 2254, *The String Representation of LDAP Search Filters*. Here are some examples:

- You want to search your directory for entries with a surname of "Doe". The attribute type for surname is `sn`, so your filter is:

  ```
  (sn=doe)
  ```

  In simple search filters, like this, you can omit the parentheses if you prefer.

- In addition, you are interested only in entries whose given name (i.e. first name) is "Jane". The attribute type for a given name is called (can you guess?) `givenname`. Our filter is now:

  ```
  (&(sn=doe)(givenname=jane))
  ```

  Note how the two filters `(sn=doe)` and `(givenname=jane)` are ANDed in a prefix notation, and the whole filter is then surrounded in parentheses.

- Suppose further you want to find either all entries with a surname of "Doe" and a given name of "Jane", or those that have a room number A1. You join the two sub-filters with a boolean OR:

```
(|(&(sn=doe)(givenname=jane))(roomnumber=A1))
```

- You want to search your directory for all names starting with the string "Smith" to find people called "Smith", as well as "Smithsonian". The asterisk allows you to specify a substring in a search:

```
(sn=Smith*)
```

A.3.6 Search scopes

When searching an LDAP directory, you specify how "deeply" within the DIT the directory server should search for you. The depth is called the *search scope*. The search scope defines the set of entries at the search base that the directory server should consider for a search operation (Figure A.4). (Remember that the search base specifies the DN in the hierarchy where your search starts.) There are three search scope values:

base — The search operation should be performed only against the entry specified as the search base DN. No subordinate entries will be considered.

one — The search operation is performed against entries that are immediate subordinates (i.e. children) of the entry specified as the search base DN. The base entry itself is not included, nor are any entries below the immediate children.

subtree — The directory searches the entry specified as the search base DN and all of its subordinates to any depth.

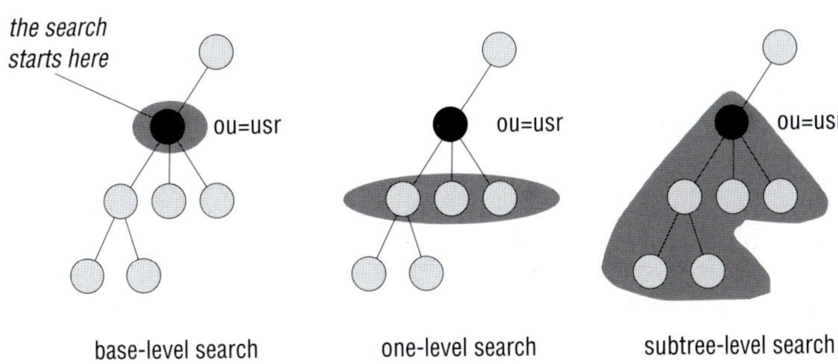

Figure A.4: Search scopes

The areas your in directory that are searched through, for the respective scopes, when you start searching at `ou=usr,dc=qupps,dc=biz` are shown in Figure A.4.

A.3.7 Searching entries

You use the ldapsearch program to search your LDAP directory from the command line. (Check the manual for your version of the ldapsearch command to determine the options you need. OpenLDAP's implementation uses -x to specify simple authentication, -b for the search base, and -LLL modifies the LDIF output to omit unnecessary comments.)

To search your directory, specify a search base, the scope level of the search (default is subtree) and the LDAP search filter to apply. The search base is where in the directory hierarchy where you want to start searching: specify the base DN of your DIT to search the entire tree, or the DN of the container you want to limit the search to.

```
$ ldapsearch -x -LLL -b "dc=qupps,dc=biz" "(sn=steward)"
dn: uid=as00,ou=usr,dc=qupps,dc=biz
objectClass: inetOrgPerson
uid: as00
givenName: Anita
sn: Steward
cn: Anita Steward
displayName: Anita Steward
telephoneNumber: +34 71989-1803
roomNumber: S6
l: Utrecht
```

You can omit the parentheses around the filter if it doesn't use the logical operators "&" or "|". Although not shown here, you typically also limit the attribute types you want returned by the directory server, specifying these as additional arguments to ldapsearch. (* means all attributes, + returns so-called operational attributes, and if you specify 1.1, ldapsearch returns just the DN.)

```
$ ldapsearch -x -LLL "(sn=steward)" givenname mail
dn: uid=as00,ou=usr,dc=qupps,dc=biz
givenName: Anita
```

In the previous example, we wanted two attribute types returned, but only the given name was returned. There are two reasons why the mail attribute might not have been returned:

1. The mail attribute type doesn't exist (so it simply cannot be retrieved), or ...

2. Due to access controls on the server, the directory refuses to return the mail attribute type unless the client is authorized. In the above example, the connection is "anonymous" (i.e. the client hasn't bound to the directory with credentials), so the server doesn't return the requested attribute type.

If we repeat the same search, authenticated as manager (using -W to have ldapsearch prompt for a password) we "see" what was hidden:

```
$ ldapsearch -x -LLL -D cn=manager,dc=qupps,dc=biz  -W ↩
                                  "(sn=steward)" givenname mail
Enter LDAP Password:
dn: uid=as00,ou=usr,dc=qupps,dc=biz
givenName: Anita
mail: as00@example.net
mail: anita.steward@example.net
```

Note how we have omitted the search base (option `-b`) in the above examples; the OpenLDAP client utilities retrieve some default settings from `ldap.conf`. This is a useful shortcut. (See the ldapsearch manual page for more information.)

A.3.8 Modifying entries

To modify entries in your LDAP directory via the command-line you typically use ldapmodify. This program expects an LDIF file describing the modifications you want performed. For example, to replace the `description` attribute type in John's directory entry and add a telephone number:

1. Create a file containing the changes you want performed:

```
$ cat john-changes
dn: cn=John Doe, ou=usr, dc=qupps, dc=biz
changetype: modify
replace: description
description: John loves LDAP!
-                                          ... a single dash ...
add: telephonenumber
telephonenumber: 555111
```

2. Submit the changes to the directory server:

```
$ ldapmodify -x -D cn=manager,dc=qupps,dc=biz  -W < john-changes
Enter LDAP Password:
modifying entry "cn=John Doe, ou=usr, dc=qupps, dc=biz"
```

The syntax for the ldapmodify command takes a bit of getting used to; its manual page contains examples which are instructive.

A.3.9 Deleting entries

Before you can delete something, you have to know what you want to delete, and you usually determine that by searching for the distinguished names of the LDAP entries you want removed from your LDAP directory.

Suppose you want to delete John's directory entry: you search your LDAP directory using ldapsearch, by specifying a filter:

```
$ ldapsearch -x -LLL 'cn=john*' 1.1
dn: uid=jc38,ou=usr,dc=qupps,dc=biz

dn: cn=John Doe,ou=usr,dc=qupps,dc=biz
```

The search returns the DNs of the matching entries. Choose the DN of the one(s) you want to delete, and then use ldapdelete:

```
$ ldapdelete -x -D cn=manager,dc=qupps,dc=biz -W ↩
                         'cn=John Doe,ou=usr,dc=qupps,dc=biz'
Enter LDAP Password:
```

Of course, if you already know the DN of the entry you want to delete, you don't have to search for it.

A.3.10 Interpreting slapd's log-file

OpenLDAP's slapd server records voluminous logging information if you want it to. We recommend however that you only log connections and operations and entries sent (and that is how silverinst.sh configured your slapd) You can do this manually by setting slapd's loglevel to "`stats stats2`" in `slapd.conf`. When queries are performed by the directory server, your system's log will show you what is happening:

```
conn=22 fd=7 ACCEPT from IP=127.0.0.1:43392 (IP=:: 389)
conn=22 op=0 BIND dn="" method=128
conn=22 op=0 RESULT tag=97 err=0 text=
conn=22 op=1 SRCH base="dc=qupps,dc=biz" scope=2 deref=0 filter="(sn=smith*)"
conn=22 op=1 SRCH attr=mail telephone
conn=22 op=1 ENTRY dn="uid=es04,ou=usr,dc=qupps,dc=biz"
conn=22 op=1 ENTRY dn="uid=ps27,ou=usr,dc=qupps,dc=biz"
conn=22 op=1 ENTRY dn="uid=fs52,ou=usr,dc=qupps,dc=biz"
conn=22 op=1 SEARCH RESULT tag=101 err=0 nentries=3 text=
conn=22 op=2 UNBIND
conn=22 fd=7 closed
```

By looking at the above log, can you guess what the client asked for? That's right:

```
$ ldapsearch -LLL -x 'sn=smith*'  mail telephone
...
```

(Note that our suggested loglevel can degrade performance; for ultimate performance, set the loglevel to 0.)

A.3.11 LDAP URLs

Some of the DNS servers require that you specify an LDAP URL (Uniform Resource Locator, RFC 4516) in their configuration (Figure A.5). An *LDAP URL* describes a an LDAP search operation, and the URL syntax is:

`ldap://`*hostport*`/`*dn*`[?`*attrs*`[?`*scope*`[?`*filter*`]]]`

where each of the components has the following meaning:

hostport the hostname, and optional port number prefixed by a colon, of the LDAP server.

dn the search base.

attrs a comma-separated list of attribute type names to request (often unused by applications).

scope the *scope* of the search (i.e. how deep the search will be). You specify it as one of the strings `base`, `one` or `sub` to mean a base-level, one-level or sub-level search respectively (default is `base`).

filter the search filter as described above.

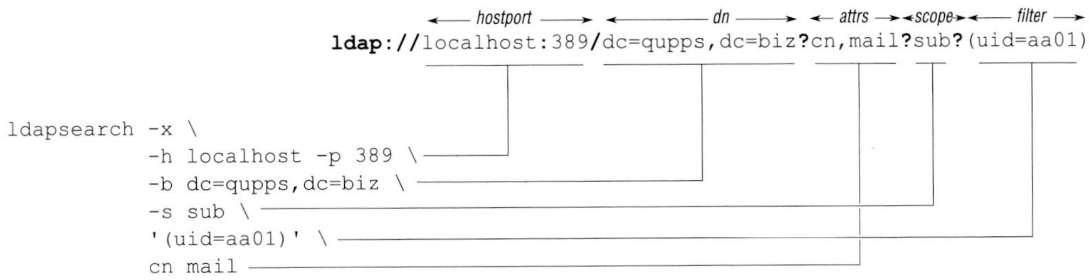

Figure A.5: Comparing ldapsearch and an LDAP URL

A.3.12 Features you will probably want to add to your OpenLDAP server

OpenLDAP is a powerful and standards-compliant directory server, and we've only covered a small portion of its capabilities in this introduction. We strongly recommend you find out what else it's capable of. Here are some examples.

Indexes

If you have applications that frequently search specific attribute types, you can index them. Indexes can greatly improve the performance of searches. For example on our machine, searching a directory with 100 000 entries on an un-indexed attribute takes 2.636 seconds, compared to 0.004 seconds for an indexed attribute.

OpenLDAP supports various types of index: `equality` (for a filter such as `sn=Doe`), `substring` (e.g. to search for `sn=Do*`, say) and `presence` (to determine if an attribute type exists, e.g. `sn=*`). If you don't index attributes, the directory server (slapd) has to scan all entries in the back-end to determine whether the filter applies to entries you are searching for.

While indexes greatly speed up searches, they do consume CPU, disk, and memory resources. You shouldn't go overboard in defining indexes, and you should remove unused indexes.

Access control

We shortly mentioned access control above. OpenLDAP has many ways to limit what users can "see" in your directory. You can grant access to a set of entries and/or attributes based on whether the client has connected anonymously, has bound with credentials, belongs to a particular group, or has connected via a particular transport (SSL, TLS, IPC socket). Consult the `slapd.access` manual for details.

Transport Layer Security

OpenLDAP supports Transport Layer Security (TLS) (as well as the non-standard LDAP over SSL) for encrypting traffic between LDAP clients and the server. To implement TLS you require X.509 certificates.

Simple Authentication and Security Layer

OpenLDAP supports Simple Authentication and Security Layer (SASL) for authenticating users. When correctly configured, OpenLDAP can also use Kerberos via SASL's GSS-API interface.

Overlays and back-ends

OpenLDAP has a large number of overlays (modules of code) with which you ensure referential integrity on the directory, enable unique values (e.g. to ensure uniqueness of attribute types), rewrite entries on the fly, etc.

Additional back-ends allow you to use a single instance of slapd to serve data retrieved from a different LDAP directory server, or even from Perl, a shell script, or an SQL database. A relatively new back-end called `config` allows you to store slapd's own configuration in such a way that you can modify it on-the-fly via LDAP, instead of having to restart slapd after changing its `slapd.conf` file.

SLAPI plug-ins

You can extend OpenLDAP's slapd directory server in a number of different ways with *SLAPI plug-ins* – functions that you write and bundle into a shared object library, that is dynamically linked to slapd. For example, you can validate data before it's stored in the directory, notify users when data in the directory changes, or forbid certain changes. Plug-ins are called by the server when specific events occur, such as before or after an LDAP `add` or `modify` operation is performed.

Replication

The duplication of all or part of a directory information tree (DIT), and the process of keeping the duplicates synchronized, are both called replication. Most LDAP servers can be configured to replicate all or any specified parts of their data.

OpenLDAP has had replication built in from its inception. OpenLDAP originally used slurpd; however, this is now deprecated and will be removed from OpenLDAP 2.4. Instead, whenever possible you should use the LDAP Synchronization Replication, called "syncrepl" for short (Figure A.6). This method is more configurable and more reliable. It also offers a pull replication initiated by slave (or consumer) servers, and a pseudo-push replication in which clients initiate the connection and the master server (provider) then automatically pushes updates down the pipe to the slave servers.

Instead of modifying the master server every time a new slave server is brought into operation (as was necessary with slurpd), syncrepl offers the following advantages:

- The master server seldom needs to be interrupted; additional slave servers can be brought online on the fly.
- You don't have to manually dump the data from the master to prime a slave; the slave can do that itself. (However, if you have low bandwidth or fragile network

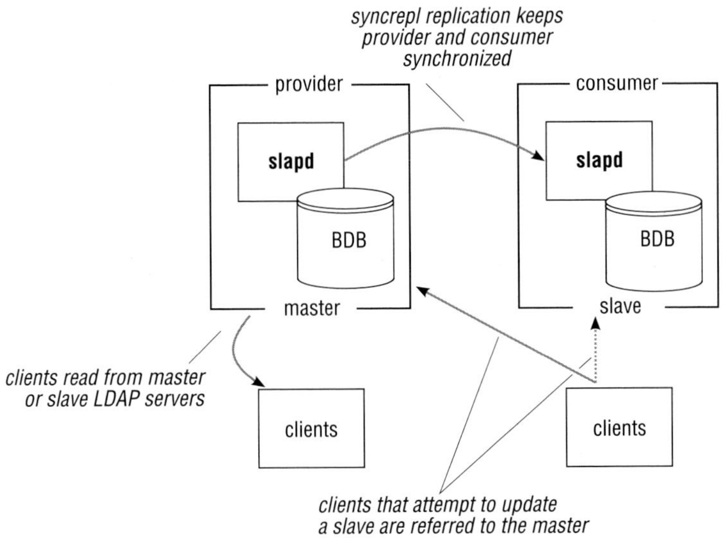

Figure A.6: OpenLDAP syncrepl

connections it might be wise to prime a slave by dumping the contents of the master directory server with slapcat and adding it to a slave with slapadd.)

- Slave servers retrieve all updates as soon as they come on-line, automatically recovering from any network outages there may have been between slave and master.

A.4 Extending your LDAP directory

We discussed in Section A.1.5, that an LDAP schema defines the set of object classes and attribute types you are allowed to use, and we said that you can extend that schema. For some of the DNS name server brands we discuss, you extend the schema of your directory server to support object classes and attribute types used by the DNS server. This is not difficult: in most cases to extend the schema for a DNS server you only have to copy a file into slapd's configuration. Nevertheless, you might want to know what goes on "behind the scenes". It is beyond the scope of this book to fully explain how that works, but we show you briefly what you have to do in order to add new objects and attribute types.

A.4.1 Objects and identifiers

The following is an example of an attribute specification, and we discuss its syntax below:

```
attributetype ( 1.3.6.1.4.1.7637.100.1.1.1 NAME 'songTitle'
    DESC 'The song title'
    EQUALITY caseIgnoreMatch
    SUBSTR caseIgnoreSubstringsMatch
    SYNTAX 1.3.6.1.4.1.1466.115.121.1.151024
    SINGLE-VALUE
)
```

Each element in the schema (object class, attribute type, and syntax) is identified by a globally unique *Object Identifier* (*OID*), commonly found in protocols described by ASN.1. In particular, OIDs are heavily used by the Simple Network Management Protocol (SNMP). OIDs are assigned by IANA, and your organization can easily obtain one by applying for a Private Enterprise Number (PEN) at `http://pen.iana.org/pen/PenApplication.page` (Note that you should *never* use other people's Private Enterprise Number to form your own OID namespace!) For example, the OID for the `sn` attribute type is 2.5.4.4, and the OID for the `mail` type is 0.9.2342.19200300.100.1.3.

LDAP objects have the following characteristics:

- Each object (class or attribute) has a unique OID assigned to it.
- Each object has a unique name assigned to it. The name is used by your client applications to find the object (e.g. `cn`, `givenname`, `songTitle`, etc.).
- Each attribute type has a *syntax* associated with it, which defines the kind of values the attribute may contain. Examples of syntaxes are 1.3.6.1.4.1.1466.115.121.1.28 for a JPEG photograph and 1.3.6.1.4.1.1466.115.121.1.15{64} for a string with a length of no more than 64 characters. You can find the list of LDAP syntaxes supported by OpenLDAP with:

```
$ ldapsearch -x -s base -b "cn=subschema" "(objectclass=*)" ldapSyntaxes
dn: cn=Subschema
ldapSyntaxes: ( 1.3.6.1.1.16.1 DESC 'UUID' )
ldapSyntaxes: ( 1.3.6.1.1.1.0.1 DESC 'RFC2307 Boot Parameter' )
ldapSyntaxes: ( 1.3.6.1.1.1.0.0 DESC 'RFC2307 NIS Netgroup Triple' )
ldapSyntaxes: ( 1.3.6.1.4.1.1466.115.121.1.52 DESC 'Telex Number' )
ldapSyntaxes: ( 1.3.6.1.4.1.1466.115.121.1.50 DESC 'Telephone Number' )
ldapSyntaxes: ( 1.3.6.1.4.1.1466.115.121.1.15 DESC 'Directory String' )
...
```

- Each attribute type has a *matching rule* associated with it, which defines the built-in methods of comparison available in the LDAP server. Examples of matching rules are `caseIgnoreMatch`, which matches strings case-insensitively, and `integerMatch` for integers. You can find the list of matching rules supported by OpenLDAP with:

```
$ ldapsearch -x -s base -b "cn=subschema" "(objectclass=*)" matchingrules
dn: cn=Subschema
matchingRules: ( 1.3.6.1.1.16.3 NAME 'UUIDOrderingMatch' SYNTAX ↩
                                                1.3.6.1.1.16.1 )
```

```
matchingRules: ( 1.3.6.1.1.16.2 NAME 'UUIDMatch' SYNTAX 1.3.6.1.1.16.1 )
matchingRules: ( 1.2.840.113556.1.4.804 NAME 'integerBitOrMatch' SYNTAX↩
                                         1.3.6.1.4.1.1466.115.121.1.27 )
...
```

- For each attribute type, you define whether the type is single-valued or multi-valued.
- You can give an optional description to an object. This description is typically displayed in clients that query your schema.
- For object classes, you then define which attributes are mandatory (MUST) and which are optional (MAY).

The formal definition of LDAP object classes and attributes types is specified in RFC 4512, and we won't discuss the specification in detail. We do however show you an example below.

A.4.2 Extending your schema

To extend the schema in your LDAP directory server, you typically perform these steps:

1. Obtain a (or use your existing) Private Enterprise Number, for naming new objects. In the examples that follow, we use the OID 1.3.6.1.4.1.7637 assigned to us, and we subclass that for object classes and attribute types.
2. We recommend you design your OID namespace hierarchy to separate object classes and attribute types. For example, you might expand your OID arc (i.e. segment) for attribute types (1.3.6.1.4.1.7637.**100**) and for object classes (1.3.6.1.4.1.7637.**101**).

   Irrespective of how you maintain your namespace, we recommend you maintain a registry (i.e. a list) of the OIDs you have issued to ensure you don't issue an OID twice. (You can do this in a simple text file.)
3. In addition to unique OIDs, you will have to give your objects names that will not clash with existing names. For example, you cannot "create" a new attribute type called `mail`. One way of ensuring that names don't clash is to prefix them with a string identifying your organization (e.g. `qupps-mail`).
4. You define the objects of your new schema in a local schema file. Section A.4.3 shows a complete example.
5. You configure your LDAP server to load the schema file. In OpenLDAP this is simply a matter of adding it to `slapd.conf`. For example, for the schema file we show you below, you would add the following line to `slapd.conf`:

   ```
   include /path/to/songs.schema
   ```
6. Restart your LDAP server so the new configuration takes effect. Note, that when restarting the server, syntax errors in schema files can prevent the server from starting.
7. Now you can create new objects for your schema.

A.4.3 A sample schema file for storing songs

We now show you a simple schema file for cataloging songs. (This file is also installed by silverinst.sh into the schema directory of your OpenLDAP installation.) This schema defines a new object class called `song` and four attribute types for `song` objects, that are defined in the schema file. There are a few points you should note:

- Each definition is in fact a single line; whitespace at the beginning of a line indicates a continuation line. Parenthesis are mandatory where we have placed them.
- Names (`NAME`) and descriptions (`DESC`) contain strings enclosed in single quotes.
- The attribute type `songGenre` is *not* described as being single-valued and is therefore multi-valued, so you may specify more than one value for the attribute type `songGenre`.
- The object class has mandatory (`MUST`) and optional (`MAY`) attribute types. The types `description` and `seeAlso` are not defined in this schema. They are "imported" from standard schemas offered by OpenLDAP – the schema files defining these attribute types are also `included` in `slapd.conf`.

Listing A.1: A schema file for songs

```
# Attribute types
attributetype ( 1.3.6.1.4.1.7637.100.1.1.1 NAME 'songTitle'
   DESC 'The song title'
   EQUALITY caseIgnoreMatch
   SUBSTR caseIgnoreSubstringsMatch
   SYNTAX 1.3.6.1.4.1.1466.115.121.1.15{1024}
   SINGLE-VALUE
   )

attributetype ( 1.3.6.1.4.1.7637.100.1.1.2 NAME 'songGenre'
   DESC 'Song Genre'
   EQUALITY caseIgnoreMatch
   SUBSTR caseIgnoreSubstringsMatch
   SYNTAX 1.3.6.1.4.1.1466.115.121.1.15{1024}
   )

attributetype ( 1.3.6.1.4.1.7637.100.1.1.3 NAME 'songArtist'
   DESC 'The singer, not the Song'
   EQUALITY caseIgnoreMatch
   SUBSTR caseIgnoreSubstringsMatch
   SYNTAX 1.3.6.1.4.1.1466.115.121.1.15{1024}
   SINGLE-VALUE
   )

attributetype ( 1.3.6.1.4.1.7637.100.1.1.4 NAME 'songYear'
   DESC 'Year of publication'
   EQUALITY integerMatch
   SYNTAX 1.3.6.1.4.1.1466.115.121.1.27
   SINGLE-VALUE
   )
```

```
# Object classes
objectclass ( 1.3.6.1.4.1.7637.101.1.1.1 NAME 'song'
   DESC 'A song'
   SUP top STRUCTURAL
   MUST ( songTitle $ songGenre $ songArtist )
   MAY (
         description $ seeAlso $ songYear
       )
  )
```

You can view the description of an object class and its associated attribute types in an LDAP browser. We show you an example in Figure A.7.

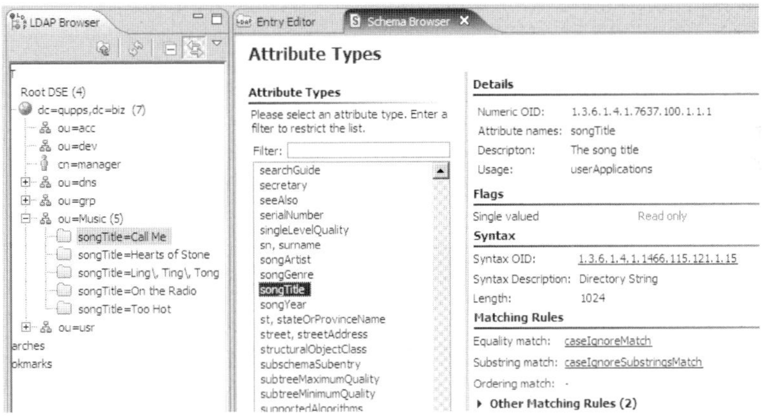

Figure A.7: An LDAP schema browser

A.4.4 A song in LDIF format

We use the schema above for storing songs[3]. Here is an sample song in LDIF:

```
dn: songTitle=On the Radio,ou=Music,dc=qupps,dc=biz
objectClass: song
songTitle: On the Radio
songGenre: Pop
songGenre: Favorite
songArtist: Donna Summer
songYear: 1980
```

Note the following:

- The attribute `songGenre` is multi-valued, so it can take on more than one value.
- The type `songYear` is optional, so you can omit it (if you can't remember when the song was written).

[3]The data we use is in no way authoritative; it was created from memory.

A.4.5 Loading and finding songs

In our directory we create a container in which we store our songs. To illustrate that the name of the container is independent of the entries it contains, we won't call it songs, but "Music". The LDIF to add the container is:

```
$ cat music.ldif
dn: ou=Music, dc=qupps,dc=biz
ou: Music
objectclass: organizationalunit

$ ldapadd -x -D cn=manager,dc=qupps,dc=biz  -W < music.ldif
```

We also add the songs themselves, in LDIF format, with ldapadd:

```
$ ldapadd -x -D cn=manager,dc=qupps,dc=biz  -W < songs.ldif
```

A.4.6 Finding entries with Perl's Net::LDAP

Section A.3.7 showed how you use ldapsearch to search your directory. To show you that you can quite easily create a custom program to do that, we use Perl's Net::LDAP module. Here is the sample program:

Listing A.2: Searching the directory for songs with Net::LDAP: songl

```
#!/usr/bin/perl
use Net::LDAP;

my ($msg, @entries, $e, $filter, $st, $sa, $sy, @sg);

die "Usage: $0 filter\n" unless ($#ARGV >= 0);
$filter = $ARGV[0];

my $ldap = Net::LDAP->new('ldap.qupps.biz', port => 389, version => 3);
$msg = $ldap->bind();
$msg->code && die("Can't bind to directory: " . $msg->error);

$msg = $ldap->search(
        base    => 'ou=Music,dc=qupps,dc=biz',
        scope   => 'one',
        filter  => "$filter",
        attrs   =>  [ qw(songTitle songGenre songArtist songYear) ],
);
die("search failed with " . $msg->code()) if $msg->code();

my $count = 1;
foreach $e ($msg->entries) {
        $st     = $e->get_value('songTitle');
        $sa     = $e->get_value('songArtist');
        $sy     = $e->get_value('songYear') || '????';
        @sg     = $e->get_value('songGenre');

        printf "%2d. %s %-20s %-20s %s\n",
                        $count++, $sy, $st, $sa, join(':', @sg);
}
```

Our small songl (song list) program expects an LDAP filter on the command line. For example, to find all the songs, run:

```
$ songl objectclass=song
 1. 1980 On the Radio          Donna Summer         Pop:Favorite
 2. 1980 Too Hot               Kool & The Gang      Pop
 3. 1984 Hearts of Stone       Charms               Soft
 4. 1980 Call Me               Blondie              Rock
 5. ???? Ling, Ting, Tong      Charms               Rock
```

We can also search with more complex filters. To search for all pop songs written in 1980:

```
$ songl '(&(songGenre=pop)(songyear=1980))'
 1. 1980 On the Radio          Donna Summer         Pop:Favourite
 2. 1980 Too Hot               Kool & The Gang      Pop
```

Note how we quote the filter to avoid meta-characters being interpreted by the shell.

That concludes our introduction to LDAP and to OpenLDAP.

Summary

- Entries in an LDAP directory are organized in a hierarchical tree. Each entry is identified by a `DN`, a distinguished name. Each component of a `DN` is called a relative distinguished name (`RDN`) (e.g. `ou`=dev).
- Each entry has one or many attribute types, each with one or many values associated with it. Each entry must have exactly one structural object class that specifies which attribute types an object may have.
- LDAP has a well-defined API and is supported by many applications and vendors. It is often faster than a relational database system, at least for search and read operations.
- LDAP entries are represented in a text format called `LDIF` which is also used to manipulate your LDAP directory.
- An LDAP directory tree is easily replicated and distributed.
- You typically extend the schema of a directory server by adding definitions of object classes and attribute types to it with the definition of new schema elements, from which you build LDAP objects.

Notes and further reading

- The OpenLDAP project and its documentation are hosted at `http://www.openldap.org/`
- *Understanding and Deploying LDAP Directory Services*, by Tim Howes, Mark C. Smith, and Gordon S. Good (Mcmillan) is a comprehensive tutorial with a thorough treatment of LDAP directory services.

Appendix

B Use $INCLUDE and fix your SOA

One of the most common errors when working with zone master files is forgetting to increment the serial number in a zone's Start of Authority (SOA) record. Time and time again, system administrators add records and reload the zone, only to find that secondary servers have not transferred the changes. The reason: a secondary server initiates a zone transfer only if the zone's serial number on the master server is higher than the serial number on the slave. To overcome this (and to protect ourselves from our own forgetfulness) we have implemented a system we consider foolproof. You can use this for BIND name servers, and with slight modifications, for NSD too.

1. Choose a top-level directory for your zone files. We use `/var/named`, but you can use whatever is convenient.

2. In this directory create a subdirectory for each letter of the alphabet. Store files for each domain in the subdirectory corresponding to the first letter of the domain name. For example, store files for qupps.biz in directory `q`. (You don't have to organize your zone files this way, but we find it works well.)

3. We name our zone files *domain*`.zone`. So in the `zone` clause in `named.conf` we have, for example:

```
zone "qupps.biz" {
   type master;
   file "q/qupps.biz.zone";
};
```

The zone file itself (i.e. `q/qupps.biz.zone`) uses `$INCLUDE` directives to include two files, as follows. The included files are shown in bold. Paths in the `$INCLUDE` directives are relative to named's working directory, as specified in the `directory` option.

```
$TTL 3600
$ORIGIN .

$INCLUDE q/qupps.biz.soa        ; the SOA

$ORIGIN qupps.biz.

qupps.biz.        NS nsa.qupps.biz.
                  NS nsb.qupps.biz.
                  NS nsc.qupps.biz.

$INCLUDE q/qupps.biz.rr         ; the records
```

The two files that are included are:

`soa` The file *domain*`.soa` contains only the Start of Authority (SOA) record:

```
qupps.biz. 86400 IN SOA ns1.qupps.biz.  h.qupps.biz. (
                  2008020208       ; Serial
                  10800     ; Refresh
                  900       ; Retry
                  604800    ; Expire
                  3600 )    ; Minimum TTL
```

`rr` The file *domain*`.rr` contains the other resource records for the zone:

```
                                A    92.168.1.20
                                MX   10 mail.qupps.biz.
nsa          604800             A    10.1.1.1
nsb          604800             A    10.1.2.1
www3                            A    10.1.1.2
```

This appears a bit complicated, but it isn't really. You typically create the `soa` file once, and forget about it. When you add, modify or delete a resource record, you edit the *domain*`.rr` file.

4. A `Makefile` (for GNU make) does the rest. It builds the `.zone` file from its corresponding `.soa` and `.rr` files if they were modified more recently than the `.zone`, by running fixserial.pl on the `.soa` file (see below).

Listing B.1: `Makefile` for fixing SOA in zone files automatically

```
1 .SUFFIXES: .zone .soa .inc
2 ZONESDIR=/var/named/?
3 # change the list of SOA files into a list of ZONE files
4 # by replacing '.soa' suffix with '.zone'
5 zones =  $(patsubst %.soa,%.zone,$(wildcard $(ZONESDIR)/*.soa))
6
7 all: $(zones)
8         rndc reload
9 # for NSD:
10 #        nsdc rebuild
11 #        nsdc reload
12
13 %.zone: %.soa %.rr
14         fixserial.pl $(basename $@).soa > $(basename $@).soa.fix &&↩
15              mv $(basename $@).soa.fix $(basename $@).soa
16         touch $@
```

The `Makefile` works as follows:

- Line 13: *domain*`.zone` depends on *domain*`.soa` and *domain*`.rr`.
- Lines 5–7: check all the files in the `a`, `b` , `c`,... directories below the top-level directory (`$ZONESDIR`) to see if they've changed.
- Lines 13–16: For any zone where the `.soa` or the `.rr` file has changed, run the fixserial.pl program.
- Line 8: invoke rndc (or optionally nsdc) to reload the name server.

Note that the `Makefile` doesn't concatenate the `.soa` and `.rr` files because they are both `$INCLUDE`d in the `.zone`.

5. Whenever you modify *domain*.soa or *domain*.rr, you run make. The `Makefile` builds the *domain*.zone file: it runs fixserial.pl on the `soa` file to "fix" the serial number in it. A typical session to update a zone will look like this:

```
$ edit q/qupps.biz.rr
$ make
fixserial.pl q/qupps.biz.soa > q/qupps.biz.soa.fix &&↩
              mv q/qupps.biz.soa.fix q/qupps.biz.soa
touch q/qupps.biz.zone
rndc reload
```

The fixserial.pl *program*

Our program fixserial.pl reads a zone file (in our case simply an SOA record) and "fixes" its serial number, setting it to a value in *YYYYMMDDnn* format.

Listing B.2: fixserial.pl "fixes" a serial number in a zone file

```
#!/usr/bin/perl
# fixserial.pl (C)2008 by Jan-Piet Mens
# Read SOA from zone file and set new serial number. Prints result to stdout.

use POSIX qw(strftime);
use Net::DNS;
use Net::DNS::ZoneFile::Fast;
use strict;

die "Usage: $0 zonefile\n" unless ($ARGV[0]);

my $zonefile = $ARGV[0];
my $today = strftime("%Y%m%d", localtime);

my $zone = Net::DNS::ZoneFile::Fast::parse(file => $zonefile);

foreach my $rr (@$zone) {
        if ($rr->{type} eq 'SOA') {

                my $n;

                $_ = $rr->{serial};
                if (/(\d+)(\d\d)/) {
                        my $olddate = $1;
                        $n = ($olddate ne $today) ? -1 : $2;
                }
                my $serial = sprintf("${today}%02d", ++$n);

                $rr->{serial} = $serial;
        }
}
foreach my $rr (@$zone) {
        $rr->print;
}
```

Appendix

C BIND SDB

Here we give you the full source code for two items that we discussed in Chapter 8:

- The utility for the special LDAP object class called `dNSZoneAXFR`, to generate ACLs for inclusion into your `named.conf` when using the BIND-sdb-LDAP driver.
- A simple load-balancing driver for BIND SDB.

C.1 Generate zone clauses for BIND-sdb-LDAP

In Section 8.3.9 we discussed a small utility to generate an `include` file for zones defined for BIND-sdb-LDAP. This is the program, and you can download it from the Web site (☞ D083):

Listing C.1: Generate zone clauses for BIND SDB from LDAP

```
#!/usr/bin/perl
# sdbldap2bind.pl (C)2008 by Jan-Piet Mens
# Create an include file for BIND's 'named.conf' with all zones (dNSZone
# objects), adding 'allow-transfer' stanzas if the zone entries have the
# appropriate attribute types.

use strict;
use Net::LDAP;

my $server = 'localhost';
my $DNSbase = 'ou=dns,dc=qupps,dc=biz';
my $TTL    = 3600;        # default RR TTL

my $ldap = Net::LDAP->new( $server ) or die "$@";

my $mesg = $ldap->bind;

$mesg = $ldap->search(
               base   => $DNSbase,
               filter => '(&(objectClass=dNSZone)(relativeDomainName=@))',
               attrs  => [ qw(zonename dnszoneaxfracl) ],
            );

$mesg->code && die $mesg->error;

foreach my $e ($mesg->entries) {
    my $dn = $e->dn();
    my $zone = $e->get_value('zonename');
    my @acl = $e->get_value('dnszoneaxfracl');
```

```
    $dn =~ s/^relativedomainname=[^,]+,//ig;

    print <<EndHead;
zone "$zone" {
    type master;
    database "ldap ldap://$server/$dn $TTL";
EndHead
    if ($#acl >= 0) {
        print "\tallow-transfer {\n";
        foreach my $a (@acl) {
            if ($a =~ /^[\d]+/) {
                print "\t\t$a;\n";
            } else {
                print "\t\t\"$a\";\n";
            }
        }
        print "\t};\n";
    }

    print "};\n\n";
}

$mesg = $ldap->unbind;
exit 0;
```

C.2 Simple BIND SDB load-balancer driver

In Section 8.5.1 we developed a simple load-balancing driver for BIND SDB, and we discussed how you compile and link it to named. Here is the full source code, which you can also download from the book's Web site (☞ D084). The code consists of three files: `load.h`, `load.c`, and a sample `named.conf`.

C.2.1 load.h

Listing C.2: Sample BIND SDB load balancer: `jpload.h`

```
#include <isc/types.h>

isc_result_t jpload_init(void);
void jpload_clear(void);
```

C.2.2 load.c

Listing C.3: Sample BIND SDB load balancer: `jpload.c`

```
#include <config.h>
#include <string.h>
#include <stdio.h>

#include <isc/print.h>
#include <isc/result.h>
#include <isc/util.h>
#include <isc/mem.h>
#include <dns/sdb.h>
#include <dns/log.h>
#include <dns/lib.h>
#include <named/globals.h>

#include <isc/file.h>
#include <isc/lib.h>
#include <isc/log.h>
#include <isc/msgs.h>
#include <isc/msgcat.h>
#include <isc/region.h>

#include "jpload.h"

static dns_sdbimplementation_t *jpload = NULL;

struct jpinfo {
        char *path;                  /* file name containing IPV4 (A) address */
        char *mname;                  /* name of primary NS for this zone */
};

static isc_result_t
jpload_lookup(const char *zone, const char *name, void *dbdata,
              dns_sdblookup_t *l)
{
        isc_result_t res;
        struct jpinfo *jpi = dbdata;

        UNUSED(zone);

        printf("*** jpload_lookup start: zone=%s name=%s\n", zone, name);

        if (strcmp(name, "@") == 0) {
                /*
                 * If authority() is not defined, issue RR for SOA
                 * and for NS here.
                 */

        } else if (strcmp(name, "www") == 0) {
                char buf[BUFSIZ];
                FILE *fp;

                res = ISC_R_FAILURE;
                if ((fp = fopen(jpi->path, "r")) != NULL) {
```

```
                        if (fgets(buf, sizeof(buf) - 1, fp) != NULL) {
                              buf[strlen(buf) - 1] = '\0';        /* strip nl */

                              res = dns_sdb_putrr(l, "a", 60, buf);
                              if (res != ISC_R_SUCCESS)
                                    res = ISC_R_FAILURE;
                        }
                        (void)fclose(fp);
                  }
                  return (res);
      } else if (strcmp(name, "filename") == 0) {
                  res = dns_sdb_putrr(l, "txt", 60, jpi->path);
                  if (res != ISC_R_SUCCESS)
                        return (ISC_R_FAILURE);
      } else  if (strcmp(name, "dns1") == 0) {
                  res = dns_sdb_putrr(l, "A", 100, "127.0.0.1");
                  if (res != ISC_R_SUCCESS)
                        return (ISC_R_FAILURE);
      } else  {
                  return (ISC_R_NOTFOUND);
      }
      return (ISC_R_SUCCESS);
}

/*
 * lookup() does not return SOA or NS records, so authority() must be defined.
 */

static isc_result_t
jpload_authority(const char *zone, void *dbdata, dns_sdblookup_t *l) {
      isc_result_t res;
      struct jpinfo *jpi = dbdata;

      UNUSED(zone);

      res = dns_sdb_putsoa(l, "dns1", "root.dns1", 7);
      if (res != ISC_R_SUCCESS) {
            return (ISC_R_FAILURE);
      }

      res = dns_sdb_putrr(l, "ns", 86400, jpi->mname);
      if (res != ISC_R_SUCCESS) {
            isc_log_iwrite(dns_lctx,
                        DNS_LOGCATEGORY_DATABASE,
                        DNS_LOGMODULE_SDB, ISC_LOG_ERROR,
                        isc_msgcat, ISC_MSGSET_GENERAL,
                        ISC_MSG_FAILED, "dns_sdb_putrr");
            return (ISC_R_FAILURE);
      }

      return (ISC_R_SUCCESS);
}

/*
 * An example of 'allnodes' which is called for a zone transfer; note
 * that most of this is static data
```

```
 */

static isc_result_t
jpload_allnodes(const char *zone, void *dbdata, dns_sdballnodes_t *an) {

        isc_result_t res;
        struct jpinfo *jpi = dbdata;
        static const char **tp, *texts[] = {
                        "These words will be individually quoted",
                        "\"its fleece was white as snow\""
                };

        UNUSED(zone);

        printf("*** jpload_allnodes start: zone=%s \n", zone);

        res = dns_sdb_putnamedrr(an, "filename", "txt", 1800, jpi->path);
        if (res != ISC_R_SUCCESS)
                return (ISC_R_FAILURE);

        res = dns_sdb_putnamedrr(an, "@", "NS", 100, "dns1");
        if (res != ISC_R_SUCCESS)
                return (ISC_R_FAILURE);

        res = dns_sdb_putnamedrr(an, "dns1", "A", 100, "127.0.0.1");
        if (res != ISC_R_SUCCESS)
                return (ISC_R_FAILURE);

        for (tp = texts; tp && *tp; tp++) {
                res = dns_sdb_putnamedrr(an, "poem", "TXT", 86400, *tp);
                if (res != ISC_R_SUCCESS)
                        return (ISC_R_FAILURE);
        }

        res = dns_sdb_putnamedrr(an, "googl", "cname", 3600, "www.google.com.");
        if (res != ISC_R_SUCCESS)
                return (ISC_R_FAILURE);

        res = dns_sdb_putnamedrr(an, "imap", "a", 3600, "192.168.2.1");
        if (res != ISC_R_SUCCESS)
                return (ISC_R_FAILURE);
        return (ISC_R_SUCCESS);
}

static isc_result_t
jpload_create(const char *zone, int argc, char **argv, void *driverdata,
                void **dbdata)
{
        struct jpinfo *jpi;

        UNUSED(zone);
        UNUSED(driverdata);

        printf("*** jpload_create start\n");

        if (argc != 2)
```

```
                return (ISC_R_FAILURE);
        jpi = isc_mem_get(ns_g_mctx, sizeof(struct jpinfo));
        if (jpi == NULL)
                return (ISC_R_NOMEMORY);

        if ((jpi->path = isc_mem_strdup(ns_g_mctx, argv[0])) == NULL)
                return ISC_R_NOMEMORY;
        if ((jpi->mname   = isc_mem_strdup(ns_g_mctx, argv[1])) == NULL)
                return ISC_R_NOMEMORY;

        printf("*** jpload_create end\n");

    *dbdata = jpi;
        return (ISC_R_SUCCESS);
}

static void
jpload_destroy(const char *zone, void *driverdata, void **dbdata)
{
        struct jpinfo *jpi = *dbdata;

        UNUSED(zone);
        UNUSED(driverdata);

        isc_mem_free(ns_g_mctx, jpi->path);
        isc_mem_free(ns_g_mctx, jpi->mname);
        isc_mem_put(ns_g_mctx, jpi, sizeof(struct jpinfo));
}

/*
 * This zone supports zone transfer, so allnodes() is defined.
 */
static dns_sdbmethods_t jpload_methods = {
        jpload_lookup,                /* lookup */
        jpload_authority,        /* authority */
        jpload_allnodes,        /* allnodes */
        jpload_create,                /* create */
        jpload_destroy                /* destroy */
};

/*
 * Wrapper around dns_sdb_register().
 */
isc_result_t
jpload_init(void) {
        unsigned int flags;

        flags = DNS_SDBFLAG_RELATIVEOWNER | DNS_SDBFLAG_RELATIVERDATA;
        return (dns_sdb_register("jpload", &jpload_methods, NULL, flags,
                                ns_g_mctx, &jpload));
}

/*
 * Wrapper around dns_sdb_unregister().
 */
void
```

```
jpload_clear(void) {
        if (jpload != NULL)
                dns_sdb_unregister(&jpload);
}
```

C.2.3 named.conf

Listing C.4: Sample BIND SDB load balancer: `named.conf`

```
zone "load.local" {
  type master;
  database "jpload /var/load/balance.ip dns1";
  //          ^            ^                ^
  //          |            |                +- mname
  //          |            +------------------ filename
  //          +------------------------------- driver name
};
```

Appendix

D Bind DLZ

Here we give you the full source code for two items that we discussed in Chapter 9:

- The utility that loads BDBHPT databases from a MySQL database.
- Helper functions for automatically creating PTR resource records.

D.1 Load BDBHPT from an SQL database

In Section 9.9 we discussed Bind DLZ's Berkeley DB High Performance Database driver (BDBHPT), and we explained that you have to create your own tools for populating its database. We have created a program, mydns2bdbhpt.pl, that you can use as a basis for writing your own.

This program reads MySQL database tables, and "dumps" their content into individual Berkeley DB databases for use by Bind DLZ's BDBHPT driver (Figure D.1). We've chosen to use the database schema used by the MyDNS name server (Chapter 5), but you can easily modify the program to use a different schema.

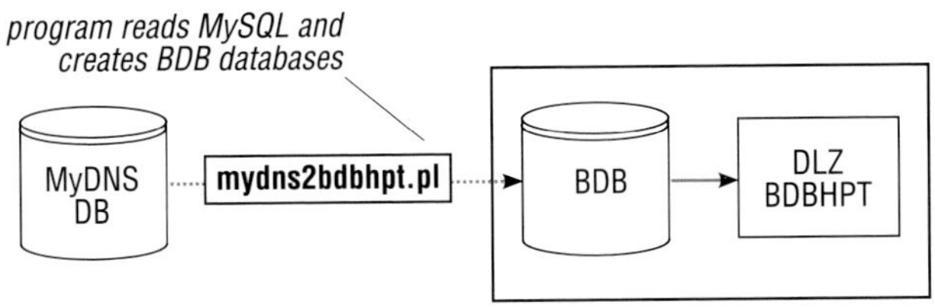

Figure D.1: Create BDB databases from MySQL

The mydns2bdbhpt utility performs the following steps:

1. Initialize the connection to MySQL and `PREPARE` the `SELECT` statements for retrieving zones and their data.
2. Initialize the Berkeley DB databases.
3. Enumerate all zones and add their reversed names to the `DNSzone` database.
4. For each zone, enumerate all resource records, and add them to the `DNSdata` database, simultaneously creating the `DNSaxfr` database for zone transfers.

5. Add permission to transfer each zone by specifying three static IP addresses in the `DNSclient` database.

Listing D.1: Convert SQL data to BDB databases for DLZ's BDBHPT driver

```
#!/usr/bin/perl

use strict;
use BerkeleyDB;
use DBI;

my $dsn         = 'DBI:mysql:mydns:127.0.0.1';
my $dbpath      = '/var/spool/myns';
my $dbfile      = 'DLZ.db';

my $dbh = DBI->connect($dsn, "dnsadmin", "hah!")
    or die "Can't connect to $dsn";

my $soaq        = "SELECT id,origin,ns,mbox,serial,refresh,retry,expire,minimum,ttl";
$soaq          .=     " FROM soa ORDER BY origin";
my $sth         = $dbh->prepare($soaq);

my $rrq         = "SELECT name,type,data,aux,ttl FROM rr WHERE zone = ?";
my $rrst        = $dbh->prepare($rrq);

my (%DNSdata, %DNSzone, %DNSaxfr, %DNSclient, $rid);

&initBDB('P');

$sth->execute();

# Find all zones

while (my $soa = $sth->fetchrow_hashref) {
    my $line;
    my $zone = $soa->{origin};

    $zone =~ s/\.$//;    # Remove trailing period

    # Add a zone; the key is a reversed zone name and its value is empty

    $DNSzone{reverse $zone} = "";

    # Add the zone's data. First the SOA ...

    $line = $soa->{ttl} . ' ';
    $line .= 'SOA ';
    $line .= $soa->{ns} . ' ';
    $line .= $soa->{mbox} . ' ';
    $line .= $soa->{serial} . ' ';
    $line .= $soa->{refresh} . ' ';
    $line .= $soa->{retry} . ' ';
    $line .= $soa->{expire} . ' ';
    $line .= $soa->{minimum};

    $DNSdata{"$zone @"} = rec("@ $line");
```

```
    # ... and then all the other RR

    $rrst->execute($soa->{id}) or warn;
    while (my $rr = $rrst->fetchrow_hashref) {

        my $host = $rr->{name};

        $host = '@' if (!$rr->{name});

        $line = "$host ";
        $line .= $rr->{ttl} . ' ';
        $line .= $rr->{type} . ' ';
        $line .= $rr->{aux} . ' ' if ($rr->{type} eq 'MX');

        if ($rr->{type} eq 'TXT') {
            $line .= '"' . $rr->{data} . '"';
        } else {
            $line .= $rr->{data};
        }

        $DNSdata{"${zone} ${host}"} = rec($line);

        # Add zone/host pointers to the AXFR data, taking care
        # to ensure key/value uniqueness for this database

        if (!defined($DNSaxfr{$zone}) && ($DNSaxfr{$zone} ne "$host")) {
            $DNSaxfr{$zone} = $host;
        }

    }

    # Allow AXFR for clients? This should use the optional 'xfer'
    # column of MyDNS, but we use 3 static addresses.

    $DNSclient{$zone} = '127.0.0.1';
    $DNSclient{$zone} = '192.168.1.20';
    $DNSclient{$zone} = '192.168.1.164';
}

untie %DNSdata;
untie %DNSzone;
untie %DNSaxfr;
untie %DNSclient;

$sth->finish();
$rrst->finish();
$dbh->disconnect();
exit;

# Return a record for BDBHPT containing a unique BDB replication
# id, a single SPACE and the data.
sub rec {
    my ($rr) = @_;

    $rid++;           # give unique record-id
```

```
    return "${rid} ${rr}";
}

sub fatal {
    my ($dbname) = @_;
        die "Cannot create $dbfile:$dbname: " .  $BerkeleyDB::Error . "\n";
}

sub initBDB {
    my $mode = shift;

    my %DBflags = (
       C => DB_INIT_CDB | DB_INIT_MPOOL | DB_CREATE,
       T => DB_INIT_TXN | DB_INIT_MPOOL | DB_INIT_LOCK | DB_INIT_LOG | DB_CREATE,
       P => DB_PRIVATE  | DB_INIT_MPOOL | DB_CREATE,
    );

    my $BDB = new BerkeleyDB::Env
        -Home        => $dbpath,
        -Flags       => $DBflags{$mode},
        -ErrFile     => *STDERR,
        -Verbose     => 1 ;

    tie %DNSdata, 'BerkeleyDB::Hash',
        -Env         => $BDB,
        -Flags       => DB_CREATE,
        -Property    => DB_DUP | DB_DUPSORT,
        -Filename    => "$dbpath/$dbfile",
        -Subname     => "dns_data"
        or fata('dns_data');

    tie %DNSzone, 'BerkeleyDB::Btree',
        -Env         => $BDB,
        -Flags       => DB_CREATE,
        -Filename    => "$dbpath/$dbfile",
        -Subname     => "dns_zone",
        or fata('dns_zone');

    tie %DNSaxfr, 'BerkeleyDB::Hash',
        -Env         => $BDB,
        -Flags       => DB_CREATE,
        -Property    => DB_DUP | DB_DUPSORT,
        -Filename    => "$dbpath/$dbfile",
        -Subname     => "dns_xfr",
        or fata('dns_xfr');

    tie %DNSclient, 'BerkeleyDB::Hash',
        -Env         => $BDB,
        -Flags       => DB_CREATE,
        -Property    => DB_DUP | DB_DUPSORT,
        -Filename    => "$dbpath/$dbfile",
        -Subname     => "dns_client",
        or fata('dns_client');
}
```

You can download the program from the book's Web site (☞ D095).

D.2 Helper functions for automatically creating PTR records

In Section 9.10.4, on page 253 we discussed how you can automatically create PTR records in Bind DLZ, using three MySQL functions. We show these three functions here.

1. Function `revip4()` takes a dotted-decimal IPv4 address and reverses it:

```
mysql> SELECT revip4('192.168.1.4');
+-----------------------+
| revip4('192.168.1.4') |
+-----------------------+
| 4.1.168.192           |
+-----------------------+
```

Listing D.2: Custom MySQL function `revip4()` in Bind DLZ

```
-- revip4: return a reversed dotted-quad (JPM)

DELIMITER $$
CREATE FUNCTION revip4 (quad CHAR(15)) RETURNS CHAR(15)
BEGIN
        DECLARE hexip CHAR(15);
        DECLARE invip CHAR(15);

        SET hexip = LPAD( HEX(INET_ATON(quad)), 8, '0');
        SET invip = CONCAT(
                        MID(hexip, 7, 2),
                        MID(hexip, 5, 2),
                        MID(hexip, 3, 2),
                        MID(hexip, 1, 2));

        RETURN INET_NTOA(  CONV(invip, 16, 10) );
END $$
DELIMITER ;
```

2. Function `ip4octet()` uses MySQL's `inet_aton()` function to return the rightmost octet of an IPv4 address:

```
mysql> SELECT ip4octet('192.168.1.4');
+-------------------------+
| ip4octet('192.168.1.4') |
+-------------------------+
| 4                       |
+-------------------------+
```

Listing D.3: Custom MySQL function `ip4octet()` in Bind DLZ

```
-- ip4octet: return the fourth octet of a dotted-quad (JPM)

DELIMITER $$
CREATE FUNCTION ip4octet (quad CHAR(15)) RETURNS CHAR(15)
BEGIN
     RETURN CONV(RIGHT(HEX(INET_ATON(quad)), 2), 16, 10);
END $$
DELIMITER ;
```

3. Function `inarpa4()` returns the in-addr.arpa zone name for a dotted-decimal IPv4 address. It calls `revip4()` to reverse the IPv4 dotted decimal, slices off everything before the first period in the resulting string, and appends in-addr.arpa:

```
mysql> SELECT inarpa4('192.168.1.4');
+------------------------+
| inarpa4('192.168.1.4') |
+------------------------+
| 1.168.192.in-addr.arpa |
+------------------------+
```

Listing D.4: Custom MySQL function `inarpa4()` in Bind DLZ

```
-- inarpa4: return the in-addr.arpa address for an IPv4 (JPM)

DELIMITER $$
CREATE FUNCTION inarpa4 (quad CHAR(15)) RETURNS CHAR(128)
BEGIN
     RETURN CONCAT(
       MID(revip4(quad),
            LOCATE('.', revip4(quad)) + 1,
            LENGTH(quad)
       ), '.in-addr.arpa');
END $$
DELIMITER ;
```

If you use a different brand of name server with an SQL back-end, you can modify the code above to suit.

Appendix

E Perl DNS name servers

In Chapter 15 we discussed how you use Perl to create your own DNS name server program, and we showed you an example in Section 15.3. In the following sections, we show you:

1. The full source code for that example.
2. A sample server using Net::DNS::Nameserver.
3. A sample server using Net::DNS::Server.

E.1 Stanford::DNSserver

This is the full source code for the program clidnsd.pl in Section 15.3, pages 365–368.

Listing E.1: Perl DNS Nameserver: Stanford::DNSserver

```
#!/usr/bin/perl

use IO::Socket;
use Sys::Syslog;
use Sys::Hostname;
use Stanford::DNS;
use Stanford::DNSserver;
use Net::LDAP;

require 'dnssrv.pl';

my $ldapsrv      = '_ldap._tcp.qupps.biz';
my $ldapbase     = 'ou=usr,dc=qupps,dc=biz';

my $myname       = hostname();
my $tld      = 'info.qupps.biz';
my $atld     = 'users.qupps.biz';
my $ttl      = 3600;
my $ld;

foreach my $srv (dnsSRV($ldapsrv)) {

    my $hostport = ${$srv}{address} . ":" . ${$srv}{port};
    print "Trying to connect to ", ${$srv}{target}, " at $hostport\n";
    $ld = Net::LDAP->new($hostport);

    last if (defined($ld));
}
```

```
$ld->bind() or die "$0: Can't bind to directory at $_";

$ns = new Stanford::DNSserver (
    listen_on => ["127.0.0.1"],
    port      =>         53,
    defttl    =>         60,
    debug     =>          1,
    daemon    =>       "no",
    pidfile   => "/tmp/example.pid",
    logfunc   => sub { print shift; print "\n" },
    exitfunc  => sub {
            print "Bye!\n";
            $ld->disconnect;
            });

# Add static answers for SOA, NS, and A
$ns->add_static("$tld",
     T_SOA, rr_SOA($myname, "hostmaster.$tld",
           time, 3600, 3600, 86400, 0));
$ns->add_static("$tld", T_NS, rr_NS($myname));

my $myaddr = inet_ntoa((gethostbyname($myname))[4]);
$ns->add_static("$tld", T_A,
    rr_A(unpack('N', inet_aton($myaddr))));

# Set up handler for dynamic requests
$ns->add_dynamic("$tld" => \&userreq);

# Start serving answers...
$ns->answer_queries();

sub userreq {
    my ($domain, $host, $qtype, $qclass, $dm, $from) = @_;

    print "DOMAIN=[$domain], HOST=[$host], QT=[$qtype] FROM=[$from]\n";

    $dm->{rcode} = NOERROR;

    $host =~ s/[\W]//g;      # Sanitize
    if (!$host) {
        $dm->{rcode} = SERVFAIL;     # No username specified
        return;
    }

    if ($qtype == T_A || $qtype == T_ANY) {

        my @iplist = dnsADDR(9, "$host.$atld");

        for my $ip (@iplist) {
            # push each IP back into Stanford::'s reply

            $entry = unpack('N', inet_aton($ip));
            $dm->{answer} .= dns_answer(QPTR, T_A, C_IN, $ttl, rr_A($entry));
            $dm->{ancount} += 1;
        }
```

```
    }

    if ($qtype == T_TXT || $qtype == T_ANY) {

        my $msg = $ld->search(base => $ldapbase,
                filter => "(&(objectclass=person)(userid=${host}))",
                attrs => [ qw(cn telephonenumber) ]);
        if ($msg->code) {
            $dm->{rcode} = SERVFAIL;
            return;
        }
        my @entries = $msg->entries;

        foreach my $e (@entries) {
            my $cn = $e->get_value('cn') or 'unknown';
            my $tel = $e->get_value('telephonenumber') or 'unknown';

            $dm->{answer} .= dns_answer(QPTR, T_TXT, C_IN,
                $ttl, rr_TXT("name: $cn"));
            $dm->{ancount} += 1;
            $dm->{answer} .= dns_answer(QPTR, T_TXT, C_IN,
                $ttl, rr_TXT("phone: $tel"));
            $dm->{ancount} += 1;
        }
    }

    # If no answers available, return NXDOMAIN

    if (! $dm->{ancount} ) {
        $dm->{rcode} = NXDOMAIN;
    }
}
```

Listing E.2: Handling Service (SRV) queries in Perl

```
#!/usr/bin/perl

use strict;
use Net::DNS;
use Net::DNS::RR;

my $reso = Net::DNS::Resolver->new(
    nameservers     => [ qw(127.0.0.1) ],
    recurse     => 0,
    debug       => 0,
    port        => 53,
);

#my @ldaphosts = dnsSRV('_ldap._tcp.qupps.biz');
#
#foreach my $srv (@ldaphosts) {
#       print "Target: ", ${$srv}{target}, "\n";
#       print "Priority: ", ${$srv}{priority}, "\n";
#       print "Port:    ", ${$srv}{port}, "\n";
#       print "Address ", ${$srv}{address}, "\n\n";
#}
```

```
sub byprio {
    my %a = shift;
    my %b = shift;

    $a->{priority} <=> $b->{priority};
}

sub dnsSRV {
    my ($domain) = @_;
    my @results = ();

    my $query = $reso->query($domain, 'SRV');

    if ($query) {
        my $n = 0;
        foreach my $rr ($query->answer) {

            $results[$n++] = {
                    'target'    => $rr->target,
                        'port'      => $rr->port,
                        'address'   => dnsADDR(1, $rr->target),
                        'priority'  => $rr->priority,
                    };
        }
    } else {
        print "dnsSRV: query failed: ", $reso->errorstring,"\n";
    }

    return sort byprio @results;
}

sub dnsADDR {
    my ($count, $domain) = @_;
    my @results;

    my $query = $reso->query($domain, 'A');

    if ($query) {
        foreach my $rr ($query->answer) {
            push(@results, $rr->address);
            last unless ($count--);
        }

    } else {
        print "dnsADDR: query failed: ", $reso->errorstring,"\n";
    }

    return @results;
}

1;
```

E.2 Net::DNS::Nameserver

The Perl module Net::DNS::Nameserver, created by Michael Fuhr, implements a DNS server class. The example program below listens on port 9953 and responds with hard-coded answers to queries for Address (A) records and Text (TXT) records. No matter what domain you specify, it returns 192.168.1.34 as an answer for all A queries, and `"hello cruel"` and `"world"` for all TXT queries. Something like this could be useful if you are a Web hoster and provide identical answers for queries on many hundreds of domains.

Listing E.3: Perl DNS Nameserver: Net::DNS::Nameserver example

```
#!/usr/bin/perl -w

use strict;
use Net::DNS::Nameserver;

my $serial = 1;

sub handler {
    my ($qname, $qclass, $qtype, $peer) = @_;
    my ($rcode, @ans, @auth, @add);
    my $ttl = 3600;
    my $rdata;

    if ($qtype eq 'A' || $qtype eq 'ANY') {
        $rdata = '192.168.1.34';
        push @ans, Net::DNS::RR->new("$qname $ttl $qclass A $rdata");
        $rcode = "NOERROR";
    }

    if ($qtype eq 'TXT' || $qtype eq 'ANY') {
        $rdata = '"hello cruel"';
        $qtype = 'TXT';
        push @ans, Net::DNS::RR->new("$qname $ttl $qclass $qtype $rdata");

        $rdata = '"world"';
        push @ans, Net::DNS::RR->new("$qname $ttl $qclass $qtype $rdata");
        $rcode = "NOERROR";
    }

    if ($qtype eq 'AXFR') {
        push @ans, Net::DNS::RR->new(
              "$qname $ttl $qclass SOA localhost. ns.localhost. \
                                  $serial 86400 10 10 10");
        push @ans, Net::DNS::RR->new("$qname $ttl $qclass NS localhost");
        push @ans, Net::DNS::RR->new("$qname $ttl $qclass A 127.0.0.1");
        $serial++;
        $rdata = '"hello cruel"';
        push @ans, Net::DNS::RR->new("$qname $ttl $qclass TXT $rdata");
    }

    # Set 'aa' flag on the answer
    return ($rcode, \@ans, \@auth, \@add, { aa => 1 });
}
```

```
my $ns = Net::DNS::Nameserver->new(
    LocalPort    => 9953,
    ReplyHandler => \&handler,
    Verbose      => 1,
) || die("Can't create nameserver object: $!");

$ns->main_loop;
```

If you start the example as it is, and send it the two queries (one for TXT and the other for an A) you will see the program print diagnostics, thanks to the Verbose mode setting. The answers to the queries are as expected:

```
$ dig @127.0.0.1 -p 9953 www.example.com txt
;; ->>HEADER<<- opcode: QUERY, status: NOERROR, id: 11690
;; flags: qr aa rd; QUERY: 1, ANSWER: 2, AUTHORITY: 0, ADDITIONAL: 0

;; ANSWER SECTION:
www.example.com.        3600    IN      TXT     "hello cruel"
www.example.com.        3600    IN      TXT     "world"

$ dig @127.0.0.1 -p 9953 something.de a
;; ->>HEADER<<- opcode: QUERY, status: NOERROR, id: 8755
;; flags: qr aa rd; QUERY: 1, ANSWER: 1, AUTHORITY: 0, ADDITIONAL: 0

;; ANSWER SECTION:
something.de.           3600    IN      A 192.168.1.34
```

The project has its own site at `http://www.net-dns.org/`

E.3 Net::DNS::Server

Luis E. Muñoz has written Net::DNS::Server, a set of Perl modules that you can use to implement a DNS name server. Individual functions you write provide answers to specific query types. For example, in the listing below, the A() function handles A queries, and the TXT() function processes TXT queries.

Listing E.4: Perl DNS Nameserver: Net::DNS::Server example

```
#!/usr/bin/perl -w

use strict;
package Net::DNS::Method::Sample;
use Net::DNS::Method;
use Net::DNS;

our @ISA = qw(Net::DNS::Method);

sub new { bless [], $_[0]; }

sub A {
    my $self = shift;
    my $q = shift;
    my $a = shift;
```

```
    # 'qclass' => 'IN', 'qname' => 'www.qupps.biz', 'qtype' => 'A'

    return NS_STOP if ($q->qtype eq 'ANY');

    $a->header->rcode('NOERROR');
    if ($q->qname eq 'xxddd.de') {
        $a->push('answer', new Net::DNS::RR $q->qname . ' 10 IN A 127.0.0.1');
    } else {
        $a->push('answer', new Net::DNS::RR $q->qname . ' 1800 IN A 10.0.12.1');
    }
    return NS_OK;
}

sub TXT {
    my $self = shift;
    my $q = shift;
    my $a = shift;

    $a->header->rcode('NOERROR');
    $a->push('answer', new Net::DNS::RR $q->qname . ' 89 IN TXT "hello world"');
    return NS_OK;
}

package main;

use Net::DNS;
use Net::DNS::Method;
use Net::DNS::Server;

my $method = Net::DNS::Method::Sample->new;

my $server = new Net::DNS::Server ('127.0.0.1:9553', [ $method ])
    or die "Cannot create server object: $!";

while (my $n = $server->get_question()) {

    foreach (0..$n) {
        $server->process;

        $server->send_response();
        my $question = $server->q();
        my $answer = $server->answer();
    }
}
```

Appendix

F User Defined Functions in MySQL

In MySQL you extend the functionality of the database system with *User Defined Functions (UDFs)*. You compile UDFs as object code and add them to the database via the `CREATE FUNCTION` statement. (Read read the documentation at `http://dev.mysql.com/doc/refman/5.0/en/adding-functions.html` for details.)

We discuss two User Defined Functions in the following sections:

A. A UDF to raise an error in a database trigger (Section F.1).

B. A UDF that automatically adds a zone clause to a `.conf` file when you insert a new zone in a back-end's database table (Section F.2).

F.1 A – Raise an error in a MySQL trigger with a UDF

In Section 6.9.6 we defined a trigger to catch illegal inserts of CNAME records when there is already a different record on the same domain. The trigger deliberately used non-existent procedure calls in MySQL to simulate an error, and we saw that doing so doesn't really work, because the simulation doesn't produce errors that abort transactions.

In order to really cause an error, we define a UDF to implement the SQL `RAISE ERROR` functionality that MySQL lacks.

F.1.1 The source code of the `raise_error()` UDF function

The UDF consists of two small C functions:

- `raise_error_init()` is invoked whenever MySQL calls the UDF, to perform initialization. By definition (i.e. this is the way MySQL works), if the init function returns an error, MySQL aborts the SQL statement with an error message and does not call the UDF's main or deinitialization functions. Our function *always* returns a failure code to MySQL, because that is the only way MySQL can be signaled to return an error to the caller.

- `raise_error()` simply returns 0 because it will never actually be called, because the init function (`raise_error_init()`) will always purposely produce an error. We have to define it though, so that we can "attach" our UDF to MySQL, and to satisfy the linker.

Listing F.1: User Defined `RAISE ERROR` Function for MySQL

```
/*
 * raise_error(): MySQL UDF by Jan-Piet Mens, based on an
 * idea by Roland Bouman in the MySQL forums
 * Usage: SET @error := raise_error('My message');
 */

#include <string.h>
#include <mysql.h>

#define E_NOSPEC "Unspecified error raised\0"

my_bool raise_error_init(UDF_INIT *initid, UDF_ARGS *args, char *message)
{
    unsigned int n;

    if (args->arg_count == 1 && args->arg_type[0] == STRING_RESULT) {
        n = strlen(args->args[0]) + 1;
        n = (n > MYSQL_ERRMSG_SIZE) ? MYSQL_ERRMSG_SIZE : n;
        memcpy(message, args->args[0], n);
    } else {
        memcpy(message, E_NOSPEC, strlen(E_NOSPEC)+1);
    }
    return 1;
}

long long raise_error(UDF_INIT *initid, UDF_ARGS *args, char *is_null, char *error)
{
    return 0;
}
```

F.1.2 Install your UDF

To install your new User Defined Function in MySQL:

1. Compile the code and link it as a shared object library. We call it `libudf_raise.so`.
2. Copy the `libudf_raise.so` library into a directory which will be found by the loader. The following `Makefile` handles both steps:

```
CFLAGS=-I/usr/include/mysql
LDFLAGS=-L/usr/lib64/mysql
DESTDIR=/usr/lib64/mysql
SONAME=libudf_raise.so

$(SONAME): udf_raise.c
        gcc -fPIC $(CFLAGS) -shared -o $(SONAME) \
                udf_raise.c $(LDFLAGS) -lmysqlclient

install: $(SONAME)
        install -m755 $(SONAME) $(DESTDIR)/$(SONAME)
```

3. Create the function in MySQL, and specify the name of your shared library (without its path name, because MySQL searches for the shared object file in standard directories):

```
mysql> CREATE FUNCTION raise_error RETURNS INT SONAME 'libudf_raise.so';
```

4. Test your User Defined Function:

```
mysql> SELECT raise_error();
ERROR:
Unspecified error raised

mysql> SELECT raise_error('Oops, this cannot happen');
ERROR:
Oops, this cannot happen
```

5. To fully remove the function from the data dictionary if you decide not to use it any more, `DROP` the function (and remove the shared library containing the UDF):

```
mysql> DROP FUNCTION raise_error;
```

You can use this function whenever you want to raise an error within an SQL procedure or trigger. Download the code from the book's Web site (☞ D291).

F.1.3 Create the trigger

The trigger used is almost identical to the original trigger defined in Section 6.9.6, but instead of calling undefined procedures, it invokes the UDF:

Listing F.2: Trigger uses `raise_error()` UDF

```
-- cnametrigger.sql by Jan-Piet Mens
-- Requires raise_error() UDF

DELIMITER $$

CREATE TRIGGER pdnsCNAMEtrigger
  BEFORE INSERT ON records
  FOR EACH ROW
BEGIN
  DECLARE nrows INTEGER;

  IF NEW.type = 'CNAME' THEN
    SELECT COUNT(*) INTO nrows
      FROM records
      WHERE name = NEW.name;

    IF nrows > 0 THEN
      -- there is an RR already (including CNAME):
      -- don't insert this one!
      --
      SET @error = raise_error('Other data exists: CNAME not inserted');
    END IF;

  ELSE --        NEW.type <> 'CNAME'
    SELECT COUNT(*) INTO nrows
```

```
        FROM records
        WHERE name = NEW.name
          AND type = 'CNAME';

      IF nrows > 0 THEN
         -- there is already a CNAME: don't insert!
         --
         SET @error = raise_error('CNAME exists: won\'t insert other data');
      END IF;
    END IF;

END $$
DELIMITER ;
```

F.1.4 Testing the trigger in PowerDNS

```
mysql> SELECT id,name,type,content FROM records WHERE domain_id = 100011;
+---------+-----------+-------+-------------------------+
| id      | name      | type  | content                 |
+---------+-----------+-------+-------------------------+
| 1000173 | jp.xa     | SOA   | 1 1800  900 604800 86400 |
| 1000174 | jp.xa     | NS    | dns.jp.xa               |
| 1000176 | dns.jp.xa | A     | 192.168.1.11            |
| 1000177 | www.jp.xa | CNAME | www.qupps.biz.          |
+---------+-----------+-------+-------------------------+

mysql> INSERT INTO records (domain_id, name, type, content) VALUES
     >   (100011,'dns.jp.xa', 'CNAME', 'www.example.');
ERROR:
Other data exists: CNAME not inserted

mysql> INSERT INTO records (domain_id, name, type, content) VALUES
     >    (100011,'www.jp.xa', 'A', '127.0.0.3');
ERROR:
CNAME exists: won't insert other data
```

That completes our `raise_error()` UDF. Now we move on and show you a more complex example, that updates a file in a file system.

F.2 B – Use a UDF to update a file in the file system

Sections 3.1 and 7.2 explained that you can use a name server with a database back-end as a stealth server to a slave NSD or BIND. That is easy to set up, but there is one problem: in both NSD and BIND slaves, you have to configure the list of zones they serve, in their respective configuration files (`nsd.conf` or `named.conf`). In particular, if you add a new zone to the stealth server, the NSD or BIND slave will *not* serve that zone until you add it to the `.conf` file. So adding a zone is a three-step process:

1. Add the zone to your back-end database.
2. Edit the `.conf` file for NSD or BIND, and insert the slave zone. In the following we assume you configure these zones in a file called `zones.incl` that you include in your name server's configuration.

3. Reload the master (stealth) name server so that it performs an AXFR zone transfer.

The program in Section 6.9.3, page 154, automatically enumerates the zones in your back-end database to create a `zones.incl` file, but how do you invoke the program? There are several options:

- Try to remember to launch it manually. This is error-prone – if you forget, your master name server won't serve the zone.
- Periodically run the program via cron. This is wasteful of resources if you have many zones. You need a mechanism that creates the list of zones only when you add or remove a zone from the database.

We love automation (because we're lazy) so we use a database trigger, a User Defined Function, a pinch of make and a squeeze of cron (Figure F.1) to automate the whole process.

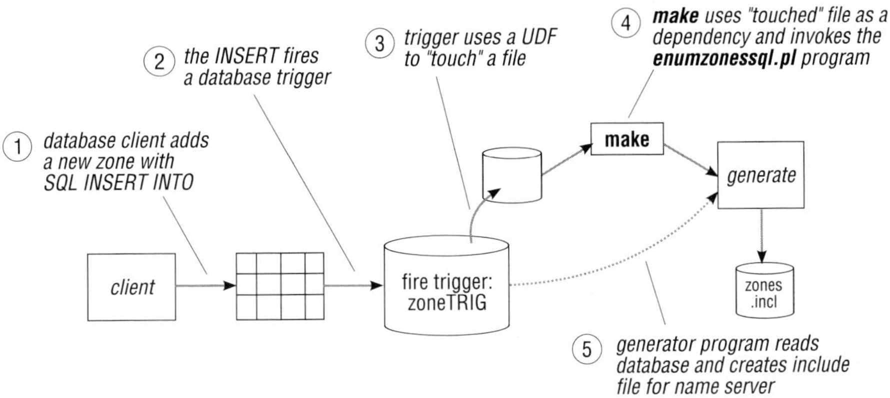

Figure F.1: Trigger an update to a file via MySQL with a UDF

1. With your chosen database client (e.g. MySQL command-line client, Web interface, Perl utility, etc.) you create a zone in your database by performing an SQL `INSERT` into the appropriate table.
2. The `INSERT` on the table fires a database trigger:

```
DELIMITER $$

CREATE TRIGGER zoneTRIG AFTER INSERT ON domains
FOR EACH ROW
BEGIN
      SET @error = newzone(NEW.name);
END $$
DELIMITER ;
```

   This example is for the table used by PowerDNS; adapt the table and column name for your brand of name server accordingly.

3. The trigger calls a MySQL UDF for each inserted row in the table, passing to the UDF the name of the newly added zone. This is not required, but we do it to show you how you can pass values to a UDF.

Listing F.3: UDF that "touches" a file on the file system

```
/* newzone.c (C)2008 by Jan-Piet Mens.  MySQL UDF */

#include <stdio.h>
#include <string.h>
#include <my_global.h>
#include <my_sys.h>
#include <mysql.h>
#include <m_string.h>

#define TOUCHFILE        "/var/nsd/zones.trig"

static pthread_mutex_t LOCK_zonefile;

/* mysql> CREATE FUNCTION newzone RETURNS INTEGER SONAME "newzone.so";  */

my_bool newzone_init(UDF_INIT *iid, UDF_ARGS *args, char *message)
{
        if (args->arg_count != 1 || args->arg_type[0] != STRING_RESULT) {
                strmov(message,"Need a STRING arg");
                return 1;
        }

        iid->max_length = 21;
        iid->maybe_null = 0;

        pthread_mutex_init(&LOCK_zonefile, MY_MUTEX_INIT_SLOW);
        return 0;
}

void newzone_deinit(UDF_INIT *iid)
{
        pthread_mutex_destroy(&LOCK_zonefile);
}

longlong newzone(UDF_INIT *iid, UDF_ARGS *args, char *isnull, char *error)
{
        uint len;
        char buf[512];
        FILE *fp;

        if (!args->args[0] || !(len = args->lengths[0])) {
                *isnull = 1;
                return 0;
        }

        len = (len >= sizeof(buf)) ? sizeof(buf) - 1 : len;

        memcpy(buf, args->args[0], len);
        buf[len] = 0;
```

```
        pthread_mutex_lock(&LOCK_zonefile);

        if ((fp = fopen(TOUCHFILE, "a")) != NULL) {
                fprintf(fp, "%s\n", buf);
                fclose(fp);
        }

        pthread_mutex_unlock(&LOCK_zonefile);
        return 1L;
}
```

The UDF "touches" (i.e. modifies) a file on the file system, and the name of the newly added zone is appended to the file contents. Install the UDF as we showed you in Section F.1.2. (We repeat the steps below, for ease of reference.)

4. Periodically, via cron, you launch make, like this:

```
$ cd /var/nsd && make -s -f Makefile.dns
```

`Makefile.dns` has a dependency on the file `zones.trig`, which is"touched" by the UDF, so make knows that it has to do something when the file's modification time changes: it calls the program that generates the `zones.incl` file.

5. This last step is where the enumzonessql.pl program retrieves a list of all zones in your back-end database, creates the `zones.incl` file and reloads your name server. The `Makefile.dns` we use is:

```
zones.incl: zones.trig
        enumzonessql.pl > /tmp/zf.$$ && mv /tmp/zf.$$ /var/nsd/zones.incl
```

6. You should append any additional steps you require (e.g. nsdc rebuild, rndc reload, etc.) to this `Makefile.dns`.

We set up and install the system as follows. This example is for the NSD name server; adapt for BIND as necessary:

```
# cd /path/to/newzone
# make
# cp newzone.so /usr/lib64/newzone.so

# cd /var/nsd
# touch zones.trig
# chown mysql:mysql zones.trig

# mysql ourpdns
mysql> CREATE FUNCTION newzone RETURNS INTEGER SONAME "newzone.so";
mysql> SOURCE /path/to/newzone/newzone.sql;
mysql> INSERT INTO domains (name, type) VALUES ('example.net', 'NATIVE');
mysql> quit

# ls -l zones.trig
-rw-r--r-- 1 mysql mysql 12 May 10 00:05 zones.trig
# cat zones.trig
example.net
```

```
# make -f Makefile.dns
enumzonessql.pl > /tmp/zf.$$ && mv /tmp/zf.$$ /var/nsd/zones.incl
# make -f Makefile.dns
make: 'zones.incl' is up to date.
```

Note the following:

- It is trivial to modify the trigger to support MyDNS' or Bind DLZ's database back-end tables instead of PowerDNS as we have done here.
- You can also add a trigger that fires when you update or delete a zone in your database.
- Remember that your UDF function operates as part of the MySQL server's address space, so if it doesn't behave, it can crash the database server. Furthermore, the UDF runs with the permissions of the MySQL daemon, so any files it needs must be accessible by the MySQL user (typically `mysql`).
- We could easily have launched make from the UDF proper, but because then a make problem might crash our database server, we prefer not to. You could launch make by using `fork()` / `exec()` (or `system()`).
- If you use PostgreSQL as your back-end database, you don't have to add a function to it. PostgreSQL can generate notifications with its `NOTIFY` command, and you create a client program that receives the notification and acts upon it. This method is more than adequate to implement something similar to what we've just described (see `http://www.postgresql.org/docs/8.1/static/sql-notify.html`).

That completes our short discussion of User Defined Functions and how you implement them in MySQL.

Appendix

G Bits and pieces

Besides name-to-address and address-to-name mapping, the DNS can be (and is) used for a number of interesting things. The following sections introduce some of these, mostly using tools we have discussed in the preceding chapters.

G.1 Using the DNS to store arbitrary (configuration) strings

If you look at the pmc program we developed in Section 19.8.1, you'll see it uses a compiled-in URL, containing both the host address and the the full pathname of its related pms server. Now suppose you have to move the pms service for some reason so its URL changes. You have a number of choices:

- If the host's address changes, the solution is easy: you change the A or CNAME record to the new machine.
- If the host's name changes, it gets a bit more difficult, although you may be able to create a CNAME for the old name, pointing to the new name. (However, the Web server on the new host will have to recognize the new name as being valid.)
- If the location of the resource changes from `/pms.php` to `/support/pms.cgi` say, it gets even more difficult. The solution is to have the Web server redirect the URL to its new location, but you may not have the permissions to alter the Web server's configuration.

A different approach is not to hard-code the URL, but alter the pmc program to use a URL supplied externally, in a configuration file, for example. That solves one set of problems, but now you have to find a way to distribute the revised configuration file to all the clients, which is easier said than done.

Using the DNS solves all the problems. We store the URL in a TXT record that we configure in our DNS, and then alter pmc to retrieve the TXT record from the DNS. We can change the URL once, in our DNS, and all copies of pmc can pick up the new value very easily (Figure G.1). Isn't that a neat solution? The next section shows you how to implement this.

G.1.1 Use TXT records to configure an application

Section 2.3.3 explained that a DNS Text (TXT) resource record can contain arbitrary strings, limited in length to 255 octets. So, for example, to store the URL of our application, we could create a TXT record such as:

```
pmsURL.qupps.biz.    600    IN    TXT       "http://webbin.qupps.biz/pms.php"
```

and the pmc client program can retrieve that value by looking up the TXT record for the domain name pmsurl.qupps.biz (Figure G.1). (Recall that domain names are case-insensitive.) We configure individual records in our DNS for each configuration variable we need. In some respects, our TXT record is functioning like an SRV record.

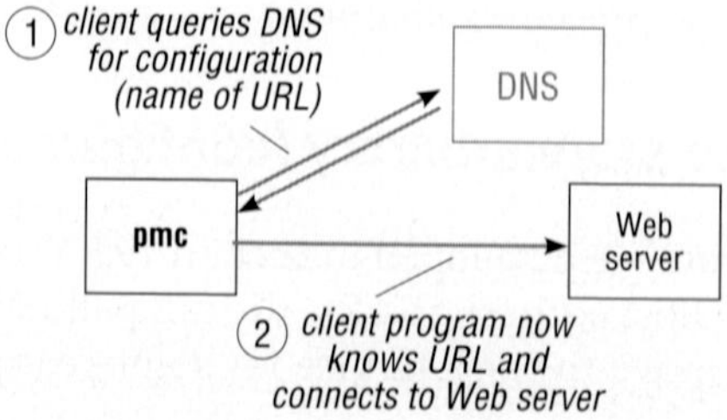

Figure G.1: Application queries the DNS for configuration data

G.1.2 A more sophisticated solution

RFC 1464, *Using the Domain Name System To Store Arbitrary String Attributes*, specifies how to associate arbitrary string information with attributes in a TXT record. The TXT record's *rdata* has the syntax:

"*attribute-name=attribute-value*"

For instance, a sample TXT resource record set could contain:

```
zoo.qupps.biz.    86400   IN  TXT  "animal=Leopard"
zoo.qupps.biz.    86400   IN  TXT  "animal=Pussycat"
```

Coming back to our example, we want the pmc client to retrieve the URL from the DNS, so we create an entry for it in our DNS zone:

```
$ dig pmsservice.qupps.biz  txt
;; ANSWER SECTION:
pmsservice.qupps.biz.    600  IN    TXT      "desc=poor man's ddns"
pmsservice.qupps.biz.    600  IN    TXT      "enabled=true"
pmsservice.qupps.biz.    600  IN    TXT      "url=http://webbin.qupps.biz/pms.php"
```

Note the following points:

- The TXT record with the `enabled=` keyword illustrates how you could globally (and remotely) disable an application (e.g. during downtime for maintenance) – an interesting concept.

- Recall that a DNS server will return the records in the RRset in "pseudo-random" order, so you have to search for your *attribute-name=* record in the RRset.
- Remember that TXT records in the DNS shouldn't contain sensitive information because they are visible to anybody, for the asking.

The code required to query a TXT record is simple, although we don't implement all RFC 1464 semantics here: (Download this Perl example, and another example in the C programming language, for *nix and Microsoft Windows, from the book's Web site (☞ D311).)

Listing G.1: Query TXT RR for pms URL

```
#!/usr/bin/perl
use strict;
use Net::DNS;

my $domain = "pmsservice.qupps.biz";
my $key    = "uRL";                          # attribute requested
my $val    = "?";
my $res    = Net::DNS::Resolver->new;        # create resolver object

my $query = $res->search($domain, 'TXT');    # perform query
die "query for $domain failed: ", $res->errorstring, "\n" unless ($query);

foreach my $rr ($query->answer) {            # RRset
        if ($rr->type eq 'TXT') {
                my $txt =  $rr->txtdata;

                if ($txt =~ /^${key}.*="?(.*)"?$/i) {
                        $val = $1;
                        last;
                }
        }
}
print "value = [$val]\n";
```

The only application we're aware of that uses TXT records like this is the clamav anti-virus system (`http://www.clamav.net/`). It uses a TXT record to publish the version number of its signature database. clamav clients query the DNS:

```
$ dig current.cvd.clamav.net txt
current.cvd.clamav.net. 900   IN   TXT "0.93.1:46:7531:1214123341:1"
```

to decide if they need to download a new version of the signature database.

G.2 A DNSBL to look up country-codes

The domain countries.nerd.dk hosts DNSBLs in which you look up IP addresses to determine the country in which that address is located. Andreas Plesner Jacobsen created the service (see `http://countries.nerd.dk/`). The data set is rebuilt every day from a variety of sources: the Regional Internet Registries (RIPE, ARIN, APNIC, AFRINIC), with some manual additions. Jacobsen makes the zone available over the public DNS, and also as files in rbldnsd format that you can download and periodically synchronize if you make heavy use of the service.

The hostnames used for the DNS zones at countries.nerd.dk are based on the country code top-level domain (ccTLD) names for each country – de for Germany, ca for Canada, us for USA, etc. To access a country-specific DNSBL zone, use *cctld*.countries.nerd.dk: for example, the server au.countries.nerd.dk contains the zone for Australia. Or you can use zz.countries.nerd.dk, which contains the data for all countries.

As with all DNSBLs, you take the IP address you want to look up, reverse the octets, and append the domain of the blacklist. For example, if your IP address is 84.60.111.207, you query for the following domain:

```
$ dig +short 207.111.60.84.zz.countries.nerd.dk txt
"de"
```

The zone provides answers to queries both as A and TXT records:

- The address in the reply for an A record contains the ISO 3166 country code number encoded in the last two octets of the answer. For example, Spain has a numeric ISO code 724, so if you look up a Spanish address, the returned IP is 127.0.**2**.**212** ((2 * 256) + 212 = 724). Whereas, if you look up an address assigned to Germany (country code 276), the returned IP is 127.0.**1**.20 ((1 * 256) + 20 = 276).

  You'll find a list of the two-letter country codes and decimal values used by this blacklist at `http://ftp.ics.uci.edu/pub/ietf/http/related/iso3166.txt`, and the IP addresses in the 127/8 network at `http://countries.nerd.dk/isolist.txt`.

- The TXT record returns the lower-case two-letter ISO 3166 country-code.

The maintainer uses this blacklist in his mail server to block e-mail from specific countries, but you can also use it, for example, to determine which countries your Web server visitors arrive from, and we'll show you how to do that now.

G.2.1 Mirror and serve the blacklist

If you make heavy use of the list, you should set up your own DNS server to serve the blacklist, as we discussed in Section 16.4. (Remember that rbldnsd can serve multiple DNSBLs simultaneously.)

To create your own zone, proceed as follows:

1. Choose a specific directory for the zone files retrieved by rsync. For example:

   ```
   # mkdir /var/spool/geo
   # chown nobody /var/spool/geo
   # cd /var/spool
   ```

2. Set up rsync to mirror the particular list you're interested in:

   ```
   $ rsync rsync://countries-ns.mdc.dk/zone/zz.countries.nerd.dk.rbldnsd  geo/
   ```

   You typically set up rsync to run via cron (but not too frequently, say once a day).

3. Choose a name for the zone. We choose qupps.geo. (Because we'll only be using the name internally, we can use anything we like.)

4. Set up rbldnsd (Section 16.4) to serve the zone you've just chosen:

```
# rbldnsd -u nobody -p /var/run/geo.pid -t 1200 -c 60 -b 127.0.0.3/53 \
          qupps.geo:ip4set:zz.countries.nerd.dk.rbldnsd
```

   Note how we use an address on the loopback interface. Note also the format of the last argument to rbldnsd: `ip4set` is the data type of the file you mirrored in step 2 above, and the rest is the filename.

5. Perform a test query to see that everything is running:

```
$ dig @127.0.0.3 +short 207.111.60.84.qupps.geo
127.0.1.20
```

G.2.2 Using your new country blacklist

Here are some ideas for using your new blacklist:

- Configure your mail servers to use this list to either block e-mail from specific countries (not recommended) or to add a message header containing the country of origin, so your users can simply satisfy their curiosity, or configure their e-mail clients to junk messages from a specific country.
- Provide language-specific information on a Web site, according to the visitor's location.
- Analyze your Web server log files, so see where your visitors come from. We show you how to do this now.

Determine country of origin in Apache log files

The Apache web server is typically configured to log, in a file called `access_log`, an entry for every resource it serves, like this:

```
192.0.100.2 - - [21/Jun/2008:00:00:24 +0200] "GET /feed/ HTTP/1.0" 302 21 blog.fupps.c...
192.168.1.4 - - [21/Jun/2008:00:04:00 +0200] "GET /category/blackberry HTTP/1.1" 400 926...
192.0.10.109 - [21/Jun/2008:00:07:55 +0200] "GET /category/syncml/page/3/ HTTP/1.1" 400 9...
192.0.18.213 - - [21/Jun/2008:00:10:10 +0200] "GET /extensions/whatmon HTTP/1.1" 200 206...
```

The first "word" on each line is the IP address of the client that retrieved the resource. We can create a small program that uses our new geo-DNSBL to find out which country the request came from.

Listing G.2: Determine geographic location of Apache clients

```
#!/usr/bin/perl
# Read IP addresses from first field of Apache logfile and determine country

use strict;
use Net::DNS;

my $domain = "qupps.geo";
my $res    = Net::DNS::Resolver->new(          # create resolver object
        nameservers => [qw(127.0.0.3)] );

my ($ip, $rev, $query);
my %ipcache;                                    # cache identical IP
my %countrylist;                                # count countries

while (<>) {
        chomp;
        s/\s.*$//;                              # leaves only IP

        if (defined($ipcache{$ip = $_})) {
                $countrylist{$ipcache{$ip}}++;  # IP seen; incr.counter
                next;
        }

        my ($a, $b, $c, $d) = split(/\./, $_, 4);
        $rev = "$d.$c.$b.$a.$domain";

        $query = $res->search($rev, 'TXT');     # perform query
        if ($query) {
                my $rr = ($query->answer)[0];
                if ($rr->type eq 'TXT') {
                        $ipcache{$ip} = $rr->txtdata;
                        $countrylist{$rr->txtdata}++;
                }
        } else {
                warn "query $rev failed: ", $res->errorstring, "\n";
        }
}
foreach my $country (keys %countrylist) {
        print $countrylist{$country} . " " . $country . "\n";
}
```

The program caches queries itself, and prints a list of *frequency / country* pairs to `stdout`:

```
$ apachelog < /var/log/htttpd/access_log | sort -n
...
42 nl
52 fr
93 uk
208 cn
776 de
...
```

That completes our discussion of this special DNSBL.

G.3 Automatic DNS NOTIFY with OpenLDAP and slapi-dnsnotify

Stefan Walter has created a package that consists of an OpenLDAP SLAPI plug-in called slapi-dnsnotify and a stand-alone program called notify-dns-slaves (Figure G.2). This combination lets you set up your LDAP directory server to:

1. Automatically increment a serial number in the zone's LDAP directory entry when you modify a zone, and then ...

2. Automatically send out DNS NOTIFY requests to the corresponding zone's slave name servers, using the ancillary notify-dns-slaves utility.

Neither of these functions is provided by PowerDNS' or BIND SDB's LDAP back-ends – which is why the plug-in was needed.

Walter created the plug-in to have a zone's serial number updated automatically whenever he updated a zone's data, irrespective of *how* he updated the data. (You could easily add that functionality in a Web front-end, say, but that wouldn't notice when you added a record with an LDAP editor.) Furthermore, instead of waiting until a slave server checks for a fresh copy of the zone, he wanted the (BIND) slaves to be notified about the zone's modification immediately.

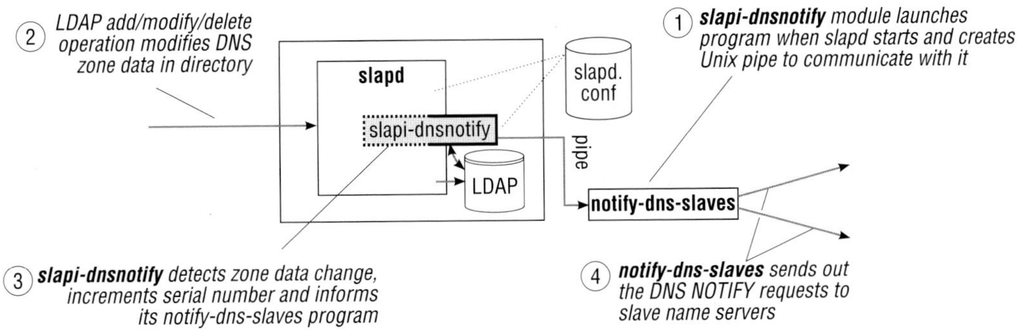

Figure G.2: slapi-dnsnotify architecture

After building the plug-in as described in its documentation, you configure the plug-in by adding it to `slapd.conf`:

```
plugin postoperation /usr/local/lib/slapi-dnsnotify.so plugin_init \
      base-dn=dc=qupps,dc=biz \
      zone-attribute =associatedDomain \
      soa-attribute =sOARecord \
      ns-attribute =nSRecord \
      enable-auto-serial \
      notify-delay =10
```

When slapd starts up, it instantiates the SLAPI plug-in, loading it from the shared library specified in the plugin statement. The plug-in launches a single child process, notify-dns-slaves, and sets up a UNIX pipe to communicate with notify-dns-slaves.

The plug-in assumes an LDAP entry is a zone if it has an `sOARecord` attribute (but you can configure a different attribute). Information about the zone (the zone's name and its Name Servers) is taken directly from the LDAP entry containing the `sOARecord`:

```
dn: dc=qupps.biz,ou=pdns,ou=dns,dc=qupps,dc=biz
dc: qupps.biz
objectClass: dcObject
objectClass: dNSDomain2
objectClass: domainRelatedObject
sOARecord: ns1.qupps.biz. hostmaster.mens.de. 17 10800 900 604800 3600
NSRecord: ns1.qupps.biz
NSRecord: ns2.qupps.biz
mXRecord: 10 mail.qupps.biz
aRecord: 192.168.1.20
dNSTTL: 86400
associatedDomain: qupps.biz
```

When the plug-in detects a modification or addition of an LDAP directory entry, it updates the zone's serial number, extracts the corresponding NS records from the LDAP entry, and communicates those via the pipe to the notify-dns-slaves program. This sends the DNS NOTIFYs, efficiently over a single datagram socket, to the specified (slave) servers, without blocking for each NOTIFY.

Because of the automatic slave server notification, the slaves are quickly informed when a zone changes, and they retrieve the zone via an AXFR zone transfer.

You can get slapi-dnsnotify and its documentation from `http://memberwebs.com/stef/software/slapi-dnsnotify/`.

Appendix

H Scripting PowerDNS Recursor with the Lua programming language

Two weeks before this book was delivered to the printers, a new version of PowerDNS Recursor was released. This version includes scripting capabilities, using the Lua language. You can use this to create or modify on the fly answers to queries received by PowerDNS Recursor. We give you a (very) short introduction to Lua, an overview of how PowerDNS Recursor uses it, and explain how you use Lua functions to manipulate DNS queries.

H.1 A (very) short overview of Lua

Lua is a powerful, fast, light-weight, embeddable scripting language, designed by Waldemar Celes, Roberto Ierusalimschy, and Luiz Henrique de Figueiredo in 1993.

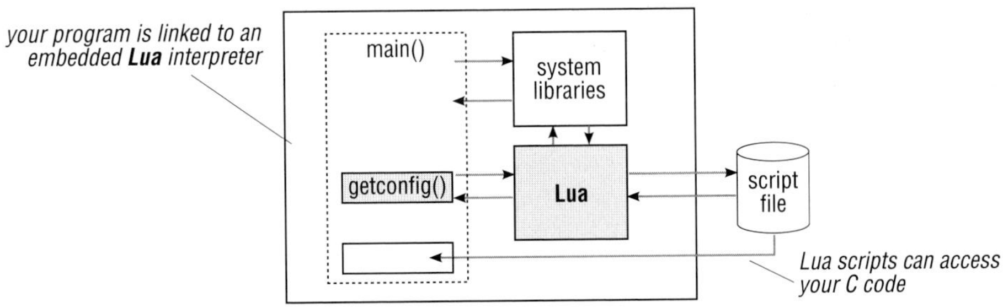

Figure H.1: You can embed Lua in your applications

It has much of the functionality found in a modern scripting language: scope, control structures, iterators, and standard libraries for processing strings, performing mathematical operations and interacting with a machine's environment. Tables are the the only data-structuring mechanism in Lua. Tables are dynamic: they grow when data is added to them (by assigning a value to a hitherto non-existent field) and shrink when data is removed from them (by assigning `nil` to a field). You can use a table as an array (indexed from 1), an associative array (sometimes called a hash or a dictionary), a record, etc. The contents of tables in Lua can include any combination of types. Tables' keys can be of any Lua value, including a function or another table. (For a complete description of the Lua language, see `http://www.lua.org/manual/5.1/`, and the book *Programming in Lua* at `http://www.lua.org/pil/`. There is also a very lively and helpful mailing list at `http://www.lua.org/lua-l.html`.)

Lua is portable (it runs on a variety of platforms), it is small, it is free software, and it is used in a large variety of applications including games (World of Warcraft, SimCity 4), productivity tools (Adobe Photoshop Lightroom, LuaTeX), window managers (Ion), databases (MySQL Proxy), networking utilities (Nmap, Wireshark), and even in some Olivetti printer firmware.

We said, that Lua is embeddable – it is designed to be used from within your own programs. But why would you do that? Lua effectively gives your application a "macro language". Lua scripts can extend the host application's own capabilities, but the host language can also extend Lua – C functions can call Lua functions and vice versa (Figure H.1).

We show you a small example in the next section. (Skip this if you don't enjoy programming.)

H.1.1 Example – embedding Lua into your program

Many programs have some sort of configuration file, where you store information your program needs. Let's assume your program needs a configurable directory name; you might code something like this in your C program, and write a `getconfig()` function to parse `our.conf` and extract the value you need:

```
char *spooldir = getconfig("our.conf");
printf("Using directory: %s\n", spooldir ? spooldir : "<undefined>");
```

Let's look at the function `getconfig()`, which we've Lua-enabled:

Listing H.1: Lua-enabled `getconfig()` function retrieves a variable

```
char *getconfig(const char *configfile)
{
    lua_State *L = lua_open();
    const char *cf;

    luaL_openlibs(L);

    if (luaL_loadfile(L, configfile) || lua_pcall(L, 0, 0, 0))
        bail(L, "can't run configuration file: %s", lua_tostring(L, -1));

    lua_getglobal(L, "SPOOLDIR");
    cf = lua_tostring(L, -1);
    lua_close(L);

    return (cf == NULL) ? NULL : strdup(cf);
}
```

This initializes Lua and loads Lua's libraries. After Lua has loaded `our.conf` and syntax-checked it, `getconfig()` retrieves the value of `SPOOLDIR` from Lua, and returns a copy of that value to the caller, or `NULL` on failure.

Let us now have a look at three different versions of the `our.conf` configuration file:

1. Our first version isn't terribly exciting (but it is a complete, if trivial, Lua program):

```
SPOOLDIR = "/var/spool"
```

When run, our program prints:

```
Using directory: /var/spool
```

Note how the double quotes (") have disappeared. (Remember: Lua is *interpreting* the file's content, and for Lua this is a string constant.)

2. Lets add some Lua variables and functions to `our.conf`: (Names are self-explanatory; the "`..`" is a string concatenation operator.)

```
t = os.getenv("HOME")                                  -- is $HOME set?
t = t or os.getenv("TEMP")                             -- for Windows
SPOOLDIR = t .. "/work"  .. '/' .. (os.date("%Y-%m-%d")) -- strftime(3)
```

   and the *same* program, run on our system, now prints:

```
Using directory: /home/jpm/work/2008-06-29
```

3. This time we *append* the following lines to `our.conf`'s content:

```
http = require "socket.http"                       -- load library
url  = "http://www.qupps.biz/~jpm/cf"              -- URI
body, code = http.request(url)                     -- perform request
if code == 200 then                                -- success
        local line = string.gsub(body, "\n", "")   -- strip newlines
        SPOOLDIR = line
end
```

   Our program now sets `SPOOLDIR` as in step 2, but if the HTTP request succeeds (i.e. the URL can be retrieved), that overwrites the variable's value. Note that we modified only our configuration file, *not* our application program.

This small example shows a bit of the power you get when your application embeds Lua. Even in such a trivial task as reading a configuration file, Lua adds a wealth of functionality. (Our tiny program now has a tremendous "configuration back-end" – think `/etc/profile` just for us.)

H.2 Add Lua scripting to PowerDNS Recursor

PowerDNS Recursor supports Lua scripts in versions 3.1.7 onwards, and the binary packages on its Web site (`http://www.powerdns.com`) include Lua-support.

PowerDNS Recursor's scripting lets you configure it to modify DNS replies, using one or both of the following functions, which you define in the Lua script (Figure H.2):

preresolve This is called *before* the caching server attempts to resolve a DNS query (i.e. before any upstream servers are contacted). If this function provides an answer, it overrides the answer the public Internet could have provided otherwise.

nxdomain This function is called *after* the resolution has occurred, if the answer resulted in an NXDOMAIN status (not found). You can use nxdomain() to override the "not found", by supplying a "found it after all" answer.

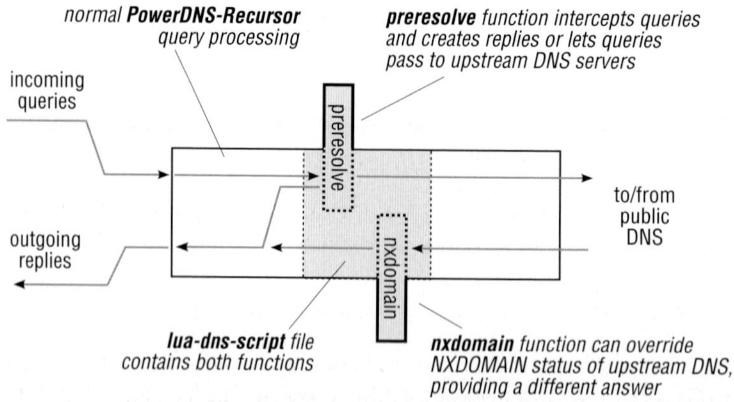

Figure H.2: How PowerDNS Recursor uses the Lua script functions during query processing

Possible scenarios for using Lua functions in your PowerDNS Recursor server include:

- Load balancing within your own organization. You can implement a preresolve function that answers a query for a specific hostname from a list of addresses managed by your Lua script. (Note that this load-balancing is used by your internal hosts only, because it is implemented on your caching server, and not on your Internet-facing authoritative servers.)

- Catch typos. You know that your general manager always mistypes www.qupps.biz (he uses an "s" instead of the "z"), so you add an nxdomain script that returns the correct address anyway. (It avoids you having to answer his questions about the reliability of your Web servers…)

- Advertisement blocking. You want to "protect" your users from certain Web sites, so you configure a preresolve function that catches queries for those and returns a harmless address, say 127.0.0.1 instead. Fredrik Danerklint has implemented such a system, using an externally acquired `hosts` file[1], together with an optional patch to PowerDNS Recursor. The patch adds a call-lua-function that dumps statistics of the function's use and lets you load new hosts (see `http://www.fredan.org/os/`). (If you want to block such domains for Web browsers only, you can use squid instead.)

H.2.1 Configure PowerDNS Recursor to use Lua scripts

Before attempting to get scripts running, we recommend you configure PowerDNS Recursor normally and get that working (Section 17.3), because the additional level of complexity introduced by scripting can make errors difficult to find. Then:

1. Create your Lua script, containing a preresolve and/or an nxdomain function. You can name the file however you want to. (We've called it `qupps.lua`.)

[1]Danerklint doesn't maintain the `hosts` file himself; note the terms of use (which are included in the file itself).

2. Configure your `recursor.conf` file to use the script, by specifying its full pathname:

```
lua-dns-script =/etc/powerdns/qupps.lua
```

3. Restart PowerDNS Recursor, and ensure no errors are reported. (A faulty Lua script will prevent PowerDNS Recursor from starting.)

4. To modify the script's behavior, edit and save the script file, and use rec_control (Section 17.3.2) to reload it at runtime (i.e. without restarting the server):

```
# rec_control reload-lua-script
ok - loaded script from '/etc/powerdns/qupps.lua'
```

   If the script cannot be compiled when you reload it (e.g. it contains syntax errors), PowerDNS Recursor keeps the currently running script loaded, and warns you there is a problem:

```
Retaining current script, error from '/etc/powerdns/qupps.lua': ↩
    Error loading LUA file '/etc/powerdns/qupps.lua': ↩
    /etc/powerdns/qupps.lua:5: '=' expected near 'ret'
```

5. You can disable the script entirely, by removing it from PowerDNS at run-time, and you can reload it again later, if you want:

```
# rec_control unload-lua-script
unloaded current lua script
```

H.2.2 Writing a Lua function for PowerDNS Recursor

PowerDNS Recursor calls the script function(s) for each query it receives, passing them (a) the IP address of the requesting client (b) the requested domain name, and (c) the numeric query type (Table H.1). (Note that the domain name is always fully qualified and always ends in a dot.)

Your Lua functions have access to the query codes through a table called `pdns`. For example, if your function wants to return a CNAME to PowerDNS Recursor, you can use the numeric constant 5 or the value `pdns.CNAME` – they are equivalent.

qtype	*qcode*	*qtype*	*qcode*	*qtype*	*qcode*
A	1	SOA	6	TXT	16
NS	2	PTR	12	SRV	33
CNAME	5	MX	15	ANY	255

Table H.1: Common query types and codes

If your function decides to handle a request, it must return a result code of 0 together with a Lua table containing records to be put in the DNS reply. If, on the other hand, your function decides *not* to handle this request (for example because it realizes it shouldn't be overriding an NXDOMAIN for this particular query), it must return -1 and an empty table, indicating that PowerDNS Recursor should proceed "as normal" for this request – i.e. as if your function weren't there.

H.2.3 Example – Override an NXDOMAIN

Recall that our CEO mistypes frequently, and we want to please him. We create a simple Lua function in the file `qupps.lua`, to override an NXDOMAIN for the domain www.qupps.bis (note the "s" at the end):

Listing H.2: Example Lua function for nxdomain

```
function nxdomain( ip, domain, qtype )
    if domain == 'www.qupps.bis.' then
        return 0, {{ qtype = pdns.A, content = '192.168.1.20' }}
    end
    return -1, {}         -- unhandled
end
```

This nxdomain function checks if the domain name (note the trailing period) equals what we are searching for, and if so, it returns 0 (indicating it has handled the query) and a Lua table with a single DNS A reply in it (irrespective of whether the original query was for an A record).

H.2.4 Example – Redirect a domain

This example uses the preresolve function to intercept a domain: it returns a CNAME whenever *something*.someyyplace.com is queried:

Listing H.3: Example Lua function for preresolve

```
function preresolve( ip, domain, qtype )
    ret = {}                    -- create table
    if                          -- for someyyplace.com, return CNAME for any query
        string.find(domain, "^someyyplace.com.$") or
        string.find(domain, "[%p]someyyplace.com.$") then
            ret[1] = { qtype = pdns.CNAME, content = "www.qupps.biz" }
            return 0, ret
    end
    return -1, ret              -- nothing to do; tell Recursor to handle it
end
```

Note the following points:

- If you need both preresolve and nxdomain handling, add both functions to the same Lua script file.
- If preresolve doesn't handle the query (i.e. it returns -1), nxdomain is invoked (if you've configured it, and if the query returns NXDOMAIN).
- Within your Lua script, you can use `matchnetmask()` (a function provided by PowerDNS Recursor) to match querying clients (consult the documentation at `http://doc.powerdns.com/recursor-scripting.html`).
- Carefully consider whether you need to implement scripting in your caching server, and test it thoroughly before deploying it.

Glossary

ACE	ASCII Compatible Encoding
ACL	Access Control List
AJAX	Asynchronous JavaScript and XML
API	Application Programming Interface
ASCII	American Standard Code for Information Interchange
ASN.1	Abstract Syntax Notation number 1
AXFR	Zone Transfer
BDB	Berkeley database
BOOTP	Boot Protocol
BSD	Berkeley Systems Distribution
ccTLD	Country-Code Top-Level Domain
CDB	Constant Database
CEST	Central European Standard Time
CGI	Common Gateway Interface
CLI	command-line interface
CPAN	Comprehensive Perl Archive Network
CRL	Certificate Revocation List
CVS	Concurrent Version Control System
DBI	Database Interface (Perl)
DHCP	Dynamic Host Configuration Protocol
DLV	DNS Look-aside Validation
DMZ	Demilitarized Zone
DNSBL	DNS Black-list
DNSSEC	DNS Security Extensions
DNS	Domain Name Service
DSN	Database Source Name
EDNS0	Extension Mechanisms for DNS
FAQ	Frequently Asked Questions
FQDN	Fully Qualified Domain Name
FTP	File Transfer Protocol
GHz	Gigahertz
GID	group ID
gTLD	generic Top-Level Domain
HMAC	Hash Message Authentication

IANA	Internet Assigned Numbers Authority
ICANN	Internet Corporation for Assigned Names and Numbers
IDN	Internationalized Domain Name
IMAP	Internet Message Access Protocol
IOU	I Owe You
IPC	Interprocess Communication
IP	Internet Protocol
ISC	Internet Software Consortium
ISO	International Standards Organization
ISP	Internet Service Provider
IXFR	Incremental Zone Transfer
KSK	Key Signing Key
LAN	Local Area Network
LDAP	Lightweight Directory Access Protocol
LDIF	LDAP Data Interchange Format
LOC	location
MIME	Multipurpose Internet Mail Extensions
MTA	Mail Transfer Agent
MUA	Mail User Agent
NAS	Network Attached Storage
NFS	Network File System
NIC	network interface card
NIC	network information center
NSD	Name Server Daemon
NSS	Name Service Switch
NTP	Network Time Protocol
ODBC	Open Database Connectivity
OID	object Identifier
PAM	Pluggable Authentication Modules
PGP	Pretty Good Privacy
PHP	Hypertext Preprocessor
PID	process ID
PPP	Point to Point Protocol
RAID	Redundant Array of Inexpensive Disks
RBL	Real-time Black-List
RDBMS	Relational Database Management System
RDN	Relative Distinguished Name
REST	Representational State Transfer
RFC	Request For Comments
RR	resource record
RRset	resource record set
RSA	Rivest, Shamir, Adleman
RSS	Really Simple Syndication
SASL	Simple Authentication and Security Layer
SHA	Secure Hash Algorithm

S/MIME	Secure MIME
SMTP	Simple Mail Transfer Protocol
SNMP	Simple Network Management Protocol
SOA	start of authority
SOHO	Small-Office/Home-Office
SPOF	single point of failure
SQL	Structured Query Language
SRV	service
SSH	secure shell
SSL	Secure Sockets Layer
SVG	Scalable Vector Graphics
TAI	Temps Atomique International
TCP	Transmission Control Protocol
TLD	Top-Level Domain
TLS	Transport Layer Security
TSIG	Transaction Signatures
TTL	Time to Live
UDF	User Defined Function
UDP	User Datagram Protocol
UID	user ID
URI	Uniform Resource Identifier
URL	Uniform Resource Locator
UTF	Unicode Transformation Format
WAN	Wide-Area Network
RPC	Remote Procedure Call
XML	eXtensible Markup Language
ZSK	Zone Signing Key

Index

In the index, many terms are marked with a small superscript (as in access-control[Unbound], for example), to indicate the program or brand of server the item relates to, or in which chapter the term appears. Page numbers in italics indicate where terms are defined. Variable names (e.g. `$UID`) are sorted under their initial letter, not under "$".

Colophon

This book was produced with Open Source tools. I am *extremely* grateful to my editor for not forcing me to use an ugly word processor; quite on the contrary, he actually suggested I do not.

- We used the LaTeX document preparation system on *nix to produce the camera-ready copy of what you hold in your hands (`www.latex-project.org`).
- We wrote every word in vi or rather a newer incantation thereof called vim (`www.vim.org`).
- We created the figures throughout the book in scalable vector graphics (SVG) with InkScape, converting them to encapsulated Postscript (EPS) for inclusion in the LaTeX source (`www.inkscape.org`).
- make is an invaluable tool that we used extensively for "compiling" the book as well as converting SVG diagrams to EPS (`http://www.gnu.org/software/make/`).
- The screen shots were made and manipulated with GIMP, the GNU Image Manipulation Program (`www.gimp.org`).
- We placed all the files that make up the book (diagrams, screen shots, example programs, etc.) under control of subversion, the revision control system (`subversion.tigris.org`) running with the Apache Web server (`httpd.apache.org`).
- While "in transit", we worked on a copy of the subversion working set that we kept synchronized with unison (`www.cis.upenn.edu/~bcpierce/unison`).
- Instead of wasting paper, we used xdvik to preview drafts of the book's chapters[2] (`xdvi.sourceforge.net`).

LaTeX produced the completed book as a Device Independent File (DVI) which we converted to Postscript and then PDF, which the printers used as camera ready copy.

[2]and that is how Alexandra kept track of the book's progress.

ALSO PUBLISHED BY UIT

Exim by Example

Getting started, with configurations for common scenarios

Jason Meers

Key benefits

1. Get a working Exim mail system up and running quickly.
2. Use ready-made configurations for all the most common scenarios.
3. Use separate easily-edited files so non-experts can adapt configurations to specific local needs.

Why is this book special?

This is the first book to explain the Exim SMTP mail server for the beginner. It is also ideal for readers who have experience of other mail servers, but now wish to switch to Exim. It provides ready-made configurations for all the most common requirements, allowing the reader to have a sophisticated and fully functioning mail system with the minimum of effort.

Description

- *Exim by Example* explains each step of getting Exim up and running as your organization's mail server. It includes detailed instructions for installation on the most popular Linux platforms.
- Teaches Exim through a series of increasingly-complex configurations. New features are added gradually; as they are introduced, the book explains them and how they fit into the overall picture.
- Provides and explains ready-made configurations for all the most common requirements: from a simple system suited to a small organization, to a mail hub handling multiple domains and relaying to many internal servers.
- Also includes information on the Dovecot POP/IMAP server so you can have a fully functioning mail system ready to use.
- Of particular interest to Windows users is how to use Exim as a secure, Internet-facing, front-end to internal Microsoft Exchange systems.

ISBN: 9780954452988
Approx. 288 pages
Publication date: May 2009

ALSO PUBLISHED BY UIT

The Exim SMTP Mail Server

Official Guide for Release 4

Philip Hazel

Second edition

E-mail is the most widely used applications, and Exim is one of the most widely used mail servers, handling mail for tens of millions of users daily.

Exim is free software. It's easy to configure. It's scalable, running on single-user desktop systems as well as on ISP servers handling millions of users. (It's the default server on many Linux systems, and it's available for countless versions of UNIX.)

Exim is fast, flexible, and reliable. It is designed not to lose messages even if your server machine crashes. It can be used as a secure Internet-facing front-end to other, proprietary, mail systems used internally in your organization.

Exim supports lookups from LDAP servers, SQL databases, and other data sources, letting you automate maintenance and configuration. It can work in conjunction with other tools for virus-checking and spam-blocking, to reject unwanted e-mails before they even enter your site.

This book will help you deploy Exim as your SMTP e-mail server throughout your organization, and to configure, tune, and secure your Exim systems.

Praise for the First Edition

"The book is simply amazing. I find the format/style/whatever 100 times better than [other documentation]."

"If there's even a whiff of a chance of you having to come into contact with Exim or its runtime configuration, then I can do nothing else but strongly recommend this book. The detail's there in spades, it reads very well, and is a fine complement to the reference manual."

"The book exceeds my expectations."

"Well presented and easy to follow"

"An excellent book that is very well written"

"So well written I learn new things every time I open it"

ISBN: 9780954452971
xviii + 622 pages

ALSO PUBLISHED BY UIT

The Joy of X

The architecture of the X window system

Niall Mansfield

This is a reprint of the 1993 classic, describing the architecture of the X window system – the de facto standard windowing system for Linux, UNIX and many other operating systems. The book has three sections:

1. X in a nutshell – a quick overview.
2. How X works, in detail, and how the user sees it.
3. Using the system, system administration, performance and programming.

The book is written in a clear, uncomplicated style, with over 200 illustrations. For maximum accessibility, it has a flexibile, modular structure that makes it easy to skip to the sections that interest you. The book has been widely recommended as a course text.

Niall Mansfield founded the European X window system User Group. He also wrote *The X window system: a user's guide*, and the widely acclaimed *Practical TCP/IP*.

Praise for This Book

"If you are new to the X Window System environment, we strongly suggest picking up a book such as The Joy of X" **Eric Raymond, in the *Linux XFree86 HOWTO***

"I find this book extraordinary. It's one of the first books on X which addresses questions of information systems policy with respect to the X Window System...It will advance the case of X and open systems by making the interesting issues more accessible" **Oliver Jones**

"a great little book called The Joy of X by Niall Mansfield that taught me much of what I know." **Jeff Duntemann's ContraPositive Diary**

"My personal touchstone when looking for a broad introduction to all things X is The Joy of X ... by Niall Mansfield" **Peter Collinson**

ISBN: 9781906860004
xii + 372 pages
Publication date: February 2009

ALSO PUBLISHED BY UIT

Practical TCP/IP

Designing, using, and troubleshooting TCP/IP networks on Linux and Windows

Niall Mansfield

New second edition

Key benefits

1. Explore, hands-on, how your network really works. Build small test networks in a few minutes, so you can try anything out without affecting your live network and servers.
2. Learn how to troubleshoot network problems, and how to use free packet sniffers to see what's happening.
3. Understand how the TCP/IP protocols map onto your day-to-day network operation – learn both theory and practice.

Praise for the First Edition

"Before this book was released I was eagerly searching for a book that could be used for my Linux-based LAN-course. After the release of this book I stopped my searching immediately"
Torben Gregersen, Associate Professor, Engineering College of Aarhus.

"Accuracy is superb – written by someone obviously knowledgable in the subject, and able to communicate this knowledge extremely effectively."

"You won't find a better TCP/IP book!"

"An excellent book for taking your computer networking career from mediocre to top notch."

"Covers TCP/IP, and networking in general, tremendously."

"This book has been touted as the 21st-century upgrade to the classic TCP/IP Illustrated (by Richard W. Stevens) These are big boots to fill, but Practical TCP/IP does an impressive job. In over 800 pages of well-organized and well-illustrated text, there is no fat, but rather a lean and – yes – practical treatment of every major TCP/IP networking concept."

"It's an ideal book for beginners, probably the only one needed for the first and second semesters of a university networking course. ... (But it is not a book just for beginners. ...)"

ISBN: 9780954452964
Approx. 700 pages
Publication date: March 2009

Web site for this book

Register your book: receive updates, notifications about author appearances, and discounts on new editions. *www.uit.co.uk/register*

Resources for your book: examples, exercises, source code, downloadable index, downloadable searchable text, and more. *www.uit.co.uk/resources*

News: forthcoming titles, events, reviews, interviews, podcasts, etc. *www.uit.co.uk/news*

Join our mailing lists: get e-mail newsletters on topics of interest. *www.uit.co.uk/subscribe*

Order books: order online. If you are a bookstore, find out about our distributors or contact us to discuss your particular requirements. *www.uit.co.uk/order*

Send us a book proposal: if you want to write – even if you have just the kernel of an idea at present – we'd love to hear from you. We pride ourselves on supporting our authors and making the process of book-writing as satisfying and as easy as possible. *www.uit.co.uk/for-authors*

UIT Cambridge Ltd.
PO Box 145
Cambridge
CB4 1GQ
England

E-mail: *inquiries@uit.co.uk*
Phone: **+44 1223 302 041**